INTERNATIONAL LAW IN AN ORGANIZING WORLD

BOOKS IN ENGLISH BY WILLIAM L. TUNG:

China and Some Phases of International Law (1940)
Cases and Other Readings on International Law (1940)
The Political Institutions of Modern China (1964)
International Law in an Organizing World (1968)

INTERNATIONAL LAW IN AN ORGANIZING WORLD

William L. Tung

Professor of International Law
Queens College, The City University of New York

THOMAS Y. CROWELL COMPANY
New York Established 1834

Library of Congress Catalog Card Number: 68–13388

Manufactured in the United States of America

Dedicated to the Men and Women of All Countries
Who Work for International Peace
through the Rule of Law

FOREWORD

BY QUINCY WRIGHT

This volume is distinctive among the many which have appeared in the field of international relations in the last few years because it integrates the principles of international law and international organization with due consideration to international politics. It also gives consideration to the varied points of view of Occidental and Oriental states, old and new states, Communist and anti-Communist states on the subject.

Professor Tung is in an unusually favorable position to write such a book. Born in China, he completed his undergraduate education there and then did graduate work in the United States, receiving a doctorate in political science at the University of Illinois and completing a year of post-doctorate research at Yale. He has taught international law and international relations in both China and the United States. He has also had much practical experience in administration, politics, and foreign affairs. He was a member of the Convention which framed the Provisional Constitution of China in 1931, Chairman of the Municipal Council of Peiping by popular election, 1933–34, and during World War II he served as Counsellor of the Supreme National Defense Council of China, on a committee of three which codified administrative laws of China, as Secretary General of the Ministry of Information, and as a member of the Legislative *Yuan*. After the war he was Director of the Department of American Affairs of the Chinese Ministry of Foreign Affairs, Vice-Minister of Foreign Affairs, and Ambassador to the Netherlands. After the Chinese Communist Revolution of 1949, he came to the United States, where he engaged in educational, journalistic, and civic work, becoming a naturalized citizen.

Dr. Tung's major interest has been in international relations and Chinese affairs, on which he has written a number of books in both Chinese and English. His book on *China and Some Phases of International Law,* followed by a case book on international law, both published in 1940, have been widely used, and his book on *The Political Institutions of Modern China,* published in 1964, provides unbiased information on both the Nationalist and Communist governments of China.

The present book is organized primarily according to the usual categories of international law, with full references to the sources and a well-chosen bibliography. However, it emphasizes the dynamic character of that law as indicated by the title and the role of developing international organization in the transition from the traditional international law of the nineteenth century, designed to maintain the sovereignty of states including the right to make war, to the new international law, accepted by most states in the great conventions of the twentieth century, attributing legal personality to international organizations and designed to assure the peaceful settlement of international disputes, to outlaw war, to protect human rights, and to promote the self-determination of peoples, the end of colonialism, and international cooperation for the economic, social, and cultural welfare of all mankind.

Dr. Tung, however, is aware that this transition has not been fully achieved. Though war may be outlawed, hostilities have recurred, both civil and international. The emancipation of colonies has proceeded rapidly but a few colonies still remain. Human rights have been proclaimed but they are not respected or protected in many parts of the world. There has been much international cooperation in the United Nations, the specialized agencies, and regional organizations, but vast differences exist between the rich and the poor nations, between the developed and the underdeveloped nations, between the Communist and the anti-Communist nations, both on the progress achieved and on the appropriate goals and methods of cooperation. Dr. Tung thoroughly understands the conditions of power politics, the heritage of a long tradition by which states have sought to maintain security and protect national interests by self-help and military power. He appreciates that this situation hampers progress in realizing the purposes and principles of the United Nations Charter intended to establish a new international law of peaceful coexistence and cooperation among all states.

As a textbook of international law, the book is notable for its carefully worded and well-documented statements of the law as it was traditionally and as it has been declared by the United Nations

Charter and other generally accepted treaties. The book is thoroughly up to date. The work of the United Nations International Law Commission and recent codification conferences is set forth. The problems of air space, outer space, the high seas, the continental shelf, statelessness, asylum, disarmament, atomic energy control, treaties, collective security, and United Nations peace-keeping and its financing are dealt with at length. The structures, functions, and procedures of the United Nations, the specialized agencies, international conferences, national foreign offices, and diplomatic services are outlined with indications of their roles in developing international law. Much attention is given to the procedures available for the peaceful settlement of international disputes and the need for making them more effective.

A feature of the book is the attention given to the ideas on international law of China, India, and other Asian countries, of the Soviet Union and other Communist countries, and of the new countries of Asia and Africa as well as of the European and American states among whom modern international law developed. Dr. Tung points out, however, that both China and India recognized principles of international law before the classics of Vitoria, Suarez, Gentilis, Ayala, and Grotius gave form to the discipline in sixteenth- and seventeenth-century Europe. The book will be of value both as a text for students and as a critical treatise for advanced scholars.

The author recognizes that if international law is to perform its function of establishing peaceful coexistence, justice, and cooperation among the states of the world with diverse economics, politics, and ideologies, it must be universal and all states must be convinced that its general observance would assure the security and protect the fundamental interests of each. The establishment of a "world safe for diversity," in the words of the late President Kennedy, is difficult in a world inured to power politics in which different peoples have different images of the ideal world of the future. The establishment of the new international law of the United Nations Charter and adequate organizations and procedures to keep it up to date and to apply it in practice may be the price of human survival in the atomic age, and sound expositions of international law have a role to play in this establishment. Dr. Tung's wide knowledge of international affairs, comprehensive sweep, and tolerant attitude make his work an important contribution to the development of international law. It should be well received by international lawyers in all countries.

PREFACE

For centuries, philosophers, jurists, and statesmen have persistently advocated the rule of law in the community of nations, which is being gradually united through international and regional organizations for the maintenance of international peace and the promotion of common welfare. In this process of integration, international law lays down basic principles and rules governing the relationship among states and thus builds an important foundation for the functioning of international organization, which, as one of its principal objectives, is to work for the observance of international law and its further development and codification. These two subjects, international law and international organization, are, therefore, so closely interrelated that neither can be treated fully without discussing the other. This is the basic approach of the present work: to describe how international law has been developed and applied in a world which is in the process of being organized.

The international community has undergone vital changes in the twentieth century. The existence of Communist governments in various countries is a fact. As a matter of international expediency, states with divergent political systems are expected to move from passive coexistence to active collaboration, notwithstanding their ideological differences. Existing longer in history as a socialist state and having more contact with Western nations than other Communist countries do, the Soviet Union has made known her viewpoint on many phases of international law. Wherever sources are available, Communist interpretation and application of international law are presented in this work, just as other widely accepted rules are.

The recent emergence of many new states in Asia and Africa has created new dimensions in international law. Among their declared policies are national sovereignty and equality, self-determination, decolonization, non-discrimination, as well as human rights. Although many of the new nations are preoccupied with domestic problems at present, they will eventually play a determining role in the forum of world politics. An attempt is therefore made to explore their views on various aspects of international law. With a few exceptions, they are found to be mainly in accord with commonly recognized principles and the established order of the international community.

Rudimentary rules and regulations governing interstate relations long existed in China, India, and Egypt, but modern international law had its origin in Western Europe. The contribution made by many Western states to the development of international law cannot be overemphasized. Nonetheless, contrary to traditional conviction deep-rooted in the Western world, European and American states do not appear to have any higher law-abiding spirit in international affairs than countries in other continents whenever their national interests are affected. Comments on a number of major events are made with the dual purpose of pointing out what international law really is and what commission or omission of action constitutes a violation. While upholding the same fundamental principles, states in the Western tradition have diversified views on certain aspects of international law. Such variations are also indicated, whether they are evidenced in the writings and practices of Continental Europe, Latin America, Great Britain, or the United States.

In spite of different backgrounds, traditions, and political systems, states are generally in common agreement on most principles of international law. Through the conclusion of law-making treaties, acts of international conferences, and efforts of international organizations, the trend of international law has been definitely moving from diversity to universality. In recent years, several international conventions have been adopted governing diplomatic and consular relations, as well as state jurisdiction over air, water, and land domain. Other important subjects are either prescribed in the United Nations Charter or are in the process of being codified, such as the settlement of international disputes and the law of treaties respectively. Certain phases of international law have been developed through custom, but are further clarified by the provisions in bilateral and multilateral treaties. All of these are discussed under appropriate topics. Essential rules governing the use of force or war and the status of neutrality are summarized, but these are subject to revision in order to adapt to changing concepts and circumstances.

The establishment of the League of Nations was epoch-making in its approach to international cooperation and collective security. The United Nations has continued and expanded these activities.

Coordinated with the specialized agencies, the achievements of this organization in economic and technical cooperation and assistance are unique in history. The failure of the United Nations to agree on the control of armaments and other important matters, to settle a number of major disputes, and to restore peace in certain troubled areas is not so much the fault of the Organization itself as it is the result of the selfish motives of states which place their national interests above the common welfare of the international community. The success of any organization depends upon the efforts of all its members. For examination of the interrelationship between the United Nations and international law, it is necessary to explain briefly its historical background, purposes and principles, membership and organization, administrative and voting procedures, as well as functions and activities. Such description is made under separate chapters whenever desirable and also with other topics wherever pertinent.

Although the jurisdiction of the two world courts is limited, their contributions to the legal settlement of international disputes through judicial decisions and advisory opinions have had far-reaching consequences. National courts of many countries also deserve credit for their judicious interpretation and application of international law. Decisions and opinions of both international and national tribunals are noticed, in order to show how the courts fit abstract rules to concrete cases, and thus aid in the development and enforcement of international law.

Individuals have not yet been given full recognition as subjects of international law, but they have been increasingly treated as such in many respects. In this work, the general rights and duties of individuals, as well as human rights and fundamental freedoms, are emphasized. The rule of law in the international community depends not only on political leaders and judges, but also on students and other persons interested in international affairs. Jeremy Bentham rightly stated that an ideal rule of law should be understood by the people who are expected to observe it. This maxim can be applied equally well to municipal law and to international law in the present community of nations. It is for this purpose, and also for these students and people, that this book is chiefly designed.

The brief treatment in this book of legal issues and judicial decisions, political disputes and problems, as well as the programs and activities of the United Nations and related agencies, is merely to illustrate the development and application of international law in this organizing world. No attempt is made to discuss these in any exhaustive manner. For a comprehensive and thorough study of these subjects, reference must be made to law reports, standard casebooks of international law, current works on international politics and diplomacy, special treatises on international and regional organizations, and pertinent collections of documentary materials.

For the convenience of readers, an index of cases has been prepared, which gives pagination both in the present work and in different casebooks. The Covenant of the League of Nations, the Charter of the United Nations, and the Statute of the International Court of Justice are embodied in the Appendix, because they are constantly referred to in the present work. Additional references are suggested in footnotes at the beginning of each major topic. Special treatises and articles are also recommended as supplementary readings. The selection is bound to be arbitrary, because limitation of space and consideration of research facilities available to the general reader do not permit the inclusion of many other works equally valuable. References already described in footnotes are not repeated in the bibliography, which lists only those works cited in the text in abbreviations and a limited number of others selected for their general interest or importance. Full titles of abbreviations can be found either in A Note on Abbreviations or in the bibliography.

In preparing this book, I am deeply indebted to three friends: Dean James Edward Tobin of Queens College, who has rendered a painstaking but indispensable contribution to its editorial improvement; Dr. Clarence A. Berdahl of Southern Illinois University, who with the late Professor James W. Garner first stimulated my interest in the study of international law and organization and jointly supervised my doctoral dissertation at the University of Illinois three decades ago, has spent considerable time in examining the substance of each topic and making many important suggestions; Dr. Quincy Wright, Professor Emeritus of the University of Chicago, who has not only graciously consented to write the Foreword but has also made most valuable comments on every chapter, particularly on my exposition of the application of traditional international law to new situations under the United Nations system. I am most grateful to my wife, Portia, for her encouragement and assistance in checking bibliographical materials. To the United Nations librarians for their courtesy and help, and to the editorial staff of the College Department of Thomas Y. Crowell Company, I wish to express my sincere appreciation. Finally, my deep gratitude is acknowledged to the Administration of The City University of New York for providing research assistance and facilities. While extending my warm thanks to all who have directly or indirectly contributed their efforts toward the completion of this work, I am solely responsible for the presentation of facts and views contained herein.

W.L.T.

Jamaica Hills, New York
July 15, 1967

CONTENTS

CHAPTER 14. WAR OR THE USE OF FORCE UNDER TRADITIONAL INTERNATIONAL LAW 426

CHAPTER 15. RELATIONS BETWEEN BELLIGERENTS AND NEUTRALS UNDER TRADITIONAL INTERNATIONAL LAW 459

A NOTE ON ABBREVIATIONS

Abbreviated forms of official and unofficial publications frequently referred to in this work are given their full titles in the bibliography. Symbols of United Nations documents follow those in the *List of United Nations Document Series Symbols* (United Nations, 1965). Certain organizations and titles are indicated both by full name and abbreviation on first appearance in the text. Abbreviations of law reports and others often used in the footnotes but not included in the bibliography are listed below, with the exception of those which are familiar from common usage and should easily be recognized by readers.

A/	Symbol of UN General Assembly documents, combined with Arabic numerals, usually followed by Roman numerals to indicate the number of the session.
A.C.	Appeal Cases (Law reports of the British House of Lords and Judicial Committee of the Privy Council), 1891– .
All Eng. L.R.	*All England Law Reports*, 1935– .
App. Cas.	Appeal Cases (Great Britain), 1875–1890.
Bingham	English Common Pleas Reports.
Black	United States Supreme Court Reports, 1861–1862.
Burrow	Burrow, English King's Bench Reports.
C.	Command Papers (Great Britain), –1899.
C. Rob.	C. Robinson's Admiralty Reports (Great Britain), 1799–1808.
Ch.	Court of Chancery or Chancery Reports (Great Britain), 1891– .

Cmd.	Command Papers (Great Britain), 1919–1956.
Cmnd.	Command Papers (Great Britain), 1957– .
Co. Rep.	Coke's Reports (Great Britain), 1572–1616.
Cranch	United States Supreme Court Reports, 1801–1815.
D.L.R.	Dominion Law Reports (Canada), 1912– .
Dallas	United States Supreme Court Reports, 1787–1800.
Doc.	Document.
Dodson	Dodson's Admiralty Reports (Great Britain), 1811–1822.
E/	Symbol of UN Economic and Social Council documents.
Ellis & Ellis	Ellis and Ellis, Queen's Bench Reports (Great Britain), 1856–1861.
ESC	Economic and Social Council of the United Nations.
Ex. D.	Exchequer Division (Great Britain), 1875–1880.
F.	*Federal Reporter* (United States), 1880–1924.
F.2d	*Federal Reporter* (United States), 2nd series, 1924– .
Fed. Supp.	*Federal Supplement* (United States, containing decisions of U.S. District Court and Court of Claims reports), 1932– .
GA	General Assembly of the United Nations.
Howard	United States Supreme Court Reports, 1843–1860.
I.C.J.	International Court of Justice.
I.C.J. Reports	International Court of Justice, *Reports of Judgments, Advisory Opinions and Orders*, 1947– .
Int. Law Com.	International Law Commission of the United Nations.
J.C.L.	*Journal of Comparative Legislation.*
J.D.I.	*Journal de droit international privé,* sometimes cited as *Clunet.*
K.B.	King's Bench (Great Britain), 1901–1952.
LN	League of Nations.
L.T.R.	*Law Time Reports* (Great Britain), 1859–1947.
Misc.	New York Miscellaneous Reports, 1892– .
N.Y.	New York State Reports.
N.Y.S.	New York Supplement Reporter, 1888– .
Nielsen's Report	*American and British Claims Arbitration,* under Agreement of August 18, 1910, Report of Fred K. Nielsen, 1926.
P.C.I.J.	Permanent Court of International Justice.

P.C.I.J., Ser. A	Judgments and Orders, 1922–1930.
P.C.I.J., Ser. A/B	Judgments, Orders, and Advisory Opinions, 1931–1940.
P.C.I.J., Ser. B	Advisory Opinions, 1922–1930.
Peters	United States Supreme Court Reports, 1828–1842.
Probate	Probate, Divorce, and Admiralty Division, British High Court of Justice.
Q.B.	Queen's Bench (Great Britain), 1891–1901, 1952– .
Q.B.D.	Queen's Bench Division (Great Britain), 1875–1890.
Res.	Resolution.
R.G.D.I.P.	*Revue générale de droit international public.*
R.I.A.A.	United Nations, *Reports of International Arbitral Awards,* 1948– .
S/	Symbol of UN Security Council documents.
SC	Security Council of the United Nations.
S.D.N.Y.	United States District Court for the Southern District of New York. Other district courts are abbreviated in the same manner.
Spinks	Spinks' *Ecclesiastical and Admiralty Reports* (Great Britain), 1853–1855.
Spinks' *Prize Cases*	Spinks' *Prize Cases* (Great Britain), 1854–1856.
Stat.	United States *Statutes-at-Large.*
Supp.	Supplement.
T/	Symbol of UN Trusteeship Council documents.
TC	Trusteeship Council of the United Nations.
T.L.R.	*Times Law Reports* (Great Britain), 1884–1952.
UN	United Nations.
U.S.	United States Supreme Court Reports, 1875– (reports before 1875 cited by name of reporter).
W.L.R.	*Weekly Law Reports* (Great Britain), 1953– .
W. Robinson	W. Robinson's Admiralty Reports (Great Britain), 1838–1952.
Wallace	United States Supreme Court Reports, 1863–1874.
Wheaton	United States Supreme Court Reports, 1816–1827.

CHAPTER 1

THE FOUNDATIONS OF INTERNATIONAL LAW

I. *THE NATURE AND SCOPE OF INTERNATIONAL LAW* [1]

§1. THE ESSENCE OF INTERNATIONAL LAW

International law is a body of principles and rules commonly observed by the members of the international community in their dealings with one another and with their nationals.[2] It is international law which provides "a legal basis for the orderly management of international relations." [3] The term 'law of nations,' a translation of '*droit des gens,*'

1. General texts on this subject: O'Connell, I, pp. 1–8,37–88; Oppenheim, I, §§1–10,20–25,37b–62; Jessup, Ch. I; Fenwick, *Principles,* Chs. I–III,V; Brierly, Ch. I, §§3–4; II, §§5–8; Hyde, I, §§1–2b; Friedmann, Chs. 7,11; Moore, *Digest,* I, §§1–2; Hackworth, *Digest,* I, §§1,7–8; Whiteman, *Digest,* I, §§1,11–12; Schwarzenberger, I, Chs. 1–2; Starke, Chs. 1,4; Hershey, Chs. I, III–V; Kelsen, Ch. V; Kaplan & Katzenbach, Chs. 1–3; Gould, Chs. 1–4; Svarlien, Chs. 3,5; Whitaker, Chs. 1–2; von Glahn, Chs. 1,3–4; Jacobini, pp. 1–3,10–21,30–34; Schuschnigg, Chs. 1–2,4; Soviet *Text,* Ch. I, §§1,3–6,8; Ch. II; Lawrence, §§1–13,50–57; Le Fur, §§1–123n; Fauchille, I, §§5–31,40–44,71–86; Hall, pp. 5–16; Korowicz, Ch. I.

2 L. Oppenheim classifies international law into universal, general, and particular, on the basis of scope of application. *International Law,* 8th ed., I, p. 5. See also the observations made by Myres S. McDougal and Associates in their *Studies in World Public Order* on the traditional concept of a universal law and the existence of regional diversities (New Haven, 1960), pp. 4–5.

3 Jessup, p. 16. For the meaning of international relations, see Quincy Wright, *The Study of International Relations* (New York, 1955), Ch. I; also

is often used interchangeably with 'international law.' Some writers prefer the term 'international public law' to emphasize the clear distinction from 'international private law' or 'conflict of laws.' One distinguished jurist suggests the term 'transnational law,' including "all law which regulates actions or events that transcend national frontiers." [4] On the whole, the term international law is still commonly used. Even though there are almost as many definitions of international law as there are textbook writers, differences lie chiefly in phraseology rather than in substance.[5]

The gaining of independence by formerly dependent territories in recent decades has had a profound impact on world affairs. The membership of international society has expanded from a comparatively small region, generally limited in historical community to Western Christianity. Now a practically universal community of nations exists.[6] These new states have associated themselves with various international and regional organizations on the basis of sovereign equality, with special emphasis on human rights and fundamental freedoms, as well as anti-colonialism.[7] Certain traditional concepts as previously conceived by Western states for the furtherance of their interests are not likely to be popular with the Communist and the emergent nations. Particularly distasteful to them are tags like superior and inferior races, or civilized and half-civilized states,[8] vestiges of imperialistic or colonial arrogance.

Stanley H. Hoffmann, *Contemporary Theory in International Relations* (Englewood Cliffs, N.J., 1960), pp. 4–6. In his treatise, *The Study of International Law* (New York, 1966), Percy E. Corbett holds that international law must not lose its identity in the broader field of international relations. For a more comprehensive discussion, reference may be made to H. Lauterpacht, *The Function of Law in the International Community* (Oxford, 1933); William D. Coplin, *The Functions of International Law: An Introduction to the Role of International Law in the Contemporary World* (Chicago, 1966).

[4] Philip C. Jessup, *Transnational Law* (New Haven, 1956), p. 2.

[5] With respect to certain new methodologies for the study of international law, including policy science, functionalism, systems theory, and phenomenological perspectives, see Richard A. Falk, "New Approaches to the Study of International Law," 61 *Am. Jour. Int. Law* (1967), pp. 487–495. See also Georg Schwarzenberger, *The Inductive Approach to International Law* (London, 1965).

[6] See C. Wilfred Jenks, *The Common Law of Mankind* (London, 1958), pp. 2–3.

[7] *Cf.* Charles De Visscher, *Theory and Reality in Public International Law* (English translation by P. E. Corbett, Princeton, 1957), pp. 92–93.

[8] See, for instance, J. Lorimer, *The Institutes of the Law of Nations* (London, 1883–1884, 2 vols.), I, pp. 157–158, 162; Lawrence, pp. 3–4, 82–83; Hershey, p. 201.

It is only natural that nations with different historical backgrounds and political systems are not favorably disposed toward norms developed chiefly by the capitalist countries of the West. Meanwhile, they have to adhere to the established order for the purpose of entering into diplomatic and economic relations with the other members of the international community. The emergent nations of Asia and Africa have made exceptions to certain norms, but in general have accepted the prevailing rules of international law. Immediately after the October Revolution, the Soviet Union found it advantageous to rely on international law against foreign intervention and also in other dealings useful to the Communist cause.[9] Other socialist countries have, more or less, shared the pragmatic approach of the Soviet Union. To the Marxists, international law, like any other law, is an instrument for the execution of national policies.[10]

Attempts have been made by some writers in Communist China to suggest two systems of international law: socialist international law applying to socialist countries and another, to bourgeois countries. But this view has not been shared by other Chinese jurists, who hold that current international law reflects the transition from capitalism to socialism.[11] What, then, are the essential principles of international law acceptable to Communist China? Peking has endorsed, at least in theory, the five principles embodied in the Sino-Indian Agreement of April 29, 1954. These principles are: (1) respect for territorial integrity and sovereignty, (2) non-aggression, (3) non-interference in domestic affairs, (4) equality among nations, and (5) mutual benefit and peaceful coexistence.[12] According to normal interpretation, these principles are

[9] See J. N. Hazard, *Law and Social Change in the USSR* (Toronto, 1953), p. 275.

[10] Thus, diversified interpretations of certain rules of international law in the interest of national expediency have weakened the rule of law in the international community. In their study, "The Identification and Appraisal of Diverse Systems of Public Order," Myres S. McDougal and Harold D. Lasswell concluded that "obviously today it is more accurate to speak of international *laws* or multi-national law than of international *law*." 53 *Am. Jour. Int. Law* (1959), p. 10.

[11] See Hungdah Chiu, "Communist China's Attitude toward International Law," 60 *ibid.* (1966), pp. 252–256; also *Soviet Yearbook of International Law,* 1958, p. 544; Jerome A. Cohen, "Chinese Communist Attitudes toward International Law—and Our Own," a paper read at the 61st Annual Meeting of the American Society of International Law on April 28, 1967, to be published in its 1967 *Proceedings.*

[12] See *People's China,* July 16, 1954 (Supp.); Tang Tsou, "Mao Tsetung and Peaceful Coexistence," in George A. Lanyi and Wilson C. McWilliams (eds.), *Crisis and Continuity in World Politics* (New York, 1966), pp. 661–672.

basically in conformity with the rules of international law prevailing in Western countries. However, Communist China's policy differs in content and scope from the Soviet policy of peaceful coexistence with the West.[13] This attitude is largely due to China's frustrated relationship with other major powers ever since the middle of the nineteenth century.[14]

There is, as yet, no consensus of opinion among the Communist jurists on the nature and functions of international law, but the definition given in the Soviet text of *International Law* serves as the representative point of view of the socialist countries:

> International law can be defined as the aggregate of rules governing relations between States in the process of their conflict and cooperation, designed to safeguard their peaceful coexistence, expressing the will of the ruling classes of these States and defended in case of need by coercion applied by States individually or collectively.[15]

This Soviet definition of international law may be disagreeable in phraseology, but is not essentially different from what has been practiced in the Western world.[16] In the opinion of the Soviet jurists, "the purpose of present-day international law is to promote peaceful coexistence and cooperation between all states regardless of their social systems." [17] This one-system theory of international law makes it possible to move gradually from diversity to universality.[18] It has, however, been seriously questioned whether the principle of coexistence can really take the place of the policy of "world revolution," the ultimate goal of Marxism.[19]

[13] *Cf.* the meaning of peaceful coexistence as defined in the 1961 Program of the Russian Communist party. See J. F. Triska (ed.), *Soviet Communism: Programs and Rules* (San Francisco, 1962), pp. 65–66; Nikita S. Khrushchev, "On Peaceful Coexistence," 38 *Foreign Affairs* (1959), pp. 1–18.

[14] See William L. Tung, *The Political Institutions of Modern China* (The Hague, 1964), pp. 20–21.

[15] Soviet *Text*, p. 7.

[16] *Cf.* Edward McWhinney, "Peaceful Coexistence and Soviet-Western International Law," 56 *Am. Jour. Int. Law* (1962), pp. 951–970.

[17] Soviet *Text*, p. 11. For further details, see Grigory I. Tunkin, *Coexistence and International Law* (*Recueil*, The Hague, 1958).

[18] According to Stephen M. Schwebel, formerly Assistant Legal Adviser of the Department of State, the Russian contribution to international law is exaggerated by the Soviet jurists. See his "The United Nations and the Challenge of a Changing International Law," *Proceedings* of Am. Society of Int. Law, 1963, pp. 83–89.

[19] See Warren Lerner, "The Historical Origins of the Soviet Doctrine of Peaceful Coexistence," 29 *Law and Contemporary Problems* (Autumn

National attitudes toward international law should not be solely guided by foreign policy,[20] even though particular phases of international law might be developed among certain states or regions due to their historical background and divergent practices. Like municipal law, international law is not static, but is flexible enough to be duly adjusted to the changing structure of the international community.[21] Through constant development and codification, especially since the beginning of the twentieth century, international law has made slow but steady progress to meet the demands of the family of nations.

§2. DISTINCTION FROM OTHER RELATED SUBJECTS

International private law Different from international law or international public law, international private law is really part of the municipal law of each state, because it deals with private rights of individuals concerning domicile, marriage, and the validity of contracts or wills. However, many international commercial transactions today involving state organs and international agencies can no longer be considered as private in nature and may fall appropriately within the field of international public law.[22] Rules and regulations of less importance or of a technical nature, such as those concerning sanitation, transportation, and communications, are generally treated under the subject of 'international administrative law,' which may be called a branch of international law.[23]

International comity Another distinction should be made between international comity and international law.[24] International com-

---

1964), pp. 865–870; also Leon Lipson, "Peaceful Coexistence," *ibid.*, pp. 871–881.

[20] There is, however, no question about the impact of policy on law as expounded by Myres S. McDougal and Florentino P. Feliciano in their monumental work, *Law and Minimum World Public Order: The Legal Regulation of International Coercion* (New Haven, 1961).

[21] See Josef Laurenz Kunz, "The Law of Nations, Static and Dynamic," 27 *Am. Jour. Int. Law* (1933), pp. 630–650; Oliver J. Lissitzyn, *International Law Today and Tomorrow* (Dobbs Ferry, N.Y., 1965).

[22] See Oppenheim, I, pp. 6–7.

[23] See Friedmann, pp. 161–162. A full discussion of the subject can be found in C. W. Jenks, *The Proper Law of International Organizations* (London, 1962), Pt. II.

[24] In the *American Banana Co. v. the United Fruit Co.* (1910), the decision of the U.S. Supreme Court was guided by the principle of comity of nations. 213 U.S. 347. In *Hilton v. Guyot* (1895), the same court defined the 'comity of nations' as the "recognition which one nation allows within

ity relates to a voluntary courtesy extended by one member of the international community to another as a matter of reciprocity or convenience; for instance, extradition of ordinary fugitives in the absence of express provisions of treaties. Such an act is not required by the rules of international law, but is motivated by international comity.[25]

Relationship with municipal law It is also important to note the relationship between international law and municipal law, which pertains to national constitutions, statutes, and judicial decisions. In one way or another, modern states have gradually recognized international law as part of the law of the land. This practice of the so-called doctrine of 'incorporation' has been evidenced in both constitutions and decisions of national tribunals.[26] As early as 1764, a British court decided that the law of nations in its full extent was part of the law of England.[27] In deciding the case of *The Charming Betsy* in 1804, Chief Justice Marshall emphasized the importance of construing Congressional acts in conformity with the rules of international law.[28] Justice Gray declared in *Paquete Habana and the Lola* in 1900: "International law is part of our law and must be ascertained and admitted by the

---

its territory to the legislative, executive, or judicial acts of another nation, having due regard both to international duty and convenience, and to the rights of its own citizens or of other persons who are under the protection of its laws." 159 U.S. 113.

[25] The extradition of Horace G. McKinley by the Chinese government to the United States in the absence of an extradition treaty is an example. See the exchange of notes between American Minister Rockhill in Peking and Prince Ch'ing of China on March 12 and 19, 1907. *U.S. For. Rel.*, 1908, pp. 129–130. Of course, a state is not obligated to observe international comity in case of conflict with national interests. See *Collco Dealings Ltd. v. Inland Revenue Commissioners*. Great Britain, House of Lords, 1961. [1962] A.C. 1.

[26] *E.g.*, Art. 1, §8, Par. 10, of the Constitution of the United States; Art. 26 of the Constitution of the French Republic of 1946; Art. 10 of the Constitution of the Italian Republic of 1947; Art. 141 of the Constitution of the Republic of China of 1946; Art. 98, Par. 2, of the Constitution of Japan of 1946. The constitutions of many other countries in Europe and Latin America have also recognized international law as an integral part of their respective municipal laws. The Constitution of the United States empowers Congress to punish offenses against international law or the law of nations. It is clear that the monistic doctrine has gradually taken the place of the dualistic view with respect to the relationship between international law and municipal law. For details, see Oppenheim, I, pp. 37–38.

[27] *Triquet v. Bath*, Great Britain, Court of King's Bench, 1764. 3 Burrow 1478.

[28] 2 Cranch 64.

courts of justice and appropriate jurisdiction as often as questions of right depending upon it are duly presented for their determination." [29] In *West Rand Central Gold Mining Co. v. The King* (1905), Chief Justice Alverstone further clarified the relationship between international law and municipal law in the following words:

> It is quite true that whatever has received the common consent of civilized nations must have received the assent of our country, and that to which we have assented along with other nations in general may properly be called International Law, and as such will be acknowledged and applied by our municipal tribunals when legitimate occasion arises for those tribunals to decide questions to which doctrines of international law may be relevant.[30]

In some exceptional cases, national tribunals have upheld the precedence of statute law over customary international law.[31] Generally, international law is applied by the national courts.[32] Such application is supported to a considerable extent in the writings of prominent jurists.[33] In the view of Soviet publicists, "both the rules of international law and those of domestic origin should have the same binding force for all organs and nationals of the countries concerned." [34] It follows, therefore, that "by promulgating a law clearly contrary to international law, the government concerned commits a violation of inter-

[29] 175 U.S. 677.

[30] Great Britain, King's Bench Division, 1905. [1905] 2 K.B. 391.

[31] For instance, *Mortensen v. Peters,* Scotland, High Court of Judiciary, 1906 (8 Session cases, 5th Ser., 93); *Head Money Cases,* U.S. Supreme Court, 1884 (112 U.S. 580). However, in the first case, the British government acknowledged Parliament's error by remitting the fine. In the other, the agreements in question are not law-making treaties.

[32] See *The Maria,* Great Britain, High Court of Admiralty, 1799, 1 C. Rob. 340.

[33] On the supremacy of international law, see Felice Morgenstern, "Judicial Practice and the Supremacy of International Law," 27 *British Yearbook of International Law* (1950), pp. 42–92. For judicial practices of different states with respect to the relationship between international law and municipal law, *cf.* Quincy Wright, *The Enforcement of International Law through Municipal Law in the United States* (Urbana, 1916); C. M. Picciotto, *The Relation of International Law to the Law of England and of the United States* (London, 1915); Edwin D. Dickinson, "The Law of Nations as Part of the National Law of the United States," 101 *University of Pennsylvania Law Review* (October 1952), pp. 26–56; (April 1953), pp. 792–833; Ruth D. Masters, *International Law in National Courts, a Study of the Enforcement of International Law in German, Swiss, French and Beligian Courts* (New York, 1932).

[34] Soviet *Text,* p. 15.

national law, for which the State concerned is responsible under international law." [35]

There is no evidence to prove that Communist China and other socialist countries hold a position contrary to that commonly accepted on the relationship between international law and municipal law. Due to their resentment against past colonial rule and non-participation in the initial development of international law, the new nations have shown a certain reluctance to accept all the existing rules alien to their historical tradition. They have, however, gradually reconciled themselves to the established system without disregarding their national aspirations.[36]

§3. EARLY DEVELOPMENT AND PRESENT SCOPE

As international law chiefly governs the relations among states, it was not well developed before the emergence of the modern state system in Europe. Rudimentary rules regulating interstate relations may, however, be found in ancient China and other countries in the East.[37] According to Soviet publicists, it was not "the States of the Mediterranean basin," but "China, India, Egypt and other ancient Eastern States which should be considered as the birth-places of International Law." [38] They have pointed out that certain rules of international law could be found "in ancient Chinese documents dating back to 2500 B.C." [39] On the basis of all available sources, international law

[35] *Loc. cit.*

[36] They question some rules of international law adopted by Western states while they were under colonial status. For the impact of international law on national law, see Myres S. McDougal and associates, *Studies in World Public Order* (New Haven, 1960), pp. 157–236.

[37] Records of customary rules of international law as practiced during the Chou dynasty (1122–249 B.C.) may be found in *Tso Chuan* and the *Annals of the Spring and Autumn* by Tso Chiu-ming and Confucius respectively. Reference may also be made to J. Escarra, *La Chine et le droit international* (Paris, 1931). For brief summaries, see Ch'eng Te-hsu, "International Law in Early China," 11 *Chinese Social and Political Science Review* (1927), No. 1, pp. 38–56; No. 2, pp. 251–270; W. A. P. Martin, "Traces of International Law in Ancient China," 14 *International Review* (January 1883), pp. 63–77. However, China did not enter into formal relationship with any Western state until 1689, when the Sino-Russian Treaty of Nerchinsk was concluded for the delimitation of boundaries between the two countries. For details, see Vincent Chen, *Sino-Russian Relations in the Seventeenth Century* (The Hague, 1966), Chs. VIII, IX.

[38] Soviet *Text,* p. 27.

[39] *Ibid.*, p. 28. For the dominant position of the Chinese Empire and its relationship with neighboring states, see J. J. G. Syatouw, *Some Newly Established Asian States and the Development of International Law* (The Hague, 1961), p. 36.

was probably developed simultaneously in both the East and the West of the ancient world.[40]

Published in 1494, the *Consolato del Mare* is perhaps the earliest collection of maritime laws as practiced in the Mediterranean. The Treaties of Westphalia of 1648 are generally regarded as the turning point of European history from the Thirty Years' War to the establishment of the modern state system.[41] International law has since developed rapidly owing to the valuable work of jurists and law-making conferences, and the conclusion of a large number of multilateral instruments with binding effect upon the signatories. These include the rules of neutrality laid down by the League of Armed Neutrality of 1780,[42] the Declaration of Paris of 1856,[43] the Geneva Convention of 1864 for the Amelioration of the Condition of the Wounded in War,[44] and the Hague Conventions of 1899 and 1907.[45]

[40] Reference may be made to Coleman Phillipson, *The International Law and Custom of Ancient Greece* (London, 1911), 2 vols.; Ragner Numelin, *The Beginnings of Diplomacy* (New York, 1950); S. V. Visvanātha Aiyar, *International Law in Ancient India* (London, 1925).

[41] The Treaties of Westphalia were negotiated among the Catholic and Protestant states at Münster and Osnabrück in 1644–1648, by which the legal equality of states was recognized in spite of their religious and other differences.

[42] The League of Armed Neutrality was originally organized by Russia, Denmark, and Sweden against English maritime interference. Prussia, Portugal, Holland, the Kingdom of the Two Sicilies, and the Emperor of the Holy Roman Empire joined later. The League laid down certain rules of war and neutrality, including rights of neutral vessels, restrictions of contraband goods, and conditions for blockade.

[43] The Declaration was adopted by the Congress of Paris after the end of the Crimean War, embodying a number of maritime rules of war and neutrality: (1) privateering is and remains abolished; (2) neutral flag covers enemy's goods, with the exception of contraband of war; (3) neutral goods, with the exception of contraband of war, are not liable to capture under enemy's flag; (4) a blockade, to be binding, must be effective—that is to say, maintained by a force sufficient really to prevent access to the coast of the enemy. See 46 *Br. & For. St. Papers,* p. 136.

[44] The Geneva Convention was concluded as a result of public demand for humanitarian action in wartime. The complete lack of facilities to care for the dead and wounded at the battle of Solférino in 1859 between France and Austria was fully described by a Swiss in his book, *Un Souvenir de Solférino* (Geneva, 1862). Aroused by public opinion, the Swiss government called the Geneva Conference in 1864, which signed the Convention. The International Red Cross was created to conduct various activities provided for in the Convention. For the text of the Convention, see *Supplement* to *Am. Jour. Int. Law* (1907), pp. 90–95.

[45] Called by Russia, the two Hague Peace Conferences were epoch-

International and regional organizations have been established and treaties and agreements among states have been concluded with greater frequency in the twentieth century. Multilateral conventions and resolutions of the General Assembly of the United Nations are regarded by all nations as effective means of developing international law. In addition to written agreements, there exist customary rules developed through centuries of general acceptance and practice.[46] Modern international law has extended from the formal structure of state relationship to active cooperation among nations for the common welfare of mankind, and from a limited number of European states to a world-wide community of developed and developing nations. Thus, international law today serves not only to preserve the order and stability of the world but also to meet the changing concepts and needs of mankind as a whole.

In recent decades, the scope of international law has been constantly expanding to cover non-political matters, especially in economic, social, labor, educational, legal, and technical fields.[47] Through treaties and conventions, many subjects formerly within the exclusive jurisdiction of domestic legislation are now regulated by rules of international law. With the exception of certain matters vitally important to national interests and not yet ripe for common agreement, states with divergent ideologies, economic levels of achievement, and religious backgrounds are working together through various intergovernmental and non-governmental organs to formulate rules and regulations for mutual

---

making not only in the large number of participating states but also in the adoption of important conventions, declarations, recommendations, and wishes. Among these are the Convention for the Pacific Settlement of International Disputes and several conventions and declarations respecting rules of land and maritime warfare. Establishment of the Permanent Court of Arbitration was decided by the First Hague Conference in 1899. For details, see A. P. Higgins, *The Hague Peace Conferences and Other International Conferences concerning the Laws and Usages of War* (Cambridge, England, 1909); J. B. Scott, *The Reports to the Hague Conferences of 1899 and 1907* (Oxford, 1917); Joseph H. Choate, *The Two Hague Conferences* (Princeton, 1913).

[46] Most treatises on international law published before World War II were based on the Western state system, of which the policy of balance of power was an essential element. See Quincy Wright, *A Study of War* (Chicago, 1942), II, pp. 743 ff. For further details of the historical development of international law, see Brierly, pp. 1–93; Hershey, Chs. III–V; and Arthur Nussbaum, *A Concise History of the Law of Nations*, rev. ed. (New York, 1954).

[47] *Cf.* C. W. Jenks, "The Scope of International Law," 31 *British Yearbook of International Law* (1954), pp. 1–48.

observance.[48] It is evident that, due to the development of international law and organization, nations are gradually becoming united in an otherwise divided world, even though the public may be less aware of such accomplishments than of discord in the international community.

II. *SOURCES AND EVIDENCES OF INTERNATIONAL LAW* [49]

§4. CUSTOM AND TREATIES AS PRIMARY SOURCES

There are two primary sources of international law: (1) custom and (2) treaties. Other sources are considered as subsidiary sources or only as evidences where rules of international law are manifested. The Statute of the International Court of Justice lists the following as sources of law to be applied by the Court in deciding cases: (1) international conventions, whether general or particular, establishing rules expressly recognized by the contesting states; (2) international custom, as evidence of a general practice accepted as law; (3) general principles of law recognized by states; (4) judicial decisions and the teachings of the most highly qualified publicists of the various nations, as subsidiary means for the determination of rules of law. It is understood that judicial decisions have no binding force except between the parties and for the particular case. According to the Statute, the Court may also decide a case *ex aequo et bono* if the parties agree to it.[50]

Custom and usage Before the emergence of enacted laws, the

[48] For instance, the General Assembly unanimously adopted a resolution on December 17, 1966, establishing a United Nations Commission on International Trade Law for the progressive harmonization and unification of the law of international trade. For its text, see Office of Public Information of the United Nations, *Resolutions of Legal Interest Adopted by the General Assembly at Twenty-first Session, 20 September–20 December 1966,* pp. 137–142, GA res. 2205 (XXI).

[49] General texts on this subject: O'Connell, I, pp. 8–36; Oppenheim, I, §§11–19c, 55–57; Fenwick, *Principles,* pp. 62–66, 84–98; Brierly, Ch. II, §4; Hyde, I, §3; Friedmann, Chs. 10–12; Hackworth, *Digest,* I, §§3–6; Whiteman, *Digest,* I, §§4–10; Schwarzenberger, I, Ch. 2(I); Starke, Ch. 2; Hershey, Ch. II; Kelsen, Ch. IV(A); Kaplan & Katzenbach, Ch. 9; Gould, Ch. 5; Whitaker, Ch. 3; Von Glahn, Ch. 2; Jacobini, pp. 3–10, 21–30; Soviet *Text,* Ch. I, §2; Schuschnigg, Ch. 3.

[50] For the provisions of the Statute on the sources, see Arts. 38, 59. For a comparison of sources between international law and private law, see H. Lauterpacht, *Private Law Sources and Analogies of International Law* (London, 1927), pp. 1–9.

conduct of communities was guided by customs and usages.[51] While these two terms are often used together, there is some distinction. Before attaining the status of a custom, a usage has to go through a sufficient period of time to indicate that it has received the common sanction of the members of the family of nations. This principle is well illustrated in *The Paquete Habana and the Lola* (1900).[52] Tracing an ancient usage concerning the exemption of coastal fishing vessels together with their cargo and crew from capture as prize of war, the United States Supreme Court concluded that through centuries of practice by the states such usage had ripened into a custom worthy of recognition as a rule of international law. Custom as an important source of international law is generally recognized by jurists in both East and West.[53]

Natural justice and morality Prior to and in the absence of customs and treaties, reason, natural justice,[54] and morality have been considered, at least in principle, as the guiding ideas in international relations.[55] However, the assent of states to such ideas is necessary in

[51] For a full discussion of the subject, see John Hosack, *On the Rise and Growth of the Law of Nations, as Established by the General Usage and by Treaties, from the Earliest Time to the Treaty of Utrecht* (London, 1882). Many provisions of international treaties are declaratory of long-established usages and customs recognized by the states as rules of international law. See Quincy Wright, "Custom as a Basis for International Law in the Postwar World," 2 *Texas International Law Forum* (Summer 1966), No. 2; Oliver J. Lissitzyn, *International Law Today and Tomorrow* (Dobbs Ferry, N.Y., 1965), pp. 34–37.

[52] 175 U.S. 677.

[53] A monograph entitled *Custom in Present International Law* (Warsaw, 1964) was recently published by a Polish scholar, Karol Wolfke, whose approach to the subject is not essentially different from that of Western jurists. In tracing the foundation of Hans Kelsen's legal theory, Quincy Wright observed: "In his earlier works he based international law on the *grund norm—pacta sunt servanda*—but, unsatisfied with such a natural law foundation for a system of positive law, in his later works [*e.g., Principles of International Law,* 1952 ed.] he based international law on the fact that nations have accepted custom as a source of positive law, and custom has established the constitution of the society of nations requiring observance of treaties, mutual respect for territory, and other rules of order." Wright, "Toward a Universal Law for Mankind," 63 *Columbia Law Review* (March 1963), p. 439.

[54] For the relationship of justice to law and politics, see Hans Kelsen, *What Is Justice? Justice, Law and Politics in the Mirror of Science* (Berkeley, 1957).

[55] This principle was emphasized in *La Jeune Eugenie,* U.S. Circuit Court, First Circuit, 1822. 2 Mason 409.

order to create a binding effect.[56] With the emergence of Communist countries, it is more difficult to expect a uniform standard of ethics in international dealings. Even though international expediency is still an important factor in world politics today,[57] morality and legal order should eventually prevail in the international community. Exceptions in practice notwithstanding, the Asian community in general is noticeably characterized by a moralistic approach to law, domestically or internationally.

International treaties and acts of international conferences and organizations While custom reflects the tacit consent of the community of nations, treaties demonstrate the express agreement of contracting parties. Modern states, especially the Soviet Union and many newly independent countries whose participation in the development of customary international law is of comparatively recent origin, have given increasing importance to treaties.[58] Undoubtedly treaties constitute the most important source of international law. Unlike bilateral treaties, many multilateral instruments have law-making effect. Under this category are, for example, the Hague Conventions of 1899 and of 1907,[59] the Covenant of the League of Nations, and the Charter of the United Nations. International congresses or conferences have played an important role in the development of international law, especially their adoption of legally binding resolutions and conclusions of law-making treaties.[60] So have the decisions of international and regional organizations.[61]

[56] See *The Antelope*, U.S. Supreme Court, 1825. 10 Wheaton 66.

[57] For further discussion on international morality, see Hans J. Morgenthau, *Politics among Nations*, 3rd ed. (New York, 1960), Chs. 15–16.

[58] For the Soviet concept of treaties as a principal source of international order, see J. F. Triska and R. M. Slusser, *The Theory, Law, and Policy of Soviet Treaties* (Stanford, 1962), Ch. 1. While recognizing the importance of international custom as "a primary and the most important means of creating norms of international law" for the nineteenth century, the majority of Soviet authors consider treaties as the principal source of international law. *Ibid.*, p. 420, note 80. Likewise, the People's Republic of China lays a strong emphasis on treaties. See *infra*, Ch. 11, note 7.

[59] For the shortcomings of the Hague Conventions, see Fenwick, *Principles*, p. 95.

[60] Among these are the Congress of Vienna of 1814–1815, the two Hague Peace Conferences of 1899 and 1907, the Paris Peace Conference of 1919, and the United Nations Conference on International Organization, San Francisco, 1945.

[61] For instance, many resolutions of the General Assembly of the United Nations are not necessarily declaratory of existing rules of international law but have far-reaching consequences to its future development.

When states adopt certain uniform stipulations regulating their relations either through their own legislation or by the conclusion of or accession to a multilateral instrument, recognition is given to a new rule of international law of which the courts are bound to take judicial notice. The decision of the United States Supreme Court in the case of *The Scotia* in 1872 was guided by this principle.[62] The Court ruled that the universal adoption of the new maritime regulations by the principal maritime nations of the world manifested a general recognition of their status as a new rule in that respect.

Many rules of international law incorporated in treaties are evolved from traditional customs.[63] While the Eastern European countries and the emergent nations in Asia and Africa have more or less shared the Soviet view of accepting decisions of international organizations as evidences or, in some cases, as sources of international law, Communist China takes a different attitude. Here again, the divergence is perhaps influenced by international reality, because Peking does not have a seat in the United Nations.[64]

§5. SUBSIDIARY SOURCES AND EVIDENCES

General principles of law recognized by states In addition to custom and treaties as sources of international law, the Statute of the International Court of Justice includes general principles of law recognized by states.[65] This was also provided in the Statute of the Permanent Court of International Justice, which applied general principles of law in *Mavrommatis Palestine Concessions* in 1924,[66] *Chorzów Factory Case* in 1928,[67] and *Diversion of Water from the Meuse* in 1937.[68] Corollaries of general principles of law have also been referred to in *Eastern Extension, Australasia and China Telegraph Co.*, U.S.-Great Britain, Claims Arbitration, in 1923.[69] Many states have attempted to invoke general principles of law to change a status quo deemed inequitable if not illegal.[70] Equity as a general principle of law has been

[62] 14 Wallace 170.

[63] For further discussion of the law of treaties, see *infra*, Ch. 11.

[64] See Hungdah Chiu, *op. cit.*, pp. 257–259; Byron S. Weng, "Communist China's Changing Attitude toward the United Nations," 20 *Int.* Organization (1966), pp. 677–704. However, references to the United Nations Charter can be found in the Sino-Afghanistan Treaty of 1960 and some early treaties concluded between Communist China and other states.

[65] Art. 38(1c).

[66] P.C.I.J. (1924), Ser. A, No. 2.

[67] P.C.I.J. (1928), Ser. A, No. 17.

[68] P.C.I.J. (1937), Ser. A/B, No. 70.

[69] Nielsen's Report, 73.

[70] On ideologies of the status quo, see Hans J. Morgenthau, *op. cit.*, pp. 90–91.

emphasized by the international tribunals.[71] In the view of Soviet publicists, "principles reflected neither in international treaties nor in international custom cannot be considered 'general principles'." [72] In any event, general principles of law will be applied only when primary sources are not sufficient to provide a basis for a court decision.[73]

Judicial decisions Subsidiary means for the determination of rules of international law include decisions of international and national tribunals. The judgments or awards of the Permanent Court of Arbitration,[74] the Permanent Court of International Justice, the International Court of Justice, and the Mixed Claims Commissions [75] certainly are evidence of the prevailing rules of international law and become a guide for future cases.[76] The advisory opinions delivered by the two world courts carry considerable weight in interpreting and developing international law.[77] The decisions of national courts show how international law is understood in a particular country and will be received, not as authority, but with respect.[78]

[71] *Diversion of Water from Meuse* just cited is one of the instances. See also *Cayuga Indians Claims,* U.S.-Great Britain Arbitration, 1926. Nielsen's Report, 203, 307.

[72] V. M. Koretsky, *General Principles of International Law* (Kiev, 1957), quoted from Soviet *Text,* p. 12.

[73] For a thorough discussion of the general principles of law, refer to Chen Bin, *General Principles of Law as Applied by International Courts and Tribunals* (London, 1953).

[74] For instance, *Pious Fund Arbitration,* U.S. v. Mexico, 1902 (Scott, Hague Court Reports, p. 3); *North Atlantic Coast Fisheries Case,* U.S. v. Great Britain (Scott, *ibid.,* p. 146).

[75] Among others, two arbitration cases between the United States and Great Britain definitely contributed to the development of international law: *Alabama Claims* in 1872 (Malloy, *Treaties,* I, p. 717); and *Bering Sea Fisheries Case* in 1893 (*ibid.,* I, p. 751).

[76] As stated before, Art. 59 of the Statute of the International Court of Justice stipulates that decisions of the Court have no binding force except between the contesting parties and in respect of the particular case. H. Lauterpacht, *The Development of International Law by the International Court* (New York, 1958), discusses most comprehensively the various phases of the subject. It is a revised and enlarged edition of his previous work, *The Development of International Law by the Permanent Court of International Justice* (London, 1934).

[77] For further details of the jurisdiction of the court, see *infra,* §190.

[78] This opinion was delivered by Chief Justice Marshall in 1815 in *Thirty Hogheads of Sugar v. Boyle.* 9 Cranch 191. Further references may be made to Ruth Masters, *International Law and National Courts* (New York, 1932); Richard A. Falk, *The Role of Domestic Courts in International*

Writings of international lawyers Due to the impartiality of the most highly qualified publicists, their writings are well respected and regarded as subsidiary means for the determination of rules of international law by the International Court of Justice.[79] The authority of their opinions has long been recognized by national courts. In the *Paquete Habana* case, Justice Gray stated in 1900: "Where there is no treaty, and no controlling executive or legislative act or judicial decision, resort must be had to the customs and usages of civilized nations; and, as evidence of these, to the works of jurists and commentators who, by years of labor, research, and experience, have made themselves peculiarly well acquainted with the subjects of which they treat." [80] However, he also cautioned that "such works are resorted to by judicial tribunals, not for the speculations of their authors concerning what the law ought to be, but for the trustworthy evidence of what the law really is." [81] In *West Rand Central Gold Mining Co. v. The King*, the British court made practically the same comment in 1905.[82]

Opinions of statesmen and national laws Statements made by government leaders are usually taken into careful consideration to ascertain their attitudes toward the interpretation and application of international law. In the *Legal Status of Eastern Greenland*,[83] the Permanent Court of International Justice decided in 1933 that a declaration by the Foreign Minister of Norway concerning the recognition of Danish sovereignty over Eastern Greenland was binding upon Norway. Because of their important positions and official capacity, statesmen may not only interpret but also affect the existing rules of international law by making declarations or other communications on matters within their competence. National laws, regulations, and decrees sometimes have profound impact on the development of international law. The

---

Legal Order (Syracuse, 1964); Charles Pergler, *Judicial Interpretation of International Law in the United States* (New York, 1928); and D. R. Deener, *The United States Attorneys General and International Law* (The Hague, 1957). Caution must be exercised not to overemphasize judicial opinions, which are, after all, only *obiter dicta*.

[79] Art. 38(1d) of the Statute. [80] 175 U.S. 677.

[81] This view was shared by the report of the Subcommittee of the Committee of Experts for the Progressive Codification of International Law of the League of Nations. C.196.M.70.1927.V. The importance of the teachings of publicists is further evidenced in the decision of the British Judicial Committee of the Privy Council in *In re Piracy Jure Gentium*, 1934. [1934] A.C. 586.

[82] [1905] 2 K.B. 391. [83] P.C.I.J. (1933), Ser. A/B, No. 53.

three neutrality acts of the United States (1935–1937), the Lend Lease Act of March 11, 1941, and President Truman's proclamation of 1945 concerning the continental shelf are conspicuous examples. But, however important these subsidiary means may be for the determination of rules, the primary sources of international law are still custom and treaties.[84]

§6. TRADITIONAL SCHOOLS OF INTERNATIONAL LAW

Writers on international law are generally classified into three schools in accordance with their relative emphasis on its divergent bases and sources. The Naturalists consider natural law as the sole basis of international law, with Samuel Pufendorf (1632–1694) as their leader.[85] On the other hand, the Positivists uphold the importance of positive law as an outcome of custom and treaties. This school was led by Richard Zouche (1590–1660) and expounded by Cornelius van Bynkershoek (1673–1743).[86] According to the Positivists, natural law is vague and ill defined.[87] Midway between the two schools are the Grotians, who draw from both natural and positive laws as sources. Among the important followers of Hugo Grotius (1583–1645) are Christian Wolff (1679–1754) and Emerich de Vattel (1714–1767).[88] Grotius published his famous work *De Jure Belli ac Pacis* in 1625, during the Thirty Years' War. He advocated humanitarian principles and emphasized the distinction between just and unjust wars. There are a number of distinguished forerunners of Grotius, including Vitoria (1480–1546),

[84] For a more exhaustive discussion of the sources of international law, *cf.* G. A. Finch, *The Sources of Modern International Law* (Washington, D.C., 1937).

[85] Professor of the Law of Nature and Nations at Heidelberg University, Pufendorf denied the existence of positive law. For the influence of the doctrine of the law of nature, see Brierly, pp. 16–25.

[86] Professor of Civil Law at Oxford, Zouche was really the founder of the Positivist school, whose cause was further elaborated by the Dutch jurist van Bynkershoek and the German philosopher Johann Jakob Moser (1701–1785).

[87] Hans Kelsen led the so-called Neopositivist school with an attempt to make a clear distinction between natural and positive laws as shown in his book *Principles of International Law* (New York, 1952).

[88] Wolff was a German philosopher and Professor of the Law of Nature and Nations at the University of Halle. Advocating national independence and equality of states, Vattel popularized international law more than Grotius did.

Ayala (1548–1584), Suarez (1548–1617), and Gentilis (1552–1608).[89] Professor of Civil Law at Oxford University, Gentilis published *De Jure Belli* in 1598; it exercised an important influence on Grotius. But the most popular book during the formative period of international law in the West was probably Vattel's *Le droit des gens, ou principes de la loi naturelle appliqués à la conduite et aux affaires des nations et des souverains,* which went through numerous editions after 1758.[90]

The divergent emphases of these various schools of international law only reflect the trend of prevailing circumstances at the time. Modern practice of states tends to lay increasing stress on custom and treaties based upon tacit or express consent. Natural law has made historical contributions, but does not meet the changing structure of the twentieth century for development toward a really universal international law.[91]

III. *THE UNIVERSALITY AND SANCTIONS OF INTERNATIONAL LAW* [92]

§7. INTERNATIONAL LAW AS TRUE LAW

Unlike municipal law, international law is neither enacted through a law-making body nor enforced by a sovereign authority. In the light of John Austin's arbitrary definition of law, the question has been raised whether international law can be considered as true law.[93] The answer is in the affirmative. In every state, customary law has always emerged earlier than written law and becomes a part of the law of the

[89] While Vitoria and Suárez also deduced international law from natural law, Ayala and Gentilis drew mainly from positive sources.

[90] For a description of early international lawyers and their writings, see Oppenheim, I, pp. 79–114. A biographical sketch of the important writers can be found in Whitaker, *Politics and Power: A Text in International Law* (New York, 1964).

[91] See Quincy Wright, *Contemporary International Law: A Balance Sheet* (New York, 1961), p. 7. In his address to the Indian Society of International Law on August 29, 1959, Jawaharlal Nehru emphasized the necessary evolution of natural law with changing technologies. 1 *Indian Journal of International Law* (1960), pp. 5, 8.

[92] General texts on this subject: Oppenheim, I, §§26–29d; Hyde, I, §§4–5a; Friedmann, Chs. 8, 18–20; Hackworth, *Digest,* I, §2; Whiteman, *Digest,* I, §3; Kelsen, Ch. I, B; Von Glahn, Ch. 5.

[93] In his *Lectures on Jurisprudence,* Campbell's 5th ed. (1911), John Austin expounded his conception of true law, which was followed by several others. For a list of writers for and against the Austinian view of law, see Hershey, pp. 18–20.

land. The basis of all law is common consent, which may be expressed in written form or tacitly accepted in unwritten form through different political processes. The increasing number of multilateral treaties and the universal application of customary rules manifest the willingness of members of the international community to accept international law as the law governing their relations with one another.[94]

After examining the legal basis and powers of the British Parliament, one eminent publicist pointed out that "all statute or written law is based on unwritten law in so far as the power of Parliament to make statute law is given to Parliament by unwritten law." [95] With respect to the law-making body, it seems that the General Assembly of the United Nations is both a political and semi-legislative organ. Although its resolutions are not legally binding, they are more often than not observed by the members of the organization, and may contribute to the development of new rules of international law. Many international conferences attended by representatives from almost all the states are, in effect, law-making bodies; [96] they have indeed adopted numerous treaties and conventions binding upon the signatories. The distinction between such conferences and the national legislature of a state is that they are not permanently established but convened for particular purposes. The international community also provides means for enforcement of international law and sanctions against violations, even though the procedures are different from those of municipal law.[97]

Necessity for the maintenance of public order in the community of nations creates international law, which has been constantly developing so as to adapt to changing circumstances.[98] Research on interna-

[94] In this respect, it is well to refer to J. L. Brierly's statement: "If, as Sir Frederick Pollock writes, and as probably most competent jurists would today agree, the only essential conditions for the existence of law are the existence of a political community, and the recognition by its members of settled rules binding upon them in that capacity, international law seems on the whole to satisfy these conditions." Brierly, p. 71.

[95] Oppenheim, I, pp. 9–10.

[96] Examples are The Hague Peace Conferences of 1899 and 1907, the San Francisco Conference of 1945 for the adoption of the Charter of the United Nations, the Geneva Conference on the Law of the Sea in 1958, and the Vienna Conferences of 1961 and 1963 for the adoption of the Conventions on Diplomatic and Consular Relations respectively.

[97] See *infra,* Ch. 1, §9; Ch. 13.

[98] For the views of McDougal and Lasswell on the appraisal of diverse systems of public order, see McDougal and associates, *Studies in World Public Order* (New Haven, 1960), Ch. I. See also Lasswell's remark on the changeability of political doctrines in his introduction to McDougal and Florentino P. Feliciano, *Law and Minimum World Public Order* (New Haven, 1961).

tional law is by no means limited to Europe and the Western Hemisphere, but is conducted in other countries as well. The trend toward universal acceptance of international law is evidenced not only in multilateral and bilateral treaties but also in its incorporation in the municipal law of many countries. In the Soviet Union, emphasis on research in international law is demonstrated in the formation of a Soviet Association of International Law and the publication of a yearbook and a standard textbook of international law. Scholars in India and many other states have also done extensive research. The enthusiastic support given by the members of the United Nations to a resolution adopted by the General Assembly on December 18, 1962, for the promotion of study and teaching of international law includes that given by the new nations.[99] All these cannot be interpreted in any other way than as general recognition of international law as true law.

Divergent opinions on particular phases of international law by the socialist and emergent nations do not affect the validity of international law. In deciding cases on the basis of the same statutes, municipal tribunals of different levels may deliver conflicting judgments; even in the highest courts of states, there are dissenting opinions. Yet the validity of the statutes so invoked is not denied because of diverse interpretations. The same conclusion should be drawn with respect to international law. The wholehearted support of the newly independent states for further study and development of international law at the United Nations and particularly at the Sixth Committee of the General Assembly is most encouraging. Admittedly international law at this stage is still incomplete. But no law is perfect and the difference is only a matter of degree.

§8. THE UNIVERSALITY OF INTERNATIONAL LAW

There was general apprehension at the time of the Russian Revolution that a state founded on Marxism and world revolution could not possibly follow the principles of international law. It did not, however, take the Soviet Union long to realize the improbability in the foreseeable future of overthrowing the established order of the world. Moscow has since adopted a flexible policy of coexistence to an extent not contradicting its national interests. The Eastern European countries, in like manner, have been getting along with the existing order and rules of international law. Despite hostile statements from time to time, Communist China has thus far been cautious in dealings with other nations, and has generally observed the normal standards of international rela-

[99] GA res. 1816 (XVII).

tions. The Communist states differ from the West in many respects, particularly in their policies toward nationalization and confiscation of properties. Contrary to general public belief, they are not alone in refusing to submit disputes to the International Court of Justice for adjudication.[100] Whatever divergent opinions they may hold toward particular phases of international law, such diversity is still within the general orbit of universality.[101]

The question has been raised whether international law is merely a body of diversified rules based on regional practices, religious beliefs,[102] and political and economic interests. Much has been written on Anglo-Saxon, Continental, and Latin-American concepts of international law.[103] Admittedly different historical backgrounds, national traditions, and interests have inevitably influenced approaches to certain phases of international law, such as the Latin-American inclination to grant political asylum and objection to forcible collection of public

[100] Less than half the states have accepted compulsory jurisdiction of the Court. The United States reservation of domestic jurisdiction under a self-judging condition has made her acceptance practically nugatory.

[101] See Georg Schwarzenberger, "The Impact of the East-West Rift on International Law," 36 *Grotius Society* (1950), pp. 229–269; also Ann van Wynen Thomas, *Communism versus International Law* (Dallas, 1953); Bernard A. Romundo, *The (Soviet) Socialist Theory of International Law* (Washington, D.C., 1964). For the Soviet view on international law, reference may be made to T. A. Taracouzio, *The Soviet Union and International Law* (New York, 1935) in addition to the Soviet *Text.*

[102] See works on the relationship between different religions and international law, including John Eppstein, *The Catholic Tradition of the Law of Nations* (Washington, D.C., 1935); M. Khadduri, *War and Peace in the Law of Islam,* 2nd ed. (Baltimore, 1955).

[103] In addition to digests and official documents, a number of books are available representing the views of Western countries, including C. C. Hyde, *International Law Chiefly as Interpreted and Applied by the United States,* 2nd ed. (Boston, 1945), 3 vols.; John H. Wigmore, *A Guide to American International Law and Practice* (New York, 1943); H. A. Smith, *Great Britain and the Law of Nations* (London, Vol. I, 1932; Vol. II, 1935); N. MacKenzie and L. H. Laing (eds.), *Canada and the Law of Nations* (Toronto, 1938); J. G. Castel (ed.), *International Law as Interpreted and Applied in Canada* (Toronto, 1965); Angelo Sereni, *The Italian Conception of International Law* (New York, 1943); H. B. Jacobini, *A Study of the Philosophy of International Law as Seen in Works of Latin American Writers* (The Hague, 1954). Some Scandinavian points of view may be found in Alf Ross, *A Textbook of International Law* (London, 1948). D. P. O'Connell, *International Law in Australia* (London, 1966), also manifests a Western concept of international law even though Australia is geographically located in the East.

debts. Serious disagreements have even existed between Great Britain and the United States concerning the principles of the freedom of the seas and neutral rights and duties. Through the shifting of national interests and the increasing need of a general standard in their dealings, nations have gradually adjusted themselves to work out common rules by mutual concessions and compromises. There is little evidence to show that the disparity among the nations has resulted in serious differences in interpretation and application of international law. On the contrary, they have contributed, in one way or the other, to its steady development toward further standardization and universality in spite of occasional violations.

States recently emancipated from imperialistic domination or newly independent from colonial rule have a deep-rooted sentiment against any vestige of imperialism and colonialism. They advocate immediate self-determination of dependent territories, abolition of unequal treaties, and sovereign right of expropriation and protection of national resources. At the Economic and Social Council and other organs of the United Nations, they have insisted on such policies against the remnants of colonialism.[104] Such claims are certainly detrimental to the political and economic interests of the powers previously dominating the developing areas. In this connection, the powers concerned should know from their own domestic affairs that in recent decades the political, economic, and social structure of the state has undergone drastic changes and that certain phases of laws and regulations have to be amended accordingly. As advanced members of the rapidly expanding society of nations, they probably will reconcile themselves with the new circumstances and modify some of their traditional concepts of international law. At the same time, appropriate compensation should be paid for alien properties and interests nationalized or expropriated by states. This has been the practice of states which carried out such policies, even though there has been disagreement over the time and amount of payment.

To every action there is a reaction. States which have suffered from imperialistic domination or colonial rule have reasons for resentment. But bygones are bygones. With technical aid and economic assistance from the United Nations and the developed nations, international cooperation will replace antagonism and moderation will prevail in future policies. As a matter of fact, many of the emergent nations became accustomed to the norms of international law while

[104] See, *e.g.*, E/3840, E/3960, A/5803. See also GA res. 2189 (XXI), adopted at the twenty-first session of the General Assembly on December 13, 1966, under the title of "Implementation of the Declaration on the Granting of Independence to Colonial Countries and Peoples."

they were still under Western influence. Fundamentally, they have accepted the universality of the long-established rules despite the fact that they did not take part in their original formulation.[105] Their active participation in the implementation of the principles and purposes of the United Nations Charter is unmistakable evidence of their enthusiastic support of the rule of law in the international community.[106] The so-called Nehru doctrine as suggested by an Indian jurist does not contradict the prevailing rules of international law, but represents the foreign policy of India in Nehru's time: active neutralism, non-alignment, non-intervention, Asian solidarity, and anti-colonialism.[107] After comparing the different traditions of Western and non-Western states, C. Wilfred Jenks and other writers have reached the conclusion that there is enough common ground to work for a universal system of international law.[108]

[105] In summarizing the views of the Sixth Committee of the General Assembly, Judge Radhabinod Pal, Indian member of the International Law Commission of the United Nations, stated that "when a state acceded to the international community it automatically was understood to conform to its rules and institutions." On the other hand, he warned: "If numerous rules of international law did not have the active support of a large sector of the international community, the entire machinery for the peaceful solution of disputes would, it was felt, be without foundation." 9 *UN Review* (September 1962), p. 31. Judge Pal's statement represents the general sentiment of the newly independent states.

[106] Studies have been made in recent years on international law and the emergent nations, including J. J. G. Syatauw, *Some Newly Established Asian States and the Development of International Law* (The Hague, 1961); William V. O'Brien and others, *The New Nations in International Law and Diplomacy* (New York, 1965); B. V. A. Röling, *International Law in an Expanded World* (Amsterdam, 1960). Some Indian views may be found in Satyavrata R. Patel, *A Textbook of International Law* (New York, 1964). For a survey of international law as interpreted and applied by a state which has had bitter experience of imperialistic domination, see William L. Tung, *China and Some Phases of International Law* (New York & London, 1940).

[107] See Satyavrata R. Patel, *op. cit.*, p. 36.

[108] C. W. Jenks, *The Common Law of Mankind* (London, 1958), p. 169. For a penetrating examination of different attitudes toward international law by countries of major cultural and ideological orders, see Friedmann, Chs. 18–20. *Cf.* also British, American, and Soviet views on international law as briefly presented in Percy E. Corbett, *Law in Diplomacy* (Princeton, 1959), Chs. 1–3. At its meeting on December 12, 1966, the General Assembly decided to include an item entitled "Consideration of Principles of International Law concerning Friendly Relations and Cooperation among States in Accordance with the Charter of the United Nations" in the provisional agenda of its twenty-second session. GA res. 2181 (XXI).

§9. SANCTIONS OF INTERNATIONAL LAW

As to the lack of sovereign authority to enforce the rules of international law in comparison with municipal laws in individual states, it is again a difference of degree and methods.[109] For national honor and self-interest, states generally comply with international law of their own volition, because manifestation of good faith will eventually produce beneficial results.[110] A flagrant violation would incur outraged public opinion internationally and domestically.[111] Besides voluntary compliance, there are various means of compelling observance. A state which has suffered injury from another state may have recourse to such retaliatory measures as retorsion, reprisals, embargo, pacific blockade, boycott, and other forcible means. In more serious cases, the United Nations may resort to enforcement action for the restoration and maintenance of international peace in accordance with the provisions of the Charter. If necessary, military and economic sanctions may be imposed upon a recalcitrant state.[112]

Sometimes states accuse each other of violations of treaty obligations,[113] but in most cases a proper interpretation can solve their differences. Legal and political disputes may be referred respectively to the International Court of Justice and other organs of the United Nations for settlement.[114] There are, in fact, fewer violations of international law than of municipal laws. Furthermore, the breach of law by a certain state, even if unpunished, does not make the law invalid. In deciding the case of *The Prometheus* in 1906,[115] the Supreme Court of

[109] "Coercion does exist in International Law," according to the Soviet view, "but it is organized differently, and implemented in other forms." Soviet *Text,* p. 11. Roger Fisher correctly pointed out that "no more in the international than in the domestic sphere should the argument be heard that governments must be lawless because they cannot be coerced." Falk & Mendlovitz, II, p. 84, reprinted from his "Bringing Law to Bear on Governments," 74 *Harvard Law Review,* pp. 1130–1140.

[110] See Jessup, pp. 7–8. *Cf.* Percy E. Corbett, *Law and Society in the Relations of States* (New York, 1951), pp. 3–89.

[111] For the influence of law and morality on the use of force, see Richard A. Falk, *Law and Morality and War in the Contemporary World* (New York, 1963).

[112] See *infra,* §§181–188, 192–193; also the Royal Institute of International Affairs, *International Sanctions* (London, 1938).

[113] See O. J. Lissitzyn, "Western and Soviet Perspectives on International Law—A Comparison," *Proceedings* of Am. Society of Int. Law, 1959, p. 21.

[114] See *infra,* §§189–196.

[115] 2 Hongkong Law Reports 207. See also J. L. Brierly, *The Outlook for International Law* (Oxford, 1944), p. 5.

Hongkong made it clear that, under such circumstances, "the law still existed, though it might not for the time being be possible to enforce obedience to it." The prevalent belief in the West that only Communist states have violated the rules of international law does not represent the whole picture. Two American jurists have frankly pointed out that, on a number of occasions, the United States "has demonstrated an unwillingness to constrain its behavior in accord with applicable law," notably in the U-2 incident of 1960 and the Bay of Pigs invasion of 1961.[116] It must also be understood that law helps the political force maintain order but cannot eliminate breaches of order completely. As municipal laws cannot prevent revolutions, international law cannot suppress violence altogether in the community of nations.

If states do not want to risk another major war, law and order must be maintained in the world. Any dispute or situation should be solved either directly by the parties concerned or through the organs of international and regional organizations.[117] Serious disputes often result in armed conflicts, which may possibly widen from local to world scale. History has repeatedly shown that each war does not end war, but breeds a new one.[118] It is therefore to the best interest of nations to avoid the use of force and to further the development and observance of international law. Active participation in and cooperation with the United Nations, specialized agencies, and other international and regional organizations are important steps toward the rule of law. When international relations are guided by justice and order in accordance with the letter and spirit of international law, nations of diversified ideologies and political systems will reciprocally benefit. In this nuclear age, there is practically no alternative.[119]

[116] Richard A. Falk and Saul H. Mendlovitz, "Towards a Warless World; One Legal Formula to Achieve Transition," Falk & Mendlovitz, II, pp. 10–11.

[117] For further discussion, see George W. Keaton and Georg Schwarzenberger, *Making International Law Work* (London, 1946); H. Kelsen, *Peace through Law* (Chapel Hill, 1944); Quincy Wright, *The Strengthening of International Law* (The Hague, 1960).

[118] Even before World War II, many major battles were fought in Europe. For their duration and participating states, see Quincy Wright, *A Study of War* (Chicago, 1943), I, pp. 220–221.

[119] See Nagendra Singh, *Nuclear Weapons and International Law* (New York, 1959). Victor P. Karpow, First Secretary of the Soviet Embassy in Washington, recently wrote: "The only alternative we have nowadays is between peaceful coexistence and nuclear holocaust. There are no other choices." See his "The Soviet Concept of Peaceful Coexistence and Its Implications for International Law," *Law and Contemporary Problems*, 29 (Autumn 1964), p. 860.

IV. *NEW TRENDS OF INTERNATIONAL LAW IN THE TWENTIETH CENTURY*

§10. THE INTERACTION OF INTERNATIONAL LAW, INTERNATIONAL POLITICS, AND INTERNATIONAL ORGANIZATIONS

International politics represents the interplay of foreign policies of different states for the ultimate purpose of achieving national supremacy, self-preservation, or balance of power. While international law works toward the rule of law in the international community, international politics stresses national expediency and self-interest.[120] International organization is the creation of these two and cannot function without due consideration of both.[121] The maintenance of peace depends largely upon the balance between legal order and national interest.

For centuries, philosophers and statesmen have searched for world peace through law and order. But their efforts have been frustrated by strong divisive forces such as geographical barriers, dynastic contests, political domination, colonial acquisition, armament competition, economic rivalry, and ideological conflict. On the other hand, with the rapid development of science and technology, the improvement of transportation and communications, as well as the changing structure of the international community, regional self-sufficiency and historical isolation have been giving way to national interdependence. The devastating effects of the Thirty Years' War, the Napoleonic Wars, and other conflicts in Europe finally brought government leaders together to discuss the formulation of some pacific means for settling disputes and comprehensive regulations governing hostile relations.

[120] In their joint work *The Political Foundations of International Law* (New York, 1961), Morton A. Kaplan and Nicholas DeB. Katzenbach emphasize "the differences between international law in a nineteenth-century 'balance of power' system and in the contemporary loose bipolar system." Pp. 76–80. Urban G. Whitaker, Jr., makes it his purpose to prove, in *Politics and Power: A Text in International Law* (New York, 1964), "that international law performs a vital political function, and international politics serves as a cradle for the growth of the law rather than a place of confinement for it." P. xiii.

[121] For the relationship of international law with international politics and the United Nations, see Quincy Wright, *International Law and the United Nations* (New York, 1960), and *Contemporary International Law: A Balance Sheet* (New York, 1961), Chs. 4–6; John G. Stoessinger, *The Might of Nations: World Politics in Our Time,* rev. ed. (New York, 1965), Pt. III.

The Hague Conventions of 1899 and 1907 The twentieth century has been epoch-making in the development of international law and organization. The two Hague Peace Conferences were unique in the history of international legislation in that many international conventions were concluded by the participating states for the peaceful settlement of international disputes and the regulation of war and neutrality.[122] The establishment of the Permanent Court of Arbitration by the First Hague Conference paved the way for further expansion of international arbitration and adjudication. Disagreements and disputes are inevitable among states, but appropriate channels and methods should be provided for amicable solution. If occasional wars cannot yet be avoided at the present stage of human development, it is extremely important to formulate rules regulating legitimate warfare and minimizing war damage and suffering.[123] In these respects, the two Hague Conferences had remarkable success.

The emergence of the League of Nations after World War I Since the Congress of Vienna, the Concert of Europe had maintained a reasonable degree of peace in Europe for almost a century. As the balance of power was gradually upset by the rise of expansionist Germany, World War I broke out in 1914. Witnessing the devastating effects, statesmen throughout the world agreed to establish machinery for the maintenance of perpetual peace. The League of Nations came into existence in 1920.[124] Established at the same time were the Permanent Court of International Justice, the International Labor Office, and other units of lesser importance. International law survived the war and prospered in the postwar period.[125] It laid the foundation for an international organization, which, in turn, devised means for enforcement and further development.

World War II and the United Nations The League of Nations lived through twenty years of relative peace, but the harsh terms im-

[122] Texts of the various Hague Conventions with commentaries can be found in A. P. Higgins, *The Hague Peace Conferences and Other International Conferences Concerning the Laws and Usages of War* (Cambridge, England, 1909).

[123] For various conventions and regulations adopted by the Hague Conferences and other rules of the laws of war and neutrality, see *infra,* Chs. 14, 15. See also Quincy Wright and others (eds.), *Preventing World War III: Some Proposals* (New York, 1962).

[124] For details, see *infra,* §§36–39.

[125] A number of multilateral instruments were concluded toward that end, notably the General Act for the Pacific Settlement of International Disputes of 1928 and the General Treaty for the Renunciation of War of 1928.

posed upon Germany through the 1919 Treaty of Versailles created a deep sense of resentment and revenge. Great Britain and France neither seriously sought peaceful readjustment with Germany before the rise of Hitler nor prevented his march into the Rhineland by force. Japan took advantage of the European situation and invaded China in disregard of her treaty obligations. Italy conquered Ethiopia in defiance of resolutions of the League of Nations. Aggressions in both East and West merged into World War II. Again Allied statesmen realized the importance of law and order in the restoration and maintenance of international peace. Preparations for the establishment of the United Nations and several specialized agencies were made while the war was still in progress. With the inauguration of the first session of the General Assembly of the United Nations on January 10, 1946,[126] much of the constructive work started by the League of Nations was continued and expanded. The International Court of Justice took the place of the old Court. More specialized agencies and numerous subsidiary bodies were set up. Both the League Covenant and the United Nations Charter emphasize respect for justice and international law, which form the guiding principles of the two organizations.

Reasons for the setbacks in the march toward law and order There is no doubt that law and organization are stabilizing factors of international order and can help maintain it once established. Nonetheless, international peace and security cannot last if powerful political forces of the community of nations are determined to break the status quo.[127] Leaders holding responsible positions in the states which are subjects of international law and members of international organizations should be blamed for the two world catastrophes of the first half of this century. International law and organization are duty-bound to make up for the disastrous mistakes already committed. At the same time, statesmen of the major powers should exert maximum efforts to strengthen law and organization.[128] Without going into the substance

[126] The Charter of the United Nations came into force on October 24, 1945, but, due to necessary planning and preparations, the first session of the General Assembly was not held until January 10, 1946, in London.

[127] In his *The Outlook for International Law* (Oxford, 1944), J. L. Brierly cautioned that "law does not create order." However, it may be used "to underpin the fabric of order once this has been established." P. 95.

[128] In the opinion of Harold D. Lasswell, "if the active members of the world's political elite—in Washington, Moscow, Peiping, London, or elsewhere—ever expect to be better off by at least a minimum system of world public order, the world will have it at once." McDougal and Feliciano, *Law and Minimum World Public Order*, p. xxii.

of the rules, it is perhaps advisable to describe briefly the new development of international law since the turn of the century in the community of nations, which is continuously in the process of integration.[129] History is full of records of cycles of integration and disintegration of human society, but "mankind has never before achieved such a degree of law and organization as it has in the institutions that have developed since World War I." [130]

§11. NEW STATUS OF THE INTERNATIONAL COMMUNITY AND INDIVIDUAL RIGHTS

With the rapid expansion of the international community in the last two decades, the major powers in Western Europe no longer hold the predominant position in world affairs. The United States, the Soviet Union, China, and other countries in the Western Hemisphere, Asia, and Africa have exercised increasing influence in the universal society of nations.[131] Even though states are still the primary subjects of international law,[132] the United Nations has its own juridic personality.[133] The status of individuals in international law has become more important since World War II. The trial and punishment of war criminals

[129] This process of integration is fully discussed in Ernst B. Haas, *Beyond the Nation-State: Functionalism and International Organization* (Stanford, 1964). For general references on the development of international law in the twentieth century and its future, see Friedmann, Chs. 6, 22; Fenwick, *Principles,* Ch. XXXVI; James W. Garner, *Recent Developments in International Law* (Calcutta, 1925), *passim;* M. O. Hudson, "The Prospect for International Law in the 20th Century," 10 *Cornell Law Quarterly* (1925), pp. 419-459; Quincy Wright, *Research in International Law since the War* (Washington, D.C., 1930); J. B. Moore, "Fifty Years of International Law," 50 *Harvard Law Review* (1937), pp. 395–448; G. W. Keeton, "International Law and the Future," 27 *Grotius Society* (1942), pp. 31–58; F. N. Keens, "The Future Development of International Law," 29 *ibid.* (1944), pp. 35–50; Jorge Americano, *The New Foundations of International Law* (New York, 1947), *passim;* C. G. Fenwick, "The Progress of International Law in the Past 40 Years," 79 Hague *Recueil* (1951), pp. 1–71.

[130] Quincy Wright, "Toward a Universal Law for Mankind," 63 *Columbia Law Review* (March 1963), p. 441. His view is shared by H. G. Wells, James T. Shotwell, and others.

[131] For membership of the United Nations, see *infra,* §§48–53.

[132] See *infra,* §§19–23.

[133] See the Advisory Opinion on *Reparation for Injuries Suffered in Service of United Nations,* International Court of Justice, 1949. I.C.J. Reports (1949), 174.

is a departure from the traditional concept of acts of state,[134] and, in effect, has reaffirmed the concept of individuals as subjects of international law.[135] The protection of human rights by the Declaration and the two covenants has further strengthened the position and dignity of persons.[136]

There is no serious issue on the recognition of new states; but, with respect to those currently divided for political reasons, the world has been confronted with the problem of which regime should be deemed the legal government. Recognition has now been granted to the Communist governments of these divided states by the Communist countries and to the non-Communist governments by others. This policy of recognition implies approval and disapproval of the government in existence and thus further aggravates the disruptive situation of the world. Strictly speaking, recognition itself is a public policy, whereas international law is chiefly concerned with the legal consequences of recognition or non-recognition.[137] Connected with recognition by individual states is the admission of new members to the United Nations and the problem of legitimate representation.[138]

With the frequent creation of new states, the problem of succession of treaties and other rights and obligations is quite complicated.[139] So far, arrangements have generally been smoothly made with the former colonial powers. Practices are divergent in different cases and are not confined to traditional concepts. There has been some conflict of interest between the principle of sovereign right of expropriation and that of protection of foreign investments. Probably the only reconciling formula is to recognize the right of expropriation with obligation to make appropriate compensation.[140] This is a political and economic reality that must not be ignored.

Most of the new nations in the international community are inclined to adopt a neutralist or non-committed policy in a world charac-

[134] At its 123rd meeting on November 21, 1947, the General Assembly adopted resolution 177 (II), which directed the International Law Commission to formulate the Nuremberg principles and prepare for a draft code of offenses against the peace and security of mankind. For the resolution and its implementation, see *Yearbook*, Int. Law Com., 1949, pp. 282–283; 1950, pp. 30–178.

[135] See *infra*, §19.

[136] For the status of individuals, see *infra*, Ch. 8, particularly §§123–127 on human rights.

[137] See *infra*, §§24–29.

[138] See *infra*, §49.

[139] For the various phases of succession to states and governments, see *infra*, §§30–33.

[140] See *infra*, §79.

terized by the bipolarization of the United States and the Soviet Union. The new nations' historical subjection to colonial rule and the recent ascendancy of nationalism are reflected in their views on activities of the world organization and development of international law. Sovereign equality, self-determination, decolonization, non-discrimination, and human rights are among the cherished hopes of the developing nations, which collectively constitute a determining force in the General Assembly. The Charter of the United Nations has been amended to permit an increase in representation of the Afro-Asian members on the Security Council and the Economic and Social Council. The relationship between the developing and developed nations is being further strengthened by the latter's continuing efforts to render economic and technical assistance to the former. Such an unprecedented scale of mutual help among states opens a new chapter in the history of the international community.

§12. NEW CONVENTIONS ON THE SEA AND THE AIRSPACE AS WELL AS DIPLOMATIC AND CONSULAR RELATIONS

Under the auspices of the United Nations, the Conference on the Law of the Sea was held in 1958 and adopted Conventions on the Territorial Sea and Contiguous Zone, on the High Seas, on Fishing and Conservation of the Living Resources of the High Sea, and on the Continental Shelf.[141] These conventions not only have codified the customary rules of international law but also have incorporated some new principles for the guidance of states in their dealings with one another. Similar steps were taken in the Convention on Diplomatic Relations of 1961 and the Convention on Consular Relations of 1963, adopted by two United Nations conferences at Vienna.[142] To avoid secret diplomacy, states are called upon to register their treaties with the Secretariat of the International Organization.[143] The codification of the law of treaties is now under continuous discussion at the International Law Commission and some new phases have been explored.[144]

[141] See *infra,* §§88–89, 104–107. The First Conference on the Law of the Sea in 1958 was attended by representatives from eighty-six states.

[142] The United Nations Conference on Diplomatic Intercourse and Immunities was held from March 2 to April 14, 1961, attended by representatives from eighty-one states and several specialized agencies. From March 2 to April 23, 1963, the United Nations Conference on Consular Relations was attended by representatives from ninety-two states. For details, see *infra,* Ch. 9, particularly §§131, 133–138.

[143] For details, see *infra,* §165.

[144] For a full discussion of the law of treaties, see *infra,* Ch. 11.

Between 1919 and 1944, several conventions came into existence for the regulation of civil aviation.[145] Intensive research has been conducted on space law in both government and private quarters. It has also been a topic under serious study by the United Nations and its subsidiary organs. A space treaty was finally adopted on December 19, 1966.[146] International instruments on other important matters agreed upon under the auspices of the League and the United Nations are too numerous to list here. Some multilateral treaties directly concluded by states in recent decades have also developed new principles of international law.[147]

§13. NEW PRINCIPLES OF TERRITORIAL PROBLEMS

At the turn of the century, almost every part of the world's land domain was under effective occupation of different states. Even the Arctic had been claimed by several states on the ground of contiguity and continuity. In the Antarctic, however, the states concerned agreed on a new principle of international law on territorial problems. Without renouncing their previous claims, the signatories to the Antarctic Treaty of 1959 reached an accord to use the Antarctic for peaceful purposes only.[148] This remarkable principle will, in all probability, be applied to the exploration of outer space and the future occupation of planets. Acquisition of territory by means of conquest no longer is permitted by the League Covenant and the United Nations Charter, because territorial integrity is paramount to the preservation of national sovereignty and any change must be made through peaceful adjustment.[149] Besides, many phases of territorial jurisdiction, exemptions, servitudes, and restrictions have been subject to constant modification in recent decades.[150]

[145] The Convention for the Regulation of Aerial Navigation of 1919 was followed by the Havana Convention on Commercial Aviation of 1928, the Warsaw Convention of 1929, and the Chicago Convention of 1944. The Chicago Conference was held during the war and attended by representatives from fifty-two states. See *infra,* §§96–99.

[146] See *infra,* §§100–103.

[147] *E.g.,* the Geneva Conventions on Prisoners of War of 1929 and 1949, incorporating new principles of the protection of prisoners of war and also of civilians. The Kellogg-Briand Pact of 1928 drastically changed the traditional institution of war as a last resort to settle international disputes.

[148] See *infra,* §91.

[149] See Art. 2(4) of the United Nations Charter; also *infra,* §94. The Stimson Doctrine of non-recognition of any situation created by forcible means was accepted by the League of Nations in 1932.

[150] See *infra,* §§70, 80–81, 104–107.

§14. NEW CONCEPT OF THE SETTLEMENT OF DISPUTES AND THE USE OF FORCE

The foundation for the settlement of international disputes was laid by the Hague Convention for the Pacific Settlement of International Disputes and further implemented by the League Covenant and the United Nations Charter. Nations are urged to solve their differences by pacific means, for which the services of the League, the United Nations, and the world courts have been made available.[151] Resort to war as a redress was renounced in the Kellogg-Briand Pact of 1928. Under the United Nations system, the use of force to settle international disputes is permitted only if employed for the enforcement of collective measures by the Organization. The right of self-defense by individual states and regional arrangements and agencies can only be claimed under the compelling circumstances of actual armed attack. The claimant must immediately report to the Security Council, because it is the authority and responsibility of the United Nations to maintain or restore international peace and security.[152] Thus, the traditional concepts and laws of war and neutrality have undergone drastic changes in the twentieth century.[153]

Any form of violence, intervention,[154] or use of force in contradiction to the letter and spirit of the Charter and the rules of international law is no longer sanctioned by world public opinion, which is too important to be ignored by the states today.[155] It is well to quote the maxim of one eminent publicist: "Opinion creates justice, justice creates law, and law develops force for its effective maintenance." [156]

§15. NEW PHASES OF INTERNATIONAL AND REGIONAL COOPERATION

The major success of the League of Nations and the United Nations has been in non-political activities. The accomplishments of the two international organizations in economic, social, technical, and cultural fields are unique in human history. Many regional agencies and

[151] For details, see *infra,* Chs. 12, 13.

[152] See *infra,* §§189–196.

[153] For a comprehensive discussion of the laws of war and neutrality, see *infra,* Chs. 14, 15.

[154] See *infra,* §§71–73.

[155] For the binding force of international law and sanctions, see *supra,* §9.

[156] Quincy Wright, *Contemporary International Law: A Balance Sheet, rev. ed.* (New York, 1961), p. 55.

arrangements began after World War II to carry out various programs for regional cooperation.[157] Most important of all are the specialized agencies, which have established their relationship with the United Nations by individual agreements. Many conferences have been sponsored by the international and regional organizations. Multilateral and bilateral treaties have been concluded to deal with a variety of subjects. All these cooperative efforts have broadened the scope of international law and organization as never before.[158]

V. *PROGRESSIVE DEVELOPMENT AND CODIFICATION OF INTERNATIONAL LAW* [159]

§16. THE DEVELOPMENT AND CODIFICATION OF INTERNATIONAL LAW THROUGH INTERNATIONAL ORGANIZATION

As stated before, international law lays down the foundation for the objectives, procedures, and functions of international organization. At the same time, international organization strengthens international law through enforcement, development, and codification of the existing rules. Leaving aside the enforcement aspect, to be discussed elsewhere in this work,[160] a brief examination will be made of the progressive development and codification of international law under the auspices of the League of Nations and the United Nations. The expressions 'progressive development' and 'codification' are closely related, but there is a clear distinction between the two. Progressive development means "the preparation of draft conventions or subjects which have not yet been regulated by international law or in regard to which the law has not yet been sufficiently developed in the practice of states"; codification is "the more precise formulation and systematization of rules of international law in fields where there already has been extensive state practice, precedent and doctrine." [161] The Hague Conferences, the League of Nations, and the United Nations have made due contributions to both of these.

[157] See *infra,* §35.

[158] For details, see *infra,* §§153–157.

[159] General texts on this subject: O'Connell, I, pp. 27–28; Oppenheim, I, §§30–37a; Fenwick, *Principles,* pp. 99–106; Brierly, Ch. II, §§6–7; Hackworth, *Digest,* I, §9; Whiteman, *Digest,* I, §13; Soviet *Text,* Ch. I, §7.

[160] See *infra,* §§189–193.

[161] See Art. 15 of the Statute of the International Law Commission, adopted by the General Assembly on November 21, 1947, and amended on December 12, 1950, December 3, 1955, and November 6, 1961. UN Doc. A/CN.4/4/Rev.1 (1962).

§17. THE HAGUE CONFERENCES AND THE LEAGUE OF NATIONS

Lack of precision of many rules of international law and the necessity of further development have long been recognized by statesmen and jurists.[162] The Hague Conferences of 1899 and 1907 started the work on codifying the laws of peace and war. Encouraged by their success, this important movement was continued after World War I by the League of Nations.[163] Under the auspices of the League, the first Conference on the Progressive Codification of International Law was held at The Hague in 1930. The Conference adopted one convention and three protocols on nationality, which came into force in 1937. Even though there was no agreement on two other subjects under discussion, *i.e.*, territorial waters and state responsibility, this conference marked the beginning of an ambitious project undertaken by an international organization.[164]

§18. THE WORK OF THE UNITED NATIONS THROUGH ITS INTERNATIONAL LAW COMMISSION AND OTHER ORGANS

The Charter of the United Nations empowers the General Assembly to initiate studies and make recommendations for the purpose of "encouraging the progressive development of international law and its

[162] It was Jeremy Bentham who first proposed the idea of codification in the eighteenth century. See Georg Schwarzenberger, *Jeremy Bentham and the Law* (London, 1948), pp. 152–184.

[163] Reference may be made to John E. Harley, *The League of Nations and the New International Law* (Oxford, 1921); James W. Garner, "Some Observations on the Codification of International Law," 19 *Am. Jour. Int. Law* (1925), pp. 327–333; John F. Williams, *Chapters on Current International Law and the League of Nations* (London, 1929); S. D. Cole, "Codification of International Law," 12 *Grotius Society* (1927); pp. 49–60.

[164] The discussions and final reports of the Conference are recorded in 3 volumes: Vol. I, Nationality: C.73.M.38.1929.V; Vol. II, Territorial Waters: C.74.M.39.1929.V; Vol. III, Responsibility of States: C.75.M.69.1929.V. For the texts of the convention and protocols, see League Docs. C.224.M.111. 1930.V; C.225.M.112.1930.V; C.226.M.113.1930.V; C.227.M.114.1930.V; C.228.M.115.1930.V; C.229.M.116.1930.V; C.351(a).M.145(a).1930.V. For comments on nationality problems, see R. W. Flournoy, "Nationality Convention, Protocols and Recommendations Adopted by First Conference on Codification of International Law," 24 *Am. Jour. Int. Law* (1930), pp. 467–485; M. O. Hudson, "Hague Convention of 1930 and Nationality of Women," 27 *ibid.* (1933), pp. 117–122. See also M. O. Hudson, "The Prospect for Future Codification," 26 *ibid.* (1932), pp. 137–143.

codification."[165] At its first session, the General Assembly appointed a Committee on the Progressive Development of International Law and Its Codification to work out a plan for the fulfillment of this responsibility. On the basis of its report, the General Assembly adopted a resolution at its second session to establish an International Law Commission whose function is to "promote the progressive development of international law and its codification."[166] The Commission is primarily concerned with public international law, "but is not precluded from entering the field of private international law."[167] The number of Commission members has increased from fifteen to twenty-five, selected individually from experts in the field. The General Assembly has also encouraged the members and other organs of the United Nations, specialized agencies, and inter-governmental bodies to initiate studies for the common purpose of progressive development of international law and its codification.[168] Resolutions adopted by the General Assembly to initiate such studies are chiefly recommended by its Sixth Committee, which is in close collaboration with the International Law Commission.[169]

At its first session in 1949, the International Law Commission selected fourteen topics for codification, subject to additions and deletions:[170] (1) recognition of states and governments; (2) succession of states and governments; (3) jurisdictional immunities of states and

[165] Art. 13(1a) of the Charter.

[166] GA res. 174 (II). See also Art. 1(1) of the Statute of the International Law Commission; *Survey of International Law in Relation to the Work of Codification of the International Law Commission,* prepared by the Secretariat of the United Nations, November 5, 1948. A/CN.4/1.

[167] Art. 1(2) of the Statute of the International Law Commission.

[168] For the work of codification before the functioning of the International Law Commission, see the *Historical Survey of Development of International Law and Its Codification by International Conferences;* Memorandum prepared by the Secretariat of the United Nations, 1947. A/AC. 10/5. See also J. L. Brierly, "The Codification of International Law," 47 *Michigan Law Review* (1948), pp. 2–10.

[169] See Herbert W. Briggs, *The International Law Commission* (Ithaca, 1965), Pt. III, Ch. 4.

[170] Art. 18 of the Statute of the International Law Commission provides:

"1. The Commission shall survey the whole field of international law with a view to selecting topics for codification, having in mind existing drafts, whether governmental or not.

"2. When the Commission considers that the codification of a particular topic is necessary or desirable, it shall submit its recommendations to the General Assembly.

"3. The Commission shall give priority to requests of the General Assembly to deal with any question."

their property; (4) jurisdiction with regard to crimes committed outside national territory; (5) regime of the high seas; (6) regime of territorial waters; (7) nationality, including statelessness; (8) treatment of aliens; (9) right of asylum; (10) law of treaties; (11) diplomatic intercourse and immunities; (12) consular intercourse and immunities; (13) state responsibility; and (14) arbitral procedure.[171] Among the drafts prepared by the Commission and recommended by the General Assembly for codification, items 5, 6, 11, and 12 have already been discussed and adopted by special international conferences under the auspices of the United Nations.[172] In some cases, because of diversified views of the states, the General Assembly decided to postpone further consideration. Meanwhile, the Commission has been considering other topics deemed ready for codification.[173]

At its twentieth session in 1965, the General Assembly recommended that the Commission "continue the work of codification and progressive development of the law of treaties and of special missions" and "its work on state responsibility, succession of states and governments and relations between states and intergovernmental organizations." [174] Similar resolutions were adopted at the twenty-first session of the General Assembly, and an international conference on the law of treaties was scheduled for early in 1968.[175] The Secretary-General was recently asked by the General Assembly to report on the implementation of the program for assistance and exchange in the field of international law. This includes steps to encourage and coordinate existing international law programs carried out by states, organizations, and institutions, and also forms of direct assistance and exchange.[176] The General Assembly, the International Court of Justice, and other organs of the United Nations have done much toward the progressive development and codification of international law.[177] More materials on the

[171] See *Yearbook*, Int. Law Com., 1949, p. 281, "Report to the General Assembly."

[172] See *supra*, §12.

[173] See *Repertory*, U.N., I, pp. 405–432; Supp. No. 1, I, pp. 147–154; Supp. No. 2, II, pp. 119–127; also *Yearbook*, Int. Law Com., since 1949. For a summary of the annual reports of the International Law Commission and its recommendations to the General Assembly, see Herbert W. Briggs, *op. cit.*, Pt. III, Chs. 2–3.

[174] GA res. 2045 (XX).

[175] GA res. 2166 (XXI), 2167 (XXI).

[176] GA res. 2099 (XX), 2204 (XXI). For details, see *Yearbook*, UN, 1965, pp. 633–638.

[177] See Philip C. Jessup, "Development of International Law by the United Nations," 39 *Am. Jour. Int. Law* (1945), pp. 754–757; G. H. Hackworth, "The International Court of Justice and the Codification of International Law," 32 *American Bar Association Journal* (1946), pp. 81–86; H.

sources of international law have been made available by the publication of official documents.[178]

Lauterpacht, *The Development of International Law by the International Court* (New York, 1958); Yuen-li Liang, "The General Assembly and the Progressive Development and Codification of International Law," 42 *Am. Jour. Int. Law* (1948), pp. 66–97; Rosalyn Higgins, *The Development of International Law through the Political Organs of the United Nations* (New York, 1963), *passim.*

[178] See *supra,* §§4–6.

CHAPTER 2

INTERNATIONAL PERSONS, RECOGNITION, AND SUCCESSION

I. *SUBJECTS OF INTERNATIONAL LAW*[1]

§19. STATES AS PRIMARY SUBJECTS OF INTERNATIONAL LAW

International persons are primarily states to which rights and duties are generally attributed. As subjects of international law, the position of states in the international community corresponds to that of individuals under municipal law. Under normal conditions, the relationship of individuals to international law is established through states of which they are nationals. This concept is shared by the Communist countries and the emergent nations.

[1] General texts on this subject: O'Connell, I, pp. 89–133, 303–318, 353–360, 363, 385; Oppenheim, I, §§63–70, 85–111a, 168g, 288–289; Jessup, Ch. II; Fenwick, *Principles,* Ch. VI; Brierly, Chs. I, §§1–2; II, §§1–2; IV; V, §3; Hyde, I, §§6–34E; Friedmann, Chs. 13–15; Moore, *Digest,* I, §§3–18; Hackworth, *Digest,* I, §§10–17, 21–24; Whiteman, *Digest,* I, §§2, 14–51; Schwarzenberger, I, Ch. 3 (I–III, VI); Starke, Chs. 3, 5, 18, §1; Hershey, Chs. VI–VII; Kelsen, Ch. II(C); Kaplan & Katzenbach, Ch. 4; Gould, Ch. 6; Svarlien, Chs. 1, 6; Von Glahn, Ch. 6; Jacobini, pp. 36–45; Soviet *Text,* Ch. III, §§1–3; Schuschnigg, Ch. 5; Korowicz, Ch. 4; Lawrence, §§34–45; Le Fur, §§124–313; Twiss, I, §§1–11; Phillimore, I, §§71–74; Rivier, I, §§4–6; Taylor, §§120–133; McNair, I, pp. 33–66.

Subjects of international law are, however, not exclusively limited to states. Sometimes individuals may be subjects. It has long been international practice that pirates as individuals of whatever nationality may be attacked and punished by any state.[2] Individuals are also held responsible for breach of blockade and carriage of contraband.[3] After World War I, special protection of racial, linguistic, or religious minorities was negotiated at the Paris Peace Conference, resulting in the conclusion of a number of minority treaties with the newly established states. The League Council was empowered to take necessary measures for the fulfillment of the stipulations. After World War II, war criminals of the Axis Powers were tried and prosecuted by the Nuremberg and Tokyo International Tribunals on the ground that they had committed crimes against peace, the law of war, and humanity in violation of international law.[4] Thus, individuals were held responsible for acts of state.

In pursuance of the provisions of the Charter of the United Nations to promote and encourage respect for human rights and fundamental freedoms, the General Assembly adopted the Universal Declaration of Human Rights on December 10, 1948.[5] The Convention on Genocide, which came into force on January 12, 1951, reaffirms individual responsibility of persons involved in the crime of genocide whether they are government leaders, public functionaries, or private citizens.[6] In the Advisory Opinion on the *Jurisdiction of the Courts of Danzig* in 1928,[7] the Permanent Court of International Justice ruled that the parties concerned had the intention to confer rights of action on the Danzig railway officials. Thus, individuals are no longer considered as objects only but also, in many respects, as subjects of international law. On the other hand, present practice in the international community does not emphasize individuals as subjects of international law to the extent advocated by Hans Kelsen and other writers.[8]

Like the League of Nations, the United Nations is a juridic person

[2] See *infra*, §112.

[3] See Kelsen, p. 206; also *infra*, §§233–235.

[4] By the Agreement of August 8, 1945, establishing the Nuremberg Tribunal and the Charter of January 19, 1946, concerning the organization of the Tokyo Tribunal. For details, see *infra*, §226.

[5] The vote was 48 to 0. There were 8 abstentions, including Saudi Arabia, the Union of South Africa, and the Soviet bloc.

[6] See Art. IV of the Convention, which was unanimously adopted by the General Assembly on December 9, 1948. For details, see *infra*, §§123–127.

[7] P.C.I.J. (1928), Ser. B, No. 15.

[8] For a comprehensive discussion of individuals as subjects of international law, see Korowicz, Ch. VIII; also Vladimir R. Idelson, "The Law of Nations and the Individual," 30 *Grotius Society* (1944), Pt. 1, pp. 50–82.

even though it cannot be classified as a superstate or a confederation in the true sense. In the opinion of the International Court of Justice, it is "a subject of international law and capable of possessing international rights and duties." [9] The same status may be enjoyed by other international agencies and, to a lesser extent, by regional organizations.[10] When an insurrection in a country has reached the proportion of a civil war in both the material and legal senses, recognition of the status of belligerency by the parent state or the legal government or by third powers confers upon the rebels the rights and duties of a state in the conduct of war. Such a belligerent regime is treated as a subject of international law for the duration of the war.[11] In view of the above, it is safe to conclude that subjects of international law are primarily states but may also include, in many respects, individuals, international organizations, and other political entities.[12] However, there is no consensus of opinion on this. The Soviet Union considers international organization as a subject of international law in a limited sense.[13] So long as the Communist government of China is kept outside the United Nations, there is no possibility that it will so treat the world organization.

§20. CLASSIFICATION OF STATES

A state is a political entity, composed of population, territory, and a government, which exercises sovereignty internally and externally within the limit of law. Bodin's concept of the internal sovereignty of a state as absolute and unrestricted by law is no longer true.[14] External sovereignty is limited by rules of international law and by bilateral and multilateral treaties to which the state is a party. Size of population, extent of territory, and form of government are not the tests of statehood. History reveals fully how states have been evolved in various

[9] Advisory Opinion on *Reparation for Injuries Suffered in the Service of the United Nations,* I.C.J. Reports (1949), 174.

[10] See C. Wilfred Jenks, "The Legal Personality of International Organizations," 22 *British Yearbook of International Law* (1945), pp. 267–275.

[11] For details, see *infra,* §28.

[12] See Korowicz, Ch. VII; also Philip C. Jessup, "The Subjects of a Modern Law of Nations," 45 *Michigan Law Review* (February 1947), pp. 383–408.

[13] See T. A. Taracouzio, *The Soviet Union and International Law* (New York, 1935), p. 15; Jan F. Triska and Robert M. Slusser, *The Theory, Law, and Policy of Soviet Treaties* (Stanford, 1962), pp. 49–52.

[14] The term 'sovereignty' was first used by Bodin in 1576. Numerous definitions have since been introduced by political philosophers. For a thorough examination of the subject, see Korowicz, Chs. I–V. Although Bodin's concept of unrestricted sovereignty has been modified, the principle of non-intervention in matters within the domestic jurisdiction of states is generally recognized.

areas at different times.[15] The members of the British Commonwealth became independent states through a long process of evolution from dependent colonies to self-governing colonies, then dominions, and finally their present status. Since the conclusion of World War II, many independent states have emerged from former mandates, trust territories, and other dependent communities.

States may be classified, on the basis of their internal structure, as unitary or composite. A unitary state is represented by a supreme central government, such as France and Japan; a composite state is a union of several political entities, with certain internal powers reserved for themselves, to form an international person. Composite states have two forms: confederation and federal union. With a loosely organized central government and too much power reserved for the component units, confederation has proved ineffective. In a federal union, the central government is authorized by a constitution to deal with important matters of common interest, while the component entities retain certain original or non-delegated powers. A confederation from 1781 to 1789, the United States of America subsequently adopted the form of federal union. Modern states generally adopt either unitary or federal systems.[16]

International law is concerned not so much with the internal structure of a state as with its exercise of external sovereignty in the international community. The classification of states as sovereign and semi-sovereign is based on whether they are fully independent or not. With the exception of a few vassal states and international protectorates, nations today are all sovereign states.

§21. SOVEREIGN STATES

With the rapid development of nationalism and the incessant drive for decolonization, many independent states have emerged after World

[15] See *The Helena*, Great Britain, High Court of Admiralty, 1801. 4 C. Robinson 3. In reaching the decision that Algiers was a state, the British court reviewed the history of the Barbary States, which were once pirates but had elevated themselves into States of Algiers, Sally, Tripoli, and Tunis.

[16] In past history, there was a real union as another kind of composite state, for instance, the Austro-Hungarian Empire before its separation in 1918. Such a real union was composed of several internally independent states to form a single international person under one dynasty, with a joint council or common ministers in charge of important matters of mutual interest, especially national defense and foreign affairs. The so-called personal union was neither a composite state nor a separate international person, such as the Netherlands and Luxemburg from 1815 to 1890. In this case, union existed because there was one ruler, but each remained as a sovereign state and a separate international person.

War II. Most of the former administering and colonial powers have shown readiness to follow this irresistible trend. Some even felt relieved of long-standing burdens and apprehensions. With a membership more than doubled in the last two decades, the family of nations is no longer limited to Christian states as historically conceived by early writers. Admittedly, these emergent nations are still weak politically and economically. They are nonetheless sovereign states and will become more viable through a reasonable period of self-help and foreign assistance. Neither is disparity of power a new phenomenon. In the prewar community of nations, certain members were stronger and richer than others. Like the working class after the Industrial Revolution in the domestic societies, the new nations will eventually develop maturity and become the backbone of a truly universal community.

Sovereignty and independence are relative. Modern states tend to be increasingly interdependent and self-restrictive in the exercise of their external sovereignty, being bound by international law and treaties for the benefit and convenience of all. Such interdependence and self-restriction, of the states' own volition, are the very expression of their sovereign will.

Neutralized states On account of geographical location and need for self-preservation, several states in Europe have become neutralized states at one time or another by guarantee of the major powers. Belgium became a neutralized state at the time of her independence in 1831, and Luxemburg achieved the same status in 1867.[17] Their status of permanent neutrality, violated by Germany in 1914, was ultimately terminated after World War I. Switzerland has kept her neutralized status since 1815.[18] As a member of the League of Nations, Switzerland obtained recognition of her neutral position from the League Council. Because no such latitude is provided in the Charter, Switzerland has not joined the United Nations.[19] Austria proclaimed herself a permanent neutral state after the conclusion of a treaty with the Soviet Union on May 15, 1955, and received recognition as such by other major powers. The neutralization of Laos, initially self-declared on July 9,

[17] The permanent neutrality of Belgium was guaranteed by Austria, Great Britain, France, Prussia, and Russia by the Treaty of London of November 15, 1831. Austria, Great Britain, Holland, Italy, Prussia, and Russia collectively guaranteed the neutrality of Luxemburg by a treaty signed in London on May 11, 1867.

[18] The neutrality of Switzerland was guaranteed by a joint declaration of March 20, 1815, by Austria, Great Britain, France, Portugal, Prussia, Russia, Spain, and Sweden.

[19] See Oppenheim, I, pp. 245–246.

1962, was supported by thirteen powers in a joint declaration of July 23, 1962.[20]

Permanent neutralization is definitely a restriction on the freedom of action of a state, but when self-imposed for national interest is an exercise of sovereignty itself. Thus, neutralized states are also sovereign states. After World War II, a number of states, including India and the United Arab Republic, claimed to be neutralist or non-aligned states in the power struggle between the Communist and Western nations. This policy of non-entanglement, formulated for particular circumstances and without commitment to any permanent status, is fundamentally different from the traditional concept of neutralized states.[21] To a small state surrounded by strong neighbors, one-sided friendship or partisanship is sometimes considered a necessary alternative to neutrality for self-preservation.[22] Mention should also be made of the distinction between neutralized states and neutralization of a certain area, which merely prohibits the preparation for or conduct of war in the specified territory.

The Vatican Even though the Pope no longer exercises temporal power as in former times, he is the head of the Roman Catholic Church and has sovereign jurisdiction over Vatican City. However small its area and population, the Vatican is an international person of unique nature and maintains a status of neutrality in peace and war.[23]

[20] The thirteen powers which took part in the International Conference on the Settlement of the Laotian Question, 1961–1962, are Burma, Cambodia, Canada, China (People's Republic), France, India, Poland, Thailand, the Soviet Union, the United Kingdom, the United States, North Vietnam, and South Vietnam. For the Declaration and Protocol on the neutrality of Laos, see U.S. Congress (89th Cong., 1st Sess.), *Background Information relating to Southeast Asia and Vietnam* (Washington, D.C., 1965), pp. 91–99.

[21] For aspects of neutralism and non-alignment, see Ernest W. Lefever, "Nehru, Nassau, and Nkrumah on Neutralism," *Neutralism* (Washington, D.C., 1961, mimeographed copy), pp. 85–110; Peter Lyon, *Neutralism* (Leicester, England, 1963). See also pertinent articles on non-alignment in foreign affairs, in 362 *The Annals* of the American Academy of Political and Social Science (November 1965).

[22] Prince Norodom Sihanouk, Cambodian Chief of State, considered his friendship with Communist China as principally a guarantee against falling victim to annexation attempts by Vietnam and Thailand. In his opinion, "China until now has safeguarded our existence as an independent state." *The New York Times*, August 4, 1966.

[23] The present status of the Vatican is based on the Lateran Treaty of February 11, 1929, between the Holy See and Italy. For its text, see 23 *Am. Jour. Int. Law* (1929), Supp., pp. 187–195.

In his "Message for Mankind" delivered at the United Nations in October, 1965, Pope Paul VI defined his status as "the least-invested, if you wish to think of him thus, with a minuscule, as it were symbolic, temporary sovereignty, only as much as is necessary to be free to exercise his spiritual mission, and to assure all those who deal with him that he is independent of every other sovereignty of this world." [24]

The Holy See was represented at the United Nations Conference on the Law of the Sea at Geneva in 1958, the Conference on Diplomatic Intercourse and Immunities at Vienna in 1961, and the Conference on Consular Relations at Vienna in 1963. These three were all law-making conferences sponsored by the Organization and attended by representatives from almost every state in the world. As an independent state concerned with humanity and the welfare of mankind, the Vatican is naturally interested in the law and order of the world as a whole. Some states maintain diplomatic relations with the Vatican; several of them regard the Papal nuncio as dean of the diplomatic corps. In spite of a basic policy against religion, the Soviet Union has maintained informal relations with the Vatican through unofficial contacts. Generally speaking, however, the relationship between the Vatican and Communist countries are less than cordial, due to basic differences in ideology and constant friction between church and state.

§22. SEMI-SOVEREIGN STATES

Semi-sovereign states are internally autonomous but externally under the control of stronger states, especially in matters of national defense and foreign affairs.[25] The so-called vassal states and international protectorates belong to this category. With the ascendancy of nationalism in recent years, no state is willing to be subservient to another. Thus, the class of semi-sovereign states has become obsolete.

Vassal states A vassal state is under the suzerainty of a sovereign state, which acts as guardian of the former in external affairs. Such a relationship was maintained for a time between Turkey and Egypt and also between the German princes and the Holy Roman Empire. Suzerainty is not necessarily incompatible with the sovereignty of

[24] Quoted from an unofficial English translation of his address to the United Nations on October 4, 1965, in *New York Herald Tribune,* October 5, 1965.

[25] Their relationship varies in different cases. See the *Nationality Decrees Issued in Tunis and Morocco,* Permanent Court of International Justice, 1923, P.C.I.J. (1923), Ser. B, No. 4.

the vassal state. In *Statham v. Statham and the Gaekwar of Baroda,*[26] a British court concluded, on the basis of historical records, that Baroda was under the suzerainty of Great Britain, free and independent of all except the suzerain. Before her independence in 1945, Outer Mongolia, technically an integral part of Chinese territory, was practically autonomous under the suzerainty of China.[27]

International protectorate An international protectorate comes into existence when a weaker state, either voluntarily or compulsorily, puts itself by treaty under the protection of a more powerful state, but still retains its status as an international person. The relationship of France with Tunis and Morocco prior to their independence falls under this category.[28] Being two separate entities, the protectorate may be uninvolved in a war between the protecting state and a third power. Thus, the Ionian States as a British protectorate did not automatically participate in a war between Great Britain and Russia. By the Treaty of Paris of 1815, Great Britain had the power to declare war for the Ionian States, but failed to exercise it.[29]

Domestic protectorate Different from the international protectorate is the so-called domestic protectorate, such as the Cherokee Nation under the guardianship of the United States. In the judgment of the Supreme Court, the Cherokee Nation is neither a foreign state nor one of the several states of the Union.[30] All the Indian tribes are under the sovereignty and dominion of the United States.

§23. MANDATES AND TRUST TERRITORIES

The former League of Nations mandates and those later transferred to the United Nations system as trust territories have all become inde-

[26] Great Britain, Probate, Divorce and Admirality Division, 1911. [1912] Probate 92.

[27] Under the tripartite treaty of 1915 between China, Outer Mongolia, and Russia, Outer Mongolia was regarded as an autonomous entity under the suzerainty of China. However, by the Sino-Russian Treaty of 1924, Russia recognized Outer Mongolia as "an integral part of the territory of China." Notwithstanding the treaty obligations, Russia had intermittently exercised a controlling influence in the area.

[28] See the *Rights of Nationals of the United States of America in Morocco,* International Court of Justice, 1952. I.C.J. Reports (1952), 176.

[29] *The Ionian Ships,* Great Britain, Admiralty Prize Court, 1855. 2 Spinks, 212.

[30] *The Cherokee Nation v. Georgia,* U.S. Supreme Court, 1831. 5 Peters 1.

pendent nations, with the exception of South-West Africa and certain islands in the Pacific.[31] This unique achievement is due to the combined efforts of the local inhabitants and the mandatory and administering powers. Their elevation from dependent territories to full-fledged international persons must be credited to the League of Nations and the United Nations, which established and supervised the mandatory and trusteeship systems respectively.[32]

II. RECOGNITION [33]

§24. NATURE OF RECOGNITION

The existence of a state or government is independent of recognition, which is granted by other members of the international community for mutual interest.[34] When a new state or government is established in control of a defined territory and the bulk of its popula-

[31] Quincy Wright's *Mandates under the League of Nations* (Chicago, 1930) is the most authoritative treatise on the subject. For the status of South-West Africa, see the Advisory Opinion on *International Status of South-West Africa,* International Court of Justice, 1950. I.C.J. Reports (1950), 128. For a brief but enlightened discussion of the non-self-governing territories, trust territories, and League mandates, see Brierly, pp. 173–189. For further details, see *infra,* §157.

[32] See Art. 22 of the League Covenant; Chs. XII, XIII of the United Nations Charter.

[33] General texts on this subject: O'Connell, I, pp. 181–208; Oppenheim, I, §§71–75g; Jessup, Ch. III; Fenwick, *Principles,* Ch. VIII; Hyde, I, §§36–51; Moore, *Digest,* I, §§19–22, 27–75; Whiteman, *Digest,* II, Ch. III; Hackworth, *Digest,* I, §§25–56; Starke, Ch. 6; Hershey, Ch. VIII; Schwarzenberger, I, Ch. 3 (IV–V); Kelsen, Ch. III(D); Kaplan & Katzenbach, Ch. 5; Gould, Chs. 7–8; Svarlien, Ch. 7; Whitaker, Chs. 8–9; Von Glahn, Ch. 7; Jacobini, pp. 45–49; Soviet *Text,* Ch. III, §5; Sen, Ch. XVI; Lawrence, §§44–48; Le Fur, §§594–606; Despagnet, §§79–85; Fiore, §§165–182; Fauchille, I, §§195–213(9); De Louter, I, pp. 216–224; McNair, I, pp. 130–151; II, pp. 326–371.

[34] There is a distinction between recognition of states and of governments. For convenience, they are discussed together unless divergent principles and practices require separate treatment. For a thorough study on the subject, consult H. Lauterpacht, *Recognition in International Law* (Cambridge, England, 1947); T. C. Chen, *The International Law of Recognition* (New York, 1951).

tion, with sufficient stability and capability to carry out international obligations, it is generally time for other states to extend recognition, in the absence of special political considerations. Recognition does not mean approval of the origin or political institutions and programs of the new regime, which are essentially internal matters and should not be questioned by the recognizing state. This has been the general practice among states, including Great Britain and the United States from the time of Jefferson up to the beginning of the twentieth century. Insisting on change of government through constitutional process, President Woodrow Wilson adopted a non-recognition policy toward the Huerta government in Mexico in 1913 because Huerta came to power by violent means.[35] The arrogant position assumed by one state in laying down the standard of legitimacy of a new government in another was strongly refuted by the so-called Estrada Doctrine.[36]

Change of government through normal process does not require new recognition, in contrast to the transfer of power through revolution or fundamental alteration of the form of state. But recognition is a public policy and, as such, it has often been used as an instrument in international politics. The withholding of recognition of the Soviet Union by the United States for almost sixteen years was largely due to the latter's disapproval of Communist policies and programs, especially non-fulfillment of international obligations and interference with the internal affairs of other states through propaganda and subversion.[37] For a short period, the United States even maintained diplomatic relations with the Russian representative in Washington appointed by the Kerensky government, which had ceased to exist. Recognition was eventually granted to the Soviet government in 1933, largely because the European situation necessitated the solidarity of the major powers in the face of the rise of Hitler in Germany. However, the Communist

[35] The principle of non-recognition of a new government created by force was originally incorporated in the Treaty of 1907, signed by five Central American Republics. As Señor Tobar, Foreign Minister of Ecuador, publicly endorsed this principle, it was known as the Tobar Doctrine.

[36] It was named after Señor Estrada, Foreign Minister of Mexico, who, in 1930, denounced the use of recognition as a means of interfering with the domestic affairs of a foreign state. However, by the Montevideo Resolution of 1943, the American states adopted a policy of non-recognition of any new government coming to power by force through subversive activities of the Axis Powers. For a more extensive discussion of American practices, consult W. L. Neumann, *Recognition of Government in the Americas* (Washington, D.C., 1947).

[37] This was reflected in the decision of *Salimoff & Co. v. Standard Oil Co. of New York*, Court of Appeals of New York, 1933. 262 N.Y. 220.

policies and programs remained the same, with or without recognition.

Increasing conflict of national interests in recent years has stiffened the American policy of non-recognition of the People's Republic of China. The situation is much more complicated than the Soviet case in the 1930's because of the effective functioning of the government of the Republic of China in Taiwan and the United States commitment to defend Taiwan and other areas in Asia against Communist aggression. Under the prevailing circumstances, it is most unlikely that the United States will consider any step in conflict with her treaty obligations.[38]

The cold war has furthered departure from the traditional concept of recognition. Non-recognition has almost become the practice of the major powers toward certain governments due to ideological incompatibility or international rivalry, as in divided Germany, Korea, and Vietnam. On the other hand, the attitude toward the emergent nations is different. Recognition has usually been granted at the earliest moment in order to create friendly relations. Some federated states in Africa received recognition but failed to survive.[39] Meanwhile, the newly independent states expect prompt recognition. Delay on the part of the United States in extending recognition to Guinea and to the People's Republic of Zanzibar was resented by the two governments.[40] The emergent nations have not had any difficulty in receiving recognition when their international status or form of government has changed.[41]

In view of the divergent practices stated above, there is as yet no definite standard governing the policy of recognition in the community of nations. International politics is still the determining factor of the

[38] See William L. Tung, *The Political Institutions of Modern China* (The Hague, 1964), p. 317. For a discussion of the Chinese sovereignty over Taiwan, see Joseph W. Ballantine, *Formosa* (Washington, D.C., 1952); Frank P. Morello, *The International Legal Status of Formosa* (The Hague, 1966).

[39] Inevitably, there is much power politics in Africa, as well described in Gabriel A. Almond and James S. Coleman (eds.), *The Politics of Developing Areas* (Princeton, 1960).

[40] Zanzibar first changed from a sultanate to a republic and later merged with Tanganyika to form a new state, Tanzania, on April 26, 1964. The United States continued diplomatic relations with the new state by maintaining the American embassy in Dares Salaam and lowering that in Zanzibar to the status of consulate-general.

[41] The British Dominion of Ghana became a republic on July 1, 1960; the Republic of Tunisia was established after its change of status from the former kingdom on July 30, 1957. Prompt recognition was granted by the states in both cases.

attitudes of states toward recognition and non-recognition, while international law chiefly deals with their general procedures and legal consequences.

§25. MODES OF RECOGNITION

Recognition is a political decision made by the executive branch of government and binding upon the courts of the recognizing state. In *Russian Government v. Lehigh Valley Railroad Co.* (1919), a United States court went so far as to state that the court was bound by the certificate of the State Department and should not consult newspaper reports and comments about the non-existence of the Kerensky government.[42] Similar positions may be discerned in decisions of courts in Great Britain and other countries.[43] Recognition may be express—by a specific provision in a treaty,[44] or tacit—through exchange of diplomatic agents and establishment of conventional relations.[45] It must be emphasized that conclusion of, or accession to, a multilateral treaty, of which an unrecognized government is a signatory, does not produce the effect of recognition. Thus, by adhering to the Nuclear Test Ban Treaty of 1963, East Germany has not been recognized by Great Britain or the United States. Neither do limited contacts between two governments imply recognition, as in the case of the United States and Communist China. Here, diplomatic negotiations conducted through intermittent sessions at over 130 meetings by authorized representatives from Geneva to Warsaw, without recognition, are unique in diplomatic history and constitute a new precedent in international law.

Recognition is usually granted singly, but sometimes collectively. It may be said that the participating states of the Geneva Conference of 1954 granted collective recognition to Cambodia, Vietnam, and Laos. The admission of new states to the League of Nations or the United Nations does not effect their recognition by individual members of the Organization. On the other hand, an international organization may

[42] U.S., District Court, S.D.N.Y., 1919. 293 F. 133.

[43] See, *e.g.*, *Duff Development v. Kelantan*, Great Britain, House of Lords, 1924. [1924] A.C. 797. See also a later decision by the House of Lords in 1953 in *Gdynia Ameryka Linie Zeglugowe Spolka Akcyina v. Boguslawski.* [1953] A.C. 11.

[44] For instance, the Treaty of Rome between Italy and the Soviet Union on February 7, 1924, provides in Art. I: "The Power of each of the contracting parties is mutually recognized as the only legal and sovereign one in the respective countries."

[45] See Moore, *Digest*, I, p. 73.

recommend non-recognition of a state illegally created,[46] or recognition of a regime as the only legal government of a state.[47]

Although recognition is generally unconditional, there are precedents of conditional recognition, which implies assurance given by the recognized state or government for the performance or non-performance of certain acts. Thus, by the Treaty of Berlin of July 13, 1878, Bulgaria and Serbia were recognized by the major powers in Europe on condition that no religious disabilities be imposed upon their subjects.[48] In treaties with the new states of Poland, Czechoslovakia, and Yugoslavia after World War I, they were required to protect minorities in their respective territories. Similar instances may be found in recent times.[49] But recognition once given cannot be withdrawn even if the recognized state or government does not fulfill the conditions. The only resort for the recognizing state is to sever diplomatic relations or take necessary measures to enforce fulfillment.

§26. DISTINCTION BETWEEN DE FACTO AND DE JURE RECOGNITION

De jure recognition is generally full and complete in nature. If a new state or government is, in the judgment of the recognizing state, not yet in a position to fulfill all the conditions of recognition, circumstances may necessitate the grant of *de facto* recognition first. Great Britain's recognition of the Soviet Union was *de facto* in 1921, followed by *de jure* in 1924. The Carranza government in Mexico was recognized *de facto* by the United States in 1915 and *de jure* two years later.[50] When Indonesia became independent, the practice of states

[46] This was applied to the puppet state of Manchukuo set up by Japan, in accordance with the resolution adopted by the Assembly of the League of Nations on March 11, 1932.

[47] As in the case of the Republic of Korea, according to the resolution adopted by the General Assembly of the United Nations on December 12, 1948.

[48] The signatories of the Treaty were Austria-Hungary, France, Germany, Great Britain, Italy, Russia, and Turkey.

[49] By an exchange of notes between the United States and the Soviet Union on November 16, 1933, the latter agreed to refrain from interfering in the internal affairs of the former. There were conditional overtones in American recognition of the Arab Union on May 24–28, 1958. See Whiteman, *Digest*, II, p. 135.

[50] The decision of the British court in *The Arantzazu Mendi* in 1939 to grant juridical immunity to the Nationalist government of Spain, then in *de facto* control of a part of Spanish territory, was subject to severe criticism. [1939] A.C. 256.

varied in granting *de facto* and *de jure* recognition.[51] With rare exceptions, recent recognition of the emergent nations in Asia and Africa is *de jure,* because *de facto* recognition as halfway between recognition and non-recognition has proved distasteful to the recognized states. Majorie M. Whiteman has suggested that the terms '*de facto*' and '*de jure*' be applied to the political entity rather than the mode of recognition.[52] This is perhaps a sensible way to avoid ambiguity and embarrassment. The prevailing practice of the United States is to extend recognition *per se.* Serious consideration of all these aspects was made when the United States granted *de jure* recognition to the United Arab Republic in February 1958.[53]

Even though *de facto* recognition is provisional, the internal acts of the recognized authority, whether *de facto* or *de jure,* receive the same effect in the courts of the recognizing state.[54] There is, however, a slight distinction between these two forms of recognition of states when the right of succession as a result of annexation is involved. This distinction may be discerned in *Haile Selassie v. Cable & Wireless, Ltd. (No. 2)* in 1939.[55] A British court first ruled that Italy was not entitled to the assets of Abyssinia through annexation, which was then only accorded *de facto* recognition by Great Britain. This attitude changed after the British government extended *de jure* recognition to the annexation.

§27. LEGAL EFFECTS OF RECOGNITION

Only a recognized government has the capacity to sue in the recognizing state.[56] Once recognized, the effect is retroactive to the date of

[51] See J. J. G. Syatauw, *Some Newly Established Asian States and the Development of International Law* (The Hague, 1961), pp. 104–106.

[52] Whiteman, *Digest,* II, pp. 3–4.

[53] *Ibid.,* p. 4.

[54] See *A. M. Luther v. James Sagor & Co.,* Great Britain, Court of Appeal, 1921 ([1921] 3 K.B. 532); *The Arantzazu Mendi* just cited; *Bank of Ethiopia v. National Bank of Egypt and Liquori,* Great Britain, Court of Chancery, 1937 ([1937] 1 Ch. 513). See also N. D. Houghton, "Responsibility for Acts and Obligations of *de Facto* Governments," 64 *United States Law Review* (May 1930), pp. 242–256.

[55] [1939] Ch. 182.

[56] In the case of *Republic of China v. Merchants' Fire Assurance Corporation of New York,* the Circuit Court of Appeals (Ninth Circuit) ruled, in 1929, that the Republic of China was entitled to sue in the courts of the United States after recognition, which was evidenced in the conclusion of a commercial treaty between the two countries and the reception of the Chinese envoy by the United States. 30 F.2d 278. For the principle that an

inception of the new government. This principle was, for instance, applied to the recognition of the government of Nationalist China by the United States in *Republic of China v. Merchants' Fire Assurance Corporation of New York* in 1929,[57] and also to the Carranza government of Mexico in *Oetjen v. Central Leather Co.* in 1918.[58] In extending *de jure* recognition to the Finnish government on January 12, 1920, the United States considered full recognition as of May 7, 1919, the date of *de facto* recognition. However, recognition of a new government does not invalidate the legal acts of a formerly recognized *de jure* government.[59]

Suits may not be brought against a recognized government without its consent. Likewise, an unrecognized government is immune from foreign judicial process.[60] Whether the internal acts of a recognized government will be given effect by the recognizing state depends upon the nature of the acts.[61] If they are opposed to the public policy of the recognizing state, effect may not be given by the courts of the latter.[62] As a matter of international comity, validity of the internal acts of an unrecognized government may be granted without prejudice to the interests of the grantor or of friendly powers.[63] Recognition of a state or government may be withdrawn if the international person no longer exists or diplomatic relations are established with a new government.

---

unrecognized government cannot sue in the courts of the United States, see *Russian Socialist Federated Soviet Republic v. Cibrario,* United States, Court of Appeals of New York, 1923. 235 N.Y. 255.

[57] 30 F.2d 278.

[58] U.S. Supreme Court, 1918. 246 U.S.297.

[59] See *Civil Air Transport Inc. v. Central Air Transport Corp.,* Great Britain, House of Lords, 1953 ([1953] A.C.70); *Boguslaweki v. Gdynia Ameryka Linie,* Great Britain, Court of Appeal, 1950 ([1950] 1 K.B. 157).

[60] See *Wulfsohn v. Russian Socialist Federated Soviet Republic,* United States, Court of Appeals of New York, 1923. 234 N.Y. 372.

[61] Foreign tribunals are not competent to recognize or enforce any decrees of an unrecognized government. See *Digmeloff v. Civil Affairs of St.-Josse-Ten-Noode,* Belgium, Brussels Civil Court, 1928. *Annual Digest,* 1927–28, No. 45.

[62] In denying the application of confiscatory decrees without compensation by the Soviet government, a French court held that recognition of the Soviet government by France did not obligate French courts to give effect to what contravened to the public policy of France. *Russian State v. Campagnie Ropit,* France, Court of Appeal of Aix, 1925. 53 *Journal de droit international,* 667.

[63] In *James & Co. v. Second Russian Insurance Co.,* effect was not given to the nationalization decree of the unrecognized Soviet government. United States, Court of Appeals of New York, 1925. 229 N.Y. 248.

Instances are the British withdrawal of her recognition of Abyssinia when Abyssinia was annexed by Italy in 1938 and of the government of the Republic of China when Great Britain established diplomatic relations with the People's Republic on the mainland in January 1950. The legal consequences of such cases are similar to those described in connection with recognition. On the other hand, the United States long continued to maintain diplomatic relations with Estonia, Latvia, and Lithuania, after the annexation of the three Baltic states by the Soviet Union in 1940, through their representatives in Washington. Rather than grant recognition to a new government, a state may continue to receive the diplomatic representative of a previous government that has been overthrown. But such an unfriendly act is bound to create adverse political, if not legal, consequences.[64]

§28. RECOGNITION OF INSURGENCY AND BELLIGERENCY

When a political insurrection reaches the proportion of war in a material sense, the parent state or the legal government may accord a status of insurgency to the rebels, from humanitarian reasons or practical necessity. The same status may be granted by third powers. Then combatants, if captured, will be treated as prisoners of war instead of as traitors or pirates.[65] After granting the status of insurgency to the rebels, third powers have the duty to enforce neutrality laws.[66] Meanwhile, they are entitled to due respect and protection of lives and property of their nationals by the insurgents.

A status of belligerency may be granted if a rebellion reaches the proportion of a civil war in a legal sense, under a responsible government capable of carrying out its internal and external obligations.[67]

[64] See the *Russian Government v. Lehigh Valley Railroad Co.*, United States, District Court, S.D.N.Y., 1919. 293 F. 133. For further discussion of the legal effects of recognition, consult J. G. Hervey, *The Legal Effects of Recognition in International Law* (Philadelphia, 1928).

[65] See *The Ambrose Light*, United States, District Court, S.D.N.Y., 1885. 25 F. 408. When the American government had not granted any form of recognition to the Colombian insurgents, the ship carrying Colombian insurgents was deemed piratical. But it was eventually released due to implied recognition of a status of war in Colombia. The Geneva Convention of 1949 applies to all hostilities.

[66] Neutrality was proclaimed by Great Britain and the United States at the time of their recognition of the Cuban rebels with the status of insurgency in 1869 and 1895 respectively.

[67] For discussion of a civil war in a material or legal sense, see *The Three Friends*, U.S. Supreme Court, 1897. 166 U.S. 1.

Then the rebels are entitled to the same rights and duties as is a state or government with respect to the conduct of war, but not beyond that. Both contesting parties have the right of visit and search, capture of contraband, and enforcement of blockade. Informal relations may be established between the belligerents and third powers, but nothing should be done to effect recognition of the rebelling belligerent as a new state or government. The acts of military authorities of the belligerents,[68] including levying an assessment,[69] are valid, but confiscatory decrees of an unsuccessful belligerent for the furtherance of civil war have been repudiated by the United States Supreme Court.[70]

§29. PREMATURE RECOGNITION

Third powers usually exercise their discretion in deciding the time and circumstances to grant recognition of insurgency, belligerency, or a new government or state as a result of civil war or any drastic changes in another state. Premature recognition in either case, merely for national self-interest, would be a gross affront to the legal government or parent state. The injured authority may interpret premature recognition by a third power as intervention in its domestic affairs and resort to retaliatory measures. Great Britain declared war against France after the latter recognized the independence of the United States in 1778. Recognition of Panama by the United States in 1903 within three days after the declaration of independence was greatly resented by Colombia. Thus recognition should be based on not only public policy but also law and fact.

In some instances, the complaint of premature recognition has not necessarily been justified.[71] The creation of Manchukuo by Japan on February 18, 1932, was not a matter of premature recognition, but actually an act of aggression upon Chinese territory by Japan in violation of the League Covenant and other treaty obligations. The League

[68] See *Ford v. Surget,* U.S. Supreme Court, 1878. 97 U.S. 594.

[69] See *O'Neill v. Central Leather Co.,* U.S., Court of Errors and Appeals of New Jersey, 1915. 87 N.J. Law 552.

[70] *Williams v. Bruffy,* 1877. 96 U.S. 176. Among various instances of recognition of belligerency are Texas by the United States in 1836, and the Southern Confederacy by Great Britain in 1861.

[71] In spite of the American complaint of premature recognition of the status of belligerency accorded by Great Britain to the Southern Confederacy on May 13, 1861, British action was justified in view of the prevailing situation, especially the proclamation of blockade by President Lincoln on April 19 of the same year.

members were bound by its resolution of non-recognition of March 11, 1932, parallel to the Stimson doctrine of non-recognition.[72]

In wartime, the primary interest of each contesting power is to subjugate its enemy. Recognition of friendly rebelling regimes within enemy states will definitely weaken the enemy. Thus, Poland and Czechoslovakia were recognized by the Allied Powers during World War I even before their actual existence as independent states. Similar recognition was accorded the Free French Movement under General de Gaulle in World War II. In peacetime, however, recognition of independence is not generally granted until it has been achieved in fact.

The prompt recognition of the state of Israel by the United States in 1948 was resented by the Arab states, which have not yet reconciled themselves to the existence of the new nation.[73] In the case of emergent nations in recent years, recognition has been granted by the states almost on the same day as that of independence.[74] In these cases, fear of premature recognition was removed because independence had already been certified by the states previously in control of the dependent territories.[75]

[72] See William L. Tung, *China and Some Phases of International Law* (New York & London, 1940), pp. 14, 164–168.

[73] Ten minutes after the effective time of Israel's independence, President Truman granted *de facto* recognition to the Provisional Government of Israel on May 14, 1948; but it was not until January 31, 1949, that *de jure* recognition was simultaneously given to Israel and Transjordan. Here there is a delicate distinction between recognition of state and that of government. Actually, full and *de jure* recognition of the state of Israel was granted on May 14, 1948, when it was represented by a *de facto* Provisional Government.

[74] Denys P. Myers has described the American policy of recognition toward the new nations as instantaneous, at times even anticipatory. See his analysis of "Contemporary Practice of the United States relating to International Law," 55 *Am. Jour. Int. Law* (1961), pp. 703–720, on recognition of states. See also William V. O'Brien and Ulf H. Goebel, "The United States Recognition Policy toward the New Nations," in *The New Nations in International Law and Diplomacy* (edited by William V. O'Brien, New York, 1965), pp. 98–228. For a list of the newly independent nations with indications of their past and present status as well as dates of independence and of United Nations membership, see *ibid.*, pp. 224–228. Further information on the subject may be found in Max F. Millikan and Donald L. M. Blackmer (eds.), *The Emerging Nations: Their Growth and United States Policy* (Boston, 1961).

[75] Consideration of domestic political implications had caused delay in American recognition of Transjordan, whose independence had been declared by Great Britain on March 22, 1946. See Whiteman, *Digest,* II, p. 172. In view of the delicate circumstances of Guinea's independence from

III. *SUCCESSION*[76]

§30. THE CHANGE OF INTERNATIONAL PERSONALITY

New international persons may be created through establishment of a new state,[77] division of one international entity into several states,[78] or merger of several states into one.[79] Under any of these conditions, questions of succession will arise, particularly with respect to rights and obligations.[80] Succession may also occur in the case of an international person other than a state. The United Nations and the International Court of Justice were successors to the League of Nations and the Permanent Court of International Justice respectively.[81] Estab-

---

France on October 2, 1958, the United States did not extend recognition to this new state until November 1, for further clarification of the situation.

[76] General texts on this subject: O'Connell, I, pp. 423–460; Oppenheim, I, §§76–84a; Fenwick, *Principles,* Ch. VII; Moore, *Digest,* I, §§76–79, 107–133A; Hackworth, *Digest,* I, §§20, 78–82; Whiteman, *Digest,* II, Ch. IV; Starke, Ch. 10, Schwarzenberger, I, Ch. 3 (VIII); Hershey, Ch. IX; Gould, Ch. 14; Svarlien, Ch. 8; Von Glahn, Ch. 8; Soviet *Text,* Ch. III, §6; Jacobini, p. 50; Lawrence, §49; Le Fur, §§607–637; Wharton, I, §5; Nys, I, pp. 432–435; II, pp. 28–38; Pradier-Fodéré, I, §§156–163; Calvo, I, §§99–104; McNair, I, pp. 155–181.

[77] Most of the emergent nations in Asia and Africa belong to this category. Almost all of them immediately applied for membership in the United Nations. Western Samoa, whose foreign relations are conducted through New Zealand, is an exception.

[78] For instance, the separation of Austria and Hungary after World War I, Denmark and Iceland in 1944, Senegal and Mali from the Federation of Mali in 1960.

[79] The United Arab Republic was originally formed by the union of Egypt and Syria in 1958, but the latter seceded on September 28, 1961, to resume independent status. The Federation of Malaya received the support of the United Nations in its inclusion of Sabah and Sarawak as a result of a United Nations investigation, in conformity with the wishes of the people of the two states. 49 Department of State *Bulletin* 542 (1963).

[80] The complexity of the problems involving state succession makes codification into a uniform standard difficult at present, though it has been under consideration by the International Law Commission. See GA res. 2167 (XXI).

[81] In an advisory opinion on *International Status of South-West Africa* in 1950, the International Court of Justice pointed out that the function of the Mandate Commission was succeeded by the Trusteeship Council. I. C. J. Reports (1950), 128. Due to the difference in nature between states and international organizations, rules governing state succession cannot be applied to international organizations.

lishment of diplomatic relations by Western powers with states of long history but hitherto isolated from the international community, *e.g.*, China and Japan, does not confer new international personality on them. Neither does a change of government affect the continuity of state personality.[82] This principle is well illustrated in the case of *The Sapphire*,[83] in which the U.S. Supreme Court laid down the rule, in 1871, that a change of government in France did not affect state personality or national sovereignty.

The means by which a new state is created are immaterial to the status of an international person. The independence of former mandates, trust territories, colonies, and other dependent communities was achieved after World War II through either peaceful negotiation or forcible methods.[84] Some states were established under the auspices of the United Nations,[85] while others by the voluntary action of the metropole.[86] Certain nations obtained their international personality by a combination of factors.[87] Whatever the case, rights and obligations involving succession have to be settled in accordance with the stipula-

[82] Further reference may be made to K. Marek, *Identity and Continuity of States in Public International Law* (Geneva, 1954).

[83] 11 Wallace 164.

[84] Tunisia and Morocco achieved their recent independence through peaceful negotiation. They were originally independent states, but became French protectorates in 1883 and 1912 respectively. On the other hand, Algeria, Cyprus, and Indonesia used force to obtain independence.

[85] By terminating the trusteeship agreements with the administering powers, the United Nations sponsored the independence of certain trust territories, such as Cameroon, Ghana, and Tanganyika. Korea's independence was also under the sponsorship of the United Nations, but has nothing to do with the trusteeship system.

[86] Burma, Ceylon, and India are in this category.

[87] Establishment of the independent states of Libya and Somalia was influenced by a combination of factors, including recommendations of the General Assembly, pressures of the Council of Ministers, and a Soviet demand for trust territories in Africa. Besides, Great Britain and Italy were not anxious to keep these territories. See William V. O'Brien, *The New Nations in International Law and Diplomacy*, p. 215. Brief description of these two countries may be found in Agnese N. Lockwood, "Libya—Building a Desert Economy," *International Conciliation* (1957), No. 512; A. A. Castagno, Jr., "Somalia," *ibid.* (1959), No. 522. Cambodia, Laos, and Vietnam achieved independence through a long and complicated process; their destiny was decided by the Geneva Conference of 1954. The Republic of Indonesia was created under unique circumstances, starting from armed revolt, followed by United Nations mediation, and subsequently by collective recognition after a roundtable conference.

tions of individual agreements of the parties concerned. Owing to their resentment against colonialism and dissatisfaction with the status quo, the new nations do not always follow Western practice concerning the succession of rights and obligations. But there is no basic difference between their concept and traditional rules.

§31. UNIVERSAL AND PARTIAL SUCCESSION

Succession is universal when a state is totally absorbed by another either upon its own volition or through forcible annexation. The succeeding states may be a few in number, as in the partition of Poland by Austria, Prussia, and Russia. Partial succession may occur under such conditions as acquisition of a part of territory from another or secession from an existing state.[88] International personality may be substantially affected by the loss of a certain degree of independence without invoking the problem of succession.[89] Mere change of government through revolution or constitutional process does not involve the question of succession. Thus, the repudiation by the Soviet government of certain treaties and loan agreements previously concluded by the Tsarist and Provisional governments was not in conformity with the general practice of states, but was based upon its public policy in the interest of the newly established order in Russia.[90]

§32. RIGHTS AND OBLIGATIONS UNDER STATE SUCCESSION

Change of sovereignty over a territory does not immediately affect the private rights and obligations of local people.[91] There is, however,

[88] For instance, the secession of Pakistan from India. In this case, India remained as a Member of the United Nations, while Pakistan applied for a new membership.

[89] In the Advisory Opinion on the *Austro-German Customs Union Case*, the Permanent Court of International Justice concluded that the customs union between Austria and Germany would affect the independence of Austria. P.C.I.J. (1931), Ser. A/B, No. 41. See also *Terlinden v. Ames*, U.S. Supreme Court, 1902. 184 U.S. 270.

[90] Normally, a succeeding government is bound by treaty and other obligations of the preceding government of the same state. See *The Tinoco Arbitration*, Great Britain-Costa Rica, 1923. 18 *Am. Jour. Int. Law* (1924), p. 147.

[91] See *United States v. Percheman*, U.S. Supreme Court, 1833 (7 Peters 51); *German Settlers in Poland*, Permanent Court of International Justice, 1923 (P.C.I.J., 1923, Ser. B, No. 6).

much controversy over public rights and obligations.[92] As a rule, the succeeding state is entitled to all public property of the annexed state with the exception of that under servitude or easements.[93] There is no positive law governing public debts, which are in most cases assumed by the annexing state. But the United States did not accept the debts and liabilities of Texas when the latter joined the Union.[94] The Soviet Union did not hold Estonia, Poland, and Finland responsible for the debts of Imperial Russia when these states obtained independence after World War I.[95] When a state is divided, public debts are usually apportioned according to treaty provisions.[96]

Contractual obligations are generally binding upon the succeeding state if a third party is involved. In *United States v. Prioleau,*[97] the British High Court of Chancery decided in 1865 that a contract between the Southern Confederacy and a third party had to be recognized by the United States. However, contractual obligations between a vanquished state and its own nationals for the prosecution of the war may not be recognized by the annexing state. This principle was laid down by the Supreme Court of the Transvaal of the Union of South Africa in *Postmaster-General v. Taute* (1905).[98] Nevertheless, the court admitted that more and more such obligations should be assumed for humanitarian reasons. The same rule was applied to *West Rand Central Gold Mining Co. v. The King,*[99] decided by a British court in the same

[92] Many publicists hold that a succeeding state is entitled to all public rights but not necessarily bound by all obligations. For the views of many British and American writers, see D. P. O'Connell, "Independence and Problems of State Succession," in William V. O'Brien, *The New Nations in International Law and Diplomacy,* pp. 253–254.

[93] See *The Peter Pázmány University,* Permanent Court of International Justice, 1933. P.C.I.J. (1933), Ser. A/B, No. 61. In the *Free Zones of Upper Savoy and the District of Gex* (1932), the Permanent Court of International Justice regarded France as a successor to Sardinia's obligation in a territorial arrangement with Switzerland. P.C.I.J. (1932), Ser. A/B, No. 46.

[94] In the *Texas Bond Cases,* the United States-Great Britain Claims Commission rejected in 1954 a British claim on certain unpaid bonds of Texas against the United States. 4 Moore, *Int. Arb.* 3591.

[95] See T. A. Taracouzio, *The Soviet Union and International Law* (New York, 1935), pp. 22–24.

[96] *Cf. Ottoman Debt Arbitration,* Arbitration under the Treaty of Lausanne, 1925. 1 R.I.A.A. (1925), 529. For further details, consult Ernst H. Feitchenfeld, *Public Debts and State Succession* (New York, 1931).

[97] 2 Hemming & Miller, 559.

[98] Transvaal Law Reports, T.S. 582.

[99] Great Britain, King's Bench Division, 1905. [1905] 2 K.B. 391.

year, even though the petitioner was a company of the succeeding state.[100]

The succeeding state is not liable to the torts of the defunct state. Thus, in the judgment of the arbitration tribunal in the *Claim of Robert Brown,*[101] the conquering state was not obligated to right a wrong committed by the conquered state. The same principle was held by the Claims Arbitration Tribunal between the United States and Great Britain in the *Hawaiian Claims Arbitration* in 1925.[102] This rule was, however, questioned by the Permanent Court of International Justice in 1934, in the *Lighthouses Case* between France and Greece.[103]

The rights and obligations of the inhabitants of the annexed state among themselves and with the annexing state depend much upon the private laws of the locality. Generally speaking, they are not immediately affected by the transfer. In *Vilas v. City of Manila,*[104] the United States Supreme Court ruled, in 1911, that private laws continue in force unless abrogated or changed by the new ruler.[105] It must be understood, however, that law is a reflection of public order and will inevitably be subject to revisions in order to adjust itself to newly created circumstances.

§33. SUCCESSION TO TREATIES

There are positive and negative approaches to the problem of succession to treaties,[106] but the exact nature of treaty provisions in relation to the national interests of the succeeding state is perhaps the determining factor in international practice. In the interest of international order, treaty rights and obligations should be observed under normal circumstances. Generally speaking, executed or dispositive

[100] For further discussion of succession to contractual rights and obligations, see Starke, pp. 271–273; D. P. O'Connell, *op. cit.*, pp. 26–30.

[101] United States-Great Britain, Claims Arbitration, 1923. Nielsen's Report, 187.

[102] *Ibid.*, 160.

[103] *Annual Digest,* 1933–34, Case no. 36.

[104] 220 U.S. 345.

[105] *Cf. Panama Railroad Co. v. Bosse,* U.S. Supreme Court, 1919. 249 U.S. 41.

[106] Consult R. W. G. de Muralt, *The Problem of State Succession with Regard to Treaties* (The Hague, 1954); International Law Association Committee on State Succession to Treaties and Other Governmental Obligations, *The Effect of Independence on Treaties* (London, 1965); Kenneth J. Keith, "Succession to Bilateral Treaties by Seceding States," 61 *Am. Jour. Int. Law* (1967), pp. 521–546.

treaties concerning territory, servitude, and the like, are subject to devolution. With the emergence of many new nations in Africa, international practice in this respect is further diversified, but boundaries established by the former colonial powers have generally been continued. The Malagasy Republic, Congo (Brazzaville), Congo (Kinshasa), and several other countries have upheld the general continuity of treaties. On the other hand, Algeria and Israel have taken a rather negative position. Other states from the French community followed the affirmative approach in practice though they did not make any commitment in principle. Most of the former British colonies accepted the transmission of treaties on the basis of their devolution agreements.[107] Tanganyika, Uganda, and Zanzibar indicated their willingness to maintain treaties for a limited period.[108] Succeeding states may claim the right to denounce unfavorable treaties on the ground of *rebus sic stantibus*.[109] But, on the whole, the new nations have followed the general practice of states so long as it is not detrimental to their national interests.

If the succeeding state is a loosely organized union formed by several independent states, the problem of succession to treaties becomes more complicated. This situation occurred with the Arab Union.[110] The attitudes of the new nations toward succession to different kinds of treaties may be attested by their declaration in reply to an inquiry of intention by the Secretary-General of the United Nations. There is generally no question about succession to international treaties of a universal nature, such as the Conventions on the Privileges and Immunities of the United Nations and of the Specialized Agencies, adopted by the

[107] In its note of December 21, 1957, Ghana informed the United States of the formal transfer to Ghana as of March 6, 1957, "the rights and obligations of Treaties and Agreements between the United Kingdom and others in so far as the nature of these rights and obligations admitted such transfer." Whiteman, *Digest*, II, p. 153.

[108] See D. P. O'Connell, *op. cit.*, pp. 19–21.

[109] See Arnold D. McNair, *The Law of Treaties—British Practice and Opinions* (Oxford, 1961), p. 511; also *infra*, §170. The final text of the Draft Articles on the Law of Treaties, adopted by the International Law Commission in 1966, provides that these articles are "without prejudice to any question that may arise in regard to a treaty from a succession of states." For the text of the Draft Articles and commentaries, see 61 *Am. Jour. Int. Law* (1967), pp. 263–463.

[110] In its note of May 28, 1958, the Arab Union informed the United States that treaties prior to the establishment of the Union would remain binding on Jordan and Iraq but not on the Union and that only for treaties "concluded after the formation of the Union would the members 'be under the jurisdiction and authority of Arab Union Government.'" William V. O'Brien, *op. cit.*, p. 185. The Arab Union was dissolved on August 1, 1958.

General Assembly in 1946 and 1947 respectively. Many new nations acceded to such multilateral conventions applicable to them merely by signing the pertinent protocols to show their consent implicitly or expressly.[111]

The question has been raised whether commitments concerning military servitudes will survive a change of sovereignty of the servient state. The successor state is usually bound by such commitments, and has, in practice, tacitly acquiesced in the established servitude or concluded a new treaty to reaffirm the obligations assumed by its predecessors.[112] There should be no such problem in the case of change of government. When Fidel Castro came to power in Cuba, his revolutionary government notified the United States on January 6, 1959, that "all international commitments and agreements in force will be fulfilled." This policy was intended to apply to American rights in the Guantanamo naval base, later disputes notwithstanding.[113] It is extremely difficult for a state to exercise the right of military servitude in a foreign territory against the will of the succeeding state or government.[114]

[111] See the *Introduction by United Nations Secretariat to Signatures, Ratifications, Acceptances, Accession, etc., concerning the Multilateral Conventions and Agreements in Respect of Which the Secretary General Acts as Depository*. UN Doc. 1949.V.9, p. 3.

[112] For positive and negative military servitudes as well as recent practices in Morocco, the West Indies, and other areas, see Albert J. Esgain, "Military Servitudes and the New Nations," in William V. O'Brien, *op. cit.*, pp. 71–95.

[113] U.S. Department of Defense, *United States Naval Base: Guantanamo Bay, Cuba,* Statement of August 10, 1962 (3rd ed.), p. 2.

[114] For further discussion of the subject of state succession, consult D. P. O'Connell, *The Law of State Succession* (Cambridge, England, 1956); Herbert A. Wilkinson, *The American Doctrine of State Succession* (Baltimore, 1934); Arthur B. Keith, *Theory of State Succession with Special Reference to English and Colonial Law* (London, 1907).

CHAPTER 3

THE ESTABLISHMENT OF INTERNATIONAL ORGANIZATION

I. *THE EMERGENCE OF INTERNATIONAL ORGANIZATION* [1]

§34. HISTORICAL DEVELOPMENT

Farsighted philosophers, publicists, and political writers have long realized the importance of international organization to the peace and order of the world. Ever since the fourteenth century, various ideas and projects have been launched in the West, including Dante Alighieri's proposal of a world state and Pierre Dubois' plan of a confederation of political entities.[2] The concept of a world assembly of independent states on a permanent basis was presented by Emeric Crucé in 1623.[3] These early projects,[4] which were further developed by William Penn,

[1] General texts on this subject: Claude, Chs. 1–2; Blaisdell, Ch. 1; Goodspeed, Ch. 1; Leonard, Chs. 1–2; Watkins & Robinson, Chs. 1–5; Oppenheim, I, §§166–167aa; Brierly, Ch. III; Starke, Ch. 18, §§2, 4–7; Svarlien, Ch. 2.

[2] Dante Alighieri published his *De Monarchia* in the early fourteenth century (*c.* 1310–1313). For the liberation of the Holy Land, Pierre Dubois suggested the advisability of organizing a kind of league in his *De Recuperatione Terrae Sanctae* (1306).

[3] A Parisian monk, Crucé published his famous book *Nouveau cynée* in 1623.

[4] For further discussion of various peace projects, consult S. J. Hembleben, *Plans for World Peace through Six Centuries* (Chicago, 1943).

Jeremy Bentham, and others in later years, generally provided an organ representative of the states, majority voting procedure, arbitration, as well as economic and cultural cooperation. Sanctions against recalcitrant states were stipulated in some cases.[5]

The Concert of Europe marked a period of international consultation among the Great Powers from 1815 to 1914. Even though unity of purpose disappeared rapidly after the Congress of Aix-la-Chapelle in 1818, concerted efforts in time of crisis preserved peace in Europe for almost a century. But this system of consultation was not without defects, among which were lack of a written charter and of a permanent structure for regular meetings.[6] In the Western Hemisphere, an initial conference of the Inter-American states was held in 1899, with the establishment of the Pan American Union as a permanent organ in the following year.[7] This regional agency, first of its kind, made a long step toward the eventual founding of an international organization for the maintenance of peace and security in the world.

Non-political organs of international scope preceded political ones. Because of increasing interdependence among the states and the practical necessity of closer contacts, a large number of international agencies with various functions came into existence. The most notable among these were the Danube Commission (1856), the International Telegraphic Union (1865), the Universal Postal Union (1874), and the International Health Office (1907). The cross-fertilization of international law and organization further developed international and regional agencies, beginning with the technical but moving steadily toward the comprehensive.

§35. INTERNATIONAL AND REGIONAL ORGANIZATIONS

International organizations like the League of Nations and the United Nations are universal in nature. In the opinion of one eminent writer, "international organization—which ought, strictly speaking, to be called *interstate* organization—is a phenomenon of a multistate system." [8] The regional organizations have a narrower scope and are lim-

[5] For details, see Leonard, pp. 23–28.

[6] See Gerard J. Mangone, *A Short History of International Organization* (New York, 1954), pp. 40–42, 48–60; Leonard, p. 35; F. P. Waters, *A History of the League of Nations* (Oxford, 1952), p. 9.

[7] Under the leadership of Simón Bolívar, a Pan-American Conference took place as early as 1826, but it failed to achieve greater unity among the participating states.

[8] Inis L. Claude, Jr., *Swords into Plowshares*, 3rd ed. (New York, 1964), p. 17.

ited to certain geographical areas. They include the Organization of American States (OAS), the North Atlantic Treaty Organization (NATO), the Southeast Treaty Organization (SEATO), the Central Treaty Organization (CENTO), the League of Arab States (Arab League), the Organization of African Unity (OAU), the Warsaw Pact Organization, the Council of Mutual Economic Assistance (COMECON), the European Coal and Steel Community, the European Common Market, the Colombo Plan, and many other economic and technical organizations.[9] All these regional agencies should be complementary to the work of the United Nations in accordance with the provisions of the Charter.[10]

Also of international scope are the specialized agencies that deal with labor, finance, food and agriculture, public health, aviation, education, science and culture, and other technical functions. These independent agencies have established relations with the United Nations through individual agreements and have worked closely with that organization.[11] Most of the international and regional organizations are long-range in nature. But there are also temporary organizations whose life lasts for the duration of their missions. One notable instance is the International Refugee Organization (IRO), which was created in December 1946 and ceased to exist at the end of 1951. There are numerous non-governmental and governmental organizations,[12] but this work will

[9] Official publications of the various regional organizations concerning their functions and activities are available. For brief descriptions of the more important agencies, see Charles G. Fenwick, *The Organization of American States: The Inter-American Regional System* (Washington, D.C., 1963); Massimo Salvadori, *NATO: A Twentieth-Century Community of Nations* (Princeton, 1957); NATO Information Service, *The North Atlantic Treaty Organization,* 12th ed. (Paris, 1965); Andrzej Korbonski, "COMECON," *International Conciliation* (September 1964), No. 549. For further references, see Ruth C. Lawson (ed.), *International Regional Organizations: Constitutional Foundations* (New York, 1962); Political and Economic Planning (London), *European Organizations* (London, 1959); Istvan Szent-Miklosy, *The Atlantic Union Movement* (New York, 1965); Goodspeed, Ch. 16; Blaisdell, Chs. 12–13; Jacob & Atherton, Chs. 5–6; Kaplan & Katzenbach, Ch. 12; D. W. Bowett, *The Law of International Institutions* (New York, 1963), Pt. II.

[10] See Arts. 51–54 of the Charter in particular.

[11] See *infra,* §151.

[12] Further information may be found in A. J. Peaslee and D. P. Xydis, *International Governmental Organizations: Constitutional Documents* (The Hague, 1961). By GA res. 2167 (XXI), adopted by its twenty-first session, the General Assembly recommended that the International Law Commission continue its work on relations between states and intergovernmental organizations.

only discuss international organization in relation to international law.[13]

II. *THE LEAGUE OF NATIONS*[14]

§36. PREPARATION FOR ITS ESTABLISHMENT

How to establish an international organization for the maintenance of peace and security had been discussed and planned in the early part of World War I on both sides of the Atlantic. In June 1915, the League to Enforce Peace was inaugurated in Philadelphia, with ex-President William Howard Taft as president of the organization.[15] In Great Britain, Lord Bryce led the Council for the Study of International Relations to devise means for preventing future wars. The League of Nations Society was founded in England in May 1915. Many official and unofficial drafts for a future international organization were prepared in Great Britain, France, and the United States.[16] Of the Fourteen Points presented by President Wilson in his address to Congress on January 8, 1918, the last one dealt specifically with a future international organization: "A general association of nations must be formed under specific covenants for the purpose of affording mutual guarantees of political independence and territorial integrity to great and small states alike."[17]

The official drafts proposed by Great Britain, France, and the United States were kept confidential for the time being,[18] but the

[13] The law of international institutions is on the borderland of public international law, private international law, and administrative law. An authoritative study on the subject is C. W. Jenks, *The Proper Law of International Organizations* (London, 1962).

[14] General texts on this subject: Claude, Ch. 3; Goodrich, Ch. I; Goodspeed, Chs. 2–3; Eagleton, Ch. 10; Leonard, Chs. 7–9; Watkins & Robinson, Chs. 6–10; Oppenheim, I, §§167ab–167p; Soviet *Text*, pp. 329–333.

[15] At a public meeting of the League to Enforce Peace in Washington in May 1916, President Wilson and Senator Henry Cabot Lodge both spoke for the need of an international organization. Lodge eventually led the campaign against the ratification of the League Covenant by the Senate. For further discussion of the subject, see Hamilton Foley, *Woodrow Wilson's Case for the League of Nations* (Princeton, 1923).

[16] Extensive information may be found in Theodore Marburg, *Development of the League of Nations Idea* (New York, 1932), 2 vols.

[17] Indirectly related to the future organization were the principles laid down in the first four points: open diplomacy, freedom of the seas, removal of trade barriers, and reduction of armaments.

[18] Prepared by the Walter G. F. Phillimore Committee for Great Britain, the Léon Bourgeois Committee for France, and Colonel Edward M. House for the United States.

publication of General Smuts' plan for the League on December 16, 1918, invited world attention due to his important position and the broader scope of his plan.[19] After his arrival in Paris in December 1918, Wilson insisted on the incorporation of a league covenant in the peace treaties. Upon approval of his proposal, the Peace Conference appointed a covenant-drafting committee on February 3, 1919, with Wilson as its chairman. After integrating the official drafts and also proposals made by neutral countries,[20] Wilson presented the final text of the League Covenant to a plenary session of the Peace Conference on April 28, 1919.[21] The Covenant, consisting of twenty-six articles, was unanimously adopted and was incorporated into the peace settlement as Part I of the Treaty of Versailles and of all other peace treaties. The League began legal existence on January 10, 1920,[22] when the Treaty of Versailles came into effect. Sir Eric Drummond was appointed the first Secretary-General of the League, with Geneva as its headquarters.

§37. THE OBJECTIVES OF THE LEAGUE OF NATIONS

The objectives of the League of Nations were stated in the preamble of the Covenant in words which reflected lofty ideas for a future world. The Japanese proposal for equal treatment of all races and nationalities was, regrettably, not included.[23] Measures to be taken to fulfill the principles and purposes of the League were embodied in various articles of the Covenant, the essence of them being summarized below. The extent of League achievements in pursuance of its objectives will be discussed later in conjunction with the activities of the United Nations.

Maintenance of international peace and security Among positive steps for the maintenance of international peace and security were

[19] General Smuts was then Defense Minister of the Union of South Africa and later its delegate to the Paris Peace Conference.

[20] Switzerland, the Netherlands, and the Scandinavian countries raised many objections to the first draft of the Covenant because of dominance of the great powers, exclusion of defeated Germany, and lack of other desired provisions.

[21] David H. Miller, *The Drafting of the Covenant* (New York, 1928), 2 vols., is a useful reference on this subject. For the text of the League Covenant, see Appendix I.

[22] Due to necessary preparations, the first session of the League Assembly was not held until November 1920.

[23] See David H. Miller, *op. cit.*, I, p. 183. At that time there was racial discrimination against Japanese and other Asians in the United States, especially on the West Coast. But these discriminatory laws concerning immigration and naturalization as well as other restrictions have now been abolished.

reduction of national armaments, prevention of the evil effects of private manufacture of arms, and exchange of full information on such matters. A permanent commission was established to advise and assist the Council of the League in the execution of the above responsibilities. Any war or threat of war and any serious dispute would be a concern of the League, which was to take whatever action necessary to safeguard international peace. International differences would be solved through pacific means, including good offices, mediation, inquiry, conciliation, arbitration, and judicial settlement. If a member or nonmember of the League were to go to war in violation of the provisions of the Covenant, economic and military sanctions might be imposed against the aggressor.[24]

Promotion of international cooperation The League was to promote international cooperation in various fields, including commerce, labor, public health and welfare, communications and transportation, and just treatment of native inhabitants of territories under the control of members of the League. Such territories would include the mandates under the tutelage of the mandatories. A Permanent Mandates Commission was to examine the annual reports of the mandatories and submit advice to the League Council on related matters. Special efforts were also to be made to establish relations with international bureaus or commissions by the conclusion of general agreements.[25]

Respect for justice and international obligations According to the stipulations of the Covenant, members of the League were mutually obligated to respect and preserve one another's territorial integrity and political independence. President Wilson considered this to be a sure protection of small countries and the heart of the Covenant. To make this obligation more acceptable, the Assembly was empowered to advise revisions of existing treaties if they were deemed not justified any more. To prevent secret diplomacy, registration and publication of future treaties were required. Members were further obligated to abrogate and refrain from entering into any engagements inconsistent with the League Covenant. However, this obligation was not deemed to affect the validity of arbitration treaties or regional understandings like the Monroe Doctrine. The express mention of the Monroe Doctrine was insisted upon by President Wilson against the wishes of many Latin-American states.[26]

It was the ultimate purpose of the League of Nations to establish

[24] See Arts. 8–9, 11–17, of the Covenant.
[25] See Arts. 22–24 of the Covenant.
[26] See Arts. 10, 18–21, of the Covenant.

the rule of law in the community of nations. Soon after the establishment of the League there came into existence the Permanent Court of International Justice. The Court was competent to hear and determine any legal dispute of an international character submitted to it by the parties concerned and also to give advisory opinions upon any dispute or question referred to it by the Council or the Assembly. Among disputes suitable for submission to judicial settlement were interpretation of treaties, questions of international law, and facts possibly constituting a breach of any international obligation, as well as the extent and nature of the reparation for any such breach. Whether a dispute were within domestic jurisdiction would be decided in accordance with the rules of international law.[27] The League was also responsible for the progressive development and codification of international law.[28] Whatever shortcomings the League might have manifested in its actual performance, there was nothing wrong with these basic principles and purposes, which have been largely incorporated into the Charter of the United Nations.

§38. PRINCIPAL ORGANS OF THE LEAGUE OF NATIONS

The principal organs of the League of Nations were the Assembly, the Council, and a permanent Secretariat.[29] Subsidiary to these were auxiliary organs,[30] autonomous organizations,[31] and special organizations.[32]

[27] See Arts. 13, 14, 15(8), of the Covenant.

[28] See *supra*, §17.

[29] Art. 2 of the Covenant. For a survey of the League organs, see Denys P. Myers, *Handbook of the League of Nations since 1920* (Boston, 1930), Ch. II.

[30] There were four categories of auxiliary organs: (1) technical organizations: Economic and Financial Organization, Organization for Communications and Transit, Health Organization; (2) permanent advisory commissions: Military, Naval and Aerial Questions, Intellectual Cooperation, Supervisory Commission, Mandates, Control Organ for the Manufacture and Distribution of Drugs, Advisory Commission for Social Questions, Opium Commission, Permanent Central Opium Committee, Advisory Committee of Experts for Slavery; (3) temporary advisory commissions: Commission for the Study of European Union, Special Committee on Contributions in Arrears; (4) administrative or executive organizations: Advisory Commission for Refugees, Commissioner for Bulgarian Refugees (Sofia).

[31] These were the Permanent Court of International Justice and the Internationl Labor Office (Organization).

[32] *E.g.*, International Institute of Intellectual Cooperation (Paris), High Commissioner for Refugees (Jewish and others) from Germany, Institution for Unification of Private Law (Rome), International Nansen Office for Refugees, and International Center for Study of Leprosy.

All members of the League were represented in the Assembly.[33] The members of the Council were of two kinds: the permanent members consisted originally of the Principal Allied and Associated Powers,[34] namely Great Britain, France, Italy, and Japan, but later included Germany (1926) and the Soviet Union (1934); the non-permanent members were gradually increased from four to eleven, elected by the Assembly from time to time at its discretion.[35] The Secretariat was a service organ, headed by a Secretary-General, who appointed staff members in accordance with the staff regulations and with the approval of the Council.[36]

Concurrent powers of the Assembly and the Council Both the Assembly and the Council could deal with any matter within the sphere of action of the League or affecting the peace of the world. They shared the power to increase the Council members, select the Secretary-General of the League,[37] elect judges of the Permanent Court of International Justice, seek its advisory opinions,[38] settle international disputes, participate in the process of the revision of the Covenant, and perform other functions conferred on them without distinction by the Covenant and treaties. The Council was originally designed to play a predominant role, but the Assembly later became increasingly important in the League.[39]

Functions and powers of the Assembly Some powers were entrusted to the Assembly alone; others, to the Council only. Those ex-

[33] For the membership as well as its admission and withdrawal, see *infra*, §§48–53, in conjunction with the United Nations.

[34] The wording 'Principal Allied and Associated Powers' gave the impression that the League was an instrument created by the victorious powers. The original provision by designating individual states was more logical, but finally abandoned because of the uncertainty of Italy's participation after the departure of her delegation from Paris during the Peace Conference as a protest again Allied rejection of her territorial aspirations. It turned out, however, that Italy joined the League, but the United States did not.

[35] From four to six in 1922, to nine in 1926, and to eleven in 1936. See also Art. 4, pars. 1 and 2 *bis*. The term of non-permanent members was later fixed at three years.

[36] See *infra*, §152.

[37] Appointed by the Council with the approval of the Assembly.

[38] The Assembly and the Council could exercise this power separately and independently.

[39] See Arts. 3(3), 4(2, 4), 11(2), 14, 26, of the Covenant. The Council was dominated by the great powers, even though they became numerically fewer in later years. For a comprehensive survey of organization, functions, and operations, consult C. Howard-Ellis, *The Origin, Structure, and Working of the League of Nations* (Boston, 1929).

clusively under the jurisdiction of the Assembly were admission of new members; selection of rules and regulations relating to election, terms of office, and conditions of re-eligibility; control of the budget; and advice to the League on revision of treaties and consideration of international conditions potentially dangerous to world peace. The Assembly could also take part in settling international disputes referred to it by the Council,[40] or at the request of either party to a dispute.

Functions and powers of the Council As stated before, the executive powers conferred upon the Council were comparatively extensive. Among these were powers to formulate plans for reduction of armaments,[41] advise how to carry out guarantees against external aggression, and resort to collective action in case of war or threat of war. The Council had jurisdiction over expulsion of members from the League, supervision and control over mandates, and approval of Secretariat staff recommended for appointment by the Secretary-General. The Council also had power to incorporate in the League budget the expenditures of bureaus or committees placed under the direction of the League. If necessary, moving the League seat from Geneva would be at the discretion of the Council.[42] It is quite clear that the Council was intended to be the executive organ of the League.

§39. THE OUTCOME OF THE LEAGUE OF NATIONS

The objectives, functions, and powers of the League as briefly described above will be further analyzed under appropriate topics in conjunction with those of the United Nations. As an international organization, the League was the first of its kind in the experience of mankind. Being a war product created by the victorious powers for the maintenance of the status quo during the postwar period, the organization had inborn weakness. Nevertheless, for a quarter of a century the League served a useful purpose limited by prevailing circumstances. Many international disputes were settled directly or indirectly through the League.[43] Owing to lack of wholehearted support from the major

[40] See Arts. 1(2), 4(1,2 *bis.*), 6(5), 15(9,10), 19, of the Covenant. A thorough discussion of the Assembly may be found in Margaret E. Burton, *The Assembly of the League of Nations* (Chicago, 1941).

[41] With the assistance of a Permanent Military, Naval, and Air Commission as its subsidiary organ.

[42] See Arts. 6(2,3), 7(1,2), 8(4,5), 9, 10, 11(1), 12–17, 22(7–9), 24, of the Covenant. For further details, see T. P. Conwell-Evans, *The League Council in Action* (New York & London, 1929).

[43] The following were the principal disputes considered by the League Assembly or Council during the period 1920–1939: Enzeli affair, Persia-

powers, its success in regulation of armaments and other political matters was moderate. The United States' refusal to join the League and Permanent Court of International Justice further weakened the position of the organization, though the American government took parallel action against Japan during the Far Eastern crisis.[44] The League, however, achieved much in non-political fields, which will be discussed later.[45]

When World War II broke out, Switzerland was determined to maintain neutrality. In view of Germany's withdrawal from the League, the presence of League headquarters in Geneva would no longer be desirable. Part of the League staff later moved to the United States and took temporary quarters at Princeton. Some agencies managed to function in London and Washington. Montreal was chosen by the International Labor Office as its headquarters. Under extremely difficult circumstances, the League carried out some economic, social, and other tasks.

Soviet Russia, 1920; Åaland Islands, Sweden-Finland, 1921; Albanian frontier, Albania-Greece, Serb-Croat-Slovene Government, 1921–1924; Vilna, Poland-Lithuania, 1920–1922; Upper Silesian question, Germany-Poland, 1921–1922; Tunis-Morocco nationality decrees, Great Britain-France, 1922; Bulgarian armed bands on the frontier, Bulgaria-Greece, Rumania, and Serbia, 1922; Hungarian-Czechoslovak frontier, Hungary-Czechoslovakia, 1922–1923; Hungarian optants, Hungary-Rumania, 1923–1930; Jawozina District, Poland-Czechoslovakia, 1923–1924; Corfu Island, Italy-Greece, 1923; Memel dispute, Lithuania-Poland, 1923–1924; Mosul, Great Britain-Turkey, 1924–1926; expulsion of the Oecumenical Patriarch, Greece-Turkey, 1925; Demir-Kapu, Bulgaria-Greece, 1925–1926; Greco-Turkish frontier, Greece-Turkey, 1926; Gran Chaco, Bolivia-Paraguay, 1928–1935; Austro-German Customs Union, Great Britain, France-Austria, 1931; Manchuria, China-Japan, 1931–1932; Leticia, Peru-Colombia, 1932–1935; Italo-Ethiopian War, Italy-Ethiopia, 1934–1935; German rearmament, France-Germany, 1935; Uruguay-Soviet Relations, 1936; Spanish Civil War, Spain-Italy, Germany, 1936–1939; Alexandretta and Antioch, Turkey-France, 1936–1937; China War, China-Japan, 1937–1945; Russo-Finnish War, 1939. Of course, not all the disputes mentioned above were settled by the League. Many of them were eventually settled by the disputing parties themselves either in accord with League procedures or through other mutually agreed means. For further information, see Quincy Wright, *A Study of War* (Chicago, 1942), pp. 1430–1431. A brief description of the principal disputes is in John I. Knudson, *A History of the League of Nations* (Atlanta, 1938), *passim;* Leonard, pp. 136–141; Denys P. Myers, *op. cit.*, pp. 270–281.

[44] For details, consult Quincy Wright, *Legal Problems in the Far Eastern Controversy* (New York, 1941).

[45] See *infra,* §§153–157 in particular.

During the course of the war, the leaders of the Allied powers gave serious consideration to the problem of a future international organization and finally decided to start a new one as a substitute for the League. The reasons could be easily understood. The Soviet Union naturally had no intention to keep the League, from which she was expelled because of her war with Finland in 1939. Although President Wilson initiated the League, the United States never joined it. Great Britain, France, and other powers were not too enthusiastic about maintaining the World War I product. The Permanent Court of International Justice had to give way to a new one, in name if not in substance. Actually, the United Nations inherited a great many features from the League system. There are more similarities than differences between them in objectives, organization, functions, and activities.[46]

After the establishment of the United Nations, the Assembly of the League held its last meeting in April 1946, and voted to dissolve. On April 19, the League officially ceased to exist. A special Board of Liquidation completed the disposal of all assets, accounts, and other matters on July 31, 1947. In the words of Sir Robert Cecil, one of the founders of the League, "The League is dead, long live the United Nations." [47]

III. *PREPARATION FOR A NEW INTERNATIONAL ORGANIZATION* [48]

§40. EARLY DECLARATIONS

The weakness of the League of Nations in the settlement of international disputes and the catastrophe caused by World War II aroused statesmen throughout the world to search for peace through a new international organization. The London Declaration signed by the Al-

[46] For an evaluation of the League of Nations, see Arthur Sweetser, "The Non-political Achievements of the League," *Foreign Affairs* (October 1940), pp. 179–192; Alfred Zimmern, *The League of Nations and the Rule of Law, 1918–1935* (London, 1936).

[47] From his closing speech at the last meeting of the League Assembly. Sir Robert was also Vice-Chairman of the Covenant-making Committee at the Paris Peace Conference. For his observations and contributions, see his book, *A Great Experiment* (New York, 1941).

[48] General texts on this subject: Goodrich, Ch. II; Claude, Ch. 4; Goodspeed, Ch. 4; Goodrich & Hambro, pp. 1–43; Eagleton, Ch. 11, §§79–81; Leonard, Ch. 3; Watkins & Robinson, Chs. 14–15; Oppenheim, I, §168; Svarlien, Ch. 4; Soviet *Text*, pp. 333–336.

lied Powers on June 12, 1941, was the first move in that direction, emphasizing the importance of united action in war and peace.[49] When President Franklin D. Roosevelt and Prime Minister Winston Churchill announced their war aims in the Atlantic Charter on August 14, 1941, they expected the eventual "establishment of a wider and permanent system of general security." [50] The principles laid down in the Atlantic Charter were reaffirmed by the United Nations Declaration, signed at Washington on January 1, 1942, by twenty-six nations, including the United States, Great Britain, the Soviet Union, and China.[51]

The nature of a future organization was clarified at the Quebec Conference in August 1943, when the leaders of the United States and Great Britain decided that it should be a universal organ rather than a number of regional councils as originally conceived by Churchill.[52] The Moscow Declaration on General Security of October 30, 1943, was a joint statement of first importance, signed by representatives of Great Britain, China, the United States, and the Soviet Union.[53] The four

[49] The Signatories were Great Britain, Australia, Canada, New Zealand, and the Union of South Africa; the governments-in-exile of Belgium, Czechoslovakia, Greece, Luxemburg, the Netherlands, Norway, Poland, Yugoslavia; and General de Gaulle of France. For the text of the Declaration, see *Everyman's UN*, 1945–1963, p. 3.

[50] In the Atlantic Charter, the two leaders also pointed out the necessity of reduction of armaments after the war. For its text, see *Yearbook*, UN, 1946–1947, p. 2.

[51] The original signatories were U.S.A., U.K., U.S.S.R., China, Australia, Belgium, Canada, Costa Rica, Cuba, Czechoslovakia, Dominican Republic, El Salvador, Greece, Guatemala, Haiti, Honduras, India, Luxemburg, Netherlands, New Zealand, Nicaragua, Norway, Panama, Poland, Union of South Africa, Yugoslavia. The following powers were later adherents to the Declaration: Mexico, Philippines, Ethiopia, Iraq, Brazil, Bolivia, Iran, Colombia, Liberia, France, Ecuador, Peru, Chile, Paraguay, Venezuela, Uruguay, Turkey, Egypt, Saudi Arabia, Syria, Lebanon. As the Declaration was signed by governments, France and Denmark could not act at the time. They were, however, generally considered as associated with the United Nations from the very beginning. For the text of the Declaration, see *ibid.*, pp. 1–2.

[52] The regional councils would be one in each of the following areas: Europe, the Orient, and the Western Hemisphere. Conveyed to President Roosevelt in February 1943, Churchill's idea was opposed by the State Department. See Leonard, pp. 44–45.

[53] The representatives were Vyacheslav Molotov of the Soviet Union, Cordell Hull of the United States, Anthony Eden of Great Britain, and Ambassador Foo Ping-sheung of China. For the text of the Moscow Declaration, see *Yearbook*, UN, 1946–1947, p. 3.

major powers agreed on the principle of the future international organization:

> That they recognize the necessity of establishing at the earliest practical date a general international organization, based on the principle of the sovereign equality of all peace-loving states, and open to membership by all such states, large and small, for the maintenance of international peace and security.[54]

Three essential points were emphasized for the future international organization by the Moscow Declaration: (1) equality of states, (2) universal membership, and (3) peace-loving requirement. Pending its establishment, the Four Powers agreed to consult with one another and with other signatories of the United Nations Declaration. When Roosevelt, Churchill, and Stalin met at Teheran to discuss common war efforts, they declared, on December 1, 1943, that their concord would win an enduring peace which would command the good will of the world.

§41. THE DUMBARTON OAKS PROPOSALS

In order to avoid dissension between the executive and legislative branches about the future organization, President Roosevelt and Congressional leaders were determined to establish a bipartisan policy from the preparatory stage. Before the end of 1943, both the House and the Senate adopted resolutions to that effect.[55] Meanwhile, the State Department had prepared a "Possible Plan for a General International Organization," which was frankly discussed by leaders of both parties. With further support of public opinion, the United States government was encouraged to invite, in the fall of 1944, Great Britain, China, and the Soviet Union to send delegates to Dumbarton Oaks in Washington, D.C., for preliminary discussions on the future international organization.[56] At that time, the Allied Powers indicated an unprecedented

[54] Art. 4 of the Declaration, *loc. cit.*

[55] The Fulbright Resolution by the House of Representatives on September 21, 1943, and the Connally Resolution by the Senate on November 5 of the same year.

[56] The delegations were led by Under-Secretary of State Edward R. Stettinius for the United States, Permanent Under-Secretary for Foreign Affairs Sir Alexander Cadogan for Great Britain, Ambassador Andrei Gromyko for the Soviet Union, and Ambassador V. K. Wellington Koo for China. Because the Soviet Union was then not at war with Japan, two series of conferences were held: U.S.-U.K.-U.S.S.R., from August 21 to September 28; U.S.-U.K.-China, from September 29 to October 7.

willingness to promote international cooperation. Even before the discussion at Dumbarton Oaks, a number of important conferences were held for the establishment of several specialized agencies of international scope.[57]

The Dumbarton Oaks Proposals agreed upon by the four major powers covered almost every phase of the future international organization with the exception of the following, which would be subject to future decision. First, while there was general agreement on the necessity of unanimity of the permanent members in reaching decisions on non-procedural matters at the Security Council, the Soviet representative objected to the position held by Great Britain and the United States that a party to a dispute, without distinction of permanent and non-permanent members, should not participate in voting.[58] Second, the problem of trusteeship with respect to the mandated territories under the League system and the colonies of enemy states was left for future decision.[59] Third, while no question was raised about the usefulness of a world court, it could not be decided whether the court should be completely new or a continuation of the Permanent Court of International Justice. Fourth, no agreement was reached on initial membership, because Great Britain and the United States objected to the Soviet view of limiting it to states at war with the Axis Powers and including each of the sixteen republics of the Soviet Union. Aside from these undecided questions, the basic provisions of the Dumbarton Oaks Proposals were incorporated into the Charter of the United Nations.[60]

[57] The Conference at Hot Springs, Virginia, for the establishment of the Food and Agriculture Organization in May–June, 1943; the creation of the United Nations Relief and Rehabilitation Administration in November 1943; and the Bretton Woods Conference in July 1944, for the establishment of the International Bank for Reconstruction and Development and also the International Monetary Fund.

[58] According to Secretary of State Cordell Hull, the unanimity rule or the veto power was adopted primarily on account of the United States. See *Memoirs of Cordell Hull* (New York, 1948), II, p. 1662.

[59] For military reasons, the Joint Chiefs of Staff of the United States insisted on the postponement of this decision. Territorial problems could easily create dissension among the Allied Powers. It was advisable not to raise such a serious issue while victory was not yet attained.

[60] The Dumbarton Oaks Proposals were divided into twelve chapters in the following order: purposes; principles; membership; principal organs; the General Assembly; the Security Council; an International Court of Justice; arrangements for the maintenance of international peace and security, including prevention and suppression of aggression; arrangements for international economic and social cooperation; the Secretariat; amendments; transitional arrangements. See *Yearbook,* UN, 1946–1947, pp. 4–9. Also

§42. THE YALTA CONFERENCE

Roosevelt and Churchill met Stalin again at Yalta on February 4–11, 1945, to discuss vital problems concerning Germany, Japan, and postwar adjustment of certain territories in Central Europe and the Far East. They also considered several issues unsettled at the Dumbarton Oaks Conference. As a result, a basic agreement was reached on the establishment of a trusteeship system, the exclusion of permanent members involved in a controversy from voting in decision of pacific settlement of disputes at the Security Council, and the inclusion in the initial members of two Soviet republics, the Ukraine and Byelorussia, and all states which declared war against the Axis Powers. It was further decided that a United Nations Conference on International Organization would be held at San Francisco on April 25, 1945.[61]

§43. THE UNITED NATIONS CONFERENCE ON INTERNATIONAL ORGANIZATION

On behalf of the four sponsoring states,[62] the United States sent invitations to forty-six states, on March 5, 1945, to attend the United Nations Conference on International Organization, which was convened at San Francisco from April 25 to June 26, 1945. Represented by fifty delegations, the Conference conducted its official business through four general committees,[63] four commissions, and twelve technical committees under the commissions.[64] A few plenary sessions were held for

---

available are the *Dumbarton Oaks Documents on International Organization,* U.S. Department of State, Conf. Ser. 56, Publication 2192; *Dumbarton Oaks Conversations on World Organization, August 21 to October 7, 1944.* Statement of tentative proposals. London: H.M. Stationery Office, 1944 [Misc. No. 4 (1944), Cmd. 6560].

[61] For the text of the Yalta Agreement, see *Yearbook,* UN, 1946–1947, pp. 9–10. For further information, see Edward R. Stettinius, Jr., *Roosevelt and the Russians: The Yalta Conference* (New York, 1949).

[62] China, Great Britain, the Soviet Union, and the United States.

[63] The general committees were the steering, the executive, the coordination, and the credentials.

[64] Under Commission I on general principles, there were two technical committees: (1) preamble, purposes, and principles; (2) membership, amendment, and secretariat. Under Commission II on General Assembly, there were four technical committees: (1) structure and procedures; (2) political and security functions; (3) economic and social cooperation; (4) trusteeship system. Under Commission III on Security Council, there were four technical committees: (1) structure and procedures; (2) peaceful settlement; (3) enforcement arrangements; (4) regional arrangements. Under Commission IV on judicial organization, there were two technical committees: (1) International Court of Justice; (2) legal problems.

final approval of the Charter provisions. The Dumbarton Oaks Proposals and various suggestions for amendment by the participating states were first discussed at the technical committees. Committee recommendations were submitted to the respective commissions, which, in turn, referred their proposals to the plenary sessions for final decision. Only the plenary sessions and commission meetings were open to the public. On June 26, the Charter of the United Nations was adopted and signed by the fifty delegations.[65] Poland was not represented at the Conference, but later signed it as an original member. The Charter went into effect on October 24, 1945, when the five permanent members and a majority of the other signatories completed the procedure of ratification.[66] By the 'Interim Arrangements,' signed by the delegates on June 26, 1945, a Preparatory Commission was established to decide on the first session of the General Assembly, which was convened in London on January 10, 1946. Thus the United Nations came into official existence.

§44. THE CHARTER OF THE UNITED NATIONS

The United Nations Charter consists of a preamble and nineteen chapters, which are divided into 111 articles. The San Francisco Conference decided to create a new world court under the name International Court of Justice. Its Statute is based on that of the Permanent Court of International Justice and forms an integral part of the Charter.[67] In comparison with the Dumbarton Oaks Proposals, the Charter

[65] For the United Nations Conference on International Organization, see *Yearbook*, UN, 1946–1947, pp. 12–34; also *Report to the President on the Results of the San Francisco Conference by the Chairman of the United States Delegation, the Secretary of State, June 26, 1945*. Department of State Publication 2349, Conf. Ser. 71 (Washington, D.C.: Government Printing Office, 1945). Materials relating to the Conference are most extensively covered in *Documents of the United Nations Conference on International Organization, San Francisco, 1945* (New York: United Nations Information Service, 1945–1946), 16 vols. See also Grayson Kirk and Lawrence Chamberlain, "The Organization of the San Francisco Conference," 40 *Political Science Quarterly* (1945), p. 321; Norman Bentwich, *From Geneva to San Francisco. An Account of the International Organization of the New Order* (London, 1946); Leland M. Goodrich, "From League of Nations to United Nations," 1 *Int. Organization* (February 1947), pp. 3–21.

[66] For the text of the Charter, see Appendix II. Further references on its history and evaluation are Ruth B. Russell, *A History of the United Nations Charter* (Washington, D.C., 1958); Norman Bentwich and Andrew Martin, *A Commentary on the Charter of the United Nations* (New York, 1950); Leland M. Goodrich and Edvard Hambro, *Charter of the United Nations: Commentary and Documents*, rev. ed. (Boston, 1949).

[67] For the text of the Statute, see Appendix III.

made many improvements, largely to satisfy the demands of the small states.[68] Consideration and discussion of a dispute or situation at the Security Council is not subject to veto.[69] Neither is a decision by the Security Council to call a United Nations Conference to review the Charter, though the revision still requires the ratification of all the permanent members.

While the United Nations system is based upon the experience of the League of Nations, the Charter is different from the Covenant in many respects. By abandoning the unanimity rule, the voting procedure of the General Assembly and the Security Council is more flexible. Pacific settlement of local disputes through regional arrangements or agencies in conformity with the purposes and principles of the Charter is encouraged. Wherever appropriate, the Security Council may utilize these arrangements or agencies for enforcement action under its authority.[70] Such a provision makes the international and regional organizations complementary. The stipulations of the Charter on maintenance of peace and security as well as enforcement measures are more comprehensive than those of the Covenant. There is definite improvement of the mechanics for economic, social, and technical cooperation under the United Nations system. Comparisons of other features of the two international organizations will be made under different headings in the present work.[71]

IV. *PRINCIPLES AND PURPOSES OF THE UNITED NATIONS* [72]

The principles and purposes of the United Nations are embodied

[68] To the small states, the Dumbarton Oaks Proposals laid too much emphasis on the power of the Security Council, dominated by the major powers as its permanent members. Thus the Inter-American Conference on Problems of War and Peace, held in Mexico City from February 21 to March 8, 1945, expressed the view that the powers of the General Assembly and the world court should be extended and that a separate organ for international cooperation should be provided. See *Yearbook,* UN, 1946–1947, pp. 10–11.

[69] This was a concession made by Stalin after his discussion with Harry Hopkins, a special envoy sent to Moscow by President Truman.

[70] See Ch. VIII of the Charter.

[71] *Cf.* J. L. Brierly, *The Covenant and the Charter* (New York, 1947); Clyde Eagleton, "Covenant of the League of Nations and Charter of the United Nations," Department of State Publication 2442 (reprinted from the Department of State *Bulletin,* August 19, 1945).

[72] General texts on this subject: Goodrich, Ch. IV; Sohn, Ch. I; Goodrich & Hambro, Ch. I; Clark & Sohn, Ch. I; Eagleton, Ch. 11, §82; Kelsen, *UN,* Chs. 1–3; Oppenheim, I, §§168a–168b, 168e–168f; Fenwick, *Principles,* pp. 204–207.

in the first two articles and the preamble, which has equal legal force with the Charter proper. Responsibility for their fulfillment rests with the governments of the member states of the United Nations, even though the phrase "We the peoples of the United Nations" is used to emphasize the well-being and determination of mankind. During discussions and debates at the United Nations organs, these principles and purposes of the Charter have often been invoked either generally or specifically.[73] Substantially similar to those of the League of Nations, the objectives of the United Nations are summarized below and will be further considered in this work wherever appropriate.

§45. MAINTENANCE OF INTERNATIONAL PEACE AND SECURITY

The maintenance of international peace and security is one of the fundamental objectives of the United Nations. The preamble specifically emphasizes that "armed force shall not be used save in the common interest." All Members must settle their disputes by peaceful means and give the Organization every assistance to enforce collective measures against a recalcitrant state.[74] Whenever the maintenance of international peace and security demands, the Organization will ensure that non-members act in accordance with the principles of the United Nations.[75]

Collective measures must be undertaken for the prevention and removal of threat to the peace, suppression of aggression, or other breaches of peace. For the preservation of peace, every dispute or situ-

[73] In many instances, the General Assembly adopted resolutions with reference to the principles and purposes of the Charter in general, such as 109 (II) on threats to the political independence and territorial integrity of Greece, 265 (III) on treatment of people of Indian origin in the Union of South Africa, and 377 (V), the Uniting for Peace Resolution. More instances may be found in *Repertory*, UN, Supp., No. 1, I, pp. 17–19; No. 2, I, pp. 14–18.

[74] Preamble, Par. 6; Art. 2(3, 5). "The Achievement of the United Nations objectives in Korea by peaceful means" was stressed at the time of discussion at the General Assembly of the question of atrocities committed by North Korean and Chinese Communist forces against United Nations prisoners of war in Korea. GA res. 498 (V).

[75] Art. 2(6). When the Polish representative requested the Security Council to include the Spanish question in the agenda by a letter of April 9, 1946, Art. 2(6) was expressly invoked. The following articles of the Charter also refer to non-members of the United Nations: 11(2), 32, 35(2). Some articles designate 'state,' 'states,' or 'nations' in general, not limited to Members only, such as 1(2), 2(7), 14, 55, 81. Among disputes involving non-members were Greek frontier incidents in 1946, Corfu Channel in 1947, Palestine in 1953. See *Repertory*, UN, I, pp. 42–48.

ation must be amicably settled or adjusted.[76] Regional arrangements or agencies for the achievement of the above purposes may be utilized.[77] Technically speaking, no Member can remain neutral under the provisions of the Charter. While the Organization is not authorized to intervene in matters essentially within the domestic jurisdiction of a state,[78] this principle of non-intervention does not prejudice the application of enforcement measures when international peace is endangered.[79] This provision is rather ambiguous and subject to diverse interpretations under different circumstances. Controversial opinions were expressed at the Security Council, when the Spanish question and the Indonesian question were debated as to whether Article 2(7) of the Charter should be applied.[80]

[76] Art. 1(1). For details, see Chs. VI, VII of the Charter; also *infra,* §§192–193.

[77] Arts. 51–54 of the Charter. See also *infra,* §§194–196.

[78] Art. 2(7) of the Charter. Art. 15 (8) of the League Covenant uses the phrase "solely within the domestic jurisdiction." The word 'essentially' in the Charter is evidently broader in scope than 'solely.' There are many instances in which objections to United Nations action have been raised on the ground of domestic jurisdiction. They include treatment of people of Indian origin in the Union of South Africa, observance of human rights in the Soviet Union, the question of Morocco, and the question of race conflict in the Union of South Africa. But the authority of the United Nations to discuss these matters is also based on other articles of the Charter. See *Repertory,* UN, I, pp. 67–75, 81–83, 88–91, 95–101. For further discussion of this subject, see Rosalyn Higgins, *The Development of International Law through the Political Organs of the United Nations* (New York, 1963), Pt. II; U.S. Senate Commitee on Foreign Relations, Subcommittee on the United Nations Charter, *Human Rights, Domestic Jurisdiction and the United Nations Charter,* Staff Study No. 11 (Washington, D.C.: Government Printing Office, 1955); Quincy Wright, "Domestic Jurisdiction and the Competence of United Nations Organs," in the Commission to Study the Organization of Peace, *Ninth Report* (1955), pp. 42–61; M. S. Rajan, *United Nations and the Domestic Jurisdiction* (Calcutta, 1958).

[79] Art. 2(7) of the Charter.

[80] The Spanish question was of domestic nature, but, in the opinion of many delegates, it constituted a threat to the peace. The Indonesian question was also contended to be essentially within the domestic jurisdiction of the Netherlands. In a speech before the Supreme Soviet, Premier Aleksei N. Kosygin attributed the worsening Soviet-American relations to the United States war in Vietnam: "Their normalization requires of the United States an observance of the norms of international law and the ending of interference in the domestic affairs of other countries and peoples." *The New York Times,* August 4, 1966. See also *infra,* §§72–73.

§46. PROMOTION OF INTERNATIONAL COOPERATION

The preamble launches the hope of promoting "social progress and better standards of life in larger freedom." International cooperation includes, but is not limited to, matters of "economic, social, cultural, or humanitarian character." United efforts must also be exerted in the promotion and encouragement of "respect for human rights and for fundamental freedoms for all without distinction as to race, sex, language, or religion." [81] During discussion at the General Assembly of the treatment of Indians in the Union of South Africa, the question was raised whether "a policy of racial segregation (*apartheid*) is necessarily based on doctrines of racial discriminations." [82] The *apartheid* policy has been repeatedly condemned by the United Nations.

The Economic and Social Council is provided with other organs to assist it in carrying out various phases of international cooperation and bringing the specialized agencies into relationship with the United Nations.[83] The international trusteeship system, a substitute for the mandate system under the League of Nations, is another step toward fulfilling the principles and purposes laid down in the Charter. The trust territories are classified into three categories in accordance with the Charter: (1) former League mandates, (2) territories detached from enemy states, and (3) territories voluntarily transferred by states responsible for their administration.[84] Promotion of the welfare of the local inhabitants and achievement of eventual independence of these territories are the basic objectives. In this respect, the United Nations and the administering powers have been quite successful.

§47. RESPECT FOR JUSTICE AND INTERNATIONAL OBLIGATIONS

It is the high hope of the peoples of the United Nations "to establish conditions under which justice and respect for the obligations arising from treaties and other sources of international law can be maintained." [85] The territorial integrity and political independence of all states must be respected.[86] The Charter is less rigid than the League

[81] Preamble, Par. 4; Art. 1(3). [82] GA res. 44 (I).

[83] Art. 57 of the Charter. See also *infra,* §§151, 155.

[84] Art. 77 of the Charter. For details, see *infra,* §157.

[85] Preamble, Par. 3.

[86] Art. 2(4) of the Charter. In discussion at the General Assembly on promotion of stability of international relations in the Far East, the purpose "to secure the independence and territorial integrity of China" was emphasized. GA res. 383B (V). At its 857th meeting on May 23, 1960, the Security

Covenant in this respect, because the members of the United Nations are not obligated to take necessary measures for the preservation of the status quo of any state pending decision of the Security Council. On the other hand, the scope of the threat to or the use of force is much wider than that of "resort to war" as provided in the League Covenant.[87] Express stipulation for considering the revision of treaties is not found in the Charter. However, such a consideration is implied in the power of the General Assembly to recommend measures for the peaceful adjustment of any situation.[88] Registration and publication of treaties are provided for in the Charter as in the League Covenant.[89] In case of any conflict between the Charter and other international agreement, the former shall prevail.[90] In this connection, mention must be made that there is no reference to the Monroe Doctrine in the Charter, as there was in the League Covenant.[91]

The basic principles of international law as envisioned by the Charter are equality of states, equal rights and self-determination of peoples, and respect for human rights and fundamental freedoms.[92] Furthermore, the maintenance of international peace and security by whatever means must be guided by the principles of justice and international law.[93] Peace at any price or even at the sacrifice of justice is not real peace.[94] Administration of justice in accordance with interna-

---

Council discussed the complaint by the Soviet Union (U-2 incident) against incursions by the United States aircraft into the territory of other states. See *Repertoire*, SC, Supp., 1959–1963, pp. 281–282.

[87] Art. 2(4) and Ch. VII of the Charter. *Cf.* Arts. 10, 16, of the League Covenant.

[88] Art. 14 of the Charter; *cf.* Art. 19 of the Covenant.

[89] Art. 18 of the Covenant; Art. 102 of the Charter.

[90] Art. 103 of the Charter. [91] See Art. 21 of the Covenant.

[92] Preamble, Par. 2; Art. 1(2, 3) of the Charter.

[93] Art. 1(1) of the Charter.

[94] The resolution adopted by the Council of the League of Nations to recognize Italy's conquest of Ethiopia was in the interest of peace at the sacrifice of justice. See 18 LN *Monthly Summary* (1938), pp. 97–102. Similarly, the surrender of the Sudetenland to Germany did not maintain peace in Europe. See Quincy Wright, *A Study of War*, pp. 947–949. *Cf.* Charles De Visscher, *Theory and Reality in Public International Law* (Princeton, 1957), p. 328. The purpose "to secure general and full observance of the requirements of international law and of universal standards of human decency" was stressed during the discussion at the General Assembly of the question of atrocities committed by the North Korean and Chinese Communist forces against United Nations prisoners of war in Korea. GA res. 804 (VIII).

tional law falls within the jurisdiction of the International Court of Justice, which has the same powers and functions as the Permanent Court of International Justice under the League system.[95] In the development of international law and its codification, the United Nations has continued the efforts of the League and achieved a large extent of agreement on various subjects.[96]

[95] Ch. XIV of the Charter and the Statute of the Court. See also *infra*, §§189–191.

[96] A concise but systematic study of the relationship between international law and the United Nations can be found in Quincy Wright, *International Law and the United Nations* (New York, 1960). See also *supra*, §§16–18.

CHAPTER 4

THE STRUCTURE OF THE UNITED NATIONS

I. *MEMBERSHIP OF THE UNITED NATIONS* [1]

§48. THE NATURE AND KINDS OF MEMBERSHIP

Sovereign states as primary members Like the League of Nations, the United Nations possesses independent juridic personality and is itself a subject of international law.[2] Through such organizations, the international community has been gradually organized, however loosely at the present stage. Contrary to the principle of universal membership, not all political entities can automatically become members of the inter-

[1] General texts on this subject: Goodrich, Ch. V; Claude, Ch. 5; Blaisdell, Ch. 3; Clark & Sohn, Ch. II; Sohn, Chs. II–III; Wilcox & Marcy, Ch. IV; Goodrich & Hambro, Ch. II; Goodspeed, Ch. 6; Kelsen, *UN*, Chs. 4–7, 18; Eagleton, Ch. 11, §83; *Everyman's UN*, pp. 6–8; Oppenheim, I, §§168c–168e; Fenwick, *Principles*, pp. 207–212; Soviet, *Text*, pp. 335–336; Schwarzenberger, I, Ch. 10.

[2] As a juridical person, the United Nations may make claims for itself and its officials for damages suffered in the performance of their official duties. See the Advisory Opinion on *Reparation for Injuries Suffered in Service of the United Nations*, International Court of Justice, 1949. I.C.J. Reports (1949), 174. Art. 104 of the Charter of the United Nations provides that "the Organization shall enjoy in the territory of each of its Members such legal capacity as may be necessary for the exercise of its functions and the fulfillment of its purposes."

national organization. Yet membership is not limited to independent states, but also includes dominions or colonies in the case of the League of Nations and even the constituent republics of a sovereign state, such as the Byelorussian S.S.R. and Ukrainian S.S.R., in the case of the United Nations.[3] When India, Lebanon, the Philippine Commonwealth, and Syria joined the United Nations as original members, they were not yet sovereign and independent states.

Original membership as distinguished from elective membership The original members of the League of Nations were the signatories named in the Annex to the Covenant and also those listed in the Annex when they acceded to the Covenant without reservation.[4] Of the list of original members, Hedjaz and the United States never accepted membership, and Ecuador did not join the League until 1934. The original members of the United Nations are the states which signed and ratified the Charter: participating members of the United Nations Conference on International Organization at San Francisco, or the signatories to the Declaration by United Nations of January 1, 1942.[5] Poland was the only country under the second category.[6] All the original members of the United Nations signed and ratified the Charter in accordance with Article 110.

Elective members are admitted to the international organization through application. The United Nations today has more elective members than original ones, 71 to 51 out of a total membership of 122 as of July 1967.[7] Most of the elective members achieved independence after

[3] See Art. 1(2) of the League Covenant. India was a British colony when she became a member of the League of Nations. For the inclusion of the two constituent republics of the Soviet Union as members of the United Nations, see *supra*, §42.

[4] Art. 1(1). For a list of the original members of the League, see Appendix I, Annex to the League Covenant.

[5] Art. 3 of the Charter.

[6] Poland's non-participation in the San Francisco Conference was due to lack of agreement among the sponsoring powers as to which government should be recognized as the legal government of Poland.

[7] The following is a list of the Members of the United Nations as of July 1967. The asterisk indicates original membership.

Afghanistan	Belgium*	Byelorussian S.S.R.*	Ceylon
Albania	Bolivia*	Cambodia	Chad
Algeria	Botswana	Cameroon	Chile*
Argentina*	Brazil*	Canada*	China*
Australia*	Bulgaria	Central African Republic	Colombia*
Austria	Burma		Congo (Brazzaville)
Barbados	Burundi		Congo (Kinshasa)

1954. With the exception of Western Samoa, all the new states applied for membership in the United Nations and were admitted to the Organization. They are economically less developed, have a common policy of anti-colonialism, and usually associate themselves with the so-called Asian group, African group, Arab group, or Afro-Asian group.[8] This geographical alignment is by no means unnatural, because the old or original members have their own affiliations, such as the Western, Communist, and Latin-American blocs. Though these divisions have often been reflected in voting behavior, national interests in individual issues are still the determining factor of their attitudes.[9] Whether original or elective, all Members are entitled to the same rights and are under the same obligations in accordance with the provisions of the Charter, with certain exceptions and variations. These rights and duties as well as the

---

Costa Rica*
Cuba*
Cyprus
Czechoslovakia*
Dahomey
Denmark*
Dominican Republic*
Ecuador*
El Salvador*
Ethiopia*
Finland
France*
Gabon
Gambia, The
Ghana
Greece*
Guatemala*
Guinea
Guyana
Haiti*
Honduras*
Hungary
Iceland
India*
Indonesia
Iran*
Iraq*
Ireland
Israel
Italy
Ivory Coast
Jamaica
Japan
Jordan
Kenya
Kuwait
Laos
Lebanon*
Lesotho
Liberia*
Libya
Luxemburg*
Malagasy Republic
Malawi
Malaysia
Maldive Islands
Mali
Malta
Mauritania
Mexico*
Morocco
Nepal
Netherlands*
New Zealand*
Nicaragua*
Niger
Nigeria
Norway*
Outer Mongolia
Pakistan
Panama*
Paraguay*
Peru*
Philippines*
Poland*
Portugal
Rumania
Rwanda
Saudi Arabia*
Senegal
Sierra Leone
Singapore
Somali Republic
South Africa*
Spain
Sudan
Sweden
Syria*
Tanzania
Thailand
Togo
Trinidad and Tobago
Tunisia
Turkey*
Uganda
Ukrainian S.S.R.*
U.S.S.R.*
United Arab Republic*
United Kingdom*
United States*
Upper Volta
Uruguay*
Venezuela*
Yemen
Yugoslavia*
Zambia

[8] For further discussion of the new members, see J. E. S. Fawcett, "The New States and the United Nations," in William V. O'Brien (ed.), *The New Nations in International Law and Diplomacy* (New York, 1965), pp. 229–252; Paul G. Hoffman, *One Hundred Countries and One and a Quarter Billion People* (Washington, D.C., 1960).

[9] See Leroy N. Rieselbach, "Quantitative Techniques for Studying Voting Behavior in the UN General Assembly," 14 *Int. Organization* (1960), pp. 291–306.

voting privileges of the permanent members of the Security Council will be discussed under various headings of this work.[10]

§49. ADMISSION OF ELECTIVE NEW MEMBERS

Conditions of admission The qualifications of new members as laid down in the League Covenant were essentially two: (1) effective guarantees of sincere intention to observe international obligations, and (2) acceptance of League regulations on armaments and armed forces.[11] The United Nations Charter is more elaborate in the conditions required of new membership: (1) states, (2) peace-loving, (3) acceptance of Charter obligations, (4) capability to undertake these obligations, and (5) willingness to do so.[12] Such terms as 'peace-loving,' 'capability,' and 'willingness' are vague and subject to controversial interpretations. In view of these requirements, the United Nations does not follow the more desirable principle of universal membership and has, from time to time, excluded certain states from membership primarily because of political considerations and power alignments.[13]

Sometimes states fulfilling all the above-mentioned conditions have not been recommended by the Security Council for admission. It has happened that certain states could be admitted only together with others at the same time. Admission on a *quid pro quo* basis is definitely illogical even if advisable in practice. On whether additional conditions other than those expressly provided in Article 4(1) of the Charter can be attached to admission, the International Court of Justice, upon the request of the General Assembly, delivered a negative advisory opinion on May 28, 1948.[14] It should be pointed out that the conditions required

[10] See *infra*, Chs. 10, 13 in particular; Kelsen, *UN*, Chs. 5–6.

[11] See Art. 1(2) of the League Covenant.

[12] Art. 4(1) of the Charter. For the admission of new members to the United Nations and the concept of statehood in United Nations practice, see Rosalyn Higgins, *The Development of International Law through the Political Organs of the United Nations* (New York, 1963), pp. 1–42.

[13] Spain's application for membership was first turned down by the United Nations in 1946 for lack of qualifications stated in the Charter because of the relationship between the Franco government and the Axis Powers during the war. The General Assembly resolution of February 9, 1946 endorsed the view of Potsdam Declaration of August 2, 1945, on the Spanish question. This position was eventually reversed and Spain was admitted to the United Nations on December 14, 1955.

[14] *Conditions of Admission of a State to Membership in the United Nations (Charter, Article 4)*, 1948. I.C.J. Reports (1948), 57. The General Assembly accepted the advisory opinion of the Court.

of new membership are not always faithfully observed by the Members of the Organization.[15]

Admission of new states may result from division of an existing Member or merger of two Members of the United Nations. In case of division, the procedure of admission is only required for the seceding state, such as Pakistan after separation from India in 1947. In case of merger, the change is noted by the United Nations without going through the admission procedure. When the United Arab Republic was formed in 1958 by the union of Egypt and Syria, the United Nations simply noted the change after a report of the Secretary-General. A state which has withdrawn from the Organization may be readmitted, as in the case of Indonesia in 1966.[16]

The problem of representation A distinction must be made between the admission of a new member and the problem of representation as to which government of a Member state should be seated in the United Nations organs.[17] At its 325th plenary meeting on December 14, 1950, the General Assembly adopted a resolution concerning recognition by the United Nations of the representation of a Member state. It reads, in part: "Whenever more than one authority claims to be the government entitled to represent a Member state in the United Nations, . . . the question should be considered in the light of the purposes and principles of the Charter and the circumstances of each case." [18] The problem of seating the government of the People's Republic of China has been repeatedly raised at the United Nations and the specialized agencies. At the sixteenth session of the General Assembly, the issue of

[15] *Cf.* Art. 2(2) of the Charter. For further discussion of the membership of the United Nations, see Aleksander W. Rudzinski, "Admission of New Members: the United Nations and the League of Nations," *International Conciliation* (April 1952), No. 480; Leo Gross, "Progress towards Universality of Membership in the United Nations," 50 *Am. Jour. Int. Law* (1956), pp. 791–827; Benjamin Akzin, *New States and International Organizations* (Paris, UNESCO, for the International Political Science Association, 1955); Eric Stein, *Some Implications of Expanding United Nations Membership* (New York, 1956); U.S. Senate Committee on Foreign Relations, Subcommittee on UN Charter, *The Problem of Membership in the United Nations,* Staff Study No. 3 (Washington, D.C., 1954).

[16] Indonesia resumed membership on September 28, 1966, without objection from the members of the General Assembly.

[17] For recognition, representation, and credentials in United Nations practice, see Rosalyn Higgins, *op. cit.,* Pt. III; Yuen-li Liang, "Recognition by the United Nations of the Representation of a Member State: Criteria and Procedure," 45 *Am. Jour. Int. Law* (1951), pp. 689–707.

[18] GA res. 396 (V). See *Repertory,* UN, I, p. 281.

representation was considered as an important matter, which must be decided by a two-thirds majority of the General Assembly.[19] On November 29, 1966, the General Assembly again defeated a draft resolution to seat the Communist government in Peking in place of the government of the Republic of China.[20]

Procedure of admission Admission of new members to the League of Nations was simply through a two-thirds vote of the Assembly by members present and voting.[21] The Council had no voice in the decision. According to the provisions of the Charter, a new member can only be admitted to the United Nations by a decision of the General Assembly upon recommendation by the Security Council.[22] The voting procedure of the Security Council prescribes that any decision on substantive or non-procedural matters must be made by the affirmative vote of nine members,[23] including the five permanent members. Recommendation for new membership is deemed a substantive mat-

[19] Much has been written on the problem of Chinese representation. See Herbert W. Briggs, "Chinese Representation in the United Nations," 5 *Int. Organization* (1951), pp. 3–31; Benjamin H. Brown and Fred Greene, *Chinese Representation: A Case Study in UN Political Affairs* (New York, 1955); Lincoln P. Bloomfield, "China, the United States, and the United Nations," 20 *Int. Organization* (1966), pp. 653–676; a Report of a National Policy Panel established by the United Nations Association of the United States of America, "China, the United Nations and United States Policy," *ibid.*, pp. 705–723; Myres S. McDougal and Richard M. Goodman, "Chinese Participation in the United Nations," 60 *Am. Jour. Int. Law* (1966), pp. 671–727.

[20] The vote was 57 to 46, with 17 abstentions. In the opinion of many delegates, Peking has not fulfilled the conditions laid down in the Charter. On February 1, 1951, the General Assembly adopted a resolution condemning Communist China's act of aggression in Korea. GA res. 498 (V).

[21] Art. 1(2) of the Covenant. States admitted to the League of Nations were Afghanistan, Albania, Austria, Bulgaria, Costa Rica, Dominican Republic, Ecuador, Egypt, Estonia, Ethiopia, Finland, Germany, Hungary, Iraq, Irish Free State, Latvia, Lithuania, Luxemburg, Mexico, Turkey, U.S.S.R. For the original members and states invited to accede to the Covenant, see Appendix I, Annex to the League Covenant.

[22] Art. 4(2) of the Charter.

[23] According to the amended Charter which became effective on August 31, 1965, the membership of the Security Council is increased from 11 to 15. Thus decisions on substantive or non-procedural matters are to be made by an affirmative vote of 9 members, including the concurring votes of the permanent members, instead of 7 members as originally provided in Art. 27(3) of the Charter.

ter.[24] Thus any permanent member can veto any application for reasons beyond the conditions previously described. After the recommendation by the Security Council but not before, the General Assembly decides approval or disapproval of the application by a two-thirds majority present and voting. If the Security Council fails to recommend, the General Assembly may request its further consideration, but cannot act beyond that.[25] A deadlock was thus reached for some time concerning the admission of several Communist and non-Communist states and was finally solved through the so-called package deal of December 14, 1955.[26]

Unfortunately, states currently divided for political reasons, such as Germany, Korea, and Vietnam, have not been permitted to enter the United Nations as regular members by 1967. It is an irony of history that the Republic of Korea, created under the sponsorship of the United Nations, has not been accorded membership. In spite of substantial contributions to United Nations programs of economic development, the Federal Republic of Germany has been kept outside the Organization. North Korea, East Germany, North Vietnam, and South Vietnam remain non-members. When international politics conflicts with legal institutions, the latter usually suffer. Nevertheless, world peace cannot be ensured unless legal institutions prevail.

§50. WITHDRAWAL OF MEMBERSHIP

The League Covenant expressly provided that any member might withdraw from the League after two years' notice. One important condition was fulfillment of all its international obligations, including those under the Covenant at the time of withdrawal. A member might terminate membership in the League by refusing to ratify amendments which had already taken effect.[27] The right to withdraw and its terms as stipulated in the Covenant were realistic and logical.

The Charter has no provision whatsoever on this subject, even though it was seriously discussed at the San Francisco Conference. The reasons for this omission were given in a declaration of interpretation in the Report of Committee I/2, which was subsequently approved by Commission I and the plenary session of the Conference. According to this declaration, members ought always to continue their cooperation

[24] For details of voting procedure, see *infra*, §§147–150.

[25] This position was further clarified by the International Court of Justice in its Advisory Opinion on the *Interpretation of Peace Treaties of 1947 with Bulgaria, Hungary, and Rumania,* 1950. I.C.J. Reports (1950), 10.

[26] States admitted through this package deal were Austria, Finland, Ireland, Italy, Jordan, Portugal; Albania, Bulgaria, Hungary, Rumania; Cambodia, Ceylon, Laos, Libya, Nepal, and Spain.

[27] See Art. 1(3), 26(2), of the Covenant.

within the United Nations, but, at the same time, they would not be prevented from withdrawing under exceptional circumstances or as a result of disagreement on Charter amendments. In any case, however, withdrawal would carry a stigma, since such withdrawal would increase the burden for the remaining members. The San Francisco Conference, therefore, decided "to abstain from recommending insertion in the Charter of a formal clause specifically forbidding or permitting withdrawal." [28]

In the history of the League of Nations, there were sixteen withdrawals.[29] Up to 1964, there was not a single withdrawal from the United Nations. However, the prolonged quarrel between Indonesia and Malaysia and the latter's election to the Security Council as a nonpermanent member changed that record. On January 7, 1965, after the seating of Malaysia on the Security Council, Indonesia expressed her extreme dissatisfaction by withdrawing from the United Nations. This unique action was formalized by a letter of January 21 from Foreign Minister Subandrio to Secretary-General U Thant.[30] Since no required conditions were provided in the Charter, the withdrawal was to take effect on the date of notification.[31] Soon afterward, Indonesia withdrew from several specialized agencies and subsidiary organs of the United Nations, including FAO, UNESCO, and UNICEF. After almost nineteen months of absence, however, Indonesia reversed her policy as a result of a shift of power in the government. After informing the Secretary-General of her intention to rejoin the United Nations, Indonesia sent a delegation led by Foreign Minister Adam Malik to attend the twenty-first session of the General Assembly.[32]

[28] See *Report to the President on the Results of the San Francisco Conference by the Chairman of the United States Delegation, the Secretary of State* (Department of State Publication 2349), p. 49; also *Documents*, U.N.C.I.O., I, pp. 616–617, 619–620.

[29] The following is a list of withdrawals from membership in the League of Nations: Brazil, Chile, Costa Rica, Germany, Guatemala, Honduras, Hungary, Italy, Japan, Nicaragua, Paraguay, Peru, Rumania, Salvador, Spain, and Venezuela. The first notification of withdrawal was from Costa Rica on December 24, 1924, and the last, from Rumania on July 11, 1940.

[30] For the text of Indonesia's letter of withdrawal from the United Nations, see *The New York Times*, January 22, 1965.

[31] There are provisions of withdrawal from other international organs, such as the International Monetary Fund, International Bank for Reconstruction and Development, FAO, ICAO, and UNRRA.

[32] See *The New York Times*, September 29, 1966. For a critical analysis of the Indonesia withdrawal, see Egon Schwelb, "Withdrawal from the United Nations: The Indonesian Intermezzo," 61 *Am. Jour. Int. Law* (1967), pp. 661–672.

§51. EXPULSION FROM MEMBERSHIP

Expulsion from an international organization is a serious penalty, imposed only under extraordinary circumstances. According to the League Covenant, "any Member of the League which has violated any covenant of the League may be declared to be no longer a Member of the League by a vote of the Council concurred in by the Representatives of all the other Members of the League represented thereon." [33] This provision was invoked when the Soviet Union attacked Finland in 1939 in violation of obligations under the Covenant. The Council voted expulsion on December 14, 1939, with the concurrence of the representatives of all other League members.

Opposition was raised to a similar provision in the Charter at the San Francisco Conference, but expulsion of a recalcitrant member was deemed necessary under the conditions as stipulated in Article 6: "A Member of the United Nations which has persistently violated the Principles contained in the present Charter may be expelled from the Organization by the General Assembly upon the recommendation of the Security Council." The word 'persistently' emphasizes the serious nature of the Charter violation. A decision to expel a recalcitrant member may be recommended to the General Assembly by the Security Council through a majority of nine members including the concurring votes of all the permanent members in accordance with the voting procedure of the Security Council on non-procedural or substantive matters. Unlike the League Covenant, the Charter permits a permanent member to veto its own expulsion, because a member of the Security Council need only abstain from voting in cases involving pacific settlement of its disputes.[34] If a recommendation is made by the Security Council, the General Assembly may adopt a resolution to effect the expulsion by a two-thirds majority of the members present and voting.[35] Fortunately, expulsion of a member from the United Nations has never had to be considered.

§52. SUSPENSION OF MEMBERSHIP

There was no provision in the League Covenant concerning suspension of membership. According to the Charter, however, members of the United Nations may be suspended from the rights and privileges of membership under certain conditions. This may occur when the Security Council has taken preventive or enforcement action against a member, whose exercise of the rights and privileges will then be sus-

[33] Art. 16(4) of the Covenant.

[34] Art. 27(3) of the Charter.

[35] Art. 18(2) of the Charter.

pended by the General Assembly upon recommendation of the Security Council.[36] Unless and until the Security Council decides for restoration due to a change of circumstances, the state in question will remain in an awkward position.

A member may lose its voting right in the General Assembly if arrears in the payment of its financial contributions to the Organization equal or exceed the amount of contributions due from it for the preceding two years. If failure to pay is due to circumstances beyond the member's control, the General Assembly may decide to permit it to vote.[37] Here the determining power rests in the General Assembly alone. Questions may arise concerning the exact conditions beyond the control of the member and the precise scope of financial contributions. Of course, suspension of membership will not release a member from its past obligations.

In 1961, a serious question was raised whether certain expenditures authorized by the General Assembly relating to the United Nations operation in the Congo (ONUC) since 1960 and the United Nations Emergency Force in the Near East (UNEF) since 1956 constituted "expenses of the Organization" within the meaning of Article 17, Paragraph 2, of the United Nations Charter, which states that "the expenses of the Organization shall be borne by the Members as apportioned by the General Assembly." On request of the General Assembly,[38] the International Court of Justice delivered an advisory opinion in the affirmative on July 20, 1962.[39] By a resolution of December 19 of the same year, the General Assembly accepted the opinion of the Court.[40] With the support of other members, the United States attempted to invoke the application of Article 19 of the Charter, which would suspend the voting right in the General Assembly of the Soviet Union and other states. After protracted negotiations in and outside the United Nations, invocation of the article was dropped, but the issue remains unsolved.[41]

[36] See Art. 5 of the Charter.

[37] Art. 19 of the Charter. At each session of the General Assembly, its Committee of Contributions reports whether action is required to apply this article. No such action has ever been taken.

[38] By a General Assembly resolution on December 20, 1961. See *Yearbook*, UN, 1961, pp. 571–572.

[39] Advisory Opinion on *Certain Expenses of the United Nations (Art. 17, Par. 2, of the Charter).* I.C.J. Reports (1962), 151.

[40] GA res. 1854 (XVII).

[41] For the costs of several peace operations of the United Nations, see John G. Stoessinger and associates, *Financing the United Nations System* (Washington, D.C., 1964), p. 106. See also David Singer, *Financing International Organization* (The Hague, 1961), *passim.*

§53. UNIVERSAL VERSUS LIMITED MEMBERSHIP

If a world organization is the aim of the community of nations, the present system of membership of the United Nations should be reconsidered. In view of the rejection of many applicants for membership through the exercise of the veto power, even though their admission was favored by overwhelming majorities in the General Assembly and the Security Council, suggestions have been made to vest the sole authority over admission in the General Assembly as was the procedure in the League of Nations. Another proposal has been to add a new category of associated membership with restricted rights and privileges. Both would require the revision of the Charter, and none is practical. Some extremists even have suggested the expulsion of the Communist states or the withdrawal of the United States from the United Nations.[42] Either step would merely increase world tension in contradiction to the original principles and purposes of the Organization.

Perhaps the best solution is to seek an agreement among the permanent members of the Security Council and other members of the United Nations to admit any state which applies for membership and indicates its willingness to comply with the provisions of the Charter, regardless of its political system and power alignment. A state in existence is a state in fact and should be included in the international organization. Admission does not imply approval, but merely recognizes political reality. To exclude certain states from the world body not only weakens the Organization but also aggravates international friction. With vision, courage, and tolerance, the present members of the United Nations can further the cause of international cooperation by applying the principle of universal membership on the basis of mutual understanding without the necessity of amending the Charter. It must be understood, however, that universal membership is distinct from the problem of which government should be the legal representative of a member state.

II. *THE ORGANIZATION OF THE UNITED NATIONS* [43]

§54. PRINCIPAL AND SUBSIDIARY ORGANS

Principal organs There are six principal organs of the United Nations: the General Assembly, the Security Council, the Economic

[42] For details, see Wilcox & Marcy, Ch. IV.

[43] General texts on this subject: Goodrich, Ch. VI; Blaisdell, Ch. 2; Clark & Sohn, Chs. III–V, X, XIII; Sohn, Chs. IV-VII; Goodrich & Hambro,

and Social Council, the Trusteeship Council, the International Court of Justice, and the Secretariat. Corresponding to the Assembly and the Council of the League of Nations, the General Assembly and the Security Council are chiefly responsible for the maintenance of international peace and security. In a change from the League structure, the economic, social, and technical functions of the United Nations are performed by the Economic and Social Council, which coordinates all activities of the specialized agencies and other organs within its jurisdiction. The Trusteeship Council supervises the trusteeship system with powers broader than the Permanent Mandates Commission of the League of Nations, but the trust territory designated as strategic area is within the competence of the Security Council. In spite of their status as principal organs of the United Nations, both the Economic and Social Council and the Trusteeship Council are subordinate to the authority of the General Assembly.[44] The International Court of Justice and the Secretariat correspond to their counterparts under the League system, except that the Permanent Court of International Justice was a separate entity, related to but not a part of the League of Nations. Leaving the Court and the Secretariat to be discussed elsewhere,[45] the organization of the other organs is described below.[46]

Subsidiary organs Besides the six principal organs, the United Nations may establish subsidiary organs whenever necessary. Sometimes they are also called 'subsidiary bodies' or 'subordinate bodies,'[47] and they may also appear in the form of commissions, committees, and the like. Under the authority of the Charter, the Statute, or rules of procedure, the principal organs may create or discontinue them, or modify their organization and functions.[48] In the practice of the United Nations, certain agencies are established by treaties and conventions, such

---

pp. 44–56, 146–150, 199–204, 367–370, 462–465; Goodspeed, Chs. 5–6, 10; Kelsen, *UN*, Chs. 8–10; Leonard, Chs. 4, 11, 20, 26; Eagleton, Ch. 12, §§87–101; *Everyman's UN*, pp. 9–26; Oppenheim, I, §§168h–168s; Fenwick, *Principles*, pp. 212–219; Starke, Ch. 18, §8; Schwarzenberger, I, Ch. 10 (IV–V); Soviet *Text*, pp. 336–346; Satow, Ch. XXIX.

[44] See Arts. 7(1), 63, 64, 82, 83, 87, of the Charter.

[45] See *infra*, §§189–191 and 152 respectively.

[46] *Infra*, §§55–58.

[47] Art. 7(2) of the Charter. For the distinction between subsidiary organs and subsidiary bodies, see Blaisdell, p. 82.

[48] Under Arts. 22, 29, and 68 of the Charter for the General Assembly, the Security Council, and the Economic and Social Council respectively; Rule 66 of the Rules of Procedure of the Trusteeship Council; and Arts. 26, 27, and 29 of the Statute of the International Court of Justice.

as the Permanent Central Opium Board and the Drug Supervisory Body, under the designation of other organs.[49] Unlike the subsidiary organs, their creation, discontinuance, or organization is not entirely within the competence of the principal organs.

The functions of the subsidiary organs may be political,[50] economic,[51] budgetary,[52] social,[53] technical,[54] or judicial.[55] Some of these organs are on a continuing basis of operation, such as the United Nations Children's Fund (UNICEF) and many others established for relief and reconstruction.[56] But the majority, such as commissions and committees, do not have interim machinery if not in session. There is no standard for the composition of these subsidiary organs. The Interim Committee of the General Assembly is composed of all member states,[57] but others have only a small and select membership. The executive board of UNICEF includes certain non-member states as well. Some organs, such as the Technical Assistance Board, have individual

[49] The PCOB was originally set up under the Agreement of February 11, 1925, concerning the Manufacture of, Internal Trade in, and Use of Prepared Opium, which was amended by the Protocol of 1946 and approved by the General Assembly under res. 54 (I). The Drug Supervisory Body was first established under the International Convention for Limiting the Manufacture and Regulating the Distribution of Narcotic Drugs of July 13, 1931. This convention was later amended by the same protocol and approved by the General Assembly under the same resolution.

[50] For instance, the United Nations Commission for India and Pakistan created by the Security Council under a resolution adopted on January 20, 1948.

[51] Regional commissions of the Economic and Social Council are of such a nature and operate on a permanent basis.

[52] *E.g.*, the Advisory Committee on Administrative and Budgetary Questions.

[53] Commission on Human Rights, and the United Nations High Commissioner for Refugees under GA res. 428 (V).

[54] The Technical Assistance Board (TAB) under the ESC res. 222 (IX).

[55] The Administrative Tribunal and United Nations Tribunals in Libya and Eritrea.

[56] UNICEF was established under GA res. 57 (I). In the relief and reconstruction category are the United Nations Relief and Works Agency for Palestine Refugees in the Near East (UNRWA), under GA res. 302 (IV), and the United Nations Korean Reconstruction Agency (UNKRA), under GA res. 410 (V).

[57] Popularly known as the 'Little Assembly,' the Interim Committee was set up by the General Assembly in November 1947 to carry out studies and inquiries on matters of peace and security, especially during recess of the General Assembly.

experts as their members; the United Nations Mediator in Palestine is a one-man operation.

There is also a wide range of differences with respect to the powers of the subsidiary organs. UNICEF may make final decisions and conclude agreements with governments. The Disarmament Commission under the General Assembly can call international conferences.[58] The Collective Measures Committee was set up to prepare studies. The majority of these subsidiary organs have functions limited to reporting and making recommendations. Normally, a subsidiary organ is to report to the principal organ under which it is established, but there are variations. The Office of the High Commissioner of Refugees, a subsidiary organ of the General Assembly, is required to submit reports to both the General Assembly and the Economic and Social Council; the Atomic Energy Commisison (AEC),[59] established by the General Assembly, reports to the Security Council. While many subsidiary organs are on an *ad hoc* basis, some are permanent. In conclusion, the subsidiary organs vary greatly in organization, functions, procedures, and duration.[60]

Because of the nature and extent of their functions, the General Assembly, the Security Council, and the Economic and Social Council have continuously established numerous subsidiary organs under the authorization of the Charter. Based upon its own rules of procedure, the Trusteeship Council has set up only a few. The chambers of the International Court of Justice are really an integral part of it and cannot be considered as subsidiary organs. The Secretariat is a service organ with a permanent staff to carry out its functions, but it has occasionally created some subsidiary bodies to advise the Secretary-General on specific subjects, as in the case of the Review Board on Permanent Appointments.

§55. THE GENERAL ASSEMBLY

As the representative organ of the United Nations, the General Assembly consists of all the member states, each of which may have no more than five representatives and five alternates.[61] There is no limitation on the number of advisers, technical experts, and persons in similar capacity for each delegation. The designation of individual representa-

[58] The Commission was established under GA res. 502 (VI).

[59] Established under GA res. 1 (I).

[60] For details, see *Repertory*, UN, I, pp. 223–229.

[61] Art. 9 of the Charter; art. 25 of the Rules of Procedure of the General Assembly, as amended and adopted by the General Assembly on December 31, 1963 (A/520/Rev.7).

tives to any principal organ is indicated in credentials to the Secretary-General. The General Assembly elects its own President and Vice-Presidents for each session, and adopts its own rules of procedure.[62] The Main Committees of the General Assembly are its component parts rather than subsidiary organs. Their function is to consider agenda items referred to them by the General Assembly and to prepare recommendations to be submitted to plenary meetings. Every member state is represented at each of the Main Committees. There are seven: First Committee (political and security, including the regulation of armaments); Special Political Committee (special items, such as *apartheid* and the like); Second Committee (economic and financial matters); Third Committee (social, humanitarian, and cultural matters); Fourth Committee (trusteeship, including non-self-governing territories); Fifth Committee (administrative and budgetary matters); and Sixth Committee (legal matters). In principle, the General Assembly will not deliberate on any matter not yet discussed in one of the committees, but this procedure may be waived. In addition, procedural or standing committees or *ad hoc* bodies may be set up to render specific services to the General Assembly.[63]

At its regular and special sessions, the General Assembly has established subsidiary organs in the form of study committees and other organs of political, administrative, operational, legal, and judicial nature. Under the authority of the General Assembly, some of the subsidiary organs may adopt their own rules of procedure and create their own subsidiary bodies. The International Law Commission, a subsidiary organ of the General Assembly, has made substantial contributions to the development and codification of international law. The Interim Committee was challenged by a number of Members as an illegal intrusion on the powers of the Security Council and of its permanent members, but certain objections were met by modification of functions and procedures in order to avoid conflict with powers of the Security Council and the General Assembly.[64] There are many other kinds of sub-

[62] See Art. 21 of the Charter; also Rules of Procedure of the General Assembly. The Vice-Presidents have been increased to seventeen in accordance with a resolution of the General Assembly on December 17, 1963. For the sessions of the General Assembly, see *infra,* §146. For the election and functions of the presiding officers of the United Nations General Assembly and various Councils, see S. E. Werners, *The Presiding Officers in the United Nations* (The Hague, 1967).

[63] The General Committee and the Credentials Committee are procedural. The standing committees are the Advisory Committee on Administrative and Budgetary Questions and the United Nations Pension Committee.

[64] See GA res. 111 (II); *Repertory,* UN, I, pp. 675–676.

sidiary organs under the General Assembly, such as the Committee on Information from Non-Self-Governing Territories, the Scientific Committee on the Effects of Atomic Radiation, the Advisory Committee on International Conference on the Peaceful Uses of Atomic Energy, the Negotiating Committee on Extra-budgetary Funds, and the Committee of Experts on United Nations Public Information.[65] Some of the subsidiary organs, such as the Collective Measures Committee, no longer exist. To ensure maximum usefulness and avoid overlapping, it is advisable to have periodical re-evaluation of the subsidiary organs.

§56. THE SECURITY COUNCIL

The League Covenant had a flexible provision for the membership of the Council; [66] the Security Council of the United Nations originally had eleven members. The recent Charter amendment which became effective on August 31, 1965, increased the non-permanent members from six to ten, and the total membership to fifteen.[67] The ten non-permanent members are elected by the General Assembly, with due regard to their contributions to international peace and equitable geographical distribution,[68] for a term of two years and are not eligible for immediate re-election. Each member of the Security Council has one representative, who must be available at all times so as to enable the Council to function continuously.[69] The Security Council is to meet periodically and adopts its own rules of procedure.[70] The Presidency of the Council is rotated monthly among its members according to English alphabetical order.

The principle of equitable distribution of seats on the Security Council is more complicated than that of the League Council,[71] because

[65] For further details of the subsidiary organs of the General Assembly, see *Repertory*, UN, I, pp. 661–742; Supp. No. 1, I, pp. 221–239; Supp. No. 2, II, pp. 221–274.

[66] See Art. 4(1, 2) of the Covenant.

[67] Art. 23(1) of the Charter.

[68] The criteria were fully discussed at Committee III/1 of the San Francisco Conference. See *Documents* U.N.C.I.O., Reports of the Rapporteur of Committee III/1, Doc. 1050, III/1/58, p. 213.

[69] See Arts. 23 and 28 of the Charter.

[70] Provisional Rules of Procedure of the Security Council, adopted by the Security Council at its first meeting and amended up to February 28, 1950. UN Doc. S/96/Rev.4.

[71] Equitable distribution was achieved at the League Council by representation from Latin America, the Far East, the Middle East, Scandinavia, the Little Entente, and the British Commonwealth of Nations. At the first election of the Security Council, three were selected to serve for one year and the other three, for two years. Thus three members will be elected each year.

the membership of the United Nations has been rapidly increasing. Even after the amendment of the Charter, not all Members of the Organization may have the opportunity to serve on the Security Council. There was a gentleman's agreement in London in 1946 that the seats of the non-permanent members were to be distributed as follows: two from Latin America and one each from the British Commonwealth, the Middle East, Western Europe, and Eastern Europe.[72] When the number of the non-permanent members was increased to ten, the General Assembly accompanied this with a new scheme for the distribution of seats: five from Afro-Asian states, two from Latin America, one from Eastern Europe, and two from Western Europe and other states.[73] The principle of equality of states is violated by the provision for permanent members. Although the original intention was to match responsibility with power, it must be emphasized that the victorious powers of World War II may not be strong and great forever. The Security Council is further weakened by conferring the special privilege of veto power upon the five permanent members.

In pursuance of Article 29 of the Charter, the Provisional Rules of Procedure provide that "the Security Council may appoint a commission or committee or a rapporteur for a specified question." [74] Certain subsidiary organs set up by the Security Council are on a standing basis, such as the Committee of Experts and the Committee on the Admission of New Members; others are for particular purposes, like the United Nations Commission for Indonesia and the Commission of Investigation concerning Greek Frontier Incidents. Many *ad hoc* committees and subcommittees have been established by the Security Council to deal with the Spanish question, the Palestine question, and other issues. There are also a number of subsidiary organs created by the General Assembly but also under the authority of the Security Council. These include the Disarmament Commission and the United Nations Commission on Palestine.[75] Distinguished from the subsidiary organs, the Military Staff Committee is provided for by Article 47 of the Charter. Even though the Committee is empowered with comprehensive functions on military matters, it has long become impotent due to disagreement among the permanent members.[76]

[72] See *Repertory*, UN, II, p. 8. However, the Eastern European states did not always get one seat after 1950.

[73] GA res. 1991A (XVIII).

[74] Rule 28.

[75] For field commissions and other subsidiary organs under the Security Council, see *Repertory*, UN, II, pp. 123–131. See also *ibid.*, Supp., No. 1, I, pp. 243–247; No. 2, II, pp. 319–321.

[76] See *infra*, §193.

§57. THE ECONOMIC AND SOCIAL COUNCIL

The Charter originally provided in Article 61 that the Economic and Social Council should be composed of eighteen members, six elected annually by the General Assembly for a term of three years and eligible for immediate re-election.[77] As a result of a Charter amendment which came into effect on August 31, 1965, the number was increased to twenty-seven.[78] Each member of the Economic and Social Council has one representative and one vote. The permanent members of the Security Council generally have no difficulty in being elected to this Council, but this is not guaranteed by the Charter and China has recently failed of election.[79] Each representative may be accompanied by such alternates and advisers as may be necessary.[80] The Economic and Social Council elects its own President and three Vice-Presidents at each session; sessions are normally held at least twice a year. It adopts its own rules of procedure [81] and may set up necessary commissions or committees to perform various functions within its jurisdiction.

The subsidiary organs of the Economic and Social Council are generally in economic and social fields, including the promotion of human rights and related subjects.[82] Many organs were recommended

[77] In the first election, arrangements were made to ensure continuity by selecting six each for one-year, two-year, and three-year terms. Thus six members would be elected each year.

[78] At the fortieth session of the Economic and Social Council, the first after its expansion of membership, Tewfik Bouattoura, Algeria's chief delegate, was elected President. While the General Assembly had delegates from Asia and Africa as its Presidents, this was the first time that an African was elected to head the Economic and Social Council. See *The New York Times,* February 24, 1966.

[79] The problem of Chinese representation was first raised at the fifth session of the General Assembly by the Indian delegation, which submitted a draft resolution that the Central Government of the People's Republic of China be represented in substitution for the National Government of the Republic of China. It has since been a serious issue at every session of the main organs of the United Nations and of several specialized agencies. Now the Economic and Social Council has no representation of either of the two contesting governments. For the distinction of admission of new members from the problem of representation, see *supra,* §49.

[80] Rule 18 of the Rules of Procedure.

[81] Art. 72(1) of the Charter. The Rules of Procedure of the Economic and Social Council were first adopted on March 18, 1949, and last amended on December 20, 1966. UN Doc. E/4264/Add.1.

[82] Art. 68 of the Charter.

for immediate creation by the Preparatory Commisison for the implementation of the Charter.[83] Functional commissions were established to make all kinds of studies and recommendations, such as the Commission on Human Rights, Social Commission, Population Commission, Commission on the Status of Women, Transport and Communications Commission, Fiscal Commission, Statistical Commission, and Commission on Narcotic Drugs. There are also a number of subcommissions. Most important are the four regional commissions, which have broad responsibilities in their respective regions.[84]

There are other types of subsidiary organs under various categories: *Ad Hoc* Committee on Declaration of Death of Missing Persons, Committee on Negotiations with Intergovernmental Agencies on standing basis, and sessional committees on economic, social, and other matters. The functional commissions and standing committees generally remain in existence unless the Economic and Social Council decides otherwise.[85] To carry out its multiple functions, the Council has often conferred limited powers on its subsidiary organs under their terms of reference to make studies and submit recommendations.[86]

§58. THE TRUSTEESHIP COUNCIL

The Trusteeship Council is composed of three categories of membership: (1) the United Nations Members which administer trust territories; (2) the permanent members of the Security Council not administering trust territories; and (3) enough other members to make an equal division between the administering and non-administering countries, elected by the General Assembly for a term of three years and eligible for re-election. A non-member of the United Nations may be an administering authority over a trust territory, though there is no express provision for this in the Charter.[87] Unlike the Permanent Man-

[83] See *Report of the Preparatory Commission,* PC/20, Ch. 3, Sec. 4, Par. 10.

[84] For details, see *infra,* §151.

[85] For further information on the functional commissions, see the Rules of Procedure of the Functional Commissions of the Economic and Social Council, adopted by the Council's resolution 289 (X) of March 6, 1950, and amended by its resolution 481 (XV) of April 1, 1953. UN Doc. E/2425.

[86] See *Repertory,* UN, III, pp. 475–525.

[87] When Italy was made administering authority over Somaliland, she had not yet been admitted to the United Nations. However, she was then given a seat on the Trusteeship Council as an observer. This was also the practice of the League of Nations. After Japan's withdrawal from the League, she remained as the mandatory power over the Pacific Islands.

dates Commission, which consisted of individual experts and functioned under the League Council, the Trusteeship Council is represented by states. Each member of the Trusteeship Council has one representative and one vote. Members of the United Nations which are not members of the Trusteeship Council may be invited to attend the meetings of the Trusteeship Council without voting if they have proposed items on its agenda.[88] The Trusteeship Council elects its own President and Vice-President at the annual regular session and adopts its own rules of procedure.[89]

Even though the Charter has no specific provision for the creation of subsidiary organs by the Trusteeship Council, it was envisaged by the Preparatory Commission.[90] In pursuance of Rule 66, the Trusteeship Council has established a number of committees as its subsidiary organs for study and report on specific questions. Their composition and terms of reference were defined by the Council. They include the Standing Committee on Administrative Unions, Standing Committee on Petitions, and numerous drafting committees.[91] With limited functions in comparison with other political organs of the United Nations, the Trusteeship Council has no need of many subsidiary or subordinate bodies.

III. *FUNCTIONS AND POWERS OF THE UNITED NATIONS* [92]

§59. THE SCOPE OF THE PRESENT INVESTIGATION

The present investigation of the functions and powers of the United Nations is limited to the political organs; the International Court of Justice and the Secretariat will be discussed in other chapters.[93] Since many political functions of the United Nations are shared

[88] Arts. 89, 90, of the Charter; Rule 12 of the Rules of Procedure of the Trusteeship Council.

[89] UN Doc. T/1/Rev.6, adopted by the Trusteeship Council as amended up to its twenty-ninth session.

[90] See *Report of the Preparatory Commission of the United Nations,* PC/20, December 23, 1945, Ch. IV, Sec. 2.

[91] See *Repertory,* UN, IV, pp. 440–441.

[92] General texts on this subject: Goodspeed, Ch. 12; Blaisdell, Chs. 4–5; Claude, Ch. 9; Sohn, Chs. IV–VII; Goodrich & Hambro, pp. 56–84, 150–188, 204–213, 370–385, 465–473; Clark & Sohn, Chs. IV, V, X, XIII; Eagleton, Ch. 12, §§89, 92; Watkins & Robinson, Chs. 16–17; Fenwick, *Principles,* pp. 219–227; Schwarzenberger, I, Ch. 10 (I, VI).

[93] See *infra,* §§189–191, 152, respectively.

by the General Assembly and the Security Council, it seems advisable to study their concurrent powers first. As a matter of convenience and practical necessity, the actual application of the functions and powers of the General Assembly, the Security Council, the Economic and Social Council, and the Trusteeship Council will be more extensively described under different headings wherever appropriate. For these reasons, the following analysis of these individual organs is brief and introductory.

§60. CONCURRENT POWERS OF THE GENERAL ASSEMBLY AND THE SECURITY COUNCIL

The General Assembly and the Security Council are the chief political organs of the United Nations in charge of the maintenance and promotion of international peace and security. In order to achieve this objective, the Charter provides these two organs with extensive powers both separately and jointly. In this respect, the Security Council has primary but not exclusive responsibility. The General Assembly may discuss any dispute or situation, but cannot make recommendations on matters currently seized by the Security Council.[94] However, mere consideration and discussion by the General Assembly without recommendation seem permissible under the provisions of the Charter.[95] During the past twenty years, the General Assembly has adopted numerous resolutions dealing with disputes, situations, and various items, especially in connection with self-determination and human rights. In most cases, its work is complementary to rather than in conflict with the functions of the Security Council.[96]

The General Assembly may consider and make recommendations on the general principles of cooperation, such as disarmament or regulation of armaments and other matters in the interest of international

[94] Art. 12(1) of the Charter. From the very beginning of the history of the United Nations, this constitutional issue has been raised. Many questions have been considered by both organs at different times. But so long as the item is kept on the agenda of the Security Council, the General Assembly cannot make recommendations on it.

[95] When the Indonesian question was included in the agenda of the General Assembly, it was under consideration at the Security Council.

[96] See Sydney D. Bailey, *The United Nations: A Short Political Guide* (New York, 1964), Chs. IV, VI; John G. Hadwen & Johan Kaufmann, *How United Nations Decisions Are Made* (Leyden, 1960); Robert O. Keohane, "Political Influence in the General Assembly," *International Conciliation* (March 1966), No. 557. For an analytical list of measures recommended by the General Assembly, see Blaisdell, pp. 95–101.

peace and security, but any question on which action is necessary must be reported to the Security Council by the General Assembly before or after discussion.[97] As for regulation of armaments, the Security Council must formulate plans for the consideration of the Members of the United Nations.[98]

On the recommendation of the Security Council, the General Assembly may determine the admission of new members and the terms by which non-members may become parties to the Statute of the International Court of Justice.[99] In the opinion of the International Court, the General Assembly has no power to admit new members without the recommendation of the Security Council.[100] In case of failure by the Security Council to recommend, the General Assembly may send back the application to it for further consideration. According to the Charter, Members of the United Nations are *ipso facto* parties to the Statute of the Court; this was not the case with members of the League in relation to the Permanent Court of International Justice.[101] Both organs elect, independently of each other, the judges of the International Court of Justice and may request advisory opinions on legal matters from it. The other organs of the United Nations and specialized agencies may, with the approval of the General Assembly, also request advisory opinions from the International Court of Justice.[102]

Another concurrent power of major importance relates to selection of the Secretary-General of the United Nations. The Security Council has the power to recommend and the General Assembly the power finally to appoint him.[103] This procedure is also applied to renewal of an appointment. Any permanent member of the Security

[97] See Arts. 11, 24, of the Charter. It has been the earnest hope of the Members of the United Nations from the very beginning to regulate armaments. This culminated in two resolutions adopted at the first session of the General Assembly: 1 (I) and 41 (I), on atomic problems and general armaments. For details, see *infra,* §154. The word 'action' may imply enforcement action or any action under Chs. V–VIII of the Charter. Under GA res. 377 (V), it meant coercive action. There was discussion in the following years on the requirement for action by the Security Council in connection with the Spanish question and others.

[98] *Cf.* Arts. 11 and 26 of the Charter.

[99] Arts. 4(2), 93, of the Charter.

[100] Advisory opinion on *Conditions of Admission of a State to Membership in the United Nations (Charter, Article 4),* 1948. I.C.J. Reports (1948), 57.

[101] See *infra,* §189.

[102] For details, see Arts. 4–14 of the Statute of the International Court of Justice, and Art. 96 of the Charter.

[103] Art. 97 of the Charter.

Council may veto a recommendation. Although the General Assembly may disapprove the recommendation by the Security Council, it has never done so.

Controversy over the concurrent powers of the two organs has been centered in the maintenance of peace and security. When the Korean War broke out in 1950, the Security Council was able, because of the absence of the Soviet representative, to adopt effective measures against the aggression of the North Korean forces. But no further action could be taken by the Security Council after the Soviet member returned and exercised or threatened to exercise the veto power. Eventually, the Korean question was removed from the agenda of the Security Council to the General Assembly. The Uniting for Peace Resolution was adopted at the fifth session of the General Assembly on November 3, 1950,[104] and accordingly collective measures, including the use of armed force, may be recommended by the General Assembly for the maintenance of peace if the Security Council fails to exercise its primary responsibility to do so. Although the validity of this resolution has been challenged by the Soviet Union, the General Assembly acted in accordance with it in other crises, such as the Suez and Hungary in 1956, and Jordan and Lebanon in 1958. It is clear that the Security Council has 'primary' but not 'exclusive' responsibility for the maintenance of international peace and security and that the General Assembly may exercise its 'secondary' responsibility in order to avoid inaction by the United Nations.[105] The argument on respective jurisdiction was heard again when Members of the United Nations were asked to pay contributions for expenditures of peace operations decided by the General Assembly.[106]

[104] GA res. 377 (V), adopted at the 302nd plenary meeting of the General Assembly by a vote of 52 to 5, with 2 abstentions. For its text, see GA *Official Records,* Supp. No. 20, 5th Sess., p. 10; *Yearbook,* UN, 1950, pp. 193–195.

[105] See Brierly, pp. 115–118. There has been much discussion of the 'secondary' responsibility of the General Assembly *versus* the 'primary' responsibility of the Security Council ever since the early years of the United Nations. See, *e.g.,* General Assembly resolutions 111 (II), 196 (III), and 295 (IV) in connection with the establishment of the Interim Committee; 377 (V), 503 (VI), and 703 (VII) with respect to the Uniting for Peace and the establishment of a Collective Measures Committee. Of course, items may be referred by the Security Council to the General Assembly, for instance, the Spanish question in 1946.

[106] See *infra,* §193. For further references of the relationship between the General Assembly and the Security Council, see *Repertoire,* SC, 1946–1951, pp. 211–227; Supp. 1952–1955, pp. 75–81; Supp., 1956–1958, pp. 71–80; Supp., 1959–1963, pp. 123–129.

§61. FUNCTIONS AND POWERS OF THE GENERAL ASSEMBLY

Broadly speaking, the General Assembly may discuss any questions or matters within the scope of the Charter or relating to the powers and functions of any United Nations organ and may also make recommendations on those if not currently under discussion by the Security Council.[107] It is within the competence of the General Assembly to initiate studies and make recommendations to promote progressive development and codification of international law, realization of human rights and fundamental freedoms for all, and international cooperation in political, economic, social, cultural, educational, and health fields.[108] The Security Council and other organs of the United Nations are required to submit reports to the General Assembly.[109] Unlike the League Covenant, the Charter does not specifically mention revision of inapplicable treaties, but such authority is implied in the provision that the General Assembly may recommend measures for the peaceful adjustment of any situation, regardless of origin, which might impair the general welfare or friendly relations among nations.[110]

[107] Art. 10 of the Charter. The powers of the General Assembly are further emphasized by Art. 11. In the practice of the General Assembly, its recommendations are addressed not only to Member states, but also to non-members, non-governmental organizations, and individuals.

[108] Art. 13 of the Charter. This article should be read in conjunction with Art. 55 on international cooperation in the economic and social fields. Here the General Assembly transcends its political function to legal matters. By resolution 174 (II) adopted at its second session, the General Assembly established an International Law Commission, which decided at its first session in 1949 to include fourteen topics for codification.

[109] Arts. 15, 24(3), 98, of the Charter. The General Assembly usually takes note of the annual reports submitted by the Security Council without making recommendations. The International Court of Justice publishes a yearbook containing its annual work, but has never submitted reports to the General Assembly.

[110] Art. 14 of the Charter. Specific reference to revision of treaties was originally suggested. Owing to strong objections, the question is not expressly mentioned in the Charter, but is included by implication under the broad term 'peaceful adjustment.' Art. 14 was invoked when several delegations supported the Argentine proposal to consider revision of the Peace Treaty with Italy at the second session of the General Assembly in 1947. The proposal was eventually withdrawn due to many objections. This article was also referred to in the discussion of other questions, such as the Tunisian question and the question of race conflict in South Africa.

The General Assembly has the power to elect the non-permanent members of the Security Council, all the members of the Economic and Social Council, and the elective members of the Trusteeship Council.[111] It lays down regulations for the appointment of the Secretariat staff,[112] and exercises supervisory powers over the Economic and Social Council and Trusteeship Council and over the execution of trusteeship agreements for all areas not designated as strategic.[113] In these respects, the General Assembly expects to receive full cooperation and assistance from the organs concerned.[114]

The General Assembly has the power to consider and approve the budget of the United Nations, apportion contributions among the Member states, and examine the budgets of specialized agencies.[115] While the League Assembly had actual control over the budgets of the technical organizations,[116] the General Assembly limits its budgetary power over the specialized agencies to examination and recommendations. Because of the recent financial difficulty of the United Nations as a result of refusal to pay expenditures for peace operations by several Member states and the subsequent advisory opinion delivered by the International Court of Justice on July 20, 1962, on *Certain Expenses of the United Nations (Art.17, Par. 2, of the Charter)*,[117] the budget problem of the United Nations has become so important that its basis

[111] Arts. 23(1), 61(1), 86(1c). The membership of the Security Council, the Economic and Social Council, and the Trusteeship Council has been briefly mentioned under the section on the organization of the United Nations. See *supra*, §§55–58.

[112] Art. 101(1) of the Charter.

[113] Arts. 16, 60, 85, 87, of the Charter. Actually, examination of annual reports of the administering authorities and dispatch of visiting missions are performed by the Trusteeship Council. The strategic areas are under the supervision of the Security Council because of its primary responsibility for the maintenance of international peace and security.

[114] Arts. 66, 85, 87, of the Charter. Numerous functions have been performed by the Economic and Social Council under the authorization of the General Assembly. See *infra*, §§155–156. The General Assembly has approved trusteeship agreements for areas not designated as strategic, received reports from the Trusteeship Council, exercised supervisory functions, and, in some cases, even taken direct action under Art. 87 of the Charter.

[115] Art. 17 of the Charter. Actually the Secretary-General prepares the budget on an annual basis and submits it to the General Assembly for consideration and adoption.

[116] See Arts. 6(5), 24, of the League Covenant.

[117] I.C.J. Reports (1962), 151; also *Yearbook*, I.C.J., 1962–1963, pp. 77–83.

of contribution requires brief review. In accordance with the principle adopted by the General Assembly in 1946, no Member state should contribute more than one-third of the regular budget, but the United States was apportioned in the same year 39.89% of the total. The one-third rule was not put into practice until 1954. However, this ceiling is not applied to expenditures for voluntary programs and enforcement measures, for which the major powers are expected to contribute a large portion.[118] The recent financial crisis of the United Nations is not so much due to defects of the budgeting system as to political differences about peace operations in the Congo and the Middle East, which will be treated elsewhere.[119]

§62. FUNCTIONS AND POWERS OF THE SECURITY COUNCIL

With its primary responsibility for maintaining international peace and security, the Security Council has substantially more power than the General Assembly.[120] It is within the competence of the Security Council to investigate any dispute or situation which may lead to international friction and to recommend methods or terms for adjustment or settlement.[121] If there is a threat to or breach of the peace or an act of aggression, the Security Council may recommend action and call on Members to apply economic sanctions and other measures short of war with a view to maintaining or restoring peace. In extreme cases,

[118] For proposed changes of budgetary matters under Art. 17, see Wilcox & Marcy, Ch. XIV. The United States contributed a total of $326 million in 1965 to seventy-one international organizations and agencies. See the *Fourteenth Annual Report of the Department of State to the Congress on U. S. Contributions to International Organizations.* 89th Cong., 2d Sess., House Doc. No. 455.

[119] See *infra,* §193.

[120] See Arts. 11(2), 12, 24, of the Charter. With the five major powers as permanent members, it was originally thought that the Security Council could take more effective action than the General Assembly. But disappointments soon ensued when the veto power was excessively exercised. Even so, numerous questions have been submitted to the Security Council. See *Repertory,* UN, II, pp. 26–27; Supp. No. 1, I, pp. 251–252; Supp. No. 2, II, pp. 288–290. According to a summary recently issued by the United Nations, there are seventy items of which the Security Council is still officially seized. Some issues are practically fading away, while the Palestine question and the Kashmir dispute have taken much of the time of Security Council meetings. See *The New York Times,* July 10, 1966.

[121] See Chs. VI, VIII, of the Charter. For the nature of and the distinction between 'situation' and 'dispute,' see Kelsen, *UN,* pp. 366–367.

military action may be taken against an aggressor.[122] Members of the United Nations have the obligation to accept and carry out decisions of the Security Council.[123]

It is the responsibility of the Security Council to establish a system of regulation of armaments and to supervise trusteeship over territories designated as strategic areas.[124] Of course, there will always be mutual assistance with the Economic and Social Council and the Trusteeship Council whenever needed.[125] Furthermore, the Security Council may make recommendations or decide on measures to give effect to a judgment of the International Court of Justice if requested by one party on the failure of the other to fulfill its obligations.[126] Further discussion of the functions of the Security Council will be made under the subject of the United Nations and the enforcement of peace.[127]

[122] Ch. VII of the Charter deals with enforcement measures and sanctions under various circumstances.

[123] Art. 25 of the Charter. However, two exceptions are specifically mentioned in the Charter: Arts. 106, applying to measures under the responsibility of the five major powers, and 107, in relation to former enemy states. Art. 106 was invoked at the time of discussion of the United Action for Peace and the Palestine Question. No action could be taken under Art. 106 because of disagreement among the permanent members of the Security Council. Art. 107 was referred to at the General Assembly during discussion of the problem of Korean independence; human rights in Bulgaria, Hungary, and Rumania; problem of Austria; and many other occasions.

[124] Arts. 26, 83(1), of the Charter. For the regulation of armaments, the Military Staff Committee is to render assistance to the Security Council as the Permanent Military, Naval and Air Commission did to the League Council. Arts. 11 and 47 of the Charter also refer to the subject of disarmament, while Art. 8 of the League Covenant emphasizes reduction of armaments. See *infra,* §154.

[125] Arts. 65, 83(3), of the Charter. The Economic and Social Council has manifested its cooperation whenever needed, for instance, on the occasion for implementing the Uniting for Peace Resolution, 377 (V). The Economic and Social Council adopted a resolution on July 31, 1950, to effect assistance to the civilian population of Korea. The relationship between the Security Council and the trust territory of the Pacific Islands has been practically limited to approval of trusteeship agreements and transmittal of questionnaires and reports.

[126] Art. 94(2) of the Charter. Great Britain invoked this article in the *Anglo-Iranian Oil Co.* case (I.C.J. Reports, 1952, p. 93), but did not do so in the *Corfu Channel Case* (I.C.J. Reports, 1949, p. 4), when Albania refused to comply with the decision of the International Court of Justice and pay compensation.

[127] See *infra,* §§192–193.

§63. COMPARISON OF THE POWERS OF THE GENERAL ASSEMBLY AND THE SECURITY COUNCIL WITH THEIR LEAGUE COUNTERPARTS

Judging by the composition and functions of the corresponding organs of the two international organizations, the division of powers has been worked out on similar lines. The League Assembly and the General Assembly are more or less representative in character, but not nearly an international legislature. The League Council had less power than the Security Council, which has primary authority in maintaining peace and security. On the principle of power commensurate to responsibility, the major powers as permanent members have predominant influence. As stated before, the League Covenant was more flexible in its provision for both permanent and non-permanent Council membership.

According to the League Covenant, the admission of new members was exclusively within the competence of the Assembly; the Charter requires also the recommendation of the Security Council. Both organs had to concur on appointment and approval of the Secretary-General, but the order of consideration is reversed in the United Nations. Disarmament and supervision of the mandate system were chiefly within the special jurisdiction of the League Council, but such matters are now shared by the General Assembly and the Security Council. While the League Council could control the budgets of the special bureaus and technical bodies, the General Assembly lacks such absolute authority over the budgets of the specialized agencies. The League Council alone had the power to expel members; under the United Nations system, expulsion must be decided by the General Assembly upon recommendation of the Security Council.

As distinguished from the decisions of the League Council, which were legally only recommendations, the decisions of the Security Council are legally binding upon the Members of the United Nations. This is an important step toward consolidation of power in an international organization, notwithstanding the difficulty of actual application. Adoption of resolutions on important or non-procedural matters requires only a two-thirds majority in the General Assembly instead of the unanimity required in the League Assembly. Because of this, it is technically easier to reach decisions in the General Assembly than in its League counterpart, although actually the unanimity rule caused little difficulty in the League. The voting rule of the Security Council is less rigid than the unanimity rule of the League Council, since only the permanent members must concur in the decision of non-procedural matters. Had it not been for the tension between Western and Communist states resulting from the cold war, the Security Council might well have performed its functions more promptly and efficiently than the League Council. In this respect, it is evident how much the maintenance and promotion of international peace and security depend on the political climate of the community of nations. Legal institutions alone cannot achieve a utopia.

§64. FUNCTIONS AND POWERS OF THE ECONOMIC AND SOCIAL COUNCIL

The Economic and Social Council is in charge of economic and social activities. It is one of the principal organs of the United Nations, but is under the authority of the General Assembly. For the realization of the stability and well-being of the international community and with the cooperation of the Members of the United Nations, the Economic and Social Council is to promote, on behalf of the Organization: (1) higher standards of living, full employment, and conditions of economic and social progress and development; (2) solutions of international economic, social, health, and related problems; (3) international cultural and educational cooperation; and (4) universal respect for and observance of human rights and fundamental freedoms for all without distinction as to race, sex, language, or religion.[128] The United Nations has held many international conferences to discuss ways and means to achieve these objectives. Several important instruments have been concluded to effect their realization, such as the Universal Declaration of Human Rights and the Genocide Convention.[129] Condemnation of violations has been expressed in a number of resolutions adopted by the United Nations.[130]

Subject to the approval of the General Assembly, the Economic and Social Council is to conclude agreements with the specialized agencies to bring them into relationship with the United Nations. Such agencies, established by interested governments, have a wide range of

[128] Arts. 55, 56, of the Charter. There were similar provisions in the preamble and Art. 23 of the League Covenant. Other provisions of the Charter referring to the same objectives are the preamble, Arts. 1(3), 10, 13(1b), 17, 22, 59, 62–66, 68, and 71.

[129] See *infra*, §§123–127.

[130] *E.g.*, 'Observance in Bulgaria and Hungary of the Human Rights and Fundamental Freedoms,' GA res. 272 (III); 'The Question of Race Conflict in South Africa resulting from the Policies of *Apartheid* of the Government of the Union of South Africa,' GA res. 616 (VII), 721 (VIII), and others; 'The Question of the Treatment of People of Indian Origin in the Union of South Africa,' GA res. 44 (I), 265 (III), 395 (V), 511 (VI), 615 (VII), 719 (VIII).

international responsibilities in economic, social, cultural, educational, health, and related fields as defined in their basic instruments. In accordance with the terms of the agreements and by means of consultation and recommendations, the Economic and Social Council has the function of coordinating the activities of the specialized agencies. Whenever necessary, the Economic and Social Council may also make recommendations to the General Assembly and to the Members of the United Nations.[131] Appropriate steps may be taken by the Economic and Social Council to receive reports from the specialized agencies and Members of the United Nations so that it may appraise to what extent these recommendations have been acted on. The reports so obtained are to be transmitted to the General Assembly by the Economic and Social Council with its own comments.[132]

The Economic and Social Council has considerable freedom to perform its functions, but authorization and approval from the General Assembly are necessary for calling international conferences, concluding agreements with specialized agencies, and requesting the International Court of Justice for advisory opinions.[133] The Council may initiate studies and reports on matters within its competence and invite Members of the United Nations and representatives of the specialized agencies to participate in its deliberations without vote. Likewise, arrangements may be made for its representatives to attend meetings of specialized agencies. The Council may prepare draft conventions for submission to the General Assembly and call international conferences in accordance with the rules prescribed by the United Nations.[134]

[131] Arts. 57–59, 63, of the Charter. The general subjects included in the agreements between the United Nations and the specialized agencies cover a variety of subjects, such as recognition of authority, status and competence, liaison and reciprocal representation, exchange of information and documents, personnel arrangements, common fiscal and technical services, proposal of agenda items, recommendations and reports, and mutual assistance. The major objective of the United Nations is to coordinate the activities of the specialized agencies in order to achieve the basic purposes and principles of the Charter. Such coordination is effected through the General Assembly and its Main Committees, the Economic and Social Council and its subsidiary organs, and the Secretary-General of the United Nations.

[132] Art. 64 of the Charter. Reports supplied by the member governments are either in pursuance of individual resolutions or of lists of recommendations.

[133] See Arts. 62(4), 63, and 96(2), respectively. In some instances, the Economic and Social Council has reconsidered its decisions on request of the General Assembly.

[134] Arts. 62, 69, 70, of the Charter. The Economic and Social Council has made numerous studies, reports, and recommendations. Certain resolu-

The draft conventions, protocols, and agreements prepared by the Economic and Social Council are extensive and have been adopted by the General Assembly in most cases. International and regional conferences have been held by the Council. States not Members of the United Nations may send observers to attend its sessions as a matter of coordination.

Arrangements may be made by the Economic and Social Council with non-governmental organizations, international organizations, and even national organizations with the consent of the Member states concerned.[135] In accordance with the practice established by the Council Committee on Non-governmental Organizations, an organization with affiliates in at least three countries may be considered international. The application of a national organization may only be considered by the Committee when it has obtained consent from the Member government concerned. The Economic and Social Council generally requests its regional commissions to consult with organizations whose status has already been recognized.[136]

As stated before, the Security Council may request the Economic and Social Council to supply necessary information and assistance. At the request of Member states or specialized agencies, the Economic and Social Council may perform services for them with the approval of the General Assembly. It may carry out other functions assigned by the General Assembly or specified in the Charter.[137] On several occasions, the General Assembly and the Economic and Social Council have extended to non-members of the United Nations the right to request services. The technical services performed by the Expanded Program of Technical Assistance are quite extensive in scope. Others may be carried out by specially created bodies such as the United Nations Children's Fund and the United Nations Relief and Works Agency for Palestine Refugees in the Near East.

In comparison with the League Covenant, the Charter providing for the Economic and Social Council as one of the principal organs of the United Nations is a major improvement. There was no organ under the League with corresponding status and powers. Owing to practical necessity, the Economic and Financial Commission was established under the League Council in 1920 and then divided into the Economic

---

tions were adopted in spite of strong objections by several delegates, *e.g.*, consideration by the states concerned of holding a conference to discuss resumption of international Danube traffic. ESC *Official Records,* 1st yr., 3rd sess., No. 5, pp. 62–72; No. 6, pp. 73–78.

135 Art. 71 of the Charter.

136 See, for instance, its res. 414 (XIII).

137 Art. 66 of the Charter.

and Financial Committees in 1927. Other organs were set up to carry out technical functions, such as the Communications and Transit Organization, the Health Organization, and the Committee on Intellectual Cooperation. While these organs served useful purposes in their respective fields, they could not compare with the wide scope of functions of the Economic and Social Council and the specialized agencies under its coordination.

§65. FUNCTIONS AND POWERS OF THE TRUSTEESHIP COUNCIL

The chief function of the Trusteeship Council is to fulfill the basic objectives of the trusteeship system. These objectives may be summarized as follows: (1) furtherance of international peace and security; (2) advancement of the inhabitants of the trust territories toward self-government or independence; (3) respect for human rights and fundamental freedoms, and recognition of interdependence of the peoples of the world; (4) equal treatment in the trust territories of all Members of the United Nations and their nationals in the administration of justice and in social, economic, and commercial matters; and (5) maintenance of peace in the trust territories.[138] To check on the progress of the above objectives, the Trusteeship Council is to formulate and distribute questionnaires on the political, economic, social, and educational advancement of the inhabitants of the trust territories. On the basis of such information, the annual reports of the administering authorities are prepared. The Trusteeship Council not only reviews such reports but also examines petitions and makes periodic visits. Further actions may be taken in accordance with the terms of the trusteeship agreements.[139] Whenever necessary, the Trusteeship

[138] Arts. 75, 76, 84, of the Charter. The basic terms of the trusteeship system were agreed upon at the Yalta Conference, which postponed discussion of actual disposition of the territories until a later date. See Department of State, *Press Release* 239, March 24, 1947. The application of Arts. 75 and 76 to establish the international trusteeship system is detailed in Arts. 77–91 of the Charter. The Declaration regarding Non-Self-Governing Territories in Arts. 73–74 embraces similar principles and objectives as in Arts. 75 and 76, but these non-self-governing territories may still form an integral part of the states concerned. For a comparison with the League mandatory system, see Arts. 22–23 of the Covenant.

[139] Arts. 87–88 of the Charter. Supervision through regular examination of reports is an effective step toward achieving the objectives of the trusteeship system. The basic feature of the report system is similar to that of the League mandates, which were required to submit annual reports to the League Council. Petitions and periodic visits are equally important in preventing abuses and promoting public welfare of the local inhabitants.

Council may request the assistance of the Economic and Social Council and the specialized agencies.[140]

The trusteeship system applies to three categories of territories: those (1) held under the League of Nations mandates, (2) detached from enemy states, and (3) placed voluntarily under the system by states responsible for their administration.[141] The terms of trusteeship are stipulated in individual agreements between the United Nations and the administering authorities. It is assumed that a trusteeship agreement will end when its objectives are fulfilled. In practice there is none under the third category, and only one, Somaliland, under the second.[142] The Pacific Islands, formerly under Japanese mandatory in the League of Nations days and now designated as a strategic area,[143] are administered by the United States under the supervision of the Security Council, which may avail itself of the assistance of the Trusteeship Council. All other mandates under the League system except South-West Africa were assigned to several administering authorities by trusteeship agreements.[144] These trust territories are under the supervision of the General Assembly with the assistance of the Trusteeship Council. Most of the trust territories have now achieved their ultimate aim of independence.[145]

One fundamental defect of the trusteeship system is the lack of sanction against a former mandatory power which has refused to conclude a trusteeship agreement. Due to the persistent refusal of the Republic of South Africa to transfer its mandate, South-West Africa, to the trusteeship system of the United Nations, the General Assembly requested the International Court of Justice for an advisory opinion on July 11, 1949.[146] The Court held that the Union of South Africa continued to have the international obligations stated in Article 22 of the League Covenant and that competence to determine and modify the international status of South-West Africa rested with the Union of South Africa acting with the consent of the United Nations.[147] The General Assembly accepted the advisory opinion of the Court.[148] In

[140] Art. 91 of the Charter. The Rules of Procedure of the Trusteeship Council prescribe means for the application of Art. 91.

[141] Art. 77 of the Charter.

[142] Originally detached from Italy, Somaliland became a trust territory. For details, see *infra*, §157.

[143] Art. 82 of the Charter.

[144] There are no restrictions on installation of military fortifications or maintenance of military forces in trust territories as there were for the League mandates. See Arts. 79–81 of the Charter.

[145] For details, see *infra*, §157.

[146] GA res. 338 (IV).

[147] I.C.J. Reports (1950), 128.

[148] GA res. 499A (V).

spite of repeated resolutions of the United Nations, the Republic of South Africa has refused to change the status of South-West Africa.[149]

No Member state of the United Nations may be administered under the trusteeship system, because it is against the principle of sovereign equality for one Member state to be under the jurisdiction of another.[150] Also outside the trusteeship system are the non-self-governing territories, a declaration on which is embodied in the Charter. States with such territories are obliged to promote the well-being of the local inhabitants and their progressive development toward self-government.[151] Many non-self-governing territories have now achieved either complete independence or self-autonomy, although it has been difficult to agree on a clear standard to determine self-government.[152] By a resolution adopted by the General Assembly on December 14, 1960, Members of the United Nations were urged to transfer all powers to the local population of the territories.[153] The long struggle of anti-colonialism has not yet come to an end, but national independence through self-determination is an irresistible trend in the twentieth century.

IV. *PROSPECTS AND LIMITATIONS OF THE UNITED NATIONS AND OTHER INTERNATIONAL ORGANIZATIONS*

§66. COMMON FEATURES

The development and structure of international organizations from their formative period to the present time have been briefly described. The history of the League of Nations has revealed to the

[149] For the early development of the dispute and the relevant provisions of the mandate of South-West Africa, see *Repertory*, UN, IV, pp. 195–207.

[150] Art. 78 of the Charter.

[151] Ch. XI of the Charter. Discussion of non-self-governing territories along with the functions of the Trusteeship Council is merely a matter of convenience. The supervision of such territories is really within the competence of the General Assembly in accordance with Art. 10 of the Charter. See D. W. Bowett, *The Law of International Institutions* (New York, 1963), p. 71.

[152] The General Assembly formulated in 1953 a list of factors as a guide to determine whether a territory has achieved self-governing status. Puerto Rico under the United States and Surinam under the Netherlands are now considered as self-governing territories.

[153] GA res. 1514 (XV).

world what an international organization could and could not do under varying circumstances. The purposes and principles, composition and functions, and operational procedures of the United Nations are largely based upon the lessons of the League. Both the League and the United Nations have certain common features, which include promotion of mutual understanding among the states, maintenance of international peace and security, furtherance of economic and social welfare of the peoples of the world, and, above all, respect for human rights and dignity in all phases of life. But these high hopes can only be achieved through incessant efforts of the Member states. International organization at the present stage of human development is still loosely constituted and often adversely affected by power politics within the international community.

§67. BASIC LIMITATIONS

Owing to the deep-rooted tradition of balance of power,[154] emphasis on national sovereignty, and the different political and economic systems of the component members, as well as their divergent attitudes toward an international organization,[155] the United Nations cannot be expected to perform its functions in the same manner as the national government of a state. Any expectation beyond its present capabilities and possibilities is bound to cause disappointment to responsible leaders and individuals. There is a basic difference between a state and an international organization. While a national government has the

[154] Inis L. Claude, Jr., observed that "it would be too much to say that the United Nations 'presides over' the operation of the balance of power system, but its functioning does have considerable relevance to the working of that system." See his "The Management of Power in the Changing United Nations," 15 *Int. Organization* (1961), p. 234.

[155] Under the auspices of the Carnegie Endowment for International Peace, many institutions and groups have engaged in national studies on international organization, under such titles as *Australia and the United Nations*. The countries under study include Australia, Belgium, Brazil, Canada, China, Denmark, Egypt, the Federal Republic of Germany, Great Britain, Greece, India, Israel, Italy, Japan, Mexico, Pakistan, the Soviet Union, Sweden, Switzerland, Turkey, the United States, Uruguay, and Yugoslavia. The project has two concluding volumes: *L'État souverain et l'Organisation internationale* by Maurice Bourquin, and *The Nations and the United Nations* by Robert M. MacIver. Switzerland and the Federal Republic of Germany are not members of the United Nations. National policies and attitudes toward the United Nations may be found in these volumes. Works of similar nature have also been prepared by individual scholars.

authority to enforce laws of the land within its jurisdiction, the success of an international organization in gaining observance of its decisions and recommendations depends largely on the willingness and good faith of member states. Though collective sanctions may be enforced against a recalcitrant state, such efforts are difficult and have not yet proved sufficiently effective. However, the inability of the League of Nations and the United Nations to fulfill all the objectives of political nature is not the fault of the organizations, but is due to lack of sincere cooperation among the constituent members.[156]

§68. THE PROSPECTS

In spite of their shortcomings, international organizations will play a more important role in the international community. Both the League of Nations and the United Nations have done much to reduce world tension and have prevented many serious crises directly or indirectly. Their activities in the non-political fields have been remarkably successful. Since no domestic government can completely cope with disorders or prevent the commission of all crimes, it is unrealistic to expect too much from an international organization in the present world. Because of the increasing necessity of peaceful coexistence and the futility of relying on force to execute national policies, members of the international community will gradually concentrate their attention to the constructive objectives of mankind. As responsibility should be commensurate with power, the permanent members of the Security Council and especially the two superpowers have the obligation to exert their utmost efforts toward that end.[157] Further description and analysis of the achievements and failures of the League of Nations and the United Nations will be presented under different headings below.

[156] In this respect, Jeremy Bentham was not far wrong in saying that all men were brothers but all sovereign nations were enemies. See Quincy Wright, *International Law and the United Nations* (New York, 1960), p. 4. It is understood that, in the twentieth century, peoples of most states have much voice in determining the policies of their governments.

[157] See Alvin Z. Rubinstein, "More Responsibility for Russia?" Falk & Mendlovitz, III, pp. 832–837; Kaplan & Katzenbach, Ch. 13. In his analysis of the Soviet attitude toward the United Nations, Richard N. Gardner, formerly Deputy Assistant Secretary of State for International Organization Affairs, gave various instances of Soviet lack of cooperation and flagrant violations of Charter provisions; but he hoped that the Soviet Union would play a more constructive role in the United Nations. See his *In Pursuit of World Order* (New York, 1964), Ch. 2.

CHAPTER 5

FUNDAMENTAL RIGHTS AND DUTIES OF STATES

I. *FUNDAMENTAL RIGHTS OF STATES*[1]

§69. RIGHT OF SOVEREIGN EQUALITY

Certain rights are fundamental to the existence of a state. The most important is the right of sovereign equality, which means, as provided in the United Nations Charter, national sovereignty and legal equality.[2] Sovereign equality of states is the basis of the four principles

[1] General texts on this subject: O'Connell, I, pp. 319–321, 344–348; II, pp. 655–660, 913–961; Oppenheim, I, §§112–128, 141–147a, 203–208; Fenwick, *Principles,* Chs. XI, XIII (§§A–B), XX; Brierly, Ch. VI, §§4, 7; Hyde, I, §§52–57, 152–153, 218–220, 244–249; II, §§250–269; Moore, *Digest,* I, §§23–26; II, §§175–202, 209–226, 250–290; Hackworth, *Digest,* II, §§112–138, 150–159, 169–190; Whiteman, *Digest,* II, Chs. V (§10), IV, XII; Schwarzenberger, I, Ch. 4; Starke, Chs. 7, 8 (§§1–4); Hershey, Ch. X; Kaplan & Katzenbach, Chs. 6–7; Svarlien, Ch. 9; Von Glahn, Chs. 9, 10, 12, 18; Jacobini, pp. 51–66, 100–101; Soviet *Text,* Ch. V, §5; Schuschnigg, Chs. 6–7; Korowicz, Ch. VI; Sen, Ch. XV; Eagleton, Ch. 3, §§21–22; Le Fur, §§462, 469; De Louter, II, §§31–33; Wheaton-Atlay, §§95–103b; Davis, pp. 74–89; Wilson & Tucker, §§63–66; McNair, I, pp. 69–117, 186–224.

[2] See Art. 2(1) of the Charter. For consideration of a Declaration on the Rights and Duties of States prior to and in the United Nations, as well as a Draft Declaration, see UN Doc. A/CN.4/2, *Preparatory Study concerning a Draft Declaration on the Rights and Duties of States,* International Law Commission, 1948.

adopted by the General Assembly on December 16, 1963, and a Special Committee on Principles of International Law concerning Friendly Relations and Cooperation among States has been established to formulate means and standards for their fulfillment.[3] Sovereignty is essential to independence, though it is often restricted by treaties and international law for the sake of collective defense, economic cooperation, and common convenience by the states themselves. Meantime, national interdependence necessitates mutual respect for sovereign rights in states' dealings with one another.[4] No individual state or even the United Nations should interfere in the domestic affairs of another state unless the latter's internal or external policies have adversely affected the vital interests of others or international peace and security.[5]

In international law, all states are legally equal in spite of their physical differences.[6] In the words of Vattel, "a small republic is no less a sovereign state than the most powerful kingdom."[7] The principle of "perfect equality and absolute independence" was emphatically

[3] The four principles are as follows: (1) states' refraining in international relations from the threat or use of force against the territorial integrity or political independence of any state, or in any other manner inconsistent with the purposes of the United Nations; (2) states' settling their disputes by peaceful means in such a manner that international peace and security and justice are not endangered; (3) duty not to intervene in matters within the domestic jurisdiction of any state, in accordance with the Charter; (4) sovereign equality of states. See GA res. 1966 (XVIII), *Yearbook*, UN, 1963, p. 518.

[4] The abduction of Adolf Eichmann by Israeli agents in Argentina was deemed by the Security Council in June 1960 a violation of Argentina's sovereignty, but the two countries settled the dispute soon afterward. See *infra*, §122.

[5] See Art. 2(7) of the Charter. The International Law Commission prepared a draft declaration of the rights and duties of states in pursuance of resolution 178 (II), adopted by the General Assembly on November 21, 1947, but no further action has been taken. For its text, see 44 *Am. Jour. Int. Law* (1950), Supp., pp. 15–21. See also *infra*, §§193–196.

[6] For a distinction between equality in law and of fact, see the Advisory Opinion on *Minority Schools in Albania*, Permanent Court of International Justice, 1935. P.C.I.J., Ser. A/B, No. 64.

[7] Vattel, *Droit des Gens* (English translation), Introduction, Pars. 18–21. The principle of equality is evidenced in the first two articles of the United Nations Charter. The following works discuss this subject most fully: E. D. Dickinson, *The Equality of States in International Law* (Cambridge, 1920); J. Goebel, Jr., *The Equality of States: A Study in the History of Law* (New York, 1923); P. H. Kooijmans, *The Doctrine of Legal Equality of States* (Leyden, 1964).

stated by Chief Justice Marshall in *The Schooner Exchange v. McFaddon* in 1812,[8] and reaffirmed in *The Antelope* case in 1925.[9] In deciding the restoration of vessel and cargo to the Spanish owners in the latter case, the United States Supreme Court reasoned that under international law all nations are perfectly equal and no nation can rightly impose a rule upon another. Five years later, the British High Court of Admiralty enunciated the same principle in *Le Louis* that all distinct states are equal to and independent of all others.[10] The primacy of the great powers in the Security Council as permanent members and the practice of weighted voting in several international organs is based on the political reality of power commensurate with responsibility,[11] but must be deemed a departure from the principle of legal equality. On the other hand, all members of the General Assembly have equal representation regardless of their differences in size, population, budgetary contributions, and other respects.

§70. JURISDICTIONAL RIGHTS AND EXEMPTIONS

As a corollary to national sovereignty and independence, a state has, in principle, exclusive jurisdiction over its territorial domain. Such a jurisdictional right is applied to its nationals and properties, and, to a lesser extent, to resident aliens and foreign properties located therein.[12] However, certain exemptions and immunities from territorial jurisdiction have been traditionally granted by states on a reciprocal basis as a matter of mutual convenience. According to Chief Justice Marshall, it is the principle of "perfect equality and absolute independence of sovereigns" that has "given rise to a class of cases in which every sovereign is understood to waive the exercise of a part of that complete exclusive territorial jurisdiction which has been stated to be the attribute of every nation."[13] On the other hand, unilateral exemp-

[8] 7 Cranch 116. [9] 10 Wheaton 66. [10] 2 Dodson 210.

[11] See Art. 23 of the Charter. The system of weighted voting is used by the Universal Postal Union and several other agencies. The voting rights of the members of the International Bank for Reconstruction and Development and the International Monetary Fund are based upon their subscribed shares of total capital.

[12] For details, see *infra*, Chs. 6–8.

[13] *The Schooner Exchange v. McFaddon*, U.S. Supreme Court, 1812. 7 Cranch 116. In the *Sabbatino Case,* the U.S. Supreme Court ruled in 1965 that United States courts would not question the legality of a foreign government's expropriation of property within its own borders. 376 U.S. 398. For further discussion of the subject, see Joseph M. Sweeney, *The International Law of Sovereign Immunity* (Washington, D.C., 1963); C. Wilfred Jenks, *International Immunities* (London, 1957).

tions and privileges imposed by major powers on certain weaker states through the conclusion of unequal treaties are against the principle of national sovereignty. Such unequal treaties have now been abolished.[14]

Judicial exemptions The acts of a state or of its officials done under governmental authority within the realm are not subject to judicial review in the courts of another.[15] It has been contended that acts of state are subject to review in case of violation of international law.[16] In principle, a foreign state, sovereign, or diplomatic agent cannot be sued without its or his consent.[17] This rule is, however, not applied to a minor officer for a tortious act.[18] Also immune from local jurisdiction is the public property owned or operated by a state,[19] but many states are reluctant to grant immunity to the commercial engage-

[14] As a victim of such unequal treaties, China had suffered the most for almost a century. See W. W. Willoughby, *Foreign Rights and Interests in China*, 2nd ed. (Baltimore, 1927), 2 vols., Chs. 22–26, in particular; William L. Tung, *China and Some Phases of International Law* (London & New York), pp. 70–74, 136. There are, of course, many treaties which grant special rights and privileges in the territories of contracting states on a reciprocal basis.

[15] *Underhill v. Hernandez*, U.S. Supreme Court, 1897. 168 U.S. 250. In *Finck v. Minister of the Interior*, the Mixed Tribunal of First Instance in Cairo decided in 1924 that an act of state cannot in law be the basis of an action for damages on the part of an individual who was injured thereby. *British Yearbook of International Law*, 1925, p. 219. See also Eleanor W. Allen, *The Position of Foreign States before National Courts—Chiefly in Continental Europe* (New York, 1933).

[16] See Quincy Wright, "Reflections on the Sabbatino Case," 59 *Am. Jour. Int. Law* (1965), pp. 304–315.

[17] See *The Parlement Belge*, Great Britain, Court of Appeal, 1880. L.R. [1880] 5 P.D. 197. For details, see *infra*, §§139–143.

[18] See *Johnstone v. Pedlar*, Great Britain, House of Lords, 1921. 2 A.C. 262.

[19] In *Mason v. Intercolonial Railway of Canada*, the Supreme Judicial Court of Massachusetts dismissed a proceeding in 1908 on evidence that the railway in question was owned and operated by the King of Great Britain for the public benefit of Canada. 197 Mass. 349. In *New York and Cuba Mail S.S. Co. v. Republic of Korea*, a U.S. District Court, S.D.N.Y., decided in 1955 to vacate the attachment of funds belonging to the Government of Korea. 132 Fed. Supp. 684. In *Vavasseur v. Krupp*, the British Court of Appeal ruled in 1878 that it could not interfere with goods purchased by a foreign state. 9 Ch. 351. Similarly, tobacco purchased in the United States by the French government was deemed free from local taxation to defray public expenses. See *French Republic v. Board of Supervisors of Jefferson County*, United States, Court of Appeals of Kentucky, 1923. 200 Ky. 18.

ments of state agencies. Thus, trade delegations of the Communist states and government-owned commercial airplanes and merchantmen are not entitled to the same degree of privileges and exemptions as diplomatic missions and public properties for non-commercial purposes. Practices vary in different states. The more restrictive trend has been evidenced in judicial decisions and the recent conventions adopted by the United Nations Conference on the Law of the Sea at Geneva in 1958.[20]

If there are no special agreements to the contrary, foreign warships,[21] military aircraft, and armed forces once permitted to enter a territory are immune from local jurisdiction unless the members of the forces concerned commit crimes ashore while not on official duty. During and after World War II, unusual circumstances necessitated certain new practices. Allied military and maritime courts were established in Great Britain in accordance with the Allied Forces Act of 1940, Allied Powers (Maritime Forces) Act of 1941, and the United States of America (Visiting Forces) Act of 1942. According to the Status of Forces Agreement signed by the North Atlantic Powers on June 19, 1951, sending and receiving states exercise concurrent jurisdiction over members of visiting forces and civilian personnel. The United States has concluded status of forces agreements with several states, including Japan and the Republic of China, where a sizable number of American forces are stationed.[22]

[20] In *The Attualita* case, the U.S. Circuit Court of Appeals (Fourth Circuit) decided in 1916 that the sanctity of public property could not extend to property requisitioned by the state for its service. 238 F. 909. See also *Chemins de Fer Liégeois-Luxembourgeois v. État Néerlandais,* Belgium, Cour de Cassation, 1903. *Pasicrisie Belge* (1903), I, 294. For details of the Conference on the Law of the Sea at Geneva, see *infra,* §§104–107. See also Paul Shepard, *Sovereignty and State-owned Commercial Entities* (New York, 1951); T. Kochu Thommen, *Legal Status of Government Merchant Ships in International Law* (The Hague, 1962). For a gist of the State Department instructions of September 15, 1961 on the subject, see 56 *Am. Jour. Int. Law* (1962), p. 533.

[21] See *The Schooner Exchange v. McFaddon,* U.S. Supreme Court, 1912. 7 Cranch 116.

[22] George Stambuk made an interesting study of this subject in *American Military Forces Abroad, Their Impact on the Western State System* (Columbus, 1963), in which the well-publicized Girard Case in Japan was discussed. See *Wilson v. Girard,* U.S. Supreme Court, 1957. 354 U.S. 524. At the time of the Communist occupation of China's mainland in 1949, a few thousand troops under the Nationalist government crossed the border of Yunnan Province and entered Burma. Upon the complaint of the Burmese government, the General Assembly adopted on April 23, 1953, a resolution

Diplomatic immunity The head of a state temporarily present in a foreign state is immune from civil or criminal jurisdiction of the local courts. If he travels incognito, such an immunity cannot be asserted in a suit against him unless he immediately discloses his actual status. In *Mighell v. Sultan of Johore* in 1893,[23] the British Court of Appeal dismissed a suit against the sultan for breach of promise to marry upon evidence that he was the sovereign of a foreign state. A foreign sovereign cannot be sued in the courts of another state. In *De Haber v. Queen of Portugal* in 1851, a British court stressed the principle that "to cite a foreign potentate in a municipal court, for any complaint against him in his public capacity, is contrary to the law of nations and an insult which he is entitled to resent."[24] But when a sovereign institutes action before a foreign court, he subjects himself to judgment on a counterclaim.[25]

Diplomatic agents and their official personnel are also immune from civil and criminal process.[26] Such immunity applies to past and current obligations.[27] Diplomats are also entitled to innocent passage through a third state and are exempt from local jurisdiction.[28] Similar immunities are extended to officials of international organizations.[29]

---

that they should either be interned or leave Burma. Eventually they were evacuated to Formosa. See *Everyman's UN*, 1945–1963, pp. 122–123. In pursuance of the Sino-American Agreement on the Status of United States Forces in the Republic of China of August 31, 1965, which came into effect on April 12, 1966, the Chinese government exercises jurisdiction over certain civil and criminal cases involving American personnel in Taiwan. In *Public Procurator v. John A. Wilson* (1966), the Chinese District Court of Kaohsiung sentenced the defendant to twenty months' imprisonment for his crime of manslaughter in accordance with the provisions of the Chinese Criminal Code (File No.: 55th Year, Shu-772; 61 *Am. Jour. Int. Law*, 1967, p. 816).

[23] [1894] 1 Q.B. 149. [24] 17 Q.B. 196.

[25] See *Norway v. Federal Sugar Refining Co.*, United States, District Court, S.D.N.Y., 1923. 286 F. 188.

[26] See, for instance, *Magdalena Steam Navigation Co. v. Martin*, Great Britain, Court of Queen's Bench, 1859. 2 Ellis & Ellis, 94. For a full discussion of the subject, see *infra*, §§139–143.

[27] See respectively the following two cases: *Procureur Général v. Nazare Agha*, France, Cour de Cassation (Chambre Civile), 1921. 123 Arrêts de la Cour de Cassation en Matière civile, p. 271. English translation from Hudson, 421. *Musurus Bey v. Gadban*, Great Britain, Court of Appeal, 1894. 2 Q.B. 352.

[28] See *Wilson v. Blanco*, U.S., New York Superior Court, 1889 (56 N.Y. Superior Ct. 582); *Holbrook, Nelson and Co. v. Henderson*, U.S. Superior Court of City of N.Y., 1839 (4 Sandford 619).

[29] For details, see *infra*, §143.

Without the consent of his own government a diplomat cannot waive his immunity,[30] but the members of his family may do so.[31] In connection with personal immunity, the premises of a diplomatic mission and the residence of a diplomat are entitled to exterritoriality and cannot be intruded on by local authorities without permission.[32] The immunities and privileges of consular officers are not on the same footing as those of diplomats [33] and are generally provided in treaties or conventions on a reciprocal basis.[34] This brief description of exemptions and immunities merely shows certain exceptions to the jurisdictional rights of states. Diplomatic immunities and privileges will be discussed further below.[35]

II. *SELF-PRESERVATION VERSUS INTERVENTION* [36]

§71. ACTS OF SELF-PRESERVATION

Measures for the defense of national sovereignty and independence under compelling circumstances are permissible in international practice, but dictatorial interference in the rights of other states under the guise of self-preservation cannot be justified. The British seizure of the Danish fleet in 1807 and destruction of the French fleet at Oran in 1940 to prevent them from falling to enemies' hands were vindicated. On the other hand, the German invasion of Belgium in 1914 and Japanese aggression in Manchuria in 1931 could not be excused.[37] In pro-

[30] See *United States v. Benner,* U.S., Circuit Court, Eastern District of Pennsylvania, 1830. 1 Baldwin 234. For prerequisites of waiver, see *In re Republic of Bolivia Exploration Syndicate,* Great Britain, Chancery Division, 1913. [1914] 1 Ch. 139.

[31] See *Herman v. Apetz,* U.S. Supreme Court of N.Y., N.Y. County, 1927. 130 Misc. N.Y. Rep. 618.

[32] *United States v. Jeffers,* U.S., Circuit Court for the District of Columbia, 1836. 4 Cranch, Cir. Ct. Rep. 704.

[33] *Barbuit's Case,* Great Britain, Court of Chancery, 1737. Williams, Cases in Equity during the time of Lord Chancellor Talbot, 281.

[34] *United States v. Trumbull,* U.S., District Court, Southern District of Calif., 1891. 48 F. 94.

[35] See *infra,* §§139–143.

[36] General texts on this subject: O'Connell, I, pp. 321–344; Oppenheim, II, §§50–52, 129–140a; Fenwick, *Principles,* Ch. XXII; Hyde, I, §§62–84; Moore, *Digest,* VI, §§897–926; Schwarzenberger, I, Ch. 7 (I–IV); Jacobini, pp. 53–56; Soviet *Text,* Ch. III, §4.

[37] Japan's attempt to justify aggression as a legitimate measure of self-defense was refuted by the Lytton Commission of Inquiry, whose report was

testing against the British attack on *The Caroline* in American waters during the Canadian rebellion in 1837, Secretary of State Daniel Webster defined the necessary conditions of self-defense as "instant, overwhelming, and leaving no choice of means, and no moment for deliberation." [38] Webster's definition may be taken as a milestone in distinguishing an act of self-preservation from that of aggression.[39] Thus, the war crimes tribunals at Nuremberg and Tokyo rejected the plea of the German and Japanese leaders that their actions in an aggressive war were taken in self-defense.[40]

§72. GROUNDS OF INTERVENTION

Intervention is dictatorial interference by one state in the domestic affairs of another or in a difference between two other states.[41] In the past, there have been numerous interventions on various grounds, which may be summarized as follows: (1) self-preservation or self-defense as stated above; (2) action at the invitation of the lawful government or in accordance with the stipulations of a treaty; [42] (3) protection of the lives and property of nationals abroad; [43] (4) stopping cruelty and persecution in the interest of humanity; [44] (5) prevention

---

endorsed by the Assembly of the League of Nations. See League Doc. C.663.M.320.1932.VII; also William L. Tung, *op. cit.*, pp. 164–168.

[38] Moore, *Digest*, II, p. 412.

[39] For a thorough discussion of the subject, see D. W. Bowett, *Self-Defense in International Law* (New York, 1958).

[40] See *infra*, §226.

[41] For further references on intervention, see E. C. Stowell, *Intervention in International Law* (Washington, D.C., 1921); A. V. W. Thomas & A. J. J. Thomas, *Non-Intervention. The Law and Its Import in the Americas* (Dallas, 1956); Roland J. Stanger (ed.), *Essays on Intervention* (Columbus, 1964); P. H. Winfield, "The History of Intervention in International Law," 3 *British Yearbook of International Law* (1922–1923), pp. 130–149, and "The Grounds of Intervention in International Law," 5 *ibid.* (1924), pp. 149–162.

[42] The landing of American and British forces in Lebanon and Jordan in 1958 was grounded on invitations of the local governments, which had also complained to the Security Council against intervention in their domestic affairs by the United Arab Republic. See *Repertoire,* SC, Supp., 1956–1958, pp. 121–128. On legal aspects of such intervention, see Quincy Wright, "United States Intervention in the Lebanon," 53 *Am. Jour. Int. Law* (1959), pp. 112–125. United States intervention in Cuba in 1906 for the restoration of order was in accordance with the Treaty of Havana of 1903.

[43] The military expedition of the Allied Powers against China during the Boxer Uprising in 1900 was chiefly to protect the lives of their nationals.

[44] The intervention by Great Britain, France, and Russia at the time of the Greek revolt against Turkey in 1827 was of this nature.

of the establishment of a Communist regime;[45] (6) keeping other states from interfering with the affairs of certain regions under special influence of another state;[46] and (7) maintenance of the balance of power.[47] The collective intervention by the United Nations in the Congo was unique in nature, chiefly for the purpose of restoring domestic order in that country and preventing possible disturbances of international peace.

Strictly speaking, any kind of intervention by one state is detrimental to the independence of the other. Non-intervention is the normal rule of international law, with possible exceptions for self-preservation, treaty rights, and humanity. Due to the deep resentment of the population and government of the intervened state, the result of intervention is generally contrary to the original expectation of the

[45] The most notable instance was Allied intervention in Russia against the Bolshevik revolution. There was actually a certain degree of foreign intervention in the Spanish Civil War in 1936. In June 1954, Guatemala complained to the Security Council against the open aggression of Honduras and Nicaragua. In a cablegram of June 19, 1954, sent by the Guatemalan Foreign Minister to the President of the Security Council, he stated that such aggression was "at the instigation of certain foreign monopolies whose interests have been affected by the progressive policy" of the government of Guatemala. See *Repertoire,* SC, Supp., 1952–1955, pp. 119–121. The pro-Communist regime was later overthrown by a new government, which withdrew the complaint. Among recent instances of intervention are United States military action against the Viet Cong, and the landing of American forces in Santo Domingo in 1965.

[46] The Monroe Doctrine was originally declared to prevent intervention by European powers in the Western Hemisphere. When the United States insisted on arbitrating the boundary dispute between Venezuela and Great Britain, Secretary of State Olney went so far as to assert that "the United States is practically sovereign on this continent, and its fiat is law upon the subjects to which it confines its interposition." See Moore, *Digest,* VI, p. 553; Julius W. Pratt, *A History of United States Foreign Policy* (Englewood Cliffs, N.J., 1955), pp. 347–352. Other great powers have claimed at one time or another certain regions under their special influence. The essence of the Monroe Doctrine was later accepted by the Latin-American states as their general policy, particularly in the Act of Chapultepec of March 3, 1945, and the Treaty of Rio de Janeiro of September 2, 1947.

[47] This was the traditional policy of Great Britain and other nations. On various occasions, intervention by the Concert of Powers in the nineteenth century was to maintain the balance of power. The joint intervention by Russia, Germany, and France to demand that Japan restore the Liaotung Peninsula to China after the first Sino-Japanese War (1894–1895) was in order to maintain the balance of power in the Far East.

intervening state. The adverse effect of United States intervention in the Dominican Republic in 1965 has been reflected in popular dissatisfaction both in and outside that country. The unilateral declaration of neutralization of the Formosa Strait by the United States during the Korean War to prevent hostilities between the Chinese Nationalists and Communists in that area was resented by Peking as a kind of intervention in the domestic affairs of China.

Since the rise of the international Communist movement, a new type of intervention has emerged through subversive activities carried out by one state against the established order of another.[48] North Vietnam has been accused of rendering active assistance to the Viet Cong in South Vietnam. Instead of resorting to proportionate measures of retaliation by the government of South Vietnam, the United States deemed it necessary to bomb the territory of North Vietnam. American desire to prevent the spread of Communism might necessitate such a military expediency, but any sanction of this nature should properly be undertaken by the United Nations.[49]

§73. NON-INTERVENTION AND COLLECTIVE SELF-DEFENSE

The security system under the League of Nations relied upon collective measures as a substitute for individual action against any recalcitrant state. The Charter of the United Nations does not permit intervention by individual states, except in individual or collective self-defense against armed attack. It emphasizes collective security in the face of threats to or breaches of the peace, and acts of aggression.[50] Article 39 stipulates that "the Security Council shall determine the existence of any threat to the peace, breaches of the peace, or acts of aggression and shall make recommendations, or decide what measures shall be taken in accordance with Articles 41 and 42, to maintain or restore international peace and security." Such enforcement action may also be applicable to states not members of the United Nations and to

[48] Such subversive activities amount to intervention in the domestic affairs of another state and, therefore, violate international law. From the very beginning, the General Assembly has condemned indirect intervention through propaganda, subversion, and infiltration by adopting a number of resolutions on November 3, 1947, December 1, 1949, and November 17, 1950. The condemnation of such indirect means of aggression is implied in a recent resolution, adopted by the General Assembly on December 20, 1965.

[49] For further discussion of the subject, see *infra,* §196.

[50] See Arts. 10, 11, 16, 17, of the League Covenant; Ch. VII of the Charter.

political entities not recognized as states. Among cases of the United Nations action under Article 39 are Indonesia, Palestine, and Korea.

Individual or collective self-defense is permissible under the Charter if armed attack occurs against a Member of the United Nations, until the Security Council has taken necessary measures to maintain or restore international peace and security. Here, the action of self-defense is to resist immediate armed attack, not to fight a preventive war or a remote threat. Besides, measures taken by members in the exercise of this right of self-defense must be immediately reported to the Security Council and must not in any way affect the authority and responsibility of the Security Council.[51]

The United Nations is not authorized to intervene in matters which are essentially within the domestic jurisdiction of any state.[52] The doctrine of non-intervention in the internal and external affairs of another state has been endorsed by the Inter-American system,[53] which, as one of the regional organizations, is permitted by the United Nations Charter to deal with such matters relating to the maintenance of peace and security as are appropriate for regional action and consistent with the purposes and principles of the Organization.[54] The same function and responsibility may be undertaken by the Southeast Asia Treaty Organization and other regional agencies in their respective areas.[55] The principle of non-intervention was reasserted by the General Assembly in its resolution of December 20, 1965, which stresses that no state "shall organize, assist, foment, finance, incite or tolerate subversion, terrorist or armed activities directed to the violent overthrow of the regime in another state or interfere in civil strife in another state." [56] By a resolution adopted at its twenty-first session on December 19, 1966, the General Assembly called upon all states to implement the declaration on the inadmissibility of intervention.[57]

[51] Art. 51 of the Charter. The joint intervention of Great Britain and France in the Israeli-Egyptian conflict in the Suez Canal Zone in 1956 was condemned by the General Assembly even though their action was based on the ground of threat to their vital interests in that region. For details, see *Yearbook*, UN, 1956, pp. 19–62.

[52] Art. 2(7) of the Charter.

[53] Resolutions to this effect were adopted at the Montevideo Conference of 1933 and the Buenos Aires Conference of 1936.

[54] Art. 52(1) of the Charter.

[55] See *supra*, §35; *infra*, §§194–196.

[56] The resolution was adopted by a vote of 109 to 0, and, if acted upon by the Members, would eliminate the evils of direct and indirect intervention.

[57] GA res. 2225 (XXI), with 114 in favor, none against, and 2 abstentions.

§74. PEACEFUL COEXISTENCE

A corollary of non-intervention is the doctrine of peaceful coexistence.[58] Fundamentally, the Communists hold that socialism must triumph in the end, but during the transitory period they will coexist with the capitalist states. Since neither can annihilate the other by forcible means, coexistence is inevitable for the time being. Presumably originated by Lenin,[59] this concept was supported by Stalin and his successors. In the words of Khrushchev, "peaceful coexistence can and should develop into peaceful competition for the purpose of satisfying man's needs in the best possible way." [60] Peaceful coexistence attracted world-wide attention when Chou En-lai, Prime Minister of the People's Republic of China, elaborated five principles for its realization: equality of states, mutual respect for national sovereignty and territorial integrity, non-aggression, non-interference in domestic affairs of other states, and mutual benefit and peaceful coexistence. These principles were embodied in the Sino-Indian Agreement of April 29, 1954, the Sino-Soviet joint declaration of October 11, 1954, the joint statement by Prime Minister Nehru and President Ho Chi Minh of October 18, 1954, and other communiqués by leaders of different countries, including Burma, Poland, and Yugoslavia.[61] The five principles of peaceful coexistence were reaffirmed at the Asian-African Conference at Bandung in April 1955,[62] and also sponsored by the manifesto of sixty-four Communist and workers' parties in 1957.[63]

Signifying a temporary détente, this concept of coexistence certainly allayed the apprehension of the neutralist or non-committed states and would serve as an ideal substitute for the cold war if acted upon by Communist and non-Communist states alike.[64] On the original

[58] This term is widely known as *panch shila* in Hindi, derived from the Sanskrit.

[59] See V. I. Lenin, *The National-Liberation Movement in the East* (Moscow, 1957), p. 240.

[60] Nikita S. Khrushchev, "On Peaceful Coexistence," 38 *Foreign Affairs* (October 1959), pp. 1–18, at p. 4. For a more comprehensive study of Soviet utilization of this principle to support policy objectives, see Bernard A. Ramundo, *Peaceful Coexistence* (Baltimore, 1967).

[61] See J. J. G. Syatauw, *Some Newly Established Asian States and the Development of International Law* (The Hague, 1961), pp. 206–219.

[62] For details, see *China and the Asian-African Conference* (Peking, 1955). In the final communiqué of the Conference, the phrase "live together in peace" was used, substantially the same as peaceful coexistence in the opinion of Chou En-lai.

[63] See Russell H. Fifield, "The Five Principles of Peaceful Coexistence," 52 *Am. Jour. Int. Law* (1958), p. 508.

[64] Khrushchev reminded the West in 1959 that "there is only one way

proposal of the Soviet Union, the General Assembly adopted, on December 14, 1957, a resolution relating to the principles of peaceful coexistence in slightly different wording.[65] The United States and other Western Members raised no objection to it, because these principles are in conformity with the Charter of the United Nations.[66] There is no doubt, however, that the war in Vietnam reverses the precept of coexistence between peoples of different beliefs no matter how convincing the arguments for intervention by the parties concerned may be. At its twenty-first session, the General Assembly considered the report of the 1966 Special Committee on Principles of International Law concerning Friendly Relations and Cooperation among States,[67] and requested the Committee to formulate proposals on non-intervention in the domestic affairs of states. A resolution was adopted to include that item in the provisional agenda of its twenty-second session.[68]

III. *RESPONSIBILITY OF STATES* [69]

§75. THE NATURE OF STATE RESPONSIBILITY

The doctrine of state responsibility is based on the necessity of observing international obligations in accordance with the normal

---

to peace, one way out of the existing tension: peaceful coexistence." In spite of his provocative actions in Cuba and elsewhere, it was he who made the following sober remarks: "The existence of the Soviet Union and of the other socialist countries is a real fact. It is also a real fact that the United States of America and the other capitalist countries live in different social conditions, in the conditions of capitalism. Then let us recognize this real situation and proceed from it in order not to go against reality, against life itself. Let us not try to change this situation by interferences from without, by means of war on the part of some states against other states." Khrushchev, *op. cit.*, p. 18.

[65] The vote was 77 to 0, with one abstention. The resolution as finally adopted was submitted by India, Sweden, and Yugoslavia, using "peaceful and tolerant relations" and "friendly and cooperative relations." See Russell H. Fifield, *op. cit.*, pp. 504–510. For the text of the resolution, see UN Doc. A/3802, December 14, 1957.

[66] For the statement made at the General Committee on September 30, 1957, by Henry Cabot Lodge, United States Chief Delegate to the United Nations, see 37 Department of State *Bulletin* (1957), p. 693.

[67] The Committee met in New York from March 8 to April 25, 1966.

[68] GA res. 2181 (XXI), adopted on December 12, 1966, with 85 in favor, none against, and 2 abstentions.

[69] General texts on this subject: O'Connell, II, pp. 836–844, 868–910, 1019–1154, 1203–1213; Oppenheim, I, §§148–165b; Fenwick, *Principles,*

standard of the community of nations. A state is directly responsible for its international delinquency due to any act of commission or omission of its own or of its authorized agents. To a lesser extent, it is indirectly responsible for injuries to resident aliens or damages to their property as a result of lack of due diligence in protecting them.[70] The important factors for determining whether a state has exercised due diligence are time, place, and other related circumstances. Discriminatory acts and denial of justice are also reasons for complaints by foreign states and resident aliens.[71]

Full amends should be made promptly in proportion to the seriousness of the delinquency, usually in the form of apology, compensation, punishment of wrongdoers, and assurance of preventing similar occurrences. Direct and willful acts by the state are more serious than indirect responsibility. While a state has special responsibility toward foreign states, most cases involve protection of resident aliens and their property.[72]

Chs. XIV–XV; Hyde, I, §§217A–217D; II, §§269A–309A; Moore, *Digest,* VI, §§998–1063; Hackworth, *Digest,* V, §§520–546; Schwarzenberger, I, Ch. 6(V); Starke, Ch. 9; Hershey, Ch. XI; Jessup, Ch. V; Gould, Ch. 17; Svarlien, Ch. 10; Von Glahn, Ch. 14; Soviet *Text,* Ch. III, §7; Schuschnigg, Ch. 9; Le Fur, §§664–678; Vattel, III, Bk. 2, Ch. 6; Strupp & Blociszewski, §19; Calvo, III, §§1261–1298; Piédelièvre, I, pp. 317–322; McNair, II, pp. 197–322.

[70] Some writers use the terms 'original' and 'vicarious' to represent 'direct' and 'indirect' responsibility of states. See Oppenheim, I, p. 337. For a general survey of the subject, see C. Eagleton, *The Responsibility of States in International Law* (New York, 1928). With reference to state responsibility for damages, see also Marjorie M. Whiteman, *Damages in International Law* (Washington, D.C., 1937–1943), 3 vols.

[71] The segregation of Japanese children by the board of education in San Francisco in 1906 was a discriminatory act, which was later repealed after protest by the Japanese government. For the comments of Secretary of State Elihu Root, see 1 *Am. Jour. Int. Law* (1907), 273 ff. For the meaning and scope of denial of justice, see G. G. Fitzmaurice, "The Meaning of the Term of Denial of Justice," 13 *British Yearbook of International Law* (1932), pp. 93–114; A. V. Freeman, *The International Responsibility of States for Denial of Justice* (London, 1938); C. Eagleton, "Denial of Justice in International Law," 22 *Am. Jour. Int. Law* (1928), pp. 538–559.

[72] For details, see E. M. Borchard, *The Diplomatic Protection of Citizens Abroad* (New York, 1915), §§75–81, 86–96, 127–130; C. Eagleton, *The Responsibility of States in International Law,* pp. 44–94, 125–156; F. S. Dunn, *The Protection of Nationals* (Baltimore, 1932), Chs. 4–8; A. P. Fachiri, "International Law and the Property of Aliens," 10 *British Yearbook of International Law* (1929), pp. 32–55; G. H. Hackworth, "Responsibility of

The trials of war criminals after World War II by the International Military Tribunal in Nuremberg and the International Military Tribunal for the Far East in Tokyo set up a new standard of double responsibility for the state and its agents. In addition to severe punishment of the vanquished states for their responsibility in the war, civilian and military agents of the Axis Powers were held responsible for committing crimes against peace, war crimes, and crimes against humanity. Individual responsibility for official acts under the order of one's government is a departure from the traditional rules of international law.[73]

§76. SPECIAL RESPONSIBILITIES TOWARD FOREIGN STATES

As a matter of mutual respect for the independence and sovereignty of the members of the international community, a state should exercise special care to prevent acts injurious to foreign states. Thus any military expedition from its territory against the legal government of a foreign state is contradictory to its neutral status and should be prohibited. This principle is applied to both international and civil wars and any violation amounts to intervention, for which the injured state has the legitimate right to demand redress. The case of *The Alabama Claims* was based upon this established rule of international law.[74] The active assistance rendered by the United States to Cuban exiles in their invasion of the Bay of Pigs in April 1961 was nothing but intervention, the purpose of which was to overthrow the Castro government in Cuba. A more serious situation occurred in Greece from 1946 to 1949, when the Greek guerrillas received active aid from the neighboring states of Albania, Bulgaria, and Yugoslavia. In all these cases, the states concerned could not be absolved from their responsibilities.

A state is also obligated to prohibit counterfeiting foreign currency within its territory detrimental to the sovereign right of a foreign state. Thus, in *Emperor of Austria and King of Hungary v. Day and Kos-*

States for Damages Caused in Their Territory to the Person or Property of Foreigners," 24 *Am. Jour. Int. Law* (1930), pp. 500–516. At its twenty-first session, the General Assembly adopted a resolution that the International Law Commission continue its work on state responsibility. GA res. 2167 (XXI).

[73] See also *infra*, §226.

[74] United States-Great Britain, Claims Arbitration, 1872. Malloy, *Treaties*, I, 717. For the Havana Convention of 1928 on this subject, see *International Conferences of American States, 1889–1928* (Washington, D.C., 1931), p. 435.

suth,[75] the British High Court of Chancery decided in 1861 to compel the defendants to surrender plates and all money printed therefrom. The United States Supreme Court upheld the same principle in *United States v. Arjona* in 1887.[76] The traditional courtesy of government officials to refrain from making slanderous statements against foreign governments or leaders is no longer observed by states engaging in the cold war.[77] It is generally understood that a state has no obligation to enforce penal or revenue laws of foreign states.[78]

§77. PROTECTION OF RESIDENT ALIENS

An alien once admitted to a foreign state is entitled to the equal protection of its laws. If he is subject to a denial of justice by its administrative, legislative, or judicial authorities,[79] he may ask the interposition of his own government for redress.[80] Before doing so, he must exhaust all local remedies and present his claims diligently.[81] Normally

[75] 3 De Gex, Fisher & Jones, 217. [76] 120 U.S. 479.

[77] See Fenwick, *Principles,* pp. 305–306; also L. Preuss, "Responsibility for Hostile Propaganda against Foreign States," 28 *Am. Jour. Int. Law* (1934), pp. 649–668.

[78] See *Queen of Holland v. Drukker,* Great Britain, Chancery Division, 1928. [1928] Ch. 877. However, the United States-Canada Arbitration Tribunal decided in *Trail Smelter Arbitration* in 1941 that measures should be taken by a state to keep its territory from being used for economic injury to another state. 3 R.I.A.A., 1905.

[79] Denial of justice in its narrow sense is limited to deficiencies of the judicial branch. See Art. 9 of the Harvard Draft Convention on Responsibility of States. Local courts should be accessible to aliens for redress of wrongs. See *Berger v. Stevens,* Supreme Court of North Carolina, 1929. *Annual Digest,* 1929–1930, Case No. 160. Consult also C. Eagleton, "L'Épuisement des recours internes et le déni de justice, d'après certaines décisions récentes," 62 *Revue de droit international et de législation comparée* (1935), pp. 504–526; J. W. Garner, "International Responsibility of States for Judgments of Courts and Verdicts of Juries Amounting to Denial of Justice," 10 *British Yearbook of International Law* (1929), pp. 181–189; O'Connell, II, pp. 1024–1029.

[80] See *Panevezys-Saldutiskis Railway Case,* Permanent Court of International Justice, 1939. P.C.I.J. (1939), Ser. A/B, No. 76.

[81] In the *Gentini Case,* the Italy-Venezuela Mixed Claims Commission held, in 1903, that a delay in making a claim usually rendered its merit questionable, though the delay in the case considered was condoned. Ralston's *Report,* p. 724. In the case of *Don Pacifico,* an English Jew residing in Greece, Great Britain argued that the victim's failure to resort to local remedies in Greek courts was justified by legal disabilities imposed on Jews. Mixed Commission of Inquiry, 1850–1851. 39 *Br. & For. St. Papers,* p. 332.

diplomatic protection of a state extends to its nationals only,[82] but there are exceptions.[83]

If the claim by the interposing government on behalf of its national is not accepted by the state where he resides, an international claims commission is usually established to investigate and determine the merits of the case.[84] In the *De Galván* case,[85] the General Claims Commission, set up by the United States and Mexico in 1927, decided to award damages to Mexico on behalf of the mother of De Galván, a Mexican citizen killed in Texas by an American, on the ground of denial of justice by the local authorities who failed to conduct a prosecution within a period of six years. It may be said that delay of justice is a denial of justice because of the difficulty, later, of obtaining satisfactory evidence and other hardships. In conjunction with the principle of equal protection, an injured alien has no reason to claim more compensation from the receiving state than that accorded to its own nationals.[86] Compensation is generally awarded to the injured person, but sometimes it is also extended to the claimant state.[87] However, vindication or exemplary damages are not considered.[88]

Complaints have been made against the substandard judicial proc-

---

The local remedy principle was also upheld in the *Interhandel (Preliminary Objections) Case* by the International Court of Justice in 1959. I.C.J. Reports (1959), 6. In the *Ambatielos Claim,* the Greece-Great Britain Commission of Arbitration ruled in 1956 that local remedies had not been exhausted. 50 *Am. Jour. Int. Law* (1956), 674–679. See also Castor H. P. Law, *The Local Remedies Rule in International Law* (Geneva, 1961).

[82] For the determination of a person's nationality, see *infra,* §114.

[83] A state may extend diplomatic protection to aliens serving in its military forces or on its ships. An international organization may also be a claimant. See *Reparation for Injuries Suffered in Service of the United Nations,* International Court of Justice, 1949. I.C.J. Reports (1949), 174. A state does not necessarily have the right to protect a national who obtained his nationality for ultra motives. See the *Nottebohm Case,* International Court of Justice, 1953. I.C.J. Reports (1953), 111.

[84] The status of the claimant is always an important factor. See *Mavrommatis Palestine Concessions Case (Jurisdiction),* Permanent Court of International Justice, 1924. P.C.I.J. (1924), Ser. A, No. 2.

[85] *Opinions of Commissioners,* 1927, p. 408.

[86] This principle was upheld by the United States-El Salvador Claims Arbitration of the *Rosa Gelbtrunk* case in 1902. *U.S. For. Rel.,* 1902, p. 877.

[87] This was done in *The I'm Alone,* United States-Great Britain, Special Joint Commission, 1935. [1933: 1935] 3 R.I.A.A., 1609.

[88] See *Lusitania Cases,* United States-Germany, Mixed Claims Commission, 1923. *Annual Digest,* 1923–1924, Case No. 113.

ess of certain states. In the *Chattin Case,*[89] the United States-Mexico General Claims Commission ruled in 1927 against Mexico for her failure to maintain the minimum standard of justice required of civilized nations. This decision was based upon an unfair standard by demanding that a state treat aliens on a higher plane than its own nationals. At the First Conference for the Codification of International Law at The Hague in 1930, Wu Chao-chu, the Chinese delegate, criticized this kind of double standard with a subtle reminder that an alien could exercise the right of absence from a country deemed undesirable.[90] On the other hand, Great Britain and the United States generally uphold the necessity of an international standard of justice.[91] Yet the so-called minimum standard is entirely a matter of opinion. Many states in Asia, Latin America, and Africa do not agree with this concept held by the Western powers.

In time of insurrection or civil war, a state is not responsible for losses suffered by resident aliens provided it has exercised due diligence to prevent their occurrence.[92] The responsibility of a state for mob violence against aliens depends upon the circumstances under which it has exercised due diligence for their protection.[93] The refusal of responsibility by the United States for mob violence against the Chinese at Rock Springs, Wyoming, in 1885 was on the ground of the remoteness of the locality and other reasons as presented by Secretary of State Thomas F. Bayard.[94] On the other hand, severe terms have

[89] *Opinions of Commissioners,* 1927, p. 422. For further discussion on the judicial standard, see A. H. Roth, *The Minimum Standard of International Law Applied to Aliens* (Leiden, 1950).

[90] See League Doc. 351(C).M.145(C).1930.V., p. 187.

[91] See Brierly, p. 279; Hall, pp. 59–60.

[92] This is known as Calvo Doctrine, advocated by C. Calvo, an Argentine publicist. See his *Le Droit international: théorique et pratique,* 5th ed. (Paris, 1896), 6 vols., III, §1280. See also Haig Silvanie, *Responsibility of States for Acts of Unsuccessful Insurgent Governments* (New York, 1939).

[93] In *Home Missionary Society Case,* the United States-Great Britain Claims Commission decided in 1920 to reject the American claim because there was no evidence of lack of due diligence on the part of Great Britain. Nielsen's Report, 421.

[94] See Moore, *Digest,* VI, §§1023 ff. While refusing responsibility in principle, the United States government has often paid compensation to claimant states out of sympathy in cases of mob violence. See also J. W. Foster, "International Responsibility to Corporate Bodies for Lives Lost by Outlawry," 1 *Am. Jour. Int. Law* (1907), pp. 4–10; J. Goebel, Jr., "The International Responsibility of States for Injuries Sustained by Aliens on Account of Mob Violence, Insurrections and Civil Wars," 8 *ibid.* (1914), pp. 802–852.

often been imposed by the Western powers on weaker states in cases of mob violence.[95] Special protection should be rendered to foreign officers, but undue measures of retaliation against a delinquent state are unwarranted.[96]

§78. FULFILLMENT OF CONTRACTUAL OBLIGATIONS

A breach of contract by a foreign government with an alien raises the problem of state responsibility. As a rule, the injured alien should exhaust all local remedies before appealing to his own government for diplomatic representation. To avoid repeated intervention by foreign governments on behalf of their nationals, a number of Latin-American states in the late nineteenth century introduced the so-called Calvo Clause in their contracts with aliens by stipulating that any contractual disputes would be determined by the national courts according to national laws.[97] The validity of the Calvo Clause was sometimes challenged on the ground that states have the inherent right to intervene on behalf of their nationals in case of denial of justice. However, if the claims are not based upon denial of justice, contractual disputes should be adjudicated by the local courts. This principle was upheld by the United States-Mexico General Claims Commission in dismissing the claims in the *North American Dredging Co.* case in 1926.[98]

In this connection, mention should also be made of the so-called Drago Doctrine. In protest against the use of force by Great Britain, Germany, and Italy to collect public debts from Venezuela in 1902, Dr. Luis Drago, the Argentine Foreign Minister, declared that "a public debt cannot give rise to the right of intervention, and much less

[95] See William L. Tung, *China and Some Phases of International Law*, pp. 64–65.

[96] This opinion was held by the Committee of Jurists appointed by the League of Nations in connection with the assassination of General Tellini of Italy on Greek territory in 1923. General Tellini was an Italian member of an international commission surveying the boundary between Greece and Albania. In retaliation, Italy occupied Corfu Island in August 1923. Greece appealed the case to the League of Nations and the Conference of Ambassadors of Paris. A month later, Italy evacuated the island.

[97] See Calvo, III, §1280; Hackworth, *Digest*, V, p. 635; E. M. Borchard, *The Diplomatic Protection of Citizens Abroad*, §371 ff.; M. T. Manton, "Governmental Defaults in the Payment of Contractual Obligations," 68 *United States Law Review* (March 1934), pp. 131–142; Donald R. Shea, *The Calvo Clause: A Problem of Inter-American and International Law and Diplomacy* (Minneapolis: University of Minnesota Press, 1955).

[98] *Opinions of Commissioners*, 1927, p. 21.

to the occupation of the soil of any American nation by any European power."[99] This is a sound principle, but the debtor state should in turn abide by a reasonable settlement through negotiation or arbitration.[100] Generally speaking, governments are reluctant to intervene in a dispute involving public bonds, which are not as specific as individual contracts, unless there is evidence of discrimination against certain bondholders.[101]

§79. EXPROPRIATION OF ALIEN PROPERTY

Mutual convenience and international order require states to grant due respect for and protection of alien property located in their territories. With reasonable compensation and without discrimination, expropriation is permissible when it is necessary for public purposes and in accordance with treaty provisions.[102] In the dispute between Germany and Poland in the case of *Factory at Chorzów*,[103] the Permanent Court of International Justice ruled in 1928 that restitution and reparation should be made if the expropriation was in violation of a treaty. The Soviet Union has insisted on her right of expropriation without compensation. As late as 1962, the Soviet representative to the United Nations made a statement to that effect.[104] While Mexico and several other countries have upheld such a right, due compensation was made for expropriations.[105] Prompt and adequate payment is not only essential to international justice and order but also an encouragement to foreign investment when needed.[106]

[99] Moore, *Digest,* VI, p. 592. For details, see Henri A. Moulin, *La doctrine de Drago* (Paris, 1907).

[100] For the Porter Convention adopted at the Second Hague Conference in 1907, see A. P. Higgins, *The Hague Peace Conferences* (Cambridge, England, 1909), pp. 180–197.

[101] When the Portuguese government granted special treatment to British holders of gold bonds in 1924, the United States protested on the ground of discrimination against American bondholders. See Hackworth, *Digest,* V, p. 627.

[102] See the *Norwegian Shipping Claims Case* (Norway-United States), Permanent Court of Arbitration, 1922. Scott, *Hague Court Reports,* II, 39. See also *German Interests in Polish Upper Silesia* (Germany-Poland), Permanent Court of International Justice, 1926. P.C.I.J., (1926), Ser. A., No. 7.

[103] P.C.I.J. (1928), Ser. A, No. 17.

[104] See UN Doc. A/C.2/SR.834 (November 15, 1962), p. 16.

[105] See Hackworth, *Digest,* III, p. 657.

[106] In *Banco Nacional de Cuba v. Sabbatino,* a U.S. Court of Appeals affirmed in 1962 that the Cuban nationalization decree was a violation of

The most notable issues in recent years were the *Anglo-Iranian Oil Company* case between Iran and Great Britain,[107] and the nationalization of the Suez Canal by Egypt in 1956.[108] Whether such action can be justified depends upon the merits of each case. There is no agreement among states about certain international standards governing such matters, especially in view of the conflict of interests between capital-exporting and developing countries.[109] Perhaps the former should reconcile themselves to the irresistible trend of political and economic nationalism.[110] A reasonable solution is found in a resolution adopted by the General Assembly on December 14, 1962.[111] On the basis of the report of the Commission on Permanent Sovereignty over Natural Resources, the resolution incorporated both the right of expropriation and the principle of adequate compensation. Most states

---

international law. 307 F.2d 845. But the Supreme Court reversed the decision in 1964 on the act of state principle, stating that "the Judicial Branch will not examine the validity of a taking of property within its own territory by a foreign sovereign government, extant and recognized by this country at the time of the suit, . . ." 376 U.S. 398. For comments on the decision, see Quincy Wright, "Reflections on the Sabbatino Case," 59 *Am. Jour. Int. Law* (1965), pp. 304–315. The Supreme Court of Aden decided in *Anglo-Iranian Oil Co. v. Jaffarate* in 1953 that Iranian legislation was invalid on account of Iran's failure to make due compensation. 1 W.L.R. 246.

[107] *Anglo-Iranian Oil Company* (Jurisdiction), International Court of Justice, 1952. I.C.J. Reports (1952), 93.

[108] See *Documents on American Foreign Relations*, 1956 (edited by Paul E. Zinner of the Council on Foreign Relations, New York, 1957), Ch. IV, C.

[109] For the views of jurists and statesmen from the developing countries on the international standard of treatment of aliens and the requirement of "prompt, adequate, and effective compensation," see sources cited in Oliver J. Lissitzyn, "International Law in a Divided World," *International Conciliation* (March 1963), No. 542, p. 44, note 68; p. 48, note 74.

[110] In discussing traditional rules of international law developed to promote the interest of capital-exporting nations, Richard A. Falk frankly observed that such a law "will not serve the interests of a world community where capital export is no longer coincident with political power." Falk & Mendlovitz, II, p. 176; reprinted from Falk, "Historical Tendencies, Modernizing and Revolutionary Nations, and the International Legal Order," 8 *Howard Law Journal* (Spring 1962), pp. 128–151.

[111] GA res. 1803 (XVII). India and nine other Afro-Asian states voted against a Soviet amendment upholding the inalienable right of states of nationalization, expropriation, and other measures. Among the sixteen Latin-American countries rejecting the amendment were Mexico and Brazil. See UN Doc. A/PV.1193, pp. 71–76.

have paid adequate compensation in cases of nationalization, though the amount might not meet the standard of the investors. Moderation will encourge the flow of foreign capital to countries which are much in need of industrial development and economic aid.[112]

On November 25, 1966, the twenty-first session of the General Assembly adopted a resolution to implement permanent sovereignty over natural resources.[113] The Secretary-General was requested to co-ordinate the activities of the Secretariat in the field of natural resources with those of other United Nations organs and to take necessary steps to facilitate the exploitation of the natural resources of developing countries in programs for their accelerated economic growth. He is to submit a progress report on the subject at the twenty-third session of the General Assembly.[114]

[112] For further discussion of nationalization and expropriation, see B. A. Wortley, *Expropriation in Public International Law* (Cambridge, England, 1959); Samy Friedman, *Expropriation in International Law* (London, 1953); E. D. Re, *Foreign Confiscations in Anglo-American Law* (New York, 1951); G. White, *Nationalization of Foreign Property* (New York, 1961).

[113] GA res. 2158 (XXI).

[114] For details, see Office of Public Information of the United Nations, *Resolutions of Legal Interest Adopted by the General Assembly at Its Twenty-first Session, 20 September–20 December 1966*, pp. 43–46.

CHAPTER 6

STATE TERRITORY

I. *TERRITORIAL DOMAIN IN GENERAL*[1]

§80. THE SCOPE OF TERRITORIAL JURISDICTION

In principle, a state exercises exclusive jurisdiction over its territory, which consists of land, maritime domain, and airspace.[2] For the maintenance of international peace and order, states are required to show mutual respect for territorial integrity. This fundamental duty of states is expressly stipulated in the Covenant of the League of Nations,[3] the Charter of the United Nations,[4] and other international treaties.[5] In matters concerning territorial status, national courts are bound by the opinions of the political branch of the state.[6] Sometimes

[1] General texts on this subject: O'Connell, I, pp. 360–363, 463–464, 602–616; Oppenheim, I, §§169–175; Brierly, Ch. V, §§1, 4, 5; Hyde, I, §134; Moore, *Digest,* I, §125; Hackworth, *Digest,* I, §83; Schwarzenberger, I, Ch. 5(I).

[2] For jurisdictional rights and exemptions of states, see *supra,* §70.

[3] Art. 10 of the Covenant.

[4] Art. 2(4) of the Charter.

[5] For instance, the Nine-Power Treaty of February 6, 1922. The signatories of the Treaty agreed to "respect the sovereignty, the independence, and the territorial integrity of China." For its text, see *Treaties and Agreements with and concerning China, 1919–1929* (Washington, D.C., 1929), pp. 89–93.

[6] In *Williams v. Suffolk Insurance Co.* in 1839, the decision of the U.S. Supreme Court was based on the opinion of the executive branch of the government concerning the status of the Falkland Islands. 13 Peters 415.

a territory is under the condominium of two states, as was the Sudan under Great Britain and Egypt from 1898 until her independence in 1956.[7] Allied control of Germany after World War II was not in the nature of condominium, but of military occupation.[8]

§81. INTERNATIONAL SERVITUDES AND RESTRICTIONS

International servitudes are imposed by one state through treaties or otherwise on another to restrict its exercise of sovereignty over a part or the whole of its territory for the benefit of the former.[9] There are generally two kinds of servitudes: positive and negative. The right to construct railways by Russia in Manchuria and Germany in Shantung Province at the end of the nineteenth century falls under the former category,[10] while the demilitarization of Sakhalin and adjacent islands after the Russo-Japanese War and of the Rhineland as a consequence of World War I belongs to the latter.[11] There are many other instances.[12]

Restrictions of territorial sovereignty may occur in other forms, some of which no longer exist: claims of spheres of influence or interest in Asia and Africa by former imperial and colonial powers; extraterritoriality or consular jurisdiction enjoyed by Western nations

[7] See *Bencini v. Egypt and the Sudan,* Egypt, Mixed Tribunal at Cairo, 1910. 23 *Bulletin de législation et de jurisprudence égyptienne* (1911), p. 12; translation from 4 *Am. Jour. Int. Law* (1910), Hudson, 280. With the same status were Schleswig-Holstein and Lauenburg under Austria and Prussia in 1864–1866. See Abdalla A. el-Erian, *Condominium and Related Situations in International Law* (Cairo, 1952).

[8] See *infra,* §219.

[9] For details, see F. A. Váli, *Servitudes of International Law* (New York, 1958); J. B. Scott, *International Servitudes* (Washington, D.C., 1910); P. Labrousse, *Des servitudes en droit international public* (Bordeaux, 1911); H. D. Reid, *International Servitudes in Law and Practice* (Chicago, 1932); P. B. Potter, "The Doctrine of Servitudes in International Law," 9 *Am. Jour. Int. Law* (1915), pp. 627–641; A. D. McNair, "So-called State Servitudes," 6 *British Yearbook of International Law* (1925), pp. 111–127.

[10] See W. W. Willoughby, *Foreign Rights and Interests in China* (Baltimore, 1927), 2 vols., *passim,* for special rights and privileges acquired by the Western powers and Japan in China.

[11] Art. IX of the Treaty of Portsmouth of 1905; Art. 180 of the Treaty of Versailles.

[12] The Soviet-Finnish Peace Treaty of 1947 provided for the demilitarization of the Åaland Islands merely to restore the *status quo ante bellum* under the Soviet-Finnish Agreement of 1940.

in Turkey, China, Japan, Morocco, and other countries;[13] reservation of economic rights in a territory granted to another state;[14] and right of navigation of foreign ships in territorial waters and stationing of foreign troops in various parts of a state.[15] The administration of leased territories, such as the Panama Canal Zone, Guantanamo Bay in Cuba, and Kowloon from China, was practically transferred from the lessee to the lessor for the duration of the lease,[16] but, with the exception of perpetual lease, the restriction or suspension of the exercise of sovereignty on the part of the lessee is temporary.

Treaties or practices involving limitation of sovereignty should be construed strictly and may be terminated by the renunciation of the benefited party, by mutual agreement of the states concerned, or even by unilateral denunciation due to vital change of circumstances.[17] International servitudes, especially military servitudes, are conducive to severe interference in domestic affairs of other states and inherently detrimental to the principle of sovereign equality of nations.[18] In a

[13] This unilateral system, originally demanded by the Western powers on the ground of differences of judicial standard and administration, is now completely abolished. For details, consult Wesley R. Fishel, *The End of Extraterritoriality in China* (Berkeley, 1952); Hyde, II, pp. 849–871.

[14] Reservation of mining rights by the Dutch government in territory granted to Prussia is an example. See *Aix-la-Chapel-Maastricht R.R. Co. v. Thewis and Royal Dutch Government*, Germany, Oberlandesgericht of Cologne, 1914. 8 *Am. Jour. Int. Law* (1914), p. 907.

[15] The right of passage of British ships in the Kiel Canal was affirmed by the Permanent Court of International Justice in *The S.S. Wimbledon*, 1923. P.C.I.J. (1923), Ser. A, No. 1. In *The Right of Passage over Indian Territory* in 1960, the International Court of Justice decided in favor of the limited right of Portuguese nationals and merchandise to cross a certain territory of India to Portuguese enclaves. I.C.J. Reports (1960), 6. For navigation of foreign ships and stationing of foreign armed forces in China, see William L. Tung, *China and Some Phases of International Law*, pp. 1–8, 28–30.

[16] For leased territories, foreign concessions and settlements, and spheres of influence or interest, see William L. Tung, *op. cit.*, pp. 19–28. For comment on such practices by S. V. Molodtsov, see Soviet *Text*, pp. 187–188.

[17] See *infra*, §170. The neutrality of the Black Sea and restriction on Russia's armed vessels as stipulated in the Treaty of Paris of 1856 were denounced by Russia in 1878 on the ground of vital change of circumstances. See also the decision of the Permanent Court of International Justice in *Free Zones of Upper Savoy and the District of Gex* in 1932. P.C.I.J. (1923), Ser. A/B, No. 46. Here the Court reviewed the rights and obligations of states concerned, but did not expressly recognize the doctrine of international servitude.

[18] In the *North Atlantic Coast Fisheries Case*, the Tribunal of the Permanent Court of Arbitration rejected in 1910 the doctrine of international

different category is the modern practice of establishing military bases for mutual defense through special agreements, which, in effect, create a kind of reciprocally beneficial alliance. The postwar period is characterized by such engagements, which have become a source of distrust and conflict among nations, especially the Soviet Union and the United States.[19]

II. *BOUNDARIES AND TERRITORIAL WATERS*[20]

§82. BOUNDARIES

The territorial domain of a state is limited by boundaries through natural barriers or artificial means. Natural barriers usually consist of mountains, forests, deserts, the open sea, rivers, marshes, and the maritime belt; artificial boundaries are formed by geographical lines of longitude and latitude demarcated by stones, walls, trenches, canals, posts, and other landmarks.[21] State boundaries today are determined either through historical titles or by international conventions, but most boundary agreements are based on traditional lines fixed in early times.[22]

Boundary lines separated by mountains usually run along the watershed, unless such mountain ranges are located entirely in one state. The dividing line of a boundary river is normally the middle of its navigable portion or *thalweg*, generally known as the mid-channel

---

servitude. Scott, *Hague Court Reports,* 146. The Committee of Jurists of the League Council took the same attitude in the *Aaland Islands Case* in 1920. LN *Official Jour.*, Special Supp., No. 3.

[19] See Albert J. Esgain, "Military Servitudes and the New Nations," in William V. O'Brien (ed.), *The New Nations in International Law and Diplomacy* (New York, 1965), pp. 42–97.

[20] General texts on the subject: O'Connell, I, pp. 549–569, 616–651; Oppenheim, I, §§176–184, 191–202; Fenwick, *Principles,* Ch. XIX; Brierly, Ch. VI, §1; Hyde, I, §§135–187, 194–198B; Moore, *Digest,* I, §§126–157; III, §§351–371; Hackworth, *Digest,* I, §§84–91, 100–107; II, §§216–219; Whiteman, *Digest,* III, Chs. VI–VIII; Hershey, Chs. XII, XIV; Svarlien, Ch. 11; Von Glahn, Chs. 17, 19; Jacobini, pp. 71–85; Soviet *Text,* Ch. V, §§4, 6, 9, 10; McNair, I, pp. 307–379.

[21] For further details, consult S. W. Boggs, *International Boundaries* (New York, 1940); Stephen B. Jones, *Boundary-Making* (Washington, D.C., 1945).

[22] The world map has been constantly reshaped by peace treaties ending wars, notably treaties of 1648, 1815, 1919, and 1947.

rule,[23] which holds good in spite of imperceptible gain through accretion or gradual loss through aversion.[24] The boundary line in unnavigable rivers, lakes, and landlocked seas is in the middle, in the absence of special agreements. The same rule is applied to a narrow strait, which may also be divided through mid-channel or other arrangements by treaties.

Boundary disputes are not infrequent among neighboring states, but they may be settled through various pacific means, such as direct negotiation,[25] arbitration,[26] international commissions,[27] and judicial settlement.[28] While divergent versions of treaty provisions may be referred to judicial channels for correct interpretation, most boundary disputes are political in nature.[29] In recent years, boundary treaties

[23] See James W. Garner, "The Doctrine of *Thalweg* as a Rule of International Law," 29 *Am. Jour. Int. Law* (1935), pp. 309–310. The mid-channel rule may also be applied to national rivers flowing through several states. See *Iowa v. Illinois,* U.S. Supreme Court, 1891. 147 U.S. 1.

[24] See *Nebraska v. Iowa,* U.S. Supreme Court, 1892. 143 U.S. 359.

[25] Most boundary treaties have been concluded through negotiation, for instance, the Anglo-American Treaty of 1908 on the boundary between Canada and the United States.

[26] For instance, the United States arbitration of the boundary dispute between Great Britain and Venezuela in 1899, and the Alaska boundary dispute between Great Britain (Canada) and the United States in 1903.

[27] The treaties of peace after World War I provided for special commissions to settle boundary issues. It is the more common practice today to establish a joint commission in charge of investigation and demarcation of boundaries between two contending states, such as that established by China with Great Britain in 1934 concerning the former's boundary dispute with Burma.

[28] Two boundary disputes in recent years were settled by the International Court of Justice. In the *Frontier Lands Case* between Belgium and the Netherlands in 1959, the Court upheld the Belgian claim to certain frontier lands in accordance with the Boundary Convention of 1843, in spite of administrative functions performed by Dutch local officials in the disputed area. I.C.J. Reports (1959), 209. In the *Case concerning Temple of Preah Vihear* between Cambodia and Thailand in 1962, the Court decided, on the basis of an uncontested map of the frontier line, in favor of Cambodian claims to the temple area and certain objects removed from the temple by Thailand. I.C.J. Reports (1962), 6.

[29] Many postwar boundaries in Europe, such as the Oder-Neisse line between Poland and Germany, were decided on political grounds. Border clashes sometimes occur due to misunderstandings by frontier guards. According to an announcement by the Interior Minister of Thailand, General Praphas Charustathien, the conflict between the Cambodian troops and Thai policemen on June 20, 1965, was a result of a cough at the wrong

have been concluded by the People's Republic of China with Burma, Nepal, Afghanistan, and Pakistan, but the Sino-Indian boundary dispute has developed into armed conflict between the two most populous countries in the world. In such cases, it may be advisable for a third state to offer good offices and mediation to settle the dispute through mutual concessions.[30] A number of treaties have been concluded to settle boundary lines of the Soviet Union with neighboring countries, including Turkey, Iran, Afghanistan, Norway, Poland, Finland, Rumania, Hungary, and Czechoslovakia.[31] However, the territorial dispute in the border regions of the Soviet Union and Communist China has come to the fore since September 1964, and the possibility of its peaceful settlement through amicable negotiation seems more remote.[32]

---

time. See *The New York Times,* June 24, 1965. For border disputes among African countries and their relationship with OAU, see Saadia Touval, "The Organization of African Unity and African Borders," 21 *Int. Organization* (1967), pp. 102–127. In pursuance of the agreement between India and Pakistan on June 30, 1965, for a cease-fire in the Rann of Kutch, an arbitration tribunal was established to determine their boundary dispute. Hearings began in September 1966.

[30] Many documents have been issued by both governments to justify their claims, including *The Sino-Indian Boundary Question,* enlarged ed. (Peking: Foreign Languages Press, 1962); *Report of the Officials of the Governments of India and the People's Republic of China on the Boundary Question* (New Delhi: Indian Ministry of External Affairs, 1961).

[31] For an illustration, see the Treaty Governing the Soviet-Czechoslovak Frontier and the Procedures for Settling Boundary Incidents, signed on November 30, 1956. *Records of the Supreme Soviet of the U.S.S.R.*, 1957, No. 20. Of the seventeen agreements concerning boundary disputes included in *A Survey of Treaty Provisions for the Pacific Settlement of International Disputes, 1949–1962,* published by the United Nations in 1966, seven were concluded between the Soviet Union and her neighboring countries. For their texts, see pp. 780–880.

[32] For details, see *The New York Times,* September 2, 6, 19, 1964. The Communist government in Peking announced new controls of riverboat traffic using frontier ports and rivers linking China with neighboring countries. The regulations, issued by the Ministry of Communications and approved by the State Council, would affect the navigation of Soviet ships in the Amur, the Sungari, the Argun, and related waterways. Even though the Chinese government officially declared that the aim was to safeguard China's national sovereignty, facilitate navigation, and ensure safety, the new measures reflect the deteriorating relationship between the two Communist giants in contrast with the spirit of the Sino-Soviet Treaty of February 14, 1950. See *ibid.*, April 24, 25, 1966. See also Dennis J. Doolin, *Territorial Claims in the Sino-Soviet Conflict* (Stanford, 1965).

§83. BAYS AND GULFS

As distinguished from international waters, territorial waters are internal waters which are part of the territorial domain of a state.[33] Also under national jurisdiction is the maritime belt adjacent to the open sea, generally known as territorial sea or marginal sea.[34] Bays and gulfs, straits, lakes and landlocked seas, rivers, and canals may be either territorial or international, depending upon the conditions discussed below.

A bay is usually smaller than a gulf, but both are inlets of the high sea. According to the traditional rule, a bay or gulf is territorial when the headlands belong to one state and are no more than six miles apart.[35] When the headlands belong to more than one state and are more than six miles across, in the absence of special treaties, the bay is international and the maritime belt of each state is measured from the coast of the bay.[36] However, many states have claimed bays and gulfs much wider than six miles as territorial. This is especially true of many historical bays and gulfs.[37]

A wider entrance of bays than the traditional rule of six miles has

[33] For claims to authority over internal waters in general, see Myres S. McDougal and William T. Burke, *The Public Order of the Oceans* (New Haven, 1962), pp. 89–173.

[34] For details, see §§88–89.

[35] See *Commonwealth v. Manchester,* United States, Supreme Judicial Court of Massachusetts, 1890. 152 Mass. 230. For further details, consult Mitchell P. Strohl, *The International Law of Bays* (The Hague, 1963); Leo J. Bouchez, *The Regime of Bays in International Law* (Leiden, 1964).

[36] The traditional three-mile limit was upheld by the United States-Great Britain Claims Commission in *The Schooner Washington* case in 1853. The Commission compared the Bay of Fundy in this case to the Bay of Biscay and the Bay of Bengal, over which no state could have jurisdiction beyond the three-mile limit. *Report of Decisions,* p. 170.

[37] For example, the United States' Chesapeake and Delaware bays, Canada's Hudson Bay and Bay of Conception, Norway's Varanger Fiord, and France's Bay of Cancale. The Gulf of Aqaba, which is from ten to thirty miles in width and is bordered by four states, has been a principal source of conflict between Israel and the Arab states with respect to the free passage of Israeli shipping. On May 22, 1967, President Gamal Abdel Nasser of the United Arab Republic announced the blockade of the Gulf, which was condemned by Israel as a gross violation of international law and an act of aggression. In his statement of May 24, President Johnson considered the Gulf to be an international waterway and upheld Israel's right of its free, innocent passage. See *The New York Times,* May 24, 25, 1967.

been considered desirable.[38] Proposals to that effect were made by several research institutes.[39] The Geneva Conference on the Law of the Sea of 1958 defined the width of territorial bays whose coasts belong to a single state. According to this provision, a territorial bay embraces waters enclosed by a closing line between two low-water marks of its natural entrance not exceeding twenty-four miles.[40] Historical bays are excepted from this rule.

§84. STRAITS

The narrow passage connecting two large bodies of water is called a strait. A strait is territorial when it divides the territory of one state and is not more than six miles in width. If the distance exceeds six miles, the coastal state exercises jurisdiction only up to three miles from the shore. When a strait divides the land of two states, the mid-channel rule is the boundary line. Many states today have, however, claimed straits with much wider distance as territorial.[41]

Ships of all nations are entitled to innocent passage[42] through straits and this cannot be suspended, in accordance with the Convention on the Territorial Sea and Contiguous Zone of 1958.[43] No tolls may be collected for such innocent passage.[44] Foreign warships are also entitled to innocent passage through a strait which forms an international highway. This right was reasserted by the International

[38] See the opinion of the Tribunal of the Permanent Court of Arbitration in the *North Atlantic Coast Fisheries* case in 1910. Scott, *Hague Court Reports*, p. 146.

[39] For example, the recommendation of twelve miles by the Institute of International Law in 1894 and of ten miles by the Harvard Research Draft Convention of Territorial Waters in 1929.

[40] See Art. 7 of the Convention on the Territorial Sea and Contiguous Zone of 1958.

[41] The Great Belt of Denmark and the Narrow Seas of Great Britain are instances.

[42] See *infra*, §89.

[43] Art. 16(4). In upholding the right of innocent passage of Israeli ships through the Strait of Tiran and the Gulf of Aqaba, Secretary Dulles reasoned that the narrow Strait of Tiran was the sole passageway linking the Red Sea and the Gulf of Aqaba. See *The New York Times*, March 6, 1957. For the view of a Soviet international lawyer on the status of the Strait of Tiran, see Igor Blishchenko's article in *Krasnaya Zvezda* (a newspaper of the Soviet Ministry of Defense), a summary of which can be found in *The New York Times*, June 29, 1967.

[44] The collection of so-called sound dues by Denmark was exceptional and was discontinued in 1857.

Court of Justice in the *Corfu Channel Case* in 1949.[45] Hostile action by belligerents in a territorial strait of a neutral nation is not permissible.[46]

Special mention should be made of the Bosphorus and Dardanelles, two territorial straits of Turkey connecting the Black Sea with the Mediterranean. When Russia extended her border to the Black Sea in the eighteenth century, Turkey conceded free navigation to foreign merchantmen but still excluded the entrance of foreign warships in her treaties with interested powers.[47] Restrictions imposed upon Turkey by the Treaty of Lausanne of 1923 were largely abolished by the Convention regarding the Regime of the Straits signed at Montreux in 1936.[48] Now the two straits are open to navigation of merchant ships of all nations which are not at war with Turkey. The entrance of foreign warships to the straits is subject to certain regulations and international obligations and may be denied if Turkey is at war or under threat of war.[49]

§85. LAKES AND LANDLOCKED SEAS

A lake or a landlocked sea surrounded by the land territory of one state is territorial. If it is located in more than one state, the riparian states are entitled to a proportional share to be divided from the middle of the water as the boundary line.[50] The Black Sea is unique in that it was transformed from a territorial sea of Turkey into an open

[45] I.C.J. Reports (1949), p. 4.

[46] See the decision of the British High Court of Justice in the case of *The Bangor* in 1916. [1916] Probate, 181.

[47] This status was accepted by the London Convention of 1841 between Turkey on one side and Great Britain, Austria, France, Prussia, and Russia on the other. Later treaties, including the Treaty of Paris of 1856 and the Treaty of London of 1871, confirmed it with some modifications.

[48] The signatories of the Montreux Convention were Great Britain, Turkey, the Soviet Union, France, Rumania, Greece, Bulgaria, Yugoslavia, Japan, and Australia. Italy adhered to it in 1938. See LN *Treaty Series*, No. 16 (1923); Cmd. 1929; LN *Official Jour.*, 1926, pp. 951–974.

[49] For details, see Oppenheim, I, pp. 513–516. The Soviet Union raised the issue concerning the status of the two straits in 1946 and 1953. See *Izvestia*, August 13 and September 28, 1946, and *Pravda*, July 19, 1953. For further discussion on international straits, see E. Brüel, *International Straits* (London, 1947), 2 vols.

[50] See *supra*, §82. France and Switzerland are the riparian states of the Lake of Geneva. The Great Lakes belong to Canada and the United States. For the legal regime of the Great Lakes, see Don Courtney Piper, *The International Law of the Great Lakes* (Durham, N.C., 1967).

sea due to changes in the map of Europe. It is the general practice of nations that international lakes and landlocked seas connected to the open sea are open to free navigation of merchant ships of all nations.

§86. RIVERS

Rivers located in the territory of one state are national and subject to the exclusive jurisdiction of that state. Boundary rivers belong to the riparian states, their dividing line being stated previously.[51] In the absence of special treaties, other states have no right of free navigation in either national or bordering rivers. An international river which flows through several states is of a different nature. While each state has jurisdiction over the portion of the river located in its territory, it is open to navigation by merchant ships of all nations, subject to certain charges and regulations. This principle was first recognized by the Final Act of the Congress of Vienna in 1815, confirmed by the peace treaties after World War I, and reasserted by the Barcelona Convention of 1921 under the auspices of the League of Nations.[52] The most notable of the international rivers is the Danube, which long has been under the control of the riparian and interested states.[53] After World

[51] See *supra,* §82.

[52] The Barcelona Convention adopted two important statutes: one laying down general principles on international navigable waterways, and the other applying the right of transit of persons and goods. For further discussion of the principle of free navigation in international rivers and its historical background, see the *Territorial Jurisdiction of the International Commission of the River Oder* in 1929. In this case, the Permanent Court of International Justice emphasized the principle of community interests. P.C.I.J. (1929), Ser. A, No. 23. For a general survey of the subject, consult Paul M. Ogilvie, *International Waterways* (New York, 1920).

[53] First laid down by the Treaty of Paris of 1856, the principle of free navigation on the Danube and its mouths was provided in detail by a convention in 1921. Afterward, two commissions for the Danube were set up, with the European Commission in charge of the lower part of the river from Braila to the Black Sea and the International Commission, of the upper part. Since 1948, the Danube has been under the control of a single commission. At the Belgrade Conference in that year, a new convention on the regime of the Danube River was signed by the riparian states: the Soviet Union, Rumania, Bulgaria, Hungary, Czechoslovakia, and Yugoslavia. Due to discriminatory provisions against the non-riparian states, the United States, Great Britain, and France refused to sign it and considered the 1921 convention still valid. For the Soviet view of the status of the Danube, see Soviet *Text,* pp. 238–241. Consult also J. P. Chamberlain, *The Régime of the International Rivers: Danube and Rhine* (New York, 1923).

War I, many other rivers in Europe were given international status.[54]

Unlike national rivers under the absolute control of the state where they are located, international rivers are fertile sources of controversy among the riparian states. In order to avoid conflict of interests, each state bordering the river must respect the rights of others on the basis of an equitable share of river benefits. Unless adversely affected, they must not object to legitimate exploitation of its resources or development of its water system by any riparian state. Disputes arising out of conflict of interests should be referred to arbitral or judicial settlement. The establishment of an administrative agency for planning and supervision probably will be advantageous to all riparian states.[55]

§87. CANALS

Artificial waterways built in the territory of one state are national canals and subject to the sole jurisdiction of that state in the same manner as are national rivers. The openings of the Corinth Canal by Greece and the Kiel Canal by Germany up to 1914 to the commerce of all nations were under no international obligation but of their own volition. The Treaty of Versailles forced Germany to maintain free navigation on the Kiel Canal for merchantmen and warships of all nations at peace with Germany.[56]

[54] Among these rivers are the Elbe, the Oder, and the Vistula. Also regulated by international treaties and of historical interest are the Congo and Niger rivers, with their tributaries, in accordance with the General Act adopted by the Berlin Conference of 1884–1885 and replaced by a convention of September 10, 1919. The Permanent Court of International Justice dealt with these provisions in a dispute between Belgium and Great Britain over the *Oscar Chinn Case* in 1934. P.C.I.J. (1934), Ser. A/B, No. 63.

[55] In the *Lake Lanoux Arbitration* in 1957, the France-Spain Arbitration Tribunal ruled that any river project undertaken by one riparian state should take into consideration the interests of the other riparian states even though no prior consultation or agreement was necessary. 53 *Am. Jour. Int. Law* (1959), pp. 156–171. The diversion of the Jordan River has been an issue since 1953 between Israel and her neighboring Arab states. For further discussion of economic uses of international waterways, see James Simsarian, "The Diversion of Waters Affecting the United States and Canada," 32 *Am. Jour. Int. Law* (1938), pp. 488–518; Herbert A. Smith, *The Economic Uses of International Rivers* (London, 1931); Harry O. Mance, *International River and Canal Transport* (London, 1945).

[56] For the legal status of the Kiel Canal, see *The S.S. Wimbledon,* Permanent Court of International Justice, 1923. P.C.I.J. (1923), Ser. A, No. 1. But the legal position of the Kiel Canal changed again when Germany denounced the Treaty of Versailles on November 14, 1936.

The interoceanic canals, such as the Suez connecting the Red Sea with the Mediterranean and the Panama built between the Atlantic and the Pacific oceans, have different status. As international passageways, they are open to navigation by ships of all nations by payment of necessary tolls, even though they are under the territorial jurisdiction of the states where they are located.[57]

The neutralization of the Suez Canal was stipulated by the Convention of Constantinople of October 29, 1888, signed by Great Britain, France, Germany, Austria-Hungary, Russia, Spain, Italy, Holland, and Turkey. The canal must be open to free navigation of all ships of all nations at all times. It cannot be blockaded, nor is any act of hostility permitted inside and within three miles of the canal. The erection of permanent fortifications is forbidden.[58] There are certain restrictions on belligerent warships in wartime. No question arose about the passage of belligerent ships during the two world wars and the war between Italy and Ethiopia in 1935–1936. The Suez Canal is now under the control of the United Arab Republic,[59] which has persistently prohibited the passage of Israeli ships through the canal on the ground that a state of war exists between the two countries, in spite of Israeli-Arab armistice agreements.[60] This serious dispute is not simply a legal

[57] For further details of the status of international canals in general, see Edward A. Whittuck, *International Canals* (London, 1920); R. R. Baxter, *The Law of International Waterways, with Particular Regard to Interoceanic Canals* (Cambridge, 1964).

[58] See Arts. 1–7, 11, of the Convention of Constantinople.

[59] Great Britain succeeded Turkey in undertaking the defense of the Canal. Stationing of British troops in the canal zone and Egyptian obligation to render necessary assistance were based upon agreements of 1936 and 1954 respectively. Nationalization of the Suez Canal by Egypt in 1956 was followed by armed conflict with Israel, Great Britain, and France. After the intervention, the Anglo-Egyptian agreement was abrogated, but the international status of the canal has not changed. For further details, consult J. A. Obieta, *The International Status of the Suez Canal* (The Hague, 1963); Charles W. Hallberg, *The Suez Canal* (New York, 1931); Robert O. Matthews, "The Suez Canal Dispute: A Case Study in Peaceful Settlement," 21 *Int. Organization* (1967), pp. 79–101.

[60] The detention by the United Arab Republic of a Danish ship *Inge Toft* with Israeli cargo in June 1959 evidenced the determination of President Gamal Abdel Nasser to enforce a blockade against Israeli ships and cargo through the Suez Canal. It might be recalled that the principle of freedom of passage through the Suez Canal without discrimination was reasserted by the Security Council on October 13, 1956, in accordance with the provisions of the 1888 Convention, and that the United Arab Republic affirmed it in a declaration on April 24, 1957. 51 *Am. Jour. Int. Law* (1957), pp. 673–675. For details, see Von Glahn, pp. 294–298.

issue, but part of the long-standing political controversy between Israel and the Arab countries.

The international status of the Panama Canal was essentially based on the Hay-Pauncefote Treaty, concluded between the United States and Great Britain on November 18, 1901.[61] Its terms of neutralization are similar to those provided for the Suez Canal, but the United States may maintain necessary forces of military police for its protection.[62] Fortifications have been built since 1912. During the two world wars, belligerent warships were allowed to pass through the canal and its adjacent areas until the United States entered the war. The Canal Zone was leased to the United States in perpetuity for her use, occupation, and control by the Hay-Varilla Treaty of November 18, 1903, and recently Panama has manifested dissatisfaction with the present status in spite of later amendments. Bilateral negotiations for its improvement have been underway for some time. On June 27, 1967, the two governments announced that they had reached an agreement on new treaties which would govern their respective rights of control and operation of the Panama Canal.[63]

III. *THE TERRITORIAL SEA OR MARITIME BELT*[64]

§88. THE LIMIT OF THE TERRITORIAL SEA

The extensive claims over various parts of the high seas made in early times by Portugal, Spain, and the Scandinavian countries vanished before the end of the eighteenth century. It has long been recognized by states that the territorial domain of a state bordering the open sea extends one marine league or three nautical miles from the low-water mark of the shore.[65] If a new island is formed within three

[61] This treaty was to supersede the Clayton-Bulwer Treaty of 1850.

[62] Art. 3 of the Hay-Pauncefote Treaty.

[63] See *The New York Times,* June 27, 1967. The texts were withheld pending ratification by the two governments. For further details, see Norman J. Padelford, *The Panama Canal in Peace and War* (New York, 1942).

[64] General texts on this subject: O'Connell, I, pp. 523–549; Oppenheim, I, §§185–190c; Fenwick, *Principles,* Ch. XIX, §F; Brierly, Chs. V, §6; VI, §2; Hyde, I, §§142–143; Hackworth, *Digest,* I, §§92–99; Whiteman, *Digest,* IV, Ch. IX; Jacobini, pp. 75–78; Soviet *Text,* Ch. V, §7.

[65] The one-marine-league rule was generally attributed to the Dutch jurist Bynkershoek, in the early part of the eighteenth century, when coastal cannon range was limited to three nautical miles. This three-mile rule has been upheld in many judicial decisions. See, *e.g., The Elida,* Germany,

miles from the shore, the maritime belt is measured from that island.[66] However, because of considerations of modern defense, protection of fishing rights, and execution of national laws, this traditional rule is no longer universally observed. The United States, Great Britain, France, and the Soviet Union have exercised jurisdiction beyond the three-mile limit for the enforcement of revenue, sanitary, and other regulations. Several other states have extended their exclusive fishing rights up to twelve miles.[67]

At the Hague Conference for the Codification of International Law in 1930, an attempt was made to set a uniform standard. Although no agreement was reached on the width of the territorial sea, the difference among the states centered on a limit of three or six miles. The United Nations continued the effort and convened the First Conference on the Law of the Sea at Geneva in 1958. Eighty-six states were represented at the Conference, which adopted, among others, the Convention on the Territorial Sea and the Contiguous Zone.[68] The Convention merely provides detailed methods for measuring the breadth of the territorial sea,[69] leaving the limitation of mileage for future consideration.[70]

At the Second Conference on the Law of the Sea at Geneva in 1960, a joint proposal was presented by Canada and the United States, recommending a six-mile limit of the territorial sea and an additional

---

Imperial Prize Court, 1915. 1 *Entscheidungen des Oberprisengerichts,* 9; English translation from 10 *Am. Jour. Int. Law* (1916), 916. In *Queen v. Keyn,* the British High Court of Admiralty dismissed the case in 1876, not due to objection to the three-mile rule but on the ground that Parliament had not actually extended the criminal jurisdiction of the courts over the territorial sea. L.R.2 Exch. Div. 63. An act of Parliament to that effect promptly followed in 1878.

[66] See the decision of the British High Court of Admiralty in the case of *The Anna,* 1805. 5 C. Rob. 373.

[67] For national legislation and international agreements on the subject, see *Laws and Regulations on the Regime of the Territorial Sea* (The United Nations, 1957). UN Doc. ST/Leg/Ser.B/6.

[68] For its text, see UN Doc. A/Conf.13/L/52. For summary records of meetings and annexes, see UN Doc. A/Conf.13/38.

[69] See Arts. 3–13 of the Convention, which came into effect on September 10, 1964. The Convention follows the principle of straight baselines wherever possible as standard of measurement; this was upheld by the International Court of Justice in the *Anglo-Norwegian Fisheries Case* in 1951. I.C.J. Reports (1951), 116.

[70] For an evaluation of the First Conference on the Law of the Sea by Max Sorensen, see *International Conciliation* (1958), No. 520, pp. 195–255.

six-mile zone for exclusive fishing, thus extending the maximum limit to twelve nautical miles.[71] Again there were divergent opinions among the eighty-eight states represented at the Conference. The Soviet Union and many countries from Asia, Africa, and Latin America demanded a straight twelve-mile limit. Their chief consideration was protection of fishing rights and national security. This compromise proposal was eventually rejected when it fell one vote short of meeting the requirement of two-thirds approval. The developing countries were divided in their votes, while the Communist countries were solidly against adoption.[72] The failure to agree on a uniform limit of the territorial sea has encouraged nations to make unilateral declarations and conclude regional agreements extending the maritime belt and exclusive fishing right to twelve miles.[73] International controversies as a result of such conflicting claims are almost inevitable.[74]

[71] The joint proposal recommended further that any state whose vessels had made a practice of fishing in the outer six miles of the fishing zone for five years before 1958 could continue to do so for ten years from October 31, 1960. See UN Doc. A/Conf.19/C.1/L.10. For the summary records of the meetings of the second conference, annexes, and the final act, see UN Doc. A/Conf.19/8. In October 1966, President Johnson signed a bill extending the fishing zone to twelve miles from the coast of the United States. See 80 Stat. 908; *The New York Times,* October 18, 1966.

[72] The vote was 54 to 28. Among the representatives from Asia, Africa, and Latin America, 28 cast affirmative votes, and 17, negative. See *The New York Times,* April 27, 1960; also UN Doc. A/Conf.19/8, thirteenth plenary meeting (April 26, 1960), Par. 18.

[73] The new nations are especially sensitive to their sovereign rights over a much wider breadth of territorial sea. On December 13, 1957, the Indonesian government went so far as to state that "all waters around, between and connecting the islands or parts of the islands belonging to the Indonesian archipelago, irrespective of their width or dimension, are natural appurtenances of its land territory, and, therefore, an integral part of the inland or national waters subject to the sovereignty of Indonesia." It further declared that "the delineation of the territorial sea, with a width of twelve nautical miles shall be measured from straight baselines connecting the outermost points of the Republic of Indonesia." Insisting on the three-mile limit, the United States launched a strong protest against the Indonesian claims. See *The New York Times,* January 18, 1958. These claims were again incorporated in the Government Act No. 4, promulgated on February 18, 1960. For its English text, see UN Doc. A/Conf.19/5/Add.1, pp. 3–4.

[74] A serious controversy over fishing rights developed between Iceland and Great Britain because of the former's exclusion of British trawlers from fishing within a twelve-mile limit of territorial sea. For a time, Great Britain sent warships to protect British fishing in the unilaterally declared zone. Finally, Great Britain yielded to the twelve-mile limit in return for certain

Contiguous zone The First Conference on the Law of the Sea in 1958 agreed on the principle of a contiguous zone. For the enforcement of customs, fiscal, immigration, and sanitary regulations, as well as the punishment of their violations committed in its territorial domain, a coastal state may exercise such jurisdiction in a zone of the high seas contiguous to its territorial sea within the limit of twelve miles. In the absence of special treaties, two coastal states opposite or adjacent to each other may not extend their contiguous zones beyond a median line every point of which is equidistant from the nearest points on the baselines from which the breadth of the territorial seas of the two states is measured. This new rule as embodied in the Convention on the Territorial Sea and Contiguous Zone of 1958 has cleared up the confusion created by previous claims of varying distances for such purposes by different states.[75]

§89. INNOCENT PASSAGE

Ships of all nations in peacetime have the right of innocent passage through the territorial sea of a state, but hostile action is absolutely prohibited.[76] If the coastal state is a belligerent or a neutral in wartime, it may lay down regulations to forbid or restrict the passage of foreign ships through its territorial sea in the interest of national security. According to the Convention on the Territorial Sea and Contiguous Zone of 1958, passage is innocent so long as it is not prejudicial to the peace, good order, or security of the coastal state, as well as the provisions of this Convention and rules of international law. Besides traversing, innocent passage may include stopping and

---

minor privileges granted to British ships for a transitional period of three years. See *The New York Times,* February 28, 1961. In protest against a statement made by an American Deputy Secretary of Defense, Cyrus R. Vance, that the United States recognized only a three-mile limit, North Vietnam declared on September 1, 1964, that its territorial sea and airspace extended twelve miles off the coast and warned the United States to respect this limit. See *ibid.,* September 2, 1964. For jurisdiction over and width of the territorial sea, see Myres S. McDougal and William T. Burke, *The Public Order of the Oceans* (New Haven, 1962), pp. 174–564.

[75] See Art. 24 of the Convention.

[76] In *South American Steamship Company v. United States,* the United States-Chilean Claims Commission, set up under the convention of August 7, 1892, held the United States liable for damages caused by violation of the territorial waters of Chile. Moore, *Int. Arbitrations,* III, p. 3067. Innocent passage does not apply to territorial waters between the baseline from which the territorial sea is measured and the mainland.

anchoring incidental to ordinary navigation or necessary by *force majeure* or distress. Fishing vessels are not permitted to fish in the territorial sea. Even in peacetime, submarines are required to navigate on the surface and to show their flags. The coastal state may prevent any passage which is not innocent, and may even suspend temporarily the passage of foreign ships in specified areas of its territorial sea for the sake of national security.[77] Foreign ships have no right of *cabotage,* that is, navigation and trade between the ports of the coastal state.[78]

IV. *ACQUISITION AND LOSS OF TERRITORY*[79]

§90. CORRESPONDING MODES OF TERRITORIAL ACQUISITION AND LOSS

There is no unanimous opinion among jurists concerning the legal means of acquiring state territory, but the following modes have been traditionally recognized both in theory and practice: (1) discovery and occupation of *territorium nullius,* (2) accretion, (3) prescription, (4) conquest and annexation (not permitted under the United Nations Charter), and (5) cession. Leasing of territory and spheres of influence or interest affect the exercise of sovereignty and administration, but not the legal title to the territory concerned.[80]

[77] See Arts. 14–17 of the Convention.

[78] For further discussion on jurisdiction over the territorial sea, consult Philip C. Jessup, *The Law of Territorial Waters and Maritime Jurisdiction* (New York, 1927); William E. Masterson, *Jurisdiction in Marginal Seas* (New York, 1929); G. Etzel Pearcy, "Measurement of the U.S. Territorial Sea," Department of State *Bulletin,* June 29, 1959, p. 963, also issued in pamphlet form (Department of State publication 6879).

[79] General texts on the subject: O'Connell, I, pp. 465–522; Oppenheim, I, §§209–247; Fenwick, *Principles,* Ch. XVIII; Brierly, Ch. V, §2; Hyde, I, §§58, 98–106; Moore, *Digest,* I, §§80–89; Hackworth, *Digest,* I, §§57–77; Hershey, Ch. XIII; Gould, Ch. 12; Svarlien, Ch. 12; Whitaker, Ch. V; Von Glahn, Ch. 16; Jacobini, pp. 68–71, 88–89; Soviet *Text,* Ch. V, §§1–3; Lawrence, §§71–92; Le Fur, §§314–329, 685–744; Grotius, II, Bk. 2, Chs. 3–4; Vattel, III, Bk. 1, Chs. 18, 22–23; Bk. 2, Ch. 7; Bynkershoek, pp. 31–105; Taylor, §227; Gidel, III, pp. 222–325; McNair, I, pp. 285–306.

[80] For a general description of territorial claims, see Normal Hill, *Claims to Territory in International Law and Relations* (New York, 1945); R. Y. Jennings, *The Acquisition of Territory in International Law* (Manchester, 1963). As for spheres of influence or interest, Japan's claim of a special position in China on the ground of territorial propinquity and contiguity was once embodied in the Lansing-Ishii Agreement of November 2, 1917, over the protest of the Chinese government. For the exchange of notes between Lansing and Ishii and the Chinese declaration of November 12, 1917, see MacMurray, *Treaties,* II, pp. 1394–1395; also *U.S. For. Rel.,* 1917, p. 270.

Corresponding modes of losing territory may be applied: (1) dereliction, corresponding to occupation; (2) loss through the operation of nature, corresponding to accretion; (3) prescription; (4) conquest and annexation; and (5) cession. Secession through successful revolt or peaceful negotiation is a mode of losing territory which has no corresponding mode of acquisition.[81] As the other modes of acquisition and loss are analogical, the following description is limited to those of the former in order to avoid unnecessary repetition.

§91. DISCOVERY AND OCCUPATION

In former times, discovery alone could acquire the legal title of a territory. As unclaimed land diminished, the old concept changed accordingly. Now discovery may only create an inchoate title, which can be consummated through real and effective occupation.[82] But occupation may be independent from discovery, because a territory may be discovered by one state without actual possession and later occupied by another state.[83] In any event, the territory concerned must be either uninhabited or settled only by uncivilized tribes.[84]

[81] Examples of successful revolt are the British loss of the thirteen colonies in North America in 1776 and Colombia's loss of Panama in 1903. After World War II, many new states in Asia and Africa achieved their independence through peaceful negotiation with the colonial powers.

[82] This principle has been upheld by both international and national tribunals. See *The Island of Palmas (Miangas)*, Tribunal of the Permanent Court of Arbitration, 1928. Scott, *Hague Court Reports* (2nd ser.), p. 84. For a decision by a national court, see *Johnson and Graham's Lessee v. William M'Intosh*, U.S. Supreme Court, 1823. 8 Wheaton 543. With respect to her claims over the Arctic, the Soviet Union holds "that irrespective of the nationality of the discoverers or explorers, sovereignty to lands discovered automatically vests with the state within whose sphere or sector of 'terrestrial gravitation' the land is found." T. A. Taracouzio, *The Soviet Union and International Law* (New York, 1935), p. 57.

[83] Exactly this happened in the case of the Falkland (Malvinas) Islands, which involved Spain, Argentina, and Great Britain in a long controversy over their claims of discovery, abandonment, and occupation. For details, see J. Goebel, *The Struggle for the Falkland Islands* (New Haven, 1927). In protest against the recent Argentine claim, the Legislative Council of Falklands, on behalf of the local population, made it known that they have been proud to be citizens of that British colony and that constitutional association with any foreign power would be completely repugnant to them. See *The New York Times*, September 6, 1964.

[84] For further discussion on this subject, see M. F. Lindley, *The Acquisition and Government of Backward Territory in International Law* (London, 1926).

In order to be real and effective, occupation must be an express act of state followed by the establishment of a responsible administration in the territory.[85] Notification to other states is desirable but unnecessary, even though the Final Act of the Berlin Conference of 1885 made it mandatory in the case of the partition of African territory among its signatories.[86] The doctrine of hinterland (back country) held by the European powers in Africa and the theory of contiguity and continuity applied by the United States in the Oregon boundary dispute with Great Britain can only be valid if the claimed territories are under real and effective occupation.[87]

The Arctic Through discovery and occupation and the application of the theory of contiguity and continuity, the United States, the Soviet Union, Canada, Norway, and Denmark have claimed sovereignty over all the lands and islands lying within their respective polar sectors of the Arctic adjacent to their coasts.[88] This Arctic sector theory is important because of scientific research, natural resources, communications lines, and national defenses around the North Pole. Probably the various polar sectors are now considered under the effective and real occupation of the above-mentioned five states in view of their partial settlement and establishment of bases.[89]

[85] In the case of the *Legal Status of Eastern Greenland,* between Denmark and Norway in 1933, the Permanent Court of International Justice decided in favor of Denmark, because no other state claimed, up to 1931, sovereignty over that territory. P.C.I.J. (1933), Ser. A/B, No. 53. On the basis of France's continuous claim of the title of Clipperton Island, Mexico lost the case to France in 1931 through arbitration. See the *Clipperton Island Arbitration.* 26 *Am. Jour. Int. Law* (1932), p. 390. In the *Minquiers and Ecrehos Case* in 1953, the International Court of Justice denied the French claim of occupation of the islets in favor of Great Britain. I.C.J. Reports (1953), 47.

[86] Art. 34 of the Final Act. The notification was applied neither to nonsignatories of the Final Act nor to other regions of the world.

[87] The United States also claimed in 1805 the crest of watershed as her territorial limit in Louisiana by reason of effective occupation of the mouth of a river. For further details on occupation of territory, see Moore, *Digest,* I, §81.

[88] In the opinion of a Soviet writer, S. V. Molodtsov, "the term 'polar sector of a State adjacent to the Arctic' means the expanse of which the base line is the coast of the given State, the apex the North Pole and the limits to either side the meridians from the North Pole to the eastern and western frontiers of the State." Soviet *Text,* p. 191.

[89] For further discussion, consult G. Smedal, *Acquisition of Sovereignty over Polar Areas* (Oslo, 1931).

The Antarctic In recent decades, Great Britain, Argentina, Chile, Norway, and several other countries have made extensive and conflicting claims in the Antarctic region through the general application of the sector theory. Notwithstanding her contribution to the exploration in the South Polar areas, the United States has refrained from making territorial claims, but has worked since 1948 toward the internationalization of the Antarctic. On December 1, 1959, the Antarctic Treaty was signed in Washington by Argentina, Belgium, Chile, France, Japan, New Zealand, Norway, the Union of South Africa, Great Britain, the Soviet Union, and the United States.[90] The contracting parties agreed to use the Antarctic only for peaceful purposes to facilitate scientific research and international cooperation. Any military establishment or testing is prohibited, subject to mutual inspection.[91] While the Treaty does not constitute renunciation by the states of any previous rights, claims, or policies relating to territorial sovereignty in the Antarctic, no new claims may be asserted while the treaty is in force for a period of thirty years.[92] Any dispute concerning the interpretation and application of the treaty is to be resolved through peaceful means of the states' own choice, including settlement by the International Court of Justice.[93] Probably the provisions of this treaty will be applied in the future to other important but controversial areas, especially to outer space.

§92. ACCRETION

Accretion is the enlargement of the territory of a state through artificial or natural formations in its territorial waters, boundary rivers, or along its coast of the open sea. While it is permissible to construct dikes and other objects in international waters, "no state is allowed to alter the natural conditions of its own territory to the disadvantage of the natural conditions of a neighboring state territory." [94] On the other hand, natural deposits through gradual process of a river or ocean will confer on the state concerned the legal title of the newly created land, delta, or island. The island so formed within the maritime belt of a state belongs to that state and its territorial sea is to be measured from the low-water mark of the shores of the island.[95]

[90] See *The Conference on Antarctica,* Department of State publication 7060; 54 *Am. Jour. Int. Law* (1960), pp. 476–483.

[91] Arts. 1–3, 5–10. [92] Arts. 4, 12. [93] Art. 11.

[94] Oppenheim, I, p. 564.

[95] This principle was upheld by the British High Court of Admiralty in the case of *The Anna,* 1805. 5 C. Rob. 373.

§93. PRESCRIPTION

Unlike usucaption in Roman law, prescription in international law is not necessarily based upon *bona fide* possession. While no unanimity exists among publicists concerning the validity of prescription as a mode of acquiring territory, it is generally recognized in international practice, as in municipal law, for the sake of stability and order. Prescription is defined by L. Oppenheim as "the acquisition of sovereignty over a territory through continuous and undisturbed exercise of sovereignty" during a period long enough "to create under the influence of historical development the general conviction that the present condition of things is in conformity with international order." [96] Even though a territory may have been originally acquired by fraud or violence, its long and continuous possession redeems the title.[97]

There is no definite time limit in international law to bar a claim against a state in possession of a territory through prescription. Each case must be judged by its individual merit on the basis of its historical background, actual circumstances, and other important factors. In the boundary arbitration between Great Britain and Venezuela in 1899, the disputing parties recognized, in their treaty of February 2, 1897, the validity of a title after an adverse holding for fifty years.[98]

§94. CONQUEST AND ANNEXATION

Conquest of a territory without the intention of annexing it does not acquire the title of the territory; an example is the Allied occupation of Germany and Japan after World War II.[99] Forceful annexation

[96] Oppenheim, I, p. 576. According to W. E. Hall, "title by prescription arises out of a long and continued possession, where no original source of proprietary right can be shown to exist, or where possession in the first instance being wrongful, the legitimate proprietor has neglected to assert his right, or has been unable to do so." Hall, p. 143. See also O'Connell, I, pp. 487–492.

[97] In *Rhode Island v. Massachusetts*, the U.S. Supreme Court in 1846 upheld this principle, regardless of misconstruction of an original charter grant. 4 Howard 591. It was reaffirmed by the Court in *Arkansas v. Tennessee* in 1940. 311 U.S. 1. Prescription was recognized by the Permanent Court of Arbitration in *The Island of Palmas*, between the United States and the Netherlands, 1928. Scott, *Hague Court Reports* (2nd ser.), p. 84.

[98] Actually the United States forced the arbitration, against the wishes of Great Britain. For details, see Hyde, I, pp. 143–147.

[99] In *United States v. Rice*, the U.S. Supreme Court decided in 1819 that the laws of a conquered territory of a state as well as its protection and corresponding claims to allegiance were suspended during the period of conquest. 4 Wheaton 246. During the Allied occupation of Germany and

without the consent of the annexed, prevalent in the past, is unsupported by law. Thus, Italy's conquest of Ethiopia in 1935-36, followed by annexation, was condemned by the League of Nations, which imposed economic sanctions against the aggressor.[100] Neither is it legally permissible if consent is given under strong pressure. This was the case in Japan's annexation of Korea in 1910.[101]

If a territory is under the suzerainty of a state which later incorporates it as an integral part of the country, the validity of the action depends upon the wishes of the majority of the population and the international status of the incorporated territory.[102] The detachment of part of the territory of one state by another through conquest followed by the establishment of a puppet regime is really annexation under disguise. The non-recognition doctrine declared by the United States and the League of Nations was applied to such a forcible change of the status quo when Manchuria was conquered by Japan and then formed a state of Manchukuo in 1932 under the direction and protection of the conqueror.[103] The Soviet Union opposes annexation in principle, but, in

---

Japan, numerous laws and regulations were enacted to enforce the declared purposes of the Allies.

[100] See A. J. Toynbee, *Survey of International Affairs,* 1935, Vol. 2, pp. 212–239.

[101] In a note to Russia on February 5, 1904, Japan emphasized the independence and territorial integrity of Korea. However, on August 22, 1910, Korea was compelled by circumstances to sign a treaty of annexation. The mass demonstration of the Korean people at the funeral of the abdicated king on March 1, 1919, revigorated their consistent demand for Korea's independence. The question has been raised whether the incorporation of the three Baltic states as part of the Soviet Union was based on their own volition or on an act of forced annexation.

[102] The incorporation of Tibet by the People's Republic as an integral part of China was challenged on the ground of the special status of Tibet and the questionable loyalty of the Tibetans toward China. For a collection of documents, speeches, news dispatches, editorials, commentaries, and background materials relating to Tibet, see *Concerning the Question of Tibet* (Peking: Foreign Languages Press, 1959). In the opinion of the Tribunal of the Permanent Court of Arbitration in *The Island of Palmas* (1928), "suzerainty over the native state becomes the basis of territorial sovereignty as toward other members of the community of nations." Scott, *Hague Court Reports* (2nd ser.), p. 84.

[103] For Secretary of State Stimson's statement on non-recognition on January 7, 1932, see LN *Official Jour.*, Special Supp., No. 101, p. 155. Non-recognition of Manchukuo was incorporated in the Assembly resolution of March 11, 1932, and the Assembly report of February 24, 1933. China's denunciation of acquiring territory by conquest was stated by Foreign Minister Lo Wen-kan on August 29, 1932. See *ibid.*, No. 102, p. 39.

practice, her territorial expansion during and after World War II scarcely conformed to the wishes of the incorporated areas.[104]

The renunciation of war by the Kellogg-Briand Pact of 1928 virtually eliminated conquest as a legitimate means of acquiring territory. Preservation of national sovereignty and territorial integrity is one of the cardinal principles of the League Covenant and the United Nations Charter. Thus, territorial annexation in any form against the wishes of the state concerned is illegal.[105] One rare instance in recent years was India's conquest of Portuguese Goa in December 1961, chiefly on the ground of anti-colonialism.[106] No action was taken by the United Nations, which received a complaint from the Portuguese government.[107]

§95. CESSION

Cession is the formal transfer of a territory from one state to another through a variety of means. Rumania's taking possession of Dobrudja by relinquishing a portion of Bessarabia to Russia was ces-

[104] For Lenin's condemnation of annexation as violating the principle of self-determination and constituting a form of national oppression, see his *Collected Works* (Moscow), XXII, p. 320.

[105] For further discussion of the legality of acquiring territory by conquest, consult M. M. McMahon, *Conquest and Modern International Law: The Legal Limitations on the Acquisition of Territory by Conquest* (Washington, D.C., 1940); Robert Langer, *Seizure of Territory* (Princeton, 1947).

[106] The ground of anti-colonialism was emphasized by Quincy Wright in his article "The Goa Incident," 56 *Am. Jour. Int. Law* (1962), pp. 617–632.

[107] For Portugal's complaint against India's armed attack on the territories of Goa, Damao, and Diu and the proceedings at the Security Council, see *Repertoire,* SC, Supp., 1959–1963, p. 197. Subsequent to the Israeli-Arab conflict in June 1967 and Israel's capture of the Jordanian sector of Jerusalem, the Israeli government adopted municipal and administrative measures for the unification of Jerusalem. An emergency special session of the General Assembly, which was convened to discuss the Middle Eastern crisis, denounced Israel's unilateral change of the status of the city. See *The New York Times,* July 5, 15, 1967, for two GA resolutions. According to Israeli Foreign Minister Abba Eban, Israel's action was not intended for territorial annexation but for "Jerusalem's unity and Jerusalem's peace." See *ibid.,* July 13, 19, 1967. This issue was basically inseparable from the general settlement of the Israeli-Arab dispute. In view of the recurrence of hostilities in the past and their potential danger to international peace and security, the major powers should work together under the United Nations to solve the long-standing differences between Israel and the Arab states by taking into consideration their mutual rights of territorial integrity, innocent passage of international waters, as well as national independence and security.

sion through exchange.[108] The United States acquired Louisiana, Alaska, and several other places through purchase. Cession of territory through marriage settlement or testament is only of historical interest.[109] In many cases, cession has been effected by the conclusion of treaties as a result of military defeat or other important considerations. Although the territorial transfer may be a matter of necessity, the act of negotiating for and ratification of the treaty is an indication of mutual consent. Thus, a territory originally acquired through conquest may legally change hands through the formalization of a treaty. For the maintenance of the balance of power in certain regions, third parties sometimes intervene in the cession of a territory from one state to another. The joint intervention by Russia, France, and Germany demanding the restoration of the Liao-tung Peninsula to China after the first Sino-Japanese War of 1894–1895 was deeply resented by Japan.[110]

The treaty of cession usually contains provisions concerning proportionate share of public debts, option of nationality,[111] and other articles of particular importance to the states concerned. A formal government act taking possession of the ceded territory is necessary in order to prescribe the details of the new administration and rights and duties of the population.[112] Individual property rights are not immedi-

[108] The exchange was formalized by the Treaty of Berlin in 1878.

[109] The motive of King Leopold's will of 1908 bequeathing the Congo Free State to Belgium in his capacity of sovereign of both was complicated. The question was whether it was a free gift or an act of annexation in disguised form.

[110] Joint intervention took place after the signing of the Sino-Japanese Peace Treaty at Shimonoseki on April 17, 1895, but before its ratification. Japan yielded to the demand by the conclusion of another convention with China on November 8, 1895. Japan's resentment against Russia's active part in the intervention was probably one of the important factors leading to the Russo-Japanese War of 1904–1905. See Hertslet, *Treaties,* I, No. 63.

[111] The option of nationality is provided in many treaties to give the inhabitants in the ceded territory a choice between their original nationality and a new allegiance. Unless prohibited by the treaty, those choosing their original nationality can be expelled by the state which has acquired the territory, as in the case of a large number of Germans from Poland and Czechoslovakia after World War II. Extreme hardship was imposed upon many Greek and Turkish nationals as a result of a special Convention concerning the Exchange of Greek and Turkish Population, supplementary to the Treaty of Lausanne of July 24, 1923. J. B. Schechtmann, *European Population Transfers, 1939–1945* (New York, 1946), is a useful reference on the subject.

[112] On the necessity of a formal act of taking possession of the ceded territory, see *The Fama, Butler (Master),* Great Britain, High Court of Admiralty, 1804. 5 C. Rob. 106.

ately affected by the cession of territory.[113] To ascertain the wishes of the inhabitants, the ultimate destination of the ceded territory is sometimes decided by a plebiscite. The Soviet Union has also considered the plebiscite to be one of the most appropriate means of deciding territorial problems.

A plebiscite was applied to the cession of Nice and Savoy to France in 1860 and of Venice to Italy in 1866. The same principle was used to determine the destiny of the Saar Basin. When free expression is restricted, a plebiscite cannot indicate the true sentiment of the population. This was the case in the unification of Austria with Germany in 1938 when the former was occupied by German forces. An attempt was made by the United Nations to settle the Kashmir dispute between India and Pakistan by plebiscite, for which an administrator was appointed. But the proposal could not be implemented because of disagreement between the disputing parties. On January 26, 1957, Kashmir was incorporated as an integral part of India, which subsequently refused to resort to plebiscite for settling the dispute.[114]

Before the formation of the Federation of Malaysia on September 16, 1963, Indonesia challenged it as a neo-colonial plan by which Great Britain would retain influence in Southeast Asia. Joined by the Philippines, which had a latent claim over British North Borneo, Indonesia wanted to ascertain the wishes of the people of Sabah (North Borneo) and Sarawak prior to the establishment of the Federation of Malaysia. The governments of the two countries, with the agreement of the government of Malaya, requested Secretary-General U Thant on August 5, 1963, to undertake the task by a United Nations special mission, with the promise that Indonesia and the Philippines would welcome the formation of the Federation of Malaysia provided that the support of the people of the two territories was evidenced. In compliance with their wishes and on the basis of the principle of self-determination,

[113] This principle was asserted in *United States v. Percheman,* U.S. Supreme Court, 1833. 7 Peters 51. See also *Davis v. The Police Jury of the Parish of Concordia,* in which the Supreme Court ruled in 1850 that a franchise granted after the signing of the treaty of cession was invalid. 9 Howard 280.

[114] The Security Council appointed, on January 20, 1948, the United Nations Commission for India and Pakistan (UNCIP), which proposed an impartial plebiscite to settle the dispute. Notwithstanding the subsequent efforts of United Nations mediation, India considered the question closed. The dispute developed into armed conflict between the two countries in 1965. An armistice was reached on January 11, 1966, as a result of the Tashkent conference, but no peaceful settlement can be foreseen. For the text of the Indian-Pakistani Declaration of Tashkent, see *The New York Times,* January 11, 1966.

the Secretary-General dispatched a special mission to survey the sentiment of the local inhabitants. On September 14, 1963, he conveyed the finding to the governments concerned that there was no doubt about the wish of a sizable majority of the people of the two territories to join the Federation of Malaysia.[115] However, President Sukarno was determined to crush the newly formed Federation until General Suharto reversed the policy of the Indonesian government and signed a peace accord with Malaysia on August 11, 1966.

Another plebiscite is to be held, by the end of 1969, by the Papuan population in former Dutch New Guinea to decide whether they wish to remain under Indonesian rule. This former Dutch colony, West New Guinea or West Irian (its Indonesian name), was transferred to Indonesia by the Netherlands through the sponsorship of the United Nations by an agreement of August 15, 1962, between the two governments. In accordance with the agreement, the United Nations took over the administration of the territory on October 1, 1962, for an interim period and transferred the responsibility to Indonesia on May 1 of the following year.[116]

In the long-standing issue between Spain and Great Britain over Gibraltar, the expressed desire of self-government by the local population has been challenged by Spain on the ground that the present population of Gibraltar has been artifically brought in during the period of British rule for over 260 years. Spain contends that these local people should not have the right to determine the future of Gibraltar. Great Britain insists that the local residents should decide their ultimate status. This territorial issue, with its deep historical background and nationalistic significance, can only be settled through compromise.[117]

[115] In his letters to the foreign ministers of the three governments informing them of his conclusions, the Secretary-General emphasized the words "complete compliance with the principle of self-determination within the requirements of GA res. 1541 (XV), Principle IX of the Annex." For the texts of the identical letters, see *ibid.*, September 15, 1963. For a survey of Philippine claims to British North Borneo, see *ibid.*, June 23, 1962.

[116] For details, see *The New York Times,* August 16 and October 1, 1962. The General Assembly, by a vote of 89 to 0, approved the New Guinea agreement on September 21, 1962. See *ibid.*, September 22, 1962.

[117] The Spanish claim relied on one passage of the Treaty of Utrecht of 1713 that, if at any time Great Britain should give up Gibraltar, Spain would have the right to it. For the various statements made before the Special Committee on Colonialism of the United Nations, see *The New York Times,* September 24, 25 and October 1, 1964. For further discussion on plebiscites, see Sarah Wambaugh, *Plebiscites since the World War* (Washington, D.C., 1933), 2 vols.; Johannes Mattern, *The Employment of the Plebiscite in the Determination of Sovereignty* (Baltimore, 1921).

CHAPTER 7

AERIAL SPACE AND THE HIGH SEAS[1]

I. *JURISDICTION OVER AIRSPACE AND AIRCRAFT*[2]

§96. THE THEORY AND PRACTICE OF AIRSPACE BEFORE 1919

After the invention of the airplane, regulation of aerial navigation became increasingly important. In the absence of customary international law, jurists proposed different theories with respect to the control of aerial space by individual states.[3] These may be summed up as follows: First, aerial space is entirely free from state control in the same way as the high seas.[4] Second, a state has jurisdiction over the

[1] Certain aspects of aerial space and the high seas are analogical, but none is under the absolute control of a state. Hence it is appropriate to discuss them under one independent chapter together with jurisdiction over aircraft and ships.

[2] General texts on the subject: O'Connell, I, pp. 580–596; Oppenheim, I, §§197a–197f; Fenwick, *Principles,* Ch. XXI, §§A, C; Brierly, Ch. V, §8; Ch. VI, §3; Hyde, I, §§188–193F; Hackworth, *Digest,* IV, §§365–369; Whiteman, *Digest,* II, Ch. V, §§16–18; Schwarzenberger, I, Ch. 4 (V, E); Hershey, Ch. XVI; Svarlien, Ch. 15; Von Glahn, Ch. 22; Jacobini, pp. 85–87; Soviet *Text,* Ch. V, §11.

[3] For details on the law of the air, consult H. D. Hazeltine, *The Law of the Air* (London, 1911); J. M. Spaight, *Aircraft in Peace and the Law* (London, 1919); A. D. McNair, *The Law of the Air,* 2nd ed. (London, 1953); David H. N. Johnson, *Rights in Air Space* (Manchester, 1965).

[4] This view was represented by P. Fauchille and adopted by the Institute of International Law in 1906.

lower zone of the aerial space above its territory and territorial sea, leaving the higher zone completely free.[5] This is analogous to the maritime belt and the high seas. Third, aerial space is under the jurisdiction of the adjacent state subject to innocent passage for civil aircraft of other states under similar conditions as in the territorial sea.[6] Fourth, a state has absolute sovereignty over its aerial space without limitations.[7]

When World War I broke out, the theory of freedom of aerial navigation was completely disregarded by the neutrals. The governments of Switzerland, Denmark, Norway, and the Netherlands prevented the passage of belligerent aircraft above their territorial domain. Innocent passage without previous consent and forced landing without distress signals also were not tolerated. Belligerent aircraft and airmen from both sides intruding into the air domain of the neutrals were interned. Thus, practice during World War I upheld the principle of absolute sovereignty of a state over the airspace above its land and maritime domain.[8]

§97. THE PARIS CONVENTION OF 1919

In view of the terrible danger which aerial space had become during the war and its importance in time of peace, the Peace Conference at Paris drew up the Convention for the Regulation of Aerial Navigation, which was signed on October 13, 1919.[9] The Convention applied to peacetime only and was not binding on the belligerents or neutrals during war.[10] The contracting parties recognized that every state had complete and exclusive sovereignty over the airspace above its territory and territorial sea. Innocent passage of civil aircraft of other states

[5] The fundamental difficulty of this proposition is the dividing line, for which there are many suggestions, few of which are practical.

[6] J. Westlake made this proposal in 1906 at the meeting of the Institute of International Law, but it failed of adoption.

[7] This theory is based upon the maxim that whose is the soil, his it is up to the sky *(Cujus est solum ejus est usque ad caelum)*. In an executive order of 1939 regulating aerial navigation by foreign and domestic aircraft over the Panama Canal Zone, the United States claimed sovereignty over its aerial space, not without protest by the Republic of Panama. See Hackworth, *Digest,* IV, pp. 389–391.

[8] For details, consult James W. Garner, *International Law and the World War* (London and New York, 1920), 2 vols.

[9] For its text, see LN *Treaty Series,* XI, 173; Hudson, *International Legislation,* I, 359.

[10] Art. 38.

was granted, subject, however, to certain regulations as provided in the Convention and with the exception of prohibited areas.[11] The carrying of munitions and explosives was forbidden.[12] The rules governing the entrance of foreign warships into territorial waters were to be applicable to foreign military aircraft. State aircraft other than military might enter other states under special arrangements.[13]

The nationality of an aircraft was determined by its registry. It must be registered in the same state of which its owners were nationals and could not be validly registered in more than one state.[14] Civil aircraft engaged in international navigation must carry all required papers, including certificates of registration and airworthiness, licenses of the operating crews, a list of passengers, and bills of lading and manifest for cargo if any.[15] International airways might be established with the consent of the states concerned, but *cabotage* was generally to be reserved for their own aircraft.[16] The territorial state might visit foreign civil aircraft to verify necessary documents and enforce regulations.[17] In case of distress, the rules concerning the salvage of ships would be applied to aircraft.[18]

The Convention set up the International Commission for Air Navigation (CINA), under the jurisdiction of the League of Nations and in charge of administrative functions and other matters concerning the amendment of the Convention and its annexes.[19] A number of amendments were made later.[20] The Paris Convention was binding upon the signatories. Its basic provisions were embodied in the domestic legislation of many states not parties to it and remained unchanged in later conventions. The United States signed the Convention but failed to ratify it inasmuch as its administrative agency was placed under the League of Nations, of which the United States was not a member. But its basic principles were incorporated in the American Air Commerce Act of 1926 and the Federal Aviation Act of 1958. The Soviet Union did not participate in the drafting of the Paris Convention or accede to it. Following the general practice of other nations, the Soviet government claims sovereignty over the aerial space above its land and maritime domain.

§98. OTHER CONVENTIONS PRIOR TO WORLD WAR II

Bilateral and multilateral agreements were concluded between the signatories of the Paris Convention, between the non-signatories, and

[11] Arts. 1–3. [12] Art. 26. [13] Arts. 30–33. [14] Arts. 5–10.
[15] Arts. 11–13, 19. [16] Arts. 15–16, 24. [17] Art. 21.
[18] Arts. 22–23. [19] Art. 34.
[20] It was amended in October 1922, June 1923, June 1929, and December 1929.

between both signatories and non-signatories, for regulating the navigation of civil aircraft, innocent passage, and related matters. The Havana Convention on Commercial Aviation, adopted by the Sixth International Conference of American States on February 28, 1928, incorporated the basic principles of the Paris Convention for the common observation by the states in the Western Hemisphere which did not adhere to it.[21] No administrative agency was established by the Havana Convention, but provisions were made for the adoption of uniform systems and the distribution of necessary information.

The unrestricted carriage of airmail was stipulated in the Universal Postal Convention signed in London on June 28, 1929.[22] The Warsaw Convention of October 12, 1929, dealt with the problem of liability and the unification of certain rules regarding international air transportation, such as passenger tickets and luggage checks.[23] On August 12, 1933, a Sanitary Convention for Aerial Navigation was concluded at The Hague for the purpose of preventing the spread of communicable diseases by foreign aircraft.[24] The United States adhered to all the above conventions.

After the outbreak of World War II, the nations were again handicapped by the lack of regulations governing air warfare. In 1922–1923, the Commission of Jurists provided for by the Washington Naval Disarmament Conference drafted rules concerning rights and obligations of belligerent and neutral states with respect to military aircraft, but these proposals never materialized in a treaty.[25] The neutral countries insisted on the unlimited altitude of the aerial space above their land and maritime domain, and interned belligerent aircraft and their crews even in cases of forced landing. The Panama Declaration of October 3, 1939, firmly asserted the neutral rights of the states in the Western Hemisphere and warned that any flight by the military aircraft

[21] For the text of the Havana Convention, see Hudson, *International Legislation,* IV, p. 2354. The United States ratified this convention.

[22] 46 Stat. 2523.

[23] 49 Stat. 3000. The liability problem was further dealt with in the Rome Convention for Unification of Certain Rules related to Damages Caused by Aircraft to Third Parties on the Surface, which was not ratified by the United States. The limited amount of compensation to be paid by an airline for a passenger's death or injury on an international flight and the efforts of the United States to raise the legal limit were reviewed in an article by Richard Witkin in *The New York Times,* February 18, 1962. The Hague Protocol of September 28, 1955, is to amend the Warsaw Convention to double the limit of liability, but it has not yet come into effect. The United States adhered to the Warsaw Convention in 1934.

[24] 49 Stat. 3279.

[25] See Hackworth, *Digest,* I, pp. 45–46.

of belligerents over their aerial space would be a violation of their neutrality.[26]

§99. THE CHICAGO CONVENTION OF 1944

Before the end of World War II, the Civil Aviation Conference was convened in Chicago on November 1, 1944, with representatives from fifty-two states. While the war was still going on, the states envisaged the increasing importance of civil aviation in relation to the jurisdiction over aerial space. The Conference adopted one convention, three separate agreements, and a number of resolutions and recommendations on several technical matters.[27] The United States took a leading role at the Conference, but the Soviet Union neither attended it nor adhered to the Convention.

The Convention, which came into effect on April 4, 1947, covers a wide variety of subjects on civil aviation. A state exercises sovereignty over the airspace above its land and maritime domain, which includes territories under its sovereignty, suzerainty, protection, or mandate.[28] It follows the general line of the Paris Convention of 1919 in respect of the nationality of aircraft,[29] *cabotage*,[30] required documents,[31] right of search,[32] prohibited areas,[33] prevention of the spread of disease,[34] and prohibition or regulation of the use of photographic apparatus in aircraft over the territory of another state.[35] Scheduled air services are to be regulated by separate agreements. Aircraft engaged in non-scheduled international services may make non-stop flight across the territory of a contracting state and also non-traffic stops without prior permission, but they must land if this is demanded by the territorial state.[36] These provisions are not applied to aircraft used for military,

[26] 44 Department of State Conference Ser. (1940), pp. 55–56.

[27] For their texts, see Department of State publication No. 2282.

[28] Arts. 1–2 of the Convention. [29] Arts. 17–21.

[30] Art. 7. [31] Art. 29. [32] Art. 16.

[33] Art. 9. The 'air corridors' are now designated for restricted air navigation through an otherwise 'closed' airspace.

[34] Art. 14.

[35] Art. 36. This provision is similar to that in Art. 24 of the Paris Convention of 1919.

[36] Arts. 5–6. According to Art. 9, such flights by foreign aircraft may be temporarily prohibited, except those specially authorized by the territorial government. In *Public Prosecutor v. Matsumoto*, the defendant, a Japanese aircraft pilot, was prosecuted by the District Court of Taipei, China, in 1965, for illegal intrusion on Chinese airspace and landing at a Chinese airport in violation of Art. 16 of the Chinese Civil Aviation Law. File No.: 54th Yr., Yi—11165. 60 *Am. Jour. Int. Law* (1966), 412.

customs, and police services, or to aircraft without pilots.[37] The Convention prescribes, in detail, the applicability and enforcement of regulations concerning landing and departure, prosecution of violators, airport and similar charges, customs and immigration procedures, investigation of accidents, and navigation facilities and standard systems. However, these provisions in no way affect the freedom of action of the contracting states in wartime, either as belligerents or neutrals.[38]

The unique feature of this Convention is the establishment of the International Civil Aviation Organization (ICAO),[39] in charge of a much wider scope of functions than the International Commission for Air Navigation created by the Paris Convention of 1919. Composed of an assembly as a representative body and a council as an administrative agency, the ICAO aims at promoting the principles and techniques of international air navigation and fostering the planning and development of international air transport.[40] Other auxiliary machinery may be established when necessary. The headquarters of the ICAO is in Montreal. As one of the specialized agencies, it cooperates closely with the United Nations through an agreement of May 13, 1947.[41]

Besides the Convention, the Chicago Conference adopted two separate transit and transport agreements, embodying the so-called five freedoms. The International Air Services Transit Agreement lists two freedoms for scheduled international air services: (1) to fly across the territory of a contracting state without landing, and (2) to land for non-traffic purposes.[42] The International Air Transport Agreement provides for three additional freedoms for scheduled international through services by the contracting states on a reciprocal basis: (3) to put down passengers, mail, and cargo taken on in the territory of the state where the aircraft is registered; (4) to take on the same for such territory; and (5) to take on the same destined for the territory of any other contracting state and to put down the same coming from any

[37] Arts. 3–8. [38] Arts. 10–13, 15, 23–24, 26, 28–42, 89.

[39] A Soviet delegation spent two weeks in Montreal in April and May 1967, to consult on the regulations and operating procedures of ICAO, which has now 113 members. There is a possibility that the Soviet Union will become a party to the Chicago Convention of 1944. See *The New York Times,* May 4, 1967.

[40] Arts. 43–55, 67–79. The Chicago Conference also adopted an Interim Agreement on International Civil Aviation, which set up a Provisional International Civil Aviation Organization (PICAO) to carry out the objectives and functions provided for in the Convention pending its ratification.

[41] For its text, see *Yearbook,* UN, 1946–1947, pp. 741–745.

[42] For its text, see 39 *Am. Jour. Int. Law* (1945), p. 135.

such territory. These three freedoms are granted only to through services on a route constituting a reasonably direct line from and back to the homeland of the state where the aircraft is registered.[43]

While considerable progress has been made in the field of civil aviation through international cooperation, many problems remain unsettled. The Convention on the Territorial Sea and the Contiguous Zone, adopted at the First Conference on the Law of the Sea in 1958,[44] merely declares the existing rule that "the sovereignty of a coastal state extends to the air space over the territorial sea as well as its bed and subsoil." [45] Closely related to civil aviation is the right of wireless communication, for which a number of international conventions have been adopted.[46] By means of bilateral treaties, some difficulties concerning landing and innocent passage have been alleviated. On the whole, the contracting parties have observed the provisions of the various conventions and agreements, a few exceptional cases notwithstanding. The flying of an unarmed U-2 plane with photographic apparatus over Soviet territory for reconnaissance purposes was justified by the United States as a matter of necessity for national defense in view of the repeated threat of aggression by the Soviet Union, but it was definitely in violation of the territorial sovereignty of another state and the provisions of the Chicago Convention to which the United States is a signatory.[47] The Soviet fear of non-commercial and non-scheduled flights over her territory by foreign civil aircraft is probably the reason why she has not become a member of the International Civil Aviation

[43] For the text of the Transport Agreement, see *ibid.*, p. 139. For further discussion on international control of aviation and air transport, consult Bin Chen, *The Law of International Air Transport* (London, 1962); Oliver J. Lissitzyn, *International Air Transport and National Policy* (New York, 1942); K. Colegrove, *International Control of Aviation* (Boston, 1930).

[44] UN Doc. A/Conf.13/L.52. [45] Art. 2.

[46] For details, see Fenwick, *Principles*, pp. 491–495; also J. D. Tomlinson, *The International Control of Radio Communications* (Ann Arbor, Mich., 1945).

[47] After the exposure of the U-2 incident on May 1, 1960, the Soviet Union complained to the Security Council against the aggressive act of the United States, but its draft resolution was rejected at the 860th meeting on May 26, 1960, by 2 votes in favor, 7 against, with 2 abstentions. Two months later, the Soviet Union introduced another draft resolution against United States intrusion on Soviet territory by an American RB-47 plane on July 1 of the same year. At the 883rd meeting of the Security Council, the Soviet draft resolution was rejected again by 2 votes in favor, and 9 against. See *Repertoire*, SC, Supp., 1959–1963, pp. 157–158, 185–186, respectively. See also Quincy Wright, "Legal Aspects of the U-2 Incident," 54 *Am. Jour. Int. Law* (1960), pp. 836–854.

Organization (ICAO). Much less would she tolerate air reconnaissance by U-2 planes or any other aircraft with similar missions.

II. *LEGAL ASPECTS OF OUTER SPACE* [48]

§100. THE FREEDOM OF OUTER SPACE

Research in space law preceded the flight of *Sputnik* I,[49] which marked the beginning of the space age on October 4, 1957.[50] Voluminous literature has since been written by both official and private sources, but definite rules governing space remain to be formulated. Due to the variety of air density in the high atmosphere found by the International Geophysical Year, even the lowest height for the boundary of outer space is hard to determine. However, it is generally recognized that outer space is free for peaceful use by all nations in the same way as are the high seas.[51]

It is difficult to compare outer space with the Antarctic.[52] By concluding the Antarctic Treaty at Washington on December 1, 1959, the signatories agreed to open the continent to free exploitation by placing in abeyance whatever claims they may have had. On the other hand, the principle of the peaceful use of outer space precludes any legal right of claims by individual states. The advancement of space exploration by the United States and the Soviet Union has made it necessary for the United Nations to study the various aspects of the peaceful uses of outer space.[53]

[48] General texts on the subject: O'Connell, I, pp. 596–600; Fenwick, *Principles,* Ch. XXI, §B; Schwarzenberger, I, Ch. 4 (V, F); Whiteman, *Digest,* II, Ch. V, §§19–25; Jacobini, pp. 87–88. Several special treatises of exceptional value are listed elsewhere in this section.

[49] The first doctoral dissertation on space law was prepared by the Prince of Hanover at the University of Goettingen in 1953.

[50] No attempt will be made in the present work to describe the activities or techniques of space exploration. It is important to note that the satellites orbiting beyond airspace and guided missiles are not pilotless aircraft prohibited by the Chicago Convention of 1944.

[51] Encouraged by the precedent set by the International Geophysical Year, Dag Hammarskjöld, Secretary-General of the United Nations, took a courageous step in May 1958 to call upon the nations to renounce claims of jurisdiction over outer space.

[52] Philip C. Jessup and H. J. Taubenfeld made a comparative study in their *Controls for Outer Space and the Antarctic Analogy* (New York, 1959).

[53] A Staff Report of the Select Committee on Astronautics and Space Exploration (86th Cong., 1st Sess., House Doc. No. 89) prepared a valuable

§101. RECOMMENDATIONS OF THE UNITED NATIONS AD HOC COMMITTEE

Encouraged by the scientific cooperation of the International Geophysical Year, the General Assembly established an *Ad Hoc* Committee on the Peaceful Uses of Outer Space on December 13, 1958.[54] Composed of eighteen members, the Committee was to examine the organization, activities, and resources of the United Nations, the specialized agencies, as well as other international bodies concerning the peaceful uses of outer space, with a view to formulating programs of international cooperation and studying their legal aspects. The Committee divided itself into two subcommittees: technical and legal. Among the programs recommended by the Committee were the central registration of orbital elements, use of radio frequencies, and destruction or recovery of spent satellites. With respect to the organizational structure, the Committee deemed that time was not yet ready for the establishment of a new intergovernmental agency or for the concentration of all space activities in one existing organ.

After examining the legal problems, the Committee concluded that existing knowledge of the various phases of outer space did not warrant the drafting of a comprehensive code of space law, including the definitions of airspace and outer space. On the exploration of the celestial bodies, the Committee recommended that no state should claim sovereignty over them. It suggested that it was essential to give priority to six problems demanding early solution: (1) ascertaining the free exploration and use of outer space in accordance with existing or future international law or agreements; (2) determining the type and extent of liability for injury or damage caused by space vehicles; (3) allocating radio frequencies to space vehicles; (4) preventing interference between space vehicles and aircraft; (5) identifying and registering space vehicles and coordinating launchings; and (6) considering problems resulting from the re-entry, descent, and landing of space vehicles in states other than the launching places.

The work of the *Ad Hoc* Committee was first obstructed by the non-participation of the Soviet Union, Poland, and Czechoslovakia, and then by the absence of India and the United Arab Republic. The

---

study, *Survey of Space Law*, with an extensive bibliography. See also H. Peter Kehrberger, *Legal and Political Implications of Space Research. Space Law and Its Background: Political, Military, Economic Aspects and Techno-Scientific Problems of Astronautics. A Selective Bibliography of Eastern and Western Sources* (Hamburg, 1965).

[54] UN Doc. C.I/L.220/Rev.1 (1958).

frustration was largely due to the rivalry between the Soviet Union and the United States, but the Committee nevertheless completed its report in June 1959. Encouraged by these comprehensive suggestions, the General Assembly decided to continue the study by creating the United Nations Committee on the Peaceful Uses of Outer Space (UNCOPUOS) on December 12, 1959.[55]

§102. UNCOPUOS STUDIES AND THE SPACE TREATY

The work of UNCOPUOS Consisting of twenty-four members, UNCOPUOS had a larger representation from the Communist bloc than did the Ad Hoc Committee. But it did not start to work until late November 1961 because of procedural disagreement between the Soviet Union and the United States. They eventually agreed on a draft resolution, which was unanimously adopted by the General Assembly on December 20, 1961.[56] This resolution "commends to states for their guidance in the exploration and use of outer space the following principles: (a) international law, including the Charter of the United Nations, applies to outer space and celestial bodies; (b) outer space and celestial bodies are free for exploration and use by all states in conformity with internationl law and are not subject to national appropriation." [57]

UNCOPUOS studied various problems and proposals in the Legal Subcommittee and the Scientific and Technical Subcommittee. In 1962, seven proposals were submitted by the United States, the Soviet Union, and several other states for consideration, but no agreement was reached.[58] There was serious debate in the Legal Subcommittee in June 1962 over American high-altitude nuclear explosions, which were condemned by the Soviet Union as a gross violation of international law but defended by the United States on the ground of national security.[59] In spite of divergent opinions, the Committee made progress in many phases of legal problems. On the basis of its report, the General Assembly unanimously adopted a resolution on December 13, 1963,[60] which recommended nine points for the guidance of states in the exploration and use of outer space.[61]

At its final meeting of the twentieth session, the General Assembly called on UNCOPUOS to continue drafting international agreements on assistance to and return of astronauts and space vehicles and on

[55] GA res. 1472 (XIV). [56] GA res. 1721 (XVI).

[57] *Yearbook*, UN, 1961, p. 35.

[58] For details, see *Yearbook*, UN, 1962, pp. 38–45.

[59] See *ibid.*, p. 46. [60] GA res. 1962 (XVIII).

[61] For the text of the nine points, see *Yearbook*, UN, 1963, p. 101.

liability for damage caused by objects launched into outer space.[62] In the same resolution, UNCOPUOS was urged to give consideration to incorporating in international agreement form legal principles governing the activities of states in the exploration and use of outer space.[63]

The Space Treaty Negotiations for a space treaty have been carried on both in and outside UNCOPUOS. The turning point was reached in late 1966 when the two space powers, the Soviet Union and the United States, reconciled two major conflicting views: space tracking facilities and inspection visits to space stations and vehicles.[64] Instead of insisting on automatic supply to Moscow of an equal share in the vast tracking network established by the United States with many countries through bilateral agreements, the Soviet Union accepted a compromise proposal that such facilities would be arranged among the states individually on a basis of equality. To meet the Soviet desires, the United States also took a conciliatory position on inspection visits, which would only be made with reasonable advance notice on a basis of reciprocity. Because of these mutual understandings and the patient work of UNCOPUOS and its Legal Subcommittee, a space treaty was finally drafted and unanimously approved by the General Assembly on December 19, 1966.[65]

Consisting of a preamble and seventeen articles, the Space Treaty embodies principles governing the activities of states in the exploration and use of space, including the moon and other celestial bodies. It not only incorporates all nine points adopted by the General Assembly on December 13, 1963, but also includes effective dissemination of space information, reciprocal observation and inspection, and strict prohibition of military activities. The essentials of the Treaty may be summarized as follows:

(1) free exploration and use of outer space and celestial bodies

[62] GA res. 2130 (XX).

[63] The Legal Subcommittee on Peaceful Uses of Outer Space discussed various phases in September 1965, but failed to reach an accord on the text of a draft agreement. For its report, see A/AC.105/29, October 1, 1965. However, the Subcommittee renewed its efforts in 1966, which eventually led to the successful conclusion of the present space treaty.

[64] The differences were ironed out by Arthur J. Goldberg and Platon D. Morozov, representing the United States and the Soviet Union respectively.

[65] Prior to its discussion at the General Assembly, the draft treaty was first submitted to the First Committee, which approved it on December 17, 1966. GA res. 2222 (XXI). For the text of the treaty, see *The New York Times,* December 20, 1966; UN Doc. A/6621, pp. 11–18.

by the states on equal basis, for the benefit of all mankind, and in the interest of international peace and cooperation; [66]

(2) prohibition of national appropriation of outer space and celestial bodies by claim of sovereignty, occupation, or any other means; [67]

(3) state activities in the exploration and use of outer space in accordance with international law, including the Charter of the United Nations; [68]

(4) responsibility of states for activities in outer space by their governmental or non-governmental agencies, and responsibility of an international organization and participating states for their activities in outer space; [69]

(5) respect for corresponding interests of other states in outer space and conduct of appropriate consultations in case of activities potentially harmful to others; [70]

(6) retention of state jurisdiction over its objects and personnel in outer space, and return of such objects found outside the state upon the presentation of identifying data if requested; [71]

(7) liability of the state for damage to a foreign state or to its national or juridical persons by objects launched in airspace or outer space; [72]

(8) assistance to, and return of, astronauts to the state of registry of their space vehicle, in the event of accident, distress, or emergency landing; [73]

(9) prohibition of all military activities in outer space and on celestial bodies, including the placing in orbit of any objects carrying nuclear or similar weapons of mass destruction, installation of such weapons on celestial bodies, establishment of military bases or fortifications, conduct of military maneuvers, as well as testing of any weapons; [74]

[66] Art. 1 of the Treaty; Points 1–2 of GA res. 1962 (XVIII). Further reference to these two documents in this section will be only as 'Art.' and 'Point.' Art. 1 is in conformity with GA res. 110 (II) of November 3, 1947, which condemned any propaganda detrimental to the peace of the world including outer space.

[67] Art. 2; Point 3.

[68] Art. 3; Point 4.

[69] Art. 6; Point 5.

[70] Art. 9; Point 6.

[71] Art. 8; Point 7.

[72] Art. 7; Point 8.

[73] Art. 5; Point 9.

[74] Art. 4, which is based on GA res. 1884 (XVIII) of October 17, 1963. This article does not exclude the use of military personnel for scientific research or for any other peaceful purposes or of any equipment or facility necessary for peaceful exploration of celestial bodies.

(10) equal opportunity to observe the flight of space objects by agreements among the states concerned; [75]

(11) dissemination through the Secretary-General of the United Nations of all information concerning space activities; [76]

(12) inspection visits, through reasonable advance notice and on reciprocal basis, to all stations, installations, equipment, and space vehicles on celestial bodies.[77]

The last five articles of the Treaty deal with procedural matters. The above provisions apply to the activities carried out by a single signatory state or by several states jointly. Any practical questions involving the activities of international intergovernmental organizations are to be resolved by the signatories with the appropriate international organization or with one or more of its members.[78] The Treaty, made in Chinese, English, French, Russian, and Spanish, which are equally authentic,[79] is open to all states for signature in Washington, London, and Moscow. Future amendments may be made by the agreement of the majority of the signatories.[80] The Treaty will come into effect upon the deposit of instruments of ratification by five signatory states, including Great Britain, the Soviet Union, and the United States.[81] Terms of withdrawal from the Treaty are also provided.[82] There is no question that the Treaty will be ratified by almost all the states in the near future, but further details on the liability for damages and on assistance to and return of astronauts and space vehicles remain to be worked out, probably by the conclusion of separate agreements.[83]

§103. THE PROSPECT OF SPACE LAW

The United Nations has been making continuous studies on the legal and technical aspects of space exploration through its own organs and a number of specialized agencies under the coordination of the Economic and Social Council. Other intergovernmental and non-governmental organizations are also involved in the space research. UNESCO, WMO, ITU, ICAO, IAEA, and many others have directly or indirectly participated in the work. In addition, international and national scientific organizations as well as governmental agencies of several advanced nations have engaged intensively in various phases of space exploration.

As yet there is no systematic code of space law, in spite of all the

[75] Art. 10. [76] Art. 11. [77] Art. 12. [78] Art. 13.
[79] Art. 17. [80] Arts. 14, 15. [81] Art. 14. [82] Art. 16.
[83] The General Assembly requested UNCOPUOS in December 1966 to continue its work on these matters. GA res. 2222 (XXI).

efforts as stated before. The fundamental reason is the insufficiency of space knowledge at present and the unwillingness of states to be bound by rules which might turn against their national interests. In the view of Soviet experts, the formulation of space law is not incompatible with the Soviet policies of 'peaceful coexistence,' 'peaceful cooperation,' and 'disarmament.'[84] The conclusion of the Space Treaty is a very encouraging step, but future agreement on space law depends much upon continuing improvement of the relationship between the space powers and the general détente of the cold war. A United Nations conference on the exploration and peaceful uses of outer space will be held at Vienna in August 1968, in accordance with the resolution adopted by the fifth special session of the General Assembly on May 23, 1967.[85] Further phenomenal success in space exploration, such as landing on the moon and other discoveries, will necessitate the speedy draft of a space code, in which rules and regulations governing outer space will be incorporated.

[84] See Robert D. Crane, "Basic Principles in Soviet Space Law: Peaceful Coexistence, Peaceful Cooperation, and Disarmament," 29 *Law and Contemporary Problems* (1964), pp. 943–955.

[85] GA res. 2250 (V). The twenty-first session of the General Assembly originally decided that the conference was to be held in September 1967. See GA res. 2222 (XXI), adopted on December 20, 1966. But further study and necessary preparation demanded its postponement for one year. Andrew G. Haley made a systematic study of space law in his *Space Law and Government* (New York, 1963). Some important documents and proposals on space law can be found in its appendix. See also *Survey of Space Law*, House Doc. No. 89 (Washington, D.C., 1959); A Symposium on Space Law, *The JAG Journal* (February 1959); the Seventeenth Report of the Commission to Study the Organization of Peace, *New Dimensions for the United Nations* (New York, 1966), pp. 36–41; Joseph M. Goldsen (ed.), *Outer Space in World Politics* (New York, 1963). A brief presentation of the complex issues of space law can be found in The American Assembly, *Outer Space* (New York, 1962). The joint efforts of Myres S. McDougal, Harold D. Lasswell, and Ivan A. Vlasic produced a most exhaustive work in this field, *Law and Public Order in Space* (New Haven, 1964). Some scientific and technical information on space exploration is contained in a publication by the National Aeronautics and Space Administration in 1964, the *Proceedings* of the Conference on the Law of Space and of Satellite Communications, which was a part of the Third National Conference on the Peaceful Uses of Space, Chicago, May 1963 (Washington, D.C., 1964). See also Maxwell A. Cohen (ed.), *Law and Politics in Space* (Montreal, 1964); American Bar Association, *Report to the National Aeronautics and Space Administration on the Law of Outer Space* (prepared by L. Lipson and N. DeB. Katzenbach, Chicago, 1961).

III. *THE HIGH SEAS* [86]

§104. THE FREEDOM OF THE HIGH SEAS

The high seas embrace international waters which are not included in the territorial sea and national waters of individual states.[87] In spite of historical claims by many states and divergent views among publicists,[88] it now is generally recognized that the high seas do not belong to any state, which exercises jurisdiction only over persons, ships, aircraft, goods, as well as natural resources over or under such international waters in accordance with mutual agreements and the prevailing rules of international law.[89] The tests of nuclear and other weapons in the Pacific Ocean by the United States, the Soviet Union,

[86] General texts on the subject: O'Connell, I, pp. 569–579; Oppenheim, I, §§248–259, 281–287d; Fenwick, *Principles,* Ch. XXII; Hyde, I, §§227–230; Moore, *Digest,* I, §§163–173; II, §§227–233, 308–309; Hackworth, *Digest,* I, §§108–111; Whiteman, *Digest,* IV, Ch. X; Brierly, Chs. V, §7; VI, §8; Schwarzenberger, I, Ch. 5 (II); Starke, Ch. 8, §5; Hershey, Ch. XV; Svarlien, Ch. 13; Von Glahn, Ch. 20; Jacobini, pp. 78–81, 89, 92–94; Soviet *Text,* Ch. V, §8; Corbett, Ch. 4; McNair, I, pp. 229–281.

[87] The terms 'open sea' and 'high seas' are used interchangeably. The high seas include such international waters as the Atlantic Ocean, the Pacific Ocean, the Mediterranean Sea, the Caribbean Sea, the Red Sea, and the Bays of Biscay and Bengal.

[88] During the latter part of the Middle Ages, some European states made fantastic claims to various regions of the high seas, for instance, Spain over the Pacific Ocean and the Gulf of Mexico, and Portugal over the Indian Ocean and the South Pacific. Hugo Grotius advocated the doctrine of the freedom of the seas in his *Mare liberum* in 1609, but his liberal view was refuted by John Selden in his work *Mare clausum* in 1618. Special reference to the law of the sea may be found in the following valuable treatises: H. A. Smith, *The Law and Custom of the Sea,* 3rd ed. (London, 1959); McDougal and Burke, *The Public Order of the Oceans* (New Haven, 1962); A. Pearce Higgins and C. John Colombos, *The International Law of the Sea,* 4th ed. (London & New York, 1959); William McFee, *The Law of the Sea* (Philadelphia, 1950); G. Gidel, *Le Droit international public de la mer, le temps de paix* (Paris, 1932–1934), 3 vols.; C. M. Franklin, *The Law of the Sea: Some Recent Developments* (Washington, D.C., 1961).

[89] The last challenge to the freedom of the seas was by Russia in her claim of sovereignty over the Bering Sea in 1821, which was abandoned after strong resistance from the United States, Great Britain, and other powers. The United States has long been the champion of the freedom of the seas, this principle being also the second of President Wilson's Fourteen Points. On claims to shared use and competence upon the high seas, see McDougal and Burke, *op. cit.,* pp. 730–1007.

and France undoubtedly constituted a hindrance to the freedom of navigation and fishing in the test areas of the high seas.[90]

The First Conference on the Law of the Sea, attended by representatives from eighty-six states at Geneva in 1958, adopted, among others, the Convention on the High Seas, which came into effect on September 30, 1962.[91] The provisions of the Convention are generally declaratory of the established principles of international law. The doctrine of the freedom of the seas was reaffirmed and may be summarized in the following categories: (1) freedom of navigation, (2) freedom of fishing, (3) freedom to lay submarine cables and pipelines,[92] and (4) freedom to fly over the high seas.[93] Of course, all the above freedoms are subject to international regulation. A landlocked state is entitled to free access to the sea by concluding a special agreement with its adjacent coastal states, on the basis of reciprocity and free transit through their territorial domain.[94]

[90] After the conclusion of the Nuclear Test Ban Treaty in Moscow on August 5, 1963, only underground testing is permitted. Even though the Treaty came into effect on October 1, 1963, France and Communist China have not adhered to it and are not bound by its provisions.

[91] For its text, see United Nations Conference on the Law of the Sea, *Official Records,* II, pp. 135–139. UN Doc. A/Conf.13/L.53. If there is any dispute arising out of the interpretation or application of the provisions of this Convention or of other conventions adopted by the 1958 Conference on the Law of the Sea, it may be settled through the International Court of Justice, an arbitral tribunal, or a conciliation commission in accordance with the Optional Protocol of Signature concerning the Compulsory Settlement of Disputes, signed at Geneva on April 29, 1958. For the text of the Protocol, which came into effect on September 30, 1962, see UN Doc. A/Conf. 13/L.57.

[92] Art. 26 of the Convention of the High Seas. This provision does not preclude the right of a state to take reasonable measures for exploration of the continental shelf and the exploitation of its natural resources. The protection of submarine cables has been a concern of many states; this led to the International Convention for the Protection of Submarine Telegraph Cables at Paris on March 14, 1884. Twenty-six states were parties to the Convention, including Great Britain and other maritime nations. After a series of breaks of five trans-Atlantic cables in the Newfoundland area in February 1959, the United States Navy sent a boarding party to a Soviet trawler, *Novorossisk,* suspected of violating Article 2 of the 1884 Convention. In reply to a Soviet protest, the United States government declared that it was duty-bound to protect the cables in accordance with Article 10 of the Convention. See *The New York Times,* March 6, 24, 1959.

[93] During wartime, merchant ships of neutral states are subject to visit and search as well as other restrictions. For details, see *infra,* §§233–235.

[94] See Arts. 2–3 of the Convention on the High Seas. In 1962, Bolivia, a landlocked state, demanded of Chile the cession of an adjacent part of terri-

§105. ENFORCEMENT OF SAFETY MEASURES

In order to ensure safety at sea, states are required to adopt necessary measures in accordance with international standards with respect to seaworthiness of ships, manning of ships and labor conditions for crews, use of signals, maintenance of communications, and prevention of collisions.[95] Assistance must be promptly rendered to rescue persons and ships in distress because of collision or other reasons.[96] Emphasis is also laid on the prevention of pollution of the seas by discharge of oil or radioactive waste.[97] Repression of piracy and the punishment of the transportation of slaves are to be the common efforts of all nations.[98] The Convention on the High Seas prescribes, in detail, the jurisdiction over ships and the principle of hot pursuit, which will be discussed below.[99] Regulations are to be drafted concerning safety procedures of submarines meeting in the high seas.[100]

---

tory as a corridor to the sea. The controversy should have been settled in accordance with the letter and spirit of the Convention. On July 8, 1965, a convention was adopted by a United Nations conference represented by sixty-two states to help the landlocked states, concerning the means of transport, storage of goods in transit, free zones at ports, and other facilities. See *The New York Times*, July 9, 1965. On April 7, 1966, Portugal turned down a British request to block oil shipments to Rhodesia on the ground of "non-intervention in the free access to the sea of landlocked countries." See *ibid.*, April 8, 1966.

[95] Art. 10 of the Convention on the High Seas. Great Britain in 1863, the United States in 1864, and other principal maritime nations in the following years adopted uniform regulations to prevent collisions at sea. In *The Scotia* case, the U.S. Supreme Court ruled, in 1872, that universal adoption of the new maritime regulations manifested a general recognition of their status as a new rule of international law. 14 Wallace 170. Certain uniform rules on collisions and salvage at sea were adopted in two conventions at the Brussels Conference in 1910.

[96] Art. 12 of the Convention on the High Seas.

[97] Arts. 24–25. On May 4, 1967, Great Britain commenced legal proceedings against the tanker *Torrey Canyon*, wrecked on the high seas on March 18 of the same year, for her subsequent spilling into the sea tons of crude oil, polluting British harbors and coating resort beaches of Cornwall. Also named in the British claim were her two sister ships, all owned by the Barracuda Tanker Corporation, a subsidiary of the Union Oil Company of California, and all registered in Liberia. This case involves many legal questions, including the extent of liability of ships and the right of states to protect their shores. See *The New York Times*, May 5, 1967.

[98] See Arts. 13–22. [99] See *infra*, §§108–111.

[100] One of the Soviet nuclear submarines that recently sailed around the world in six weeks without surfacing tracked a United States nuclear sub-

§106. FISHING AND CONSERVATION OF LIVING RESOURCES

Initiated by the Hague Convention for the Regulation of the Police of the Fisheries in the North Sea outside Territorial Waters in 1882, several conventions on fisheries have been signed by the nations concerned. The tribunal arbitrating the *Behring [Bering] Sea Seal Fisheries Case* in 1893 adopted regulations for the protection of seals.[101] The preservation of other fisheries, including halibut and salmon, and the regulation of whaling were among other subjects of international agreements.[102]

The Convention on Fishing and Conservation of the Living Resources of the High Seas,[103] adopted by the First Conference on the Law of the Sea at Geneva on April 29, 1958, recognizes the right of the nationals of all states to engage in fishing on the high seas. Such a right is, however, subject to treaty obligations, rights and interests of other states, and provisions concerning the conservation of living resources of the high seas.[104] A coastal state has a special interest in

---

marine for more than an hour and a half. This story was revealed by Captain Igor Gromov, a Soviet officer who made the voyage, in the final article of a series of four in *Izvestia*. See also *The New York Times*, April 17, 1966.

[101] See Malloy, *Treaties*, I, 751; Moore, *Digest*, I, pp. 914–916.

[102] See also the *North Atlantic Coast Fisheries Case* (United States-Great Britain), Tribunal of the Permanent Court of Arbitration, 1910. Scott, *Hague Court Reports*, p. 146. Beginning in 1965, the United States, Canada, and sixteen European states engaged in fishing operations in the North Atlantic have participated in a Fisheries Policing Conference in London. A Convention on the Conduct of Fishing Operations in the North Atlantic, adopted by the Conference, is now open for signature from June 1 to November 30, 1967.

[103] For its text, see United Nations Conference on the Law of the Sea, *Official Records*, II, pp. 139–141. UN Doc. A/Conf.13/L.54.

[104] See Arts. 1–2 of the Convention on Fishing and Conservation of the Living Resources of the High Seas. The right of setting up conservation zones to preserve fisheries in areas contiguous to a coastal state was claimed by the United States by a presidential proclamation on September 28, 1945, and met no challenge from other nations. Since 1947, some Latin-American states have claimed a wide area adjacent to their territorial seas as conservation zones. For further discussion, see the Commission to Study the Organization of Peace, *New Dimensions for the United Nations: The Problems of the Next Decade* (17th Report, New York, 1966), pp. 39–41, 135–164); F. V. García-Amador, *The Exploitation and Conservation of the Resources of the Sea*, 2nd ed. (Leiden, 1959); Shigeru Oda, *International Control of Sea Resources* (Leiden, 1963); Stephen A. Riesenfeld, *The Protection of Coastal Fisheries under International Law* (Washington, D.C., 1942).

the preservation of living resources in any area of the high seas adjacent to its territorial sea, and may adopt unilateral measures of conservation in case of failure to reach an agreement with other states concerned.[105] The breadth of a fishing zone contiguous to a state's territorial sea was discussed at the First and Second Conferences on the Law of the Sea in 1958 and 1960, but no conclusion was reached.[106]

§107. EXPLOITATION OF NATURAL RESOURCES IN THE CONTINENTAL SHELF

The term 'continental shelf,' as commonly used today, designates the seabed and subsoil of the submarine areas adjacent to the coast of land or islands, but outside the area of the territorial sea, to a depth of 200 meters or, beyond that limit, to where the depth of the subjacent waters admits of the exploitation of natural resources.[107] In his proclamation of September 28, 1945, the President of the United States first made such a claim, which was followed by Great Britain and several Latin-American countries. Although such unilateral declarations by states were assented to by others, the concept of a continental shelf had not been universally recognized until the Convention on the Continental Shelf came into effect on June 10, 1964.

The Convention provides that a coastal state may exercise sovereign rights over the continental shelf for the exploration and exploitation of its natural resources without depending on occupation or any express proclamation. No other state may make the same claim without the express consent of the coastal state. The natural resources are the mineral and other non-living resources of the seabed and subsoil, together with living organisms belonging to sedentary species.[108]

In the absence of special agreement or other conditions, the boundary line of the continental shelf adjacent to the territories of two or more states whose coasts are opposite to each other is the median line. If the shelf is adjacent to the territories of two adjacent states, the principle of equidistance from the nearest points of the baselines is to be applied for the demarcation of their boundary.[109] The International

[105] Arts. 6–7 of the Convention. [106] See *supra*, §88.

[107] Art. 1 of the Convention on the Continental Shelf, adopted by the First Conference on the Law of the Sea at Geneva on April 29, 1958. For its text, see United Nations Conference on the Law of the Sea, *Official Records*, II, pp. 142–143. UN Doc. A/Conf.13/L.55.

[108] Art. 2 of the Convention. Sedentary species are organisms which, at the harvestable stage, either are immobile on or under the seabed or are unable to move except in constant physical contact with the seabed or the subsoil.

[109] Art. 6 of the Convention. See also Peter C. L. Anninos, *The Continental Shelf and Public International Law* (The Hague, 1953); M. W.

Court of Justice is the proper channel for the settlement of state differences concerning the delineation of the continental shelf.[110]

Coastal states may establish safety zones at a distance not exceeding 500 meters around their installations and other devices on the continental shelf for the purpose of exploration and exploitation. However, the right of a coastal state over the continental shelf must not affect the legal status of the superjacent waters as high seas or that of the air space above those waters or interfere with navigation, scientific research, fishing, conservation of living resources, and the laying or maintenance of submarine cables or pipelines.[111]

The status of the bed of the sea beyond the continental shelf has not been decided. It has been suggested that there should be a definite limit to the continental shelf and that the bed of the sea beyond the continental shelf should be under the jurisdiction of the United Nations. Consequently, states or corporations which might wish to exploit the resources of the high seas would have to obtain a concession from the United Nations. Thus, dangerous competition between states, such as occurred in the New World when America was discovered, would be avoided. Further, such a plan would contribute toward the solution of United Nations financial problems.

IV. *JURISDICTION OVER SHIPS* [112]

§108. NATIONALITY OF SHIPS

The nationality of a ship is determined by the state where it is registered. It is within the domestic legislation of each state with a mari-

---

Mouton, *The Continental Shelf* (The Hague, 1952); B. L. Barry, *The Continental Shelf* (Geneva, 1960).

[110] Two cases were submitted to the Court in February 1967: (1) *North Sea Continental Shelf, Federal Republic of Germany v. The Netherlands;* (2) *North Sea Continental Shelf, Denmark v. Federal Republic of Germany.*

[111] Arts. 3–5 of the Convention. For claims to authority in ocean areas adjacent to the territorial sea, including the control and appropriation of resources, see McDougal and Burke, *op. cit.*, pp. 565–729.

[112] General texts on the subject: O'Connell, II, pp. 661–727; Oppenheim, I, §§260–280; Fenwick, *Principles,* Ch. XVI; Hyde, I, §§221–243A; Moore, *Digest,* I, §174; II, §§203–208, 310–316, 321–335; Hackworth, *Digest,* II, §§139–149, 208–215; Schwarzenberger, I, Ch. 5 (IV); Starke, Ch. 8, §6; Svarlien, Ch. 14; Von Glahn, Ch. 21; Jacobini, pp. 90–92, 94–99; Lawrence, §§100, 102–103; Despagnet, §§422–433; Pradier-Fodéré, V, §§2376–2470, 2491–2515; Holland, *Lectures,* pp. 162–165; Calvo, I, §§385–473, 485–512.

time flag to prescribe requirements for registration of ships.[113] The flag state exercises jurisdiction over, and renders protection to, its ships, under conditions and limitations set forth by conventions and international law.[114] The Convention on the High Seas and the Convention on the Territorial Sea and the Contiguous Zone, adopted at the First Conference on the Law of the Sea at Geneva in 1958 with representatives from almost all the states at the time, stipulate various legal aspects concerning ships. As these two conventions have already come into effect, the pertinent provisions are binding upon the signatories.

According to the Convention on the High Seas, a ship sails under the flag of one state only and may not change its flag during a voyage or in a port of call unless its ownership or registry has actually been changed. A ship sailing under flags of two or more states is deemed without nationality.[115] On the other hand, if a ship is employed in the official service of an intergovernmental organization, it is permitted to fly the flag of the organization at the same time.[116] Unlike merchantmen, warships and other public ships for non-commercial uses are immune from the jurisdiction of any state other than the flag state.

§109. NATIONAL SHIPS IN FOREIGN AND INTERNATIONAL WATERS

It is pure fiction to consider ships as a floating portion of the territory of the flag state, but some states, especially Great Britain, exercise jurisdiction over national ships on the basis of that concept. Thus, a child born on an English vessel on the high seas is deemed born in

[113] For the laws and regulations of various countries on this subject, see *Laws concerning the Nationality of Ships,* prepared by the Codification Division of the Office of Legal Affairs of the United Nations Secretariat in 1955. UN Doc. ST/Leg/Ser.B/5 and Add.1. The landlocked states before 1920 made no attempt to have maritime flags. Following the Treaty of Versailles and the Treaty of St. Germain, the Declaration of Barcelona of 1921 extended flag recognition from the Allied and Associated Powers to all states parties to the Declaration, with or without seacoast. For its text, see Hudson, *International Legislation,* I, p. 662.

[114] See Arts. 5, 6(1), of the Convention on the High Seas. For a comprehensive discussion on the nationality of ships, see McDougal and Burke, *The Public Order of the Oceans,* pp. 1008–1140.

[115] For further discussion, see Robert Rienow, *The Test of the Nationality of a Merchant Vessel* (New York, 1937).

[116] Arts. 6–9 of the Convention on the High Seas. Whether a ship or an aircraft may retain its nationality after committing piracy is determined by the law of its flag state.

England.[117] The United States followed the English rule in *Crapo v. Kelly* in 1872.[118] Recognizing this traditional fiction as untenable, the Supreme Court decided in *Lam Mow v. Nagle* in 1928 that a child born of Chinese parents aboard an American vessel on the high seas was not born in the United States.[119]

In any event, the jurisdiction of a state over national ships is within the discretion of domestic legislation so long as not in conflict with the conventions and international law. States generally exercise jurisdiction over crimes committed aboard national vessels on the high seas and also in foreign waters if such offenses do not disturb the peace of the port.[120] In *Regina v. Leslie* in 1860,[121] the British Court of Criminal Appeal decided that an act legal in the state in whose waters it was committed but illegal under British law would be punished by Great Britain when the vessel reached the high seas.

§110. FOREIGN SHIPS WITHIN TERRITORIAL WATERS

Foreign ships have the right of innocent passage in territorial waters of other states. The Convention on the Territorial Sea and the Contiguous Zone stipulates, in detail, the nature and scope of innocent passage, these provisions being actually declaratory of the existing rules of international law.[122] The coastal state generally does not exercise jurisdiction over a crime committed aboard a foreign ship in its port if local peace and tranquility are not disturbed.[123] In the *Case of Antoni*, the Supreme Court of Justice of Mexico ruled in 1876 that Mexico had no jurisdiction over a manslaughter committed on a French ship in a Mexican port.[124] However, in *Wildenhus' Case* in 1887,[125] the United States Supreme Court took a different position by stating that public tranquility was disturbed by a felonious homicide committed on a Belgian ship in the port of Jersey City. It seems up to the local court to

[117] See *Marshall v. Murgatroyd*, Great Britain, High Court of Justice, 1870. 6 Q.B. 31.

[118] 16 Wallace 610. In this case, the U.S. Supreme Court held that the territory of Massachusetts itself extended to the ship on the high seas.

[119] 24 F. 2d 316.

[120] See *United States v. Rodgers*, U.S. Supreme Court, 1893 (150 U.S. 249); *Regina v. Anderson*, Great Britain, Court of Criminal Appeal, 1868 (11 Cox's Criminal Cases, 198). The British jurisdiction made no distinction between crimes committed by a British subject or by an alien on a British ship, in the case of *Queen v. Carr* in 1882 (10 Q.B. 76).

[121] Bell's Crown Cases, 220.

[122] Art. 14. See also *supra*, §89.

[123] *Cf.* Fauchille, I, Pt. II, p. 1034.

[124] 61 El. Foro, p. 194.

[125] 120 U.S. 1.

interpret whether an act constitutes disturbance of peace and tranquility of the port or is only a matter of internal discipline.

According to the Convention on the Territorial Sea and the Contiguous Zone, the coastal state exercises criminal jurisdiction over acts on board foreign ships in the territorial sea in any of the following cases: (1) consequences of the crime extending to the coastal state; (2) the nature of the crime resulting in disturbance of the peace of the country or the good order of the territorial sea; (3) the assistance of local authorities being requested by the captain of the ship or by the consul of the flag state; and (4) the suppression of illicit traffic in narcotic drugs. The coastal state has also the right to take necessary steps for arrest or investigation on board a foreign ship passing through the territorial sea after leaving internal waters. Such a right does not extend to crimes committed before the ship enters the territorial sea if it does not enter the internal waters of the state. Any arrest or investigation should take due consideration of the interests of navigation and keep appropriate contact with the consular authority of the flag state if requested by the captain of the ship.[126]

The coastal state is not to stop or divert a foreign ship passing through the territorial sea in order to exercise civil jurisdiction on board a ship, or to levy execution against or arrest the ship for the purpose of any civil proceedings in respect of obligations or liabilities not incurred by the ship itself through the territorial waters.[127] In spite of divergent practices in the past,[128] the Convention treats government ships operated for commercial purposes on the same basis as merchantmen.[129]

Warships and other government ships for non-commercial purposes enjoy immunities in foreign territorial waters. As public instrumentalities of a foreign state, they are practically floating portions of its territory. In the classic case *The Schooner Exchange v. McFadden,* in

[126] Art. 19 of the Convention on the Territorial Sea and the Contiguous Zone.

[127] Art. 20.

[128] In *Berizzi Bros. Co. v. S.S. Pesaro* in 1926, the U.S. Supreme Court upheld the immunity from local jurisdiction of an Italian government vessel engaged in commerce. 271 U.S. 562. However, this position was reversed in *Republic of Mexico v. Hoffman,* U.S. Supreme Court, 1945. 324 U.S. 30. In his study of the *Legal Status of Government Merchant Ships in International Law* (The Hague, 1962), T. Kochu Thommen concluded that their status is the same as that of private merchant ships in international law.

[129] Art. 21. At the First Conference on the Law of the Sea at Geneva in 1958, a Soviet proposal to grant immunity to government-trading ships received only ten votes. Conscious of the sovereign right of territorial jurisdiction, the new nations have been in favor of more restrictive policies. See United Nations Conference on the Law of the Sea, *Official Records,* III, First Committee, p. 132. (forty-third meeting, April 11, 1958).

1812,[130] Chief Justice Marshall dismissed the suit on the ground that the French warship *Exchange* was exempt from the jurisdiction of the United States. Of course, the coastal state may prohibit the entry of foreign warships into a port. Once they have entered, they also may be ordered to leave the territorial sea in the event of their disrespect of local laws and regulations.[131]

In *The Parlement Belge,* involving a public mailship of the Belgian government, the British Court of Appeal, in 1880, reversed the judgment of the High Court of Admiralty and upheld the ship's immunity from local jurisdiction.[132] The reason given was that it would be contrary to international law to call upon a foreign sovereign to sacrifice either his property or his independence.[133] On the other hand, the members of the crew may be punished by the coastal state for crimes committed ashore during recreation or other non-official activities.

§111. NAVIGATION ON THE HIGH SEAS

Hovering Under normal conditions and in time of peace, no state may exercise jurisdiction over foreign ships on the high seas except for cases of slave trading and piracy. In *Church v. Hubbart* in 1804,[134] the United States Supreme Court upheld the right of nations to go outside their territorial sea in self-defense to prevent the violation of their trading laws by hovering vessels. To prevent foreign merchantmen from hovering off the American coast with the intention to smuggle liquor, the United States obtained the consent of Great Britain through a treaty in 1924 to seize hovering vessels outside the territorial sea but within one hour's sailing distance from the shore by motorboat.[135]

[130] 7 Cranch 116.

[131] Art. 23 of the Convention on the Territorial Sea and the Contiguous Zone.

[132] 5 P.D. 197.

[133] Under different circumstances, the British Judicial Committee of the Privy Council contested in 1938 the traditional concept of exterritoriality of public ships, in *Chung Chi Cheung v. The King.* [1939] A.C. 160.

[134] 2 Cranch 187. The same rule was applied to *The Grace and Ruby,* United States, District Court, District of Massachusetts, 1922. 283 F. 475. *Cf.* the Brussels Convention for the Unification of Certain Rules relating to the Immunity of State-owned Vessels of 1926. Hackworth, *Digest,* II, pp. 463–465.

[135] See *Ford v. United States,* U.S. Supreme Court, 1927. 273 U.S. 593. The Anglo-American Treaty of 1924 virtually superseded the pertinent provisions of a previous statute of the United States concerning prevention of liquor smuggling. *Cf.* the decision of the U.S. Supreme Court in *Cook v. United States,* 1933. 288 U.S. 102.

Hot pursuit Another exception to the general rule of the freedom of the high seas is the seizure of a foreign ship through hot pursuit by the coastal state, which has reason to believe that the ship concerned has violated its laws and regulations.[136] According to the Convention on the High Seas, the right of hot pursuit may be exercised only by warships, military aircraft, and other specially authorized government ships or aircraft.[137] The pursuit must be commenced when a foreign ship is within the territorial waters or the contiguous zone of the pursuing state and disobeys its order to stop. It may be continued outside the territorial sea or the contiguous zone without interruption, but must cease when the ship pursued enters the territorial sea of another state. The aircraft giving the order to stop must actively continue the pursuit until the ship is arrested either by the aircraft itself or by another aircraft or a ship summoned by the pursuing aircraft. Compensation for loss or damage must be made by the pursuing state if the pursuit or arrest is not justified.[138]

Slave trading on the high seas While slavery is an internal matter of a state, slave trading on the high seas concerns the public policy of all nations. From the beginning of the nineteenth century, Great Britain worked toward abolishing the slave trade by the conclusion of bilateral and multilateral treaties.[139] In *La Jeune Eugenie* in 1822, the United States Circuit Court (First Circuit) condemned the slave trade as repugnant to the "great principles of Christian duty, the dictates of natural religion, the obligations of good faith and morality and the eternal maxims of social justice." [140] Yet the prohibition of slave trade

[136] See Herbert A. Smith, *The Law and Custom of the Sea,* 3rd ed. (London, 1959), pp. 71–72.

[137] Art. 23(4).

[138] Art. 23(1–3, 5–7). In *The Ship North v. The King,* the Supreme Court of Canada decided in 1906 that international law has recognized the practice of hot pursuit. 37 Canada Supt. Ct. Rep. 385. However, the circumstances surrounding the pursuit and sinking of a Canadian vessel, *I'm Alone,* by American patrol boats were deemed unjustified by the United States-Great Britain Special Joint Commission in 1935. Joint Final Report of the Commission, 1935. [1933: 1935] 3 R.I.A.A., 1609. For James W. Garner's comments on this case, see 16 *British Yearbook of International Law* (1935), p. 173.

[139] Among these were the Treaty of Paris of 1814, Treaty of London of 1841, General Act of the Berlin Conference on Congo of 1885, General Act of the Anti-Slavery Conference at Brussels of 1890, Convention of St. Germain of 1919, and Geneva Slavery Convention of 1926. For details, see Oppenheim, I, pp. 733–734.

[140] 2 Mason 409.

is still based upon municipal legislation and treaty provisions.[141] The Convention on the High Seas requires every state to adopt effective measures for the prevention and punishment of the transport of slaves in ships authorized to fly its flag, which may be verified by any warship on the high seas in case of suspicion. It provides further that any slave taking refuge on board any ship, whatever its flag, shall *ipso facto* be free.[142] The prohibition of slavery and slave trade in all forms is stressed in the Universal Declaration of Human Rights.[143]

Collision and salvage In the event of collision and other incidents on the high seas, penal or disciplinary proceedings may be instituted only before the judicial tribunals or administrative authorities either of the flag state or of the state whose nationals are involved.[144] The United States assumed jurisdiction in 1872 over the British steamer *Scotia,* which collided with and sank an American ship.[145] A well-known case of collision occurred on the high seas involving the French steamship *Lotus* and the Turkish ship *Boz-Kourt,* which was sunk resulting in the death of eight Turkish nationals. In deciding the case in 1927, the Permanent Court of International Justice ruled that Turkey had criminal jurisdiction over the French officer of the watch on board the *Lotus,* which entered a Turkish port.[146]

The Convention on the High Seas also provides that a master's certificate may be withdrawn by the issuing state only and that arrest or detention of the ship may be ordered only by the flag state.[147] With respect to salvage as a result of collision or other incidents on the high seas, every flag state must require the master of the ship to rescue persons in distress under circumstances permissible.[148] In deciding cases of salvage, the courts generally hold the questions at issue as *communis juris.*[149]

[141] In some early cases, the courts in the United States and Great Britain held that slave trade unlawful in municipal law was not a piratical act in international law. See *Le Louis,* Great Britain, High Court of Admiralty, 1817 (2 Dodson 210); *The Antelope,* U.S. Supreme Court, 1825 (10 Wheaton 66).

[142] Arts. 13, 22.

[143] Art. 4 of the Declaration.

[144] Art. 11(1) of the Convention on the High Seas. Previously, the maritime nations held two conferences at Brussels in 1910 and 1952, adopting a convention on collisions and another on salvage in 1910, also a convention on criminal jurisdiction over collisions in 1952.

[145] 14 Wallace 170.

[146] P.C.I.J. (1927), Ser. A, No. 10.

[147] Art. 11(2–3).

[148] Art. 12.

[149] See *Two Friends,* Great Britain, High Court of Admiralty, 1799 (1 C. Rob. 271); *Mason v. Le Blaireau,* U.S. Supreme Court, 1804 (2 Cranch 240).

§112. SUPPRESSION OF PIRACY

Piracy in international law is now associated with not only ships but also aircraft.[150] The Convention on the High Seas defines any of the following as an act of piracy:

(1) any illegal act of violence, detention, or depredation, committed for private ends by the crew or the passengers of a private ship or a private aircraft, and directed against another ship or aircraft, or against persons or property on board, on the high seas or in a place outside the jurisdiction of any state;

(2) any act of voluntary participation in the operation of a ship or an aircraft with knowledge of facts making it a pirate ship or aircraft, or of inciting or intentionally facilitating the commitment of piracy;

(3) any act of piracy committed by a public ship or aircraft whose crew has mutinied and taken control of the ship or aircraft is assimilated to an act committed by a private ship or aircraft.[151]

A pirate ship or aircraft is that under the dominant control of persons who either intend or have committed a piratic act. Every state may seize a pirate ship or aircraft or anyone taken by pirates and arrest the persons and seize the property on board to be adjudicated by its court. Visit, search, arrest, or seizure on account of piracy may be carried out only by warships or military aircraft or other public ships or aircraft authorized for that purpose. Appropriate compensation must, however, be made for loss or damage caused by any unjustified act of the state concerned.[152]

Piracy is an international crime which may be punished by any state. Thus, a pirate loses the protection of the state of which he is a national. Piracy is also applied to the mutinous crew or passengers of a ship or an aircraft, public or private, which together with goods on

[150] For traditional definitions of piracy, see Hall, §81; Lawrence, §102. It should be noted that piracy in municipal law is determined by the legislation of different states. See Harvard Research (1932, V), *A Collection of Piracy Laws of Various Countries.*

[151] See Arts. 15–16 of the Convention on the High Seas. Actual robbery was not considered an essential element of piracy by the British Judicial Commitee of the Privy Council in *In Re Piracy Jure Gentium* in 1934. [1934] A.C. 586.

[152] See Arts. 17–21 of the Convention on the High Seas. In the case of *The Marianna Flora,* the U.S. Supreme Court decided in 1826 that no damages were due a ship which resisted lawful approach with violence. 11 Wheaton 1.

board are converted for their private use.[153] It is controversial whether an act against neutral commerce committed by a ship of an insurgent not recognized as a belligerent is piracy and subject to condemnation, even though a United States District Court decided in the affirmative in *The Ambrose Light* in 1885.[154] Sometimes ruthless acts by belligerents on the high seas disregarding human life and the law of nations are condemned as piratical,[155] but such a broad expression does not represent the term 'piracy' as generally used in international law.

[153] The Brazilian government granted political asylum to the rebel crew of *Santa Maria,* a Portuguese cruise ship, because the motive of the mutiny was political. See *The New York Times,* January 24–31, 1961.

[154] Southern District of New York, 1885. 25 F. 408. When the ironclad *Huascar* under the insurgents of Peru in 1887 stopped British ships and seized coal on board, the British navy attacked the *Huascar* because of its piratic act. See Cobbett, 299. *Cf. The Magelian Pirates,* Great Britain, High Court of Admiralty, 1853. 1 Spinks 81.

[155] This broad application of piratical acts may be found in the Nyon Agreement of 1937 during the Spanish Civil War and also in President Roosevelt's order in September 1941, especially concerning ruthless submarine warfare.

CHAPTER 8

THE STATUS OF INDIVIDUALS

I. *NATIONALITY AS A LINK BETWEEN INDIVIDUALS AND THE STATE*[1]

§113. INDIVIDUALS IN INTERNATIONAL LAW

The status of individuals has become increasingly important with respect to both their rights and duties in international law. Although the Statute of the International Court of Justice recognizes only states as parties, the provisions of the United Nations Charter and other international instruments have definitely indicated a new trend of giving individuals a more prominent position.[2] Such a development is also

[1] General texts on the subject: O'Connell, II, pp. 728–750; Oppenheim, I, §§288–313a; Jessup, Ch. IV; Fenwick, *Principles,* Ch. XIII, §§C–F; Hyde, II, §§342–398; Moore, *Digest,* IV, §§372–486; Hackworth, *Digest,* III, §§220–258; Schwarzenberger, I, Ch. 5 (III); Starke, Ch. 11, §1; Hershey, Ch. XVII, §§I–III; Whitaker, Ch. 11; Svarlien, Ch. 25; Jacobini, pp. 101–107; Soviet *Text,* Ch. IV, §§1–3; Schuschnigg, Chs. 10–11; Hall, §§66–74, 87; Fauchille, I, §§410–432; Rivier, I, pp. 303–306; Stockton, pp. 175–185; McNair, II, pp. 3–39.

[2] This new trend is evidenced in many international instruments on protection of minorities and on human rights and fundamental freedoms. See *supra,* §11; *infra,* §§123–126. See also the memorandum submitted by the Secretary-General of the United Nations on February 10, 1949, *Survey of International Law in Relation to the Work of Codification of the International Law Commission.* UN Doc. A/CN.4/1/Rev.1.

supported by several prominent publicists, including H. Lauterpacht and Philip C. Jessup. But individuals today have not quite reached the status of subjects of international law. Their relationship to international law is through the link of nationality.

Nationality in its political aspect may be defined as the status of a person bound by the tie of allegiance to a state and entitled to the protection of that state.[3] While nationality is a matter of extreme significance internationally, each state may enact its own laws to prescribe conditions under which a person may acquire or lose his nationality of that state.[4] In like manner, the nationality of business corporations is determined by the municipal laws of each state. Generally the place of incorporation and the control of interests are standards of tests, which are often subject to divergent interpretations and applications by different states.[5] Such issues are properly within the sphere of private international law and not to be discussed here.

[3] The term 'nationality' may also be used in an ethnographical sense, which is not within the scope of the present discussion. The relationship of allegiance to protection was discussed as early as 1608 in *Calvin's Case*. 7 Co. Rep. 1. For further details, see *Nottebohm Case,* International Court of Justice, Preliminary Objection, 1953 (I.C.J. Reports, 1953, p. 111); Second Phase, 1955 (*ibid.*, 1955, p. 4); also *Lynch Claim,* British-Mexican Claims Commission, 1929 (*Annual Digest,* 1929–1930, p. 221). For further discussion, see H. F. van Panhuys, *The Role of Nationality in International Law* (Leiden, 1959).

[4] The exclusive right of a state to enact its own nationality laws is sometimes restricted by international obligations, as evidenced in the advisory opinion of the Permanent Court of International Justice in *Nationality Decrees Issued in Tunis and Morocco,* 1923. P.C.I.J. (1923), Ser. B., No. 4. See also E. M. Borchard, *Diplomatic Protection of Citizens Abroad* (New York, 1915), §§11, 253–262.

[5] In *Bohemian Union Bank v. Administrator of Austrian Property,* the Chancery Division of the British High Court of Justice decided in 1927 that the quasi-nationality of business associations is determined by the rule of location. 2 Ch. 175. Some states determine the national character of a business corporation from its location of home office or place of principal business operations. In *Daimler Co., Ltd. v. Continental Tyre and Rubber Co., Ltd.* (1916), the British House of Lords stressed the principle that a domestic corporation controlled by enemy aliens had the character of an enemy. 2 A.C. 307. The controversy between the United States and Switzerland in the *Interhandel Case* was centered on control of German interests in that Swiss company which, in turn, controlled the General Aniline and Film Corporation in the United States. Thus the American government contended that the company had an enemy character. See I.C.J. Reports (1959), p. 6. This controversy was eventually settled through direct negotiation of the parties concerned.

§114. ACQUISITION OF NATIONALITY

Birth Acquisition of nationality is mainly through birth, even though a person may also acquire nationality of another state by the process of naturalization and other means in accordance with the provisions of its nationality laws and regulations. The principal rules determining nationality by birth are (1) *jus sanguinis* (law of blood), and (2) *jus soli* (law of soil or place). The practices of states may be classified into three groups: (1) solely on *jus sanguinis,* (2) principally on *jus sanguinis* but partly on *jus soli,* and (3) principally on *jus soli* but partly on *jus sanguinis.*[6] It is generally agreed that the rule of *jus soli* is not applied to children born of foreign heads of states or diplomats, or of the occupation forces of an enemy state.

Naturalization Next in importance as a means of acquiring nationality is naturalization, by which an alien may become a national of a state through certain legal process in accordance with its municipal laws. Subject to certain disabilities and restrictions,[7] a naturalized national is generally entitled to the same rights and privileges as the

[6] A ready reference to nationality laws of various countries before World War II is R. W. Flournoy, Jr. and M. O. Hudson, *A Collection of Nationality Laws and Regulations of Various Countries as Contained in Constitutions, Statutes, and Treaties* (New York, 1929). For a survey of nationality laws of the Soviet Union and the Communist states in Eastern Europe, see Soviet *Text,* pp. 154–159. In *United States v. Wong Kim Ark,* the U.S. Supreme Court decided in 1898 that a person born in the United States of Chinese parents was of American nationality by birth. 169 U.S. 649. At the same time, Wong was considered a Chinese national by the Chinese government by the rule of *jus sanguinis.* Thus he had double nationality at time of birth. In the application of *jus soli,* a person born of foreign parents on an American ship outside the territorial waters of the United States was not considered an American national. See *Lam Mow v. Nagle,* U.S. Supreme Court, 1928. 24 F.2d 316. Sometimes both *jus sanguinis* and *jus soli* were applied, as in the case of *Weeden v. Chin Bow.* In deciding the case, the U.S. Supreme Court laid down the rule that a person born abroad of an American parent or parents, who had never resided in the United States, was not of American nationality. 274 U.S. 657.

[7] The Fourteenth Amendment to the Constitution of the United States provides that "all persons born or naturalized in the United States, and subject to the jurisdiction thereof, are citizens of the United States and of the State wherein they reside." But "no person except a natural-born citizen, . . . shall be eligible to the Office of President." Art. II, Sec. 1. There are other restrictions on the rights of naturalized citizens in the United States.

native-born nationals of that state. It is within the competence of domestic legislation of each state to limit the right of naturalization to certain people or races, but any discriminatory act is against international comity and will inevitably result in resentment and retaliation by the government and people of the state concerned.[8] Special consideration is usually given by a state to an alien applying for naturalization if he has been in active service of that state.[9] Naturalization in its broad sense may also include such means of acquiring nationality as marriage, legitimation, adoption, option,[10] acquisition of domicile, and active service in a foreign government. The change of nationality of the population in a certain territory as a result of cession or annexation is actually mass naturalization.[11]

Other modes A person who has lost his original nationality through naturalization or for other causes may regain it on fulfilling certain conditions. This process is called 'redintegration' or 'resump-

[8] The United States formerly limited the right of naturalization to "free white persons" according to the Acts of 1802 and 1824, and later extended it to "aliens of African nationality and to persons of African decent" by the Act of 1870. The so-called "white persons" meant people of "Caucasian race," as ruled by the U.S. Supreme Court in *United States v. Ozawa,* 1922. 260 U.S. 178. The Chinese Exclusion Acts were finally repealed by the Act of December 17, 1943.

[9] Under Title 8 of the U.S. Code, Sec. 1439, an alien who has had at least three years of active military service may apply for American citizenship. He is not required to fulfill the usual provision for five-year residence in the United States and six-month residence in a state. Nor does the usual thirty-day waiting period after filing the petition apply to him. Sec. 1447C, U.S. Code. Carlos Viera, a Havana-born resident in Miami and a survivor of the 1961 Bay of Pigs invasion, obtained American nationality in June 1964 without fulfilling the regular residence requirement. Joseph Minton, an immigration officer, stated that Viera did not break continuity of residence even though imprisoned for twenty-one months after his capture in Cuba. Normally a six-month interruption of residence by going abroad is permissible and not considered as a break in continuity of residence. See *The New York Times,* June 25, 1965.

[10] A recent example was the Protocol on Option appended to the Soviet-Czechoslovakian Agreement of 1945 on the Trans-Carpathian Ukraine.

[11] This was the process applied to the people in territories acquired by the United States. After the annexation of Lithuania, Latvia, and Estonia by the Soviet Union, Soviet nationality was conferred on the peoples of the three states by a decree of September 7, 1940. *Records of the Supreme Soviet of the U.S.S.R.,* 1940, No. 31.

tion.' Another mode of regaining his original nationality is through the revocation of a voluntary expatriation certificate. In some states, a person may keep his original nationality even if he becomes a national of another state through naturalization.[12] On the other hand, renunciation of his original nationality is required by some states in order to complete the legal process of naturalization.[13]

§115. LOSS OF NATIONALITY

Nationality may be lost through the various modes of naturalization by which a person renounces his original nationality and acquires a new nationality of another state.[14] Mass deprivation of nationality was practiced by the Soviet Union,[15] Germany, and several other countries after World War I by denationalizing a large number of their nationals abroad who were deemed undesirable elements on various grounds. Sometimes, a person may lose his nationality through revocation of his naturalization or redintegration certificate.[16] Formerly, a

[12] A British subject naturalized in a foreign state does not automatically lose his British nationality without renunciation on his part in accordance with the British Nationality Act of 1948.

[13] This is the practice of the United States and many other countries. According to the American Nationality Act of 1952, an American national naturalized in a foreign state loses his American nationality. Robert E. Webster of Ohio lost his American citizenship when he became a Soviet national. Later he wanted to return to the United States. American immigration officials advised him that he could return to the United States under the Russian immigration quota and that, if he desired to resume American nationality, he would have to meet the residence requirement for naturalization. See *The New York Times,* May 26, 1960.

[14] Sometimes a person may lose his original nationality without acquiring another. See *Rajdberg v. Lewi,* Poland, Supreme Court, 1927. *Annual Digest,* 1927–1928, No. 209. Having lost his Soviet nationality, the plaintiff became a stateless person.

[15] By decrees issued by the Presidium of the Supreme Soviet in 1945, 1946, and 1947, the Soviet Union restored Soviet nationality to those who lost Russian nationality while domiciled in Manchuria, Japan, France, Czechoslovakia, Bulgaria, Yugoslavia, and Belgium. See Soviet *Text,* p. 156. The Indonesian government recently withdrew citizenship from its former Ambassador to Peking, Djawato, who resigned in protest against the policy of the Indonesian government toward Communist China. It is not clear whether loss of citizenship will deprive him of his Indonesian nationality. See *The New York Times,* April 17, 19, 1966. On July 12, 1967, eight Greek expatriates, including actress Melina Mercouri, were deprived of Greek citizenship by the military regime in Athens on charges of "engaging in anti-national activities." See *ibid.,* July 13, 1967.

[16] The penalty of denaturalization applied to naturalized citizens as

naturalized citizen of the United States who left the country and resided in his native state for two years or in any other foreign state for five years was presumed to have renounced his nationality unless he had complied with the rules fixed by the State Department to rebut such a presumption.[17] This statute was declared unconstitutional by the Supreme Court in the case of Mrs. Angelika Schneider in 1964.[18]

The traditional principle of indissoluble allegiance has now given way to the right of voluntary expatriation by the nationals of modern states. Expatriation may be effected with or without the consent of the state of one's birth in accordance with its nationality law. But no state at war will allow its nationals to expatriate themselves whose services are urgently needed.[19]

§116. MULTIPLE NATIONALITY AND STATELESSNESS

Double or multiple nationality Due to the divergent practices of *jus sanguinis* and *jus soli*, a person may be born of double nationality. In *United States v. Wong Kim Ark*,[20] Wong was born of Chinese parents in American territory. Thus, he obtained the nationality of both countries.[21] A person may even have quadruple nationality if he is born of a Chinese father and a Turkish mother on board a British ship in an

---

practiced in the United States and other countries is also a source of statelessness.

[17] 34 Stat. 1928.

[18] Mrs. Schneider, a naturalized American, lost her nationality because she returned to Germany, her original country, and resided there. The U.S. Supreme Court, by a 5–3 vote on May 18, 1964, restored her American nationality. Probably many thousands will benefit by this decision. See *The New York Times*, May 19, 1964.

[19] Until 1870, traditional English common law denied the right of a subject to transfer his allegiance to a foreign state. China held the same principle before her promulgation of the first nationality law of 1909. For an analysis of Chinese nationality laws, see William L. Tung, *China and Some Phases of International Law* (New York & London, 1940), pp. 85–101. For an early ruling by an American court denying the right of expatriation without government consent, see *Williams' Case*, United States, Circuit Court, District of Connecticut, 1799. 2 Cranch 88. The U.S. Congress adopted a joint resolution in 1868 to declare expatriation an inherent right of all people. 15 Stat. 223.

[20] U.S. Supreme Court, 1898. 169 U.S. 649.

[21] The actress Elizabeth Taylor is another instance of double nationality, because she was born of American parents in London in 1932. For her giving up American nationality without open forswearing of allegiance, see *The New York Times*, January 10, 1965. See also Nissim Bar-Yaacov, *Dual Nationality* (London, 1961).

American port.[22] The problem of double or multiple nationality has caused considerable difficulty to the persons and states concerned, especially with respect to military service and diplomatic protection.

In order to alleviate this complicated situation, the Hague Codification Conference adopted a Convention on Certain Questions relating to the Conflict of Nationality Laws and a Protocol relating to Military Obligations in Certain Cases of Double Nationality.[23] According to the Convention, a state is not to give diplomatic protection to any of its nationals against a state whose nationality that person also possesses. Such a person with double nationality may renounce one with the consent of the state concerned.[24] The Protocol permits a person of double or multiple nationality to fulfill his military obligation in one country only, subject to the loss of nationality in other countries.[25] Although these two instruments were ratified by only a small number of states, groundwork was laid for the conclusion of bilateral treaties to incorporate these principles and for further deliberation by future international conferences.[26]

[22] This would happen through application of the rule of *jus sanguinis* by China (Art. 1 of the Chinese Nationality Law of 1929) and Turkey (Art. 1 of the Turkish Nationality Law of 1928), and that of *jus soli* by the United States or by Great Britain, which considers a British ship a floating portion of her territory.

[23] For their texts, see 24 *Am. Jour. Int. Law* (1930), Supp., p. 201; Hudson, *Int. Legislation,* V, p. 374.

[24] Arts. 4, 6, of the Convention. In *United States (William MacKenzie) v. Germany,* the Mixed Claims Commission ruled in 1926 that if a person of double nationality wanted to renounce one, he must proceed in accordance with the methods prescribed by statute. *Decisions and Opinions of the Commission,* p. 628. The Tribunal of the Permanent Court of Arbitration held the same principle in *The Canevaro Case* in 1912. Thus, a Peruvian born in Peru of Italian parents could not assert his Italian nationality, especially in view of the fact that he had chosen Peruvian rather than Italian citizenship when he ran for the Senate and occupied other public offices in the Peruvian government. Scott, *Hague Court Reports* (1916), p. 284. In its notice to bearers of American passports on July 1, 1928, the State Department warned American citizens residing in other countries whose nationality they also possessed that the United States could not protect them through diplomatic representation in view of the legal right of such countries to their allegiance. This was a departure from previous policy of the United States in the case of Christian Ernst in 1859. See Moore, *Digest,* III, p. 573.

[25] Art. 1.

[26] A number of multilateral instruments have been concluded directly or indirectly relating to the subject, including the Convention on the Nationality of Married Women of February 20, 1957, and the Optional Protocol

Statelessness A person may become stateless through deprivation of his nationality by the state of his birth, the revocation of his naturalization or redintegration certificate, or other causes. Sometimes a child is stateless at the time of his birth.[27] Much injustice has been done to such stateless persons, who may suffer all kinds of hardship and mistreatment without protection from any state.[28] The two protocols concerning statelessness, adopted by the Hague Codification Conference in 1930,[29] provide certain means toward relieving the hardship of stateless persons. Under these protocols a person born in a state whose nationality his mother possesses obtains the nationality of that state even if his father has no nationality.[30] As to the stipulation that a state which deprives the nationality of a person staying in another state is obliged to admit him upon the request of that state, it is ineffective in its actual application. The above-mentioned Convention on Certain Questions relating to the Conflict of Nationality Laws prescribes that an expatriated person does not lose his original nationality unless and until he obtains a nationality of another state.[31]

---

concerning Acquisition of Nationality of April 18, 1961. The United States-Norwegian Treaty of November 1, 1930, provides exemption from military service and other acts of allegiance of a person with nationality of both Norway and the United States by the country not of his birth, but only for temporary stay. In the Exchange of Notes annexed to the Consular Convention relative to the Possessions and Colonies of the Netherlands, signed by China and the Netherlands on May 8, 1911, the Chinese government recognized the principle that Chinese residents in the Dutch East Indies of both Chinese and Dutch nationality should be subject to the jurisdiction of the country where they were domiciled. An agreement was reached on the same subject between Indonesia and the People's Republic of China in 1955. Selection of nationality based on permanent domicile of persons of double nationality in the Soviet Union and Yugoslavia was agreed upon by the two countries in 1956. Determination of nationality without distinction of sex was emphasized in the Convention on the Nationality of Women, adopted at the Conference of American States at Montevideo in 1933.

[27] In some countries, children born of persons without any nationality are themselves stateless. Under certain circumstances, an illegitimate child may be stateless.

[28] It was reported in 1959 that there were at least eight thousand stateless persons roaming the world's seaways. They must accept low pay and remain virtually prisoners of their ships because of their unfortunate status. See *The New York Times,* July 23, 1959.

[29] See *supra,* §17.

[30] Art. 1 of the Protocol relating to a Certain Case of Statelessness.

[31] For a person who became stateless during the period between the renunciation of his original nationality and acquisition of another, see *Stoeck v. Public Trustee,* Great Britain, High Court of Justice, 1921. 2 Ch. 67.

For the mitigation of the unfortunate consequences of statelessness, certain measures were included in the Convention relating to the International Status of Refugees of 1933 and the Convention on the Status of Refugees of 1951.[32] The Universal Declaration of Human Rights of 1948 emphatically stresses the right of nationality of every person against any arbitrary deprivation.[33] The Draft Conventions of 1953 on the Elimination of Statelessness and on the Reduction of Statelessness represent the efforts of the International Law Commission of the United Nations to ensure that every person may have the nationality of the country of his birth and that states must not use deprivation of nationality as a means of punishment.[34] These principles have been incorporated into the Convention relating to the Status of Stateless Persons of September 28, 1954, and the Convention on the Reduction of Statelessness of August 30, 1961.[35]

II. *STATE JURISDICTION OVER INDIVIDUALS* [36]

§117. JURISDICTION OVER NATIONALS ABROAD

Subject to the provisions of minority treaties and other international conventions, a state has absolute jurisdiction over its resident nationals.[37] The situation is slightly different with non-resident nationals,

[32] The Convention of 1933 specially dealt with the treatment of Russian, Armenian, and assimilated refugees, who were granted the so-called Nansen passports. For the text of this Convention, see LN *Treaty Series* (1937), No. 4. The Convention of 1951 is broader in scope but does not apply to those who became refugees after January 1, 1951. UN Doc. A/Conf.2/108.

[33] Art. 15. [34] UN Docs. A/CN.4/63, A/CN.4/75.

[35] For further discussion, see P. Weis, *Nationality and Statelessness in International Law* (London, 1956); C. Seekler-Hudson, *Statelessness with Special Reference to the United States* (Washington, D.C., 1934).

[36] General texts on the subject: O'Connell, II, pp. 751–791; Oppenheim, I, §§314–326; Fenwick, *Principles,* Ch. XIII, §§G–J; Brierly, Ch. VI, §§5–6; Hyde, I, §§59–64A; Moore, *Digest,* IV, §§534–578; Hackworth, *Digest,* III, §§277–303; Starke, Ch. 11, §2; Gould, Ch. 15; Von Glahn, Ch. 13; Soviet *Text,* Ch. IV, §4; Sen, Ch. XII; Lawrence, §§93, 97–98; Grotius, II, Bk. 2, Chs. 20–21; Vattel, III, Bk. 2, Ch. 8; Pufendorf, II, Bk. 8, Chs. 1–3; Westlake, I, pp. 215–217, 252–261; Mérignhac, II, pp. 732–778; Nys, II, pp. 275–303.

[37] Under special circumstances, nationals may be kept from traveling to certain countries by being refused passports. This right of the United States government was upheld by the Supreme Court in a ruling concerning the travel ban to Cuba on May 3, 1965. See *The New York Times,* May 6,

who are, nonetheless, entitled to the protection of and bound by the tie of allegiance to their state. They have the obligation to testify in its courts,[38] and pay income taxes to their home government even though their income or property might be subject to taxation by the state of their domicile.[39] The hardship of double taxation has been recognized by various states and gradually alleviated by international agreements and domestic legislation.

With respect to criminal offenses committed by nationals abroad, they should be punished by the state where the laws have been violated, especially in view of the fact that acts illegal in one state may be lawful in another.[40] It was through consideration of this principle and of international comity that the United States Supreme Court declared it improper to expect a foreign state to enforce an anti-monopoly statute of the United States.[41] However, in *United States v. Sisal Sales Corp.* in 1927,[42] the same court assumed jurisdiction over the case because the criminal acts were committed partly in the United States and partly abroad.

§118. PROTECTION OF NATIONAL MINORITIES

The protection of national minorities is usually provided in constitutions and international conventions. Although the matter is within the competence of the domestic legislation of each state,[43] the contract-

---

1965. The part of the Internal Security Act of 1950 denying passports to members of the American Communist party and its fronts was ruled unconstitutional by the Supreme Court on June 22, 1964. See *ibid.*, June 23, 1964.

[38] In *Blackmer v. United States*, the U.S. Supreme Court decided in 1932 that an American national had the obligation to return to his country to give testimony in its courts. *Cf.* the decision of the British Court of Common Pleas in *Douglas v. Forrest* in 1828. 4 Bingham 686.

[39] See *Cook v. Tait*, U.S. Supreme Court, 1924. 265 U.S. 47.

[40] See *People v. Werblow*, U.S. Court of Appeals of New York, 1925. 241 N.Y. 55. However, crimes committed by nationals of a state in its diplomatic premises abroad (fictitious territory of that state) are under the jurisdiction of that state. See *Public Prosecutor v. Wang Min-yao and Sung Chen-wu*, China, District Court of Taipei, 1965. (File No.: 54th Yr., Shu—2107.) 60 *Am. Jour. Int. Law* (1966), p. 411.

[41] *American Banana Co. v. United Fruit* Co., U.S. Supreme Court, 1909. 213 U.S. 347.

[42] 274 U.S. 268.

[43] The protection of national minorities is affirmed in the domestic legislation of the Communist countries. See Soviet *Text*, p. 141. In Communist

ing parties are also bound by their treaty obligations.[44] After World War I, equal and just treatment of racial, religious, and linguistic minorities was guaranteed in treaties by the Allied and Associated Powers with Austria-Hungary, Bulgaria, Czechoslovakia, Greece, Poland, Rumania, Turkey, and Yugoslavia.[45] According to the Convention of November 27, 1919, between Greece and Bulgaria, people of racial, religious, and linguistic minorities were allowed to migrate freely from one state to another.[46] These minority treaties were placed under the guarantee of the League of Nations. Although many complaints were presented to and examined by the League, actual protection of the rights of national minorities depended largely on the good faith of the states concerned.

The treaties concluded by the Allied Powers with Finland, Italy, Bulgaria, Hungary, and Rumania after World War II provide broad protection of all persons against any racial, religious, or linguistic discrimination and for the promotion of human rights. These principles are also specifically embodied in the Charter of the United Nations. It should be noted that resident aliens of different racial, religious, and linguistic origins are not considered under the same category of national minorities.[47] The provisions of human rights in the peace treaties were tested during the period 1948–1950, when complaints of violations were brought before the United Nations against Bulgaria, Hungary, and Rumania. It was proved that the United Nations could do little in these cases short of forcible enforcement.[48] These two international or-

---

China, provisions to this effect may be found in the Common Program of 1949, the Constitution of 1954, and other laws and regulations. See William L. Tung, *The Political Institutions of Modern China* (The Hague, 1964), pp. 276–277, 306–308.

[44] In the Treaty of Berlin of 1878, Bulgaria, Rumania, Montenegro, and Serbia agreed not to impose religious disabilities on any of their nationals.

[45] See the Advisory Opinion on the *Jurisdiction of the Courts of Danzig*, Permanent Court of International Justice, 1928. P.C.I.J. (1928), Ser. B, No. 15. See also the Advisory Opinions of the Permanent Court of International Justice on the *German Settlers in Poland* in 1923 (P.C.I.J., Ser. B, No. 6); and the *Minority Schools in Albania* in 1935 (*ibid.*, Ser. A/B, No. 64).

[46] See the Advisory Opinion on the *Exchange of Greek and Turkish Population*, Permanent Court of International Justice, 1925. P.C.I.J. (1925), Ser. B, No. 10.

[47] For the attitude of the American states on this subject, see the Lima Declaration on Foreign Minorities of 1938. *International Conferences of American States, 1933–1940* (Washington, D.C., 1940), p. 256.

[48] See the Advisory Opinion on the *Interpretation of Peace Treaties with Bulgaria, Hungary, and Rumania of 1947*, International Court of Justice, 1950. I.C.J. Reports (1950), 65, 221.

ganizations have, however, made continuing efforts to ensure the well-being of the minorities.[49]

§119. JURISDICTION OVER ALIENS

The admission of aliens to the territory of a state is not obligatory under international law. A state may exclude all aliens or certain undesirable persons,[50] but any discrimination against the admission of any special races or nationalities is bound to create repercussions.[51] The quota system of the United States, by apportioning the number of immigrants from different countries, shows a distinctive preference of

[49] The United Nations set up a Subcommission on Prevention of Discrimination and Protection of Minorities in charge of these matters.

[50] See *Musgrove v. Chun Teeong Toy,* Great Britain, Judicial Committee of the Privy Council, 1891. [1891] A.C. 272. The U.S. Supreme Court held the same position in *Nishimura Ekiu v. United States,* 1892 (142 U.S. 651), and *Fong Yue Ting v. United States,* 1893 (149 U.S. 698). Because of her repeated statements against American policy in Vietnam, the State Department denied Mrs. Ngo Dinh Nhu's request for a six-month visit in June 1964 after the fall of President Ngo Dinh Diem in South Vietnam. See *The New York Times,* June 25, 1964. In the past, seclusion of a state represented a policy of complete isolation from the outside world and, as a result, no aliens would be welcome to that state. The reluctance of China, Japan, and Korea to receive aliens in early days was largely due to lack of understanding between the East and the West. To understand misconceptions of China's absolute seclusion and contempt for foreigners, see William L. Tung, *China and Some Phases of International Law,* pp. 56–58.

[51] Since 1880, the United States has enacted a series of laws excluding the immigration of Chinese and other specified races from Asia. The decision of the U.S. Supreme Court in the *Chinese Exclusion Case* (130 U.S. 581) in 1889 was actually in conflict with the Sino-American treaties of 1868 and 1880. Popular indignation in China culminated in the boycott of American goods in 1905. The United States eventually concluded treaties with China and Japan in 1894 and 1907 respectively to prevent immigration of laborers from these two countries. The political wisdom of the American policy of excluding the so-called unassimilable races was questionable. Aside from *apartheid* policy, the Republic of South Africa has imposed discriminatory restrictions upon Indians and Chinese and thus created deep resentment not only among those population groups but also by the governments of India and China. For arbitrary classification of Asian people of different racial origins, see *The New York Times,* August 1, 1965. The immigration policy of Australia is now under review by the order of Prime Minister Harold Holt, with the possibility of relaxing traditional restrictions against non-white immigrants. See *ibid.,* February 24, 1966.

certain races to others.[52] It is an irony of history that a land of immigrants should have imposed the strictest restrictions upon later comers who try to seek freedom and democracy in a country long advocating such causes.[53]

The enactment of immigration laws is within the competence of the legislature, which generally authorizes an immigration office to take charge of their execution and administration.[54] The determination of questions of fact by the proper administrative authorities is controlling in the absence of any abuse of discretion.[55] Once admitted, an alien is entitled to the equal protection of the laws of the country. In *Truax v. Raich* in 1915,[56] the United States Supreme Court ruled that no state might deny to any alien the ordinary means of earning a livelihood because of race or nationality. On the other hand, a state has the sovereign right to expel or deport any alien whose entry is found illegal or whose presence is opposed to its security and interests.[57] An alien cannot be

[52] The present quota system based on the Immigration Act of 1924 has long been under criticism, and a new law initiated by President Johnson through his message to Congress on January 13, 1965, is under consideration in Congress. Under the present system, even Columbus might not be able to get a visa to the United States as a quota immigrant.

[53] Reference may be made to a pamphlet, *A Nation of Immigrants,* written by John F. Kennedy when he was junior Senator from Massachusetts. An excerpt can be found in *The New York Times Sunday Magazine,* August 4, 1963. As President, Kennedy acted toward carrying out his ideas by calling on Congress to abolish the present quota system.

[54] A uniform immigration law for Central America was presented to the Conference of Ministers of Interior and Security Officials of Guatemala, El Salvador, Honduras, Nicaragua, and Costa Rica at Panama in July 1965. It would be a unique feature in international relations if the proposed law were approved by the five governments. See *The New York Times,* July 25, 1965.

[55] See *United States v. Ju Toy,* U.S. Supreme Court, 1905. 198 U.S. 253.

[56] 239 U.S. 33. Foreign students in the United States are not allowed to engage in part-time work without special approval by the immigration authorities. For the expulsion of seventeen Japanese and Korean students on this ground, see *The New York Times,* June 13, 1965. For the responsibility of states to protect aliens, see *supra,* §77.

[57] The government of Indonesia expelled a young American woman of the Peace Corps in April 1965, because "Indonesia does not need the Peace Corps," according to a government statement. *The New York Times,* September 5, 1965. See also the Pan-American Convention on the Status of Aliens of February 20, 1928. Hudson, *Int. Legislation,* IV, p. 2377. In peacetime, expulsion of an alien must be based upon justified reasons. Otherwise, his native state may make diplomatic representation on his behalf. See the *Boffolo Case,* Italy-Venezuela, Arbitration before the Italian-Venezuelan

kept from voluntary departure if he has paid taxes and fulfilled all other obligations required by the state of his temporary sojourn.[58]

The rights and duties of aliens depend upon the laws and regulations of the different countries. While political rights are generally reserved for citizens, aliens are entitled to all civil privileges, subject to certain restrictions, such as the purchase of land or the performance of certain professional practices.[59] However, such restrictions should not be applied to a particular group on racial or religious grounds.[60] Since aliens are entitled to the protection of their residing states, they are under obligation to pay taxes and to perform duties required by law. Whether they may be exempted from military service of the state of their domicile depends upon the provisions of the prevailing laws of that state and of its treaties with their home state.[61]

Mixed Claims Commission, 1903. Ralston, *Venezuelan Arbitrations*, p. 699. In wartime, a belligerent may find it necessary to expel all nationals of the enemy state or intern them for the duration of hostilities. There is a technical difference between expulsion and reconduction: the former is "an order to leave the country," while the latter is "forcible conveying away of foreigners." See Oppenheim, I, pp. 694–695.

[58] It was reported that about two hundred aircraft experts of West German nationality were barred from leaving the United Arab Republic in July 1965. The matter was complicated by certain contract obligations between the government of the United Arab Republic and Hassan Sayed Kamil, an Egyptian-born Swiss industrialist who hired the experts. See *The New York Times*, July 30, 1965.

[59] In the *Case of Nina Sukostor*, the Supreme Court of China ruled in 1933 that procedural relief would be granted an alien either by treaty or if the law of his own country gave the same privileges to Chinese nationals. *A Collection of the Decisions of the Chinese Supreme Court* [in Chinese], Ser. 24, p. 14; English translation from Tung, p. 117. See also *Jordan v. Tashiro*, U.S. Supreme Court, 1928. 278 U.S. 123. For restrictions of political and civil rights of aliens in the Soviet Union, see Soviet *Text*, p. 163.

[60] Japan strongly protested against the discriminatory nature of San Francisco's segregating Japanese students in separate schools in 1906 and of California's excluding the purchase of real estate by aliens not eligible to citizenship in 1913. See Hackworth, *Digest*, III, p. 755; 8 *Am. Jour. Int. Law* (1914), p. 571.

[61] Some states disqualify an alien from eligibility to citizenship if his exemption or discharge from military service is granted at his request on the ground of his alien status. See Section 315(a) of the United States Immigration and Nationality Act of 1952. An alien may be considered as not residing in the state for the purposes of his liability to military service. See *McGrath v. Kristensen*, U.S. Supreme Court, 1950. 340 U.S. 162. In *Polites v. The Commonwealth of Australia*, the Australian High Court decided in 1945 to give effect to a Parliamentary Act to impose military service

An alien owes temporary allegiance to the state of his sojourn and is subject to its local jurisdiction. In *Ford v. United States* in 1927,[62] the United States Supreme Court went so far as to state that an alien outside American territory conspiring to commit unlawful acts against the United States might be prosecuted when he was brought into the country.[63] According to a controversial decision of the Permanent Court of International Justice in the case of *The Lotus* in 1927,[64] a state could even institute criminal proceedings against aliens on a foreign ship on the high seas if they had committed acts producing harmful results on a ship of that state and consequently in a place assimilated to its territory.

The temporary allegiance of an alien to the state of his domicile does not cease if its territory is invaded by an enemy. Any aid to the enemy constitutes an act of treason and will be punished by the state after its recovery of the invaded territory.[65] This principle is inherent in a state's right of self-preservation. In *Joyce v. Director of Public Prosecutors* in 1946,[66] the British House of Lords upheld the decision of the lower court to convict Joyce, an American-born alien with a British passport, who committed an act of treason outside British territory by broadcasting for Germany, then at war with Great Britain. The British court emphasized the bond between Joyce and Great Britain by his possession of a British passport, which he obtained by claiming to be a British subject.

---

on resident aliens. *Annual Digest,* 1943–1945, No. 61. All resident aliens in the United States are now subject to the draft and no exemption or waiver has been granted since 1956.

[62] 273 U.S. 593.

[63] See, however, the American attitude in *The Cutting Case,* Mexico, Bravos District Court, Chihuahua, 1886. Moore, *Report on Extraterritorial Crime and the Cutting Case,* p. 9. In this case, the United States protested against the jurisdiction of a Mexican court over an American for an alleged libel committed in the United States. Although the Mexican government rejected the American demand for his release, he was set free because of withdrawal of the suit by the plaintiff.

[64] P.C.I.J. (1927), Ser. A, No. 10. The principle of this case was not adopted by the International Convention for Certain Rules relating to Penal Jurisdiction in Matters of Collision or Other Incidents of Navigation of 1952 (Brussels Convention, Cmd. 8954), nor was it approved by the Geneva Convention on the High Seas of 1958.

[65] See *De Jager v. Attorney General of Natal,* Great Britain, Judicial Committee of the Privy Council, 1907. [1907] A.C. 326.

[66] [1946] A.C. 347. For further discussion of limitations on the criminal jurisdiction of a state, see Brierly, pp. 299–304.

§120. EXTRATERRITORIAL JURISDICTION IN ASIAN AND AFRICAN COUNTRIES

This unilateral system of extraterritorial jurisdiction was imposed by Western powers on certain Asian and African countries in the past. Also known as 'capitulations' or 'consular jurisdiction,' it was practiced in Turkey, Japan, Egypt, Iran, Morocco, Thailand, and China, exempting resident aliens from the local jurisdiction of such countries.[67] Instead, Western nationals were tried by their respective consular officials and, in Shanghai and Egypt, by mixed courts.[68]

Such an intrusion on national sovereignty was justified on the ground of the fundamental differences of civil and criminal codes as well as judicial systems between the West and other countries. Nevertheless, states enjoying this privilege never reciprocated in the case of other nationals. Extremely dissatisfied with the abuses inherent in this abnormal situation, states affected struggled for its abolition.[69] Al-

[67] Extraterritorial jurisdiction was first established in the Ottoman Empire in the sixteenth century, because its laws based on the Koran could not appropriately apply to Western Christians resident in Turkey. For arguments that the origin of consular jurisdiction was based on custom as distinguished from treaty rights, see the *Rights of Nationals of the United States of America in Morocco,* International Court of Justice, 1952. I.C.J. Reports (1952), 93.

[68] Extraterritorial jurisdiction was also known as consular jurisdiction, because it was exercised by consular officials. The mixed courts in Egypt were a complicated system, fully described in J. H. Scott, *The Law Affecting Foreigners in Egypt,* rev. ed. (Edinburgh, 1908). Much literature has been written on extraterritorial jurisdiction. For a survey and bibliography, see Hyde, II, pp. 849–871. China's denunciation of the Sino-Belgian Treaty of November 2, 1865, providing for extraterritorial justification, was brought to the Permanent Court of International Justice, which upheld the Belgian contention by a provisional order of January 8, 1927. Later, the Belgian government withdrew the case as a result of the conclusion with China of a new treaty of November 22, 1928. P.C.I.J. (1927), Ser. A, No. 8; *Annual Digest,* 1927–1928, Nos. 350, 351.

[69] Through prolonged and frustrating negotiations, this unilateral system of extraterritorial jurisdiction was first abolished by Japan in 1899 and finally came to an end in 1943, when the United States and Great Britain signed treaties with China on January 11, 1943, for its relinquishment. It should be noted that, following the October Revolution, the Soviet government renounced extraterritorial jurisdiction obtained by Tsarist Russia. An analytical study of extraterritorial jurisdiction in China can be found in Shih-shun Liu, *Extraterritoriality, Its Rise and Its Decline* (New York, 1925). For a brief description of the status of aliens in China prior to 1842, see

though the subject is now of historical interest only, it has constituted a source of resentment against Western imperialism.

III. *ASYLUM AND EXTRADITION* [70]

§121. THE RIGHT OF ASYLUM

Asylum in general The so-called right of asylum is the granting of shelter and protection by one state to aliens who are political offenders or even ordinary criminals in the absence of extradition treaties.[71] While the right to grant asylum within the territorial domain is generally recognized, the practices of nations vary in extraterritorial cases either on their ships outside territorial waters or in their diplomatic and consular premises abroad. With the exception of Latin-American countries,[72] states generally refrain from granting extraterritorial asylum in order to avoid conflicting claims of national sovereignty and territorial jurisdiction of the states concerned.[73] It is noteworthy that no such right

---

V. K. Wellington Koo, *The Status of Aliens in China* (New York, 1912), pp. 63–64.

[70] General texts on the subject: O'Connell, II, pp. 792–815; Oppenheim, I, §327–340a; Fenwick, *Principles,* Ch. XVII; Hyde, II, §§310–341, 443–443A; Moore, *Digest,* II, §§291–307; IV, §§579–622; Hackworth, *Digest,* II, §§191–196; IV, §§304–348; Starke, Ch. 11, §3; Hershey, Ch. XVII, §§IV–V; Von Glahn, Ch. 15; Jacobini, pp. 99–100, 107–110, 188–189; Soviet *Text,* pp. 167–168; Sen, Ch. XIV; Schuschnigg, Ch. 12; McNair, II, pp. 40–76.

[71] This subject has been under study by the International Law Commission of the United Nations. For the surrender of ordinary criminals and extradition treaties, see *infra,* §122. The so-called *Franchise du Quartier,* an ancient custom claimed by certain embassies in Europe but completely abandoned at the end of the seventeenth century, implied "the right to prevent the arrest of persons dwelling in the vicinity of their embassy, and the exemption from octroi tax of supplies brought in nominally for their use." Satow, p. 223. The taking of bast or shelter in a foreign legation was a custom in Persia as a way of expressing grievances. An interesting incident concerning an attempt by the wives of the Shah to seek shelter in the British legation in Tehran was recorded in the *Biography of Sir Mortimer Durand,* former British Minister to Persia. See *ibid.*, p. 225.

[72] For details, consult C. Neale Ronning, *Diplomatic Asylum. Legal Norms and Political Reality in Latin American Relations* (The Hague, 1965).

[73] Among early disputes of this nature was serious friction between France and Venice over the forced surrender and persecution of three Venetians who took refuge in the French embassy in Venice in 1540. See

is provided in the Vienna Convention on Diplomatic Relations of 1961.

Territorial asylum Permission or refusal of territorial asylum is usually within the competence of domestic legislation in the absence of international agreements.[74] Almost all states have admitted aliens of one category or another seeking refuge in their territories for political and humanitarian reasons.[75] The right of asylum has been provided for in the fundamental laws of many countries after World War II, such as the French Constitution of 1946 and the Italian Constitution of 1947. The constitutions of the Soviet Union and the People's Republic of China lay special emphasis on granting asylum to foreign Communists.[76] At the same time, Western states have also extended political asylum to foreign Communists who deserted their homeland for political reasons.[77]

Stuart, p. 123. For the controversy between Colombia and Peru over Haya de la Torre, known as the *Asylum Case,* decided by the International Court of Justice in 1950, see I.C.J. Reports (1950), p. 266.

[74] For extradition treaties, see *infra,* §122.

[75] For instance, the government of Congo (Kinshasa) announced, on March 31, 1965, that it would grant asylum to Rev. Fulbert Youlou, ousted President of the neighboring Congo Republic (Brazzaville). See *The New York Times,* April 1, 1965.

[76] Art. 129 of the Soviet Constitution specifies aliens "persecuted for defending the interests of the working people, or for scientific activities, or for struggling for national liberation." The granting of asylum in China to foreign political refugees is provided in the Communist Constitution of 1931 and of 1954, and also in the Common Program of 1949. See William L. Tung, *The Political Institutions of Modern China,* pp. 161, 268, 284. For the Soviet view of the right of asylum as practiced in socialist and capitalist countries, see Soviet *Text,* pp. 164–166.

[77] There are numerous instances in the postwar period. Yuri I. Nossenko, a ranking member of the Soviet secret police attached to the Soviet delegation to the Disarmament Conference at Geneva, sought political refuge in the United States in February 1964. Semyon K. Tsarapkin, the Soviet chief delegate, accused the Swiss authorities of unwillingness to prevent the departure of Nossenko from Switzerland. See *The New York Times,* February 11, 13, 1964. A young Estonian sailor, Viktor Jaanimets, who jumped ship from Premier Khrushchev's liner, *Baltika,* in New York on October 10, 1960, was granted political asylum in the United States. Khrushchev took it philosophically with a remark that if the sailor "had approached me on shipboard, I would have given him some money for the first period until he finds a job." *Ibid.,* October 13, 1960. Vladimir Ilyich Ponomarev, a Soviet citizen working for UNESCO, was granted political asylum in Great

The Universal Declaration of Human Rights of 1948 specifically provides that "every one has the right to seek and to enjoy in other countries asylum from persecution," with the exception of cases "genuinely arising from non-political crimes or from acts contrary to the purposes and principles of the United Nations." [78] It must be understood that asylum is not to be granted to persons who have committed war crimes or genocide. In accordance with the Geneva Convention on the Status of Refugees of 1951, asylum will be given to those who are unable or unwilling to return to their original countries because of "well-founded fear of being persecuted for reasons of race, religion, nationality, membership of a particular social group or political opinions." [79]

As a clear standard of political or non-political crime is difficult to determine, some discretion must be left to the administrative and judicial authorities of the individual states. Once persons are granted asylum in another state, they must observe the laws and regulations of the receiving state and refrain from engaging in any political activities which may embarrass the relations between the host and their original countries.[80]

Taking note of the draft declaration on territorial asylum submitted by its Sixth Committee, the twenty-first session of the General Assembly paid serious attention to the subject. A resolution was unanimously adopted on December 16, 1966, to place that item on the provisional agenda of its next session with a view to the final adoption of a declaration.[81] Meanwhile, the Secretary-General was requested to transmit the draft declaration and the Committee report to Members of the United Nations for their further consideration.

Britain on November 10, 1964. *Ibid.*, November 11, 1964. The State Department announced on September 11, 1964, that Professor Heinz Barwich, a senior East German nuclear physicist long associated with Soviet research, was granted asylum in the United States. *Ibid.*, September 12, 1964. Svetlana Alliluyeva, Stalin's daughter, came to the United States on April 21, 1967. She was admitted on a visitor's visa. Thus, technically, the problem of political asylum was not invoked. However, the State Department made it clear that she would be "free to remain here as long as she wishes." *Ibid.*, April 22, 1967.

[78] Art. 14. See also M. R. Garcia-Mora, *International Law and Asylum as a Human Right* (Washington, D.C., 1956).

[79] Art. 1-A(2).

[80] After his abortive flight to Latin America on December 3, 1964, and return to Spain, Juan D. Perón, former Argentine dictator, pledged in writing to refrain from any political activity while in the territory of Spain. See *The New York Times*, December 25, 1964.

[81] GA res. 2203 (XXI).

Extraterritorial asylum In view of past abuses and complaints arising from the granting of extraterritorial asylum, even the Latin-American states have deemed it advisable to lay down certain restrictions. Thus, the Havana Convention on Asylum, adopted at the Sixth International Conference of American States in 1928, limits the right of granting asylum in diplomatic premises, warships, military camps, and military aircraft only to political offenders, under urgent circumstances, and for the shortest period indispensable to their safety.[82] In signing this Convention, the United States categorically declined to regard the so-called doctrine of asylum as part of international law.

Even though the Latin-American states have endorsed the principle in other Pan-American conventions in subsequent years,[83] the asylum granted by the Colombian embassy in Lima to a Peruvian political refugee, Haya de la Torre, developed into a serious dispute between the two countries. It was submitted to the International Court of Justice for adjudication in 1950,[84] but was not settled until his eventual departure from Lima through a safe-conduct in 1954.[85] In spite of the undesirable consequences, some embassies, particularly in Latin America, have been crowded with refugees at times of political upheaval.[86] To alleviate this situation, the embassies concerned should negotiate with the receiving state to provide the political offenders with safe-

[82] For the text of the Convention, see 20 *Am. Jour. Int. Law* (1928), Supp., p. 158.

[83] *E.g.*, the twenty American states signed in 1954 the Convention on Diplomatic Asylum at Caracas, confirming their traditional principle of asylum.

[84] I.C.J. Reports (1950), p. 266.

[85] The two countries signed an agreement in March 1954, providing Haya de la Torre with a safe-conduct, by which he succeeded in leaving Lima for Mexico City in April of the same year.

[86] President Manuel Urrutia Lleo of Cuba announced on January 7, 1959, that three hundred members of the former Batista regime taking political asylum in the embassies in Havana would be given safe-conduct to leave the country. See *The New York Times*, January 8, 1959. Many incidents occurred in 1960 alone. On February 24, seventeen Dominicans took refuge in the Brazilian embassy in Ciudad Truillo. *Ibid.*, February 25, 28, 1960. On July 5, José Miro Cardona, Cuban ambassador-designate to the United States, took refuge in the Argentine embassy in Havana, where he joined Sergio Rojas Santamarina, former Cuban ambassador to Great Britain. *Ibid.*, July 6, 1960. In the same month, there were thirty-three political refugees in the Mexican embassy in Ciudad Trujillo. *Ibid.*, August 1, 1960. These numbers seem very small in comparison with the gigantic scale of the Spanish Civil War, when there were over ten thousand political refugees in diplomatic premises in Madrid.

conducts to ensure their uneventful departure from the country to a foreign land. Such safe-conducts once issued should be honored in good faith. The persecution of Prime Minister Imre Nagy and several other political offenders by the Hungarian government after their departure from the Yugoslav embassy in Budapest with safe-conducts in 1956 created tension in the relations between Yugoslavia and Hungary.

The United States has traditionally taken an unfavorable attitude toward the practice of extraterritorial asylum,[87] although asylum was occasionally granted as temporary shelter to persons who would become victims of mob violence or other illegal acts. This was done not as an obligation under international law, but for humanitarian reasons. Cardinal Mindszenty has taken refuge in the American diplomatic premises in Budapest since the Hungarian Revolution in 1956. In May 1964, the American embassy in Bujumbura, Burundi, granted political asylum to Chi-ping Tung, a cultural attaché of the Chinese Communist embassy in Burundi.[88] In this case, the refugee was not a national of the receiving state.

§122. EXTRADITION

The basis of extradition There is no general rule of international law governing extradition, which concerns the delivery of a person by a state where he is found to another state where he has committed or has been convicted of a crime.[89] Whereas nations share the desire to have criminals tried and punished by the state where evidence is more available, the surrender of fugitives is still determined by domestic

[87] See, for instance, the United States Navy Regulations and Naval Instructions of 1913, and the Instructions issued by the State Department in 1927.

[88] Tung's defection took place only twenty-four hours after his arrival in the capital. For his statement and the accusation made by Peking, see *The New York Times*, June 2, August 5, 1964.

[89] Extradition may be granted without requiring physical presence in the state at the time of the commitment of the crime, but this is only an exception to the general rule. See *Kossekechatko and Others v. Attorney-General for Trinidad*, Great Britain, Judicial Committee of the Privy Council, 1932. [1932] A.C. 78. For a crime committed on board a ship, see *R. v. Governor of Birxton Prison, Ex Parte Kolczynski*, Great Britain, High Court of Justice, 1955. 1 Q.B. 540. However, a national of a state who has committed a crime on a foreign public ship within the territorial waters of the state is not subject to extradition to the foreign state. See *Chung Chi Cheung v. The King*, Great Britain, Judicial Committee of the Privy Council, 1939. [1939] A.C. 160. For further discussion, see S. D. Bedi, *Extradition in International Law and Practice* (Rotterdam, 1966).

legislation of the individual state in the absence of treaties.[90] Many states decline to extradite their own nationals.[91] Great Britain and the United States do not make such an exception, unless extradition treaties provide to the contrary.[92]

Reciprocity is the cardinal principle of extradition treaties. The validity of the extradition treaty between the United States and Italy was questioned by an American citizen in *Charlton v. Kelly* due to Italy's refusal to extradite her own nationals.[93] The United States Supreme Court ruled in 1913 that lack of mutuality would make an extradition treaty voidable but not void. In the absence of treaty obligations, a state may still extradite criminals to another as a matter of courtesy, which does not need to be reciprocated.[94]

No person can be tried for offenses which are not included in the extradition treaty and described in the extradition proceedings.[95] Neither is it permissible to try and punish a person for a crime different

[90] A list of extradition treaties can be found in *Harvard Research, Extradition,* Appendices. Ratification of the United States-Brazilian Treaty of Extradition on Novemebr 17, 1964, might be facilitated by the fact that Brazil had been a haven in recent years for a number of American financiers wanted in the United States. See *The New York Times,* November 18, 1964. See also *In Re Sutherland,* Australia, Supreme Court of New South Wales, 1922. 39 *New South Wales Weekly Notes,* p. 108. Here the Court ruled that the law of Australia recognized the legality of detention of convicted criminals under the law of any friendly power.

[91] Following this principle, France, Germany, and other countries punish their nationals for crimes committed abroad. Great Britain and the United States follow the principle that offenders, including their own nationals, should be tried where the crimes have been committed.

[92] Great Britain refused to extradite Alfred Thomas Wilson to Switzerland, because their extradition treaty prohibited the surrender of their own nationals. See *R. v. Wilson,* Great Britain, High Court of Justice, 1877. 2 Q.B. 42. On the same ground, a French request to extradite an American national was turned down by the United States. See *Valentine v. Neidecker,* U.S. Supreme Court, 1936. 299 U.S. 5. It should be noted that aliens in the United States and Great Britain have the privilege of *habeas corpus.*

[93] 229 U.S. 447.

[94] The surrender of Horace G. McKinley by the Chinese government to the United States in 1907 in the absence of an extradition treaty was not to be reciprocated by the American government, as shown in the exchange of notes between Prince Ch'ing and American Minister Rockhill. See *U.S. For. Rel.,* 1908, pp. 129–130.

[95] In *United States v. Rauscher* in 1886, the U.S. Supreme Court ordered the release of Rauscher because he was tried for a crime not stipulated in the Anglo-American treaty. 119 U.S. 407.

from that stated at the time of extradition.[96] It is important that the nature of a crime should be chiefly determined by the law of the country where it has been committed.[97] Extradition may be refused if the offender's act does not constitute the same crime in the country where he is found.[98]

Non-extradition of political criminals The principle of non-extradition of political criminals was non-existent before the French Revolution. As a matter of fact, many offenses stipulated in early treaties were political crimes according to modern conception. The French constitution of 1793 granted asylum to foreign exiles for the cause of liberty. On the other hand, the governments of Austria, Prussia, and Russia persisted in their mutual extradition of revolutionists. Public opinion in Great Britain, Switzerland, Belgium, France, and the United States became aroused over this reactionary practice. Belgium was the first country to enact a law in 1823 prohibiting the extradition of political criminals and to conclude a treaty with France in the following year to the same effect. Now this principle has been universally followed by other states. The refusal by the Netherlands to extradite Emperor William II to the Allied Powers after the conclusion of World War I was based upon this principle.[99]

[96] In the *Winslow* case in 1876, Great Britain insisted that a person extradited for one crime could not be tried for another. See Moore, *Digest,* IV, §596. *Cf. R. v. Corrigan,* Great Britain, High Court of Justice, 1931. 1 K.B. 527. For refusal of extradition due to insufficient evidence, see *Samuel Insull Case,* Greece, Court of Appeals, 1933. 28 *Am. Jour. Int. Law* (1934), p. 362.

[97] The exact meaning of certain legal terms is important in the determination of extradition. For the interpretation of the Spanish word '*falsificación*' in the United States-Mexican Treaty of 1861, see *Benson v. McMahon,* U.S. Supreme Court, 1888. 127 U.S. 457, 466.

[98] In the *Eisler Extradition Case* in 1949, a British court denied the United States request to extradite Eisler, because his act in the United States charged as perjury was not perjury in English law. See 43 *Am. Jour. Int. Law* (1949), pp. 487–491. A French court refused to extradite Henry Blackmer to the United States in 1928 on the ground of the difference of penalty for perjury in the two countries and the expiration of time limit for imposing the corrective penalty. *Case of Henry Blackmer,* France, Court of Paris, 1928. Hudson, p. 514. But, in *Factor v. Laubenheimer* in 1933, the U.S. Supreme Court ruled that the crime charged was extraditable even if not punishable according to the law of the state of Illinois where he was found. 290 U.S. 276.

[99] As a neutral country during World War I, the Netherlands was not bound by the Treaty of Versailles, in which the Allied demand for the Kaiser's extradition had originated. An intricate case occurred in December

Sometimes it is difficult to make a distinction between political and ordinary crimes, because, in many cases, they are mixed in nature. In complex cases, the states concerned have to take all the circumstances into consideration to determine, preferably through judicial inquiry, whether such crimes are predominantly political or ordinary.[100] Political crimes should not be limited to specific offenses against the state, but should include all offenses with political motives or purposes whether committed by one individual or a group. An exception was made by the so-called *attentat* clause, first enacted by Belgium in 1856 and followed by other states in Continental Europe, by which the murder of the head of a state and a member of his family would not be classified as a political crime. The British court decided in 1894 that an anarchist was unqualified for an exemption from extradition for political offenses, because he was totally opposed to all governments.[101]

Under the auspices of the League of Nations, a convention was signed at Geneva on November 16, 1937, to treat terrorism as an ordinary crime, but it never came into effect. After World War II, a new principle has been established to punish individuals for their responsibility in committing crimes against peace, humanity, and law of war,

---

1963, concerning the Portuguese request for extradition from the United States of Henrique M. Galvão, who came to the United States from Brazil to testify before a United Nations trusteeship committee on conditions in Portuguese African territories. He was the leader of a group of Portuguese revolutionaries who seized a Portuguese liner in the Caribbean and held it from January 23 to February 2, 1963. Then he landed the passengers in Recife, Brazil, where he resided as a political refugee. It was questionable whether the Headquarters Agreement signed between the United Nations and the United States could protect him from extradition. Fortunately, his 36-hour visit to New York ended without incident when he flew back to Brazil. See *The New York Times*, December 8, 11, 1963.

[100] See *In re Castioni*, Great Britain, Queen's Bench Division, 1890. [1891] 1 Q.B. 149. In this case, the British court decided that the acts committed by Castioni, a Swiss citizen, were to further a political uprising against the government of Switzerland, with no personal malice toward an official he shot. The United States government extradited Marcos Perez Jimenez in August 1963 for embezzlement and other ordinary crimes in Venezuela while he was President. His extradition was much criticized because of the political element involved in the case. *Perez Jimenez v. Aristeguita*, United States, Circuit Court of Appeal, Fifth Circuit, 1962. 311 F.2d 547. For his statement before the Venezuelan Supreme Court on October 10, 1965, see *The New York Times*, October 11, 1965.

[101] *In re Meuner*, Great Britain, Queen's Bench Division, 1894. 2 Q.B. 415. Different from anarchists, "communists and socialists," according to Amos S. Hershey, "stand upon an entirely different footing, for their efforts are not directed against the bases of all social organization." Hershey, p. 384.

and also for acts of genocide in accordance with the Convention on the Prevention and Punishment of the Crime of Genocide. Thus, persons who have committed or have been convicted of such crimes are not exempted from extradition.[102] Piracy is a non-political or an ordinary crime, but it is not subject to extradition and can be punished by any country.[103]

Desirability of a uniform law of extradition There was a serious controversy between Argentina and Israel in June 1960 because of the forcible abduction of Adolf Eichmann by Israeli agents in Argentina and his secret transportation to Israel for trial as a war criminal.[104] Argentina complained to the Security Council of the United Nations against Israel's violation of her territorial sovereignty. Although the dispute was eventually settled through an Israeli apology,[105] the incident

[102] Following the statement of President Roosevelt of July 30, 1943, the Moscow Conference of the Allied Powers agreed on October 30 to pursue the war criminals anywhere and to deliver them to the accusers for trial and punishment. For details, see *infra,* §226. Most Nazi leaders were captured in the territory of the belligerents at the end of the war. A number of less important ex-Nazis managed to escape from Germany to neutral countries. The Adolf Eichmann case received much publicity due to the circumstances of his arrest and transportation to Israel. Another former Nazi, Gerhard Bohne, who took refuge in Argentina, was arrested by the local authorities in March 1964, upon the request of West Germany for trial for war crimes. See *The New York Times,* March 4, 1964. Art. 7 of the Genocide Convention provides: "Genocide and the other acts enumerated in Art. III shall not be considered as political crimes for the purposes of extradition. The Contracting Parties pledge themselves in such cases to grant extradition in accordance with their laws and treaties in force." For further details of the Convention, see *infra,* §127.

[103] In the case of *Attorney-General for Hongkong v. Kwong-A-Sing* in 1873, the extradition to China of a Chinese national committing piracy was denied by the British Judicial Committee of the Privy Council. See M. T. Z. Tyau, *The Legal Obligations Arising out of Treaty Relations between China and Other States* (Shanghai, 1917), pp. 191–192.

[104] For a list of literature concerning this case, see Von Glahn, p. 249. The text of Eichmann's death sentence, read by the Presiding Justice of a Special Israeli Court on December 15, 1961, can be found in 56 *Am. Jour. Int. Law* (1962), p. 805. The court deemed that the circumstances surrounding Eichmann's abduction could not affect its jurisdiction.

[105] For the complaint by Argentina and the resolution adopted by the Security Council at its 868th meeting on June 23, 1960, see *Repertoire,* SC, Supp., 1959–1963, pp. 159–161. The incident was closed on August 3, 1960, by a joint statement issued simultaneously by the two governments, with special reference to their compliance with the Security Council's resolution

further proves the necessity of developing uniform rules of extradition in order to avoid all kinds of irregularities.[106]

Efforts toward this much-desired goal have been made by both research institutions and governments. The Institute of International Law adopted a series of rules governing extradition at the end of the nineteenth century. A most extensive study on the subject was made by the Harvard Research in International Law in 1935. Regional conventions concerning extradition were adopted by the Central American Republics in 1907 and the Seventh International Conference of American States in 1933. It is time for the United Nations to prepare a set of uniform rules governing extradition, but its success in this respect depends largely on the willingness of the states to compromise their variant claims of territorial sovereignty and extraterritorial jurisdiction.[107]

IV. *INTERNATIONAL PROTECTION OF HUMAN RIGHTS*[108]

§123. EARLY EFFORTS AND THE PROVISIONS OF THE UNITED NATIONS CHARTER

Sporadic efforts in the past to further the well-being of mankind have been recorded in many national enactments of first importance,

---

for the advancement of their friendly relations. See *The New York Times*, August 4, 1960.

[106] The Eichmann case was unique in nature, but irregularities were not lacking in the past. See, for instance, *Ker v. Illinois*, U.S. Supreme Court, 1886. 119 U.S. 436. If the irregularity of extradition is the fault of the local authorities of the requested state, the requesting state is not required to return the fugitive. See *The Case of Savarkar* (France-Great Britain), Tribunal of the Permanent Court of Arbitration, 1911. Scott, *Hague Court Reports*, p. 276. It may be well to mention a recent example of irregularity. Antoine Argoud, a former French army colonel, was convicted of rebellion against France and lived clandestinely in West Germany, where he was abducted and transported back to France in February 1963. In spite of the irregularities, France rejected Germany's demand for his return. See *The New York Times*, January 3, 1964.

[107] This subject was considered by the Committee of Experts of the League of Nations, which decided in 1926 that the time was not ready to prepare a law of extradition. See 20 *Am. Jour. Int. Law* (1926), Special Supp., pp. 242, 257.

[108] General texts on the subject: O'Connell, II, pp. 817–835; Oppenheim, I, §§340b–340c, 340h–340r; Fenwick, *Principles*, Ch. XIII, §K; Starke, Ch. 11, §4; Svarlien, Ch. 26; Von Glahn, pp. 718–725; Soviet *Text*, pp. 169–173; Corbett, Ch. 7.

such as the American Declaration of Independence of 1776, the French Declaration of the Rights of Man and the Citizen of 1789, and bills of rights as provided in the constitutions of different states. A number of international treaties and conventions were concluded for the prevention of slave-trading, protection of minorities, and improvement of labor conditions. No less important was the adoption of a Declaration of the International Rights of Man by the Institute of International Law in 1929,[109] even though it was of an unofficial nature. After the outbreak of World War II, preservation of human rights and freedoms was asserted in the Atlantic Charter and the Declaration of the United Nations in 1941 and 1942 respectively. This continuous movement culminated in the various provisions in the United Nations Charter and other international instruments.

Respect for human rights and freedoms is repeatedly stated in the Charter of the United Nations. "We the Peoples of the United Nations" are determined, according to the preamble, "to reaffirm faith in fundamental human rights" and "to promote social progress and better standards of life in larger freedom." Among the purposes and principles of the United Nations is that of achieving "international cooperation in promoting and encouraging respect for human rights and for fundamental freedoms for all without distinction as to race, sex, language, or religion." [110] The fulfillment of this task is entrusted to the General Assembly and other organs of the United Nations.[111] Again, in Article 55(c) of the Charter, "universal respect for, and observance of, human rights and fundamental freedoms for all" is reasserted as necessary for international cooperation.[112]

The Economic and Social Council of the United Nations is provided with the power to make recommendations and to set up commissions for the fulfillment of this important cause.[113] Members of the United Nations are legally obligated to take joint and separate action in cooperation with the Organization for the achievement of this purpose in accordance with the provisions of the Charter.[114] In actual practice, however, a clear definition of human rights and enforceable

[109] For its text, see 24 *Am. Jour. Int. Law* (1930), p. 560.

[110] Art. 1(3) of the Charter.

[111] See Art. 13(1b). The Afro-Asian states have been most persistent in their efforts at the General Assembly against racial discrimination. See, for instance, GA res. 1780 (XVII), December 7, 1962.

[112] See Myres McDougal, "Perspectives for an International Law of Human Dignity," *Proceedings* of Am. Society Int. Law (1959), pp. 107–132.

[113] See Arts. 62(2), 68, of the Charter.

[114] Art. 56. For comments on the binding force of the Charter provisions on this subject, see Oppenheim, I, pp. 740–741; Jessup, pp. 87–93.

provisions remains to be desired. According to a recent report of the Economic and Social Council, suppression of slavery is still a lively issue in parts of Africa and Asia.[115]

§124. UNIVERSAL DECLARATION OF HUMAN RIGHTS

In pursuance of Article 68 of the Charter, the Economic and Social Council established the Commission on Human Rights in February 1946 for the preparation of fundamental documents on human rights. On December 10, 1948, the General Assembly adopted the Universal Declaration of Human Rights.[116] Consisting of thirty articles, the Declaration embodies a long list of inalienable rights of mankind: personal, civil, political, economic, social, and cultural. It emphasizes the right to life, liberty, security, and nationality; to ownership of property; to freedom of thought, conscience, and religion; to freedom from arbitral arrest, detention, or exile; to freedom of movement, residence, and peaceful assembly and association. There are many other rights, which, if realized, would be ideal for all peoples in the world.

The Declaration itself is only recommendatory in nature, but it serves the purpose of clarifying the basic principles of human rights provided in the Charter, which is binding upon the Members of the United Nations. The essentials of the Declaration have been referred to in national legislation, judicial decisions, resolutions of the United Nations, and other international instruments.[117] The date of its adoption is now observed annually as Human Rights Day.

§125. COVENANTS ON HUMAN RIGHTS

After the Declaration of Human Rights was adopted in 1948, the Commission on Human Rights took one step further toward the preparation for an international bill of rights. At first, it contemplated a single covenant to cover all phases of human rights, with a provision for a Human Rights Committee to receive complaints. Objections were raised in the General Assembly to the inclusion of everything in one document

[115] This lengthy report reveals many accusations made by the Anti-Slavery Society, a non-governmental organization affiliated with the United Nations in consultative status, and also rebuttals by the governments concerned. See also *The New York Times,* April 17, 1966.

[116] The vote was 48 to 0, with 8 abstentions (Saudi Arabia, the Union of South Africa, and the Soviet bloc). For the text and a survey of the Declaration, see *Yearbook,* UN, 1948–1949, pp. 535–537. For the Soviet view of the Declaration, see Soviet *Text,* pp. 138–139.

[117] For details, see Starke, pp. 304–305.

and the Commission was directed to draft one Covenant on Civil and Political Rights and another on Economic, Social, and Cultural Rights.

In 1954, the Commission completed the preliminary drafts of both covenants, each of which contains a preamble, general provisions, substantive articles, and final clauses. With respect to measures of implementation, immediate steps would be taken to adopt and ensure civil and political rights, and maximum efforts would be exerted to achieve progressively economic, social, and cultural rights. These drafts were submitted to the General Assembly, which referred them to its Third Committee for further study and discussion. The United States, the Soviet Union, and many other states were unable to agree on the methods and substance of advancing human rights through international covenants.

After nineteen years of scrutiny and preparation, Members of the United Nations finally reached an agreement on all the issues involved in these instruments. On December 16, 1966, the General Assembly unanimously adopted both Covenants, "thus fulfilling one of the promises made at San Francisco in 1945 and completing the first step toward the implementation of the Universal Declaration of Human Rights." [118] The Covenant on Civil and Political Rights provides for freedom of expression, religion, movement, and peaceful assembly; protection from inhuman treatment and arbitrary arrest or detention; right to life, to a fair trial, and of minorities.[119] An Optional Protocol makes it available to persons or groups to appeal to an eighteen-member Human Rights Committee.[120] The Covenant on Economic, Social and Cultural Rights includes the right to education, work, medical care, and other social and economic benefits.[121] Both Covenants provide for self-determination and national sovereignty over natural resources,[122] and are to be legally binding upon ratifying states. However, without effective sanctions against violations, their enforcement will chiefly depend upon the willingness of the peoples and governments concerned and the pressure of world public opinion.[123]

[118] Secretary-General U Thant's New Year's Message, *The New York Times,* December 31, 1966; *UN Monthly Chronicle,* January 1967, pp. i–ii.

[119] For its text, see UN Doc. A/6546, pp. 175–197.

[120] For its text, see *ibid.,* pp. 198–202.

[121] For its text, see *ibid.,* pp. 162–174.

[122] Arts. 1, 2, of the Covenants.

[123] The most comprehensive information concerning human rights may be found in the *Yearbook on Human Rights,* published by the United Nations. See also H. Lauterpacht, *International Law and Human Rights* (London, 1950); James F. Green, *The United Nations and Human Rights* (Washington, D.C., 1956); M. Ganki, *International Protection of Human*

§126. THE EUROPEAN CONVENTION ON HUMAN RIGHTS

The European Convention for the Protection of Human Rights and Fundamental Freedoms, adopted by the members of the Council of Europe on November 4, 1950, is a regional instrument to implement the human rights provisions of the United Nations Charter and of the Universal Declaration of Human Rights.[124] The Convention has not only listed the essential rights with precise restrictions and exceptions,[125] but also provides two organs for their enforcement in the European Commission on Human Rights and the European Court of Human Rights. The Commission has the power to receive and investigate complaints submitted by the contracting parties or by individuals and non-governmental organizations, and to report to the Council of Ministers for action.[126] The decisions thus reached are obligatory on the contracting parties which have made a declaration to accept its jurisdiction. The Court has jurisdiction over cases brought up by the Commission and the signatories. It came into existence in January 1959.[127]

In the promotion and protection of human rights, this European Convention is so far the most advanced and practical. It is also important to note that no application of complaints is admissible if local remedies have not yet been exhausted.

§127. THE GENOCIDE CONVENTION

At the second part of its first session in December 1946, the General Assembly affirmed in a resolution that genocide is a crime under

---

Rights (Geneva, 1962). One well-known publicist in Communist China, Chou Keng-sheng, strongly objected to collective intervention for the protection of human rights and freedom. In his opinion, intervention on whatever grounds in domestic affairs of other states, whether by the United Nations or by regional organizations, will merely serve the interests of imperialistic powers. See his *Recent Trends in Anglo-American Thought of International Law* (Peking, 1963, in Chinese), p. 47. On October 26, 1966, the twenty-first session of the General Assembly adopted resolutions 2142 (XXI) and 2144 (XXI), with a view to eliminating all forms of racial discrimination.

[124] For its text, see 45 *Am. Jour. Int. Law* (1951), Supp., pp. 24–39. An amendment was made on March 20, 1952, and came into effect in 1953.

[125] Art. 15 of the Convention.

[126] The Commission, set up in 1954, has been empowered to receive complaints from non-governmental organizations and individuals since July 1955.

[127] The Court delivered its first judgment on November 14, 1960, in the *Lawless Case*. 56 *Am. Jour. Int. Law* (1962), pp. 171–210.

international law.[128] Serious studies were made by the Economic and Social Council with a view to preparing a draft convention. On December 9, 1948, the General Assembly discussed the draft and unanimously adopted the Convention on the Prevention and Punishment of the Crime of Genocide.[129] Its effective period of ten years will be automatically renewed for successive periods of five years for contracting parties which have not rejected it.[130]

The Convention confirms the criminality of genocide in time of peace or war. Any of the following five acts directed toward destroying a national, ethical, racial, or religious group is genocide, a crime under international law: (1) killing members of the group; (2) causing them serious bodily or mental harm; (3) deliberately inflicting measures on the group to bring about its physical destruction; (4) imposing measures intended to prevent birth within the group; and (5) forcibly transferring children of one group to another.[131] Persons committing the following acts are punishable whether they are constitutionally responsible rulers, public officials, or private individuals: (1) genocide; (2) conspiring to commit genocide; (3) direct and public incitement to commit genocide; (4) attempt to commit genocide; and (5) complicity in genocide. None of these acts are considered political crimes and thus they are not subject to extradition. The contracting parties have the obligation to ensure effective penalties for such offenders and to enforce measures for the prevention and suppression of such crimes.[132]

Despite divergent opinions on the substance and enforcibility of this Convention,[133] it has added another safeguard to the protection of human rights. But the reservations made by many states at the time

[128] GA res. 96 (I).

[129] For the text of the Convention and a brief description of its preparation, see *Yearbook*, UN, 1948–1949, pp. 953–962.

[130] Art. 14. The Convention will cease to be in force if the number of contracting parties becomes less than sixteen (Art. 15). The United States has not ratified it because of the constitutional consideration that the federal government might encroach on the powers reserved to the states and also unwillingness to extradite offenders for acts vaguely defined in the Convention but not clearly illegal under federal law. All these considerations were evidenced in the hearings before a Subcommittee on Foreign Relations, U.S. Senate, 81st Cong., 2nd Sess.

[131] Art. 2 of the Convention.

[132] See Arts. 3–8 of the Convention.

[133] According to Art. 9, the International Court of Justice is empowered to solve disputes between the contracting parties concerning the interpretation, application, or enforcement of the Convention.

of signature and ratification have weakened its binding force. An advisory opinion delivered by the International Court of Justice on May 28, 1951, has clarified the situation to a certain extent.[134]

[134] *Reservations to the Convention on the Prevention and Punishment of the Crime of Genocide,* International Court of Justice, 1951. I.C.J. Reports (1951), p. 15.

C H A P T E R 9

DIPLOMATIC RELATIONS AND IMMUNITIES

I. *INSTRUMENTALITIES IN CHARGE OF FOREIGN RELATIONS* [1]

§128. DIPLOMATIC INTERCOURSE AMONG STATES

The development of diplomatic relations The conduct of foreign relations is diplomacy, which may be defined as a means to realize the ends of a state through the execution of its foreign policies.[2] The channels of diplomatic transactions are direct negotiations between states, international conferences, and various international and regional organizations, through which mutual understandings and interests may be promoted. Diplomatic commitments are generally in the form of treaties concluded by the participating states, whose faithful observance lays down the foundation of international order and cooperation.

Egypt, China, and India conducted international and interstate relations long before the emergence of the Western state system. Special envoys were frequently sent by the states of China under the Chou dynasty (1122–249 B.C.) on ceremonial occasions and for political negotiations. Beginning with the Han dynasty (206 B.C.–221 A.D.),

[1] General texts on the subject: Oppenheim, I, §§341–357a, 418–419, 443–476; Satow, Chs. I–V; Hyde, II, §§408–410A; Gould, Ch. 9; Svarlien, Ch. 16; Jacobini, pp. 163–170; Soviet *Text,* Ch. VII, §§1–4; Sen, Chs. I–II; Stuart, Chs. 1–6; Plischke, Chs. 1–6.

[2] For other definitions of diplomacy, see Satow, pp. 1–3.

China had more contacts with other sovereign states, but her diplomatic intercourse was chiefly with states in Asia. It was not until 1689 that China signed her first treaty with a Western power, *i.e.*, the Treaty of Nerchinsk with Russia for the delimitation of boundaries between the two countries.[3]

In the Western world, the Greeks and Romans accepted ambassadors on temporary missions. They respected the right of personal inviolability.[4] The development of Italian city states gave impetus to the exchange of diplomatic envoys. Since the fifteenth century, resident embassies and diplomatic procedures were gradually established. The Congress of Vienna in 1815 laid down the foundation of modern diplomacy in the classification of diplomatic envoys and other rules, which have been generally followed by the states with little modifications.

Modern types of diplomacy The nineteenth century may be said to be the golden age of diplomacy, through which a prolonged period of peace was maintained in Europe. Many successful diplomats were tough-minded but polite-mannered. Negotiations were conducted with great patience in a quiet way. This is quite different from the twentieth century. The Soviet Union has combined diplomacy with propaganda from the very beginning.[5] The conduct of open diplomacy for the purpose of creating a favorable public opinion has its own merits. However, successful negotiations cannot be expected if the conference room is turned into a propaganda platform. Throughout the period of the cold war, nations have resorted to propaganda and counter-propaganda. While condemning psychological warfare through propaganda, Secretary John Foster Dulles himself used a number of sensational slogans, such as 'liberation' of the Communist satellites and 'massive retaliation.' There is nothing wrong with propaganda if it only tells the truth in an appropriate manner at the right moment.[6]

[3] For diplomatic relations and correspondence among the states during the Chou dynasty, consult Tso Chiu-ming and Confucius, *Tso Chuan and the Annals of the Spring and Autumn*. See also *supra*, §3.

[4] For a brief description of diplomatic relations among the Greeks and Romans, see Stuart, pp. 115–118. Further details may be found in Coleman Phillipson, *The International Law and Custom of Ancient Greece* (London, 1911), 2 vols.

[5] At Brest-Litovsk, the Soviet delegates published their speeches immediately after their delivery for propaganda purposes.

[6] For further references, see S. D. Kertesz and M. A. Fitzsimons (eds.), *Diplomacy in a Changing World* (Notre Dame, 1959); Warren F. Ilchman, *Professional Diplomacy in the United States, 1779–1939* (Chicago, 1961); Percy Corbett, *Law in Diplomacy* (Princeton, 1959).

§129. CHANNELS OF DIPLOMATIC TRANSACTIONS

The head of state Whereas the formulation of foreign policy in a modern state is generally shared by the legislature, its execution is the responsibility of the executive branch alone.[7] Whether such a power is vested in the head of state or government depends upon the constitutional provisions of different states. In *United States v. Curtiss-Wright Export Corporation,* Justice Sutherland of the Supreme Court delivered the following opinion in 1936:

> In this vast external realm, with its important, complicated, delicate and manifold problems, the President alone has the power to speak or listen as a representative of the nation. He makes treaties with the advice and consent of the Senate; but he alone negotiates. Into the field of negotiation the Senate cannot intrude; and Congress itself is powerless to invade it.[8]

The head of government In Great Britain, India, Japan, and other countries where there is a nominal head of state, the actual power of conducting foreign relations is vested with the prime minister and his cabinet. In the Soviet Union, the People's Republic of China, and other Communist countries, the prime minister is technically in charge of state affairs, but the ultimate authority is always wielded by the party and its leader or leaders. International law does not prescribe any uniform practice in respect of the division of powers in the conduct of foreign relations, this being entirely within the domestic jurisdiction of each state.

[7] The conduct of foreign relations during the American Revolution was controlled by the Continental Congress. Under the Confederation, it was performed by the Committee of Secret Correspondence from 1775 to 1777, when it was replaced by the Committee of Foreign Affairs. The Department of Foreign Affairs, established in 1781, was still responsible to the legislature. It was not until the adoption of the Constitution that the President had the power to control foreign relations in the United States. For details, see Quincy Wright, *Control of American Foreign Relations* (New York, 1922).

[8] 299 U.S. 304. It is important to note that the head of a state, once captured by the enemy as a prisoner of war, like Napoleon III during the Franco-Prussian War, is deprived of all his powers. The President of Mexico, Antonio López de Santa Anna, was captured by the Texans at the battle of San Jacinto in April 1836. He was compelled to sign a treaty recognizing Texan independence, but, on returning to Mexico, he declared it void on the ground that he had signed it under duress.

Personal diplomacy There is much discussion of the relative merits of personal diplomacy conducted by the heads of states and of governments directly. In wartime, problems of utmost importance can be settled speedily by responsible leaders rather than through the regular diplomatic channels. The meetings of the Allied leaders in Quebec, Tehran, Cairo, Yalta, and Potsdam during World War II definitely strengthened the war efforts, which might not have been accomplished by lower-level conferences.

On the other hand, much objection has been raised to the vague and secret understandings reached at Yalta between Roosevelt and Stalin in 1945. The summit conference at Geneva in 1955 discussed the subject of free elections in Germany, but its agreement has been disputed by the Soviet Union. Under normal circumstances, negotiations can be best conducted by professional diplomats. Even if circumstances necessitate high-level meetings, they should be preceded by preliminary talks through regular channels.[9] However, good-will missions by heads of states or of governments will do much to promote mutual understandings among nations.

§130. THE ROLE OF THE FOREIGN MINISTER

Organs in charge of foreign affairs Due to the complexity of international relations in modern times, the head of state or government has to entrust the conduct of foreign affairs to an intermediate organ. It is generally known as the ministry of foreign affairs, as in France,[10] China,[11] and the Soviet Union.[12] The foreign minister usually

[9] Secretary of State Dean Rusk believes that the hazards involved in summit talks outweigh any possible advantages. His view was enunciated in a speech before the Council on Foreign Relations on January 18, 1960. See Dean Rusk, "The President," 38 *Foreign Affairs* (April 1960), pp. 353–369. However, for an exchange of views on the Middle Eastern crisis and other world issues, President Johnson and Soviet Premier Aleksei N. Kosygin had a two-day conference in Glassboro, New Jersey, on June 23, 25, 1967. Although no agreement was reached, both leaders considered the talks useful. See *The New York Times,* June 24, 26, 1967. Further references on the subject can be found in Keith Eubank, *The Summit Conferences 1919–1960* (Norman, Okla., 1966).

[10] The Department of Secretaries of State was founded in France in 1547, and was reorganized into a single Ministry of Foreign Affairs in 1589.

[11] The organ in charge of foreign affairs in China has undergone many changes. For details, see William L. Tung, *China and Some Phases of International Law,* pp. 105–110.

[12] Under Tsar Ivan III, the office conducting foreign relations was called 'Chamber of Embassies.' The proper title of the organ in charge of

ranks first or second in the cabinet. In Great Britain, the Foreign Secretary or Secretary of State for Foreign Affairs takes charge of the Foreign Office.[13] The corresponding organ in the United States is the Department of State, headed by the Secretary of State.[14] Their internal organization varies in different countries according to domestic legislation, but their powers and functions are mainly the same, *i.e.*, the conduct of foreign affairs under the direction of the head of state or government. Sometimes, a prime minister holds concurrently the office of minister of foreign affairs.

The representative character of the foreign minister As the representative of his government, a statement made by the minister of foreign affairs on behalf of his government on matters within his competence has binding effect in international dealings. Thus the Permanent Court of International Justice decided, in the *Legal Status of Eastern Greenland* in 1933,[15] that the declaration of the Norwegian Foreign Minister concerning the settlement of the recognition of Danish sovereignty over Eastern Greenland was binding upon Norway. The conclusiveness of the official opinions of a foreign minister on various questions is accepted by municipal courts in numerous instances. The courts generally consider a foreign minister's statements as authoritative with respect to the recognition of a new state or government, change of state territory, the existence of hostilities or war, and other related subjects.[16]

---

foreign affairs in the Soviet Union is People's Commissary for Foreign Affairs.

[13] As early as 1253, the King's Secretary was created as a part of the royal household of Henry III. But the Foreign Office headed by a single Secretary of State for Foreign Affairs began only in 1782.

[14] The Department of Foreign Affairs, described in note 7, was reorganized by an Act of Congress of July 27, 1789. The present name of the Department of State was adopted on September 15, 1789, with Thomas Jefferson as first Secretary of State. He had a staff of five clerks, one interpreter, and two messengers, in charge of various domestic duties in addition to foreign affairs. See Moore, *Digest,* IV, pp. 780–781.

[15] P.C.I.J., Ser. A/B, No. 53.

[16] See Oppenheim, I, pp. 765–768. For the conclusiveness of the interpretation of treaties by the executive departments in the French courts, see *La Compagnie des Services Contractuels v. Tito Landi, Annual Digest,* 1935–1937, No. 216. United States courts have even gone further than their counterparts in Great Britain in extending this rule to substantive questions of law. See *Lamont v. Travelers Insurance Company,* United States, New York Court of Appeals, 1939 (281 N.Y. 362); *Ex Parte Republic of Peru,* U.S. Supreme Court, 1943 (318 U.S. 578).

The increasing responsibility of the foreign minister The twentieth century has been marked by the advancement of scientific and technical development, steady emergence of new states, constant confrontation with perplexing problems and controversies, increasing demands for interdependence and international cooperation, and frequent meetings of international and regional agencies. All these have added to the heavy responsibilities of foreign ministers, especially those of the major powers. The Secretary of State of the United States has become one of the busiest men in the world. In addition to his complicated functions in dealing with important state affairs, he has to attend endless ceremonies and social events. In order to relieve him of routine matters, there has been much discussion about the reorganization of the State Department. Nothing has, however, materialized.[17]

§131. DIPLOMATIC AND CONSULAR INSTITUTIONS

The development of diplomatic institutions Diplomatic relations may be traced back to ancient times, but diplomacy in the modern sense did not flourish in the Western world until the end of the Middle Ages in the Italian city states.[18] Besides ambassadors, others with the titles of resident, agent, chargé d'affaires were used by various states from the sixteenth to the eighteenth century. The Congress of Vienna of 1815 laid down the uniform standard of modern classification of diplomatic envoys. According to the Protocol of Vienna of March 19, 1815, "diplomatic agents are divided into three classes: that of ambassadors, legates, or nuncios; that of envoys, ministers, or other persons accredited to sovereigns; that of chargés d'affaires accredited to ministers of foreign affairs." [19] The Congress of Aix-la-Chapelle adopted,

[17] Among the proposals was the creation of a supersecretary of state and a 'traveling foreign minister.' The majority of the participants in the eighteenth American Assembly sponsored by Columbia University had serious doubts about the split-up of foreign policy operations. The participants included Dean Acheson, Henry M. Wriston, and other leaders in various fields. See *The New York Times,* October 8, 1960. See also The American Assembly, *The Secretary of State,* edited by Don K. Price (Englewood Ciffs, N.J., 1960).

[18] Dante, Petrarch, and Machiavelli were among the famous diplomats at that time. Many countries, including Russia under Ivan III, employed Italian diplomats as their representatives.

[19] Art. 1 of the Protocol, which can be found in 2 *Br. & For. St. Papers,* p. 179. The long-standing controversy of seniority and precedence was also settled by the Protocol in Arts. 2, 6, 7. Diplomatic agents on an extraordinary mission have no superiority of rank. No precedence may be claimed on account of relation of consanguinity or of family and political alliances. The order of signatures in treaties is to be decided by lots between the envoys.

on November 21, 1818, another rank, ministers resident, an intermediate class between ministers and chargés d'affaires. Legates and nuncios, as provided in the Vienna Protocol, are representatives of the Pope.[20]

Diplomatic agents of the ambassadorial and ministerial classes may claim the title 'excellency' by right and by courtesy respectively. Theoretically, ambassadors have easier access to the head of state, but most negotiations are now conducted through the minister of foreign affairs. Ministers resident are not entitled to the same honors as ministers or to the title of 'excellency.' A chargé d'affaires is accredited from one foreign minister to another.[21]

Ambassadors were exchanged only by major powers in the past. Hostile to monarchical pomp and for the sake of economy, the United States did not appoint ambassadors until 1893. The Soviet Union abolished diplomatic ranks in 1918 and designated her envoys as plenipotentiary representatives, but after having experienced grave inconvenience, envoys were later allowed to have their rank indicated in their credentials. Since May 9, 1941, the Soviet government has followed the general practice by classifying its diplomatic envoys as ambassadors, ministers, and chargés d'affaires. The class of ministers resident has never come into general use. Some other titles, such as 'agent and consul-general' and 'commissioner and consul-general,' used occasionally of persons appointed to semi-sovereign states, have become obsolete.[22]

There is no difference between a minister and an envoy, which are generally used as a double title for a diplomatic agent of ministerial rank. The word 'envoy' is often applied to any head of mission.

[20] The legates are cardinals, while the nuncios are not. See Satow, p. 162.

[21] A unique case occurred in Laos, which, due to a transition of government, recognized both Nationalist China and Communist China. Ambassador Han Lih-wu, representing the Nationalist government, presented his credentials to the King on July 20, 1962. Communist China's chargé d'affaires, Liu Chun, came to the capital earlier, but could only present his credentials to the Foreign Minister according to established protocol. Laos now has diplomatic relations with Communist China only. See *The New York Times,* July 21, 1962.

[22] Some efforts have been made in the past to codify the law on diplomatic relations. The Committee of Experts for the Progressive Codification of International Law recommended this in 1927, but the Council of the League of Nations decided to exclude the subject from the agenda of the Hague Conference for the Codification of International Law in 1930. A Convention on Diplomatic Officers was adopted by the Sixth Conference of American States at Havana in 1928, but it was not ratified by the United States. For its text, see 22 *Am. Jour. Int. Law* (1928), pp. 142–151.

The exchange of diplomatic agents is for mutual convenience, but no state is obliged under international law to follow the practice.[23] Once diplomatic relations are established, envoys of the same rank are usually sent to each other's capital. There are exceptions to this general practice. Switzerland has received ambassadors from other states, but hesitated to appoint diplomats of the same rank. The United States has no diplomatic mission at the Vatican, although the Pope is represented by a legate at Washington.[24] Special envoys for temporary missions are frequently sent by nations. The United States has, from time to time, appointed some prominent diplomats as ambassadors at large.[25] Mention should be made of the diplomatic corps, which comprises all members of the diplomatic missions in the same receiving state. It is headed by a *doyen,* the senior diplomatic envoy of the highest class in the capital. His wife is called *doyenne.* The *doyen's* function is generally limited to ceremonial matters and to the informal conveyance of information.[26]

In pursuance of the General Assembly resolution 1450 (XIV) of December 7, 1959, the United Nations Conference on Diplomatic Intercourse and Immunities was convened in Vienna from March 2 to April 14, 1961. Eighty-one states and several specialized agencies were represented. More than half were from Asia, Africa, and Latin America. The five permanent members of the Security Council and all the Communist states participated in the Conference, which was practically

[23] The establishment of legations at the capitals of China and Japan was originally imposed by the Western powers, when the two countries were very reluctant to have close contact with the West in the nineteenth century.

[24] United States representation at the Holy See started in 1848, but was interrupted in 1869 after the annexation of the Papal States by Italy. Myron C. Taylor was sent by President Roosevelt as his personal representative to the Pope in December 1939, and remained in that post until 1950. General Mark Clark was nominated by President Truman as ambassador to the Vatican in 1951. Because of domestic opposition to the establishment of formal relations with the Vatican for political and religious reasons, his name was eventually withdrawn.

[25] Philip C. Jessup and W. Averell Harriman are instances.

[26] The practice of sending joint communications by diplomatic missions in Peking to the Chinese government during the period 1912–1927, concerning matters of common interest, made the *doyen* the center of activities. The Soviet Union resented the role played by American Ambassador Francis as *doyen* of the diplomatic corps in 1918. See Soviet *Text,* p. 299. On November 3, 1960, an 'action committee' was organized by the diplomatic corps in Havana to present a memorandum to Carlos Olivares, Acting Cuban Foreign Minister, demanding for observance of diplomatic interests, which had been repeatedly violated. See *The New York Times,* November 4, 1960.

world-wide in scope.[27] It adopted, on April 14, the Vienna Convention on Diplomatic Relations, Optional Protocol concerning Acquisition of Nationality, and Optional Protocol concerning the Compulsory Settlement of Disputes, which were opened for signature of April 18, 1961.[28]

The Vienna Convention on Diplomatic Relations came into effect on April 24, 1964. It contains fifty-three articles, dealing with every phase of diplomatic missions in general accordance with established practices. Omitting the third class of ministers resident, seldom sent by nations, the Convention divides the heads of missions into three classes: (1) ambassadors or nuncios; (2) envoys, ministers, and internuncios; and (3) chargés d'affaires.[29] Here, the designation of nuncios and internuncios is provided for the representatives sent by the Vatican of ambassadorial and ministerial ranks respectively.

An embassy is headed by an ambassador and a legation, by a minister. A chargé d'affaires may be the head of either mission pending the appointment of an ambassador or minister. During and after World War II, a large embassy often has been staffed by a minister to help the ambassador dispose of important business. In such a case, the minister is not the head of a legation, but second in command in the embassy. Unlike chargé d'affaires as a permanent class, a chargé d'affaires *ad interim* is a diplomatic agent temporarily appointed in charge of a diplomatic mission in the absence of the head of that mission or at the time of the latter's inability to perform functions.[30]

The development of consular institutions A rudimentary system of consular service was developed by the Greeks and Romans. Consuls were generally selected from local residents. The first consulate in history was perhaps the one established by Pisa in the Levant in 1087. The adoption of maritime codes and the development of commerce through the wars of the Crusades necessitated the service of consular institutions, which were gradually set up in many cities and ports in

[27] The Chinese delegation represented the National Government of the Republic of China.

[28] For their texts, see respectively UN Docs. A/Conf. 20/13 and Corr.1; A/Conf. 20/11; and A/Conf. 20/12. For the text of the Final Act, see UN Doc. A/Conf.20/10. All these can be found in the *Official Records* of the United Conference on Diplomatic Intercourse and Immunities, Vienna, 1961 (A/Conf.20/14/Add.1). The International Court of Justice was designated as the organ to deal with disputes arising out of interpretation or application of the Convention, unless an arbitral tribunal or conciliation commission is preferred by the disputing parties.

[29] Art. 14 of the Vienna Convention.

[30] Art. 19(1) of the Vienna Convention.

the fifteenth century.[31] Beginning with the nineteenth century, consular officers have been exchanged more extensively by the states to take care of an increased volume of commercial and other matters.

Consular officers may be either career consuls (*consules missi*) or honorary consuls (*consules electi*).[32] There are generally four classes of consular officers: (1) consuls-general, (2) consuls, (3) vice-consuls, and (4) consular agents. The United States follows this general practice;[33] Great Britain has 'proconsuls' as the fifth class.[34] A consul-general may be the head of a large consular district or of several consular districts with several consuls under him. Otherwise, each consular district is headed by a consul and each is independent of the other. But all heads of consular posts are under the direction and supervision of their country's diplomatic mission in the same receiving state.

Following the General Assembly's resolution of December 18, 1961, the United Nations Conference on Consular Relations was held in Vienna from March 2 to April 22, 1963. It was attended by representatives from ninety-two states, eleven more than those at the Diplomatic Conference in 1961. The larger number was attributed to the emergence of newly independent states in Africa. As at the Diplomatic Conference, all the permanent members of the Security Council and all the Communist states which were members of the United Nations were represented.

The Conference adopted, on the last date, the Vienna Convention on Consular Relations, the Optional Protocol concerning Acquisition of Nationality, and the Optional Protocol concerning the Compulsory Settlement of Disputes, all of which were open for signature on April 24, 1963.[35] The Convention consists of seventy-nine articles, covering

[31] The most notable of the maritime codes was *Consolato del Mare*, drafted in the fourteenth century.

[32] See Oppenheim, I, p. 832.

[33] The first American consul was sent to France in 1780, but no consular service was organized until ten years later.

[34] According to L. Oppenheim, "the so-called proconsul is not a consul but a *locum tenens* only, during the temporary absence or illness of a consul; he possesses, therefore, consular character for such time only as he actually is the *locum tenens*." Proconsuls in the British consular service "exercise, as a rule, only the notarial functions of a consular officer." Oppenheim, I, p. 833.

[35] For the texts of these documents and the Final Act, see respectively UN Docs. A/Conf.25/12; A/Conf.25/14; A/Conf.25/15; and A/Conf. 25/13. These can also be found in the *Official Records* of the United Nations Conference on Consular Relations, Vienna, 1963 (A/Conf.25/16/Add.1). The International Court of Justice was designated as the organ to deal with

all aspects of consular relations, on the basis of the existing treaties and international practices.[36] The classification of consular officers is the same as previously described. The consulate-general, consulate, vice-consulate, and consular agency are headed respectively by a consul-general, consul, vice-consul, and consular agent.[37]

The foreign service Diplomatic and consular officers are generally under a single system, commonly known as the foreign service. Members of the foreign service may be assigned interchangeably to diplomatic missions and consular posts at the discretion of the ministry of foreign affairs with the approval of the head of state or government. The United States traditionally kept two separate services until 1924, when the Rogers Act merged them into one foreign service. American diplomatic missions are also staffed with reserve and staff officers.[38] Every state lays down foreign service regulations, including qualifications of candidates, who must pass both written and oral examinations and receive a period of training before assignment.[39]

§132. OTHER GOVERNMENT AGENTS

Government agents attached to diplomatic missions Aside from regular diplomatic and consular officers who are under the direction of the ministry of foreign affairs, other ministries or departments may also send agents abroad for specific duties. Most of them are attached to diplomatic missions under the supervision of the ambassador or

---

controversies arising out of interpretation and application of the Convention, unless the disputing parties agree to resort to an arbitral tribunal or conciliation commission. For a full discussion of the 1963 Consular Convention, see L. T. Lee, *Vienna Convention on Consular Relations* (Leiden, 1966).

[36] The Convention on Consular Agents, adopted by the Sixth Inter-American Conference at Havana in 1928, was an important step toward the codification of the law on consular relations. See Hudson, *Int. Legislation,* IV, p. 2394. The Harvard draft on this subject in 1932 is also an important contribution (Legal Position and Functions of Consuls, prepared by Quincy Wright). For its text, see 26 *Am. Jour. Int. Law* (1932), Supp., pp. 189–449.

[37] See Art. 9 of the Convention.

[38] For a survey of the development of the American Foreign Service, see Stuart, pp. 81–113; also W. Barnes and J. H. Morgan, *The Foreign Service* of the United States (Washington, D.C., 1961).

[39] For regulations of other countries, see A. H. Feller and M. O. Hudson, *Diplomatic and Consular Laws and Regulations of Various Countries* (Washington, D.C., 1933), 2 vols. The United Nations has a program for foreign service officers to train diplomats from newly independent nations. See *The New York Times,* November 10, 1963.

minister, but are directly responsible to their respective superiors of the home government. The army, navy, air, commercial, agricultural, cultural, and press attachés are not regular members of the foreign service, but are equally entitled to diplomatic immunities and privileges.[40] In view of the nature of their activities, such attachés become important instrumentalities in the conduct of foreign relations.[41]

Officials on special missions Because of their power and wealth, the major powers, especially the United States, assumed increasing responsibility in their relations with other countries during and after World War II. Among the fields of their activities are programs for economic, technical, and military aid; agreements for agricultural co-operation, cultural exchange, and transfer of surplus property; negotiations for disarmament, reduction of tariffs, stabilization of currency, and prevention of the manufacture and trading of narcotic drugs. In addition, there are other international and regional commitments which require frequent consultations and meetings.

For the performance of the above functions, which far exceed the regular duties of diplomatic and consular officers, the governments concerned generally send high-ranking officials and technical experts from related departments to various countries at different times.[42] A large number of non-diplomatic personnel are required to carry out economic, technical, and military aid programs. These officials have much to do with the execution of national security policy and foreign policy.[43] Further, agents in charge of intelligence or of other secret

[40] The number and kinds of attachés sent by each government depend on the special needs of its relations with the receiving state. In a diplomatic mission, they usually rank next to the counselor. Military attachés generally have the rank of colonel or higher.

[41] The importance of the work of military attachés has often aroused the suspicions of the receiving state, resulting in their expulsion and recall. For instance, on October 6, 1964, the Soviet Union accused three American military attachés and one British military attaché in Moscow of espionage. On December 14 of the same year, the United States ordered the expulsion of three Soviet military attachés and recalled three of her own from Moscow. See *The New York Times*, October 7, December 15, 1964.

[42] These officials are given letters of commission, but not credentials. The receiving state is usually notified of their mission through diplomatic channels. Colonel House under President Wilson and Harry Hopkins under President Roosevelt were entrusted with important negotiations with Allied leaders in wartime.

[43] These officials are sometimes instrumental in concluding treaties and agreements concerning economic, technical, and military aid with the receiving governments. Whatever immunities, privileges, or exemptions they may enjoy in the receiving state are granted through courtesy.

missions are not unusual in the international community. Despite their disguised insignificance, their role in the conduct of foreign relations cannot be neglected.[44]

Due to the increasing importance of special missions, the twenty-first session of the General Assembly discussed the subject on the basis of the report of the International Law Commission. On December 5, 1966, it decided to continue the work of codification and progressive development of international law relating to special missions by taking into consideration the views expressed by different governments. The Commission was directed to submit a final draft on the topic in its next report.[45]

Military forces abroad The occupation forces of the Allied powers in Germany and Japan after World War II had practically supreme power in directing the destiny of the two defeated nations. Considering the importance and complexity of their responsibilities, professional diplomats cannot be expected to undertake such tasks. The military aid programs of the United States, especially in Taiwan, Korea, Vietnam, Thailand, and the Philippines, have necessitated the stationing of formidable army, navy, and air forces in these areas. The development of the situation in Vietnam has even changed the function of the American forces from advisory capacity to direct action. Furthermore, American military bases are found in every strategic region in the non-Communist world. Likewise, the Soviet Union has had military forces and bases in her spheres of influence, particularly in certain Eastern European countries. The importance of the military commanders of such forces stationed abroad in the conduct of foreign relations cannot be overemphasized.[46]

Other overseas agencies The information agencies and their libraries established abroad by many nations, the trade delegations sent by the Soviet Union, the purchasing agencies of various govern-

[44] Secret agents were also sent by insurgents or belligerents in a civil war to conduct informal contacts with other countries, as done by the Continental Congress and the Southern Confederacy during the American Revolution and Civil War respectively.

[45] GA res. 2167 (XXI). For the resolution on special missions adopted by the Vienna Conference of 1961, see UN Doc. A/Conf.20/10/Add.1. For a summary of the work of the International Law Commission on the subject, see 61 *Am. Jour. Int. Law* (1967), pp. 463–466.

[46] Mention should be made of the practice of many nations, including the Soviet Union and the United States, of occasionally appointing generals and admirals as ambassadors.

ments, and numerous semi-official groups also assist in the conduct of foreign relations.[47] The Peace Corps dispatched by the United States to many developing areas is a comparatively new feature along this line. Soviet officials are also sent from agencies other than ministries of foreign affairs and of foreign trade.[48] Government officials and prominent citizens traveling abroad in a private capacity have often contributed to the furtherance of understanding and friendship between nations, even though they are not permitted to conduct official negotiations.[49] In short, the conduct of foreign relations is no longer limited to diplomatic missions, but increasingly has come to be shared by other agencies and officials in the postwar period.

II. *DIPLOMATIC MISSIONS AND CONSULAR POSTS* [50]

§133. THE EXCHANGE OF DIPLOMATIC AND CONSULAR REPRESENTATIVES

Diplomatic relations are established by the mutual consent of states.[51] Once permanent missions are exchanged on a reciprocal basis,

[47] Valuable articles on overseas agencies can be found in The American Assembly, *The Representation of the United States Abroad* (New York, 1956).

[48] Soviet agencies connected with foreign relations include "the Committee for Cultural Relations with Foreign Countries of the Council of Ministers of the U.S.S.R., the Union of Soviet Societies of Friendship and Cultural Relations with Foreign Countries, the All-Union Central Council of Trade Unions, the Soviet Red Cross and Red Crescent Society." Soviet *Text,* p. 291.

[49] The Logan Act of 1799 forbidding unauthorized citizens to conduct negotiations between the United States and other governments is still in effect.

[50] General texts on the subject: O'Connell, I, pp. 348–351; Oppenheim, I, §§360–383, 406–417, 420–433, 436–442; Fenwick, *Principles,* Ch. XXIV, §§A–E, H–I; Hyde, II, §§411–425, 444–458, 460–463A, 483–488; Moore, *Digest,* IV, §§623–656; V, §§696–701, 717–731; Hackworth, *Digest,* IV, §§370–399, 423–427, 439–460; Starke, Ch. 13; Hershey, pp. 391–400, 416–422; Svarlien, Ch. 17; Von Glahn, Ch. 23; Jacobini, pp. 170–180; Soviet *Text,* Ch. VII, §§5–9; Satow, Chs. XI–XV, XX–XXI; Stuart, Chs. 7–12, 15–20; Plishke, Chs. 7–8; Thayer, Chs. I–XVII, XX–XXIII; Sen, Chs. III–IV, VII–XI; Lawrence, §§121–131; Le Fur, §§463–474; Grotius, II, Bk. 2, Ch. 18; Vattel, III, Bk. 4, Chs. 5–9; Genet, I, pp. 149–415, 423–593; Praag, §227; Woolsey, §§86–100; *Harvard Research* (1932), I, II.

[51] See Diplomatic Convention, Art. 2; Consular Convention, Art. 2. Sir Abubakar Tawafa Balewa, Nigerian Prime Minister, stated, on November 2,

permission is granted for the opening up of consular posts. On the other hand, the severance of diplomatic relations does not automatically close the consular posts.[52] In the absence of consular posts, consular functions may be exercised by the diplomatic mission. The scope of a consular district which covers the area assigned to each consular post is normally determined by the sending state with the concurrence of the receiving state.[53] Each state may decide whether it will establish or admit consular agencies conducted by consular agents who are not heads of consular posts, and appoint or receive honorary consular officers who are not entitled to the same rights and privileges as career ones.[54]

It is not necessary that the exchange of ambassadors or ministers should immediately follow the establishment of diplomatic relations between two countries. A diplomat of lesser rank may be sent to take charge of the mission for a while. The United States and Singapore agreed to exchange ambassadors four months after the American proposal to raise its consulate-general to the status of embassy.[55] Nations without diplomatic relations may permit non-political contacts for mutual benefit, as in the trade between Japan and Communist China.[56]

The size of the diplomatic or consular staff depends upon the

---

1960, that he had rejected a personal demand from Premier Khrushchev to establish a Soviet embassy 'forthwith' in his country. He insisted that such a request could only be considered in its 'proper form' because Nigeria "will not be bullied." *The New York Times,* November 3, 1960.

[52] Generally, consulates will be maintained until the situation becomes untenable, like the American consulates in Russia after the Revolution. See Pilschke, pp. 230–231. However, consular relations with an unrecognized government are more delicate, because the request of an *exequatur* (see *infra,* §135) indirectly implies recognition, unless there is a mutual understanding to the contrary. This kind of understanding was reached between the United States and the unrecognized government of Chile in October 1924. It is impossible for states to carry out consular functions during armed conflict. All the American consulates in Germany and Italy and the consulates of these two enemy states in the United States were closed during World War II.

[53] See Arts. 3–4 of the Consular Convention.

[54] Arts. 68–69 of the Consular Convention. States are now less inclined to appoint honorary consuls. There is no such provision in Soviet consular law, which does not accept nationals other than those of the sending state as consuls in the U.S.S.R. See Soviet *Text,* p. 314.

[55] See *The New York Times,* April 5, 1966.

[56] It was reported that South Korea, long a firmly anti-Communist country, has been moving continuously toward such a policy with Communist nations. See *ibid.,* April 17, 1966.

actual need and local circumstances, and in the absence of agreements the receiving state may set a reasonable limit. Express consent by the receiving state is also necessary if a foreign mission wants to establish offices in other locations.[57] After due notification to, and without express objection by, the receiving state, the sending state may, for reasons of economy, designate either the head of a diplomatic mission or any of its members to more than one state.[58] In like manner, two or more states may appoint the same person as the head of the diplomatic mission or consular post in the receiving state.[59]

Sometimes a state may appoint a special envoy to assist the head of a permanent mission on particular occasions to carry out certain functions. With the consent of the receiving state, this practice is permissible, lack of provision in the Diplomatic Convention notwithstanding.[60] The sending state must obtain the consent of the receiving state for the appointment of a member of the administrative and technical staff to be in charge of current administrative affairs of a mission which has no diplomatic staff at the time.[61]

§134. THE APPOINTMENT OF DIPLOMATIC AND CONSULAR PERSONNEL

Qualifications of diplomatic envoys The qualifications of a diplomatic envoy and the procedure concerning his appointment are within the discretion of the sending state.[62] The increasing complexity of

[57] See Arts. 11–12 of the Diplomatic Convention; Art. 20 of the Consular Convention.

[58] Art. 5(3) of the Diplomatic Convention. The United States used to accredit one envoy to the five republics of Central America. It is still the practice today that one diplomatic envoy is concurrently accredited to several states, especially in Asia and Africa.

[59] Art. 6 of the Diplomatic Convention; Art. 18 of the Consular Convention. In general, the receiving state does not like such a practice.

[60] There were numerous instances in the past, such as the appointment of William W. Rockhill as Commissioner of the United States to China to assist the American Minister to Peking in negotiating for peace during the Boxer Uprising in 1900. The ambassador at large is in the same category while roving around various capitals. Regular envoys have felt embarrassed by the presence of some special envoys sent to carry out diplomatic functions. There is no provision on special missions in the Convention on Diplomatic Relations of 1961, but the Vienna Conference adopted a recommendation that the subject be referred by the General Assembly to the International Law Commission for further consideration. See UN Doc. A/Conf. 20/10/Add. 1 (A/Conf.20/13 and Corr. 1, pp. 89–90).

[61] Art. 19(2) of the Diplomatic Convention.

[62] While religion or race should not be taken into consideration in

diplomatic functions requires a person with professional experience; political appointment is no longer considered good practice, and many more diplomatic missions today are headed by career officers. After World War I, women have gradually entered the foreign service.[63] Appointment is generally made by the head of state or government, with the approval of the legislature if so required by the constitution. In the United States, the appointment of ambassadors, other public ministers, and consuls must be approved by the Senate, unless it is in recess.[64]

Documents ancillary to appointment When the head of a diplomatic mission or a consular post is appointed, he is provided with a commission or similar instrument as a certificate of his capacity. A diplomatic envoy is also furnished with a letter of credence (*lettre de créance*). The open copy of this document is to be sent to the minister of foreign affairs of the receiving state upon his arrival, and the sealed original copy is to be presented personally to the head of state or the foreign minister if the envoy is a chargé d'affaires.[65] The 'full powers' (*pleins pouvoirs*) is a special empowering document issued only to a diplomatic envoy who is authorized to negotiate a treaty. The consular commission, known as *lettre de provision* or notification of appointment, is transmitted to the receiving state through a diplomatic or other appropriate channel.[66] Before his departure, the diplomatic or

---

selection of diplomatic officers, the reluctance of the American government to appoint Jews as diplomats to Arab countries was recently revealed by the State Department. See *The New York Times*, March 14, 1966.

[63] Madame Maréchale de Guébriant was probably the first ambassadress. She was sent by France to accompany Princess Marie Louise de Gonzague to her fiancé, the King of Poland, in 1646. Now many states, including the United States and the Soviet Union, have accredited women as their representatives. As the Soviet representative to Mexico and Scandinavian countries, Madame Alexandra Kollontai had a long diplomatic career. Madame Vijaya Lakshmi Pandit of India headed several important missions, including Washington, London, and the United Nations.

[64] Before his election to the Presidency, Martin Van Buren was appointed American Minister to England during a Senate recess. After reconvening, the Senate rejected the confirmation. For further information on recess appointments, see Maurice Waters, *The Ad Hoc Diplomat: A Study in Municipal and International Law* (The Hague, 1963).

[65] Letters of credence or credentials for ambassadors or ministers are signed by the head of state, and those for chargés d'affaires, by the foreign minister.

[66] See Arts. 10–11 of the Consular Convention.

consular officer must have his passport visaed by the receiving state, and also by third states in transit if so required.

The personnel of a diplomatic mission A diplomatic mission consists of the head, counselors, first, second, and third secretaries, attachés, other members of the official staff, and employees needed for maintenance and service. In addition, the Soviet Union sends trade missions abroad, attached to their diplomatic missions in charge of state trade. The rank of the Soviet trade representative is below counselor but above attaché and secretary.[67] In the case of non-Communist countries, commercial counselors are entrusted with matters relating to trade.

The Convention on Diplomatic Relations of 1961 prescribes specific terms to designate different kinds of personnel in a diplomatic mission: (1) 'diplomatic agent,' either the head of the mission or a member of the 'diplomatic staff,' which indicates a person with diplomatic rank; (2) 'members of the mission,' consisting of the head and the 'members of the staff of the mission,' which include all the members of the diplomatic staff, of the administrative and technical staff, and of the service staff; (3) 'members of the administrative and technical staff,' specifying those staff members employed in the administrative and technical service; (4) 'members of the service staff,' persons in the domestic service of the mission; and (5) 'private servant,' a person in the domestic service of a member of the mission but not an employee of the sending state.[68] These classifications are important to clarify respective status, functions, immunities, and privileges.

The personnel of consular posts Likewise, the Convention on Consular Relations of 1963 classifies various consular personnel under the following categories: (1) 'consular officer,' either the head of a consular post or any person entrusted with that capacity; (2) 'consular employees,' persons employed in the administrative or technical service; (3) 'member of the service staff,' any person employed in the domestic service of a consular post; (4) 'members of the consular post,' including consular officers, consular employees, and members of the service staff; (5) 'members of the consular staff,' those consular officers other than the head of a consular post, consular employees, and members of the service staff; and (6) 'member of the private staff,' any person em-

[67] The rank of a deputy trade representative of the Soviet Union is between the first and the second secretaries. The legal status of the Soviet trade missions is prescribed in the Statute on Trade Missions and Agencies of the U.S.S.R. Abroad, September 13, 1933.

[68] See Art. 1 of the Diplomatic Convention.

ployed exclusively in the private service of a member of the consular post.[69]

Prior approval required in certain cases The receiving state must be notified of the appointees to the diplomatic mission or consular post. Prior approval is required of the military, naval, or air attachés, because of the nature of their functions and repeated incidents in the past. In principle, members of the diplomatic staff and consular officers should be the nationals of the sending state, but nationals of a third state or of the receiving state may also be appointed with the latter's consent, which may be withdrawn at any time.[70] States today seldom appoint nationals of the receiving or a third state to perform functions other than maintenance and domestic services.[71]

§135. THE AGRÉMENT, RECEPTION, AND NOTIFICATION

The agrément According to modern practice concerning the appointment of a diplomatic envoy, the sending state will first ascertain whether the appointee will be considered *persona grata* by the receiving state before formal announcement. The approval or *agrément* by the latter through the process of *agréation* is essential for a diplomatic envoy to perform his functions. There is no obligation to give reasons for refusal of *agrément*.[72] The receiving state may notify the sending

[69] See Art. 1 of the Consular Convention.

[70] See Arts. 7–8 of the Diplomatic Convention; Arts. 19–22 of the Consular Convention. The Soviet Union does not accept nationals not of the sending state as consuls in the U.S.S.R.

[71] One notable exception in the past was Anson Burlingame, American Minister to Peking. After his resignation, he accepted in 1867 an appointment by the Chinese government as a Special Envoy to the United States and European countries. He was formally received in Washington and conducted negotiations for the conclusion of an important Sino-American treaty. See *U.S. For. Rel.*, 1868–1869, pp. 493, 601. No American citizen can now be received as a foreign envoy to the United States. See Hackworth, *Digest,* IV, p. 452.

[72] This principle was also embodied in Art. 8 of the Pan-American Convention, signed at Havana on February 20, 1928. The United States did not follow the practice of seeking *agrément* until the appointment of envoys with the rank of ambassador in 1893. The most embarrassing case was that of A. M. Keiley, who was appointed by the United States as Minister to Rome in 1885 but was refused as *persona non grata.* The reason was not given, but the refusal was evidently due to his speech against Italy's annexation of the Papal States. His appointment to Vienna was turned down by the Austrian government because of his civil marriage to a Jewess. In 1891,

state at any time that a member of the diplomatic mission or of a consular post is deemed *persona non grata.* In that case, the sending state has to recall him and terminate his function. Otherwise, the receiving state may refuse to recognize his status. A person may be declared *persona non grata* even before his arrival in the territory of the receiving state.[73]

The exequatur The certificate issued by the receiving state to admit and authorize the head of a consular post to perform his functions is called the *exequatur* (to let him perform). Pending its delivery and in case of necessity, he may be admitted on a provisional basis. If required by the law of the receiving state, an *exequatur* may be requested for a consular officer other than the head of the post. In all cases, the receiving state has no obligation to give reasons for its refusal to grant *exequatur.* Once admitted, the competent authorities in the consular district should be notified, so that they will render necessary assistance and protection.[74] An *exequatur* may be revoked by the receiving state at any time.[75]

Reception When a diplomatic envoy arrives in the capital of the receiving state, he is usually greeted by the chief of protocol or his deputy.[76] He will be received later by the minister of foreign affairs,

---

China rejected former Senator Henry W. Blair as Minister to Peking on the ground that he had helped enact the Exclusion Act of 1888. In former times, some European sovereigns occasionally submitted a number of candidates as a diplomatic envoy for the receiving sovereign to choose one. In 1819, Tsar Alexander picked the second from a list of four candidates submitted by France to be French Ambassador at St. Petersburg. This practice has long been discontinued.

[73] In most cases, reasons for refusal have been too evident to need explanation. For the British rejection of Major Haggerty as an American consul on the ground of his participation in the Fenian revolts, see W. E. Hall, *A Treatise on International Law* (Oxford, 1895), p. 333.

[74] See Arts. 12–14, 19(3), of the Consular Convention.

[75] In 1793, the United States revoked the *exequatur* from a French vice-consul, Mr. Duplaine, at Boston, because of his violation of the law of the receiving state. See Moore, *Digest,* V, p. 19. For the withdrawal of *exequatur* from three British consuls in the United States during the Crimean War because of their recruiting activities, see Hall, §105.

[76] To express the close relationship between Great Britain and the United States during World War II, King George VI and President Roosevelt personally greeted American Ambassador Winant and British Ambassador Lord Halifax on their respective arrivals in 1941. But these are rare cases in diplomatic history.

who is to make necessary arrangements for his audience with the head of state to present his credentials.[77] An open copy of his credentials must be handed to the ministry of foreign affairs beforehand. Generally, there is an exchange of formal speech between the envoy and the head of state at an audience, but the ceremony varies in different capitals.[78] After this solemn occasion, he will make calls and take over his functions officially.

Precedence In the diplomatic corps, envoys of higher rank or class take precedence over those of lower: first, ambassador; second, minister; and last, chargé d'affaires.[79] Envoys of the same class take precedence in the order of date and time of taking up their functions, unless local practice in the receiving state requires precedence of the representative from the Holy See.[80] The receiving state is to be notified by the head of the diplomatic mission of the precedence of the diplomatic staff of his mission.[81]

Precedence of the heads of consular posts is also determined by rank in the following order: (1) consul-general, (2) consul, (3) vice-consul, and (4) consular agent. Precedence among the heads of consular posts in the same class is similar to the practice of the diplomatic envoys, with the date of granting *exequatur* or provisional commission

[77] In September 1964, Cambodia decided to postpone indefinitely the presentation of credentials by a new American Ambassador, Randolph A. Kidder, due to her displeasure at American alliance with South Vietnam and Thailand and to her border incidents with South Vietnam. See *The New York Times*, September 16, 1964.

[78] American practice has been marked by simplicity since the time of Washington and Jefferson, whose informality was resented by the British Minister, Anthony Merry. See John W. Foster, *A Century of American Diplomacy* (New York, 1900), p. 211. On the other hand, reception at European courts has been more ceremonial. For the reception at the Court of St. James, see Satow, pp. 150–153. The Vienna Convention on Diplomatic Relations of 1961 provides in Art. 18 that "the procedure to be observed in each state for the reception of heads of mission shall be uniform in respect of each class." It is, however, difficult to expect a state to change its traditional customs concerning ceremonial details. It should be noted that a chargé d'affaires is received only by the minister of foreign affairs.

[79] The class of minister resident, originally ranked third, had long become obsolete and was omitted by the Diplomatic Convention of 1961.

[80] See Art. 16 of the Diplomatic Convention, which states further that "alterations in the credentials of a head of mission not involving any change of class shall not affect his precedence." Sometimes a change of head of state or form of government requires new credentials for the head of the mission.

[81] Art. 17 of the Diplomatic Convention.

as the determining factor. In case of the same dates, the date of one's commission by the sending state will decide the order of precedence. Acting heads rank after all heads; honorary consular heads, after all career heads in each class. In spite of acting or honorary capacity, all heads of consular posts take precedence over other consular officers. As to the order of precedence among the consular officers of a consular post, the receiving state should be notified by the sending state through the latter's diplomatic mission or the consular post in the absence of such a mission.[82]

Notification The receiving state should be kept informed of the movement of all the personnel connected with the diplomatic mission and consular posts. Usually, the ministry of foreign affairs is the organ to receive formal notification of the following matters: (1) appointment, final departure, or termination of functions; (2) arrival and final departure of members of family, or, where appropriate, termination of family relationship; and (3) engagement and discharge of employees resident in the receiving state. Notification is also required of the appointment of a chargé d'affaires *ad interim* of a diplomatic mission or of an acting head of a consular post when the head of the mission or post is temporarily vacant or unable to perform his functions.[83] In all cases, prior notification is expected whenever possible.

§136. FUNCTIONS OF DIPLOMATIC ENVOYS

Five major functions Unlike temporary or special envoys only for the performance of specific duties, the functions of permanent missions are manifold. They may range from matters of utmost importance to merely ceremonial and social activities. For convenience of discussion, they are grouped under five categories: (1) representation, (2) protection, (3) negotiation, (4) observation, and (5) administration. In addition, certain diplomatic missions are assigned by the sending state to perform concurrently consular functions.[84] On the other hand, a consular officer may perform diplomatic functions with

[82] See Arts. 16, 21, of the Consular Convention.

[83] See Arts. 10, 19, of the Diplomatic Convention; Arts. 15, 24, of the Consular Convention.

[84] See Art. 3 of the Diplomatic Convention; Arts. 3, 70, of the Consular Convention. The receiving state must be notified of the persons in charge of the consular section of the diplomatic mission. In the exercise of consular functions, the diplomatic mission may address the local authorities of the consular district, and also the central authorities of the receiving state if local laws and international agreements so permit.

the consent of the receiving state, where the sending state is not represented by a diplomatic mission of its own or of a third state.[85]

Representation As a representative of the sending state, a diplomatic envoy should endeavor to promote friendly relations with the receiving state and to further their mutual interests in economic, cultural, and scientific fields. He is expected to observe local laws and regulations and to refrain from interfering with the domestic affairs of the receiving state.[86] Critical opinions on divisive issues should be avoided.[87] He should not engage in any professional or commercial activity for personal profit.[88] Close association with his colleagues to exchange information and good relations with government leaders and press correspondents will contribute to the success of his mission. Frequent contact with people of diversified interests and social activities is also essential to the promotion of mutual understanding.[89] The wife

[85] See Art. 17 of the Consular Convention. Diplomatic functions do not change the legal status of a consular officer. After notification to the receiving state, he may act as representative of the sending state to an intergovernmental organization and will thus enjoy the immunities and privileges due to a representative in accordance with customary international law and treaties. But such immunities and privileges do not extend to him in his exercise of consular functions.

[86] Art. 41 of the Diplomatic Convention.

[87] In his speech to the American Society of International Law on April 30, 1960, Mahomedali Currim Chagla, the Indian Ambassador to the United States, asserted that American reservations on the jurisdiction of the International Court of Justice had reduced it to "a mockery." As a distinguished jurist, he was well respected in Washington. Normally, an envoy will avoid making public pronouncements against the policies of the receiving state. See *The New York Times,* May 1, 1960. When Anastas I. Mikoyan, then a Soviet First Premier, visited Norway in June 1960, he made an offensive speech against the United States. The Norwegian Foreign Minister, Halvard M. Lange, rebuked him on the following day by quoting an old Norwegian poem: "To one's friend be a friend to him and to his friend." See *ibid.,* June 26, 1960. Evidently, the use of Norwegian soil as a platform against her ally created embarrassment to the receiving state and could hardly promote cordial relations between Norway and the Soviet Union.

[88] See Art. 42 of the Diplomatic Convention.

[89] There are many interesting cases in connection with social functions in the diplomatic field. A former French consul-general in Genoa, Jean Mezière, was awarded damages of 4,000,000 lire for an injury to his finger which kept him from hand-shaking, an "important act of diplomatic life," claimed by his lawyer. See *The New York Times,* July 27, 1959. Some state dinners were too lavish to be true. When President Eisenhower visited Brazil in March 1960, the Brazilian Foreign Ministry ordered tons of food and hundreds of cases of champagne, still wine, and whiskey for a state dinner of

of a diplomat can be of considerable assistance to the effective conduct of his diplomatic function.[90]

Protection A diplomatic envoy has a responsibility to protect the rights and interests of his country and of its nationals within the limits of treaty provisions and customary international law. Consideration of private claims of his countrymen in the receiving state, especially in time of political turmoil, is always a difficult task; no diplomatic representation should be made before the exhaustion of local remedies. Due to the conflict of nationality laws, it is impossible to protect a naturalized national from being drafted into the military service by his native country upon his return to its territory. Sometimes a diplomatic envoy is instructed to undertake the temporary protection of the rights and interests of a third state and its nationals. Prior consent of the receiving state is necessary before his taking up this additional duty.[91]

Negotiation No diplomatic function is more important than negotiation, which is not only the common channel of settling international differences, but also the most effective means of promoting mutual interests and understanding between the sending and receiving states. There is no set rule for a diplomat to follow in the conduct of negotiations, but he must be thoroughly versed in the subject and the position of the receiving state. Sincerity and tact are equally important.[92] In negotiation of treaties and participation in international con-

---

250 guests and a reception of 3,500. At the service were 460 waiters, 22 headwaiters, and 70 cooks. See *ibid.*, March 24, 1960. The United States government was reported seeking ways to make American embassies think as well as drink in an American atmosphere. American diplomats were advised to serve American wine at social parties. See *ibid.*, October 7, 1964; May 24–26, June 2, 1965. See also an interesting article, "Can Diplomats Do Business without Cocktails," *U.S. News and World Report,* September 20, 1957, pp. 54–59.

[90] For an instance of undiplomatic manners of an American hostess and the effect on her husband's career, see Maude P. Child, *The Social Side of Diplomatic Life* (Indianapolis, 1925), pp. 55–57.

[91] See Art. 46 of the Diplomatic Convention. During World War II, the diplomatic missions of Switzerland and Sweden rendered valuable services to the belligerents to protect the latter's interests in enemy states upon their request and with the consent of the belligerent states concerned.

[92] The following remark attributed to Sir Henry Wotton has been much quoted: "An ambassador is an honest man, sent to lie abroad for the good of his country." This distorted version of the proper function of a diplomat caused much embarrassment to Sir Henry Wotton and to King James I of England. See Satow, pp. 132–133.

ferences, a diplomat must be resourceful and skillful in presenting his country's views, and always prepared to make proposals and counter-proposals. In short, negotiation is a most challenging task for a diplomat, whose success or failure may affect the destiny of his country in matters of vital importance.

Observation The diplomatic mission is also a listening post for a nation. An envoy is expected to observe all political, military, economic, and social developments in the receiving state. His own government depends much upon his reports for policy-making. Owing to the increasing complexity of foreign affairs, not every report is read and fully utilized by the home government. Diplomats throughout the world have this common complaint. However undesirable this situation may be, the importance of constant and accurate reports cannot be overemphasized. The means of transmitting reports must be such as to ensure absolute secrecy, especially reports of the substance of elaborate negotiations.[93]

Administration The management of a large embassy, supervision of its personnel, and coordination of the activities of other representative agencies of the sending state is an insurmountable task for a diplomat. Besides, there are many routine functions, including the issuance and renewal of passports and visas, necessary aid to destitute nationals, assistance to all kinds of requests, and replies to various inquiries. Some diplomatic missions also perform consular functions in the absence of any consular post in the receiving state. Contrary to the general impression that it is an easy life, a diplomatic post, especially in an important country and at a difficult time, is most demanding and unrewarding.[94]

§137. FUNCTIONS OF CONSULAR OFFICERS

The scope of consular functions The functions of a consular officer are chiefly commercial, yet much more diversified than those of a diplomatic envoy.[95] Technically under the supervision of the

[93] Codes and ciphers must be kept safe at all times.

[94] See Stuart, pp. 185–188. For further details on diplomatic missions, see John W. Foster, *Practice of Diplomacy* (Boston, 1906), Chs. 1–6.

[95] In the opinion of Talleyrand, a consular officer should know a great deal more than a diplomatic envoy because he is expected to be "jack of all trades." Due to overlapping of diplomatic and consular functions and interchange of assignments, foreign service officers today receive training in both capacities.

diplomatic mission, the consular posts have independent power to perform their duties in their respective consular districts. Under special circumstances and with the consent of the receiving state, a consular officer may exercise his functions outside his consular district or even in another state.[96] Upon the request of a third state and subject to the permission of the receiving state, a consular post may carry out consular functions on behalf of a third state, including the protection of the latter's consular premises and archives.[97] If the sending state neither has a diplomatic mission nor is represented by one of a third state, a consular officer may be concurrently authorized, with the consent of the receiving state, to perform diplomatic functions.[98]

Four major functions of consular officers Although the duties of consular officers of different countries vary to a certain extent according to their domestic legislation and treaty provisions, they may be grouped under the following four categories: (1) furtherance of friendly relations and commercial interests, (2) protection of nationals and their interests, (3) supervision of navigation and shipping, and (4) performance of notarial and administrative services. There are other functions specially entrusted by the sending state within the limits of local laws and treaty provisions.[99] Now only of historical interest, the exercise of consular jurisdiction or extraterritoriality in certain countries in Asia and Africa was one of the most burdensome duties of consular officers.[100]

[96] See Arts. 3, 6, 7, of the Consular Convention. While consular posts are technically under the supervision of the diplomatic mission, they generally report to and receive instruction from the ministry of foreign affairs.

[97] See Arts. 8, 27, of the Consular Convention. This is the practice under exceptional circumstances, when the consular relations between the third state and the receiving state are severed.

[98] See Art. 17 of the Consular Convention.

[99] See Art. 5 of the Consular Convention. A consular officer cannot do everything for his nationals. It is interesting to quote a passage from a State Department publication (No. 5893) about this:

"Your consulate does not change money for tourists who find the bank closed.

"It does not storm the jails and release erring citizens from the local police.

"It does not pass out funds to citizens who go broke abroad.

"It does not grant patent rights to inventors, sponsor art shows, or endorse new philosophies. . . ."

[100] See *supra*, §81.

Furtherance of friendly relations and commercial interests The cultivation of friendly relations is the responsibility of both diplomatic and consular officers, who are also expected to further the development of commercial, economic, cultural, and scientific relations between the sending and receiving states. Such a development should be reported to the home government, which will then distribute the useful information to interested parties.[101] A consular officer should be fully familiar with local rules and regulations and also treaty provisions, especially concerning trade and navigation. He certifies the shipping invoices of all goods from his consular district to his country, and is thus in the position to know the current commercial relations between the two countries. It is also his duty to see that the local authorities have imposed no discriminatory measures against his country and nationals, and to solve difficulties, if any, to the satisfaction of all parties concerned.

Protection of nationals and their interests One of the most important functions of a consular officer is to protect the rights and interests of his nationals and to render whatever assistance necessary within the limits of local laws and treaty provisions.[102] A consular officer should impress upon his countrymen residing in the consular district the necessity of observing local laws and regulations; it is also his duty to seek legal redress on behalf of their interests and to ensure appropriate representation and fair trial if apprehended. But he can only expect the local authorities to apply the same standard of justice accorded to their own citizens. Nor is he permitted to perform his protective functions in conflict with the provisions of local laws.[103]

[101] See Arts. 5(b, c) of the Consular Convention.

[102] See Art. 5(a) of the Consular Convention. For a decision upholding the right of a consular officer to protect the interests of his country, see *Von Thodorovich v. Franz Josef Beneficial Association,* United States, Circuit Court, Pennsylvania, 1907. 154 F. 911. In the present discussion, nationals include both individuals and bodies corporate of the sending state. Failure of local authorities to grant appropriate protection and redress will justify diplomatic representation. See Hyde, II, pp. 1333–1334.

[103] See Art. 5(e, g, h, i) of the Consular Convention. In *Rocca v. Thompson,* the U.S. Supreme Court ruled in 1912 that foreign consular officers in the United States were not empowered with the right of local administration of the estates of their deceased countrymen to the exclusion of those entitled to administer as provided by the laws of the state in the United States. 223 U.S. 317. For further details of consular officers in the United States, consult J. I. Puente, *The Foreign Consul: His Juridical Status in the United States* (Chicago, 1926).

As to his duty to assist nationals in difficulties, the list is endless: helping nationals stranded in his consular district for one reason or the other; locating relatives and friends as well as lost articles; receiving and forwarding mail; taking care of problems involving the sick and the dead; settling family disputes; and so forth. All these matters require a considerable amount of his time, and in many cases are very unrewarding. Of course, he cannot possibly comply with requests which do not fall within his competence and authority.

Supervision of navigation and shipping The supervision of, and assistance to, ships and aircraft as well as crews of the sending state are within the competence of a consular officer in his consular district. The provisions of the Vienna Convention on Consular Relations of 1963 are merely declaratory of existing practices. Without prejudice to the powers of the receiving state, he examines and legalizes ships' papers, takes statements about the voyage, investigates incidents if any, and settles disputes involving the master, the seamen, or passengers.[104] However, his jurisdiction over internal affairs of the ships ends when peace and tranquility of the port are disturbed and local authorities assume jurisdiction.[105] The complexity of seamen's problems and the relief to those destitute or stranded abroad challenge the best talents and maximum patience of both diplomatic and consular officers.

Performance of notarial and administrative services In accordance with the practices of nations and the provisions of the Vienna Convention on Consular Relations of 1963, a consular officer is to act as notary, civil registrar, and in other capacities of similar nature, and also to perform certain functions of administrative category. One of his routine duties is the issuance and renewal of passports to his nationals and visas to persons who wish to enter his country.[106] Within the provisions of international agreements and municipal laws, he transmits judicial and extra-judicial documents or executes letters rogatory or commissions to take evidence for the courts of the sending state.[107] He registers the birth of children of his countrymen born in his consular district, and scrutinizes cases concerning the nationality law of his country and immigration regulations. In addition, the routine administration of a large consulate or consulate-general is by no means easy.

[104] See Art. 5(k, l) of the Consular Convention.

[105] See *supra,* §110.

[106] The granting or withholding of a visa is within the competence of the consul, whose decision is not reviewable. See *Licea-Gomez v. Pilliod,* United States, District Court, N.D. of Illinois, 1960. 193 Fed. Supp. 577.

[107] See Art. 5(d, f, j) of the Consular Convention.

§138. THE TERMINATION OF DIPLOMATIC AND CONSULAR REPRESENTATION

Provisions of the Vienna Conventions The Vienna Convention on Diplomatic Relations of 1961 lays down two major causes for the termination of a diplomatic mission: recall by the sending state and dismissal by the receiving state. Conclusive evidence of either action is the receipt of notification by the receiving or sending state as the case may be.[108] Similar procedures are provided in the Vienna Convention on Consular Relations of 1963, except that it adds the withdrawal of the *exequatur* as another cause of termination of consular representation.[109] Withdrawal of this document is, in effect, a form of dismissal.

Major causes of termination The death of a diplomatic or consular officer automatically ends his term of office. Temporary missions may also be terminated upon the expiration of the specified period or the fulfillment of certain objectives. Termination of permanent representatives may be caused in any of the following ways, except that the change of the head of state or the form of government does not affect consular officers.

Recall by the sending state Recall may occur at the expiration of his term of office in the post, attainment of retirement age, resignation of his own volition for one reason or another,[110] transfer to another state or in the same state from one post to another due to change of rank,[111] or dissatisfaction with his service by the home government. Recall may also happen at the request of the receiving state if it considers the diplomatic or consular officer *persona non grata*.[112]

[108] See Art. 43 of the Diplomatic Convention. The Pan-American Convention of 1928 listed five causes, some of which concerned the termination of temporary missions (Art. 25).

[109] See Art. 25 of the Consular Convention.

[110] It is now the practice in the United States that, upon a change of Presidency, all political appointees to ambassadorial or ministerial posts are to submit their resignations, which may not necessarily be accepted by the new President. It has also been suggested that career heads of missions should follow the same practice; this might be convenient to the new administration, but would affect the morale of the foreign service.

[111] Sometimes the rank of a diplomatic envoy is temporarily raised for a coronation, royal marriage, or other state ceremony. After the temporary mission, he reverts to his original rank in the same post.

[112] One notable instance was the American demand in 1792 for Citizen Genêt's recall, which was followed by the French request for the recall of

Dismissal by the receiving state When a diplomatic or consular officer has become extremely undesirable to the receiving state, the latter may withdraw its recognition of his official status and demand his departure from its territory within a specified period. This, however, occurs only in serious cases.[113] Otherwise, his function may be terminated through recall by his home government upon the request of the receiving state.[114]

Gouverneur Morris, American Minister to Paris. See Moore, *Digest*, IV, pp. 488–490. Interference in domestic affairs through propaganda against the democratic tradition of the American states is prohibited in accordance with the "Norms concerning Diplomatic and Consular Functions," adopted by the Foreign Ministers Conference at Havana in 1940. *International Conferences of American States, 1933–1940*, p. 351. No nation can tolerate interference with its domestic matters by a foreign diplomatic agent, who will be deemed *persona non grata* if he violates this precept.

[113] The arrest and expulsion of Count Luxburg, German Minister to Buenos Aires, by the Argentine government in 1917 was due to his involvement in a plot to sink Argentine ships on their way to Europe. The serious nature of his conspiracy necessitated his immediate dismissal and detention in order to prevent further action against the national interest of the receiving state. See 12 *Am. Jour. Int. Law* (1918), pp. 135–140. In recent years, dismissal of military attachés and secretaries on the ground of illegitimate activities has been frequent: American expulsion of Nikolai I. Kurochkin, third secretary of the Soviet embassy in Washington, in June 1958 (*The New York Times*, June 8, 1958); Soviet seizure and dismissal of Russell A. Langelle, attaché of the American Embassy in Moscow, in October 1959 (*ibid.*, October 18, 20, 27, 1959); Cuba's dismissal of Edwin L. Sweet and William G. Friedemann, two attachés of the American Embassy in Havana, in June 1960 (*ibid.*, June 17, 18, 1960); American expulsion of two Cuban consular officers, Carlos Manuel Lazaro Felix Sanchez y Basquet and Berta Louisa Pla y Badia, in June 1960 (*ibid.*, June 19, 1960); Poland's dismissal of Mme. Marie E. Greindi-Czetwertynska, an attaché of the Belgian Embassy at Warsaw, in November 1959 (*ibid.*, November 5, 1959); and Swiss dismissal of two Soviet diplomats, whose names were not disclosed, in May 1960 (*ibid.*, May 12, 1960). For the expulsion of two first secretaries of the United Arab Republic Embassy in Rome, Abdel Moneim el-Neklawy and Selim Osma el-Sayed, because of their air abduction of a man in a trunk on November 17, 1964, see *ibid.*, November 18, 19, 1964.

[114] If the sending state does not act after a request for recall of its envoy, he may be dismissed by the receiving state, as in the case of Lord Sackville, British Minister to Washington, because of his alleged involvement in the American Presidential election of 1888. See Moore, *Digest*, IV, p. 536. Recently, two Soviet Embassy officers in Ottawa, H. E. Bytchkov of the Commercial Section and V. N. Poluchkin, a chancery clerk, were expelled by the Canadian government on espionage charges. The Soviet

Change of head of state or form of government The death or abdication of a sovereign or a drastic change in the form of government through revolution in either the receiving or sending state usually requires new letters of credence in the case of diplomatic envoys above the rank of chargé d'affaires; the latter is not accredited to the head of state but to the minister of foreign affairs. Such a change has no effect on consular officers. The orderly transition of office of the head of state, such as the inauguration of a new President in the United States, does not require new credentials for the envoys.[115] On the other hand, a new envoy is often appointed after a drastic revolution to replace the old one with a view to re-establishing friendly relations between the two states.[116]

The closing of the diplomatic mission or the consular post When war breaks out between sending and receiving states, their diplomatic missions automatically come to an end.[117] Severance of diplomatic relations without leading to war temporarily suspends the diplomatic missions, but consular posts will continue to function. On the other hand, the closing of the mission or withdrawal of the diplomatic staff does not necessarily constitute a break in relations.[118] Both diplomatic

Embassy rejected the accusation. See *The New York Times,* May 9, 1965. On October 13, 1961, the Soviet Union recalled its Ambassador to the Netherlands, Panteleimon K. Ponomarenko, who was declared *persona non grata,* and ordered the expulsion of the Dutch Ambassador to Moscow, Henri A. Helb, in retaliation. This incident was a result of a fist fight between Dutch police and Soviet diplomats at an Amsterdam airfield over the departure of Mme. Aleksei Golub, whose husband had defected to the West. See *The New York Times,* October 14, 1961.

[115] There were some exceptions, one of which happened in 1873 when President MacMahon succeeded President Thiers in France. New letters of credence were issued to the French envoy to Berlin on the instigation of Germany.

[116] When the Chinese Communist government was established in Peking on October 1, 1949, General N. Roshin, former Soviet Ambassador to the Nationalist government, was appointed as first Soviet Ambassador to Peking. But this was an exception to general practice.

[117] During the two world wars, diplomatic envoys were either escorted to the border or allowed to remain in the country under surveillance by the authorities of the receiving state. After severance of diplomatic relations, third states are usually entrusted to take care of the interests of the states so affected.

[118] Iran closed her legation in Washington and consulate in New York in 1936, without breaking relations with the United States. After mistreatment of American officials in Brazzaville, the United States withdrew her embassy staff from the Congo Republic without severing diplomatic relations. See *The New York Times,* August 14, 1965.

and consular relations are terminated as a result of the extinction of the receiving or the sending state.[119] A consular post is sometimes closed due to change of consular district or for other reasons decided by the sending or receiving state. The closing of consulates may be demanded by a third state after its military occupation of the receiving state.

Farewell audiences and letters of recall Before leaving his post, the head of a diplomatic mission above the rank of chargé d'affaires may ask an audience under normal circumstances for the presentation of his letter of recall.[120] The head of the receiving state will then address the head of the sending state with compliments of the envoy's conduct and regrets at his recall. This is the so-called recredential (*lettre de récréance*). More often the letter of recall is delivered by his successor at the time he presents his credentials. There is no general rule governing these ceremonial or procedural matters, but the tendency is toward less formality.

III. *DIPLOMATIC IMMUNITIES AND PRIVILEGES* [121]

§139. THE BASIS AND EXTENT OF IMMUNITIES AND PRIVILEGES

The legal foundation of immunities and privileges The principle of extending special immunities and privileges reciprocally granted by states to their diplomatic representatives is to ensure the independence and convenience in the performance of their official functions.[122]

[119] When Latvia, Lithuania, and Estonia were incorporated by the Soviet Union in 1940, the United States and several other countries continued to receive their diplomatic envoys as a protest against the annexation.

[120] No private audience will be asked in the event of severance of diplomatic relations or outbreak of war.

[121] General texts on the subject: O'Connell, II, pp. 962–1016; Oppenheim, I, §§384–405, 417a, 434–435; Fenwick, *Principles,* Ch. XXIV, §§F, G, I; Hyde, II, §§426–443A, 459, 464–482; Moore, *Digest,* IV, §§657–669; V, 702–716; Hackworth, *Digest,* IV, §§400–418, 428–438; Starke, Ch. 18, §3; Hershey, pp. 401–413, 422–424; Von Glahn, Ch. 11; Jacobini, pp. 180–191; Soviet *Text,* pp. 301–304, 306, 313, 347–348; Satow, Chs. XVI–XIX; Sen, Chs. V–VI; Schuschnigg, Ch. 13; Clark & Sohn, Annex VI; Thayer, Chs. XVIII–XIX; Stuart, Chs. 14–15, 21; Plischke, Ch. 9.

[122] While immunities are essential to the performance of official functions, accord of privileges is merely a matter of convenience. An important reference on the subject is the *Laws and Regulations regarding Diplomatic and Consular Privileges and Immunities,* prepared for the use of the International Law Commission of the United Nations in 1958 in its work on diplomatic and consular intercourse and immunities. It contains the laws and regulations of various countries. UN Doc. ST/Leg/Ser.B/7.

This practice may be traced back to ancient times, and, through custom and treaties, has been followed by all members of the international community.[123] Immunities and privileges are accorded to a lesser extent to consular officers. In commercial treaties and consular conventions, the special status of consular officers is usually embodied in the most-favored-nation clause on the basis of reciprocity.[124] The Vienna Convention on Diplomatic Relations of 1961 and that on Consular Relations of 1963 are declaratory of existing rules and practices with respect to diplomatic immunities and privileges, which are reciprocally accorded by the states without discrimination.[125]

The beginning and end of immunities and privileges The receiving state grants immunities and privileges to persons entitled to them at the moment of their entry into its territory, or upon receiving notification of their appointment if they are already in its territory. Such immunities and privileges will continue to subsist for a reasonable period after the termination of their services.[126] Immunity does not cease in respect of official acts in the exercise of their functions.[127] In the event of the death of a diplomat, the members of his family entitled to immunities and privileges will continue to enjoy them for a reasonable period.[128]

[123] For further references, consult E. R. Adair, *The Extraterritoriality of Ambassadors in the Sixteenth and Seventeenth Centuries* (London, 1929); A. S. Hershey, *Diplomatic Agents and Immunities* (Washington, D.C., 1919).

[124] For the basis of the immunities and privileges due to consuls, see *United States v. Trumbull,* U.S., District Court, S.D. of California, 1891. 48 F. 94.

[125] Art. 47 of the Diplomatic Convention; Art. 72 of the Consular Convention.

[126] In *Laperdix and Penquer v. Kouzouboff and Belin,* the Court of Paris of France asserted in 1925 that "the principle of diplomatic immunity, developed in the interest of governments and not in the interest of diplomats, does not survive the mission." 53 J.D.I. (1926), 64; English translation from Briggs, 778. For immunity from past and current obligations, see *Procureur Général v. Nazare Agha,* France, Cour de Cassation (Chamber Civile), 1921 (123 *Arrêts de la Cour de Cassation en matière civile,* p. 271; English translation from Hudson, 421); *Musurus Bey v. Gadban,* Great Britain, Court of Appeal, 1894. [1894] 2 Q.B. 352.

[127] This principle is also evidenced in the decision of *Salm v. Frazier,* France, Court of Appeals of Rouen, 1933. *Annual Digest,* 1933–1934, No. 161.

[128] Art. 39 of the Diplomatic Convention; Art. 53 of the Consular Convention.

Temporary presence in third states It is also the general practice that a third state grants the right of innocent passage to diplomats in transit, unless they travel incognito or their presence in its territory is deemed undesirable.[129] Persons entitled to immunities and privileges are generally permitted to enjoy the same in a third state,[130] which also accords necessary freedom and protection to their official correspondence and communications in transit.[131] In time of war, however, some belligerents have imposed unreasonable restraints and even committed flat violations, regardless of the established practice of nations.[132]

§140. THE RIGHT OF INVIOLABILITY AND PROTECTION

The extent and necessity of inviolability The right of inviolability is essential to the proper exercise of the functions of foreign representatives. It extends to the person of diplomatic and consular officers,[133] their premises, archives, and documents.[134] The same right

[129] Pierre Soulé, American Minister to Madrid, while landing at Calais, France, in 1854, was stopped to keep him from going to Paris because of his hostile attitude toward Emperor Napoleon III. In 1926, Madame Kollontay, Soviet Ambassador to Mexico, was refused innocent passage by the United States.

[130] No immunity can, however, be expected if the diplomat conspires to violate narcotics laws, like Mauricio Rosal, former Guatemalan Ambassador to Belgium. Rosal was arrested in the United States on October 3, 1960, and was dismissed by his own government the next day. See *The New York Times,* December 15, 1960.

[131] Immunity has been granted by the United States to foreign diplomats accredited to other countries and traveling over its territory. See *Holbrook, Nelson and Company v. Henderson,* U.S., Superior Court of City of New York, 1839 (4 Sandford 619); *Wilson v. Blanco,* U.S., N.Y. Superior Court, 1889 (56 N.Y. Supp. 582); *Bergman v. De Sieyes,* U.S., Circuit Court of Appeals, 1948 (170 F.2d 360). See also Art. 40 of the Diplomatic Convention; Art. 54 of the Consular Convention.

[132] See Stuart, pp. 270–274; Satow, pp. 248–253.

[133] For the principle that consular officers are entitled to special protection by the local government in order to perform their functions without interference, see *Mexico (Mallén Claim) v. United States,* General Claims Commission, 1927. Opinions of Commissioners (1927), p. 254.

[134] Arts. 22, 24, 29, 45, of the Diplomatic Convention; Arts. 27, 31, 33, 59, 61, of the Consular Convention. The inviolability of consular premises only applies to the part exclusively used for the work of the consular post. Concerning the inviolability of archives and documents of a consular post headed by an honorary consular officer, the Vienna Convention of 1963 has

is applied to the residence of diplomatic agents, known as *franchise de l'hôtel,* as well as their papers and correspondence.[135] The receiving state must take appropriate steps to prevent any attack on their person, freedom, or dignity. Any infraction of this right constitutes a serious offense.[136] But if any diplomatic and consular officer abuses this right by committing acts of violence or conspiring against the receiving state, he can be put under restraint.[137]

Diplomatic premises are entitled to special protection and may not be entered without the consent of the head of the mission or post except in case of fire or other disaster requiring prompt protective action. The premises, furnishings, and other property, as well as means of transport, are immune from search or requisition. The Vienna Convention on Consular Relations allows the receiving state to make necessary expropriation of those belonging to a consular post, but all possible

---

a restrictive provision that they must be kept separate from other papers and documents (Art. 61). On April 6, 1927, the Peking government of China, then under the control of Chang Tso-lin, searched the Soviet Embassy in Peking and found many documents revealing Soviet involvement in the Communist revolution in China. In *Rose v. The King,* the Canadian Court did not uphold the inviolability of diplomatic documents under special circumstances. [1947] 3 D.L.R. 618. The United States has uncovered wired microphone systems in the embassy premises in Moscow, Warsaw, and other Communist capitals. This practice is hardly in conformity with the right of inviolability, but the receiving states denied any knowledge of it. See *The New York Times,* November 3, 1964; *Long Island Press,* November 10, 1964.

[135] Arts. 30–31 of the Diplomatic Convention. In *United States v. Jeffers,* the U.S. Circuit Court for the District of Columbia decided in 1836 that local authorities may not enter the premises of a foreign mission or the residence of a diplomat without the consent of the head of the mission or of the diplomat concerned. 4 Cranch, Cir. Ct., Rep. 704.

[136] The most noted incident was the arrest of the Russian Ambassador, M. de Mathveof (Matveof or Mattueoff), in the street of London in 1708, to enforce payment of his debts. Due to the seriousness of the case, England promptly enacted the Act 7 Anne for Preserving the Privileges of Ambassadors, and expressed deep regrets to Peter the Great. Briggs, 763. In *Respublica v. Longchamps,* the U.S. Court of Oyer and Terminer at Philadelphia asserted in 1784 that an assault upon a diplomatic agent is a more serious offense than one upon an ordinary person. 1 Dallas 111. It is an established principle that a foreign envoy is entitled to special protection from insult. See Moore, *Digest,* IV, p. 629.

[137] This happened to Gyllenburg, Swedish Minister to England, in 1716, and to Prince Cellamare, Spanish Ambassador to France, in 1718. Such incidents have been rare in modern times.

steps must be taken to avoid impeding the performance of consular functions, and adequate compensation must be promptly paid.[138]

International law is violated when the receiving state permits mass demonstrations and forced entry into premises for the official use of diplomatic missions and consular posts and considerable damage to their property and belongings.[139] Even during severance of diplomatic and consular relations or armed conflict between the receiving and sending states, each must respect and protect the premises, property, and archives of the other. Their custody may be entrusted to a third state if the parties to the conflict raise no objection. Persons entitled to immunities and privileges other than nationals of the receiving state and their families are allowed to leave at the earliest possible moment. The receiving state should render whatever assistance and facilities are necessary for departure.[140]

The question of asylum and self-jurisdiction As described above, the right of asylum in diplomatic missions is not a general rule of international law, but a common practice in many states on humanitarian

[138] Art. 22 of the Diplomatic Convention; Arts. 31, 59, of the Consular Convention. The controversy between the United States and the Soviet Union over the Kasenkina case in 1948 involved the right of local police to enter the Soviet Consulate-General in New York. The former Russian schoolteacher was set free and lived in the United States until her death in 1960. This incident led to the closing of the Soviet consulates-general in New York and San Francisco and the American consulate in Vladivostok.

[139] Such demonstrations and riots have become recurrent, especially against the United States official establishments in Moscow, Cairo, and Jakarta. The receiving states have usually expressed regrets and paid some compensation, but it would be much better to adopt effective means to prevent these incidents. For the forced entry of five hundred Indonesian students to the Dutch Legation and damage to furniture and valuable paintings, see *The New York Times*, May 8, 1960. On April 26, 1965, a mob of twenty thousand Cambodians attacked the American Embassy and ripped down the American flag. See *ibid.*, April 27, 1965. A United States Court of Appeals recently issued a temporary restraining order against the Washington Police Department, directing it to permit a silent demonstration five hundred feet from the South Vietnamese Embassy. The reason cited by the police for denying permission for the demonstration was that this would put it right across the street from the Luxemburg Embassy in Washington. The Court held that the nearness of one embassy to another should not be used to frustrate the right of political protest, which is a mere demonstration without violence or riots. See *ibid.*, April 15, 1966. There is no doubt about the difference between peaceful demonstration and violence or riots.

[140] Arts. 44–45 of the Diplomatic Convention; Arts. 26–27 of the Consular Convention.

ground and regional understandings.[141] While a diplomatic envoy has the authority to supervise his subordinates, he is not entitled to exercise absolute self-jurisdiction over his retinue. No receiving state today will allow him to arrest and try a member of his staff or his countrymen.[142]

§141. IMMUNITY FROM LOCAL JURISDICTION

The legal basis of immunity The so-called right of exterritoriality confers on diplomatic personnel immunity from local jurisdiction. In other words, persons with diplomatic status are, to a varying degree, exempted from enforcement of local laws of the receiving state and also of third states in transit. They are, however, under no circumstances immune from the jurisdiction of their own sending state. On the basis of exterritoriality, a child born of a diplomatic or consular officer does not automatically acquire the nationality of the receiving state by the operation of its nationality law. An optional protocol concerning acquisition of nationality was adopted by the United Nations Conference on Diplomatic Relations in 1961 and also by the Conference on Consular Relations in 1963.[143] The extent of immunity enjoyed by diplomats and consular officers is not the same, and will be treated separately whenever necessary.

Immunity due to diplomatic officers A diplomatic agent enjoys absolute immunity from criminal jurisdiction,[144] and also from civil and

[141] See *supra,* §121. The Pan-American Convention of 1928 on asylum is a kind of regional understanding among the American states. The Soviet Union holds that the inviolability of diplomatic premises "does not give the right forcibly to detain therein any person or to give refuge therein to persons in respect to whom decisions regarding arrest have been taken by the authorized organs of the Union of Soviet Socialist Republics or of Union Republics." Art. 4 of the Statute of 1927, quoted from Soviet *Text,* p. 302.

[142] When Marquis de Rosny represented France as a ceremonial envoy to England for the accession of James I to the throne in 1603, he had one of his retinue arrested and condemned for murder by a jury of Frenchmen traveling with him. The convicted man was, however, pardoned by the King of England. After his organization of Hsing-chung Hui in 1894, Sun Yat-sen intensified his revolutionary activities against the Manchu government in China. During a trip to London in 1896, Sun was kidnapped by a Manchu agent and confined in the Chinese legation. Due to the intercession by the British government, he was subsequently released.

[143] See, respectively, UN Docs. A/Conf.20/11 and A/Conf.25/14.

[144] Although a diplomat is exempted from criminal jurisdiction, he may be expelled by the receiving state in extreme cases. This happened to Mendoza, Spanish Ambassador to England, in 1586, and to De Bass, French

administrative jurisdiction, with the following exceptions: [145] (1) a real action relating to his own private immovable property; (2) an action relating to succession in which he is involved as executor, administrator, heir, or legatee as a private person; and (3) an action relating to his private professional or commercial activity. Measures in execution of the above must not infringe the inviolability of his person or of his residence. He is not obliged to give evidence as a witness.[146] The immunity from local jurisdiction also excludes the authorities of the receiving state from holding an inquest into the cause of the death of a diplomat without the permission of the head of the mission.

Immunity due to consular officers The immunity accorded to a consular officer is not as extensive as that to a diplomatic agent.[147] In case of a grave crime and pursuant to a decision by competent judicial

---

Ambassador to England, in 1654. In most cases, delinquent diplomats have been recalled at the demand of the receiving state. Before the United States entered World War I, several diplomats from Germany and Austria-Hungary to Washington were recalled upon the demand of the American government because of their violations of American laws: Constantin Dumba, Austro-Hungarian Minister to Washington; Captain von Papen and Captain Boy-Ed, Military and Naval Attachés of the German embassy in Washington. Diplomatic immunity does not extend to a non-diplomat who has committed a crime in the premises of a diplomatic mission. See *Nikitschenkoff Case,* France, Cour de Cassation (Crim.), 1865. *Journal du Palais* (1866), p. 51; English translation from Briggs, 787.

[145] In *De Meeus v. Forzano,* the Italian Court of Cassation ruled in 1940 that diplomatic privilege is indivisible and that exemption from civil jurisdiction even in respect of private acts constitutes the necessary foundation for the exercise of public functions. *Annual Digest,* 1938–1940, No. 164. See also *Magdalena Steam Navigation Co. v. Martin,* Great Britain, Court of Queens Bench, 1959. 2 Ellis & Ellis, 94.

[146] Art. 31 of the Diplomatic Convention. At the trial of Charles J. Guiteau for the assassination of President Garfield in 1881, the Venezuelan Minister at Washington was instructed to appear as a witness. See Moore, *Digest,* IV, p. 644. The Pan-American Convention of 1928 emphasizes exemption from all civil and criminal jurisdiction (Art. 19).

[147] In *Barbuit's Case,* the British Court of Chancery asserted in 1737 that a consul was not entitled to the same privileges and immunities as ambassadors. Williams, *Cases in Equity during the Time of Lord Chancellor Talbot,* 281. There is no doubt that a consular officer is not entitled to diplomatic immunity for crimes committed not in connection with his official functions. See *Bigelow v. Princess Zizianoff,* France, Court of Appeal of Paris, 1928. *Gazette du Palais,* May 4, 1928, No. 125; English translation from 23 *Am. Jour. Int. Law* (1929), p. 172.

authority, a consular officer is liable to arrest or detention pending trial. In the execution of a judicial decision of final effect, he may be committed to prison or subjected to other forms of restriction of his personal freedom.[148] However, criminal proceedings must be conducted with the respect and consideration due to his official position. The sending state must be notified of his necessary appearance before competent authorities, as stated above.[149]

A consular officer or employee is not amenable to the jurisdiction of the judicial or administrative authorities of the receiving state in the exercise of his official functions,[150] but he is subject to civil action arising out of a contract in his private capacity or by a third party for damage caused by his vehicle, vessel, or aircraft.[151] When called upon to attend as witness in the course of judicial or administrative proceedings and concerning matters not connected with his official functions or disclosure of official documents, he is obliged to give evidence.[152] A limited degree of immunity is also applied to honorary consuls for convenience of exercise of their official functions.[153]

Waiver of immunity Diplomatic immunity may be waived by the sending state, but this must always be express. Waiver of immunity from jurisdiction in civil or administrative proceedings does not imply waiver of immunity to execution of the judgment. In either case, a separate waiver is required. Initiation of proceedings by a person enjoying immunity precludes him from invoking immunity to any counterclaim directly connected with the principal claim.[154]

[148] In 1917, the German consul-general at San Francisco was convicted of conspiracy to destroy munitions and sentenced to a fine and imprisonment.

[149] Arts. 41–42, 63, of the Consular Convention.

[150] In *Mazzucchi v. United States Consulate,* the Italian Court of Appeals at Naples (Labor Magistrate) ruled, in 1931, that examination of the official functions of foreign consular officers is not within the jurisdiction of courts of the receiving state. 72 *Monitore del Tribunali* (1931), p. 621; English translation from Hudson, pp. 434–435.

[151] Art. 43 of the Consular Convention. See also Hackworth, *Digest,* IV, p. 272.

[152] See Art. 44 of the Consular Convention. Such evidence may be taken at his office or residence, or in a written statement. If he declines to give evidence, no coercive measures or penalty may be imposed on him. For the American position, see Hyde, II, pp. 1344–1345.

[153] See Arts. 58, 63, of the Consular Convention.

[154] See Art. 32 of the Diplomatic Convention; Art. 45 of the Consular Convention. The principle that immunity cannot be waived without the consent of the sending state is well illustrated in *United States v. Benner,* U.S., Circuit Court, E.D. of Pennsylvania, 1830. 24 F. 1084. In *Herman v.*

During the deliberation of the United Nations Conference on Diplomatic Intercourse and Immunities in 1961, much concern was expressed over the claims of diplomatic immunity, which, in certain cases, deprive other persons of appropriate remedies. At its twelfth plenary meeting on April 14, the Conference adopted the following resolution:

> Recommends that the sending state should waive the immunity of members of its diplomatic mission in respect of civil claims of persons in the receiving state when this can be done without impeding the performance of the functions of the mission, and that, when immunity is not waived, the sending state should use its best endeavors to bring about a just settlement of the claims.[155]

It is understood that this recommendation applies to all persons enjoying diplomatic immunity whether in diplomatic missions or consular posts. There really is no reason why states cannot comply with this recommendation, which, if observed, will go a long way toward remedying injustices suffered by persons because of claims of diplomatic immunity. For the safety of all concerned, diplomats should waive immunity in all cases involving violations of traffic regulations, and be treated on the same basis as other residents in the receiving state.[156]

§142. EXEMPTIONS AND PRIVILEGES

Exemption from taxes and other obligations The privilege of exemption from national, regional, and municipal dues and taxes is

---

Apetz, the Supreme Court of New York ruled, in 1927, that members of a diplomat's domestic suite may waive immunity without the consent of his sending state. 130 Misc. N.Y. Rep., 618. For further discussion of waiver of immunity under various conditions, see *Dickinson v. Del Solar,* Great Britain, King's Bench Division, 1929 ([1930] 1 K.B. 376); *In re Republic of Bolivia Exploration Syndicate,* Great Britain, Chancery Division, 1913 ([1914] 1 Ch. 139); *In re Suarez (Suarez v. Suarez),* Great Britain, Chancery Division, 1917 ([1918] 1 Ch. 176).

[155] See UN Doc. A/Conf.20/10/Add.1, Pt. II—Consideration of Civil Claims.

[156] It was reported that the director of traffic in Rio de Janeiro deflated the tires of diplomatic cars parked in the wrong places. The American ambassador to Brazil, Lincoln Gordon, fell victim to the flat-tire campaign on July 8, 1964. See *The New York Times,* July 9, 1964. Due to new parking regulations applying to diplomats, cars in Washington owned by diplomats received many parking tickets. In retaliation, Manila police ticketed thirty American embassy cars on March 31, 1964. The State Department expects American diplomats abroad to comply with local traffic regulations. See *ibid.,* March 7, April 1, 1964.

applied to diplomatic and consular premises, residences of the head of the diplomatic mission and career head of the consular post, fees and charges levied by the diplomatic mission or consular post, as well as all diplomatic and consular personnel and members of their families. They are also exempted from customs duties and inspection, but not from taxes on private incomes and services as well as other indirect taxes.[157]

Diplomatic and consular personnel and members of their families are also exempted from the following: social security provisions; all personal services; all public services of any kind; military obligations, including requisitioning, military contributions, and billeting; registration of aliens, residence and work permits.[158] With respect to insurance against third-party risks, the Consular Convention of 1963 specifically provides that all members of the consular post must comply if required by laws and regulations of the receiving state.[159]

Other facilities and privileges The receiving state is obliged to accord full facilities to diplomatic missions and consular posts for their performance of official functions and to render whatever assistance necessary for acquisition of premises and accommodations for their members.[160] They are entitled to freedom of movement in the receiving

[157] See Arts. 23, 28, 34, 36, of the Diplomatic Convention; Arts. 32, 39, 49–51, 60, 62, 66, of the Consular Convention. Customs duties, charges for storage, cartage, and similar services are not exempted. If there are serious grounds for suspicion that certain articles in the personal baggage of a person with diplomatic status are prohibited by law or controlled by quarantine regulations, inspection may be conducted in the presence of him personally or of his authorized representative. There have been abuses of diplomatic privileges and exemptions, including importation of narcotic drugs. In a circular note to all diplomatic missions in Washington on October 4, 1963, the Department of State moved to restrict tax-free purchases of automobiles by foreign diplomats in order to prevent the abuse of profit through resale within a short period. See *The New York Times,* October 31, 1963.

[158] Arts. 33, 35, of the Diplomatic Convention; Arts. 46–48, 52, 65, 67, of the Consular Convention. See also Hyde, II, p. 1340.

[159] Art. 56.

[160] Because of increasing demand for premises for embassies in Washington and for missions to the United Nations in New York as well as accommodations for their members, it is difficult to expect satisfactory results in every case in spite of assistance by the authorities concerned. Some newly independent states in Africa have been disturbed by racial incidents in restaurants. In this respect, also, the Soviet Union is not entirely absolved from racial prejudices according to statements made by African students who returned from Moscow in 1961. See *The New York Times,* July 12, 16, 1961; *U.S. News & World Report,* March 27, 1961, pp. 78–79.

state, with the exception of certain areas prohibited or regulated for reasons of security or in retaliation against travel restrictions in the sending state.[161] Respect for and protection of freedom of communication is essential to the performance of diplomatic and consular functions. Official correspondence, diplomatic or consular bags, and couriers are inviolable.[162] To ensure freedom of religious worship, the right of chapel must be respected. It is also a general practice that the flag and emblem or coat of arms of the sending state may be used on the diplomatic and consular premises as well as on the residence and means of transportation of the head of the mission or post.[163]

In the exercise of consular functions, a consular officer expects local authorities to facilitate his communication and contact with his countrymen, especially if arrested or committed to prison or custody pending trial or if detained in any other manner. Whatever information involves the interests of the sending state and its nationals must be conveyed by competent local authorities to the consular post, including deaths, guardianship or trusteeship, shipwrecks, and air accidents. Normally, a consular officer deals with the local authorities in the consular district, but, circumstances permitting, he may address the competent central authorities of the receiving state.[164]

§143. PERSONS ENTITLED TO DIPLOMATIC IMMUNITIES AND PRIVILEGES

Members in diplomatic and consular service The classification and designation of the members of diplomatic mission and consular posts have already been described.[165] A full list of persons at the service

[161] The United States, the Soviet Union, and several other countries have imposed restrictions on traveling by diplomats for reasons of security and in retaliation. For a survey of these incidents, see *The New York Times*, October 30, 1963. Members of Communist-bloc delegations in New York are restricted to travel within a 25-mile radius of Columbus Circle in retaliation for travel restrictions imposed on American diplomats in Communist countries. But they may travel outside the limit by notifying the United States delegation to the United Nations several days in advance. For some unpleasant incidents as a result of these restrictions, see *ibid.*, March 24, 1966.

[162] See Arts. 21, 25–27, of the Diplomatic Convention; Arts. 28, 30, 34–35, of the Consular Convention. There have been many violations, especially in wartime, by delay of messages and restrictions of movement.

[163] See Art. 20 of the Diplomatic Convention; Art. 29 of the Consular Convention.

[164] See Arts. 36–38 of the Consular Convention.

[165] See *supra*, §§131, 133–134. According to L. Oppenheim, these officers may be classified as (1) members of the official staff, including coun-

of the diplomatic mission must be furnished to the ministry of foreign affairs of the receiving state. The diplomatic list is conclusive evidence of diplomatic immunity and privileges.[166] To the same effect is a statement from the minister of foreign affairs or other appropriate government authorities.[167] The immunities and privileges accorded to diplomatic and consular officers are also extended to their families and, to a lesser extent, to other staff and members of their families as provided in the Vienna Conventions on Diplomatic and Consular Relations.[168]

Members of the administrative and technical staff and their families are entitled to the same, except that their immunity from civil and administrative jurisdiction is limited to official acts performed within the course of duty.[169] Members of the service staff may enjoy immunity in respect of their official acts and also exemption from dues and taxes on their emoluments. Private servants may enjoy a certain degree of immunity and privileges at the discretion of the receiving state, and

---

selors, secretaries, attachés, legal advisers, interpreters, and the like; (2) persons in private service; (3) members of their families; and (4) couriers. Oppenheim, I, pp. 809–810.

[166] In *Assurantie Compagnie Excelsior v. Smith* (1923), the British Court of Appeal relied on the diplomatic list to ascertain the official position of Smith, a clerk at the American Embassy in London. 40 T.L.R. (1923), 105. See also *United States ex rel. Casanova v. Fitzpatrick*, United States, District Court, S.D.N.Y., 1963. 214 Fed. Supp. 425.

[167] In *Engelke v. Musmann*, the British House of Lords decided, in 1928, that the statement of the attorney-general, made at the instance of the Foreign Office, on the diplomatic status of Herr Engelke was conclusive. [1928] A.C. 433.

[168] Claims of immunity by members of diplomats' families from local jurisdiction over criminal or irresponsible acts have caused much embarrassment to diplomatic missions and local authorities. In some cases, immunity has been waived, for example, Carlos Waddington, son of the Chilean Minister to Belgium in 1906; in others, injustices were committed without remedy. The careless driving of David P. Hearne, son of the Irish Ambassador to the United States, created a sensation in Washington in November 1959. Finally, the Ambassador ordered him home to Ireland. See *The New York Times*, November 14, 18, 22, 1959; *U.S. News & World Report*, November 30, 1959, p. 83.

[169] In *Soc. Arethusa Film v. Reist* (1953), the Italian Tribunal of Rome decided that unofficial acts of a chancelor at the American Embassy in Rome were not immune from civil jurisdiction. 49 *Am. Jour. Int. Law* (1955), p. 102. By a decree of March 27, 1956, the Soviet Union has extended diplomatic immunities and privileges to clerical and auxiliary personnel on a reciprocal basis.

may be exempted from dues and taxes on their emoluments if they are not its nationals or permanent residents. Because of implications arising out of the right of exterritoriality, states are not inclined to accept their own nationals as diplomatic or consular officers of another state.[170] If a diplomatic agent is a national or permanent resident in the receiving state, he may enjoy immunity from jurisdiction and inviolability only for official acts. It is up to the receiving state to determine the extent of immunity and privileges enjoyed by other members of the staff of the mission and private servants if they are its nationals or permanent residents.[171] Practice varies in different states, particularly about private servants, whose audacity in claims of immunity is sometimes equaled only by their absurdity.[172]

Immunities and privileges enjoyed by consular officers are accorded to their families, but not to families of honorary consular officers or of consular employees at a consular post headed by an honorary consular officer. If the consular officers are nationals or permanent residents of the receiving state, they may enjoy immunity and inviolability only for official acts and certain essential privileges. The receiving state can limit the extent of immunities, privileges, and facilities to other members of the consular post who are its nationals or permanent residents. The same rule applies to their families.[173]

The head of state The head of state is the sole representative of the nation and enjoys all immunities and privileges when traveling

[170] In deciding *In re Baiz* in 1890, the U.S. Supreme Court found it a maxim in many countries not to receive their own nationals as foreign diplomats who, if accepted, would be amenable to local laws as to persons and property. 135 U.S. 403.

[171] See Arts. 37–38 of the Diplomatic Convention. In *Macartney v. Garbutt* (1890), a British Court ruled that a British subject appointed to a foreign diplomatic mission was entitled to diplomatic immunity unless he had been notified otherwise. [1890] 2 Q.B. 368. The immunity of a permanent resident employed as a domestic servant in a foreign diplomatic mission was recognized by the U.S. Court of Appeals (District of Columbia Circuit) in *Carrera v. Carrera*, 1949. 174 F.2d 496.

[172] See Moore, *Digest*, IV, p. 655. In deciding *Heathfield v. Chilton*, Lord Mansfield of the British Court of King's Bench delivered the following opinion in 1767: "The law of nations, though it be liberal, yet does not give protections to screen persons who are not bona fide servants to public ministers, but only make use of that pretence in order to prevent their being liable to pay their just debts." 4 Burrow 2015.

[173] See Arts. 53, 58, 71, of the Consular Convention.

abroad.[174] It makes no difference whether he is an absolute monarch or constitutionally elected.[175] He himself and his family and retinue are entitled to special protection, exempted from criminal and civil jurisdiction, as well as from all taxes and other obligations required by local laws.[176] Even if he travels incognito, his status must be fully respected after disclosure of his real position.[177] He is not, however, allowed to exercise jurisdiction over members of his retinue or to protect a fugitive in his residence. Immunities and privileges may not be granted to a deposed sovereign, but are fully accorded to a head of state temporarily in exile because of enemy occupation of his territory.[178]

Other government agents Besides persons in diplomatic and consular service, other government officials are often sent abroad on special missions of a ceremonial, political, or technical nature. Delegates, advisers, and experts to international conferences are frequently

[174] In *Statham v. Statham and Gaekwar of Baroda,* the British Court of Probate, Divorce, and Admiralty Division decided, in 1911, that the ruler of an Indian state was immune from local jurisdiction in a divorce case. [1912] Probate 92.

[175] A regent is also entitled to the same immunities and privileges.

[176] See *DeHaber v. Queen of Portugal,* Great Britain, Queen's Bench, 1851. 17 Q.B. 196. The immunity of the head of state from civil jurisdiction does not apply to a case where he himself is a plaintiff. Then he subjects himself to a judgment on a counterclaim or setoff, which should not exceed the amount awarded him, in consideration of the unenforceability of the judgment. See *Kingdom of Norway v. Federal Sugar Refining Co.,* U.S., District Court, S.D.N.Y., 1923 (266 F. 188); *State of Russia v. Banker's Trust Co.,* U.S., District Court, S.D.N.Y., 1933 (4 Fed. Supp. 417). Immunities and privileges are also due to the head of government. When Premier Moise Tshombe of Congo flew to Cairo to attend a conference of non-aligned nations in October 1964, he was detained in a palace guest house until his departure. He was considered *persona non grata* by President Gamal Abdel Nasser. For this incident and Secretary of State Dean Rusk's indirect criticism, see *The New York Times,* October 7–10, 1964.

[177] In *Mighell v. Sultan of Johore,* the British Court of Appeal dismissed, in 1893, the proceedings for want of jurisdiction. The Sultan of Johore was originally accused of promise of marriage under the name of Albert Baker, but he disclosed his real status after being sued. [1894] 1 Q.B. 149.

[178] A French court exercised civil jurisdiction over Queen Isabella of Spain in the 1870's, when she lived in Paris after being dethroned. On the other hand, the British courts treated the exiled heads of states of Allied Powers with full honors and respect. Even high officials of the Allied governments and authorities temporarily situated in England were accorded diplomatic immunities and privileges in accordance with the Diplomatic Privileges (Extension) Act of 1941, which was extended by the Act of 1944.

appointed outside the ministry of foreign affairs and its establishments abroad. While their official status is determined by the sending states, they are usually accorded appropriate immunities and privileges if their mission is of diplomatic nature. The Pan-American Convention of 1928, while designating these officers as extraordinary to be distinguished from regular or ordinary diplomatic officers, makes no distinction between them in respect of their rights, prerogatives, and privileges.[179] It should be noted that officials other than diplomats sent abroad by an unrecognized government may not be accorded immunities and privileges.[180]

International organizations and their officials Like the League of Nations, the United Nations is an international person, possesses juridical personality,[181] and enjoys "in the territory of each of its Members such privileges and immunities as are necessary for the fulfillment of its purposes." [182] The League Covenant conferred, in specific terms, diplomatic immunities and privileges upon representatives of its member states and its officials when engaged in official business.[183] Like-

[179] See Arts. 2, 9.

[180] In *Fenton Textile Association v. Krassin and Others,* the British Court of Appeal refused to accord immunity to the Soviet Trade Delegation in 1922, when the Soviet government had not yet been recognized by Great Britain. 38 T.L.R. 259. After conclusion of the Temporary Commercial Agreement between the two countries on April 16, 1930, diplomatic immunities and privileges were conferred on the head of the trade delegation and his two deputies.

[181] Art. 104 of the United Nations Charter stipulates that "the Organization shall enjoy in the territory of each of its Members such legal capacity as may be necessary for the exercise of its functions and the fulfillment of its purposes."

[182] Art. 105(1). This was later implemented by Art. 1, Sec. 1, of the General Convention of 1946. For the legal status and immunities of the United Nations, see Kelsen, *UN,* Ch. 13.

[183] See Art. 7(4) of the League Covenant. The details were stipulated in two agreements between the Secretary-General of the League of Nations and the Swiss government in 1921 and 1922. See LN *Official Jour.*, 1926, pp. 1422 ff. For court decisions confirming the right to enjoy diplomatic immunities and privileges of League officials, see *V. v. D,* Switzerland, Tribunal of the First Instance of Geneva, 1926 (54 J.D.I., 1927, pp. 1175–1178; English translation from Briggs, p. 801); *Swiss Confederation v. Justh,* Switzerland, Federal Assizes, First District, 1927 (40 *Revue pénale Suisse,* 1927, p. 179; English translation from Hudson, p. 426). For further references, consult Martin Hill, *Immunities and Privileges of International Officials: The Experience of the League of Nations* (Washington, D.C., 1947).

wise, the United Nations Charter provides that these officials "shall similarly enjoy such privileges and immunities as are necessary for the independent exercise of their functions in connection with the Organization." [184]

In pursuance of Article 105(3) of the Charter, the General Assembly adopted, by a resolution on February 13, 1946, a Draft Convention between the United Nations and the United States of America for the Establishment of Its Headquarters and a General Convention on Privileges and Immunities of the United Nations, both of which provide, in detail, the legal status of the Organization and its officials. The Headquarters Agreement was concluded between the United Nations and the United States on June 26, 1947, with provisions based upon the Draft Convention.[185] The inviolability of premises, property, and archives, as well as other privileges and exemptions, are similar to those accorded diplomatic missions.[186] The Secretary-General may waive the immunity of any official of the Organization without prejudice to its interests. If the Secretary-General himself is involved, the Security Council has the right to waive his immunity.[187] Members of the missions to the United Nations with diplomatic status are also accorded immunities and privileges.[188]

[184] Art. 105(2).

[185] GA res. 22A (I). For texts of the Conventions, see *Yearbook*, UN, 1946–1947, pp. 104–107, 100–104, respectively. The Headquarters Agreement and the General Convention are embodied in the UN *Treaty Series*, Vol. 11, No. 147, p. 11, and Vol. 1, No. 4, p. 15, respectively. A supplementary agreement concerning the Headquarters was signed between the United Nations and the United States and came into effect on February 9, 1966 (*ibid.*, Vol. 554, No. 147). For further discussion of the legal status of the Headquarters, consult C. W. Jenks, *Headquarters of International Institutions: A Study of Their Location and Status* (London, 1945). See also the Advisory Opinion on *Reparation for Injuries Suffered in Service of the United Nations*, International Court of Justice, 1949. I.C.J. Reports (1949), 174.

[186] Art. 7(5) of the League Covenant provides that "the buildings and other property occupied by the League or its officials or by Representatives attending its meetings shall be inviolable." The Headquarters Agreement prohibits United States officers from entering the headquarters district to perform any official duties without the consent of the Secretary-General, whose permission is also necessary for the service of legal process within the headquarters district. Sec. 9(a).

[187] See Sec. 20 of the Convention on Privileges and Immunities of the United Nations.

[188] Serious abuses of diplomatic immunities and privileges by members of missions to the United Nations will result in expulsion by the United

Because of the necessity of reaching certain agreements with Switzerland, a non-member state, in order to define the status of the United Nations and its personnel in Swiss territory, an Interim Arrangement on Privileges and Immunities of the United Nations was concluded between the Secretary-General of the United Nations and the Swiss Federal Council, and approved by the General Assembly on December 14, 1946.[189]

Members of the International Court of Justice are also entitled to diplomatic privileges and immunities when engaged on the business of the Court as stipulated in its Statute.[190] By an exchange of letters between the President of the Court and the Foreign Minister of the Netherlands on June 26, 1946, an agreement was reached on the details.[191] Another Convention on the Privileges and Immunities of the Specialized Agencies was adopted by the General Assembly on November 21, 1947, in respect of the representatives to, and officials of, the various agencies.[192] The premises used by delegations to international

States. On October 30, 1963, the United States ordered the departure of three members of the Soviet Mission to the United Nations within two days, because of their involvement in espionage. The Soviet Mission called the American ouster order a "deliberate provocation." See *The New York Times,* October 31, 1963.

[189] See *Yearbook,* UN, 1946–1947, pp. 249–250. The protection of government officials sent by states to attend international conferences imposes a most demanding task on local governments concerned. When M. Vorowsky, a Soviet observer to the Lausanne Conference in 1923, was assassinated, the Soviet government launched a strong protest against Switzerland, followed by serious strain in relations between the two countries.

[190] Art. 19 of the Statute. The same privileges and immunities were accorded to members of the Permanent Court of International Justice. The Hague Convention for the Pacific Settlement of International Disputes stipulated that members of the contemplated arbitration tribunal were to enjoy diplomatic immunities and privileges in the performance of their official functions.

[191] For the texts of the letters, see *Yearbook,* UN, 1946–1947, pp. 242–244.

[192] UN Doc. ST/Leg/4. See Kuljit Ahluwalia, *The Legal Status, Privileges and Immunities of the Specialized Agencies of the United Nations and Certain Other International Organizations* (The Hague, 1964). Further information on diplomatic immunities and privileges of the international organization and its officials can be found in C. M. Crosswell, *Protection of International Personnel Abroad: Law and Practice Affecting the Privileges and Immunities of International Organization* (New York, 1952); *Handbook on the Legal Status, Privileges and Immunities of the United Nations,* prepared by the Secretariat of the United Nations (ST/Leg/2, September 19, 1952).

organizations are inviolable, and are generally accorded diplomatic immunities, privileges, and exemptions.[193]

Municipal laws have been enacted by states for the enforcement of the provisions of these international instruments,[194] which are generally observed despite some controversies with respect to the extent and effect of immunities and privileges.[195] The most serious issues were raised by violation of the espionage laws of the United States by persons employed by the Secretariat of the United Nations.[196] Practices

[193] New York state law at first exempted from local taxation property used by delegations to the United Nations if situated within a twelve-mile radius of United Nations Headquarters. This limitation was later extended to fifteen miles, but the delegations from Ghana, Liberia, Indonesia, and the Soviet Union were still outside the radius. They protested that the law in question was contrary to the Headquarters Agreement because of the geographical restriction, which was eventually removed by the state legislature. See *The New York Times,* March 18, December 20, 1959.

[194] See *Laws and Regulations regarding Diplomatic and Consular Privileges and Immunities,* UN Legislation Series, Vol. VII, 1958. ST/Leg/Ser. B/7. See also D. W. Bowett, *The Law of International Institutions* (New York, 1963), pp. 281–295. In *Curran v. City of New York,* a New York court held, in 1947, that the Charter of the United Nations was part of the municipal law of the United States and that no further legislation was needed to provide immunity from taxation. 77 N.Y.S.2d 206; *Annual Digest,* 1947, No. 74.

[195] Immunity from a charge of speeding by a United Nations employee driving the Secretary-General became an issue in *Westchester County v. Ranollo,* City Court of New Rochelle, N.Y., 1946. In the opinion of the court, the defendant was not entitled to immunity as a matter of law without a trial of the issue of fact. The Legal Adviser of the State Department differed. Later, the Secretary-General paid the fine, without pressing the principle of immunity. However, in *City of New Rochelle v. Page Sharp,* a New York court upheld the immunity of a secretary of the Australian Mission to the United Nations on a similar charge. 44 *Am. Jour. Int. Law* (1950), 418.

[196] See *United States v. Coplon and Gubitchev,* U.S., District Court, S.D.N.Y., 1950. 8 Fed. Supp. 915. In this case, Gubitchev was a Soviet national temporarily employed as a member of the Secretariat of the United Nations. Although he was a third secretary of the Soviet delegation, he lost that status after a change of employment. As a United Nations employee, he was entitled to immunity from local jurisdiction in relation to his official acts. His name was never transmitted by the Secretary-General for inclusion in the diplomatic list of persons enjoying immunity and privileges in accordance with the Headquarters Agreement. Thus, he was sentenced to fifteen years in prison by the court. The sentence was, however, suspended on condition that he leave the United States forever. In *United States v. Melekh* (1960), the U.S. District Court (S.D.N.Y.) decided that a Soviet national employed at the United Nations on non-diplomatic status was not immune from local jurisdiction for espionage activities. 190 Fed. Supp. 67.

vary in different states concerning the treatment of international officials of their own nationalities.[197]

[197] Immunity was denied by a French court to Joseph Avenol, a French national then in the service of the League of Nations as Secretary-General, in an action for maintenance brought by his wife. See *Avenol v. Avenol, Annual Digest,* 1935–1937, No. 185; 77 *Décisions des Juges de Paix* (1935), p. 237. A Swiss court also denied immunity to a League employee of Swiss nationality. In *United States v. Keeney,* a claim of immunity by a former employee of the United Nations Secretariat of American nationality was denied by a U.S. District Court. 111 Fed. Supp. 233; 47 *Am. Jour. Int. Law* (1953), p. 715.

C H A P T E R 1 0

INTERNATIONAL DELIBERATION AND ADMINISTRATION

I. *INTERNATIONAL DELIBERATION THROUGH CONFERENCES* [1]

§144. FUNCTIONS OF INTERNATIONAL CONFERENCES

The promotion of understanding and the settlement of disputes among states are generally effected through negotiation, which may be conducted bilaterally or multilaterally, depending on the nature and scope of the subjects concerned. By means of written communications or personal contacts and consultations, negotiation is the most common and important method of international transaction. Secretary Charles Evans Hughes rightly said that "an hour of direct negotiation between responsible Ministers is often worth months of written communications." [2] However, direct negotiation by individual governments has

[1] General texts on the subject: Oppenheim, I, §§477–485; Hershey, Ch. XX; Satow, Chs. VII–VIII, XII; Plischke, Chs. 13–14; Schwarzenberger, I, Ch. 9 (V); Jacobini, pp. 156–160; Soviet *Text,* pp. 320–329; Claude, Ch. 15; Leonard, Ch. 5; Eagleton, Ch. 8.

[2] Plischke, p. 385.

inherent limitations. In discussing matters involving the interests of many states, there is almost no alternative to international conferences, with the characteristic advantages of collective deliberation and personal meetings among government representatives.

In former times, the term 'congress' was used for international gatherings to conclude peace, transfer territory, or discuss other important matters.[3] Now the word 'conference' is generally applied to such occasions: for instance, the two Hague Peace Conferences of 1899 and 1907, the Paris Peace Conference after World War I, and the San Francisco Conference in 1945 for the establishment of the United Nations.[4] Only technical meetings of an international nature are sometimes designated as congresses. For practical purposes, there is no difference between these denominations.

International conferences are held for specific purposes and are promptly adjourned after completion of the task.[5] Numerous conventions and agreements have been adopted in this way.[6] Many international issues of first magnitude have been settled directly or indirectly.[7] Due to the complexity of international transactions in the twentieth century, the main organs of the League of Nations and of the United Nations have held regular, special, and emergency sessions.[8] International organizations and other political entities are sometimes represented at international conferences, although the chief participants are states. While no state is obligated to attend any conference in which it is not interested, increasing interdependence among the members of

[3] For instance, the Congress of Westphalia (1648), the Congress of Vienna (1814–1815), the Congress of Aix-la-Chapelle (1818), and the Congress of Berlin (1878).

[4] According to Sir Ernest Satow, the word 'conference' was first used at the London Conference to discuss Greek Affairs in 1827–1832. See Satow, p. 304.

[5] Unlike other international gatherings, the International Conferences of American States have been convened periodically. For details, see *International Conferences of American States, 1889–1928; 1933–1940; 1942–1954* (Washington, D.C., 1931, 1940, and 1958 respectively).

[6] The Paris Declaration of 1856 and the Hague Conventions of 1899 and 1907 are instances. It was estimated that 257 lawmaking conventions were concluded during the period 1864–1914. See Manley O. Hudson, *International Legislation,* I, p. xxxvi.

[7] These were the Conferences of London in 1831 and 1867 which recognized the independence of Belgium and Luxemburg respectively, the Congress of Vienna of 1814–1815 which reshaped Europe after the Napoleonic Wars, the Conference of Algeciras in 1906 which settled the Morocco issue, and many others.

[8] See *infra,* §146.

the international community requires further cooperation through direct consultations in this manner.

§145. THE CONDUCT OF INTERNATIONAL CONFERENCES

Unlike the periodical sessions of permanent international organs with established procedures, the convocation of an international conference is much more complicated. First of all, the governments concerned exchange views on the nature and scope of the conference. Then they have to agree on sponsoring state or states, date and place, participating parties, and agenda.[9] The number of representatives, advisers, and technical experts sent by states is flexible and has varied at different conferences; one is invariably appointed as the head of the delegation. Whatever the size of the delegation, each state has only one vote, with the exception of a few organizations where multiple or weighted voting is practiced.[10] This practice is based upon the principle of the equality of states. Each conference determines its own rules of procedure, by which decisions can be reached by simple majority, absolute majority, or unanimity.

In former times, precedence was deemed extremely important by states; it is now generally determined according to the alphabetical order in French or English of the participating states. The same method may also be used to decide seating at the conference table.[11] The chief delegate of the host country of an international conference was usually

[9] The meeting place is not necessarily in the sponsoring state. The two Hague Peace Conferences, called by Russia, were held at The Hague. Geneva, London, Washington, and other important cities are often selected as sites for international gatherings because of their geographical locations, modern accommodations and facilities, and other considerations. There is no fixed pattern of procedure governing international conferences. Different from those of other peace conferences were the methods adopted by the San Francisco Conference for Japan in 1951 and the Paris Conference in 1946 for Italy, Bulgaria, Hungary, Finland, and Rumania. Less formal but extremely important are summit meetings, which have become popular among world leaders since World War II.

[10] Among these are the Universal Postal Union and the International Bank for Reconstruction and Development.

[11] For former disputes over seating by diplomats in Europe, see Satow, pp. 312–313. At the Foreign Ministers Conference of France, Great Britain, the United States, and the Soviet Union in May 1959 in Geneva, there was much fuss about whether the conference table should be square or round. See *The New York Times*, May 12, 1959. For controversy between the Western and Communist delegates at the Geneva Disarmament Conference over such matters of protocol in March 1960, see *ibid.*, March 16, 1960.

honored by being its chairman or president, but modern practice tends toward adopting a rotation system among the delegates by alphabetical order or other means.[12] As a chief guiding figure of the meetings, an experienced chairman can contribute a great deal toward the success of a conference.

Each conference decides its own rules of procedure. Routine business is conducted by a secretariat. The secretary-general and most of the secretariat staff are usually chosen from the officials of the host country. The establishment of commissions, committees, and subcommittees for the purpose of deliberation is determined by the nature and importance of the conference. A *rapporteur* is often appointed by a committee to summarize the discussions reported to plenary sessions. The official record of the proceedings is circulated to the delegations, with appendixes of other documents.[13] With respect to the official languages of an international conference, French was predominant before World War I, but now English has become more popular. The United Nations has adopted English, French, Spanish, Chinese, and Russian as official languages.[14]

§146. REGULAR AND SPECIAL SESSIONS OF THE UNITED NATIONS ORGANS

The General Assembly Unlike international conferences of a temporary nature, the main organs of the United Nations meet periodically according to the Charter provisions and their rules of procedure. The General Assembly meets in annual regular sessions and also in special sessions. The latter may be convened by the decision of the General

[12] At the Hague Conferences of 1899 and 1907, a Russian was elected president and the Foreign Minister of the Netherlands, honorary president. The presidency was rotated at the San Francisco Conference in 1945 among the chief delegates of the Big Four. At the Geneva Disarmament Conference in March 1960, the Western and Communist delegates adopted the rotation system of chairmanship by alphabetical order, with the representative of the Secretary-General of the United Nations sitting at the head of the table for the first day. See *ibid.*, March 16, 1960.

[13] For further references on international conferences, consult V. D. Pastuhov, *A Guide to the Practice of International Conferences* (Washington, D.C., 1954); F. S. Dunn, *The Practice and Procedure of International Conferences* (Baltimore, 1929); N. L. Hill, *The Public International Conference* (Stanford, 1929).

[14] English and French are the working languages, and also Spanish in the General Assembly and the Economic and Social Council. In the International Court of Justice, English and French are official languages. At the Inter-American conferences, Spanish is naturally most popular. Numerically, more people in the world speak Chinese than any other language.

Assembly itself, or at the request of the Security Council, a majority of the members of the United Nations, or one member of the United Nations with the concurrence of the majority.[15] The Secretary-General is to convoke the special session within fifteen days after receipt of a request.

If the special session is emergency in nature, it may be called within twenty-four hours at the request of the Security Council on the vote of any nine [16] of its members. If the Security Council fails to act, due to lack of unanimity of the permanent members, on a threat to peace, breach of the peace, or act of aggression, a majority of the United Nations members may likewise request the Secretary-General to convene an emergency special session in accordance with the Uniting for Peace Resolution adopted by the General Assembly at its fifth session on November 3, 1950.[17] Several emergency sessions have been held to discuss the Hungarian question and the Suez Crisis in 1956, the complaints of Lebanon and Jordan in 1958, the Congo situation in 1960, and the Middle Eastern crisis in 1967. However, collective measures, as provided in the Resolution, were not invoked on any of these

[15] See Art. 20 of the Charter; Rules 1–10 of the Rules of Procedure of the General Assembly. UN Doc. A/520/Rev.7, embodying amendments and additions adopted by the General Assembly up to December 31, 1963. Rule 1 provides that "the General Assembly shall meet every year in regular session commencing on the third Tuesday in September." The exact date has not been strictly observed. According to Rule 6, any session of the General Assembly may be adjourned temporarily and resumed at a later date. This has been the practice of many sessions. The most recent special session of the General Assembly convened on April 21, 1967. The Assembly of the League of Nations was originally expected to meet every three or four years, but, because of practical necessity, it met annually after its establishment. Five special sessions of the Assembly were held.

[16] The number was any seven until the Security Council was enlarged to fifteen by Charter amendment.

[17] GA res. 377 (V). According to that Resolution, the General Assembly may recommend collective measures to Members if the Security Council has failed to exercise its primary responsibility for the maintenance of international peace and security. Such collective measures may include the use of force in the event of a breach of the peace or act of aggression. But recommendations of the General Assembly are not legally binding upon the Members of the United Nations as are decisions of the Security Council. For discussion of the Middle Eastern crisis, an emergency special session of the General Assembly was convened on June 17, 1967. In his letter to Secretary-General Thant on June 15, 1967, Ambassador Arthur J. Goldberg questioned the necessity of the emergency session on the ground that the Security Council was still seized of the matter. See *The New York Times,* June 16, 1967.

occasions. All sessions are held at the headquarters of the United Nations unless decided otherwise by the General Assembly at its previous session or requested by a majority of the members of the United Nations.[18]

The Security Council The meetings of the Security Council are held periodically at the seat of the Organization or any other place of its own decision. The President of the Security Council, whose office is rotated monthly among its members, has the authority and responsibility to call a meeting at the request of a member of the Council after consultation with its other members.[19] In an urgent crisis, an emergency meeting must be held as soon as possible,[20] because undue delay may result in the failure of prompt action to fulfill Council functions.[21]

The Economic and Social Council The Economic and Social Council normally holds two regular sessions a year at United Nations headquarters unless decided otherwise by its previous session or at the request of a majority of its members. Special sessions are held by the decision of the Council itself, or at the request of a majority of its members, the General Assembly, or the Security Council. If the request is made by the Trusteeship Council, any member of the United Nations, or a specialized agency, a special session of the Council will likewise be held, on the condition that the Council's President and two Vice-Presidents agree to it.[22]

[18] See Rule 3 of the Rules of Procedure of the General Assembly. The General Assembly first met in London in January 1946.

[19] For details, see Rules 1–2, 4–5, of the Provisional Rules of Procedure of the Security Council, adopted by the Security Council at its first meeting and amended up to February 28, 1950. UN Doc. S/96/Rev.4. See also Art. 28 of the Charter.

[20] See Rule 3.

[21] When Moussa L. Keita of Mali was President of the Security Council in April 1966, he was criticized by its other members for delays caused by prolonged consultation with African members. On November 20, 1965, the Security Council adopted a resolution to call on all states to impose an oil embargo against Rhodesia, but the resolution did not authorize the use of force. In order to prevent oil shipments through Portuguese Mozambique, Great Britain requested the Security Council to discuss the matter and seek approval for the use of force whenever necessary. Because of Mr. Keita's delay of two days before calling a meeting, the United States formally filed a letter, on April 22, 1966, protesting his irregular procedure. See *The New York Times,* April 8, 23, 1966.

[22] For details, see Art. 72 of the Charter; Rules 1–6 of the Rules of Procedure of the Economic and Social Council, adopted by the Council on March 18, 1949, and amended up to April 1, 1953. UN Doc. E/3063.

The Trusteeship Council The Trusteeship Council meets in one regular session each year. Special sessions are held at the request of the General Assembly, the Security Council, or a majority of its members, or in accordance with a decision of its previous session. They also may be called upon the request of the Economic and Social Council or of any member of the Trusteeship Council with approval by a majority of its members. Meetings are held at the headquarters of the United Nations, unless otherwise decided at its previous session or at the request of a majority of its members.[23]

The increasing burden of international meetings Besides the regular and special sessions of the main organs of the United Nations, many international conferences have been held under its auspices. These meetings, and the printing costs associated with them, make up no small part of United Nations expenses. Thus, a special committee of fourteen experts advised the United Nations recently to halt the rapid increase in both, in order to reduce the financial burden on the Organization.[24] The problem of proliferation of publications was seriously discussed at the twenty-first session of the General Assembly in December 1966, "with a view to suggesting possible ways and means of achieving possible economy in extent and cost."[25] According to a report of the Secretary-General, international meetings held at the United Nations headquarters in Geneva alone have increased from 2,375 in 1960 to 4,052 in 1965. As the number is expected to rise, he asked for a new building to accommodate them.[26] These meetings are also most time-consuming, especially the general debate at the regular sessions of the General Assembly.[27] This is probably a necessary evil of international parliamentary practice for deliberation on matters of mutual interest among states.

[23] See Art. 90 of the Charter; Rules 1–7 of the Rules of Procedure of the Trusteeship Council, adopted by the Council as amended up to its twenty-ninth session. UN Doc. T/1/Rev.6.

[24] See *The New York Times,* July 21, 1966. For further information on the documentation workload of the United Nations Secretariat and the printing expenses, see UN Docs. A/4223 and A/6343 respectively.

[25] GA res. 2247(XXI).

[26] See *The New York Times,* July 31, 1966.

[27] According to the report of the *Ad Hoc* Committee on the Improvement of the Methods of Work of the General Assembly on May 28, 1963, the number of meetings of the General Assembly devoted to general debates had increased from thirteen at the tenth session to twenty-nine at the seventeenth session. Thus, the work of the main committees and the General Assembly as a whole had been slowed down. See GA *Official Records,* Eighteenth Session, Annexes, Agenda Item 25, A/5423.

II. *THE VOTING PROCEDURES OF INTERNATIONAL ORGANS*[28]

§147. THE LEAGUE ASSEMBLY AND COUNCIL

In order to have a clear understanding of the voting procedure of the political organs of the United Nations, it is advisable to review briefly the practice at the League of Nations. The meetings of the League Assembly were of two kinds: a regular session once a year and special sessions whenever necessary. Each member state could send three representatives, but had only one vote. Each League Council member had one representative and one vote.[29] With the exception of procedural matters, including the appointment of investigation committees, decisions of both organs were reached by unanimous vote.[30]

Whereas a simple majority was applied to procedural matters at Assembly meetings, a two-thirds majority was required in admission of new members, the election of non-permanent members of the Council, decisions on their terms of office and conditions of re-eligibility, and other important matters.[31] A report by the League Council on the settlement of international disputes was considered a substantive matter. In this case, the disputing parties could not participate in the voting.[32] Amendment to the Covenant required ratification by a majority of the League members, including all members of the Council.[33] This was additional evidence that Council members commanded a more important position than other League members.

[28] General texts on the subject: Clark & Sohn, Chs. IV–V; Goodrich & Hambro, pp. 188–198, 213–236, 385–405, 474–475; Claude, Chs. 7–8; Sohn, Chs. IV, §1; VII, §1; Kelsen, *UN*, Chs. 9, §2(B); 10, §2(B); Wilcox & March, Chs. X–XI.

[29] Arts. 3(4), 4(6), of the Covenant.

[30] See Art. 5(1–2) of the Covenant. On the basis of his experience in, and observation of, the League of Nations, Sir Robert Cecil concluded that the unanimity rule was a good precedent and had not constituted an obstacle to coercive actions of the League. See Robert Cecil, *A Great Experiment* (New York, 1941), pp. 72, 94.

[31] See Art. 4(2 *bis.*) of the Covenant. One such important matter was waiver of preliminary action by a regular Assembly committee before presenting a matter for Assembly deliberation. Further details can be found in LN Doc. C.356.M.158.1923.V.

[32] See Art. 15(6) of the Covenant.

[33] Art. 26 of the Covenant.

§148. THE GENERAL ASSEMBLY OF THE UNITED NATIONS

Each member of the General Assembly may send as many as five representatives, but has only one vote.[34] The voting procedure of the General Assembly depends upon the nature of questions: important ones by a two-thirds majority present and voting and others by a simple majority.[35] This is quite a departure from the traditional procedures of international organizations, including the League of Nations, which required unanimity in decisions of important or substantive matters.[36]

According to the Charter, important questions to be decided by the General Assembly are the following: (1) recommendations on the maintenance of international peace and security, (2) election of non-permanent members of the Security Council, (3) election of members of the Economic and Social Council, (4) election of those members of the Trusteeship Council which are not concurrently administering powers or permanent members of the Security Council,[37] (5) admission of new members to the United Nations, (6) suspension of rights and privileges of membership and expulsion of members,[38] (7) questions relating to operation of the trusteeship system, (8) budgetary questions, and (9) others to be decided as important by the General Assembly by a majority of the members present and voting.[39]

[34] See Arts. 9(2), 18(1), of the Charter.

[35] See Art. 18(2–3) of the Charter. Methods of voting are provided, in detail, in the Rules of Procedure of the General Assembly of December 31, 1963. According to Rule 89, "the General Assembly shall normally vote by show of hands or by standing, but any representative may request a roll-call." However, "all elections shall be held by secret ballot," and "there shall be no nominations." (Rule 94.) Under Rule 67, "the General Assembly shall not, unless it decides otherwise, make a final decision upon any item on the agenda until it has received the report of a committee on that item." This is a sound principle to ensure more mature deliberation at committee meetings. The General Assembly may, however, waive this requirement whenever it deems necessary.

[36] For further references, consult Wellington Koo, Jr., *Voting Procedures in International Political Organizations* (New York, 1947); U.S. Senate Committee on Foreign Relations, Subcommittee on the United Nations Charter, *Representation and Voting in the United Nations General Assembly* (Washington, D.C., 1954).

[37] See Art. 86(1c) of the Charter; also *supra,* §58.

[38] See Arts. 5–6, 19, of the Charter; also *supra,* §§51–52.

[39] See Art. 18(2–3) of the Charter. There have been frequent discussions at the General Assembly on the nature of questions, for instance, treatment of Indians in the Union of South Africa, the question of South-West Africa,

In voting on all questions at the General Assembly, whether important or not, the majority is of the members present and voting; thus the total does not include those absent or abstaining from voting. On the other hand, a two-thirds majority of all members of the United Nations is required in determining the date and place for convening a General Conference of the Members of the United Nations for a review of the Charter. The same rule is applied to amendment to and also ratification of the Charter. In the case of ratification, the two-thirds majority of the members must include all permanent members of the Security Council.[40]

The rule of one vote for each member state, regardless of its size, population, and contributions, is based upon the principle of the legal equality of states.[41] In the experience of voting behavior in the General Assembly, especially in recent years, such legal equality often results in practical inequality. Various proposals have been made to remedy the situation by changing the present system into weighted voting on the basis of population or financial contributions to the United Nations, or by adopting a combination of weighted voting and the cur-

---

admission of new members, and information concerning non-self-governing territories. For details, see *Repertory*, UN, I, pp. 574–586. On December 20, 1965, the General Assembly decided, by a vote of 59 to 45, that only a simple majority was required to adopt a resolution calling for the removal of military bases from non-self-governing territories. A matter of such a nature involving the maintenance of international peace and security has been considered an important question. For Arthur J. Goldberg's criticism of this resolution supported by the Afro-Asian group, see *The New York Times*, December 23, 1965.

[40] See Arts. 108–109. The Charter has been amended in Arts. 23, 27, and 61. The amendments were called for in G.A. res. 1991 (XV-III), and came into effect on August 31, 1965. The non-permanent members of the Security Council were increased from seven to ten and the members of the Economic and Social Council, from eighteen to twenty-seven. Revisions were accordingly made in Arts. 23, 27, and 61 of the Charter. Effective January 1966, the two Councils have been organized according to the amended membership. By GA res. 2101 (XX), the General Assembly decided to amend Art. 109(1), increasing the number of the Security Council members from seven to nine. A General Conference of the Members of the United Nations for the purpose of reviewing the Charter has not been held. According to Art. 26(2) of the Covenant, "no such amendments shall bind any Member of the League which signifies its dissent therefrom, but in that case it shall cease to be a Member of the League." There is no express withdrawal provision in the Charter, but the same right of withdrawal is probably implied. See *supra*, §50.

[41] For further discussion of the subject, see Bengt Broms, *The Doctrine of Equality of States as Applied in International Organizations* (Helsinki, 1959).

rent system. While every suggestion has its merits, none can be put into practice under the prevailing circumstances.[42]

The division of member states into different blocs or groups as a result of international rivalry and other reasons is often evidenced in voting behavior in the General Assembly. The Soviet bloc *vis-à-vis* the Western nations, the neutral bloc, the Latin-American group, and the Afro-Asian bloc have sometimes put their bloc or group interest above the merits of individual cases.[43] The consideration of national expediency rather than of justice has greatly undermined the primary purpose of the establishment of the United Nations. The new nations generally vote together on issues involving anti-colonialism, self-determination, and economic or technical aid.[44] As the great powers no longer have controlling influence in the General Assembly, they tend to rely more on the Security Council, where they occupy a privileged position as permanent members.

§149. THE SECURITY COUNCIL OF THE UNITED NATIONS

In the Security Council, each member has one vote. Criticism to the contrary notwithstanding, the voting procedure of the Security Council is less rigid than that of the League Council. Whereas a unanimity rule was adopted by the League Covenant in the Council's decision of non-procedural or substantive matters,[45] the Security Council only requires an affirmative vote of nine members including the concurring votes of the permanent members.[46] One permanent member has indeed exercised excessive veto power in the past, but other permanent members have also cast negative votes jointly, if not so often separately. According to the joint statement made by the Sponsoring

[42] See GA *Official Records*, 359th meeting (October 11, 1950), p. 98. For the proposals made by John Foster Dulles, Greenville Clark, and Louis B. Sohn, and other comments, see Wilcox & Marcy, Ch. VI. See also Clark & Sohn, Ch. IV; The Commission to Study the Organization of Peace, *New Dimensions for the United Nations: The Problems of the Next Decade* (17th Report, New York, 1966), pp. 7–23. For a full description of the sessions, agenda, debates, decisions, election, and other procedures of the General Assembly, see Sydney D. Bailey, *The General Assembly* (New York, 1960), Chs. 3–9.

[43] For further details, consult Thomas Hovet, Jr., *Bloc Politics in the United Nations* (Cambridge, 1960).

[44] For a survey of coalitions, groups, or blocs in the General Assembly, see Sydney D. Bailey, *op. cit.*, Ch. 2. See also Hayward R. Alker and Bruce M. Russett, *World Politics in the General Assembly* (New Haven, 1965).

[45] See Arts. 5(1), 11, 15, of the Covenant.

[46] See Art. 27(3) of the Charter. Prior to 1966, the required number of affirmative votes was seven instead of nine. As stated before, the amendments to the Charter came into effect on August 31, 1965.

Governments of the San Francisco Conference on June 7, 1945,[47] the adoption of the rule of unanimity of the permanent members in the decision of substantive matters was chiefly due to their primary responsibility for the maintenance of international peace and security. It was held that power should be commensurate with responsibility.

While a permanent member may veto a decision of substantive nature, any seven non-permanent members may likewise exercise this right. The veto may also occur when some non-permanent members, with the support of a number of permanent members, cast seven negative votes. There is nothing wrong in the so-called veto system itself. In comparison with the League Covenant, the Charter provision in this respect seems more flexible.[48] In both documents, any member state which is a party to a dispute must abstain from voting.[49]

A Member of the United Nations, even if not a member of the Security Council, may participate without voting in the discussion of any question which the Security Council considers to affect the Member's special interests. A non-member of the United Nations must be invited to participate, without voting, in the discussion of a dispute to which it is a party, on conditions laid down by the Security Council. In the former case, the invitation is permissible, but applied to a wider scope than a dispute; while that in the latter is mandatory, even though restricted to disputes only.[50]

[47] The sponsoring governments were China, Great Britain, the Soviet Union, and the United States. Their joint statement was later subscribed to by France. The statement represents a reasonable interpretation of the veto provision, though its binding effect on other members is subject to question. For its text, see *Repertory*, UN, II, pp. 104–106. Up to November 5, 1966, the veto power was invoked by the Soviet Union 104 times, France 4, Great Britain 3, China 2, and the United States none. See *The New York Times*, November 5, 1966.

[48] For further discussion of the veto power, see Christian Chassériau, *Le Veto en droit international* (Paris, 1948); Eduardo Jiménez de Aréchaga, *Voting and the Handling of Disputes in the Security Council* (New York, 1950); U.S. Senate Committee on Foreign Relations, Subcommittee on the United Nations Charter, *The Problem of the Veto in the United Nations Security Council* (Washington, D.C., 1954); Dwight E. Lee, "The Genesis of the Veto," *Int. Organization* (February 1947), pp. 33–42; Arlette Moldaver, "Repertoire of the Veto in the Security Council, 1946–1956," *ibid.* (Spring 1957), pp. 261–274; Norman J. Padelford, "The Use of the Veto," *ibid.* (June 1948), pp. 227–246.

[49] See Art. 15(7) of the Covenant; Art. 27(3) of the Charter.

[50] See Arts. 31–32 of the Charter. Art. 31 of the Charter corresponds to Art. 4(5) of the League Covenant, which reads: "Any Member of the League not represented on the Council shall be invited to send a Representative to sit as a member at any meeting of the Council during the considera-

On procedural matters, decisions of both the League Council and the Security Council require only a majority vote. Because of the flexible provision for Council membership, the League Covenant did not specify the exact number to constitute 'a majority.' The Charter requires, in this respect, an affirmative vote of nine members of the Security Council, whether permanent or not.[51]

The distinction between substantive and procedural matters is sometimes very ambiguous. The question whether a particular matter is procedural or not is itself considered a substantive question, and is therefore subject to veto. Thus there is the so-called double veto. Because of considerable dissatisfaction among small nations about the dominance of major powers during the course of discussion at the San Francisco Conference, compromises were made to expand the scope of procedural matters in the final text of the Charter. Attempts have also been made by the General Assembly to restrain the use of the veto power, but these have not secured the approval of all the permanent members.[52]

Decisions under Articles 28–32 of the Charter are governed by procedural vote. These include the internal organization of the Security Council for continuous function, the arrangement of its periodic meetings and also meeting places other than the seat of the Organization, the establishment of subsidiary organs necessary for the performance of Council functions,[53] and the adoption of the Council's rules of procedure, including the method of selecting its president. Also considered as procedural are decisions to invite any Member of the United Nations which is not a member of the Security Council to participate without vote in the discussion of any question specially involving its interest or any dispute to which it is a party. If the disputing party is not a member of the United Nations, the Security Council's decision on the conditions for its participation is also by procedural vote.[54]

---

tion of matters specially affecting the interests of that Member of the League." But, in accordance with Art. 4(6) of the Covenant, the representative so invited has the right to vote. Art. 32 of the Charter and Art. 17 of the Covenant are all applied to non-members of the Organization. For the application of Arts. 31 and 32, see *Repertory,* UN, II, pp. 165–170, 187–189; Supp., No. 1, I, pp. 287–288, 290; No. 2, II, pp. 331–335.

[51] See Art. 5(2) of the Covenant; Art. 27(2) of the Charter.

[52] See GA res. 117 (II), 267 (III); *Repertory,* UN, II, p. 67.

[53] The establishment of a subcommittee on the Laos situation at the 847th meeting of the Security Council on September 7, 1959, was decided as procedural at the objection of one permanent member. See *Repertoire,* SC, Supp., 1959–1963, pp. 91–92.

[54] For the basis and procedures relating to such participation, see Ch. III in *Repertoire,* SC, 1946–1951; Supp., 1952–1955, 1956–1958, and 1959–1963.

According to the provisions of the Statute of the International Court of Justice, the election of judges or the appointment of the members of the Conference as envisaged in Article 12 of the Statute are governed by procedural vote. The same rule is applied to deciding a date and place for holding a General Conference of the Members of the United Nations to review the Charter,[55] and also to amendment to the Charter. Nevertheless, ratification of an amendment requires the concurring votes of the permanent members.[56] Since amendment without ratification does not have any legal effect, no revision of the Charter can be made without the approval of all the permanent members.

From past experience, the following matters are considered procedural in nature even though this is not expressly provided in the Charter: inclusion of an item in the agenda, order of items on the agenda, adjournment of a meeting, conduct of business, and the removal of an item from the list of matters of which the Security Council is seized. On the other hand, certain matters are borderline and have been subjects of debate in the Security Council. Controversy was raised by a certain permanent member even in the decision of matters distinctly procedural in nature, such as the invitation of a non-member to participate in the discussion and postponement of consideration,[57] both of which were decided by the Security Council to be procedural. However, the establishment of subsidiary organs for the elucidation of fact was decided by the Security Council, on May 24, 1948,[58] as substantive in respect of the Czechoslovak question.

Also subjects of contention but finally decided by the Security Council to be substantive are the following: retention of a question on the list of matters of which the Security Council is seized,[59] recommendations to the General Assembly on admission to membership in the United Nations,[60] and request to the General Assembly pursuant

[55] See Art. 109(3) of the Charter.

[56] See Arts. 108–109 of the Charter. According to Art. 26 of the League Covenant, amendments to the Covenant would take effect when ratified by a majority of the members of the League, including all the members of the Council. See also Kelsen, *UN*, Ch. 10.

[57] For instance, the invitation of Canada, a non-member of the Security Council, to participate in the consideration of the first report of the Atomic Energy Commission at its 50th meeting on July 10, 1946; the decision of the Security Council at its 57th meeting on August 29, 1946, concerning postponement of the voting on the application of Albania and the Mongolian People's Republic.

[58] See Art. 29 of the Charter; also *supra*, §§54, 56.

[59] The decision of the Security Council on June 26, 1946, concerning the Spanish question is an example.

[60] See *supra*, §49.

to Article 12 of the Charter to consider and make recommendations with regard to a dispute or a situation. Whereas the distinction between these two is not clear, a situation may be considered as a potential dispute.[61] The unanimity rule of the permanent members applies to all substantive matters except decisions involving a permanent member as a disputing party in the process of the pacific settlement of disputes.[62]

If a permanent member is involved in a dispute, it must abstain from voting in the decision at the Security Council. However, mere interest of a permanent member in a dispute cannot constitute legal ground for its exclusion from voting, because a dispute before the Security Council is applied to the parties directly affected.[63] Abstention of a permanent member for whatever reason is not considered a veto. The absence of a member of the Security Council, permanent or non-permanent, has the same effect as an abstention.[64] Thus, the validity of the decisions taken at the meetings of the Security Council in June and July 1950 on the complaint of aggression upon the Republic of Korea in the absence of the Soviet representative was upheld despite the challenge of the Soviet Union.[65]

[61] For instance, the decision of the Security Council on September 15, 1947, on the Greek Frontier Incidents question. According to the definition given by the Permanent Court of International Justice in the *Mavrommatis Palestine Concessions* case in 1924, "a dispute is a disagreement on a point of law or fact, a conflict of legal views or of interests between two persons." P.C.I.J. (1924), Ser. A, No. 2, p. 11. On the other hand, a situation "is a state of affairs which has not yet assumed the nature of a conflict between parties but which may, though not necessarily, come to have that character." Goodrich & Hambro, p. 249.

[62] See Art. 27(3) of the Charter. For an analytical summary of practice concerning the distinction between procedural and all other matters, see *Repertory,* UN, II, pp. 68–87; Supp., No. 1, I, pp. 271–272; No. 2, II, pp. 309–310; also Ch. IV of *Repertoire,* SC, 1946–1951; Supp., 1952–1955, 1956–1958, 1959–1963.

[63] The question was raised at the 558th meeting of the Security Council, on September 1, 1951, in connection with the Palestine dispute, as to whether the five permanent members should abstain from voting because of their manifest interest in the Israeli complaint against restrictions on shipping in the Suez Canal imposed by Egypt. Eventually, all the permanent members participated in the voting.

[64] For details, see Kelsen, *UN,* pp. 241–243.

[65] After failure of the Soviet objection to the participation of the representative from the Republic of China in the Security Council, the representative of the Soviet Union absented himself from all the meetings of the Security Council from January 17 to August 1, 1950.

Strictly speaking, the absence of the representative of a permanent member of the Security Council from its meetings might be considered an infraction of the Charter, which requires that each member of the Security Council must be represented at all times at the seat of the United Nations.[66] This provision is to ensure the continuous functioning of the Security Council, but occasional absence of both permanent and non-permanent members has occurred.

As a situation is a potential dispute but may not develop into a dispute, a member of the Security Council involved in a controversy may contend that it is only a situation and is thus not required to abstain from voting. Furthermore, the requirement of abstention is limited to pacific settlement of disputes and is not applicable to actions with respect to threats to peace, breaches of peace, and acts of aggression. This loophole has certainly weakened the collective system of the United Nations.

In all probability, neither the Soviet Union nor the United States would have joined the United Nations without the veto provision, which may be called a necessary evil in the present stage of international relations.[67] Any amendment to the Charter for its abolition would probably not be ratified by either state, especially in view of the present power alignment in the General Assembly. Certain improvements can be or have already been made. The General Assembly has, on several occasions, assumed the responsibility of maintaining international peace and security under the authority of the Uniting for Peace Resolution of 1950. Regional arrangements and agencies have also undertaken such tasks in their respective areas in conformity with the provisions of the Charter.[68]

Self-restraint on the part of the permanent members themselves is essential to the efficient functioning of the Security Council. They should refrain from exercising the veto power in the pacific settlement of disputes and other issues not vital to their national interests.[69] They

[66] See Art. 28(1) of the Charter. Art. 4(3) of the League Covenant lacks such an express requirement.

[67] See *supra,* §§41–42.

[68] See Arts. 51–54 of the Charter; also *infra,* §§194–196.

[69] Since the establishment of the United Nations, the General Assembly has adopted a number of resolutions, urging the permanent members of the Security Council not to impede the effective and prompt action of the Council by use of the veto power. These resolutions include 40 (I), December 13, 1946; 117 (II), November 21, 1947; 267 (III), April 14, 1949. In the opinion of Secretary Dulles and many others, no veto should be used in the regular procedures for the pacific settlement of disputes. See *Review of the Charter,* Senate Hearings, 83rd Cong., 2nd Sess., Pt. I, p. 18.

should also abstain from voting voluntarily on certain questions when they have no intention to commit themselves by casting affirmative votes. It has also been suggested that the Charter be revised so that a veto can only be exercised by two negative votes of the permanent members. This is impractical, because the amendment will not meet the approval of all the permanent members and thus will not be adopted.[70] Since abuse of the veto is largely due to political dissension among the major powers, any fundamental solution must be preceded by the relaxation of international tension.[71]

§150. OTHER UNITED NATIONS ORGANS

Unlike the voting procedure of the General Assembly and the Security Council, that of the Economic and Social Council and the Trusteeship Council is comparatively simple and clear. Each member of either Council has one vote. Decisions are made by a majority of the members present and voting.[72] As the functions of these two organs are less controversial, a complicated voting procedure is unnecessary. Decisions of the International Court of Justice are made by a majority of the judges present. In case of a tie, the President of the Court or the judge acting in his place is to have a casting vote.[73]

III. *INTERNATIONAL ADMINISTRATION* [74]

§151. FUNCTIONAL AGENCIES IN CHARGE OF SUPERVISION AND ADMINISTRATION

Responsibilities of the functional agencies Consideration has been given to the powers and functions of the main organs of the League and the United Nations as well as to their similarities and dif-

[70] For a discussion of the veto problem, see Wilcox & Marcy, Ch. X.

[71] See also McDougal and associates, *Studies in World Public Order,* pp. 718–760.

[72] See Arts. 67, 89, of the Charter. The provisions of these articles are implemented by Rules 60–70 of the Rules of Procedure of the Economic and Social Council and Rules 36–43 of the Rules of Procedure of the Trusteeship Council.

[73] See Art. 55 of the Statute of the Court; also *infra,* §189.

[74] General texts on the subject: Goodrich, Ch. VII; Claude, Ch. 10; Blaisdell, Chs. 7, 17; Clark & Sohn, Ch. XV; Wilcox & Marcy, Ch. XIII; Goodrich & Hambro, Ch. XV; Goodspeed, Chs. 11, 13; Kelsen, *UN,* Chs. 11, 16; Leonard, Ch. 6; Eagleton, Chs. 7; 12,§§106–109; 13; *Everyman's UN,* pp. 467–552; Satow, Ch. XXX; Friedmann, Ch. 17; Starke, Ch. 18,§9; Oppenheim, I, §§340–340gh; Soviet *Text,* pp. 345–346, 348–359; Schwarzenberger, I, Chs. 10 (III), 11 (I).

ferences.[75] To sum up, all political activities, including the settlement of disputes and regulation of armaments, are within the competence of the General Assembly and the Security Council.[76] The maintenance of international peace and security falls primarily under the jurisdiction of the Security Council, but the General Assembly may discuss any questions or matters within the scope of the United Nations Charter and may make recommendations except on disputes or situations undertaken by the Security Council. In addition, the General Assembly has supervisory power over the Economic and Social Council and the Trusteeship Council.[77] Through various meetings and subsidiary bodies, these two political organs have performed their multiple functions.[78] The Trusteeship Council is to supervise the trust territories other than strategic areas,[79] which are under the competence of the Security Council.[80] The administration of justice is the responsibility of the International Court of Justice, which will be fully discussed elsewhere.[81]

The Economic and Social Council and the specialized agencies The present description of the functional organs is concentrated in the Economic and Social Council and specialized agencies, whose successful performance in supervision and administration has contributed much to the achievements of the United Nations. Under the authority of the General Assembly, the Council is responsible for the economic and social activities of the United Nations.[82] Its work is assisted by many subsidiary bodies in the form of commissions and committees.[83] There are four regional economic commissions under the direction of the Council to carry out functions in their respective regions: (1) the Economic Commission for Europe (ECE), (2) the Economic Commission for Asia and the Far East (ECAFE), (3) the Economic Com-

[75] See *supra,* §§36–38, 54–65. [76] See *infra,* §§154, 192–193.

[77] Except over strategic trusteeships, for which the Security Council has responsibility.

[78] See Arts. 10, 12(1), 24(1), of the Charter; also *supra,* §54. Further references on the maintenance of peace and security by the United Nations can be found in John W. Halderman, *The United Nations and the Rule of Law. Charter Development through the Handling of International Disputes and Situations* (Dobbs Ferry, N.Y., 1966).

[79] For the promotion of the political independence of dependent territories, see *infra,* §157.

[80] For details, see Arts. 75, 77, 82–83, of the Charter.

[81] See *infra,* §§189–191; also Arts. 92–93, 96, of the Charter.

[82] See Art. 62 of the Charter; also *infra,* §§155–156.

[83] See *supra,* §57; also *Everyman's UN,* p. 15.

mission for Latin America (ECLA), and (4) the Economic Commission for Africa (ECA).[84]

For the efficient execution and coordination of its activities, the Economic and Social Council is authorized, subject to the approval of the General Assembly, to enter into agreements with various specialized agencies, which have wide international responsibilities in economic, social, cultural, educational, health, and related fields.[85] Their names, headquarters, and dates of entering agreements with the United Nations are listed as follows:

International Labor Organization (ILO), Geneva, December 14, 1946
Food and Agricultural Organization (FAO), Rome, December 14, 1946
United Nations Educational, Scientific and Cultural Organization (UNESCO), Paris, December 14, 1946
International Civil Aviation Organization (ICAO), Montreal, May 13, 1947
International Bank for Reconstruction and Development (Bank or IBRD), Washington, November 15, 1947
International Monetary Fund (Fund or IMF), Washington, November 15, 1947
Universal Postal Union (UPU), Berne, July 1, 1948
World Health Organization (WHO), Geneva, July 10, 1948
International Telecommunication Union (ITU), Geneva, January 1, 1949
World Meteorological Organization (WMO), Geneva, December 20, 1951
International Finance Corporation (IFC), Washington, February 20, 1957
Intergovernmental Maritime Consultative Organization (IMCO), London, January 13, 1959
International Development Association (IDA), Washington, March 27, 1961

Besides the thirteen listed above, the International Refugee Organization (IRO), established in 1946 with headquarters in Geneva, entered into agreement with the United Nations on November 19, 1948, but ceased operations in 1951. The proposed International Trade Organization (ITO) has never come into existence. Neither the General Agreement on Tariffs and Trade (GATT) nor the International Atomic Energy Agency (IAEA) is a specialized agency, though both are closely related to the United Nations.[86]

[84] They were established respectively on March 28, 1947; March 28, 1947; February 25, 1948; and April 29, 1958.

[85] See Arts. 57–59, 63, of the Charter. For a general discussion of international administration and of the United Nations system in particular, see Norman L. Hill, *International Administration* (New York, 1931); Walter R. Sharp, *Field Administration in the United Nations System* (New York, 1961); A. Loveday, *Reflections on International Administration* (London, 1956).

[86] For a brief description of the specialized agencies, see *Everyman's UN*, Pt. III; D. W. Bowett, *The Law of International Institutions*, Ch. 4.

Legal status of the specialized agencies The legal status of each of these specialized agencies is derived from a treaty among the member states.[87] A state not a member of the United Nations may be a member of one or more of the specialized agencies, which have entered into relationship with the United Nations through individual agreements and report their work annually to the Economic and Social Council. Separate and autonomous, these agencies have their own membership, organization, functions, and budgets. Some of them, such as ITU and UPU, were established before the League of Nations. ILO appeared immediately after World War I together with the League of Nations. A few came into being before the conclusion of World War II, but most of them are postwar products. Despite their differences in function and size, they have certain common features: an assembly or a conference as a policy-making body represented by all members; an executive or supervisory organ in the form of council, board, or committee; and a secretariat headed by a secretary-general or director-general.

Relationship of the specialized agencies to the United Nations Through close cooperation with the specialized agencies which work extensively with non-governmental or private international organizations, the Economic and Social Council has achieved its maximum results in economic, social, technical, and other fields. One unrealistic suggestion heard from time to time is that the specialized agencies should be consolidated under the Economic and Social Council with a unified budget, somewhat similar to the relationship of the League of Nations with its technical organizations. It must be remembered that members of different specialized agencies are not always members of the United Nations. Consolidation under the United Nations would create a complicated situation. Besides, past achievements in non-political fields by the United Nations are due to the decentralization of these agencies in their relationship with the United Nations.[88] It is

[87] For details see Kuljit Ahluwalia, *The Legal Status, Privileges and Immunities of the Specialized Agencies of the United Nations and Certain Other International Organizations* (The Hague, 1964).

[88] See U.S. Senate Committee on Foreign Relations, Subcommittee on the United Nations Charter, *The United Nations and the Specialized Agencies* (Washington, D.C., 1955). On prewar international unions, consult Paul S. Reinsch, *Public International Unions: Their Work and Organization* (Boston, 1911). A large degree of coordination has been achieved through the Administrative Committee on Coordination (ACC), consisting of the administrative heads of the specialized agencies and the Secretary-General of the United Nations, who is designated its Chairman.

hoped that more agencies will be established in other fields for further advancement of the objectives and purposes of the Charter.[89]

§152. THE SECRETARY-GENERAL AS THE CHIEF ADMINISTRATIVE OFFICER OF THE UNITED NATIONS

The importance of the Secretary-General The Secretariat is composed of a Secretary-General, appointed by the General Assembly upon the recommendation of the Security Council, and such staff as the Organization may require. As chief administrative officer of the United Nations, the Secretary-General acts in that capacity at all meetings of the General Assembly, the Security Council, the Economic and Social Council, and the Trusteeship Council, which may also entrust him with other functions.[90] He is to bring to the attention of the Security Council any matter which in his opinion may threaten international peace and security.[91] The annual report submitted by him to the General Assembly is much more than a factual summary. The power of the Secretary-General of the United Nations exceeds that of the Secretary-General of the League of Nations.

The first Secretary-General of the League was James Eric Drummond, who was succeeded by Joseph Avenol in 1933.[92] Neither exercised such political influence on the international organization and world affairs as did Trygve Lie or Dag Hammarskjöld as Secretary-General of the United Nations. Serving from February 1, 1946, Lie imbued the position of the Secretary-General with high prestige. After Lie's resignation on November 10, 1952, Hammarskjöld succeeded him on April 10, 1953. Believing in quiet diplomacy, Hammarskjöld moved cautiously but steadfastly toward the center of United Nations politics until his tragic death on September 18, 1961. First elected as Acting

[89] The United Nations has employed two methods of creating new specialized agencies under Art. 59 of the Charter: (1) international conferences, as in the case of WHO and IMCO; and (2) setting up special committees to submit reports to the Economic and Social Council, as in the case of IRO.

[90] See Arts. 97–98 of the Charter.

[91] See Art. 99 of the Charter. The Secretary-General so acted on the Korean question and the Spanish situation. Under the League system, the Secretary-General could call a meeting of the Council only when requested by a member state. He can do so on his own initiative in the practice of the United Nations.

[92] When Joseph Avenol resigned his post on July 26, 1940, Séan Lester, Deputy Director-General, acted as Secretary-General of the League.

Secretary-General on November 3, 1961, then as Secretary-General on November 30, 1962, U Thant has been performing his functions in a more reserved manner. Upon the recommendation of the Security Council, the General Assembly, on December 3, 1966, approved him to another term of office ending December 31, 1971.

The procedure for his appointment The Charter does not stipulate the terms of office of the Secretary-General, but the General Assembly adopted a resolution on January 24, 1946, to make it five years, subject to reappointment for another term.[93] The recommendation of the candidate for Secretary-General by the Security Council requires an affirmative vote of nine members, including the five permanent members, any of which may, therefore, block the nomination. For the approval of his appointment by the General Assembly, only a simple majority is needed.[94] The General Assembly can decline to approve a nominee recommended by the Security Council, but it has no authority to appoint a person not recommended by the Security Council. While the tenure of the Secretary-General is secure, the displeasure of a permanent member toward him may cause extreme inconvenience to his smooth functioning, as experienced by both Lie and Hammarskjöld in the past.[95]

Functions of the Secretary-General Responsibilities of the Secretary-General are referred to in various articles of the Charter.[96] The Statute of the International Court of Justice sets forth certain functions of the Secretary-General, who is also entrusted with depository and other duties with respect to a number of international agreements. The express and implied functions of the Secretary-General may be summarized as follows:

(1) general administrative functions connected with meetings,

[93] GA res. 11 (I). The League Assembly in 1931 fixed the term of the Secretary-General at ten years, but Drummond resigned in 1933 and Avenol in 1940.

[94] The vote in both organs is taken by secret ballot in accordance with GA res. 11 (I). See also Rule 142 of the Rules of the Procedure of the General Assembly and Rule 48 of the Provisional Rules of Procedure of the Security Council.

[95] For the adverse attitude of the United States and the Soviet Union toward the Secretariat in 1952 and 1960, see John G. Stoessinger, *The United Nations and the Superpowers* (New York, 1965), Ch. 3.

[96] Arts. 7(1), 12, 20, 73e, 97–102(1), 110, of the Charter. See also Goodrich & Hambro, pp. 491–512.

communications, integration of United Nations activities, coordination of specialized agencies and other intergovernmental organizations, preparation of work and implementation of decisions, provision of facilities and general services, and organization and supervision of the International Secretariat;

(2) technical functions concerning collection of information and preparation of studies, operational programs particularly in the field of technical assistance, as well as procedural or legal advice;

(3) financial functions concerning his advice to United Nations organs on the financial implications of any proposals, preparation of the budget, collection of contributions, control of expenditure, custody of United Nations funds, and handling special accounts for United Nations programs financed from sources other than the regular budget;

(4) political functions in the capacity of representing the United Nations as its spokesman, negotiating agreements on behalf of the Organization, consulting with or advising individual delegations or governments upon their request, taking the initiative in making his views known or in attempting to reconcile the opposing views of member states, and rendering assistance on request of the General Assembly, either directly or by appointing a commission, in the settlement of differences between member states.[97]

In the last decade, the General Assembly and the Security Council have increasingly relied on the Secretary-General to implement decisions for the settlement of important disputes. In the Suez Canal crisis in 1956 and the Congo situation in 1960, the political role of the Secretary-General was performed under most difficult circumstances. Dag Hammarskjöld even sacrificed his life on his mission to the Congo in order to restore peace in that country. There has been much talk about the different styles of the three Secretaries-General in performance of their official functions. Actually, their differences are more

[97] According to the report of the Preparatory Commission, the functions of the Secretary-General are classified into six categories: (1) general administrative and executive functions, (2) technical functions, (3) financial functions, (4) organization and administration of the International Secretariat, (5) political functions, and (6) representative functions. The representative functions are actually either political or administrative in nature, and the organization and administration of the International Secretariat may be grouped under the first category. For further details, see *Repertory*, UN, V, pp. 119–172. See also Kelsen, *UN*, Ch. 11. For further details on the functions of the Secretary-General, see Stephen M. Schwebel, *The Secretary-General of the United Nations* (Cambridge, 1952); Elmore Jackson, "The Developing Role of the Secretary-General," 11 *Int. Organization* (1957), pp. 431–445.

apparent than real and largely the result of the changing circumstances of the United Nations from one period to another. Of course, no two persons would react to a situation exactly in the same way.[98]

The organization of the Secretariat The Secretariat of the United Nations has undergone many changes since its establishment.[99] The 'troika' proposal, submitted by the Soviet Union, to set up a three-man directorate and to give each of the three the veto power, reflected her distrust of the Secretary-General. As such a system would weaken the effectiveness of this important office, it did not receive much support from other member states.[100]

Members of the staff of the Secretariat are governed by the Staff Regulations established by the General Assembly and supplemented by the Staff Rules provided by the Secretary-General. Their duties, obligations, and privileges are embodied in these rules and regulations.[101] The staff is expected to meet the highest standard of efficiency, competence, and integrity. Both the Secretary-General and his staff are responsible only to the organization and cannot seek or receive instructions from any government or any other authority. Their international character must be respected by the Member states.[102] When staff members are recruited, due respect is to be paid to geographical distribution. Men and women are both eligible.[103] Because of conven-

[98] For a lively description of the performances of Trygve Lie, Dag Hammarskjöld, and U Thant, see Blaisdell, pp. 108–121; H. G. Nicholas, *The United Nations As a Political Institution,* 3rd ed. (New York, 1967), pp. 166–184. See also Trygve Lie, *In the Cause of Peace* (New York, 1954); Andrew W. Cordier and Wilder Foote (eds.), *The Quest for Peace* (Dag Hammarskjöld Lecture Series, New York, 1965); Joseph P. Lash, *Dag Hammarskjöld* (London, 1962); Wilder Foote (ed.), *Dag Hammarskjöld: Servant of Peace* (New York, 1962); U Thant, *Toward World Peace* (Addresses and Public Statements, 1957–1963, selected by J. Baal-Teshuva, New York, 1964).

[99] See the United Nations, *Organization of the Secretariat,* revised July 25, 1961. UN Doc. ST/SGB/124. For an analytical treatment of the subject, see Sydney D. Bailey, *The Secretariat of the United Nations* (New York, 1962).

[100] See John G. Stoessinger, *The United Nations and the Superpowers,* pp. 52–54; Sydney D. Bailey, "The Troika and the Future of the UN," *International Conciliation* (May 1962), No. 538.

[101] For the text, see UN Doc. ST/SGB/Staff Rules/1, March 16, 1962.

[102] See Art. 100 of the Charter. It is understood that staff members are forbidden to commit subversive activities against a Member state.

[103] See Arts. 8, 101(3), of the Charter. Art. 8 is implemented by the Staff Regulations of the United Nations. The equitable participation of

ience of recruitment and urgent need of staff in the early years, American nationals have been predominant in the Secretariat, but the situation has been gradually changed. There has been a rapid increase of Africans on the Secretariat staff in recent years.[104]

As a service organ of the United Nations, the Secretariat has fulfilled its responsibilities exceedingly well. The morale of the staff has been high, even when a loyalty problem was raised by the United States government about certain American citizens serving in the United Nations. Among the essential factors are job security under appropriate legal protection, home leave privileges, and high pay and other fringe benefits.[105] However one may evaluate the work of the United Nations, the administrative efficiency of the Secretariat as an international civil service is beyond criticism.[106]

---

women on the staff of the United Nations is under constant review by the Commission on the Status of Women. Other organs, such as the Review Board on Permanent Appointments, may also do something to facilitate progress.

[104] According to an announcement by the United Nations on February 15, 1966, there are 50 percent more Africans on the staff than three years ago. For African complaints and actual figures, see *The New York Times,* February 15, 16, 1966.

[105] For legal protection, see Byung Ghul Koh, *The United Nations Administrative Tribunal* (Baton Rouge, La., 1966). Because the United Nations cannot be taxed for the employer's share of social security like a private concern, American nationals employed by the United Nations Secretariat had to pay a higher percentage as if they were self-employed. The matter was brought to the attention of the Secretary-General for readjustment. See *The New York Times,* April 17, 1966.

[106] For further details on the International Secretariat, reference may be made to Royal Institute of International Affairs, *The International Secretariat of the Future* (London, 1944); Chester Purves, *The International Administration of an International Secretariat* (London, 1945); Egon F. Ranshofen-Wertheimer, *The International Secretariat: A Great Experiment in International Administration* (Washington, D.C., 1945); Carnegie Endowment for International Peace, *The United Nations Secretariat* (New York, 1951); U.S. Senate Committee on Foreign Relations, Subcommittee on the United Nations Charter, *The Status and Role of the Secretariat of the United Nations* (Washington, D.C., 1954); Stephen M. Schwebel, "The International Character of the Secretariat of the United Nations," 30 *British Yearbook of International Law* (1953), pp. 71–115; Maxwell Cohen, "The United Nations Secretariat—Some Constitutional and Administrative Developments," 49 *Am. Jour. Int. Law* (1955), pp. 295–319; C. Wilfred Jenks, "Some Problems of an International Civil Service," 3 *Public Administration Review* (1943), pp. 93–105; Frank R. Scott, "The World's Civil Service," *International*

IV. *INTERNATIONAL COOPERATION* [107]

§153. CONTRIBUTIONS OF THE INTERNATIONAL ORGANIZATIONS IN GENERAL

At the periodic meetings of the organs of the League of Nations, the United Nations, and other international organizations, leaders of the member states may exchange their ideas either personally or through their authorized representatives. Arguments and disagreements on different issues notwithstanding, there is opportunity in this open channel to discuss ways and means of reducing international tension and creating a climate for positive negotiation and cooperation. The general public is only familiar with the direct accomplishments of international organizations and not fully aware of their indirect contributions. The following is only a brief evaluation of what has been done by the League of Nations and the United Nations under four headings: (1) security and disarmament, (2) economic and technical cooperation, (3) social and cultural advancement, and (4) promotion of political independence and self-government. Certain efforts, such as the development and codification of international law, have already been described. The settlement of political and legal disputes will be discussed fully elsewhere.[108]

§154. MUTUAL SECURITY AND DISARMAMENT

The importance of disarmament talks The relationship between disarmament and security has long puzzled mankind, but the truth is that competition for armaments will result in less security in the international community. The frustrated negotiations for disarmament in recent decades, interrupted only by two world wars, have indeed exhausted the patience of statesmen. Yet a subject of vital im-

---

Conciliation (January 1954), No. 496; Georges Langrod, *The International Civil Service: Its Origins, Its Nature, Its Evolution* (Leiden, 1963).

[107] General texts on the subject: Goodrich, Chs. X–XIII; Claude, Chs. 13, 16, 17; Blaisdell, Chs. 8–11, 15; Clark & Sohn, Chs. IX, XI, XII, Annex I, Annex IV; Sohn, Ch. VIII, §§2–3; Wilcox & Marcy, Chs. VII–IX; Goodrich & Hambro, Chs. IX, XI–XII; Goodspeed, Chs. 9, 12, 14–15; Leonard, Chs. 16, 18–27; Jacob & Atherton, Chs. 8–9, 12–20; Eagleton, Ch. 14; *Everyman's UN*, pp. 180–395; Oppenheim, II, §§25h–25l; Fenwick, *Principles*, Ch. XXV; Falk & Mendlovitz, IV, Chs. 1–5; Schwarzenberger, I, Ch. 10 (V–E).

[108] See *supra*, §§16–18; *infra*, §§189–196.

portance to national security naturally requires careful consideration of all pertinent factors. Hasty decisions would not make a lasting peace. Although disarmament conferences have not yielded concrete results, the continuing discussion of the regulation and reduction of arms and armaments is itself a positive step. It is, therefore, encouraging that nations keep on talking about disarmament either independently or collectively through the United Nations.[109]

The League of Nations and regulation of armaments Disarmament talks preceded the establishment of international organizations. The Hague Peace Conferences of 1899 and 1907 showed a realization of the importance of reducing the arms burden even though no agreement was reached.[110] When the League of Nations was established, reduction of armaments was recognized in the Covenant as essential.[111] To study the problem it created a Temporary Mixed Commission, which, in 1923, submitted a Draft Treaty of Mutual Assistance to the Assembly.[112] In the following year, the Assembly produced the Protocol for the Pacific Settlement of International Disputes, generally known as the Geneva Protocol of 1924.[113] The Protocol provided for a system of pacific settlement of international disputes and planned a general disarmament conference. The Council of the League of Nations set up, in 1925, the Preparatory Disarmament Commission, with the purpose of preparing a draft convention for arms reduction, to be sub-

[109] For politics and diplomacy of disarmament, see John W. Spanier and Joseph L. Nogee, *The Politics of Disarmament* (New York, 1962); Donald G. Brennan (ed.), *Arms Control, Disarmament, and National Security* (New York, 1961); Joseph Nogee, "The Diplomacy of Disarmament," *International Conciliation* (January 1960), No. 526.

[110] The First Hague Peace Conference, originally held to limit arms competition, adopted a resolution to restrict military expenses. The Second Hague Conference recognized the seriousness of the problem, but arms reduction was not included in its agenda. Prior to these two conferences, certain bilateral treaties were concluded for the same purpose, including the Rush-Bagot Agreement of 1817 between Great Britain and the United States to limit the number and size of war vessels on the Great Lakes. For the early movement for disarmament, see Merze Tate, *The Disarmament Illusion: The Movement for Limitation of Armaments to 1907* (New York, 1942).

[111] Art. 8 of the Covenant.

[112] The Treaty failed of adoption because of objection by Great Britain and other states.

[113] This Geneva Protocol was ratified by a significant number of states, but some of its coercive provisions were distasteful to Great Britain and the Dominions.

mitted to a disarmament conference. These steps were favorably received by the major powers in Europe after the conclusion of the Locarno Treaties in 1925 and the admission of Germany to the League in 1926, and hopes were high for genuine progress toward substantial reduction of armaments.

Naval disarmament and renunciation of war Mention should be made of the independent efforts of the naval powers toward disarmament at this juncture. Called on the initiative of the United States, the Washington Naval Conference of 1921–1922 concluded a five-power agreement on capital ships,[114] with a view to gradually reducing naval armaments. Other conferences were held at Geneva in 1927 and at London in 1930.[115] Such continuous discussion was useful, even though there were no significant agreements. No less important was the universal accession to the General Treaty for the Renunciation of War or the Kellogg-Briand Pact of 1928,[116] and the unanimous adoption by the ninth Assembly of the League of the General Act for the Pacific Settlement of International Disputes.[117]

The Disarmament Conference Sponsored by the League of Nations, the Disarmament Conference met in Geneva from February to December 1932 and then from January 1933 to June 1934; sixty-four states were represented.[118] Despite the high expectations of the world, no agreement on disarmament was reached. The international situation was turning from bad to worse, largely due to the expansionist policies of Hitler and Mussolini and the eventual withdrawal of Japan and

[114] Great Britain and the United States at a parity of 5 to 5, Japan at 3, and France and Italy at 1.67.

[115] While the Geneva Conference accomplished nothing because of Anglo-American disagreement, the London Conference produced a treaty by which Great Britain, the United States, and Japan agreed to suspend the construction of certain warships until December 1936.

[116] Art. 2 of the Kellogg-Briand Pact provided that "the settlement or solution of all disputes or conflicts, of whatever nature or of whatever origin they may be, which may arise among them, shall never be sought except by pacific means." However, the Pact was weakened from the very beginning by reservations made by several major powers, and then completely discarded by Japan, Italy, and Germany when they started a war of aggression.

[117] Although only twenty-three states acceded to the General Act of 1928, some of its provisions were incorporated in a number of bilateral treaties.

[118] Some non-members of the League also participated in the Conference, including the Soviet Union and the United States.

Germany from the League. After the adjournment of the Conference, the major powers devoted their resources to an arms race, which led to the world conflagration in 1939.[119]

The United Nations and the regulation of armaments When victory over the Axis Powers was in sight in 1945, the Allies started to plan future security and arms regulation through the United Nations. On military measures, the Security Council has much broader power than its League counterpart. The Military Staff Committee as provided in the Charter is "to advise and assist the Security Council on all questions relating to the Security Council's military requirements for the maintenance of international peace and security, the employment and command of forces placed at its disposal, the regulation of armaments, and possible disarmament." [120] The General Assembly may also consider the principles concerning disarmament and regulation of armaments and make such recommendations to the Members or to the Security Council.[121] Thus, in the fall of 1946, the General Assembly adopted a resolution, entitled 'Principles Governing the General Regulation and Reduction of Armaments,' which included a recommendation that the Security Council should accelerate the placing at its disposal of the armed forces stipulated in Article 43 of the Charter.

The Military Staff Committee consists of the chiefs of staff of the permanent members of the Security Council or their representatives.[122] In its "Report on the General Principles governing the Organization of the Armed Forces Made Available to the Security Council by Member Nations of the United Nations," it listed a number of important points of disagreement among its members, including (1) contributions of the permanent members, (2) location of armed forces, (3) provision of assistance and facilities, and (4) withdrawal of armed forces after implementation of the work. Neither the Committee nor the Security Council could settle these fundamental differences. Notwithstanding the Uniting for Peace Resolution adopted by the General Assembly in 1950, the absence of military contingents available to the United Nations has caused considerable difficulty in fulfilling the responsibility of the United Nations to maintain international peace and security.

Control of atomic energy To ensure the use of atomic energy for peaceful purposes alone, the General Assembly unanimously

[119] For a brief description of League efforts toward security and disarmament, see Denys P. Myers, *Handbook of the League of Nations since 1920* (Boston, 1930), Ch. IV. See also Hans J. Morgenthau, *Politics among Nations* (New York, 1960), pp. 391–411.

[120] Art. 47(1). See also Arts. 26 and 43 of the Charter.

[121] See Art. 11(1) of the Charter.

[122] See Art. 47(2) of the Charter.

adopted a resolution on January 24, 1946, to establish the Atomic Energy Commission (AEC), which began its work on June 14 of the same year. Consisting of all the members of the Security Council and Canada, the Commission faced a serious disagreement between the American and Soviet plans. The United States representative, Bernard Baruch, called for the control of all phases of the use and development of atomic energy, while Andrei Gromyko offered a Soviet draft convention forbidding the production and use of atomic weapons. Having reached an impasse, the AEC discussions were suspended in January 1950.[123]

Reduction of conventional armaments The problem of regulation and reduction of conventional armaments was entrusted to the Commission for Conventional Armaments, which was created by the Security Council on February 13, 1947, in pursuance of the General Assembly resolution of December 14, 1946. The Commission consisted of all the members of the Security Council and began work on March 24, 1947. When the Commission rejected the Soviet plan embodying the prohibition of atomic weapons and the General Assembly turned down the Soviet proposal to reduce the land, naval, and air forces of the permanent members of the Security Council by one-third during a year, a deadlock was reached. The Soviet representative vetoed the Commission report in the Security Council and, in April 1950, refused to participate in further discussions because of the dispute over the representation of China. Under the circumstances, the Commission suspended its work.

Continuing efforts of the Disarmament Commission On January 11, 1952, the General Assembly decided on the merger of the Atomic Energy Commission and the Commission for Conventional Armaments into one Disarmament Commission. Composed of all the members of the Security Council plus Canada, the new Commission was to prepare proposals for the disclosure, verification, and balanced reduction of all armed forces and armaments, effective international control of atomic energy, and procedure and timetable for giving effect

[123] By that time, the Soviet Union refused to participate in further deliberation because of the presence of the representative from the Republic of China. There were four fundamental differences between the Soviet plan and that supported by the majority of the AEC members: (1) timing of a convention authorizing atomic weapons, (2) ownership principle and national sovereignty, (3) international inspection, and (4) use of the veto in the Security Council. For a summary of these differences, see Goodspeed, pp. 290–291. See also Frederick Osborn, "The USSR and the Atom," 5 *Int. Organization* (1951), pp. 480–498.

to the disarmament program.[124] Numerous proposals and counter-proposals submitted to the Commission and its subcommittee could not solve the differences between the Western powers and the Soviet Union. Their disagreement was complete in 1957, especially on the question of verification and control.[125]

At its thirteenth session in 1958, the General Assembly decided that the Disarmament Commission should, for 1959 and on an *ad hoc* basis, be composed of all eighty-two members of the United Nations. Before the enlarged commission met, the major powers, as a result of their Foreign Ministers Conference, reported the creation of a new Ten-Nation Disarmament Committee, composed of five Western and five Communist powers.[126] The Commission welcomed the resumption of disarmament negotiations through the Committee, which would keep the Commission informed about its progress. The Committee held its first meeting in Geneva on March 15, 1960, and adjourned on June 28 of the same year, when the Communist representatives withdrew from the Committee meeting because of serious disagreement with the Western proposals.

The eighty-two-member Disarmament Commission met in August 1960, but produced no agreement. However, as a result of further consideration at the United Nations and continued discussions among the major powers, the General Assembly, on December 20, 1961, unanimously adopted a Soviet-American joint draft resolution to set up a

[124] Great Britain, France, and the United States proposed, in 1952, to set a ceiling for the armed forces of the five permanent members of the Security Council: between 1,000,000 and 1,500,000 each for China, the United States, and the Soviet Union; and between 700,000 and 800,000 for Great Britain and France. This tripartite proposal was rejected by the Soviet representative because of its failure to prohibit bacterial warfare and other weapons of mass destruction. Instead, he proposed a one-third overall reduction in the armed forces and armaments of the major powers. In this connection, reference may be made to two government publications: U.S. Senate Committee on Foreign Relations, Subcommittee on Disarmament, *Control and Reduction of Armaments: A Decade of Negotiations, 1945–1956* (Washington, D.C., 1956); *Documents on Disarmament, 1945–1959* (Department of State Publication No. 7008, 1960), 2 vols.

[125] For the importance of arms inspection and control, see Seymour Melman (ed.), *Inspection for Disarmament* (New York, 1958); The American Assembly, *Arms Control* (edited by Louis Henkin, Englewood Cliffs, N.J., 1961); Lawrence S. Finkelstein, "Arms Inspection," *International Conciliation* (November 1962), No. 540.

[126] Canada, France, Great Britain, the United States, and Italy on one side; the Soviet Union, Bulgaria, Czechoslovakia, Poland, and Rumania on the other.

new Eighteen-Nation Disarmament Committee. Thus, eight more members were added to the original Ten-Nation Committee.[127] This expanded Committee has met intermittently since March 14, 1962. Although no agreement is in sight and France has long abstained from the meetings, it serves a useful channel for continued discussion of this vital issue. So long as the door for negotiations is kept open, mutual understanding on certain basic problems concerning the reduction and regulation of arms and armaments may be reached.[128]

Restriction of nuclear tests and weapons The question of discontinuing nuclear tests has been continuously discussed by the General Assembly and the Disarmament Commission. The test moratorium effective from November 3, 1958, as agreed upon by Great Britain, the United States, and the Soviet Union ended on August 31, 1961. The sixteenth session of the General Assembly was deeply concerned over the resumption of tests by the nuclear powers. A resolution was adopted on November 8, calling upon the states to negotiate at the Conference on the Discontinuance of Nuclear Weapons Tests at Geneva. On April 16, 1962, an eight-nation memorandum was submitted, urging the nuclear powers to reach an early agreement banning nuclear weapons tests.[129] The seventeenth session of the General Assembly considered the eight-nation memorandum to represent a sound basis for negotiation and urged the Disarmament Commission to renew its efforts toward the cessation of tests.

Because of the increasing pressure of world public opinion and courageous moves by the leaders of the nuclear powers, a test ban treaty was concluded in Moscow by Great Britain, the United States, and the Soviet Union on August 5, 1963, banning nuclear weapons tests

[127] Brazil, Burma, Ethiopia, India, Mexico, Nigeria, Sweden, and the United Arab Republic.

[128] Further references on disarmament may be made to Bernhard G. Bechhoefer, *Postwar Negotiations for Arms Control* (Washington, D.C., 1961); Changes G. Bolté, *The Price of Peace: A Plan for Disarmament* (Boston, 1956); Philip van Slyck, *Peace: The Control of National Power* (Boston, 1963), pp. 123–186; Quincy Wright, "Conditions for Successful Disarmament," 7 *The Journal of Conflict Resolution* (September 1963), pp. 286–292, and 1 *The Journal of Arms Control* (October 1963), pp. 380–386. *The United Nations and Disarmament 1945–1965* published by the United Nations in 1967, includes also a postscript on development in 1966 and early 1967.

[129] The memorandum was prepared by Brazil, Burma, Ethiopia, India, Mexico, Nigeria, Sweden, and the United Arab Republic.

in the atmosphere, in outer space, and under water.[130] The Treaty came into effect on October 10 of the same year and has been acceded to by almost every nation. However, the refusal of France and the People's Republic of China,[131] two other nuclear powers, to adhere to the treaty and the failure to forbid underground tests have considerably weakened the effectiveness of the treaty. Nevertheless, it is a major step toward the universal and complete ban of all nuclear weapons tests.

The effects of atomic radiation and the prevention of wider dissemination of nuclear weapons have been subjects of serious discussion at the General Assembly. Through the efforts of the United Nations and the cooperation of the nations concerned, the principle of peaceful uses of outer space has been well established. With the establishment of the International Atomic Energy Agency (IAEA) in 1957, the contribution of atomic energy to world peace, health, and prosperity has been accelerated.[132] The membership of the Agency is open to all states, and its Board of Governors and Secretariat take charge of general administration. Important matters are discussed at the annual meeting of the General Conference, representing all its members. IAEA has continuously worked to further the development of nuclear power for peaceful purposes, to promote the use of radioisotopes in industrial, agricultural, and medical fields, and to give technical assistance and information wherever needed.

The prevention of the spread of nuclear weapons to nations other than the nuclear powers is a matter of the utmost urgency. Sponsored by the United States and the Soviet Union, the General Assembly adopted a resolution on November 2, 1966, appealing to all states to take effective steps and conclude a treaty toward that end.[133] However,

[130] The text of the Treaty Banning Nuclear Weapon Tests in the Atmosphere, in Outer Space and Under Water can be found in Disarmament Commission *Official Records* (Supplement for January to December 1963, UN Doc. DC/207–208), pp. 53–55.

[131] See Anthony A. D'Amato, "Legal Aspects of the French Nuclear Tests," 61 *Am. Jour. Int. Law* (1967), pp. 66–77; Hungdah Chiu, "Communist China's Attitude toward Nuclear Tests," *The China Quarterly*, January–March 1965, pp. 96–107.

[132] See *supra*, §§100–103. In his address to the eighth session of the General Assembly on December 8, 1953, President Eisenhower proposed the joint contribution by the states of normal uranium and fissionable materials to an international agency, which would be set up under the supervision of the United Nations. His proposal was endorsed by the General Assembly on December 4, 1954. The statute of IAEA was approved on October 26, 1956, and the Agency came into being on July 29, 1957.

[133] The resolution was adopted by 100 to 1. Nineteen states were absent, Cuba abstained, and Albania voted no. See *The New York Times*, November 3, 1966. The Treaty for the Prohibition of Nuclear Weapons in Latin

world security and disarmament are inseparable. Nuclear weapons are only part of national armaments, which, as a whole, should be reduced and regulated in order to ensure international peace and security.

§155. ECONOMIC AND TECHNICAL COOPERATION

Achievements of the League of Nations The League of Nations, the United Nations, and other international and regional organizations have been most successful in non-political fields. The complexity of modern economic and technical problems has made the nations more interdependent than before. After the conclusion of World War I, the League was confronted with various economic problems, including tariffs, depression, access to raw materials, customs formalities, and financial reconstruction. To accelerate the cooperative efforts of the nations, the League called the World Economic Conference in 1927, the International Monetary Conference in 1933, and other conferences in technical fields, all of which yielded moderate success.

Although budget limitations kept the League from undertaking large-scale technical aid to less developed areas, it succeeded in assisting the economic reconstruction of Austria, Bulgaria, Greece, and Hungary. China received assistance for currency reforms. The League also aided Rumania, Estonia, and other countries for various purposes. As a result of consultations and conferences directly or indirectly through the League, many conventions and statutes were concluded for the furtherance of international cooperation in the economic and technical fields.[134]

America was opened for signature on February 14, 1967. It is hoped that the present negotiation for a nuclear nonproliferation treaty can reach a successful conclusion in the near future. According to George W. Ball, former Under-Secretary of State, the proposed treaty has its basic weakness in that the non-nuclear powers will be forced to enter into an act of self-abnegation not to develop or acquire nuclear weapons, while the nuclear powers maintain their advantageous position for all practical purposes. See *ibid.*, May 4, 1967. For further details, see U.S. Arms Control and Disarmament Agency, *Sixth Annual Report to Congress, January 1, 1966–December 31, 1966* (Washington, D.C., 1967, Publication No. 37).

[134] They covered a variety of subjects, including a convention and statute on navigable waterways of international concern (1921), a convention on simplification of customs formalities (1923), a protocol for arbitration of commercial disputes (1923), a convention and statute on the international regime of railways (1923), a convention and statute on maritime ports (1926), and a convention on import and export prohibitions and restrictions (1927). For a summary of promotion of international cooperation by the League of Nations, see Denys P. Myers, *op. cit.*, Ch. III, §§1–2.

Expanded programs of the United Nations The United Nations has been continuing and expanding the work of the League. While certain problems remain unsolved, new activities have been carried out. The policies laid down by the General Assembly are executed by the Economic and Social Council through close coordination with the specialized agencies. Numerous recommendations in economic and technical fields have been made to member states for their observance and performance. In addition, the United Nations has sponsored international and regional conferences to discuss commercial and financial policies, matters concerning population and migration, full employment, food and agriculture, land and agrarian reform, communications and transport, economic development and industrialization, and conservation and utilization of resources.

The United Nations launched a vast program of technical assistance to developing countries with a view to solving the above-mentioned questions. There are two kinds of technical assistance programs: (1) a regular program financed from the regular United Nations budget; and (2) an expanded program financed largely by voluntary contributions of the member governments and carried on by the United Nations and its related agencies.[135] In addition to the necessary funds and experts assigned for different projects, provision is also made for training local technicians and supplying equipment, information, and other facilities. Such services are also rendered by the specialized agencies and the four regional economic commissions, all under the coordination of the Economic and Social Council.

In order to facilitate public and private investments in the developing countries, several methods have been applied, such as the stimulation of international flow of public and private capital to finance productive enterprises, the full utilization of exports proceeds, and the increase of the United Nations Special Fund to provide more grants-in-aid and low-interest loans on flexible terms.[136] The recent merger of

[135] For further details on technical assistance, consult Walter R. Sharp, *International Technical Assistance: Programs and Organization* (Chicago, 1952).

[136] For further details on the efforts of the United Nations toward economic cooperation, reference may be made to Paul G. Hoffman, *One Hundred Countries and One Quarter Billion People* (Washington, D.C., 1960); Office of Public Information of the United Nations, *Landmarks in International Cooperation* (New York, 1965); P. L. Yates, *So Bold an Aim: Ten Years of International Cooperation toward Freedom from Want* (Rome, 1955); Harold Courlander, *Shaping Our Times: What the United Nations Is and Does* (New York, 1960); Eugene P. Chase, *The United Nations in Action* (New York, 1950); Gerard J. Mangone (ed.), *UN Administration of*

the Special Fund and the Expanded Technical Assistance Program into the United Nations Development Program will certainly increase efficiency in providing aid and capital to developing countries.[137]

§156. SOCIAL AND CULTURAL ADVANCEMENT

The work of the League of Nations The social and humanitarian activities of the League of Nations were quite broad in scope. The functions of its Health Organization covered prevention of the spread of epidemics, interchange of public health officials, reorganization of health services in various countries, and specialized studies of cancer, tropical diseases, infant mortality, health insurance, and other related subjects. The League also exerted its efforts, through different organizations and conferences, to suppress the opium trade and obscene publications, to suppress traffic in women, and to promote labor standards and welfare. Repatriation of war prisoners and displaced persons and relief and rehabilitation of refugees were among the important accomplishments of the first international organization.[138]

Economic and Social Programs (New York, 1966); Richard N. Gardner, *In Pursuit of World Order: U.S. Foreign Policy and International Organizations* (New York, 1964), Pt. II; David C. Coyle, *The United Nations and How It Works* (New York, 1966), pp. 1–87.

[137] The merger, decided by the General Assembly, took effect January 1, 1966. Paul G. Hoffman, a dominant figure in the United Nations aid program, was appointed Administrator; David Owen, former Executive Director of the Expanded Technical Assistance Program, became Coordinator. On January 19, 1966, the Governing Council of the United Nations Development Program approved eighty-two pre-investment development projects at a total cost of $254.5 million, of which the Development Program would finance $104.1 million and the member governments, the remainder of the cost. See *The New York Times*, January 20, 1966. According to the Development Assistance Committee of the Organization for Economic Cooperation and Development, with headquarters in Paris, public and private aid to the developing countries was $10.98 billion in 1965, up about $1 billion from 1964. See *ibid.*, July 20, 1966. These aid programs and peace operations imposed a heavy financial burden on the Organization. The financing problem of the United Nations has become increasingly important. For a summary of the subject, see John G. Stoessinger, "Financing the United Nations," *International Conciliation* (November 1961), No. 535. For a more comprehensive study of the problem, consult Stoessinger *et al.*, *Financing the United Nations System* (Washington, D.C., 1964).

[138] War prisoners alone numbered approximately one-half million, belonging to twenty-six countries. There were a million and a half each of Russian refugees in Europe and Asia, and Greek and other refugees evacu-

The cultural activities of the League of Nations were undertaken mainly by the International Committee on Intellectual Cooperation in the following directions: (1) improving the material condition of intellectual workers, (2) building up international contacts among various elements of the intellectual professions, and (3) promoting peace through educational and cultural cooperation.[139] No less than forty countries established national committees of intellectual cooperation. Among other international organs created for advancing cultural cooperation with the support of member governments were the International Institute of Intellectual Cooperation in Paris and the International Institute for the Unification of Private Law in Rome.[140] The cultural work of the League of Nations has been continued and much expanded by UNESCO.

Continuing efforts of the United Nations United Nations social activities are even more extensive than those of the League. The Social Commission of the Economic and Social Council advises on general social questions and recommends practical measures. As a result of World War II, the Arab-Israeli conflict, and the Korean War, serious refugee and relief problems arose. This tremendous task was first undertaken by the United Nations Relief and Rehabilitation Administration (UNRRA),[141] and followed by the International Refugee Organization (IRO).[142] After two decades, the work is still unfinished, and now is performed by the United Nations High Commissioner for

---

ated from Asia Minor to Greece, as well as three hundred thousand Armenian refugees. Beginning in the 1930's, a large number of refugees poured out of Nazi Germany, Austria, and Czechoslovakia. The International Relief Union at Geneva, established by a convention and statute of July 12, 1927, sent its agents to work wherever disasters occurred. See Denys P. Myers, *op. cit.*, Ch. III, §§3, 5–7, 9.

[139] Among the Committee members, first twelve and later increased to fifteen, were world-famous scientists and scholars, including Einstein, Bergson, and Madame Curie.

[140] For a summary of intellectual cooperation under the League of Nations, see *ibid.*, Ch. III, §4.

[141] Beginning its activities in 1943 on the basis of a forty-four-nation agreement, UNRRA carried out extensive activities in China and Central and Eastern Europe. It was largely financed by the United States, with headquarters in Washington. Its work was continued by IRO in 1947.

[142] Unlike UNRRA, IRO was a specialized agency of the United Nations. Established by the General Assembly in the fall of 1946, IRO began further identification and relief of refugees and displaced persons in 1947.

Refugees (UNHCR),[143] United Nations Relief and Works Agency for Palestine Refugees in the Near East (UNRWA),[144] and United Nations Commission for the Unification and Rehabilitation of Korea (UNCURK).[145] The United Nations Children's Emergency Fund (UNICEF), created by the General Assembly on December 11, 1946, has shifted its emphasis from emergency relief to permanent programs of child welfare. Financed by voluntary contributions from governments and individuals, UNICEF has achieved unique success in services to children throughout the world.

In connection with refugees and relief and the promotion of general welfare, the United Nations has engaged in programs of housing and planning. But, due to limitation of funds, only moderate success can be expected. By raising labor standards and extending technical assistance, ILO has successfully improved the working and living conditions of millions of workers in different countries. Attention is also paid to the promotion of trade-union rights, the abolition of forced labor, and the control of narcotic drugs.[146]

The United Nations has worked unceasingly to promote women's rights in the political, economic, social, and educational fields. As early as 1946, the Commission on the Status of Women was established to further this objective. Recommendations, draft resolutions, and other

[143] Created in December 1950 by the General Assembly, UNHCR took over the unfinished work of IRO in January 1951. With headquarters in Geneva, the High Commissioner for Refugees has three main functions: international protection, promotion of permanent solution, and emergency aid.

[144] UNRWA was created after about one million Arabs became refugees as a result of the Arab-Israeli Palestine hostilities.

[145] The General Assembly established the United Nations Korean Reconstruction Agency (UNKRA) early in the Korean War for relief, rehabilitation, and reconstruction in Korea. It continued to function until 1960. For a survey of the refugee problem, see James M. Read, "The United Nations and Refugees—Changing Concepts," *International Conciliation* (March 1962), No. 537. See also A. Grahl-Madsen, *The Status of Refugees in International Law* (Leiden, 1966). For the Protocol relating to the Status of Refugees, see GA res. 2198 (XXI), December 16, 1966.

[146] For further details on United Nations efforts to promote general welfare, consult Robert E. Asher *et al.*, *The United Nations and Promotion of the General Welfare* (Washington, D.C., 1957). On the relationship between the United Nations and the United States and the Soviet Union in economic and social activities, see L. K. Hyde, Jr., *The US and the UN: Promoting the Public Welfare* (New York, 1960); Harold K. Jacobson, *The USSR and UN's Economic and Social Activities* (Notre Dame, 1963).

instruments have been adopted by the United Nations organs and governments concerned.[147] As described before, the United Nations has also taken effective steps to promote human rights and fundamental freedoms by adopting a Universal Declaration and also two covenants on the subject. Genocide is declared by the 1948 convention to be a crime under international law in time of peace and war.[148]

The most important objective of the United Nations Educational, Scientific and Cultural Organization is to further collaboration among nations in education, science, and culture. Its activities are much more extensive than the work of the International Committee for Intellectual Cooperation and other agencies in League days. As an international clearinghouse for the exchange of information and material relating to education, science, and culture, UNESCO has broadened the work of education, encouraged cooperation among scientists and scientific organizations, and promoted welfare and mutual understanding of artists, writers, and others engaged in cultural pursuits. As a specialized agency, UNESCO has responded to the requests of member governments to participate in the United Nations Expanded Technical Assistance Program, to provide hundreds of experts, and to carry out various scientific and educational projects in many developing countries.[149]

§157. PROMOTION OF POLITICAL INDEPENDENCE OF DEPENDENT TERRITORIES

The League mandates and United Nations trusteeship system Both the League of Nations and the United Nations should be commended for their accomplishments in promoting the political independence of dependent territories. Under the League mandatory system, there were three classes of mandates under the administration and assistance of certain advanced nations as mandatories.[150] The Permanent Mandates Commission, set up by the League Council on November 29, 1920, was to receive and examine the reports from the

[147] See *Yearbook*, UN, 1965, pp. 465–477.

[148] See *supra*, §§125, 127.

[149] For the work of UNESCO and other specialized agencies, see *Everyman's UN*, Pt. III.

[150] See Art. 22 of the League Covenant. For details, see Quincy Wright, *Mandates under the League of Nations* (Chicago, 1930). The following two works deal with the mandates and trusteeship system: H. Duncan Hall, *Mandates, Dependencies and Trusteeship* (Washington, D.C., 1948); R. N. Chowdhuri, *International Mandates and Trusteeship Systems* (The Hague, 1955).

mandatories and submit its conclusions and recommendations to the Council.[151]

The United Nations trusteeship system applies to three categories of territories: (1) those formerly held under the League mandates, (2) those detached from enemy states as a result of World War II, and (3) those placed voluntarily under trusteeship by states responsible for their administration.[152] In practice, all trust territories were limited to former League mandates with the exception of Somaliland, which was detached from Italy, a former enemy state. The administering authority of a trust territory may be a single state or a group of states,[153] under the terms stipulated in the trusteeship agreements. The General Assembly, with the assistance of the Trusteeship Council, is to carry out the supervisory functions over the trusteeship system, but trust territories designated as 'strategic areas' are under the competence of the Security Council.

The independence of former mandates and trust territories The League mandates were in three classes. Class A consisted of territories formerly belonging to the Turkish Empire and were put under the following mandatories: Palestine (Great Britain), Trans-Jordania (Great Britain),[154] Syria (France), Lebanon (France),[155] and Mesopo-

[151] The League Council dealt with various mandate questions, including territorial status, nationality, military recruiting, equality of treatment, and liquor traffic. According to a recent decision of the International Court of Justice on South-West Africa (Ethiopia and Liberia—Republic of South Africa), individual members of the League of Nations had no right to challenge the execution of a mandate, because "the position of a mandatory country caught between the different expressions of view of some forty or fifty states would have been untenable." I.C.J. Reports, 1966, p. 4. For the text of a summary from the registry of the International Court of Justice on its decision in the case of South-West Africa, see *The New York Times,* July 19, 1966.

[152] The non-self-governing territories, as stipulated in Ch. XI of the United Nations Charter, are outside the international trusteeship system. Members of the United Nations have, however, accepted the obligation to promote the well-being and self-government of the peoples in their colonies and other dependencies and also to transmit regularly information to the United Nations until the territories attain a full measure of self-government. For a list of non-self-governing territories and their changing status, see *Everyman's UN,* pp. 341–369. For provisions of the United Nations Charter on non-self-governing territories and peoples, see Arts. 73–74 of the Charter. See also Kelsen, *UN,* Ch. 16.

[153] Nauru is the only instance.

[154] Palestine and Trans-Jordania under one mandate.

[155] Syria and Lebanon under one mandate.

tamia or Iraq (Great Britain). These areas reached such a state of development that all became independent states and members of the United Nations. Thus, only Class B and Class C of the League mandates and Somaliland were put under the United Nations trusteeship system, as shown in the list below.

TRUST TERRITORY	LEAGUE MANDATE (Class and Mandatory)	ADMINISTERING AUTHORITY
Nauru	Class C—Great Britain and Australia	Australia (on behalf of Australia, New Zealand, and Great Britain)
New Guinea (former German Pacific Islands south of the equator)	Class C—Australia	Australia
Territory of the Pacific Islands—the Marshalls, Marianas (except Guam), and Carolines (former German Pacific Islands north of the equator)	Class C—Japan	U.S.A.
Western Samoa	Class C—New Zealand	New Zealand
South-West Africa	Class C—Union of South Africa	
Cameroons	Class B—France	France
Cameroons	Class B—Great Britain	Great Britain
Ruanda Urundi	Class B—Belgium	Belgium
Togoland	Class B—Great Britain	Great Britain
Togoland	Class B—France	France
Tanganyika	Class B—Great Britain	Great Britain
Somaliland [156]		Italy

[156] Somaliland and the former British Protectorate of Somaliland were united to form an independent state, the Republic of Somalia, on July 1, 1960.

Trust territories formerly in Class B of the League mandate system, located in Central Africa, became independent one after another.[157] Due to their small area and sparseness of population, certain territories in Class C remain under the administration of more advanced nations.[158] These are Nauru, New Guinea, and the former Japanese-mandated islands in the Pacific. The status of South-West Africa has been unique, because of the persistent refusal by the Union (now Republic) of South Africa to place it under the international trusteeship system as recommended by the General Assembly.[159] On October 27, 1966, the General Assembly adopted a resolution proclaiming the termination of the mandate of the Republic of South Africa over South-West Africa and putting the territory under the "direct responsibility of the United Nations." [160] This was the most drastic step taken by the General Assembly toward the solution of this long-standing issue. An *Ad Hoc* Committee of fourteen members was appointed to study the problems and means of implementation of the resolution, and to report to the fifth special session of the General Assembly, which convened on April 21, 1967.[161] Being unable to reach a general agreement in its report, the Committee submitted three different proposals.[162]

[157] The French Cameroons achieved independence on January 1, 1960. The British Northern Cameroons joined the Federation of Nigeria on June 1, 1961; and the southern part merged with the Republic of Cameroon on October 1, 1961. Belgian Ruanda Urundi formed two independent states, Rwanda and Burundi, on July 1, 1962. French Togoland became independent on April 27, 1960. British Togoland joined the Gold Coast to form a new state, Ghana, on March 6, 1957. British Tanganyika became independent on December 9, 1961.

[158] Western Samoa, a Class C mandate and later trusteeship under the administering authority of New Zealand, became independent on January 1, 1962.

[159] For a summary of the frustrated negotiations of the United Nations with the Union of South Africa on the question of South-West Africa and the advisory opinion on the *International Status of South-West Africa,* see *Everyman's UN,* pp. 380–387, 415–416, 419.

[160] The vote was 114 to 2, with 3 abstentions. The United States and the Soviet Union voted for the resolution; Portugal and the Republic of South Africa cast negative votes; France and Great Britain abstained. See *The New York Times,* October 28, 29, 1966.

[161] Another important item on the agenda of this fifth special session of the General Assembly was the peace-keeping problem, which was also controversial in nature. By GA res. 2249(V), adopted on May 23, 1967, the Special Committee on Peace-Keeping was requested by the General Assembly to continue its work. See also *infra,* §193, on the peace-keeping operation of the United Nations.

[162] The essentials of the three proposals are: (a) to use force, if necessary, to take over South-West Africa from the Republic of South Africa;

After a prolonged discussion, the Assembly adopted, on May 19, a resolution providing for the appointment of a United Nations commissioner and an eleven-member Council for the administration of South-West Africa.[163] The resolution was predominantly supported by Afro-Asian and Latin-American groups, while the Western powers and almost all the Communist countries abstained from voting.[164] The Soviet Union preferred complete independence of South-West Africa to United Nations interim administration of the territory; the United States wished that the Assembly could take a more unanimous and realistic step; Great Britain considered that real barriers could not be removed by words alone and that Members had an obligation to the United Nations and to the people of South-West Africa "to avoid self-deception and the raising of false hopes." [165] It can be seen that the Assembly resolution contains no coercive measures and the Security Council is not expected to take such actions in view of the expressed attitude of the permanent members. Since the Republic of South Africa was opposed to the resolution, it is most unlikely that she would give up her control over South-West Africa at the present time.

The Trusteeship Council has been working hard toward its own liquidation.[166] Due credit should be given to the Permanent Mandate Commission of the League of Nations, which laid down a sound foundation for its successor. The efforts of the mandatories and the ad-

---

(b) to induce the Republic of South Africa to give up the former League mandate through peaceful means; and (c) to establish a United Nations body to administer South-West Africa without special reference to the use of force. For details, see UN Doc. A/6640.

[163] GA res. 2248(V). On June 13, the Assembly elected Constantin Stravropoulos, Under Secretary for Legal Affairs of the United Nations Secretariat, as Acting Commissioner and the following states as Council members: Chile, Colombia, Guyana, India, Indonesia, Nigeria, Pakistan, Turkey, the United Arab Republic, Yugoslavia, and Zambia. See *The New York Times,* June 14, 1967.

[164] The vote was 85 to 2, with 30 abstentions. The Republic of South Africa and Portugal cast two negative votes. Yugoslavia gave support to the resolution. Five Member states were absent from voting: Albania, Gambia, Lesotho, the Maldive Islands, and the Dominican Republic.

[165] *The New York Times,* May 20, 1967.

[166] Further references on the United Nations trusteeship system can be found in Charmian E. Toussaint, *The Trusteeship System of the United Nations* (New York, 1956); James N. Murray, Jr., *The United Nations Trusteeship System* (Urbana, Ill., 1957); U.S. Senate Committee on Foreign Relations, Subcommittee on the United Nations Charter, *The United Nations and Dependent Territories* (Washington, D.C., 1955).

ministering authorities have also contributed to the early independence of the dependent territories.[167]

Self-determination and decolonization are the banners of the Afro-Asian peoples, whose aspirations have received support from both the United States and the Soviet Union.[168] The resolution adopted by the General Assembly on December 14, 1960, entitled 'Declaration on the Granting of Independence to Colonial Countries and Peoples,' wholeheartedly endorsed this irresistible movement.[169] It urged the states concerned to transfer the powers in their trust and non-self-governing territories to the local peoples "in accordance with their freely expressed will and desire, without any distinction as to race, creed or color." [170] On December 13, 1966, the twenty-first session of the Gen-

[167] On many occasions the General Assembly has urged a speedy end of colonialism. Great Britain, the greatest colonial power in history, closed her Colonial Office on August 1, 1966. Administrative jurisdiction passed to the Commonwealth Office under a new Dependent Territories Division. There are still some colonies left. It is interesting to quote a remark made by Sir Charles Jeffries, who had been with the Colonial Office for forty years before retirement: "When I joined the office in 1917 I scarcely imagined that I should live to write its obituary notice. In those days it seemed to be about the most permanent institution in the world, dealing with an empire on which the sun never set and was not likely to set in any foreseeable future." *The New York Times,* August 1, 1966.

[168] According to Lenin, colonies were "dependencies with a population having no legal rights." In his study of *The Soviet Union and International Law* (New York, 1935), T. A. Taracouzio pointed out that "as a natural consequence of their attitude towards self-determination in general, communists champion the cause of colonies against their imperialistic overlords." P. 33. G. L. Tunkin, Director of the Treaty and Legal Department of the Soviet Ministry of Foreign Affairs, stated, in 1962, that "modern international law is anti-colonial in its direction." Quoted in Oliver J. Lissitzyn, "International Law in a Divided World," *International Conciliation* (March 1963), No. 542, p. 18. For a survey of the United Nations and dependent peoples and colonialism, see Emil J. Sady, *The United Nations and Dependent Peoples* (Washington, D.C., 1956); Harold K. Jacobson, "The United Nations and Colonialism: A Tentative Appraisal," *Int. Organization* (Winter 1962), pp. 37–56. See also Muhammad Aziz Shukri, *The Concept of Self-Determination in the United Nations* (Damascus, 1965).

[169] GA res. 1515 (XV). For its text, see *Yearbook,* UN, 1960, pp. 49–50. A committee of twenty-four has been set up to supervise the implementation of the Declaration. It is called the Special Committee on the Situation with Regard to the Implementation of the Declaration on the Granting of Independence to Colonial Countries and Peoples.

[170] *Ibid.,* p. 49. Jointly sponsored by the General Assembly's Special Committee on Colonialism and the Special Committee on Apartheid, an

eral Assembly reaffirmed the importance of the Declaration and condemned activities which have impeded its implementation.[171]

---

international seminar on racial discrimination and colonialism was to be held in the latter part of summer 1967.

[171] GA res. 2189 (XXI). For a general discussion of the importance of United Nations declarations, see Obed Y. Asamoah, *The Legal Significance of the Declarations of the General Assembly of the United Nations* (The Hague, 1966).

CHAPTER 11

THE LAW OF TREATIES[1]

I. *THE NATURE AND SCOPE OF TREATIES*

§158. THE FUNCTION OF TREATIES

International treaties are agreements between two or more states for mutual observance and execution of stipulated rights and obligations.[2] Through the express consent of the member states as provided in their constituent instruments, international and regional organizations may also conclude treaties with individual states and among them-

[1] General texts on the subject: O'Connell, I, pp. 211–299; Oppenheim, I, §§486–581; Jessup, Ch. VI; Fenwick, *Principles,* Ch. XXIII; Brierly, Ch. VII; Hyde, II, §§489–551; Moore, *Digest,* V, §§734–780; Hackworth, *Digest,* V, §§461–517; Schwarzenberger, I, Ch. 6; Starke, Ch. 14; Hershey, Ch. XXI; Gould, Chs. 10–11; Svarlien, Ch. 18; Whitaker, Ch. 4; Von Glahn, Ch. 24; Jacobini, Ch. 6; Soviet, *Text,* Ch. VI; Satow, Chs. XXIII–XXVII; Sen, Ch. XVII; Schuschnigg, Ch. 14; Rosalyn Higgins, Pt. V; Lawrence, §§132–134; Le Fur, §§416–448; Grotius, II, Bk. 2, Chs. 15–16; Vattel, III, Bk. 2, Chs. 12–17; Wolff, II, Ch. 4; Halleck, I, pp. 296–302; *Harvard Research* (1935), III. Reports of the International Law Commission on the law of treaties can be found in *Yearbook*, Int. Law Com. For a brief description of the reports and texts of the final Draft Articles with commentaries, adopted by the International Law Commission in 1966, see *infra,* note 9. The Draft contains 75 articles, hereafter cited as Int. Law Com.'s Draft Aritcles. In accordance with GA res. 2166(XXI), December 5, 1966, the first session of an International Conference on the Law of Treaties will be held early in 1968 and the second session, a year later.

[2] See Arts. 1, 2(a), 3–5, of Int. Law Com.'s Draft Articles.

selves.[3] The capacity to enter into international treaties is an attribute of state sovereignty,[4] but semi-sovereign states may exercise such a power to the extent expressly or impliedly permitted by the protecting or suzerain states.[5] There is some similarity between treaties in international law and contracts in municipal law; states may sign contracts with individuals or corporate bodies, but "any contract which is not a contract between states in their capacity as subjects of international law is based on the municipal law of some country." [6]

The increasing importance of treaties as the foundation of international relations and also as the primary source of international law is universally recognized by the members of the family of nations. One of the fundamental objectives of the United Nations is "to establish conditions under which justice and respect for the obligations arising from treaties and other sources of international law can be maintained." [7] In this respect, there is a consensus of opinion among the Communist and non-Communist countries, divergent interpretation and application of certain treaties notwithstanding.[8] The new nations have not departed

[3] The United Nations has concluded agreements with the United States regarding its headquarters, with Switzerland concerning its privileges and immunities, and with specialized agencies.

[4] See *The S.S. Wimbledon* (Great Britain *et al.*—Germany), Permanent Court of International Justice, 1923. P.C.I.J.(1923), Ser. A, No. 1.

[5] For instance, Tunis and Morocco were signatories to the International Sanitary Convention of 1926 before their independence.

[6] See *Serbian Loans Case,* Permanent Court of International Justice, 1929. P.C.I.J. (1929), Ser. A, No. 20/21, p. 41. See also *Anglo-Iranian Oil Co. (Jurisdiction),* International Court of Justice, 1952. I.C.J. Reports (1952), p. 93.

[7] Preamble of the United Nations Charter, Par. 3. See also Art. 38 of the Statute of the International Court of Justice.

[8] See Soviet *Text,* pp. 247–248. During the period 1917–1957, the Soviet Union concluded 2,516 international agreements, of which 2,086 were bilateral. See Jan F. Triska and Robert M. Slusser, *The Theory, Law, and Policy of Soviet Treaties* (Stanford, 1962), p. 4. For Soviet treaties in early years, see T. A. Taracouzio, *The Soviet Union and International Law* (New York, 1935), Ch. IX. Since its establishment on October 1, 1949, the People's Republic of China has concluded over 1,000 bilateral and multilateral agreements with both Communist and non-Communist states, chiefly on economic, cultural, and technical matters. For further details of the Chinese attitude toward treaties, consult the two papers presented at the 61st Annual Meeting of the American Society of International Law on April 28, 1967, to be published in its 1967 *Proceedings:* Hungdah Chiu, "Chinese Views on the Law of Treaties"; Douglas M. Johnston, "Analysis of Chinese Treaty Practice."

from this concept even though they are not entirely happy with the established order created by treaties before their independence. For almost two decades, the United Nations, chiefly through its International Law Commission, has worked incessantly for the codification of the law of treaties on the basis of its established principles and practices, and has completed the final texts of the draft articles.[9]

There is almost no limit to the scope of subjects of international treaties, which may deal with political, economic, commercial, social, cultural, and various scientific and technical matters. The list of the kinds of treaties is almost endless, including military alliance,[10] regulation of armaments, conduct of warfare, conclusion of peace, guarantee of neutrality, settlement of disputes, boundaries, extradition, diplomatic and consular relations, navigation and shipping, airways, customs, copyrights, taxation, immigration, labor conditions, social welfare, cultural exchange, economic and technical assistance, refugee problems, weights and measures, communications, and other specific topics. International interdependence and cooperation make it necessary for states to conclude hundreds of treaties, which not only regulate their dealings with one another but also promote their mutual convenience and interest. Like contracts in domestic life, treaties are absolutely essential to the relations in the international community.

[9] See reports on the law of treaties in *Yearbook*, Int. Law Com., since 1950, successively submitted by *rapporteurs* J. L. Brierly, H. Lauterpacht, G. G. Fitzmaurice, and H. Waldock. The Commission, at sessions in 1962, 1963, and 1964, adopted, respectively, Pts. I, II, and III of the draft articles on the law of treaties. Pt. I consists of twenty-nine articles, on the conclusion, entry into force, and registration of treaties; Pt. II, twenty-five articles, on the invalidity and termination of treaties; Pt. III, nineteen articles, on the application, effects, modification, and interpretation of treaties. The Commission re-examined the draft articles in 1965 and 1966, and, at its eighteenth session, adopted the final text and commentaries. See 61 *Am. Jour. Int. Law* (1967), pp. 255–285 for the text of 75 draft articles, pp. 285–463 for commentaries. Further discussion will be made at the twenty-second session of the General Assembly in order to facilitate the conclusion of a convention on the law of treaties. For an authoritative summary by Sir Humphrey Waldock, Special *Rapporteur* on the Law of Treaties for the International Law Commission from 1961–1966, see his "The International Law Commission and the Law of Treaties," 4 *UN Monthly Chronicle* (May 1967), pp. 69–76.

[10] Some treaties cover a wide range of subjects other than military alliance, such as the Treaty of Friendship, Alliance and Mutual Assistance between the Soviet Union and the People's Republic of China on February 14, 1950. In spite of the worsening relationship between the two Communist giants, this treaty is technically not void.

§159. THE TERMINOLOGY OF TREATIES

The word treaty is used as a common term for an international instrument or engagement, which may be under a different designation. In recognizing variations, the Permanent Court of International Justice stated in the *Austro-German Customs Union Case* in 1931 that international engagements may be under the title of "treaties, conventions, declarations, agreements, protocols, or exchange of notes." [11] If the substance is a treaty, it should be treated as such.[12]

Different titles In international practice, the titles generally employed to designate treaties include the following: (1) 'agreement,' used interchangeably with the term 'treaty,' but in a less formal way;[13] (2) 'arrangement,' still less formal than an agreement; [14] (3) 'convention,' more specific than a general agreement; [15] (4) 'protocol,' less formal and more restricted than a convention; [16] (5) 'declaration,' a statement of principles but equally binding; [17] (6) 'final act' or 'general act,' seldom used, but no less important than a treaty; [18] (7) 'exchange of

[11] P.C.I.J. (1931), Ser. A/B, No. 41. See also Art. 2(a) of Int. Law Com.'s Draft Articles.

[12] See *B. Altman & Co. v. United States*, U.S. Supreme Court, 1912. 224 U.S. 583.

[13] Example: the Anglo-French Agreement of January 30, 1951, regarding rights of fishing in areas of the Ecrehos and Minquiers. Art. 102 of the United Nations Charter refers to "every treaty and every international agreement." A resolution adopted by the General Assembly on December 14, 1946, clarifies further: "every treaty or international agreement, whatever its form and descriptive name." Briggs, p. 836. For an attempt by the International Law Commission to make a distinction between 'treaty' and 'agreement' by *rapporteur* Waldock, see UN Doc. A/CN.4/144, p. 13.

[14] Example: the Anglo-American Arrangement for the Disposal of Certain Pecuniary Claims of May 19, 1927.

[15] Example: the Geneva Convention of 1949 on the treatment of prisoners of war.

[16] Example: the Protocol of 1925, concerning the use in war of asphyxiating, poisonous, and other gases.

[17] Example: the Declaration of Paris of 1856, for the regulation of war on sea. Sometimes a declaration is considered as an integral part of a treaty. See *Ambatielos Case (Jurisdiction)*, International Court of Justice, 1952. I.C.J. Reports (1952), 28.

[18] Examples: the Final Act of the Congress of Vienna of 1815; the General Act for the Pacific Settlement of International Disputes, adopted by the ninth Assembly of the League and in effect as of August 16, 1929. These terms are also used to summarize or enumerate the proceedings of an international conference.

notes' or 'exchange of letters,' generally as a supplement to a treaty, but also used independently with the same effect as a treaty; [19] (8) 'pact,' narrower in scope than a treaty, but equally important; [20] (9) '*modus vivendi,*' temporary arrangement pending the conclusion of a treaty on the subject; [21] (10) '*compromis,*' a special agreement stipulating necessary procedures for settling a dispute through arbitration; [22] and (11) 'concordat,' designating an agreement with the Pope.[23]

A multipartite instrument may also be designated as a 'charter,' 'covenant,' 'statute,' 'constitution,' or 'regulation.' [24] There are still others, used only occasionally or for specific purposes.[25] On the other hand, many expressions used in diplomatic correspondence, such as 'note,' [26] 'memorandum,' [27] 'aide-mémoire,' [28] 'note verbal,' [29] and 'procès-verbal,' [30] are not in the nature of treaties. Much confusion has been created by the different designations for instruments which, in substance, are treaties. As reporter of the *Draft Convention on the Law of*

[19] Example: the Sino-American Air Transport Agreement and Exchange of Notes, December 20, 1946.

[20] Examples: the Kellogg-Briand Pact of 1928; the Soviet-French Non-Aggression Pact of November 29, 1932.

[21] Example: the Anglo-Soviet Temporary Commercial Agreement, signed at London on April 16, 1930.

[22] Example: the Anglo-American Treaty of Washington of 1871 for the *Alabama Claims* arbitration at Geneva in 1872. Art. 40(1) of the Statute of the International Court of Justice and Art. 52 of the Convention for the Pacific Settlement of International Disputes of 1907 provide for the conclusion of a *compromis* or special agreement.

[23] For the nature of a concordat and its distinction from the Lateran Treaty of February 11, 1929, between the Holy See and Italy, see Satow, pp. 343–344.

[24] Examples: the Charter of the United Nations, the Covenant of the League of Nations, the Statute of the International Court of Justice, the Constitution of UNESCO of 1946, the Hague Regulations of 1907 respecting the laws and customs on land warfare. For further details, see Satow, pp. 324–364; G. G. Wilson, *International Law,* 9th ed. (New York, 1935), pp. 208–211.

[25] Cartels and sponsions are instances. See *infra,* §218.

[26] Notes are correspondence between the minister of foreign affairs and diplomatic representatives. First-person notes are written in the first person and signed; third-person notes are not signed but initialed in the lower-right-hand corner of the last page of text.

[27] A written statement on any subject from the ministry of foreign affairs to a diplomatic mission and vice versa, not signed but initialed.

[28] An informal summary of a diplomatic interview or of events, not signed but initialed.

[29] An unsigned document of the same nature as an aide-mémoire.

[30] The minutes of the proceedings of a diplomatic conference.

Treaties, prepared for the Harvard Research in International Law in 1935, James W. Garner commented:

> The names actually employed today for the designation of instruments comprised under the generic term treaties are already numerous, and in recent years there has been a marked tendency to multiply them and to employ them without discrimination and without regard to the rules of logic and consistency.[31]

In the practice of the United Nations, there is a trend to use 'agreement' for bilateral treaties and 'convention' for multilateral instruments.

Forms of treaties Normally, a treaty contains a preamble, principal provisions, final clauses, and sometimes annexes. The contracting parties, the names of their authorized representatives, and the purposes of the treaty are contained in the preamble. Next in order are the substantive provisions, which are followed by miscellaneous articles on the duration of the treaty and procedures for ratification, adhesion, revision, renewal, and termination. Finally come the signatures of the authorized representatives. But there is no standard setup for treaties; they may differ very much in form, content, and many other respects.[32] They have, however, one characteristic in common. To be binding they must be written. Although history records some oral commitments,[33] both theory and practice consider only written instruments under the definition of treaties.[34]

§160. THE CLASSIFICATION OF TREATIES

Regardless of the different denominations, treaties may be classified under several categories on the basis of the number of contracting parties, the scope of application, and the nature of functions. Bilateral or bipartite treaties are concluded by two parties.[35] Those with more

[31] Cited from Briggs, p. 838.

[32] See Arnold McNair, *The Law of Treaties—British Practice and Opinions* (Oxford, 1961), pp. 20–30.

[33] For instance, the oral treaty of alliance of 1697 between Peter the Great of Russia and Frederick III, Elector of Brandenburg. In the *Legal Status of Eastern Greenland,* the Permanent Court of International Justice held, in 1933, that an oral declaration by a foreign minister on a subject within his province has legal effect. P.C.I.J. (1933), Ser. A/B, No. 53.

[34] This same view was held by James W. Garner in the Harvard Research in International Law previously described, and by J. L. Brierly in his proposal to the International Law Commission of the United Nations on the law of treaties. See Art. 3(b) of Int. Law Com.'s Draft Articles.

[35] Example: the Sino-American Treaty of Peace, Friendship, and Commerce of 1858. Most of these treaties are concluded by two states. The

than two contracting parties are called multilateral or multipartite treaties, which may be international or regional in scope, or functional in nature and not subject to geographical classification.[36] Again, there are many important multilateral treaties with law-making effect. The Hague Conventions of 1899 and 1907, the Covenant of the League of Nations, and the Charter of the United Nations belong to this category. The signatories are bound by the principles and rules laid down in these instruments.

There also are executed and executory treaties. The former disposes of the subject matter once and for all, such as boundary conventions; while the latter is continuous, for instance, treaties of commerce and navigation.[37] In the United States, there are executive agreements, concluded by the President without the approval of the Senate as required for regular treaties.[38] Many of these executive agreements deal with matters of extreme importance, such as the Anglo-American Destroyers-Naval Bases Arrangement of September 9, 1940, and the Yalta Agreement of February 11, 1945.[39] The legal status of the executive agreements is within the domestic jurisdiction of the United States.[40]

Soviet Union has consistently considered bilateral treaties more advantageous than multilateral ones. See E. A. Korovin, "Soviet Treaties and International Law," 22 *Am. Jour. Int. Law* (1928), p. 753.

[36] Regional treaties include the North Atlantic Security Treaty of April 4, 1949, the Warsaw Pact of Friendship, Cooperation, and Mutual Assistance of May 14, 1955, and many Inter-American treaties. The Five-Power Treaty on Naval Limitation, signed at Washington on February 6, 1922, is functional in nature.

[37] For details, see Fenwick, *Principles*, p. 519.

[38] See *United States v. Curtiss-Wright Export Corp.*, U.S. Supreme Court, 1936. 299 U.S. 304.

[39] For the United States practice of making treaties and congressional-executive or presidential agreements, see Myres S. McDougal and associates, *Studies in World Public Order* (New Haven, 1960), pp. 404–717; Quincy Wright, *Control of American Foreign Relations* (New York, 1922); Elbert M. Byrd, Jr., *Treaties and Executive Agreements in the United States* (The Hague, 1960), in which their separate roles and limitations are discussed.

[40] Part of the statement prepared by the Secretariat of the United Nations on American practice concerning the conclusion of treaties, on the basis of information supplied by the United States government, is pertinent:

"The subject of so-called Executive agreements is a complex one. A clear understanding of the subject, however, requires first of all the pointing out that the term 'Executive agreement' is itself a misnomer as applied to all 'international agreements other than treaties.'

"Actually, such agreements may be considered broadly in three classes: (1) agreements or understandings entered into with foreign governments,

Treaties may be classified by function as political,[41] economic, and related to other fields previously mentioned. The so-called most-favored-nation treaty is a misnomer. In most of the commercial treaties of the nineteenth century, there is a provision of most-favored-nation clause, by which one contracting party may be entitled to the most-favored-nation treatment granted by the other contracting party to third states on the same subject matter.[42] In conclusion, the designation and classification of treaties do not have practical significance. It is their substance, effect, and application that bind the contracting parties and create international obligations.

II. *THE CONCLUSION, RATIFICATION, AND REGISTRATION OF TREATIES*

§161. THE CONCLUSION OF TREATIES

Parties to a treaty are limited to states and public organizations composed of states, whose treaty-making power and process are governed by the provisions of their fundamental laws and statutes.[43] There

pursuant to or in accordance with, specific direction or authorization by the Congress; (2) agreements or understandings, made with foreign governments but not given effect except with the approval of the Congress, by specific sanction or implementation; and (3) agreements or understandings made with foreign governments by the Executive solely under and in accordance with the Executive's constitutional power." *Laws and Practices concerning the Conclusion of Treaties* (UN Doc. ST/Leg/Ser.B/3, 1952), p. 130.

[41] An important reference on political treaties is the United Nations, *Systematic Survey of Treaties for the Pacific Settlement of International Disputes, 1928–1948* (New York, 1949), which covers extensively all amicable means, including conciliation, arbitration, and judicial settlement.

[42] On the relation of United States commercial treaties to international law, see Robert R. Wilson, *United States Commercial Treaties and International Law* (New Orleans, 1960), particularly Chs. IV–VII, on property protection, natural resources, internal taxation, companies, and judicial remedies. See also the same author, *The International Standard in Treaties of the United States* (Cambridge, 1953), Chs. I(4), III.

[43] The treaty-making power of the United Nations is expressly stipulated in Arts. 43, 57, 63, of the Charter. Implied powers may also be found in other articles, including 17, 64, 66, 75, 77, 79, 85, 88, 104, 105. The International Law Commission did not include international organizations in the draft articles on treaties until H. Lauterpacht became *rapporteur*. Hans Kelsen is inclined to limit the treaty-making power of the United Nations to specific provisions of the Charter. See Kelsen, *UN*, p. 330. In the opinion of Rosalyn Higgins, "both practice and judicial decision have shown Kelsen's

is an increasing number of international agreements concluded by the United Nations and other international organizations. Through the General Assembly, the Security Council, the Economic and Social Council, the Trusteeship Council, and the Secretariat, the United Nations has entered into many bilateral treaties with states, specialized agencies, and public organizations, in a much more extensive way than the League of Nations did. The Organization has also concluded many multilateral treaties. The conduct of negotiations and the signing are entrusted to the Secretary-General or other authorized organs or agents of other international organizations. The specialized agencies have concluded agreements among themselves and with other entities.[44]

The present discussion will concentrate on the procedures in which states are the principal participants in the negotiation and conclusion of treaties. Normally, the head of state or government is vested with the treaty-making power. In the past, sovereigns met personally at important conferences and concluded treaties by themselves.[45] Due to the complexity of modern transactions, the ministers of foreign affairs or other duly authorized representatives have long been empowered to conduct negotiations, which, if successful, will be followed by the signing of a treaty. Usually, the contracting parties issue instruments called 'full powers' (*pleins pouvoirs*) to their authorized representatives, who will present them for examination before signing.[46] Technical agreements of minor importance may be concluded by the ministries or departments under whose jurisdiction the subject matter falls.[47]

---

view to be untenable." Higgins, *The Development of International Law through the Political Organs of the United Nations* (London, 1963), p. 243. For a general discussion of the treaty-making power, see Hans Blix, *Treaty-Making Power* (London, 1960.)

[44] On the capacity of international organizations to make treaties, see J. Schneider, *Treaty-Making Power of International Organizations* (Geneva, 1959); Hungdah Chiu, *The Capacity of International Organizations to Conclude Treaties, and the Special Legal Aspects of the Treaties so Concluded* (The Hague, 1966).

[45] The Holy Alliance was originally concluded at Paris in 1815 by the Sovereigns of Austria, Russia, and Prussia and later assented to by almost all Christian rulers in the European continent; the Yalta Agreement, by the leaders of the United States, Great Britain, and the Soviet Union.

[46] For details, consult J. M. Jones, *Full Powers and Ratification* (Cambridge, England, 1946); Arts. 6–7 of Int. Law Com.'s Draft Articles. See also Arts. 8–9, for adoption and authentication of the text of treaties.

[47] This is the practice of many states, including the United States, Norway, and the Republic of South Africa. Thus, in the conclusion of the Postal Convention of 1928, several states were represented by their postal administrations.

A treaty is concluded as soon as mutual consent is manifested in the acts of duly authorized representatives, although it will not come into effect before ratification.[48] Modern states, as a rule, require approval of treaties by the legislative branches of government as essential to ratification.[49] Multilateral treaties negotiated at international conferences generally follow the same process.[50] A treaty is not binding upon the contracting state if its representative exceeds his power in concluding it.[51]

Languages used in treaties In a bilateral treaty, it is up to the contracting parties to decide on the language to be employed. Unless otherwise agreed upon, the languages of the two states are equally authentic.[52] In multilateral treaties, Latin was the language in the Middle Ages. At the beginning of the sixteenth century, French gradually replaced Latin. English was introduced as a diplomatic language early in the twentieth century. At the Congress of Vienna in 1815, all copies of the General Treaty of Vienna were written in French.[53] The

[48] See *Philippson v. Imperial Airways, Ltd.*, Great Britain, House of Lords, 1939. [1939] A.C. 332.

[49] For the practice of different states, consult *Laws and Practices concerning the Conclusion of Treaties,* prepared by the United Nations, with a select bibliography of the law of treaties. UN Doc. ST/Leg/Ser.B/3, 1952.

[50] There are some modifications in various treaties. See *supra,* §§144–145.

[51] The case of Nicholas P. Trist has often been used for illustration. Actually, his negotiation for a peace treaty with Mexico in 1848 was not in excess of his power. On the contrary, he conformed to official instructions from Washington. President Polk's dissatisfaction with Trist was attributed partly to the latter's disregard of his recall. See Julius W. Pratt, *A History of United States Foreign Policy* (Englewood Cliffs, N.J., 1955), pp. 259–262.

[52] Sometimes the authenticity of a treaty may be affected by linguistic error. In depositing the instrument of ratification of the Genocide Convention, the Chinese government pointed out the lack of uniformity of the Chinese texts with other texts and submitted a revised copy to the Secretary-General. See GA *Official Records,* 6th Sess., 6th Committee, p. 312. By resolution 691 (VII), the corrected copy was transmitted to the states concerned, with a request to inform the Secretary-General of their acceptance or rejection. In this case, the problem of authenticity should not be a serious issue, because there are still four authentic texts in English, French, Spanish, and Russian.

[53] Art. 120 of the General Treaty of Vienna of 1815 emphasized, however, that the use of French in this Treaty would not exclude in future conventions other languages previously employed in the diplomatic relations of the signatory powers.

trend has changed since the conclusion of World War I. Both French and English were used with equal authenticity in the Peace Treaty with Germany and in the Covenant of the League of Nations. The Charter of the United Nations was written in five official languages: English, French, Chinese, Russian, and Spanish.[54]

In connection with language, order of signature has been another issue in diplomatic practice. Following the accepted usage of 'alternat,' each representative signs first on the copy for his own state. But sometimes an alphabetical order of French or English is used instead.[55] In a multilateral treaty, one original text with the signatures of the authorized representatives is deposited with the government where the signing takes place, and a certified copy is supplied by that government to other contracting parties.[56]

§162. RATIFICATION OF TREATIES

Ratification is the approval or confirmation by the appropriate authorities of the signatory state, according to its constitutional process, of a treaty concluded by its plenipotentiary.[57] Once a treaty is signed, the contracting parties have a moral but not a legal obligation to ratify it. Generally, a treaty becomes effective on the date of its ratification.[58] A treaty has no binding effect upon states which have not ratified it,[59]

[54] See Art. 111 of the Charter. With respect to interpretation of treaties in two or more languages, see Art. 29 of Int. Law Com.'s Draft Articles.

[55] Alphabetical order may also have variations. The United States was arranged under the letter *E* (États-Unis) at the First Hague Conference in 1899, but changed to *A* (Amérique) at the Second Hague Conference in 1907.

[56] For further details, see Satow, pp. 329–332.

[57] A comprehensive discussion on the subject can be found in José S. Camara, *The Ratification of International Treaties* (Toronto, 1949); Francis O. Wilcox, *The Ratification of International Conventions* (London, 1935), which deals systematically with the relationship of the ratification process to the development of international legislation.

[58] See *Haver v. Yaker*, U.S. Supreme Court, 1869. 9 Wallace 32. Again, there are variations. The Soviet-Swiss Commercial Treaty of March 17, 1948 provides: "The Treaty is subject to ratification in the shortest possible time and comes into force twenty days after the exchange of the instruments of ratification which shall take place in Berne." Cited from Soviet *Text*, p. 266. The Locarno Treaties of 1925 required the admission of Germany into the League of Nations as prerequisite for their coming into effect.

[59] See *The Eliza Ann*, Great Britain, High Court of Admiralty, 1813. 1 Dodson 244.

but the process of ratification is not required by all states nor applied to all treaties. It depends entirely on the provisions of their domestic laws.

Many important treaties have become effective on the date of signature, without the necessity of ratification. These include the Anglo-Japanese Treaty of Alliance of 1905, the Protocol of Mutual Assistance of 1936 between the Soviet Union and Outer Mongolia, the Anglo-Polish Treaty of Alliance of 1939, and the Four-Power Agreement of 1945 on the prosecution and punishment of major war criminals. A multilateral treaty may come into effect upon the deposit of a certain number of ratifications.[60] The requirement for the United Nations Charter was the ratification by the majority of the signatory states, including the five powers designated to become permanent members of the Security Council.[61] Instruments of ratification of treaties concluded under the auspices of the League of Nations and of the United Nations are deposited in the Secretariat of the respective organizations.

There is no time limit for ratification unless specified in the treaty, but prolonged delay may defeat the purpose of the treaty.[62] Provision is often made in a treaty that it be ratified as soon as possible. Ratification is often effected by an exchange of the instruments of ratification, which, in the case of a multilateral treaty, are usually deposited with the government of the contracting state where the signing of the treaty has taken place.

Reasons for refusal of ratification vary with different treaties, but they are generally based on the following grounds: change of circumstances, failure to meet the approval of the proper authorities, or procedural or substantial errors concerning the conclusion and text of the treaty. Domestic politics sometimes play an important part. Conditional ratification of a treaty is, in effect, a refusal of ratification, unless the contracting parties choose to negotiate for the new proposals.[63] So-

[60] In the Draft Articles on the Law of Treaties, the International Law Commission provides that the consent of a state to be bound by a treaty is expressed by signature, ratification, acceptance, approval, or accession (Arts. 10–12). See also Arts. 21, 22, 24, for further provisions concerning the entry into force and non-retroactivity of treaties.

[61] According to Art. 110 of the Charter, its ratifications were deposited with the government of the United States, which then notified all the signatory states and the Secretary-General of the United Nations of each deposit.

[62] For reasons which have caused delay in ratification of many law-making treaties, see LN Doc. A.10.1930.V. For the obligation of a state not to frustrate the object of a treaty prior to its entry into force, see Art. 15 of Int. Law Com.'s Draft Articles.

[63] The first Hay-Pauncefote Treaty failed to come into effect when the British government refused to accept its revised text as amended by the United States Senate on December 20, 1900. However, the two countries

called partial ratification is sometimes applied to a multilateral treaty, "if one or more provisions of the treaty which have been signed without reservation are exempted from ratification, or if an amending clause is added to the treaty during the process of ratification." [64] Strictly speaking, ratification under such circumstances is not partial or conditional.

§163. RESERVATIONS

A reservation is not a refusal of ratification, but a conditional approval or acceptance of a treaty by a signatory state, which exempts itself from being bound by certain provisions of the treaty in its relation with other contracting parties. Such a reservation may be made by endorsing a statement upon the treaty itself, in the instrument of ratification, or in any other form collateral to the treaty. Strictly speaking, no reservation can be effective without the express or tacit approval of the other contracting parties.[65] However, the concept of absolute integrity of a multilateral treaty is sound in principle, but difficult to fulfill in practice.

Any reservation weakens the effectiveness of a treaty and complicates its application. Green H. Hackworth made the following observation for clarification:

> Whether a multilateral treaty may be regarded as in force as between a country making a reservation and countries accepting such reservation, but not in force as regards countries not accepting the reservation, depends upon whether the treaty as signed is susceptible of application to the smaller group of signatories.[66]

---

started a new negotiation, which resulted in successful conclusion and ratification of the second Hay-Pauncefote Treaty in 1901. See Julius W. Pratt, *op. cit.*, pp. 398–400.

[64] Oppenheim, I, p. 912. When France excepted twenty-three articles from ratification of the General Act of the Brussels Anti-Slavery Conference of 1890, no objection was raised by the other contracting parties. In 1934, Ecuador created an interesting precedent when she decided to assume her original membership in the League by ratifying the Covenant without ratifying the Treaty of Versailles in which the Covenant was embodied. See LN *Official Jour.*, 1934, p. 1468. See also Art. 14 of Int. Law Com.'s Draft Articles.

[65] *Cf.* Harvard Research in International Law, Treaties. 29 *Am. Jour. Int. Law* (1935), 843 *et seq.* Many reservations were adopted by the United States Senate to the League Covenant and the Statute of the Permanent Court of International Justice, in spite of its eventual failure to approve the two instruments. See also GA *Official Records,* 1951, Supp., No. 9, for the report of the International Law Commission.

[66] Hackworth, *Digest,* V, p. 130.

In order to avoid complications, the contracting parties may make reservations impermissible or certain parts of the treaty not subject to reservations.[67]

There is no established rule of international law governing the effect of reservations. After the conclusion of the Genocide Convention, the United Nations faced the problem of many reservations made by the signatory states at the time of ratification.[68] On November 16, 1950, the General Assembly decided to request the International Court of Justice for an advisory opinion on a number of questions on the *Reservation to the Convention on the Prevention and Punishment of the Crime of Genocide.* The Court was quite divided on this matter. However, on May 28, 1951, it was able, by a vote of 7 to 5, to deliver an advisory opinion, which is summarized below.

When objection to a reservation by a state is made by one or more contracting parties but not by others, that state can be regarded as being a party to the Convention on the condition that the reservation is compatible with the object and purpose of the Convention. But the state or states which have objected to its reservation may consider that reserving state not a party to the Convention. The same legal effect is applied to the objections raised by signatory states but only at the time of their ratification. Objections made by states which are entitled to sign or accede to the Convention but have not yet done so have no legal effect whatsoever.[69]

While upholding the principle that no reservation can be effective against any state without its consent, the majority of the Court emphasized the nature of the contents and the desirability of flexible application of a multilateral treaty. This attitude is almost identical with the Inter-American rule on reservations.[70] It seems that the Soviet Union,

[67] The Convention on Damage Caused by Foreign Aircraft to Third States on the Surface, signed at Rome on October 7, 1952, permits no reservations whatsoever. Arts. 1–3 of the Geneva Convention on the Continental Shelf of 1958 are not subject to reservations. See Starke, p. 350. The General Assembly, on January 12, 1952, adopted a number of recommendations on reservations. See 46 *Am. Jour. Int. Law* (1952), Supp., p. 66.

[68] Soviet reservations reflect a consistent policy of objection to compulsory jurisdiction of the International Court of Justice and to limitation of the Convention's application to metropolitan countries only. In the view of the Soviet government, the Convention should be extended to colonies. See Soviet *Text,* p. 270.

[69] I.C.J. Reports (1951), p. 15. For Brierly's view on reservations which differ from the opinion of the Court, see his special report to the International Law Commission in 1951. UN Doc. A/CN.4/41; A/CN.4/L.9.

[70] For the opinion of the Governing Board of the Pan-American Union, see 45 *Am. Jour. Int. Law* (1951), Supp., p. 111.

the United States, and the developing countries all prefer this view to the so-called unanimity doctrine.[71]

In its Draft Articles on the Law of Treaties, the International Law Commission stipulated the formulation of reservations,[72] acceptance of and objection to reservations,[73] as well as procedure regarding reservations.[74] In respect of legal effects of reservations, the Commission agreed on the following provision:

[71] For the Soviet view on treaty reservations, see Jan F. Triska and Robert M. Slusser, *op. cit.*, pp. 82–88.

[72] The text of Art. 16 is as follows: "A state may, when signing, ratifying, accepting, approving or acceding to a treaty, formulate a reservation unless:

"(a) The reservation is prohibited by the treaty;

"(b) The treaty authorizes specified reservations which do not include the reservation in question; or

"(c) In cases where the treaty contains no provisions regarding reservations, the reservation is incompatible with the object and purpose of the treaty."

[73] Art. 17 provides, in detail, for acceptance of and objection to reservations as follows:

"1. A reservation expressly or impliedly authorized by the treaty does not require any subsequent acceptance by the other contracting states unless the treaty so provides.

"2. When it appears from the limited number of the negotiating states and the object and purpose of the treaty that the application of the treaty in its entirety between all the parties is an essential condition of the consent of each one to be bound by the treaty, a reservation requires acceptance by all the parties.

"3. When a treaty is a constituent instrument of an international organization, the reservation requires the acceptance of the competent organ of that organization, unless the treaty otherwise provides.

"4. In cases not falling under the preceding paragraphs of this article:

"(a) Acceptance by another contracting state of the reservation constitutes the reserving state a party to the treaty in relation to that state if or when the treaty is in force;

"(b) An objection by another contracting state to a reservation precludes the entry into force of the treaty as between the objecting and reserving states unless a contrary intention is expressed by the objecting state;

"(c) An act expressing the state's consent to be bound by the treaty and containing a reservation is effective as soon as at least one other contracting state has accepted the reservation.

"5. For the purposes of paragraphs 2 and 4 a reservation is considered to have been accepted by a state if it shall have raised no objection to the reservation by the end of a period of twelve months after it was notified of the reservation or by the date on which it expressed its consent to be bound by the treaty, whichever is later."

[74] According to Art. 18, the procedure regarding reservations is as follows:

1. A reservation established with regard to another party in accordance with Articles 16, 17 and 18:

(a) Modifies for the reserving state the provisions of the treaty to which the reservation relates to the extent of the reservation; and

(b) Modifies those provisions to the same extent for such other party in its relations with the reserving state.

2. The reservation does not modify the provisions of the treaty for the other parties to the treaty *inter se*.

3. When a state objecting to a reservation agrees to consider the treaty in force between itself and the reserving state, the provisions to which the reservation relates do not apply as between the two states to the extent of the reservation.[75]

The legal situation is entirely different in respect of a bilateral treaty, which becomes invalid if one contracting party objects to a reservation made by the other. In this connection, confusion must be avoided with the term 'understandings,' which merely state the views of the ratifying state on certain provisions of a treaty as a kind of advanced interpretation or interpretative reservation. If the understandings are not inconsistent with the substance of the treaty, no dissent is expected from the other contracting party.[76]

§164. ACCESSION, ACCEPTANCE, AND APPROVAL [77]

Different from ratification is the term 'accession,' which indicates the formal act of a state in entering into an existing treaty. For all prac-

---

"1. A reservation, an express acceptance of a reservation, and an objection to a reservation must be formulated in writing and communicated to the other states entitled to become parties to the treaty.

"2. If formulated on the occasion of the adoption of the text or upon signing the treaty subject to ratification, acceptance or approval, a reservation must be formally confirmed by the reserving state when expressing its consent to be bound by the treaty. In such a case the reservation shall be considered as having been made on the date of its confirmation.

"3. An objection to the reservation made previously to its confirmation does not itself require confirmation."

[75] Art. 19. Reservations may be withdrawn in accordance with the provisions of Art. 20:

"1. Unless the treaty otherwise provides, a reservation may be withdrawn at any time and the consent of a state which has accepted the reservation is not required for its withdrawal.

"2. Unless the treaty otherwise provides or it is otherwise agreed, the withdrawal becomes operative only when notice of it has been received by the other contracting states."

[76] For a full discussion on the subject, see Hackworth, *Digest*, V, §484.

[77] The consent of a state to be bound by a treaty may be expressed by acceptance, approval, or accession. For details, see Arts. 11–13 of Int. Law. Com.'s Draft Articles.

tical purposes, there is no difference between 'accession' and 'adherence,' which are often used interchangeably. Accession may be effected through the invitation of the original signatories, as of the North Atlantic Treaty of 1949,[78] or in accordance with the stipulated terms of the international instrument. Thus, any peace-loving state able and willing to accept the obligations of the United Nations Charter may apply for membership in the Organization, which will approve its admission by a decision of the General Assembly upon recommendation of the Security Council.[79] Here the consent of the Member states is indirectly expressed through these two organs of the United Nations. According to modern practice, a state may accede to a treaty either before or after its coming into force and with or without conditions, depending upon the nature and substance of the treaty.[80]

In recent years, the term 'acceptance' has been used, as in the Constitution of UNESCO, and that of 'approval,' as in the Constitution of WHO.[81] In these cases, non-signatory states may become parties to the respective constitutions under the following conditions: (1) signature without reservation as to acceptance or approval; (2) signature subject to reservation or approval followed by acceptance; and (3) acceptance. No state will accept a treaty if its terms cannot be approved. Nor will a state accede or adhere to a treaty if it is not acceptable.[82] However, in the practice of the United Nations, the term 'approval' is preferred. The Economic and Social Council concludes agreements with the specialized agencies, subject to the approval of the General Assembly,[83] which also exercises routine authority over agreements entered into by other organs and the Secretary-General. Ap-

[78] Greece and Turkey were invited to accede to the North Atlantic Treaty in 1951 by the original signatories in accordance with Art. 10 of the Treaty.

[79] Art. 4 of the Charter. See also *supra*, §49.

[80] The Kellogg-Briand Pact of 1928 came into effect first, before it was open for accession to other states. In his report to the International Law Commission on the law of treaties, H. Lauterpacht indicated some opposite practices. In certain treaties, accession is necessary to their coming into effect, such as the Revised General Act for the Pacific Settlement of International Disputes and the Convention on the Privileges and Immunities of the United Nations of 1946. The government of a non-signatory party may enter GATT "on terms to be agreed between such government and the contracting parties." Art. 33. For more examples, see Satow, pp. 367–368.

[81] Art. 15 of the Constitution of UNESCO and Art. 79 of the Constitution of WHO.

[82] See Satow, pp. 370–371; Yuen-li Liang, "The Use of the Term 'Acceptance' in United Nations Treaty Practice," 44 *Am. Jour. Int. Law* (1950), pp. 342–346.

[83] Art. 63 of the United Nations Charter.

proval by the General Assembly in these cases is largely a formality. Thus, the act of United Nations approval is slightly different from that of state ratification.

The recent emergence of many new states has raised the question whether they should notify the contracting parties to such multilateral conventions applicable to them of their intention to be bound by these conventions. As the protocols amending such conventions provided that they were open for signature only to the states parties to those conventions and as the new states had signed those protocols applicable to them, it was deemed by the United Nations Secretariat that their signatures constituted an implicit acknowledgment of being bound by these conventions. Some of the new states had even made express declarations to this effect under their signatures. Further notification to the contracting parties was, therefore, considered unnecessary.[84] Recently, the General Assembly laid down various procedures for the accession of states to multilateral treaties.[85]

§165. REGISTRATION OF TREATIES

Registration of treaties with the secretariat of an international organization is of recent origin. Fully aware of the problems and suspicions that arose out of the secret treaties entered into by the Allied and Associated Powers during World War I, the drafters of the League Covenant worked out a plan to avoid such secrecy. Article 18 of the Covenant requires that "every treaty or international engagement entered into hereafter by any Member of the League shall be forthwith registered with the Secretariat and shall, as soon as possible, be published by it." As a sanction against failure to fulfill this obligation, the same article provides that "no such treaty or international engagement shall be binding until so registered." A similar requirement is stipulated in the United Nations Charter, but more flexible in wording:

> 1. Every treaty and every international agreement entered into by any Member of the United Nations after the present Charter comes into force shall as soon as possible be registered with the Secretariat and published by it.

[84] For details, see *Introduction by United Nations Secretariat to Signatures, Ratifications, Acceptances, Accession, etc., concerning the Multilateral Conventions and Agreements in Respect to Which the Secretary-General Acts as Depository*. UN Doc. 1949.V.9, p. 3.

[85] See *Resolutions of the General Assembly concerning the Law of Treaties: Memorandum prepared by the Secretariat,* February 14, 1963. UN Doc. A/CN.4/154, pp. 15–16.

2. No party to any such treaty or international agreement which has not been registered in accordance with the provisions of paragraph 1 of this Article may invoke that treaty or agreement before any organ of the United Nations.[86]

Comparing the phraseology of the pertinent provisions of the Covenant and the Charter, there is no material difference between 'engagement' and 'agreement' and between 'forthwith' and 'as soon as possible.' But the non-invocation of an unregistered treaty or agreement before any organ of the United Nations is not as rigid a sanction as non-binding, because whatever cannot be invoked before the United Nations may still be binding upon the contracting parties elsewhere. According to the Charter, default of registration will make the treaty unenforceable before the United Nations, but not void.[87] While obligatory for Member states, the requirement of registration cannot be imposed on non-members, which have, therefore, no right to invoke failure of registration as a legal ground for release from treaty obligations.[88]

The Secretariat of the League and of the United Nations is designated as the organ for registration, the function of which is purely ministerial, with no authority of approval or disapproval of the treaties so registered. Non-members of the United Nations are also invited to transmit treaties and agreements entered into both before and after the date of coming into force of the United Nations Charter for filing and publication, with the exception of those already published by the League of Nations *Treaty Series*.[89] For the implementation of Article 102 of the Charter, the General Assembly adopted, on December 14, 1946, Regulations on the procedure for registration.[90] In addition to a

[86] Art. 102 of the Charter, which came into force on October 24, 1945; Art. 75 of Int. Law Com.'s Draft Articles. See also Arts. 71–74 of the Draft Articles, for procedures concerning depositories, notifications, and corrections.

[87] See Hyde, II, §491.

[88] See *Pablo Nájera Case*, France-Mexico, Mixed Claims Commission, 1928. *Annual Digest*, 1927–1928, No. 271. Because the Franco-Mexican Claims Convention of September 25, 1924, failed to be registered, Mexico declared it not binding. But the Commission ruled that Mexico, as a non-member of the League of Nations, had no right to invoke Art. 18 of the Covenant.

[89] In accordance with GA res. 23 (I), adopted by the General Assembly at its first session. From 1920 to 1944, the League of Nations *Treaty Series* published 204 volumes, containing 4,822 international instruments registered with the League Secretariat in original languages and also in English and French translations.

[90] GA res. 97 (I), later amended by 364B (IV) and 482 (V). For the

monthly list, the texts of all international instruments registered with the United Nations Secretariat are published in the United Nations *Treaty Series*.[91]

According to Article 1 of the Regulations, registration may be effected by any signatory party as soon as but not before the entering into force of a treaty or international agreement. The United Nations Secretariat has been flexible in interpreting the term 'entry into force.'[92] Multilateral instruments are registered with the Secretariat, preferably by the government in custody of the original copies. Subject to Article 1 of the Regulations, treaties or international agreements are registered *ex officio* by the United Nations in the following cases: (1) where the United Nations is a contracting party; (2) where the United Nations has been authorized by the treaty or agreement to effect registration; and (3) where the United Nations is the depository of a multilateral instrument.[93]

Subject to the same conditions, registration may be effected by a specialized agency with the United Nations Secretariat: (1) where the constituent instrument of the specialized agency provides for such registration; (2) where the treaty or agreement has been registered with the specialized agency pursuant to the terms of its constituent instrument; and (3) where the specialized agency has been authorized by the treaty or agreement to effect registration.[94] Treaties and international agreements other than those subject to registration under Article 1 of the Regulations may be filed and recorded with the United Nations Secretariat for publication under the similar procedure governing registration.[95]

---

text of the Regulations to Give Effect to Article 102 of the Charter of the United Nations, concerning registration and publication of treaties and international agreements, see *Repertory,* UN, V, pp. 283–292. For the position of the Secretariat on registration of certain types of international agreements, see *ibid.*, pp. 295–296.

[91] The first volume of the United Nations *Treaty Series* was issued in October 1947.

[92] Exceptions may be found in UN *Treaty Series,* Vol. 17 (1948), I, No. 281, p. 273; Vol. 30 (1949), I, No. 452, p. 145; Vol. 31 (1949), I, No. 485, p. 435; Vol. 55 (1950), I, No. 814, p. 194. See *Repertory,* UN, V, p. 296.

[93] Art. 4(1) of the Regulations.

[94] Art. 4(2) of the Regulations.

[95] Art. 10 of the Regulations. Treaties or international agreements requiring registration are those entered into by one or more Members of the United Nations after the coming into force of the Charter on October 24, 1945. Art. 1(1) of the Regulations.

III. *THE VALIDITY, EFFECTS, AND INTERPRETATION OF TREATIES*

§166. THE VALIDITY OF TREATIES

It is a cardinal rule of international law that treaties must be observed (*pacta sunt servanda*). A state has the moral and legal obligation to carry out the terms agreed upon by itself.[96] The binding force of a treaty is determined by the following conditions: (1) properly concluded and ratified; (2) physically enforceable; (3) free from duress, fraud, and error; and (4) consistent with customary international law and other international obligations. A treaty may be declared invalid if it is not in conformity with the above conditions.

First of all, the party to a treaty must have legal capacity of contracting, and the treaty must be duly signed by its authorized representative and eventually ratified in accordance with the constitutional process of that state.[97] Default of registration of a treaty with the Secretariat of the United Nations does not make it invalid, but it becomes unenforceable before the organs of the United Nations. Second, the object of the treaty must be within the possibility of physical fulfillment. Otherwise, the treaty has to be declared null and void.

Third, a treaty must not be signed under coercion or duress. The use of force or intimidation to compel the head of state or government or his plenipotentiary to accept harsh terms is against the basic principle of free consent in the conclusion of a treaty.[98] No treaty is valid if the person who affixes his signature is under captivity or other circumstances making it impossible to exercise his free will. On the other hand, the conclusion of a humiliating peace treaty through military defeat cannot be considered as coercion or duress in this sense. Furthermore, deliberate misrepresentation or important errors of fact make the treaty lose its binding force upon the contracting parties.[99]

[96] In *United States v. Ferris,* a U.S. District Court (Northern District of California) held, in 1927, that a treaty should be scrupulously observed by the parties on various grounds, including "a decent respect for the opinions of mankind, national honor, harmonious relations between nations, and avoidance of war." 19 F.2d 925. See also Art. 23 of Int. Law Com.'s Draft Articles.

[97] The Twenty-One Demands imposed by Japan on China in 1915 were never approved by the Chinese Parliament and thus became null and void. See William L. Tung, *The Political Institutions of Modern China,* pp. 63–64.

[98] For examples, see Fenwick, *Principles,* p. 529.

[99] If the documents or maps used for the demarcation of the boundary

Fourth, a treaty in conflict with the customary rules of international law is voidable when a third party intervenes. If it is inconsistent with other international obligations, the state or states adversely affected may object to its validity.[100] The League Covenant stresses the obligation of its Members to abrogate their treaties or understandings inconsistent with the terms of the Covenant and not to enter into such treaties in the future.[101] The United Nations Charter specifically provides: "In the event of a conflict between the obligations of the Members of the United Nations under the present Charter and their obligations under any other international agreement, their obligations under the present Charter shall prevail." [102] Both the Covenant and the Charter are multilateral treaties of law-making nature, and, therefore, supersede the inconsistent obligations of Member states under previous international engagements.

In addition to the above-mentioned conditions, a treaty is expected to be in conformity with normal standards of morality and justice, which may constitute a matter of argument among nations because of their different background and political systems. Nevertheless, a treaty providing unilateral advantage to one party without reciprocity to the other is on an unequal basis; examples are extraterritoriality and uniform tariff, which created popular resentment in Japan, China, and other countries against Western imperialism. This unpleasant memory remains in the mind of many people even after the treaties' abolition.[103]

---

between two states have significant errors or are fraudulently produced, the treaty concluded on the basis of such documents or maps is *ab initio* null and void. See the comments of James W. Garner as reporter on the Harvard Draft on the Law of Treaties, 29 *Am. Jour. Int. Law* (1935), p. 1129.

[100] When Russia concluded the Preliminary Peace Treaty with Turkey in 1878, Great Britain protested on the ground of its inconsistency with the Treaty of Paris of 1858 and the London Convention of 1871. Japan's invasion of Manchuria in 1931 and subsequent establishment of the puppet state of Manchukuo led strong protests from the United States and culminated in the Stimson Doctrine of non-recognition because of Japan's violation of the Open Door policy, the Nine-Power Treaty, and other international obligations. For further reference on the validity of treaties, see Arts. 39–50, 61, 65, of Int. Law Com.'s Draft Articles.

[101] Art. 20 of the Covenant.

[102] Art. 103 of the Charter. The International Law Commission adopted a special provision for application of successive treaties relating to the same subject matter.

[103] The present policy of Communist China is partly attributable to her reaction to foreign encroachments since the middle of the nineteenth century. For a full discussion, see M. T. Z. Tyau, *The Legal Obligation Arising out of Treaty Relations between China and Other States* (Shanghai, 1917),

Thus, justice and morality are essential to any harmonious and long-lasting agreement.

§167. EFFECTS OF TREATIES

A treaty is binding upon the contracting parties either from the date of signature or ratification, depending upon the intention, subject matter, and circumstances. When a treaty involves cession of a territory, the ceding state is not supposed to convey part of the land to individuals or to grant franchises to them during the period between signing and ratification. Otherwise, the conditions of the ceded territory would be materially changed.[104] Be that as it may, a peace treaty is so important that it should not become effective until the date of its ratification.[105] In *Haver v. Yaker*, the United States Supreme Court held in 1869 that the retroactive principle of relating back to the date of signature was only applicable to the rights of the governments involved and that it might not be invoked to deprive individuals of their rights vested in the interim.[106]

The effect of a ratified treaty on national laws and judicial proceedings varies in different states.[107] Taking the Constitution of the United States for example, Article VI(2) provides that the federal Constitution, the laws of the United States, and all the treaties made under the authority of the United States are the supreme law of the land. Thus self-executing treaties may supersede prior acts of Con-

---

pp. 1–21; also William L. Tung, *Imperialism and China* (Shanghai, 1929, in Chinese, available at Stanford University), Pt. II. Germany's demand for revision of the Treaty of Versailles on May 17, 1933, on the ground of its injustice and lack of logic was not entirely without reason.

[104] In *Davis v. the Police Jury of the Parish of Concordia*, the U.S. Supreme Court ruled, in 1850, that the cession of land was binding on signing the treaty which became retroactively absolute on ultimate ratification and that no valid grants of land could be made by the ceding state in the interim. 9 Howard 280.

[105] See *The Eliza Ann*, Great Britain, High Court of Admiralty, 1813. 1 Dodson 244.

[106] 9 Wallace 32. Art. 24 of Int. Law Com.'s Draft Articles reads: "Unless a different intention appears from the treaty or is otherwise established, its provisions do not bind a party in relation to any act or fact which took place or any situation which ceased to exist before the date of the entry into force of the treaty with respect to that party."

[107] According to Art. 25 of Int. Law Com.'s Draft Articles, "unless a different intention appears from the treaty or is otherwise established, the application of a treaty extends to the entire territory of each party."

gress.[108] It is also recognized that treaties take precedence over state statutes.[109] Furthermore, a Congressional act enacted to give effect to valid treaties supersedes inconsistent federal or state statutes.[110] A treaty once ratified is binding upon the courts of the contracting states,[111] and any domestic law in conflict with the provisions of a treaty should be revised. Although a treaty is binding upon the contracting parties, sometimes a change of form of government makes its execution impossible.[112]

Normally, a treaty is not binding upon a state which is not party to it, except to the extent accepted by that state.[113] This principle was upheld by the Permanent Court of International Justice in *Free Zones of Upper Savoy and the District of Gex* in 1932.[114] On many occasions, a third state may be indirectly affected by certain treaties, such as the most-favored-nation clause in commercial treaties and new rules of international law formulated by law-making treaties.[115]

The joint intervention by Russia, France, and Germany against the cession of Liaotung Peninsula to Japan by China as provided in the Sino-Japanese Peace Treaty of April 17, 1895, was motivated by the

[108] See *General Electric Co. v. Robertson,* United States, Circuit Court of Appeals, Fourth Circuit, 1929. 21 F.2d 214. For the effect of self-executing treaties on the rights of nationals of one state against another, see the advisory opinion on the *Jurisdiction of the Courts of Danzig,* Permanent Court of International Justice, 1928. P.C.I.J. (1928), Ser. B, No. 15.

[109] See *People v. Gerke and Clark,* United States, Supreme Court of California, 1955 (5 Cal. 381); *United States v. Belmont,* U.S. Supreme Court, 1937 (301 U.S. 324).

[110] See *Missouri v. Holland,* U.S. Supreme Court, 1920. 252 U.S. 416.

[111] See *United States v. Schooner Peggy,* U.S. Supreme Court, 1801. 1 Cranch 103. In *Foster and Elam v. Neilson,* the U.S. Supreme Court held, in 1829, that a treaty was a contract between two nations, not a legislative act. However, the Court went further to state that a treaty was "to be regarded in courts of justice as equivalent to an act of the legislature, whenever it operates of itself without the aid of any legislative provision." 2 Peters 253.

[112] Many treaties are affected by drastic revolution in a contracting state, followed by a change of policy of the succeeding government. However, in the *International Status of South-West Africa,* the International Court of Justice held, in 1950, that mandate provisions in the treaty between the League Council and South Africa were not decisively affected by the extinction of the League. I.C.J. Reports (1950), 128.

[113] For divergent opinions on the effect of treaties on third states, see R. F. Roxburgh, *International Conventions and Third States* (London, 1917).

[114] P.C.I.J. (1932), Ser. A/B, No. 46.

[115] On treaties providing for rights and obligations for third states, see Arts. 30–34 of Int. Law Com.'s Draft Articles.

national interests of the three powers in the Far East. Subsequently, Japan yielded to their demand by retroceding Liaotung Peninsula to China.[116] Sometimes third states are benefited by a bilateral treaty between other countries, as in the Hay-Pauncefote Treaty of 1901, which stipulated that the Panama Canal must be open to vessels of all nations.[117] Several provisions of the League Covenant and of the United Nations Charter involve the rights and duties of non-members.[118] According to the advisory opinion of the International Court of Justice on *Reparation for Injuries Suffered in Service of the United Nations* in 1949, the United Nations has the right to bring an international claim against non-members.[119]

§168. THE INTERPRETATION OF TREATIES

Treaties are made after a long and careful process of preparation, negotiation, conclusion, and eventual ratification. The contracting parties are expected to observe in good faith the terms agreed upon by themselves. However, disputes occasionally arise as to the precise meaning of certain provisions; these require interpretation through appropriate channels. Interpretation through municipal laws and judicial decisions of one contracting party cannot bind the other.[120]

Before the establishment of the Permanent Court of International Justice, states usually resorted to arbitration for the interpretation of treaties. In the Root treaties in 1908, the United States also designated the Permanent Court of Arbitration at The Hague as the proper channel in the interpretation of such treaties. Now, in addition to the International Court of Justice, the political organs of the United Nations provide dynamic interpretation of international conventions which are not limited to those to which the Organization is a party or concluded un-

[116] For texts of pertinent treaties, see Hertslet, *Treaties*, I, Nos. 62, 63. See also H. B. Morse, *The International Relations of the Chinese Empire* (New York, 1918), III, p. 47.

[117] According to the Harvard Research in International Law on the Law of Treaties, "if a state assumes by a treaty with another state an obligation which is in conflict with an obligation which it has assumed by an earlier treaty with a third state, the obligation assumed by the earlier treaty takes priority over the obligation assumed by the later treaty." 29 *Am. Jour. Int. Law* (1935), Supp., p. 1024, Art. 22(c).

[118] See, *e.g.*, Art. 17 of the Covenant and Art. 2 of the Charter.

[119] I.C.J. Reports (1949), 174.

[120] See *Ministère v. King*, France, Court of Cassation (Criminal Chamber), 1912. 117 *Arrêts de la Cour de Cassation et Matière Criminelle*, p. 189; translated from French, Hudson, p. 469. See also *The David J. Adams*, United States-Great Britain, Claims Arbitration, 1921. Nielsen's Report, 526.

der its auspices.[121] Some technical bodies of international agencies and regional courts may also be asked to perform this function.[122]

Direct negotiation is still the best way to settle disputes arising out of the interpretation of treaties. In modern treaties, two or more languages are usually employed and are equally authentic. A comparison of the successive drafts in different languages, the minutes of conferences, and the diplomatic correspondence is helpful in ascertaining the original meaning of the ambiguous part of the treaty.[123] As a matter of fact, detailed explanations and definitions of various terms are usually embodied in the final act or protocol annexed to a multilateral treaty.
embodied in the final act or protocol annexed to a multilateral treaty.

Caution must be exercised not to rely excessively on documents of prior negotiations; these, already assimilated into the treaty, cannot be used to contradict the definitive wording of the treaty. Sometimes a common construction of ambiguous provisions can be secured through interpretation by the original plenipotentiaries authorized to conclude the treaty. If an agreement can be directly reached by the contracting parties, recourse to arbitral or judicial tribunals may be avoided. Special provisions are usually made in bilateral and multilateral treaties concerning controversies over their interpretation and application.

International law has no precise rules governing the interpretation of treaties, but some established principles may be found in practice. First of all, a treaty must be liberally construed so as to effectuate the intentions of the parties on the basis of equality and reciprocity. This is the criterion generally followed by international and national tribunals.[124] In the interpretation of ambiguous wording, the logical mean-

[121] For details, see Rosalyn Higgins, pp. 302–309.

[122] For instance, the Executive Directors and Board of Governors of the International Monetary Fund; the Court of Justice of the European Coal and Steel Community, the European Economic Community, and the European Atomic Energy Community, in accordance with the Treaties of 1951 and 1957.

[123] As the English text of the United Nations Charter was completed first, it may be relied upon more heavily than other texts which were prepared on the basis of the English text. Technically, however, all the texts are equally authentic.

[124] See, *e.g.*, *Jurisdiction of the Courts of Danzig*, Permanent Court of International Justice, 1928 (P.C.I.J., 1928, Ser. B, No. 15); *Austro-German Customs Union Case*, Permanent Court of International Justice, 1931 (P.C.I.J., 1931, Ser. A/B, No. 41). The U.S. Supreme Court decided many cases on the same principle: *Geofroy v. Riggs*, 1890 (133 U.S. 258); *Tucker v. Alexandroff*, 1902 (183 U.S. 424); *Askura v. City of Seattle et al.*, 1924 (265 U.S. 332); *Nielsen v. Johnson*, 1929 (279 U.S. 47); *Kolovrat v. Oregon*, 1961 (366 U.S. 187).

ing is to be preferred to the less logical,[125] the plain and general meaning to the technical unless clearly used in the technical sense,[126] and the consistent meaning to that inconsistent with the obligations of international law and previous treaties toward third parties.[127]

If there is a conflict between different treaties concluded by the same contracting parties, the later treaty usually prevails. When inconsistent provisions of the same treaty are interpreted, specific permissions or prohibitions take precedence over general provisions.[128] Treaties containing the most-favored-nation clause should be interpreted liberally as to the application of the clause to third states.[129] As stated before, the League Covenant and the United Nations Charter take precedence over other international treaties concluded by Member states.[130]

[125] When Great Britain invoked her Treaty of Guarantee with Holland of 1756, asking assistance from Holland at the time of war with France, Holland insisted that such a guarantee could be applied only for defense and that any other interpretation would be inconsistent with international law. See Hall, §111.

[126] See the advisory opinion of the International Court of Justice on the *Constitution of the Maritime Safety Committee of the Intergovernmental Maritime Consultative Organization,* 1960. I.C.J. Reports (1960), 150.

[127] See, *e.g., Georges Pinson Case,* France-Mexico, Mixed Claims Commission, 1928. *Annual Digest,* 1927–1928, p. 426.

[128] For further reference on interpretation of treaties, see Arts. 27–29 of Int. Law Com.'s Draft Articles.

[129] See *Santovincenzo v. Eagan, Public Administrator,* U.S. Supreme Court, 1931. 284 U.S. 30. There are traditionally two kinds of most-favored-nation clause: the conditional form applied by the United States and the unconditional one, by Great Britain and other nations. The United States reversed its policy in 1923 when she adopted the unconditional form in a treaty with Germany. According to George G. Wilson, there still are treaties retaining conditional treatment as in the case for consular officers, and unconditional treatment for commerce. See Wilson, *International Law,* 9th ed. (New York, 1935), p. 223. The unconditional most-favored-nation clause provides reciprocally for most-favored-nation treatment without regard to the question whether a favored third state has been accorded the favor gratuitously or in return for special compensation. See, *e.g., John T. Bill Co., Inc. v. United States,* United States, Court of Customs and Patent Appeals, 1939. 104 F.2d 67. For a conditional most-favored-nation clause, see *Whitney v. Robertson,* U.S. Supreme Court, 1888. 124 U.S. 190.

[130] Art. 20 of the Covenant; Art. 103 of the Charter. On a number of occasions, discussion at the United Nations took place on Art. 103: Switzerland's application as a party to the Statute of the International Court of Justice, undertaking of collective measures by Member states as reported by the Collective Measures Committee, the Czechoslovak question at the Secu-

The Second Hague Conference in 1907 recommended compulsory arbitration for the settlement of international disputes, especially those arising out of the interpretation and application of treaties.[131] Of the four major functions of the Permanent Court of International Justice and now of the International Court of Justice in settling legal disputes, interpretation of treaties is ranked at the top.[132] In deciding contentious cases or delivering advisory opinions, the Court is to apply, first, international conventions, whether general or particular, establishing rules expressly recognized by the contesting states.[133] Even though the decision of the Court has no binding force except upon the parties for the particular case,[134] it has laid down guiding principles for the interpretation of treaties.[135] Sometimes opinions of the judges are so divergent that the ruling is made only by a bare majority, as in the *Austro-German Customs Union Case*.[136]

---

rity Council in 1948, and the compatibility of several regional arrangements. In the last instance, there was no decision as to their compatibility. This has been a sensitive question to many states. In order to avoid possible misunderstanding by states in the Western Hemisphere, the League Covenant provides in Art. 21: "Nothing in this Covenant shall be deemed to affect the validity of international engagements, such as treaties of arbitration or regional understandings like the Monroe doctrine, for securing the maintenance of peace." No similar provision was included in the United Nations Charter, which permits, in Art. 52, the existence of regional arrangements or agencies provided that their activities are consistent with the purposes and principles of the United Nations.

[131] See A. P. Higgins, *The Hague Peace Conferences and Other International Conferences concerning the Laws and Usages of War* (Cambridge, England, 1909), p. 27.

[132] See Art. 36 of the Statute. See also Yi-ting Chang, *The Interpretation of Treaties by Judicial Tribunals* (New York, 1933). For discussion of the interpretation of treaties in general, see also Tsune-chi Yu, *The Interpretation of Treaties* (New York, 1927).

[133] Art. 38 of the Statute. [134] Art. 59 of the Statute.

[135] See, *e.g.*, *Interpretation of the 1919 Convention concerning Employment of Women at Night*, Permanent Court of International Justice, 1932 (P.C.I.J., 1932, Ser. A/B, No. 50); *Territorial Jurisdiction of the International Commission of the River Oder*, Permanent Court of International Justice, 1929 (P.C.I.J., 1929, Ser. A, No. 23); *Interpretation of Peace Treaties of 1947 with Bulgaria, Hungary, and Rumania*, International Court of Justice, 1950 (I.C.J. Reports, 1950, pp. 65, 221).

[136] P.C.I.J. (1931), Ser. A/B, No. 41. The opinion was delivered by a bare majority of 8 to 7. The majority deemed the union incompatible with the Geneva Protocol; six of the eight held it also incompatible with the Treaty of St. Germain. In the opinion of the seven dissenting judges, the proposed union would be incompatible with neither.

IV. *ENFORCEMENT, REVISION, SUSPENSION, AND TERMINATION OF TREATIES*

§169. THE ENFORCEMENT OF TREATIES

Once a treaty comes into effect, it must be enforced by the contracting parties in good faith. In reaffirming the principle of *pacta sunt servanda,* the United Nations Draft on the Law of Treaties stipulates that "good faith, *inter alia,* requires that a party to a treaty shall refrain from any acts calculated to prevent the due execution of the treaty or otherwise to frustrate its objects." [137] It further emphasizes that the failure of any state to comply with its obligations "engages its international responsibility, unless such failure is justifiable or excusable under the general rules of international law regarding state responsibility." [138] It is up to the domestic law of each state to decide whether the procedure of proclamation, promulgation, or publication of a ratified treaty is required. Except for self-executing treaties,[139] laws must be enacted by the contracting parties for the implementation and execution of every international instrument which comes into effect.

In several cases, the courts of the United States held that an act of Congress would prevail if it were inconsistent with a prior treaty.[140] According to Green H. Hackworth, "the treaty still subsists as an international obligation although it may not be enforceable by the courts or administrative authorities." [141] Even though the treaty concerned is not repealed or abrogated, the very fact of its unenforceability by the courts or administrative authorities is untenable in international law.[142]

[137] UN Doc. A/CN.4/167 and Add.1–3, p. 7, Art. 55(2); Third Report on the Law of Treaties by Sir Humphrey Waldock, Special *Rapporteur,* 1964. Art. 23 of Int. Law Com.'s Draft Articles reads: "Every treaty in force is binding upon the parties to it and must be performed by them in good faith."

[138] *Ibid.*, Art. 55(4).

[139] For instance, the Anglo-American Treaty of 1924 setting a one hour's traverse limit is a self-executing treaty, because no legislation is needed for its execution. See *Cook v. United States,* U.S. Supreme Court, 1933. 288 U.S. 102.

[140] See, *e.g., Taylor v. Morton,* United States, Circuit Court, District of Massachusetts, 1855 (2 Curtis 454); *Cook v. United States,* just cited. For further references, see R. R. Wilson, *The International Law Standard of Treaties of the United States* (Cambridge, 1953); Moore, *Digest,* V, §§735–736.

[141] Hackworth, *Digest,* V, p. 186.

[142] The validity of the United States-Japanese Security Treaty of 1951 was raised in the Japanese courts in 1959. Seven left-wing Japanese unionists

President Wilson should be commended for upholding the sanctity of treaties. When he found that certain provisions in the Panama Canal Act of 1912 were in conflict with the Anglo-American Treaty of 1901, he requested Congress to repeal them "for the redemption of every obligation without quibble or hesitation." [143]

The application of treaties to dependent territories of the contracting parties has become a controversial issue since World War II. Formerly, there was no question about such application, unless there was a special provision to the contrary. Recent practice has been that, in order to cover their dependent territories, treaties concluded by colonial powers must include a 'colonial clause' or 'territorial application clause.' Now states are inclined to omit such a provision, because they expect the complete independence of their colonies in the near future.[144]

For the enforcement of treaty obligations, states in the past resorted to the use of oaths, holding hostages, pledging valuables, and other compulsory means, which have long become obsolete.[145] After World War I, a revenue charge was made against Germany to enforce her payment of war indemnities. Following the defeat of Germany and Japan in 1945, the Allied Powers occupied their territories for the en-

---

and students were arrested after their demonstration on July 8, 1957, against extension of runways to accommodate jet planes, on charges of trespassing on the United States Air Force base at Tachikawa near Tokyo. The Tokyo District Court acquitted the seven defendants on March 30, 1959, on the ground that the stationing of American forces in Japan violated Article 9 of the Japanese Constitution. That article forbids Japan to maintain "land, sea and air forces as well as other war potential." The prosecution appealed directly to the Supreme Court of Japan, which ruled unanimously on December 16, 1959, that the stationing of American forces in Japan and the maintenance of Japanese units were legal under the Constitution. The Court decided, however, that Japan's judiciary lacked the right to pass on the legality of treaties as such international commitments are a political matter. The Court, therefore, ordered the retrial of the case. See *The New York Times,* April 1, December 16, 1959.

[143] Hackworth, *Digest,* V, p. 164. Lack of federal power cannot be considered a legal excuse not to implement a treaty. Other contracting parties would not support this argument, though the United States attempted to introduce the so-called 'federal clause' in the Convention on the Suppression of the Traffic in Persons and the Draft International Covenant on Human Rights. See UN Doc. E/CN.5/115/Add.I, A/1620.

[144] Yuen-li Liang, "Colonial Clauses and Federal Clauses in United Nations Multilateral Instruments," 45 *Am. Jour. Int. Law* (1951), p. 108; also Rosalyn Higgins, pp. 309–316.

[145] For past practices, see Oppenheim, I, pp. 930–931.

forcement of peace terms. Sometimes the execution of a treaty is guaranteed by a third party.[146]

Under the collective system of the League of Nations and the United Nations, economic and military sanctions may be imposed against a recalcitrant state whose violation of treaty obligations has endangered international peace and security.[147] Upon the complaint by the government of the Republic of China of Soviet breach of treaty obligations, the General Assembly discussed the issue at its sixth session in 1950. It decided that "the U.S.S.R., in its relations with China since the surrender of Japan, has failed to carry out the Treaty of Friendship and Alliance between China and the U.S.S.R. of 4 August 1945." [148] No action, however, followed. It is clear that no matter how effective the enforcement measures may be, the upholding of treaty sanctity and international order depends mostly on voluntary and faithful observance by the contracting parties.[149]

§170. REVISION OF TREATIES AND THE DOCTRINE OF *Rebus Sic Stantibus*

Treaties are concluded for the regulation of relations between the contracting parties. After a lapse of time, certain modifications may be necessary because of changing circumstances. Recognizing the advisability of reviewing existing treaties, the League Covenant provides: "The Assembly may from time to time advise the reconsideration by Members of the League of treaties which have become inapplicable and the consideration of international conditions whose continuance might endanger the peace of the world." [150] In other words, strict maintenance of the status quo may not necessarily serve the best interests of the contracting parties. While there is no express stipulation for treaty revision in the United Nations Charter, it is implied in Article 14: "The General Assembly may recommend measures for the peaceful adjust-

[146] Guarantee by the League of Nations of the execution of the Minority Treaties of 1919 was unique. The Locarno Treaties of 1925 were guaranteed collectively by Belgium, Great Britain, France, Germany, and Italy, for the maintenance of the territorial status quo of the Franco-German-Belgian frontier.

[147] See Arts. 16–17 of the Covenant; Ch. VII of the Charter.

[148] GA res. 505 (VI). See GA *Official Records,* 6th Sess., 1st Committee, 502nd and 503rd meetings. For Western complaints of Soviet treaty violations, see Triska and Slausser, *op. cit.*, p. 395.

[149] For further references on treaty enforcement, consult S. B. Crandall, *Treaties, Their Making and Enforcement* (Washington, D.C., 1916); P. S. Wild, *Sanctions and Treaty Enforcement* (Cambridge, 1934).

[150] Art. 19 of the League Covenant.

ment of any situation, regardless of origin, which it deems likely to impair the general welfare or friendly relations among nations." [151]

Although states, compelled by inevitable circumstances, occasionally have resorted to unilateral denunciation of treaties, revision by mutual consent through some flexible means is the normal procedure.[152] Thus, modern treaties often incorporate provisions for their modification or termination because of a changed situation.[153] If the procedure of modification is provided in a treaty, any contracting party may inform the other of its intention by a formal notification.[154] Revision may be effected by conclusion of a special agreement or protocol,[155] or by negotiation of a new treaty.

Rebus sic stantibus In spite of divergent views of international lawyers toward the doctrine of *rebus sic stantibus,* there is increasing recognition that revision or termination of a treaty is necessary in case of vital change of circumstances. In 1926, the Permanent Court of International Justice took jurisdiction of the case *Denunciation of the Treaty of November 2nd, 1865,*[156] when the government of the Republic of China applied that doctrine and unilaterally denounced the Sino-

[151] An attempt was made in 1947 to have the General Assembly discuss revision of the Peace Treaty with Italy on the basis of Art. 14 of the Charter. For proposals made by the International Law Commission, see Arts. 35–38 of its Draft Articles.

[152] The conclusion of a new treaty with Russia on March 13, 1871, by the Signatory Powers of the Treaty of Paris of 1856 was practically to comply with the Russian demand for revision of the status of the Black Sea, even though they insisted on the principle that the abrogation of a treaty must get the consent of the other contracting parties. The necessity of revision through mutual consent and the danger of unilateral denunciation were emphasized in the Havana Convention on Treaties of 1928 (*International Conferences of American States, 1889–1928,* p. 416), and the Harvard Research in International Law in its Draft Convention on the Law of Treaties in 1935 (Art. 28).

[153] For instance, Art. 30 of the United States-Polish Treaty of 1931. Such provisions can be found in many commercial treaties, international labor conventions, and the economic aid agreements between the United States and other countries in 1948. See Hudson, p. 496.

[154] See *Lepeschkin v. Gossweiler & Co.,* Switzerland, Federal Tribunal, 1923. 49 *Official Reports,* Pt. I, p. 188; translation from Briggs, p. 931.

[155] Examples are the United States-Turkish Agreement of 1937 changing the date of payment provided in previous agreements; the Protocol of 1938 changing the tonnage of warships originally provided in the Treaty for the Limitation of Naval Armaments, signed in London on March 25, 1936.

[156] P.C.I.J. (1927), Ser. A, No. 8.

Belgian Treaty of 1865, which provided for extraterritoriality. Upon the application of the Belgian government, the Court issued a provisional order on January 8, 1927. But the case was later withdrawn, because a new treaty was satisfactorily concluded between the two governments on November 22, 1928.[157] Thus, the Court had no opportunity to deliver a judgment on the doctrine of *rebus sic stantibus.* Nor did it lay down any rule in *Free Zones of Upper Savoy and the District of Gex* in 1932,[158] because the changes relied upon by France in opposition to Switzerland had no bearing on the whole body of circumstances.

The doctrine of *rebus sic stantibus* was invoked by Germany in her denunciation of the Treaty of Versailles of 1919 with respect to disarmament (Part V) and demilitarization of the Rhineland (Article 43) in 1935–1936. Arguments on the ground of vital change of circumstances were made at the Security Council when it discussed the Anglo-Egyptian Treaty of 1936 and the Franco-Tunisian Convention of 1935, but no resolutions were adopted on the basis of the doctrine.[159] Panama has repeatedly expressed its dissatisfaction with the United States-Panamanian Treaty of 1903, granting the United States, in perpetuity, the use, occupation, and control of the Panama Canal Zone. In this case, the United States has indicated her willingness to negotiate a revision of the treaty.[160]

The Soviet Union is a strong supporter of the abolition of unequal treaties,[161] but the Communist standard as to which treaties are equal or not is different from that of other countries. States which suffered from the abuses of extraterritorial jurisdiction were resentful of this inequitable system imposed upon them by unequal treaties. It is also natural that newly independent states are not disposed to be bound by treaties, previously concluded by colonial powers when these treaties are detrimental to their political and economic interests.

The International Law Commission discussed at length the principle of fundamental change of circumstances. After a careful examination of divergent opinions concerning the principle as evidenced in customary international law, writings of jurists, decisions of international and national courts, practices of states, and comments from different

[157] Its text can be found in LN *Treaty Series,* Vol. 87 (1929), pp. 287–295. For details, see William L. Tung, *China and Some Phases of International Law,* pp. 174–175.

[158] P.C.I.J. (1932), Ser. A/B, No. 46.

[159] These two disputes were brought to the Security Council in 1947 and 1958 respectively. See SC *Official Records,* 2nd year, 175th and 176th meetings; 13th year, 819th–821st meetings.

[160] See *supra,* §87. [161] See Soviet *Text,* p. 248.

governments, it adopted the following provision in its final text of the Draft Articles on the Law of Treaties:

> 1. A fundamental change of circumstances which has occurred with regard to those existing at the time of the conclusion of a treaty, and which was not foreseen by the parties, may not be invoked as a ground for terminating or withdrawing from the treaty unless:
>
> (a) The existence of those circumstances constituted an essential basis of the consent of the parties to be bound by the treaty; and
>
> (b) The effect of the change is radically to transform the scope of obligations still to be performed under the treaty.
>
> 2. A fundamental change of circumstances may not be invoked:
>
> (a) As a ground for terminating or withdrawing from a treaty establishing a boundary;
>
> (b) If the fundamental change is the result of a breach by the party invoking it either of the treaty or of a different international obligation owed to the other parties to the treaty.[162]

It can be seen that the conclusion of the International Law Commission in respect of the principle of *rebus sic stantibus* is that "the principle, if its application were carefully delimited and regulated, should find a place in the modern law of treaties." [163] The exact scope and extent of its application, delimitation, and regulation will undoubtedly constitute serious subjects to be discussed at the future international conference of plenipotentiaries on the law of treaties.

The world has undergone drastic changes since the turn of the century. Recognition must be given to necessary revision or termination of existing treaties if the subsequent circumstances have been vitally changed. The problem is what kind of change may be considered vital and what international organ should be used to decide such disputable cases. In the Report by the Secretary-General of the United Nations in 1950, on Treaties for the Protection of Minorities,[164] some clarification was made on 'change of circumstances.' It was proposed that the application of the doctrine of *rebus sic stantibus* must be limited to the disappearance of or substantial change from certain factual conditions existing at the time of the conclusion of the treaty, and that the change must be so substantial as to render its application morally and politically impossible.

According to the Report, if the state invoking the claim cannot obtain the consent of the other contracting party, it may secure recogni-

[162] Art. 59.

[163] Commentary of Art. 59, Par. (6). For its full text, see 61 *Am. Jour. Int. Law* (1967), pp. 428–435.

[164] UN Doc. E/CN.4/367 (April 7, 1950), pp. 36–38, 71. For its summary, see Hudson, pp. 495–496.

tion of the validity of its claim from a competent international organ, such as one of the appropriate organs of the United Nations or the International Court of Justice.[165] It seems that the criterion laid down in the above proposals is quite reasonable. As the subject concerns interpretation of treaties, it is appropriately within the competence of the International Court of Justice.[166]

§171. SUSPENSION, REDINTEGRATION, AND RENEWAL OF TREATIES

Suspension Treaties may be suspended due to existence of war, non-observance or violation by one contracting party, and vital change of circumstances. War does not terminate all treaties; some of them, regulating the relationship between belligerents and between belligerents and neutrals, only come into operation in wartime. Many bilateral and especially law-making multilateral treaties are merely suspended for the duration of war. Non-observance or violation of a treaty by one contracting party makes the treaty voidable but not void.[167]

Vital change of circumstances can also justify the state adversely affected in suspending performance of the treaty temporarily, pending further negotiation or settlement by a competent international tribunal.[168] Mutual consent and proper notification are normally required for the suspension of treaties.[169] The provision for withdrawal in multi-

[165] Turkey succeeded in 1936 in her demand for termination of the Treaty of Lausanne of 1923, regulating the Straits of the Dardanelles and Bosphorus on the ground of vital change of circumstances in Europe since the conclusion of the treaty. The Powers concerned complied with the wishes of Turkey, replacing it with a new treaty at the Montreaux Conference in 1936.

[166] Further references on the subject can be found in C. Hill, *The Doctrine of "Rebus Sic Stantibus" in International Law* (Columbia, Mo., 1934); E. C. Hoyt, *The Unanimity Rule in the Revision of Treaties: A Re-Examination* (The Hague, 1959); Yu-hao Tseng, *The Termination of Unequal Treaties in International Law* (Shanghai, 1931).

[167] See *Charlton v. Kelly,* U.S. Supreme Court, 1913. 229 U.S. 447. This also depends on whether the breach or violation is substantial or trivial. See Hall, p. 408.

[168] See Arts. 27–28 of the Draft Convention of the Harvard Research in International Law on Law of Treaties, 1935. 29 *Am. Jour. Int. Law* (1935), Supp., p. 662. In his proclamation of August 9, 1941, President Roosevelt declared the suspension and inoperation of the International Load Line Convention of 1930 for the duration of the emergency and because of changing conditions. See Hackworth, *Digest,* V, pp. 354–355.

[169] See *Renault v. Roussky-Renault Co.,* France, Court of Appeals of Paris, 1926. *Journal du Palais* (1927), II, 1: translation from Briggs, p. 929.

lateral treaties is a realistic approach; it releases the obligations of unwilling parties under such conditions as not to affect the treaties as a whole.[170]

Redintegration and reconfirmation Suspended, expired, or canceled treaties may be revived through the process of redintegration. By mutual consent of the contracting parties and special provisions in a peace treaty,[171] a treaty suspended during the war may be redintegrated.[172] Different from redintegration is the term 'reconfirmation,' which reassures, in a new treaty, the validity of a part or the whole of a previous treaty after a change of circumstances.

Renewal Many treaties are concluded for a definite duration, after which they expire and lose binding force. Sometimes provision is made for automatic renewal for another period by mutual consent of the contracting parties.[173] This may be effected by an exchange of notes or other diplomatic instruments. The scope of the provisions for renewal may be applied to an entire treaty or only part of it. The Soviet-Finnish Treaty of Friendship, Cooperation and Mutual Assistance of 1948 was

---

See also *Lepeschkin v. Gossweiler & Co.*, Switzerland, Federal Tribunal, 1923. 49 *Official Reports*, Pt. I, p. 188; translation from Briggs, p. 931. For provisions of Int. Law Com.'s Draft Articles on suspension of treaties, see Arts. 54–58, 62–63, 68.

[170] Art. 1(3) of the League Covenant provides: "Any Member of the League may, after two years' notice of its intention so to do, withdraw from the League, provided that all its international obligations and all its obligations under this Covenant shall have been fulfilled at the time of its withdrawal." In the history of the League, sixteen nations served such notices at different times. Art. 13 of the North Atlantic Treaty of 1949 provides a different means of withdrawal or denunciation: "After the treaty has been in force for twenty years, any party may cease to be a party one year after its notice of denunciation has been given to the Government of the United States of America, which will inform the Governments of the other parties of the deposit of each notice of denunciation." For withdrawal under the United Nations Charter, see *supra*, §50.

[171] The victorious powers have usually made the decisions as to which treaties would be revived. See Arnold D. McNair, *The Law of Treaties: British Practice and Opinions* (Oxford, 1938), p. 551.

[172] According to Art. 35(b, c) of the Harvard Research in International Law on the Law of Treaties in 1935, unless contrary provision is made at the end of the war, suspended treaties will again come into operation. The same principle is applied to parts of such a treaty if such parts are clearly independent of the other parts. 29 *Am. Jour. Int. Law* (1935), p. 1183.

[173] For instance, the Treaty of Washington for the Limitation of Naval Armament of 1922.

originally concluded for a duration of ten years, which was later extended for another ten years by the Soviet-Finnish Protocol of September 19, 1955.[174] There are, however, no definite forms, scope, duration, or procedures regulating the renewal of treaties. International law leaves the contracting parties complete freedom in that respect.

§172. THE TERMINATION OF TREATIES

Expiration With the exception of treaties concerning boundaries and cessions, most treaties relating to commerce, navigation, and the like have a definite duration.[175] Unless otherwise stipulated or renewed in time, a treaty will lose its binding effect on the contracting parties at the time of its expiration.[176] A treaty may, however, be terminated before its expiration through renunciation, denunciation, dissolution, impossibility of fulfillment, or outbreak of war. Other means of termination can be generally grouped under the above categories.[177] Sometimes consent to the termination of a treaty may be implied from the attitude of the contracting parties.[178]

Renunciation For the maintenance or furtherance of peaceful relations, a beneficial party to a treaty may, by the consent of the other, renounce its special advantages and rights. Renunciation usually takes

[174] See Soviet *Text*, p. 273.

[175] The Anglo-American Treaty of November 19, 1794, is unique in that its first ten articles are of permanent nature and the others, with the exception of the twelfth, for a duration of twelve years. See Art. XXVIII. For the text of the Treaty, see Malloy, *Treaties, I*, pp. 590–606.

[176] Many modern treaties have a provision similar to the following: "The treaty shall remain in force until the expiration of one year from the day on which either of the contracting parties shall give notice of its intention to terminate the treaty."

[177] According to the Havana Convention on Treaties of February 20, 1928, treaties cease to be effective:

(1) When the stipulated obligation has been fulfilled.
(2) When the length of time for which it was made has expired.
(3) When the resolutory condition has been fulfilled.
(4) By agreement between the parties.
(5) By renunciation of the party exclusively entitled to a benefit thereunder.
(6) By total or partial denunciation, if agreed upon.
(7) When it becomes incapable of execution.

See Manley O. Hudson, *International Legislation*, p. 2382. See also Arts. 51–53, 56–67, of Int. Law Com.'s Draft Articles.

[178] See *S. E. v. G. and Gen.*, Germany, Reichsgericht, 1925. 111 *Entscheidungen des Reichsgerichts in Zivilsachen*, 40; translation from Briggs, p. 902.

place in a new treaty. As an expression of wartime solidarity and future friendship, the United States and Great Britain signed separately a new commercial treaty with China on January 11, 1943, surrendering their extraterritorial rights acquired through previous treaties.[179]

Denunciation Due to vital change of circumstances and other important factors, a treaty may be denounced by one contracting party, but unilateral denunciation is not generally sanctioned by international practice.[180] As stated before, violation of a treaty by one party makes the treaty voidable but not void. Germany's denunciation of the Treaty of Versailles in 1935–1936 did not make the treaty invalid.[181] Instead, Germany was accused by the League Council of committing a breach of international law by unilateral repudiation of treaty obligations.

Dissolution Dissolution of a treaty by consent of the contracting parties may be effected by a new treaty or declaration.[182] A clear example is the dissolution of the Covenant of the League of Nations. Question may arise out of the abrogation of a commercial treaty between two countries pending the conclusion of a new one. Here their relationship with respect to pertinent matters will be governed by the customary rules of international law.[183] Unlike other multilateral trea-

[179] For the texts of the treaties, see Yin Ching Chen (ed.), *Treaties and Agreements between the Republic of China and Other Powers* (Washington, D.C., 1957), pp. 140–155. Soviet renunciation of territorial and legal privileges acquired by Tsarist Russia in China was never fulfilled. The statements of renunciation were made by G. V. Chicherin, Soviet Commissar of Foreign Affairs, in 1918, and by L. M. Karakhan, Acting Commissar of Foreign Affairs, in the same year.

[180] On May 7, 1955, the Soviet government denounced the Anglo-Soviet Treaty of 1942 and the Franco-Soviet Treaty of 1944, on the grounds of British and French participation in NATO and its inclusion of West Germany. Fidel Castro denounced in 1960 the Treaty of Reciprocal Assistance as incompatible with the Cuban Revolution. See also *Denunciation of the Treaty of November 2nd,* 1865, Permanent Court of International Justice, 1927. P.C.I.J. (1927), Ser. A, No. 8. See also Arts. 53, 59 of Int. Law Com.'s Draft Articles.

[181] Germany denounced Arts. 160 and 173 of the Treaty of Versailles, concerning limitation of armed forces and conscription, on March 16, 1935, and also Arts. 42 and 43, on the demilitarization of the Rhineland, on March 7, 1936.

[182] This happened to the Clayton-Bulwer Treaty of 1850, as a result of the conclusion of the Hay-Pauncefote Treaty in 1901. Malloy, *Treaties,* I, p. 782.

[183] See *Hooper v. United States,* U.S., Court of Claims, 1887. 22 Court of Claims, 408.

ties, the League Covenant and the United Nations Charter expressly or implicitly provide for withdrawal and expulsion as other means for dissolution of relationship between the Member states and the two international instruments.[184]

Impossibility of fulfillment Because of physical, legal, or other changes subsequent to the conclusion of a treaty, its fulfillment may become impossible. This may happen with the physical extinction of a special object, disappearance of a special purpose, or change of a concept of international law, for example, the abolition of privateering and prohibition of slave-trading. The same consequence may result from the extinction or drastic alteration of the status of one of the contracting parties, or even of a third state which forms the special object of the treaty.[185] On the other hand, normal political transition in the contracting parties does not necessarily affect the validity of a treaty.[186] Even in the case of absorption, a treaty may still be valid if the new state continues to carry out its obligations.[187]

Outbreak of war Although there is no definite rule governing termination of treaties between belligerents after the outbreak of war, it is generally agreed that treaties are abrogated only when necessary.[188] Executory treaties relating to alliance, commerce, navigation, and treaties exclusively for peacetime purposes are terminated.[189] Executed or dispositive treaties for cession, boundaries, and others of permanent nature are merely suspended.[190] So are multilateral instruments, especially law-making treaties.

[184] For details, see *supra*, §§50–51.

[185] When Korea was annexed by Japan in 1910, the status of Korea was changed both as a contracting state and as a third party to international treaties.

[186] See *Shehaden et al. v. Commissioner of Prisons, Jerusalem, et al.*, Palestine, Supreme Court, 1947. 14 Palestine L.R. (1947), 461.

[187] See *Terlinden v. Ames*, U.S. Supreme Court, 1902. 184 U.S. 270.

[188] See *Techt v. Hughes*, U.S. Court of Appeals of New York, 1920. 229 N.Y. 222. See also Hyde, II, pp. 1529–1535. In case of an aggressor state, Art. 70 of Int. Law Com.'s Draft Articles provides that "the present articles are without prejudice to any obligation in relation to a treaty which may arise for an aggressor state in consequence of measures taken in conformity with the Charter of the United Nations with reference to that state's aggression."

[189] Thus, a treaty of friendship and commerce is abrogated by war. See *Karnuth v. United States*, U.S. Supreme Court, 1929. 279 U.S. 231.

[190] In *Society for the Propagation of the Gospel v. New Haven*, the U.S. Supreme Court held, in 1823, that vested rights under a permanent treaty

Severance of diplomatic relations generally does not affect treaties between the contracting parties.[191] What will happen to the terminated and suspended treaties after cessation of hostilities depends on the intention of the belligerents, especially the victorious powers.[192] The traditional principles of the state of possession at the end of war (*uti possidetis*) and before the war (*status quo ante bellum*) no longer hold good, because modern peace treaties stipulate all the details with many variations.[193] The operation of international conventions relating to war and neutrality will be discussed elsewhere.[194]

---

relating to territorial and other national rights are not extinguished by war. 8 Wheaton 464. Nor does a treaty cease to be valid in regard to nationals of enemy states insofar as its contents have already become part of the municipal law of the state. See *S.H.H. v. L.Ch.*, Germany, Reichsgericht, 1914. 85 *Entscheidungen des Reichsgerichts in Zivilsachen,* 374; translation from Hudson, p. 474.

[191] See Art. 65A of the United Nations Draft on the Law of Treaties. UN Doc. A/CN.4/167 and Add.1–3 (1964), p. 44. See also Art. 60 of Int. Law Com.'s Draft Articles.

[192] For details, see S. H. McIntyre, *Legal Effect of World War II on Treaties of the United States* (The Hague, 1958); Coleman Phillipson, *Termination of War and Treaties of Peace* (London, 1916).

[193] For instance, the Treaty of Versailles of 1919 had special provisions concerning the continuance, redintegration, and abrogation of treaties to which Germany was a party prior to the war. The Peace Treaty with Japan in 1951 also contains detailed provisions of this kind. See 46 *Am. Jour. Int. Law* (1952), Supp., pp. 71–76, 86–87.

[194] See *infra,* Chs. 14, 15, particularly §§202–203.

CHAPTER 12

SETTLEMENT OF INTERNATIONAL DISPUTES

I. *INTERNATIONAL PRACTICE AND LEGAL PROVISIONS* [1]

§173. METHODS IN GENERAL PRACTICE

Ever since the emergence of state system, there have been international disputes. Through mutual understanding and active cooperation by responsible leaders of different governments, such occurrences may be reduced, but cannot be eliminated altogether. To prevent political differences from developing into armed conflict, various means have been adopted for their pacific settlement. As every method has its own merits, the choice of which to use depends on the nature of each particular issue. The classification of disputes into legal and political or justiciable and non-justiciable is more academic than practical, because clear distinctions are not always possible; certain cases, for example, involve both political and legal controversies.[2]

Procedures followed by states to settle their disputes may be divided into two categories: amicable, and non-amicable or compulsive. Sometimes a combination of methods is used in order to achieve the desired purpose. Among the amicable methods are negotiation, good

[1] General texts on the subject: Oppenheim, II, §§1–3; Fenwick, *Principles*, Ch. XXVI, §§I–O; Brierly, Ch. VIII, §§5–6; Jacobini, pp. 193–196.

[2] Amos S. Hershey observed that "legal claims have often been made a pretext for disguised political aggression." For his opinion on the distinction between political and legal disputes, see Hershey, p. 457.

offices, mediation, conciliation, commission of inquiry, arbitration, and judicial settlement.[3] When all these are exhausted, states often appeal to compulsive means, but short of war, such as retorsion, reprisals, embargo, boycott, pacific blockade, and intervention. Various diplomatic pressures may also be exerted to impress upon the other party that failure of settlement can lead to serious consequences.[4] War is still the last recourse for redress, though it has been much restricted by various international agreements. However, coercive measures lack precise rules and are easily subject to abuse. The Charter permits the use of force only for self-defense by individual states or regional agencies and arrangements, or for collective action enforced by the United Nations.[5]

§174. IMPORTANT PROVISIONS IN INTERNATIONAL INSTRUMENTS

The Hague Conventions Whereas the practice of states to settle their disputes by pacific means precedes any multipartite treaties on the subject, the two Hague Peace Conferences of 1899 and 1907 formulated the first systematic rules in the Convention for the Pacific Settlement of International Disputes.[6] It filled the gap between states without bilateral agreements, provided means to solve their differences, and served as a guideline for maintenance of peace and prevention of violence.

The League Covenant The Covenant of the League of Nations went one step further by providing collective action for settling international disputes. Any war or threat of war was declared a common concern to the League, but matters solely within the domestic jurisdiction of states were excepted.[7] Members of the League might call upon the Assembly or the Council to discuss any serious differences even if they were not directly involved.[8] When the contending parties had exhausted their resources of direct negotiation and other means to adjust their dispute, they should submit it to arbitration, judicial settlement,

[3] Emphasizing "the possibility of coexistence and cooperation," Soviet publicists recognize the advisability of employing amicable means to settle disputes "between states with differing social systems." Soviet *Text,* p. 377.

[4] Upon the decisions of the Security Council, severance of diplomatic relations and demonstration of force are sanctioned by the United Nations Charter in Arts. 41 and 42 respectively.

[5] See, in particular, Arts. 39, 51, of the Charter.

[6] For details, see J. B. Scott, *The Hague Conventions and Declarations of 1899 and 1907* (New York, 1915), pp. 41–88.

[7] Arts. 11(1), 15(8), of the Covenant.

[8] Art. 11 of the Covenant.

or inquiry by the League Council or Assembly.[9] Procedures for arbitration and inquiry were provided, and the Permanent Court of International Justice was named as the proper channel of judicial settlement.[10]

Members of the League agreed that they would not go to war with a disputing party which complied with the recommendations of the Council or the Assembly.[11] If no report with such recommendations could be agreed upon by the appropriate League organ, states might take whatever actions necessary for the maintenance of right and justice.[12] The parties at variance should agree "in no case to resort to war until three months after the award by the arbitrators or the judicial decision, or the report by the Council." [13] Thus, the League could not guarantee a complete prevention of war after a cooling-off period of three months.

Collective measures, including military and economic sanctions, might be enforced by the League against an aggressor: Article 16 applied to members and Article 17, to non-members.[14] However, the final decision of enforcing military sanction was up to individual states, because the responsibility of the Council in this respect was limited to recommendations.[15] Although economic sanctions were obligatory, they proved ineffective during the Italo-Ethiopian War of 1935–1936. This was not the fault of the League system but of its members, which only gave lukewarm support to its resolutions.

Throughout the history of the League, it was confronted with approximately sixty disputes. Thirty-five were settled through peaceful means generally in accordance with League procedure. This meager success was attributed to consideration by the contending parties that

[9] See Arts. 12, 15, of the Covenant.

[10] The Court was constituted in 1921. See also Arts. 13–15 of the Covenant.

[11] Art. 15(6, 9, 10) of the Covenant.

[12] Arts. 12(1), 15(7), of the Covenant. See also the report of the Special Commission of Jurists appointed by the League Council in 1924. LN *Official Jour.* (1924), p. 524.

[13] Art. 12(1) of the Covenant. The same would apply to a report made by the Assembly. See Art. 15(10) of the Covenant.

[14] The Soviet Union was expelled from the League because of her attack on Finland in 1939. By the application of Art. 17, League Members were entitled to the same protection through collective sanction against non-members as that under Art. 16 against other Members.

[15] Art. 16(2) reads: "It shall be the duty of the Council in such case to recommend to the several Governments concerned what effective military, naval or air force the Members of the League shall severally contribute to the armed forces to be used to protect the covenants of the League."

the League might act if they could not solve their differences.[16] However, after its failure to stop Japan's invasion of China in 1931 and Italy's of Ethiopia in 1935–1936, the usefulness of the League as an international organ to maintain collective security was severely affected.

The Kellogg-Briand Pact The General Treaty for the Renunciation of War of 1928, generally known as the Kellogg-Briand Pact, was a courageous attempt to condemn war as an instrument of national policy.[17] The Pact aimed at the renunciation of war; this went beyond the League Covenant and other international instruments.[18] But it failed to provide for specific means for the settlement of international disputes or for sanctions against its violation. It remained doubtful whether the Pact also applied to wars for collective action enforced by the League or self-defense by the signatory states, and to resort to force short of war.[19] The Pact was virtually suspended during World War II;[20] its revival after the restoration of peace is questionable.

The General Act for the Pacific Settlement of International Disputes The League Assembly adopted, on September 26, 1928, the General Act for the Pacific Settlement of International Disputes, which came into effect on August 16, 1929.[21] To supplement the Kellogg-

[16] See Quincy Wright, *A Study of War* (Chicago, 1942), pp. 1430–1431.

[17] It was initially negotiated between Foreign Minister Aristide Briand of France and Secretary of State Frank B. Kellogg of the United States. Signed at Paris on August 27, 1928, by fifteen governments and ultimately adhered to by sixty-five states, the Treaty is also known as the Pact of Paris. For its text, see LN *Treaty Series,* Vol. 94, p. 57.

[18] These include the Hague Convention of 1907 for the Limitation of the Employment of Force for the Recovery of Contract Debts, the Locarno Treaty of 1925 for mutual security against the use of force, and the resolution adopted by the Pan-American Conference in February 1928 against wars of aggression.

[19] Soon after conclusion of the Kellogg-Briand Pact, hostilities between the Soviet Union and China broke out in Manchuria in 1929 because of a dispute over the Chinese Eastern Railway. The right of self-defense was given by the Soviet Union as the legal ground for her use of force. See A. J. Toynbee, *Survey of International Affairs,* 1929, pp. 344–369.

[20] In declaring war against Germany on September 3, 1939, France and Great Britain denounced Germany's invasion of Poland as a violation of the Kellogg-Briand Pact. LN *Official Jour.*, 1939, p. 386.

[21] For its text, see LN *Treaty Series,* Vol. 93, p. 343. See also *Resolutions Adopted by the Assembly of the League of Nations, September 26, 1928, relating to the Pacific Settlement of International Disputes, Non-*

Briand Pact on outlawry of war, the General Act was intended to augment the machinery for peaceful settlement of disputes through conciliation, judicial settlement, and arbitration. Conciliation was generally recommended as the first step, to be followed by arbitration if the former failed. If the dispute involved a conflict between the states as to their respective rights, judicial settlement would take place. However, reservations made by the states acceding to the Act limited its usefulness. The Act as a whole was a codification of technical procedures concerning pacific settlement of international disputes, which have been adopted in a number of bilateral treaties.[22] The General Assembly of the United Nations adopted, on April 28, 1949, the Revised General Act for the Pacific Settlement of International Disputes, which is not substantially different from the 1928 Act.[23]

The United Nations Charter The Charter of the United Nations is an improvement over the above-mentioned international instruments. For pacific settlement of disputes, it provides that the disputing parties "shall, first of all, seek a solution by negotiation, enquiry, mediation, conciliation, arbitration, judicial settlement, resort to regional agencies or arrangements, or other peaceful means of their own choice." [24] In prohibiting the use of force and resort to war, the Charter emphasizes collective action against threats to the peace, breaches of the peace, and acts of aggression.[25] The United Nations collective action includes

---

Aggression and Mutual Assistance (UN Doc. A/AC.18/43, March 11, 1948); *History and Analysis of the General Act for the Pacific Settlement of International Disputes, September 26, 1928* (UN Doc. A/AC.18/56, May 4, 1948).

[22] For details, consult Max Habight, *Postwar Treaties for the Pacific Settlement of International Disputes* (Cambridge, 1931).

[23] Because the League of Nations and the Permanent Court of International Justice as originally provided for in the 1928 Act ceased to function, appropriate revisions were made in order to restore the efficacy of the Act. For the text of the Revised Act, see UN *Treaty Series,* Vol. 71, No. 912, p. 101. Only a few states acceded to it.

[24] Art. 33(1) of the Charter.

[25] For details, see Ch. VII of the Charter. At the meeting of the Special Committee on Principles of International Law concerning Friendly Relations and Cooperation among States in April 1966, consensus was reached on the principle that "every state has the duty in its international relations to refrain from the threat or use of force" and that "wars of aggression constitute international crimes against peace for which there is a responsibility under international law." UN Doc. A/AC.125/7. See also Julius Stone, *Aggression and World Order* (London, 1958).

boycott, embargo, severance of diplomatic relations, blockade, demonstrations, and the use of force.[26] The procedure and effectiveness of the United Nations in settling international disputes are discussed in the following chapter.

Other multilateral treaties In addition to the League Covenant, the Kellogg-Briand Pact, the General Act for the Pacific Settlement of International Disputes, and the United Nations Charter, there are a number of multilateral treaties which provide for good offices and mediation, conciliation and commission of inquiry, arbitration, or judicial settlement. According to the survey made by the United Nations,[27] such treaties concluded during the period 1928–1948 are mostly under the Inter-American system. Some of them are limited to the procedure of conciliation, such as the Convention of Inter-American Conciliation of January 5, 1929, and the Inter-American Anti-War Treaty of Non-Aggression and Conciliation of October 10, 1933. The Inter-American Treaty on the Prevention of Controversies of December 23, 1936, binds the signatory states to establish permanent bilateral mixed commissions composed of their representatives.

Arbitration as the only means of settling disputes is provided in the General Treaty of Inter-American Arbitration of January 5, 1929, and the Treaty of Central American Fraternity of April 12, 1934. The Statute of the International Court of Justice of June 26, 1945, deals exclusively with judicial settlement. Both adjudication and conciliation are prescribed in the Brussels Pact of March 17, 1948. The Inter-American Treaty on Good Offices and Mediation of December 23, 1936, limits itself to these two procedures. Settlement of disputes

[26] See Arts. 41, 42 of the Charter. For further discussion of the subject, see Hans Kelsen, *Collective Security under International Law* (Newport, R.I., 1956).

[27] *Systematic Survey of Treaties for the Pacific Settlement of International Disputes, 1928–1948* (The United Nations, 1949). The United Nations published, in 1966, *A Survey of Treaty Provisions for the Pacific Settlement of International Disputes, 1949–1962*. Different from the previous survey in both substance and classification, it embodies treaties concerning the general obligation to settle disputes by pacific means and those providing for an obligation to resolve the differences arising out of particular treaty arrangements. However, "the number of treaties made exclusively for the pacific settlement of international disputes has decreased sharply. Only eight treaties of this type have been concluded in the fourteen-year period (1949–1962) covered by the present survey." P. 2.

through mediation and arbitration is stipulated in the Pact of the Arab League of March 22, 1945.

In addition to comprehensive procedures of conciliation, arbitration, and judicial settlement as provided in the General Act of 1928, the American Treaty of Pacific Settlement or Pact of Bogotá of April 30, 1948, also provides good offices and mediation.[28] International treaties and regional arrangements concluded in recent years do not cover all pacific means, but are limited to one or a few for the settlement of disputes among the signatories. Further conclusion of multilateral treaties of this nature seems unnecessary, especially in view of the existence of the United Nations Charter and many bilateral treaties with detailed provisions. Thus, during the period 1949–1962, only a few treaties of this type were concluded. The notable examples are the European Convention for the Pacific Settlement of Disputes of April 29, 1957,[29] and the Protocol of the Commission of Mediation, Conciliation and Arbitration of the Organization of African Unity of July 21, 1964.[30]

§175. GENERAL STIPULATIONS IN BILATERAL TREATIES

Conciliation, arbitration, and judicial settlement In 1949, the United Nations made available a systematic survey of treaties for the pacific settlement of international disputes concluded by the states during the period 1928–1948. With the exception of a few multilateral instruments, all others were bilateral treaties, with stipulations concerning conciliation, arbitration, and judicial settlement. Most of them provide for the three methods simultaneously, while others adopt one or two of the procedures. The majority of the signatory states agreed to include all disputes, but some limited the application to disputes of a legal nature or under treaty provisions. According to a subsequent survey published by the United Nations in 1966, only eight treaties were concluded exclusively for the pacific settlement of international disputes during the period 1949–1962,[31] while many other treaties were concerned in more general terms with the settlement of disputes and

[28] The texts of all these treaties can be found in *Systematic Survey of Treaties for the Pacific Settlement of International Disputes, 1928–1948*, Pt. II.

[29] It came into force on April 30, 1958. For the text, see *A Survey of Treaty Provisions for the Pacific Settlement of International Disputes, 1949–1962* (The United Nations, 1966), pp. 59–68.

[30] It is the first multilateral treaty of this kind for Africa. For its text, see *ibid.*, pp. 78–84.

[31] See *ibid.*, pp. 1–2.

friendship.[32] Thus the present analysis is based on the vast majority of such treaties embodied in the previous survey.

Sixteen categories In spite of their diversification, they may be classified as follows: (1) judicial settlement of all disputes; (2) conciliation and judicial settlement of all disputes; (3) judicial settlement of legal disputes and arbitration of other disputes; (4) judicial settlement of legal disputes and conciliation and arbitration of other disputes; (5) conciliation of all disputes, judicial settlement of legal disputes, and arbitration of other disputes; (6) judicial settlement of legal disputes and conciliation of other disputes; (7) conciliation of all disputes and judicial settlement of legal disputes; (8) conciliation and judicial settlement of legal disputes; (9) judicial settlement of legal disputes; (10) conciliation and arbitration of all disputes; (11) arbitration of all disputes; (12) conciliation of all disputes and arbitration of legal disputes; (13) arbitration of legal disputes; (14) arbitration of disputes as to treaties; (15) conciliation of all disputes; and (16) special provisions for the settlement of disputes by peaceful means. Although most of the treaties dealt with disputes only, some extended to 'questions,' 'differences,' 'disputes and conflicts,' 'disputes or conflicts,' and 'differences or disputes.' Whatever the case, signatory states were generally required to try to settle their disputes through negotiation before recourse to conciliation, arbitration, or adjudication.[33]

Exclusion of certain disputes In the settlement of disputes through the procedures of conciliation, arbitration, or adjudication, most of the bilateral treaties had reservations. In other words, certain disputes were excluded, especially those concerning prior events, within the exclusive competence of states, relating to sovereign rights or territorial status, concerning private claims, or involving the interests of third parties. In arbitration treaties, the United States usually excludes any dispute depending upon or involving the American traditional policy of the Monroe Doctrine. Another common exception has been applied to disputes to be settled in accordance with special provisions in other agreements, which are not limited to those already concluded by the contracting parties, but also include, in some cases, future commitments.[34] All these reservations have weakened the effectiveness of treaties for the settlement of disputes.

[32] For their texts, see *ibid.*, pp. 5–84.

[33] See *Systematic Survey of Treaties for the Pacific Settlement of International Disputes, 1928–1948*, pp. 3–23.

[34] See *ibid.*, pp. 23–49. For the texts of these treaties, see *ibid.*, pp. 331–1175.

II. *SETTLEMENT THROUGH AMICABLE MEANS* [35]

§176. NEGOTIATION

Negotiation is the normal procedure of administering foreign relations among states and also the most common method of resolving their differences.[36] Less tangible than other pacific means, negotiation may be conducted bilaterally or multilaterally, through regular diplomatic channels or summit meetings, at the capitals of the parties concerned or in a third state, for the conclusion of treaties, or for the maintenance or restoration of peace.[37] On many occasions, international disputes have been eventually settled through negotiation after the failure of other means.[38]

[35] General texts on the subject: O'Connell, II, pp. 1155–1166; Oppenheim, II, §§4–25aj; Fenwick, *Principles,* Ch. XXVI; Brierly, Ch. VIII, §§1–4; Hyde, II, §§552–585A; Moore, *Digest,* VII, §§1064–1088; Hackworth, *Digest,* VI, §§547–558; Starke, Ch. 15, §§1–2; Hershey, Ch. XXII; Gould, Ch. 18; Svarlien, Ch. 19; Von Glahn, Ch. 25; Jacobini, pp. 196–210; Soviet *Text,* Ch. IX, §§1–6; Schuschnigg, Ch. 15, §§1–4; Eagleton, Ch. 9; Corbett, Ch. 6; Lawrence, §§220–221; Le Fur, §§781–872; Vattel, III, Bk. 2, Ch. 18; Liszt, §38; Maine, pp. 210–218; Westlake, *Papers,* pp. 572–589; Holland, *Studies,* pp. 130–150.

[36] See Moore, *Digest,* VII, p. 2; Hackworth, *Digest,* VI, p. 1. Art. 33 of the Charter lists negotiation as the first step to settle disputes. In many multilateral treaties, constant consultation on important questions by the signatories is obligatory. These include the Nine-Power Treaty of 1922, the treaties of friendship, cooperation and mutual assistance between the Soviet Union and the Eastern European countries in 1948, the Sino-Soviet Treaty of Friendship, Alliance and Mutual Assistance of 1950, the North Atlantic Treaty of 1949, and the Warsaw Treaty of Friendship, Cooperation and Mutual Assistance of 1955.

[37] Normally, negotiation should precede any other means for settling international disputes. See *Mavrommatis Palestine Concessions (Jurisdiction),* Permanent Court of International Justice, 1924. P.C.I.J. (1924), Ser. A, No. 2. See also Ivo D. Duchacek (ed.), *Conflict and Cooperation among Nations* (New York, 1960), Pt. V.

[38] During the Sino-Soviet conflict over the Chinese Eastern Railway in Manchuria in 1929, the Soviet government declared that the dispute could only be settled through direct negotiations, which eventually took place and resulted in the signing of a protocol on December 22, 1929. See A. W. Griswold, *The Far Eastern Policy of the United States* (New York, 1938), pp. 396–398.

§177. GOOD OFFICES AND MEDIATION

Good offices are the services rendered by a third state or states to bring about negotiations between the disputing parties for the settlement of their differences. Although the disputants have no obligation to accept such services, many international disputes have been solved in this way. The serious conflict between the Netherlands and Indonesia was averted in 1947 through the efforts of a Committee of Good Offices appointed by the Security Council.[39] The Tashkent talks between the Pakistan President Mohammad Ayub Khan and Indian Premier Lal Bahadur Shastri were made possible by the good offices of Soviet Premier Aleksei N. Kosygin and resulted in the Indian-Pakistani Declaration of January 10, 1966, on the withdrawal of troops from areas occupied during the Kashmir conflict. The Soviet Premier was invited to witness this declaration.[40]

Mediation is the consequence of a tender of good offices, and consists of the actual transmission of suggestions, which may be declined by the parties at variance. The United Nations Mediator appointed by the General Assembly in 1948 was instrumental in preventing worsening of the Palestine crisis.[41] The conclusion of the Treaty of Portsmouth for the termination of the Russo-Japanese War in 1905 was due to the good offices and mediation of President Theodore Roosevelt.[42] Theoretical distinctions notwithstanding, good offices and mediation are not always distinguishable in diplomatic practice and treaties.[43]

According to the Covenant and the Charter, any Member may bring to the attention of the League and the United Nations any situation or dispute which might endanger international peace and security.[44] Thus, an international organization may also offer good offices and mediation to the contending parties. These procedures are specially provided in the Inter-American Treaty on Good Offices and Mediation

[39] See SC *Official Records,* 2nd year, No. 103.

[40] See *The New York Times,* January 11, 1966.

[41] According to the General Assembly resolution of May 15, 1948, the Mediator was to promote a peaceful adjustment of the Palestine situation.

[42] See Julius W. Pratt, *A History of United States Foreign Policy,* pp. 442–444.

[43] See Hyde, II, p. 101; Oppenheim, II, p. 10. The Good Offices Committee for the Korean Hostilities and the Good Offices Committee on South-West Africa, appointed by the United Nations in 1951 and 1957 respectively, were also entrusted to seek means to avert hostilities and to reach a peaceful settlement in addition to rendering good offices.

[44] Art. 11 of the Covenant; Arts. 34–35 of the Charter.

of December 23, 1936, and also incorporated in the Pact of the Arab League of March 22, 1945, and the Pact of Bogotá of April 30, 1948.

§178. CONCILIATION AND COMMISSION OF INQUIRY

While conciliation is a development of international commissions of inquiry, there is a distinction between the two: inquiry is to ascertain the facts only; conciliation goes one step further to propose an accord, even though the disputing parties have no obligation to accept it. The Hague Convention for the Pacific Settlement of International Disputes stipulates an international commission of inquiry.[45] The League Covenant provides not only for fact-finding, but also for recommendations in the nature of conciliation.[46] The United Nations Charter provides for both conciliation and inquiry as pacific means for settling international disputes.[47]

In the *Dogger Bank Case* between Great Britain and Russia in 1905, a commission of inquiry was set up in accordance with the Hague Convention to find the facts and fix the responsibility of the Russian fleet in its sinking and damaging a few British fishing vessels and causing the death and injury of several fishermen off the Dogger Bank in the North Sea during the Russo-Japanese War.[48] When Japan invaded Manchuria on September 18, 1931, China appealed to the League for action. At the Council meeting on December 10, a resolution was adopted to send a Commission of Inquiry with Lord Lytton as Chairman.[49] After reviewing the Commission's report,[50] the Assembly established a Special Committee of Nineteen to seek some conciliatory measures for settlement of the Sino-Japanese dispute. The League ef-

[45] Pt. III of the Convention. See A. P. Higgins, *The Hague Peace Conferences*, pp. 107–121.

[46] See Arts. 11, 15, of the Covenant. A resolution on conciliation was adopted by the Third Assembly of the League, and several bilateral treaties were concluded on this basis.

[47] See Art. 33 of the Charter.

[48] Scott, *Hague Court Reports*, 403. The Commission was composed of British, Russian, American, French, and Austrian admirals. It determined that the act of the Russian fleet was not justifiable. On the basis of the report, Russia paid £65,000 to Great Britain as compensation.

[49] LN *Official Jour.*, Vol. 12 (1931), Pt. 2, pp. 2291, 2374–2375. The Commission was composed of Count Aldrovandi (Italian), General Henri Claudel (French), Lord Lytton (British), Major-General Frank R. McCoy (American), and Heinrich Schnee (German). Wellington V. K. Koo and Isaburo represented the Chinese and Japanese governments respectively as assessors to assist the Commission.

[50] For its text, see LN Doc. C.663.M.320.1932.VII.

forts of conciliation did not succeed in this case, and soon afterward Japan decided to withdraw from the League.[51]

Machinery of conciliation and inquiry is provided in the General Act for the Pacific Settlement of International Disputes and many bilateral and multilateral treaties.[52] Secretary of State William Jennings Bryan concluded thirty conciliation treaties during the period 1913–1914.[53] Among the unique features of the Bryan treaties are provisions for a permanent commission and a cooling-off interval of one year, during which no hostilities can be initiated pending the investigation of the commission. Many other bilateral treaties were concluded by European and Latin-American countries, representing the general sentiment of states in favor of conciliation.

The American Treaty of Pacific Settlement, signed at Bogotá on April 30, 1948, provides for commissions for investigation and conciliation.[54] Prior to the Bogotá Pact, the Inter-American system provided for conciliation as sole means in several treaties.[55] Conciliation and judicial settlement are stipulated in the Treaty of Brussels, concluded between

[51] For the futile conciliation efforts of the League, see the statement made by the President of the Assembly at its sixteenth plenary meeting on February 21, 1933. LN *Official Jour.*, Special Supp., No. 112, p. 13. See also William L. Tung, *China and Some Phases of International Law,* pp. 164–168.

[52] In the General Act of 1928 and many other international instruments, conciliation and other peaceful means are provided for as alternative procedures. The four Arbitration Conventions embodied in the Locarno Treaty of 1925 provide for conciliation as a preliminary step for settling disputes between contending parties. Other treaties make a distinction between legal and non-legal disputes: the former are to be settled by conciliation and the latter, by arbitration or judicial settlement.

[53] Among the Bryan treaties which came into effect in that period were eleven with Latin-American countries, nine with European countries, and one with China. Other conciliation treaties were negotiated by Secretaries Kellogg and Stimson.

[54] The Inter-American Treaty for Reciprocal Assistance of September 2, 1947, provides for consultation of foreign ministers. *International Conferences of American States, 1942–1954,* p. 200. A commission of inquiry is provided in the Gondra Treaty (Treaty to Avoid or Prevent Conflicts between the American States) of 1923, and investigation and conciliation are introduced to the General Convention of Inter-American Conciliation of 1929. For texts, see *International Conferences of American States, 1889–1928,* pp. 285, 455.

[55] The Convention of Inter-American Conciliation of January 5, 1929, the Inter-American Anti-War Treaty of Non-Aggression and Conciliation of October 10, 1933, and the Inter-American Treaty on the Prevention of Controversies of December 23, 1936.

Belgium, France, Great Britain, Luxemburg, and the Netherlands on March 17, 1948. The Soviet Union has extensively applied conciliation for settling international disputes.[56] Above all, the services of the United Nations for conciliation and inquiry may be resorted to by all states.

§179. ARBITRATION

Arbitration is a more effective means of settling international disputes through a legal decision of one or more persons chosen by the disputing parties.[57] The head of a third state or other person may be requested to be an arbitrator, but the normal agency is a commission or tribunal. In the case of a mixed commission, it is generally composed of two national commissioners and an umpire. The award is based upon the rules of international law, but justice or equity, or *ex aequo et bono,* may be applied.[58] The subject of the dispute, scope of jurisdiction, guiding principles, and rules of procedure are prescribed in a special *compromis* or in a general arbitration treaty.[59] Except when there are stipulations to the contrary, an award is binding upon the parties at variance.[60]

[56] For instance, the Convention on Conciliation Procedure with Germany in 1929. Similar conventions were concluded in 1932 with Poland and France. Conciliation is also provided for in many agreements for the settlement of boundary disputes. See Soviet *Text,* pp. 383–384.

[57] Unless otherwise agreed upon by the states, submission of disputes to arbitration is not compulsory. See *Eastern Carelia Case,* Permanent Court of International Justice, 1923. P.C.I.J. (1923), Ser. B, No. 5.

[58] In *Free Zones of Upper Savoy and the District of Gex* (1932), the Permanent Court of International Justice had the legislative function of stipulating the detailed future status of the areas concerned. P.C.I.J. (1932), Ser. A/B, No. 46. Arbitration commissions may be given large latitude of power to decide cases on the basis of both law and equity.

[59] The method of arbitration to settle disputes is often provided in treaties of commerce. General treaties of arbitration may be bilateral or multilateral. Sometimes a special treaty is concluded for a particular dispute. The Treaty of Washington of May 8, 1871, which provides for four distinct arbitrations including the *Alabama Claims,* is perhaps the most important arbitration treaty. For further details on arbitral procedures, see C. M. Bishop, *International Arbitral Procedure* (Baltimore, 1930); H. M. Cory, *Compulsory Arbitration of International Disputes* (New York, 1932); K. S. Carlston, *The Process of International Arbitration* (New York, 1946).

[60] There are only a few arbitration cases where one contending party failed to carry out an award. In her dispute with Mexico in the *Chamizal Arbitration,* the United States refused to accept the award made by the International Boundary Commission in 1911. 5 *Am. Jour. Int. Law* (1911),

The institution of arbitration originated in ancient times, but modern practice began with the Jay Treaty of November 19, 1794, and the Treaty of Ghent of December 24, 1814, between Great Britain and the United States.[61] Stimulated by the *Alabama Claims* arbitration in 1872,[62] many other disputes were successfully settled through this means.[63] In adopting the Convention for the Pacific Settlement of International Disputes, the Hague Conference of 1899 established the Permanent Court of Arbitration at The Hague.[64] It is composed of persons competent in questions of international law, no more than four appointed by each signatory, with a term of six years subject to renewal. For each case the disputing parties select a number of arbitrators from the panel to form a tribunal.[65] While not a permanent court in the regular sense, it has rendered more than twenty awards.[66] Many impor-

p. 785. Any award through irregular process or in excess of power is not valid. Thus, Great Britain and the United States were not bound by the award rendered by the King of Holland in the Northeastern Boundary Dispute between the two countries, because the decision exceeded the original terms of the *compromis*. See Moore, *Digest,* VII, §1082.

[61] The Jay Treaty provided for three arbitrations: (1) a boundary issue, (2) claims on account of confiscated debts, and (3) neutral rights and duties. The Treaty of Ghent, which ended the War of 1812, involved the issues of the ownership of certain islands and the ascertainment of boundaries.

[62] Arbitration under the Treaty of Washington of May 8, 1871. Malloy, *Treaties,* I, p. 717.

[63] For instance, the *Bering Sea Seal Fisheries Case* between Great Britain and the United States in 1893 (Malloy, *Treaties,* I, p. 751), and the Alaska Boundary dispute between the United States and Canada in 1903. In the latter case, Lord Alverstone, Chief Justice of England and one of the British arbitration members, was decisive in reaching a decision favorable to the United States. See Philip C. Jessup, *Elihu Root* (New York, 1938), I, pp. 389–401.

[64] Further improvement of the organization and procedure of the Court was made at the Second Hague Conference in 1907.

[65] Usually each party chooses two from the panel, only one of whom can be its own national. Then an umpire is selected by the four arbitrators. In addition to the Court proper, the Permanent Court of Arbitration includes the Permanent Council as a supervisory body represented by the diplomatic envoys of the signatories accredited to the Netherlands, and the International Bureau, serving as the registry of the Court.

[66] The Court still exists, though it has been inactive since 1932. For a list of cases decided by the Court, see Oppenheim, II, pp. 40–41. The first case, submitted to the Court by the United States and Mexico, was the *Pious Fund Arbitration* in 1902, involving Mexico's obligations to Jesuit missions in California. Scott, *Hague Court Reports,* pp. 3–17. See also Soviet *Text,* p. 388.

tant disputes have been settled in that manner, including the *North Atlantic Coast Fisheries Case* in 1910 [67] and *The Island of Palmas (Miangos)* in 1928.[68]

The Hague Convention and the Permanent Court of Arbitration gave further impetus to international arbitration, and resulted in many more bilateral treaties.[69] Mixed arbitral tribunals and mixed claims commissions after World War I disposed of thousands of cases.[70] Arbitration is provided in the League Covenant,[71] the Locarno Treaties of 1925, the General Act for the Pacific Settlement of International Disputes of 1928, several arbitration treaties in the Western Hemisphere,[72] and the Charter of the United Nations.[73] The Arab states agreed to settle their disputes through arbitration when they concluded the Pact of the Arab League on March 22, 1945.

Among topics selected by the International Law Commission for codification in 1949 was arbitral procedure. The latest draft was referred by the General Assembly on November 14, 1958, to the Members for consideration and adoption.[74] Arbitration is generally accepted by

[67] Scott, *Hague Court Reports*, p. 146. [68] *Ibid.* (2nd Ser.), p. 84.

[69] The United States and Great Britain deserve credit for concluding many more arbitration treaties than other countries, not including abortive ones negotiated by Secretaries Hay and Knox. Secretary Elihu Root concluded twenty-five arbitration treaties in 1908–1909. During the period 1925–1929, Secretary Kellogg renewed efforts to conclude bilateral treaties of arbitration.

[70] For details, see Von Glahn, p. 463. Several arbitration tribunals were established after World War II, including the Arbitral Tribunal on German External Debts under the Agreement of February 27, 1953.

[71] See Art. 15 of the Covenant.

[72] The General Treaty of Inter-American Arbitration of 1929 is the most noteworthy. For its text, see *International Conferences of American States, 1889–1928* (Washington, D.C., 1931), p. 458. The early efforts of the Inter-American Conferences culminated in many treaties and resolutions providing for arbitration. For the texts of early treaties, see W. R. Manning, *Arbitration Treaties among the American Nations to the Close of the Year 1910* (New York, 1924).

[73] Art. 33 of the Charter. For further discussion of the historical development of arbitration, consult J. H. Ralston, *International Arbitration from Athens to Locarno* (Stanford, 1929); A. M. Stuyt, *Survey of International Arbitration, 1794–1938* (The Hague, 1939); J. L. Simpson and H. Fox, *International Arbitration: Law and Practice* (New York, 1959).

[74] For Model Rules on Arbitral Procedure proposed by the International Law Commission in 1958 and commentary, see 53 *Am. Jour. Int. Law* (1959), Supp., pp. 239–252; also *Yearbook*, Int. Law Com., 1958, II, pp. 1–15 (UN Doc. A/CN.4/113).

the major powers. Great Britain and the United States have been champions of this method. France and the Republic of China are favorably disposed to it.[75] The Soviet Union has, on several occasions, shown readiness to use arbitration for settling international disputes.[76]

§180. JUDICIAL SETTLEMENT

Adjudication through an international court, which is a permanent tribunal with a fixed number of judges, has a definite advantage over arbitration in its corporate continuity and in the consequent possibility of its building up a consistent body of case law. As early as 1907, the Second Hague Peace Conference proposed an International Prize Court and prepared a draft convention for the creation of a Court of Arbitral Justice.[77] Neither of these materialized. In the same year, a Central American Court of Justice was established at Cartago in Costa Rica for a period of ten years. Although the Court was only of a regional nature and not renewed,[78] it was the first of its kind and served as a forerunner of an international judicial tribunal.[79]

The Covenant of the League of Nations authorized the Council to formulate plans for the establishment of a Permanent Court of International Justice with jurisdiction to hear contentious cases and give advisory opinions.[80] The Advisory Committee of Jurists, appointed by the Council in February 1920, proposed a Draft Statute of the Court, which was eventually adopted by the Assembly on December 13, 1920.[81] The Statute came into effect in September 1921, when the Protocol of Signature of the Statute was ratified by twenty-eight states.[82] The United States and the Soviet Union were not parties to

[75] For Chinese practice, see William L. Tung, *op. cit.*, pp. 168–171.

[76] For Soviet practice, see Oliver J. Lissitzyn, "International Law in a Divided World," *International Conciliation* (March 1963), No. 542, pp. 28–29.

[77] See Manley O. Hudson, *The Permanent Court of International Justice, 1920–1942* (New York, 1943), Chs. 4–5.

[78] The parties to the Court were Costa Rica, Guatemala, Honduras, Nicaragua, and El Salvador. It heard ten cases and met an insurmountable difficulty in enforcing an award against Nicaragua, which concluded a treaty with the United States in violation of the rights of Costa Rica.

[79] In 1923, the same five states signed another treaty in Washington, providing for an International Central American Tribunal, but it was never established.

[80] See Art. 14 of the Covenant.

[81] For its text, see LN *Treaty Series,* 6 (1921), pp. 391–413.

[82] The Statute was amended in 1928–1929, and the Second Protocol was submitted for ratification to the states parties to it.

the Statute.[83] The Court stood the test of time, and delivered several judgments against great powers in favor of small ones. Formally dissolved by the final Assembly of the League on April 18, 1946, its function was taken over by the International Court of Justice.

The question whether there should be a new court was not decided at the Dumbarton Oaks Conference. The United Nations Committee of Jurists met in Washington in April 1945 to prepare a Draft Statute. On the basis of the Committee's report and in consideration of certain political reasons, the United Nations Conference at San Francisco finally decided to establish a new court, called the International Court of Justice, and adopted a new Statute,[84] similar to that of the Permanent Court. The General Assembly and the Security Council, voting concurrently on February 6, 1946, elected the fifteen judges of the new court, which held its first meeting on April 3 of the same year. The International Court of Justice is actually a continuation of the Permanent Court, which had built up an impressive record of jurisprudence and procedure.

Many bilateral treaties provide for settling disputes through the International Court of Justice. Adjudication is stipulated, among other methods, in the General Act for the Pacific Settlement of International Disputes of 1928, the Brussels Pact of 1948, and the Pact of Bogotá of the same year. As the International Court of Justice is the principal but not exclusive judicial organ of the United Nations,[85] other international and regional courts may also be instituted for the purpose of adjudication.[86] In the interest of international peace and order, states should have more recourse to the world court for settlement of their legal disputes. The organization and functions of the International Court of Justice will be discussed in the following chapter.[87]

[83] The United States had been expected to become a party to the Statute of the Permanent Court, but the Senate failed to approve the reservation-padded protocol of adherence. The Soviet Union entered the League in 1934, but it did not become a party to the Statute of the Permanent Court.

[84] For its text, see Appendix III.

[85] See Arts. 7, 92, of the Charter; Art. 1 of the Statute of the International Court of Justice.

[86] Art. 95 of the Charter provides: "Nothing in the present Charter shall prevent Members of the United Nations from entrusting the solution of their differences to other tribunals by virtue of agreements already in existence or which may be concluded in the future." There is now a Court of Justice of the European Communities under the treaties of 1951 and 1957.

[87] See *infra,* §§189–191.

III. *SETTLEMENT THROUGH NON-AMICABLE MEANS*[88]

§181. RETORSION

Retorsion is an unfriendly act taken by one state against another in retaliation; it is not necessarily in kind, but should be in the same proportion. The imposition of high tariffs and discriminatory immigration are often a source of resentment. In the case of *The Frances and Eliza,*[89] retorsion was carried out by excluding shipping. Because of the cold war, the Communist and Western powers have imposed travel restrictions in their territories and frequently demanded the recall of diplomats for one reason or other. These are typical instances of retorsion, which, if not properly restrained, may endanger international peace and security.[90]

§182. REPRISALS

Reprisals in peacetime are the employment of various means short of war by one contending party to apply pressure on the other for the settlement of their disputes. Wartime reprisals are resorted to by one belligerent in retaliation against illegal acts of warfare by its enemy, which may eventually be compelled to conform with the laws of war. When diplomatic redress is exhausted, measures of reprisals are often employed.[91] But such retaliation should bear some proportion to the magnitude of the injury suffered and the amount of force necessary to obtain reparation. In the *Naulilaa Case* between Portugal and Germany in 1928,[92] concerning the responsibility of Germany for damage

[88] General texts on the subject: Oppenheim, II, §§26–52; Fenwick, *Principles,* Ch. XXVII; Hyde, II, §§586–595A; Moore, *Digest,* VII, §§1089–1099; Hackworth, *Digest,* VI, §§559–561; Jessup, Ch. VII; Starke, Ch. 15, §3; Hershey, Ch. XXIV; Gould, Ch. 19; Von Glahn, Ch. 26; Jacobini, pp. 210–222; Schuschnigg, Ch. 15, §5.

[89] U.S. Supreme Court, 1823. 8 Wheaton 398. For further details, see Moore, *Digest,* VII, §1090.

[90] *Cf.* Art. 2(3) of the Charter.

[91] Reprisals are not necessarily inconsistent with the existence of peace between the contending parties. See *William Gray, Administrator, v. United States,* U.S., Court of Claims, 1886 (21 *Court of Claims Reports,* p. 340); *Perrin v. United States,* U.S., Court of Claims, 1868 (4 *ibid.,* p. 543). The practice of granting 'letters of marque' to nationals to perform acts of reprisals had been discontinued by the end of the eighteenth century.

[92] *Annual Digest,* 1927–1928, No. 360, p. 256. In the *Don Pacific* case, Greece refused to pay compensation for damage to a British subject living in Athens caused by a riot in 1847. In retaliation, Great Britain blockaded

caused in the Portuguese colonies of South Africa, the Special Arbitration Tribunal condemned the German reprisals as unjustified and excessive. Of the same nature was the Italian bombardment and temporary occupation of Corfu Island in 1923, because of Greek refusal to pay compensation for the assassination of an Italian member of a boundary commission sent by the Conference of Ambassadors to delimit the border between Albania and Greece. The Italian retaliation was far too excessive.[93]

In retaliation against the subversive activities of Soviet consulates, trade missions, and labor organizations along the Chinese Eastern Railway in Manchuria, the Chinese government raided consulates and closed other agencies in the area in 1929. Meanwhile, many Chinese nationals were arrested in the Soviet Union. In consequence of these reprisals, Sino-Soviet diplomatic relations were ruptured and not resumed until December 13, 1932.[94] The United States claimed that American air strikes against North Vietnam beginning on February 7, 1965, were in retaliation against the latter's infiltration of Communist forces to South Vietnam and military assistance to the Viet Cong.[95] It must be remembered that reprisals by means of force are not in conformity with the letter and spirit of the United Nations Charter.[96]

§183. NONINTERCOURSE AND BOYCOTT

Nonintercourse Nonintercourse is the suspension of relationship, commercial or otherwise, between two states and their nationals. The American Nonintercourse Act of March 1, 1809, repealed the previous Embargo Act of 1807 by legalizing American trade with all ports in the world except those under British and French control.[97] As a

---

the Greek coast and captured Greek vessels. The Mixed Commission of Inquiry (1850–1851) deemed the British reprisals unjustified and excessive. See 39 *Br. & For. St. Papers*, p. 332.

[93] Italy held Greece responsible for the assassination. When Greece offered to submit the dispute to the League of Nations, Italy chose direct military action. Eventually, Greece paid indemnity and Italy evacuated Corfu.

[94] See *China Year Book*, 1931, pp. 495–496; 1933, pp. 655–656.

[95] See Quincy Wright, "Legal Aspects of the Vietnam Situation," 60 *Am. Jour. Int. Law* (1966), pp. 750–769.

[96] *Cf.* Art. 2(3–4) of the Charter. For further discussion on retaliation in general, see H. S. Colbert, *Retaliation in International Law* (New York, 1948).

[97] For details, see A. C. Clauder, *American Commerce as Affected by the Wars of the French Revolution and Napoleon, 1793–1812* (Philadelphia, 1932), p. 180.

forcible measure, nonintercourse is provided for in the League Covenant and the United Nations Charter for the enforcement of collective sanctions.[98]

Boycott Boycott is partial nonintercourse, which is sometimes resorted to by the people or government of one state for the redress of grievances against another. According to Paul Fauchille, "the process of boycott was recognized in 1919 by most states as a means of legitimate pressure, which could, and even should, under certain circumstances, be employed by the Government."[99] Dissatisfied with the inaction of Switzerland after the assassination of Vatzlav Vorovsky, a Soviet delegate to the Lausanne Conference, the Soviet government imposed an economic boycott against Switzerland in 1923.[100] As a legitimate measure of peaceful resistance, the Chinese government declined any responsibility for a boycott movement against foreign goods,[101] which first occurred in 1905 against the United States because of the discriminatory nature of American exclusion laws.[102]

After Japan's invasion of Manchuria in 1931, the Chinese people organized a long-range and nation-wide boycott against Japanese goods. Notwithstanding their patriotic motivation, boycott agitators will be punished if they use violence and intimidation against personal rights and freedom. In the case of *Ko Yun-ting and Others* in 1931, the Shanghai District Court found the defendants guilty for excessive acts in enforcing boycott.[103] The legitimacy of the Chinese boycott was challenged by Japan, but the League of Nations deemed it a lawful reprisal on the basis of the Report of the Commission of Inquiry.[104]

[98] See Art. 16(1) of the Covenant; Art. 41 of the Charter.

[99] Fauchille, I, Pt. 3, p. 702.

[100] It was enforced by a Soviet decree promulgated on June 20, 1923. See T. A. Taracouzio, *The Soviet Union and International Law*, pp. 300–301.

[101] See V. K. Wellington Koo, *Memoranda Presented to the Lytton Commission*, I, pp. 53–54. Paul Fauchille authoritatively stated that "a state cannot compel her nationals or her residents to carry on commerce with the citizens of a given country when they do not wish to do so." Fauchille, I, Pt. 3, p. 701.

[102] See *U.S. For. Rel.*, 1905, pp. 204–234, 368.

[103] William L. Tung, *Cases and Other Readings on International Law*, p. 228. See also Koo, *Memoranda*, I, p. 429.

[104] This conclusion was reached by the Committee of Nineteen appointed by the League to examine the Report of the Lytton Commission on Japan's invasion of Manchuria, and was made public on October 1, 1932. See Koo, *op. cit.*, I, pp. 52–53. For further details, see William L. Tung, *China and Some Phases of International Law*, pp. 177–181. A most thorough

Boycott is provided for in the League Covenant and the United Nations Charter as one of the collective measures of economic sanction.[105]

§184. EMBARGO

Embargo, in its narrow sense, is the detention of national or foreign ships in port,[106] but it may be broadly applied to "the detention within the national domain of ships or other property otherwise likely to find their way to foreign territory." [107] The American Embargo Act of 1807 forbade the exporting of any goods from the United States to Great Britain.[108] The prohibition by the Chinese government against exporting merchandise from Manchuria to Siberia in 1918 was to enforce an embargo against the Bolshevik Revolution.[109] A more recent example is the United States arms embargo, effective January 1, 1964, against the Republic of South Africa, because of the latter's *apartheid* policy.

Both the League Covenant and the United Nations Charter provide for embargo as a kind of collective sanction.[110] Among the enforcement measures against Italy during the Italo-Ethiopian War recommended by the Coordinating Committee of the League in 1935 was

---

treatise on the Chinese boycott is C. F. Remer and W. B. Palmer, *A Study of Chinese Boycott, with Special Reference to Their Economic Effectiveness* (London, 1933).

[105] Art. 16 of the Covenant; Art. 41 of the Charter. For further discussion of boycott, consult Robert Michels, *Le boycottage international* (Paris, 1936).

[106] In *The Boedes Lust,* the British High Court of Admiralty ruled, in 1804, that the seizure of a Dutch vessel would have been a mere civil embargo, terminable upon reconciliation of the disputing parties. However, because of the ensuing declaration of war, the vessel was treated as if it had been enemy property at the time of the capture. 5 C. Rob. 233. The United States Congress, by an Act of December 22, 1807, enforced a general embargo on all shipping in retaliation for the seizure of merchant ships by Great Britain and France. 2 *Stat.* 451.

[107] Hyde, II, p. 1671. For further discussion on different kinds of embargo, see Oppenheim, II, pp. 141–142.

[108] See L. M. Sears, *Jefferson and the Embargo* (Durham, N.C., 1927), p. 103.

[109] See the Dispatch sent by American Minister Reinsch at Peking to the Secretary of State, January 28, 1918. *U.S. For. Rel.,* 1918, Russia, III, p. 172. For the Chinese embargo against British trade with Canton during the fourth decade of the nineteenth century because of the smuggling of opium by British merchants, see H. H. Morse, *The International Relations of the Chinese Empire,* I, pp. 195, 199, 257–258.

[110] Art. 16 of the Covenant; Art. 41 of the Charter.

an embargo on export of war materials and other specified goods to Italy.[111] As one of the means of imposing collective sanctions against Communist China and North Korea during the Korean War, the General Assembly called on the Members of the United Nations in 1951 to enforce an embargo on arms and strategic materials to areas under their control.[112] The decision of the Foreign Ministers Conference under the Inter-American system in January 1962 to enforce trade and arms embargo on Cuba was challenged by the latter on the ground that the action was not authorized by the Security Council of the United Nations.[113]

§185. PACIFIC BLOCKADE

Different from war blockade,[114] pacific blockade is imposed in peacetime by one of the contending parties to prevent the access to or egress from the ports or coasts of another. Notwithstanding lack of unanimity among international lawyers as to its validity, pacific blockade has been a well-established practice ever since the second quarter of the nineteenth century.[115] The blockade of the Greek coast by Great Britain, France, and Germany in 1827,[116] and the British blockade of the river and port of Canton in 1839 and 1857,[117] are some early instances.[118]

[111] By the end of January 1936, fifty-two nations accepted the application of sanctions by arms embargo and severance of financial relations with Italy, fifty agreed to embargo key raw materials, and forty-six consented to mutual financial support in the application of sanctions. But Italy could trade with the United States, a non-member of the League of Nations. After the conquest of Ethiopia, the sanctions were lifted.

[112] The resolution was adopted by a vote of 47 to 0, with 13 abstentions.

[113] The Conference, held at Punta del Este, Uruguay, acted under the Inter-American Treaty of Reciprocal Assistance, signed at Rio de Janeiro on September 2, 1947. The Rio Pact provides that collective measures to halt aggression in the hemisphere are binding on all members if voted by a two-thirds majority.

[114] See *infra*, §234.

[115] See Moore, *Digest*, VII, pp. 135–142; Hackworth, *Digest*, VI, pp. 156–159.

[116] This happened during the Greek revolt against Turkish rule. The three powers blockaded the Greek coast, then occupied by Turkey, to help Greece win her independence.

[117] See *Br. & For. St. Papers*, Vol. 29 (1840–1841), p. 1069; Vol. 34 (1845–1846), pp. 1260–1261; Vol. 47 (1856–1857), p. 560.

[118] In the same category was the British action in the *Don Pacific* case in 1850. See note 92.

The blockade of Formosa by France in 1884 was a pacific blockade in fact, even though France later considered herself at war with China after British protest against France's interference with ships of third states in peacetime.[119] Of the same nature was the blockade of the Venezuelan coast in 1902–1903 by Great Britain, Germany, and Italy to secure payment of their claims.[120] When Japan started full-scale hostilities against China on July 7, 1937, she did not declare war but enforced naval blockade of the Chinese coast.[121] Technically, it might be called pacific blockade, especially since only Chinese ships were affected.

In accordance with general practice after 1850,[122] when one contesting party enforces a blockade of the coast of another, only the ships of the blockaded or the blockading state are affected. In case of their attempt to break the blockade, such ships may be captured and sequestrated, but must be restored after termination of the dispute. Both the United States and Great Britain have taken the position that ships of third states should not be disturbed.[123] According to the League Covenant and the United Nations Charter, blockade as an instrument of col-

[119] See *Br. & For. St. Papers,* Vol. 75 (1883–1884), p. 494; Vol. 76 (1884–1885), pp. 1020, 1080.

[120] The *Venezuelan Preferential Case* was later submitted to the Permanent Court of Arbitration in 1904, to determine whether Great Britain, Germany, and Italy were entitled to preferential treatment out of customs revenues assigned by Venezuela to pay its obligations. The Court approved the preference. Scott, *Hague Court Reports,* p. 56.

[121] China eventually declared war against Japan on December 9, 1941, after Japan's attack on Pearl Harbor.

[122] "Before 1850," according to L. Oppenheim, "ships of third states were expected to respect a pacific blockade, and such as tried to break it were seized and restored at the termination of the blockade without compensation." Oppenheim, II, p. 147. See also Fenwick, *Principles,* pp. 640–641.

[123] Great Britain protested against French interference with the shipping of third states when France blockaded Formosa in 1884. When the Venezuelan coast was blockaded in 1902, the United States took the same attitude. For further discussion, see A. E. Hogan, *Pacific Blockade* (Oxford, 1908). Great Britain and the United States protested to the Chinese government against its blockade of the Chinese coast under Communist control in 1948, not so much because it interfered with the ships of third states, but because it was ineffective. In the opinion of the two governments, the Declaration of Paris of 1856 should be applied to the Chinese closure of ports, which, in effect, was blockade, and which, to be binding, must be effective. However, the Chinese government did not consider the closure of ports a war blockade.

lective sanction may affect the shipping of other Members of the international organizations and even of non-members.[124] Except in self-defense, individual states under the United Nations system are not permitted to resort to forcible measures, including pacific blockade, which may endanger international peace and security.[125]

President Kennedy's quarantine proclamation The 'quarantine' measures proclaimed by President Kennedy on October 24, 1962, entitled "Interdiction of the Delivery of Offensive Weapons to Cuba," [126] were, in fact if not in name, a pacific blockade, except that the blockade extended beyond the coast of Cuba and directly affected the shipping of other countries.[127] The American action to prevent further shipping of Soviet missiles and other offensive weapons to Cuba was based upon the principle of national self-defense and regional security in accordance with the Rio Pact of 1947. Strictly speaking, the Soviet Union was not a third party, because the threat to international peace and security involved Soviet missiles on Cuban territory. The nature of modern weapons and the urgency of the circumstances would necessitate the immediate adoption of preventive measures, which, in order to be effective, had to affect the shipping of other countries.

Recourse to pacific blockade for individual or regional self-defense is permissible under the United Nations Charter in face of an armed attack,[128] which might have been imminent in view of the speedy installation of Soviet missiles and other offensive weapons on the territory of Cuba, which is geographically close and politically hostile to the United States. Under normal circumstances, it would be illegal to use force to meet the threat of force. But, fortunately, the subsequent development of this serious incident made the use of force unnecessary.[129]

[124] In his report to the League Council in 1927, the Secretary-General of the League remarked that "third states may be led . . . to acquiesce in the application of the pacific blockade to their own ships." LN *Official Jour.*, 1927, p. 839. See also Arts. 2(6), 42, of the Charter.

[125] See Art. 2(3) of the Charter.

[126] The word 'quarantine' was used by President Franklin D. Roosevelt in his Chicago speech against Japan's invasion of China in 1937. For the text of President Kennedy's quarantine proclamation, see 57 *Am. Jour. Int. Law* (1963), Supp., pp. 512–513.

[127] It was probably because of these divergences from the traditional pattern of pacific blockade that the American government used the word 'quarantine' to avoid technical complications.

[128] See Art. 51 of the Charter.

[129] First of all, ships of Communist countries made no attempt to break the 'quarantine.' Then, after the good offices of Secretary-General U Thant

After the American intention of enforcing quarantine was made known to states in the Western Hemisphere, the Council of OAS, acting as the Provisional Organ of Consultation, met and adopted a resolution on October 23, 1962, recommending that its member states take necessary measures to halt military supplies to Cuba and calling for immediate dismantling and withdrawal from Cuba of all missiles and other offensive weapons.[130] The action of OAS was based upon the Inter-American Treaty of Reciprocal Assistance or the Rio Pact of 1947 for regional collective defense, and, according to the Charter, should have been reported immediately to the Security Council.[131] In fact, the Cuban situation was brought before the Security Council prior to the resolution of OAS.[132]

Although quarantine measures under compelling circumstances are permissible,[133] constant aerial reconnaissance over the air space of Cuba by U-2 flights is in violation of national territorial sovereignty. Despite reasons of self-defense, such a surveillance, if necessary, should have been conducted under the authority of the United Nations. It should also be noted that explicit or implied permission to use the territory of one state for recruiting troops or other purposes by the rebels of another state for the purpose of overthrowing its existing government is also a violation of international law. The action of the United States both before and at the time of the Bay of Pigs invasion

---

and direct negotiations between President Kennedy and Premier Khrushchev, the Soviet government agreed, on October 28, 1962, to dismantle and ship back the Russian missiles. For details, see *The Cuban Crisis: A Document Record* (New York, 1963), Foreign Policy Association, headline series, No. 157; David L. Larson (ed.), *The "Cuban Crisis" of 1962* (Boston, 1963); Quincy Wright, "The Cuban Quarantine," 57 *Am. Jour. Int. Law* (1963), pp. 546–565.

[130] The vote was 19 to 0. See also Arts. 3, 6, of the Rio Pact of 1947.

[131] See Art. 51 of the Charter.

[132] Under normal circumstances, no enforcement action should be taken by regional agencies or arrangements without authorization from the Security Council. In view of imminent danger to the security of the United States and peace of the Western Hemisphere, Art. 53 of the Charter was not applicable to this alarming situation. However, Judge Philip C. Jessup wrote in 1947: "Under the Charter, alarming military preparations by a neighboring state would justify a resort to the Security Council, but would not justify resort to anticipatory force by the state which believed itself threatened." Jessup, p. 166.

[133] A highly pro-Soviet view of the Cuban missile crisis can be found in Ludwik L. Gelberg, *Kryzys Karaibski 1962 roku* [*The Crisis in the Caribbean in 1962*] (Warsaw, 1964). For a systematic analysis and a selected bibliography of the 'quarantine' and the missile crisis, see Von Glahn, pp. 508–516.

was not flawless. There might have been some ground for Cuba to argue that the installation of missiles was also a kind of self-defense to prevent a large-scale intervention from her colossal neighbor.

In order to avoid the recurrence of such serious incidents, which could easily lead to a major confrontation, states should, more than ever, resort to the United Nations for settlement of their disputes.

§186. DIPLOMATIC PRESSURES

An injured state sometimes gets satisfaction from an offending state through strong protests or by severing diplomatic relations.[134] Diplomatic pressures are not forcible means and permissible under the Charter,[135] but they are not necessarily effective in impressing the parties at variance to make amends. The practice of delivering an ultimatum with the threat to use force now becomes a concern of the United Nations, because such an action will inevitably endanger international peace.[136]

§187. INTERVENTION

Interference with the domestic affairs of another state is inconsistent with the principle of territorial integrity and national independence, and is expressly prohibited by the United Nations Charter.[137] There is another kind of intervention, by which a third state dictates terms for the settlement of disputes between two other states.[138] The intervening state may be one or several.[139] Such interventions may constitute

[134] China's severance of diplomatic relations with Germany on March 14, 1917, after failure of earlier protests against German submarine attack on neutral ships, was one of many examples. See *China Year Book*, 1938, p. viii.

[135] See Art. 41 of the Charter.

[136] See Art. 2(3) and Ch. VII of the Charter. Recourse to ultimatums produced different results in the following two instances: the Austro-Hungarian ultimatum to Serbia did not get satisfaction from the latter, but led to the outbreak of World War I. On the other hand, President Yüan Shih-kai accepted Japan's Twenty-one Demands after the receipt of the latter's ultimatum on May 7, 1915, even though the Demands were never ratified by the Chinese Parliament.

[137] See Art. 2(4) of the Charter. For discussion of intervention in general, see *supra*, §§72–73.

[138] See Oppenheim, II, p. 150.

[139] A classical instance of joint intervention without actual use of force was the dictatorial interference of Russia, France, and Germany in the peace terms of the Sino-Japanese Treaty of 1895, demanding that Japan restore Liaotung Peninsula to China.

threats to, or breaches of, the peace and become an immediate concern of the United Nations.[140]

§188. DEMONSTRATION OF FORCE AND ACTS OF WAR

The show of force is the threat to use force, by which states may achieve desired results, otherwise unsuccessful through diplomatic channels.[141] The United Nations Charter includes demonstration of force as one of the enforcement measures.[142] On the other hand, the actual use of force, such as bombardment and occupation of the territory of another state, even though for temporary purposes and without the intention of going to a full-fledged war, is no longer permitted by the Charter except for individual or regional self-defense and for collective action by the United Nations.[143]

[140] See Ch. VII of the Charter.

[141] For instance, the American dispatch of forces to the Mexican border in 1864, putting strong pressure on France to evacuate her troops from Mexico. In a different category are military parades on national holidays, because they are not designed to settle any particular dispute.

[142] See Art. 42 of the Charter.

[143] See *supra,* §71, particularly for the definition of self-defense by Secretary Webster. For details, see *infra,* §§193–196.

CHAPTER 13

THE UNITED NATIONS AND THE ENFORCEMENT OF PEACE

I. *THE ROLE OF THE INTERNATIONAL COURT OF JUSTICE*[1]

§189. THE ORGANIZATION OF THE COURT

For the maintenance and enforcement of international peace, the United Nations relies chiefly on its principal organs. While the General Assembly and the Security Council deal with political issues,[2] legal matters are within the competence of the International Court of Justice insofar as the parties to a dispute have accepted its jurisdiction. As the principal judicial organ of the United Nations, it is the successor to

[1] General texts on the subject: O'Connell, II, pp. 1166–1202; Oppenheim, II, §§25ab–25ag; Fenwick, *Principles,* Ch. XXVI, §O; Kelsen, pp. 522–547; Schwarzenberger, I, Ch. 9 (II); Jacobini, pp. 205–210; Soviet *Text,* Ch. IX, §6; Whitaker, Chs. 5–6; Schuschnigg, Ch. 16; Satow, Ch. XXXII; Sohn, Ch. IX, §2; Wilcox & Marcy, Ch. XII; Goodrich & Hambro, Ch. XIV; Goodspeed, Ch. 10; Blaisdell, Ch. 14; Clark & Sohn, Ch. XIV, Annex III; Kelsen, *UN,* Ch. 15; Eagleton, Ch. 12, §§102–105; Watkins & Robinson, Ch. 12; Leonard, Ch. 15; *Everyman's UN,* pp. 395–423.

[2] See Art. 7(1) of the Charter. The political role of the Economic and Social Council, the Trusteeship Council, and the Secretary-General of the United Nations is not as important as that of the General Assembly and the Security Council.

the Permanent Court of International Justice.[3] Its Statute forms an integral part of the Charter.[4]

Composed of fifteen judges elected concurrently by the General Assembly and the Security Council,[5] the Court began to function at The Hague in April 1946. In electing the judges, not only their personal qualifications but also their fair representation of the main forms of civilization and of the principal legal systems of the world are to be taken into consideration.[6] While no two judges may be of the same nationality, there is no guarantee of equitable geographical representation at the Court. The term of the judges is nine years, but they may be re-elected.[7] Once elected, no judge can be removed unless, in the unanimous opinion of other judges, he has ceased to fulfill his functions.[8]

The Court elects its President and Vice-President for a three-year term, but they may be re-elected. For the performance of routine administrative matters, a Registrar and other officials are appointed.[9] A quorum of nine judges is required to constitute the Court, which may form one or more chambers with three or more judges to deal with particular cases.[10] A chamber of five judges is annually constituted to hear and determine cases by summary procedure. A judgment thus given by any of the chambers is considered as rendered by the Court.[11]

[3] The Permanent Court of International Justice was closely related to, but not a component of, the League of Nations. For judicial settlement of international disputes by the Permanent Court, see *supra,* §180. For further details, see Manley O. Hudson, *The World Court, 1921–1934* (Boston, 1934), Ch. I–V; the same author, *The Permanent Court of International Justice, 1920–1942* (New York, 1943); A. S. Bustamente Y. Sirven, *The World Court* (New York, 1926).

[4] See Art. 92 of the Charter. The Court is the principal but not the exclusive judicial organ of the United Nations. Thus, Art. 95 of the Charter further provides: "Nothing in the present Charter shall prevent Members of the United Nations from entrusting the solution of their differences to other tribunals by virtue of agreements already in existence or which may be concluded in the future." For the text of the Statute of the International Court of Justice, see Appendix III.

[5] For procedures of nomination and election, see Arts. 4–14 of the Statute. The judges were first elected on February 6, 1946.

[6] Art. 9 of the Statute.

[7] To maintain continuity of the Court, the terms of the judges were arranged at the first election in the following manner: five serving three years; five, six years; and five, nine years. See Art. 13 of the Statute.

[8] See Art. 18 of the Statute. [9] See Art. 21 of the Statute.

[10] For instance, labor cases and cases relating to transit and communications.

[11] For details, see Arts. 26–29 of the Statute.

The decision of the Court is reached by a majority of the judges present.[12]

§190. THE JURISDICTION OF THE COURT

Parties to the Statute The Court decides contentious cases between states which may or may not be Members of the United Nations or parties to the Statute. A Member of the League did not become *ipso facto* a party to the Statute of the Permanent Court of International Justice; an example was the Soviet Union. The provision of the Charter is different in that all Members of the United Nations are *ipso facto* parties to the Statute of the International Court of Justice. Non-members may also become parties on conditions to be determined in each case by the General Assembly upon recommendation of the Security Council.[13] Examples are Switzerland, Liechtenstein, and San Marino. In accordance with a resolution adopted by the Security Council on October 15, 1946, the Court may also be open to states not parties to the Statute under conditions fixed by the Security Council.[14]

Although public international organizations are not parties in cases before the Court, they maintain close relationship with it. Either at their own initiative or upon the request of the Court, they may present information relevant to cases. Likewise, the Court is to notify the organization concerned if the construction of its constituent instrument or of an international convention adopted by the organization is in question in a case before the Court.[15] It seems strange that, as a subject of international law with the capacity to put forward an international claim, the United Nations cannot be a party in cases before its own Court.[16]

Compulsory jurisdiction and reservations As for compulsory jurisdiction, the Statute of the Court contains an 'optional clause.' By a resolution of June 25, 1945, the General Assembly recommended that Members of the United Nations proceed as soon as possible to make

[12] In case of a tie, the President or the presiding judge has a casting vote, as in the *Case of S.S. Lotus,* Permanent Court of International Justice, 1927 (P.C.I.J., Ser. A, No. 10).

[13] Art. 93 of the Charter.

[14] See SC *Official Records,* First Year, Second Series, No. 19, p. 467.

[15] See Art. 34 of the Statute.

[16] Differences between the Organization and a Member state may be solved through an advisory opinion of the Court as provided in the General Convention on the Privileges and Immunities of the United Nations of 1947.

declarations under Article 36 of the Statute to accept the obligatory jurisdiction of the Court.[17] Declarations made by states under the Statute of the previous court and still in force are deemed as effective between the parties to the Statute of the International Court of Justice.[18] On this basis, the Court rejected the argument by Thailand in her dispute with Cambodia over the *Temple of Preah Vihear* in 1961.[19] In the dispute between Israel and Bulgaria over the *Aerial Incident of July 27, 1955,* the Court upheld Bulgaria's contention that the period of her acceptance of compulsory jurisdiction of the Court had expired in 1946.[20]

Declarations may be made unconditionally, or on condition of reciprocity on the part of several or certain states, or for a certain period.[21] It is regrettable that many states have attached a great many reservations to their acceptance of compulsory jurisdiction.[22] The United States excluded "disputes with regard to matters which are essentially within the domestic jurisdiction of the United States of America as determined by the United States of America."[23] Similar

[17] The declarations are to indicate the adherence of the states to the 'optional clause' in accordance with Art. 36(2) of the Statute. While providing for voluntary jurisdiction in principle, the Statute of the Permanent Court appended a protocol. States adhering to the protocol would accept obligatory jurisdiction of the Permanent Court subject to specified reservations. For a summary of decisions of the International Court on the optional clause, see Starke, pp. 375–376. At the Special Committee on Principles of International Law concerning Friendly Relations and Cooperation among States in April 1966, consensus was reached on the principle that "legal disputes should as a general rule be referred by the parties to the International Court of Justice." UN Doc. A/AC.125/6.

[18] See Art. 36(5) of the Statute. In the *Nottebohm Case,* the International Court of Justice ruled, in 1953, that subsequent expiration or denunciation of the declaration by one party could not deprive the Court of jurisdiction over a case previously submitted to it for adjudication. *Preliminary Objections,* 1953. I.C.J. Reports (1953), p. 111.

[19] *Case concerning the Temple of Preah Vihear, Judgment on Preliminary Objections,* International Court of Justice, 1961. *Ibid.* (1961), p. 17.

[20] *Ibid.* (1959), p. 127.

[21] See Art. 36(2–5) of the Statute.

[22] By a resolution adopted on November 17, 1947, the General Assembly emphasized "the desirability of the greatest possible number of states accepting their jurisdiction with as few reservations as possible."

[23] This so-called Connally Amendment, a self-judging form of reservation, invited severe criticism in the United States and abroad, but it did not weaken the Court to such a great extent as many people might think. In spite of reservations by other states, the United States should repeal the

reservations were made by France, Great Britain, and India, but have now been abandoned. Most states, including the Soviet Union, have not accepted compulsory jurisdiction.[24]

The reluctance of Communist countries to rely on adjudication for settling international disputes might be due to their concern that the majority of the judges of the Court, who were born and trained in Western tradition, could not be absolutely impartial.[25] But "every member of the Court shall, before taking up his duties, make a solemn declaration in open court that he will exercise his powers impartially and conscientiously." [26] Furthermore, with the emergence of many new states, the General Assembly and the Security Council have been inclined to elect judges of more diversified background and geographical distribution.

The new states have been favorably disposed to judicial settlement of legal disputes and have, during a comparatively short period, submitted several cases to the Court.[27] However, the recent decision on South-West Africa might discourage the African states from having greater recourse to the Court. By a vote of 8 to 7, the Court dismissed the complaint by Ethiopia and Liberia against the *apartheid* policy of the Republic of South Africa in the former mandated territory of South-West Africa. Without passing on the merits of the dispute, the ruling was based on the technical ground that Ethiopia and Liberia did not have sufficient legal interest in the claim.[28]

Amendment and, by doing so, would enhance the prestige of the Court at least psychologically if not materially. See also Judge Lauterpacht's opinions in the *Norwegian Loans Case* (I.C.J. Reports, 1957, p. 9), and the *Interhandel Case, Preliminary Objections* (*ibid.*, 1959, p. 6).

[24] For further discussion of the optional clause and reservations, see Brierly, pp. 355–361. See also R. P. Anand, *Compulsory Jurisdiction of the International Court of Justice* (London, 1961).

[25] See T. A. Taracouzio, *The Soviet Union and International Law*, p. 296.

[26] Art. 20 of the Statute.

[27] For details, see Ibrahim F. I. Shihata, "The Attitude of New States toward the International Court of Justice," 19 *Int. Organization* (1965), pp. 203–222.

[28] In a lengthy dissent, Judge Philip C. Jessup considered the decision completely unfounded in law. I.C.J. Reports, 1966, pp. 323–442. See also Richard A. Falk, "The South West Africa Cases: An Appraisal," 21 *Int. Organization* (1967), pp. 1–23. For a summary of the Court's decision on July 18, 1966, see *The New York Times*, July 19, 1966. Several cases have been submitted to the Court by states in Asia, Africa, and Latin America, including Cambodia, Thailand, Cameroon, Honduras, Nicaragua, Colombia, and Peru.

Legal disputes The jurisdiction of the Court comprises all legal disputes parties refer to it and all matters specially provided for in the Charter and existing treaties.[29] The following are considered legal disputes: (1) interpretations of treaties; (2) questions of international law; (3) facts which, if established, would constitute a breach of an international obligation; and (4) the nature or extent of reparation to be made for breach of an international obligation.[30] In deciding such cases in accordance with international law, the Court is to apply: (1) international conventions, establishing rules expressly recognized by the disputing parties; (2) international custom, as evidence of a general practice accepted as law; and (3) the general principles of law. As subsidiary means for the determination of rules of law, the Court also relies on judicial decisions and the writings of distinguished publicists.[31]

The Court may also decide a case *ex aequo et bono* if the contesting parties agree to it, but the Court has been extremely cautious about possible involvement in political complications.[32] If there is a dispute as to whether the Court has jurisdiction, the matter is to be decided by the Court.[33] However, the Court cannot take jurisdiction over a case which is referred to it by one party without the consent and submission of the other.[34] In the absence of a legal interest by the plaintiff state or the refusal of the defendant to accept its jurisdiction, the Court cannot decide the merits of a case.[35] In the *Case of Monetary Gold Removed*

[29] Art. 37 of the Statute provides that whenever a treaty in force refers a matter to the Permanent Court, it is to be referred to the present Court.

[30] Art. 36(1–2) of the Statute. [31] Art. 38(1) of the Statute.

[32] See Art. 38(2) of the Statute. Because of political implications, the world equity tribunal and similar proposals referred to by Clark and Sohn are difficult to be put into practice. See Clark & Sohn, Ch. XIV, Annex III(B, C).

[33] See Art. 36(6) of the Statute. For the procedure of the Court, see Ch. III of the Statute. The Court is authorized by many multilateral and bilateral treaties to decide questions arising out of their interpretation and applications. In the *South-West Africa Cases* just cited (Ethiopia and Liberia—Republic of South Africa, 1966), the Court ruled that the duty of the Court "is to apply the law as it finds it, not to make it." Referring to the humanitarian principles invoked by the complainants, the Court emphasized that it was "necessary not to confuse the moral ideal with the legal rules." See *The New York Times*, July 19, 1966.

[34] Such a case must be removed from the Court's list; for instance, the United States application against the Soviet Union concerning the *Aerial Incident of September 4, 1954*. I.C.J. Reports (1958), p. 158.

[35] See *South-West Africa Cases*, International Court of Justice, 1966. *Ibid.* (1966), p. 4.

from Rome in 1943, Italy argued that the International Court lacked jurisdiction because of the absence of Albania, another interested party.[36] Finally, the Court cannot rule on matters exclusively within the domestic jurisdiction of a state.[37]

The binding effect of judgments The decision of the Court is binding on the parties in respect of that particular case.[38] The judgment is final and without appeal,[39] but revision of the judgment is provided for in Article 61 of the Statute under prescribed conditions. Among the judgments delivered by the Permanent Court of International Justice, there was probably only one occasion when a contending party failed to carry out an award.[40] The enforcement measures as provided in the Covenant were not applied.[41]

The Charter stipulates that if any party fails to perform the obligations under a judgment, the other party may have recourse to the Security Council, which may make recommendations or decide upon measures of enforcement.[42] Most judgments have been complied with by the disputing states. There are, however, a few exceptions. As yet, the responsibility of the Security Council to execute judgments has not been tested, because no contesting party has requested it to do so.[43]

[36] *Ibid.* (1954), p. 19.

[37] See *The Right of Passage over Indian Territory Case: Preliminary Objections,* International Court of Justice, 1960. *Ibid.* (1957), p. 125. For further discussion of the procedure and jurisdiction of the Court, consult J. H. Ralston, *The Law and Procedure of International Tribunals* (Stanford, 1926; supplement, 1936); Ibrahim F. I. Shihata, *The Power of the International Courts to Determine Its Own Jurisdiction* (The Hague, 1965).

[38] See Art. 94(1) of the Charter; Art. 59 of the Statute.

[39] See Art. 60 of the Statute.

[40] In the dispute between Greece and Belgium concerning the *Société Commerciale de Belgique,* Greece did not comply with the decision of the Permanent Court to honor the awards. P.C.I.J. (1939), Ser. A/B, No. 78. In *The S.S. Wimbledon* case, failure to execute the judgment was not due to refusal by Germany but based on a ruling of the Reparations Commission. *Ibid.* (1923), Ser. A, No. 1.

[41] Art. 13(4) of the Covenant provides: "In event of any failure to carry out such an award or decision, the Council shall propose what steps should be taken to give effect thereto."

[42] See Art. 94(2) of the Charter.

[43] In the *Corfu Channel Case* in 1949, Albania refused to pay compensation to Great Britain in accordance with the decision of the International Court of Justice. I.C.J. Reports, 1949, p. 4. In the *Temple of Preah Vihear,* Thailand refused to evacuate forces from the Temple awarded to Cambodia by the International Court in 1962 (Merits). *Ibid.*, 1962, p. 6. After Iran's failure to carry out the 'interim measures of protection' decided by the

Advisory opinions In addition to the decision of contentious cases, the International Court has the function to deliver advisory opinions on legal questions at the request of the General Assembly, the Security Council, or other organs of the United Nations and specialized agencies authorized by the General Assembly.[44] Opinions are given in open court. Although these judicial opinions have no binding effect, they carry considerable moral weight and are generally respected by the organs concerned. When a request for an advisory opinion is made by a specialized agency, the Economic and Social Council must be informed. In principle, the General Assembly may attach conditions to the authorization or revoke it at any time.

As advisory opinions are limited to legal questions, the most difficult task is to distinguish them from political matters. Sometimes the Court may refuse to give an advisory opinion if it may be decisive of a controversy and thus directly affect an interested party without its previous consent. This precedent was established by the Permanent Court of International Justice in the *Eastern Carelia Case* in 1923.[45] On the other hand, the Court has no hesitancy in giving an advisory opinion on a subject within its competence such as the interpretation of treaty provisions, in spite of the argument that the request for such an opinion is political in nature, as in *Certain Expenses of the United Nations (Art. 17, Par. 2 of the Charter)*, 1962.[46]

International Court in the *Anglo-Iranian Oil Company* case in 1952, Great Britain appealed to the Security Council for action. But a subsequent decision of the Court ruled that it lacked jurisdiction of the case. Thus, the enforcement question was dropped. *Ibid.* (1952), p. 93.

[44] See Art. 96 of the Charter. The Economic and Social Council, the Trusteeship Council, and most of the specialized agencies have been so authorized, though few requested advisory opinions from the Court. The General Assembly has more often availed itself of this opportunity, but not all advisory opinions can be followed by action, due to political considerations. The most noted example is *Certain Expenses of the United Nations (Art. 17, Par. 2 of the Charter)*, International Court of Justice, 1962. I.C.J. Reports, 1962, p. 151. In the League of Nations, all advisory opinions given by the Permanent Court of International Justice were requested by the League Council.

[45] P.C.I.J. (1923), Ser. B, No. 5. This case involved a dispute between the Soviet Union and Finland. The League of Nations asked the Permanent Court to deliver an advisory opinion without the consent of the Soviet Union, which had not yet joined the League.

[46] I.C.J. Reports, 1962, p. 151. In entertaining UNESCO'S request for an advisory opinion on the *Judgments of the Administrative Tribunal of ILO*, the Court held that the views of both parties should be heard. See *ibid.* (1956), p. 77.

§191. PROPOSALS FOR IMPROVEMENT

Because of the importance of the International Court in the settlement of legal disputes, many proposals have been made to improve its present status. One suggestion is that parties to the Statute should accept compulsory jurisdiction without attaching reservations. By doing so, the Soviet Union and many other states which have not filed or renewed declarations accepting compulsory jurisdiction would make more use of the Court. Meanwhile, the jurisdiction of the Court would be broadened by eliminating such reservations as have been made by the United States and others. This suggestion is theoretically sound but impossible in practice under the prevailing international situation. Since decisions of certain legal questions may result in grave political implications, parties at variance will be most reluctant to let an independent court decide their destiny on delicate issues. The Soviet Union, which has persistently held that the jurisdiction of the International Court should be on a voluntary basis, is not likely to become a party to such a statute. While admitting that the Court has given several correct judgments and well-founded opinions, Soviet jurists are of the opinion that the Court has infringed the powers of the Security Council and has adopted a hostile attitude toward the People's Democracies.[47]

Another proposal is to extend the sphere of advisory opinions. There is actually no lack of legal provisions in this respect; these depend on the practical application of the United Nations organs and the specialized agencies. Again, advisory opinions are not binding and their effect will be determined by the willingness of the organs concerned to accept and carry them out. A more drastic idea is to authorize the Court, by a revision of the Charter, to have jurisdiction over political disputes which cannot be settled by the General Assembly and the Security Council. Such a move is absolutely impractical in the international community today. Other proposals include extension of Court jurisdiction over international organizations and individuals, but these are premature under present circumstances.

In conclusion, there is nothing fundamentally wrong with the present Statute of the International Court. What should be improved is the political relationship among the states. The rule of law is possible only when the members of the international community are willing to abide by it. On the basis of many important judgments and opinions delivered by the two world courts, both have achieved modest success in judicial settlement of international disputes.[48] In their contributions

[47] See Soviet *Text*, pp. 393, 396.

[48] For further details, consult Manley O. Hudson, *International Tribunals: Past and Future* (Washington, D.C., 1944); S. Rosenne, *The Interna-*

toward the development of international law, the two international tribunals have impressive records.[49]

II. *THE ROLE OF UNITED NATIONS POLITICAL ORGANS* [50]

§192. PACIFIC SETTLEMENT

Any dispute of potential danger to international peace and security is of deep concern to the United Nations, which requires the parties at variance to seek a solution by themselves through pacific means. Thus, in the questions of Tunisia in 1952 and the 'Appointment of a Governor for the Free Territory of Trieste' in 1953, the Security Council refrained from discussing their substance and left them to be settled directly by the parties concerned.[51]

In addition to negotiation, inquiry, mediation, conciliation, arbitration, and judicial settlement, the Charter includes "other peaceful means of their own choice," such as recourse to regional agencies or arrangements.[52] Non-members are also expected to act in accord with United Nations principles in order to maintain international peace and security.[53] Except for application of enforcement measures,[54] matters

---

tional Court of Justice: An Essay in Political and Legal Theory (Leiden, 1957); O. J. Lissitzyn, *The International Court of Justice: Its Role in the Maintenance of International Peace and Security* (New York, 1951); U.S. Senate Committee on Foreign Relations, Subcommittee on the United Nations Charter, *The International Court of Justice* (Washington, D.C., 1954); Julius Stone, "The International Court and World Crisis," *International Conciliation* (January 1962), No. 536.

[49] Further references may be made to E. Hambro, *The Case Law of the International Court* (Leiden, 1952); H. Lauterpacht, *The Development of International Law by the International Court* (New York, 1958); A. M. Stuyt, *The General Principles of Law as Applied by International Tribunals to Disputes on Attribution and Exercise of State Jurisdiction* (The Hague, 1946).

[50] General texts on the subject: Oppenheim, II, 25b–25ge, 52a–52fd; Fenwick, *Principles,* Chs. XXVI, §N; XXVII, §J; Friedmann, Ch. 16; Satow, Ch. XXXI; Hershey, Ch. XXIII; Soviet *Text,* Ch. IX, §7; Kelsen, pp. 509–519; Kaplan & Katzenbach, Ch. 11; Kelsen, *UN,* Chs. 14, 19; Goodrich, Chs. VIII–IX; Claude, Chs. 11–12, 14; Blaisdell, Chs. 6, 16; Sohn, Chs. VIII, §§1, 4; IX, §1; Goodspeed, Chs. 7–8; Eagleton, Chs. 17–18; Leonard, Chs. 10, 12–13; Clark & Sohn, Chs. VI–VII, Annex II; Wilcox & Marcy, Chs. V–VI; Jacob & Atherton, Chs. 3–4, 7, 10–11; Goodrich & Hambro, Chs. VI–VII; *Everyman's UN,* pp. 29–180.

[51] See *Repertory,* UN, II, pp. 207–209.

[52] Art. 33(1) of the Charter. [53] See Art. 2(6) of the Charter.

[54] For details, see Ch. VII of the Charter.

essentially within the domestic jurisdiction of a state are not within the competence of the United Nations.[55]

The primary responsibility of the Security Council in the maintenance of peace and security does not exclude the authority of the General Assembly to discuss questions within the scope of the Charter. Both organs have the authority to deal with any international dispute or situation, but, without the request of the Security Council, the General Assembly is not to make any recommendations on disputes or situations already under the consideration by the Security Council.[56] It should be noted that a situation is a potential dispute; it may or may not develop into a dispute.[57] On several occasions, the Security Council has removed cases from its agenda and referred them to the General Assembly, for example, the Greek question in 1947.[58]

Unlike decisions of the Security Council, resolutions adopted by the General Assembly are recommendations, which have no binding force on the Members.[59] Thus, any recommendation on which action is necessary must be referred to the Security Council either before or after discussion at the General Assembly.[60] Meanwhile, the General Assembly and the Secretary-General of the United Nations may bring

[55] See Art. 2(7) of the Charter. Domestic jurisdiction does not extend to obligations incurred by a state through an international agreement to which it is a party. See *Nationality Decrees Issued in Tunis and Morocco,* Permanent Court of International Justice, 1923. P.C.I.J. (1923), Ser. B, No. 4.

[56] See Arts. 10, 12(1), of the Charter. While Art. 35 is often used to bring disputes and situations before the Security Council, Arts. 10, 11, and 14 are invoked to refer such matters to the General Assembly.

[57] Art. 34 of the Charter states, in part: ". . . any situation which might . . . give rise to a dispute. . . ." Among questions submitted as disputes are the Syrian and Lebanese questions in 1946 (SC *Official Records,* 1st year, 1st Ser., No. 1, 19th meeting, p. 271) and the Iranian question in the same year (*ibid.,* No. 2, 26th meeting, p. 27). There are also many instances submitted as situations, including the Spanish question in 1946 (*ibid.,* No. 2, 32nd meeting, p. 122) and the Czechoslovak question in 1948 (*ibid.,* 3rd year, Nos. 36–51, 268th meeting, p. 101).

[58] Consequently, the General Assembly adopted res. 109 (III), establishing the United Nations Special Committee on the Balkans.

[59] Despite their legal weakness, recommendations adopted by the General Assembly are sometimes of great importance. In urging Albania, Bulgaria, and Yugoslavia to cease giving any assistance to guerrillas fighting in Greece, the General Assembly adopted resolution 193 (III) in 1948, which pronounced the condition a threat to peace.

[60] See Art. 11(2). Without decisions of the Security Council, Members of the United Nations may decide whether or not to act on the General Assembly recommendations. This is equally true of the Uniting for Peace Resolution of November 3, 1950.

to the attention of the Security Council any matter potentially dangerous to international peace and security.[61] Any dispute or situation may be brought before the Security Council or the General Assembly by any Member of the United Nations. Even a non-member may do so if it is involved in such a dispute and accepts in advance the obligation of pacific settlement with respect to that particular case.[62] This rule was acted upon by Thailand in 1946 and Hyderabad in 1948 in their disputes with France and India respectively.[63]

The Security Council may investigate any dispute or situation in order to determine its nature and, whenever necessary, call upon the disputing parties to solve their differences directly through pacific means.[64] Upon their failure to reach a settlement, the dispute must be referred to the Security Council.[65] After due consideration of their unsuccessful efforts, the Security Council may recommend appropriate methods or procedures of adjustment. The question was raised whether the General Assembly could investigate matters within its own jurisdiction at the time of its establishing an Interim Committee. While Article 34 explicitly gives the Security Council such a power, there is no provision in the Charter prohibiting the General Assembly from doing so.[66] However, any dispute of a legal nature should be referred to the International Court of Justice.[67]

[61] See Arts. 11(3), 99, of the Charter.

[62] See Art. 35(2) of the Charter. Art. 35 is implemented by Rules 1–9 of the Provisional Rules of Procedure of the Security Council on submission of a dispute or a situation. Once included in the agenda, the Security Council is seized of it.

[63] The same was applied to Albania in her dispute with Great Britain in 1947, when she was not a member of the United Nations.

[64] See Arts. 33(2), 34, of the Charter. Investigation has often been conducted through a subcommittee as provided in Art. 29 of the Charter. In discussing the problem of retaining the Iranian question on the agenda in 1946, the majority of the Security Council held that the Council was entitled to concern itself with a question even after agreement between the disputing parties, since continuing circumstances might endanger international peace.

[65] See Art. 37 of the Charter. Either party may refer the dispute to the Security Council. When the Egyptian question was submitted to the Security Council, both Arts. 35 and 37 were invoked.

[66] See GA res. 111 (II); also 196 (III) and 295 (IV), concerning the "Re-establishment of the Interim Committee of the General Assembly."

[67] The Security Council adopted a resolution on April 9, 1947, on the dispute between Albania and Great Britain, which reads, in part, as follows: "Recommends that the United Kingdom and Albanian Governments should immediately refer the dispute to the International Court of Justice in accordance with the provisions of the Statute of the Court."

Consideration by the Security Council may be made at its own initiative or upon the request of the disputing parties.[68] Objections have sometimes been raised to consideration by the Security Council of matters as essentially of a domestic nature and not dangerous to international peace.[69] At the same time, the Security Council may arbitrate a dispute under the authority of Article 38 of the Charter if the parties at variance so desire. Methods often resorted to by the United Nations organs for pacific settlement of disputes are good offices and mediation,[70] conciliation and commission of inquiry,[71] and judicial settlement.[72] The Security Council may decide on measures of enforcement if the dispute has developed into such a dimension as to constitute a threat to the peace, a breach of the peace, or an act of aggression.[73] The dispute between the Netherlands and Indonesia in 1949 was of such a serious nature that the Security Council called upon both parties to cease all kinds of hostilities with a view to reaching pacific settlement.[74]

[68] See Arts. 36, 38, of the Charter.

[69] Such arguments were chiefly based on Arts. 2(7), 33(1), and 107 of the Charter. For illustrations, see *Repertory*, UN, II, pp. 199–210.

[70] The Security Council set up a Committee of Good Offices in 1947 and a Commission of Investigation and Mediation in 1948 in connection with the Indonesian situation and Kashmir, respectively.

[71] Following the appointment of a Mediator in 1948, a Commission of Conciliation was constituted to deal with the Palestine question.

[72] For instance, the *Corfu Channel Case* between Great Britain and Albania in 1949. I.C.J. Reports, 1949, p. 4.

[73] For details, see Ch. VII of the Charter; also *infra,* §193.

[74] Resolution of January 28, 1949. For details on the political role of the General Assembly and the Security Council, see H. F. Haviland, Jr., *The Political Role of the General Assembly* (New York, 1951); T. J. Kahng, *Law, Politics and the Security Council* (The Hague, 1964). For further references on the maintenance of international peace and pacific settlement of disputes, consult U.S. Senate Committee on Foreign Relations, Subcommittee on the United Nations Charter, *Pacific Settlement of Disputes in the United Nations* (Washington, D.C., 1954); Leland M. Goodrich and Anne P. Simons, *The United Nations and the Maintenance of International Peace and Security* (Washington, D.C., 1955); H. G. Nicholas, *The United Nations as a Political Institution* (London & New York, 1967); Ernest A. Gross, *The United Nations: Structure for Peace* (New York, 1962); Charles A. McClelland (ed.), *The United Nations: The Continuing Debate* (San Francisco, 1960); Hans J. Morgenthau (ed.), *Peace, Security and the United Nations* (Chicago, 1946); Ivo D. Duchacek (ed.), *Conflict and Cooperation among Nations* (New York, 1960); Norman J. Padelford and Leland M. Goodrich, *The United Nations: Accomplishments and Prospects* (New York, 1965); Philip C. Jessup, *Parliamentary Diplomacy* (89 Hague *Recueil,* 1956); Richard N. Gardner, *In Pur-*

§193. ENFORCEMENT ACTION [75]

Members of the United Nations are obliged to settle their disputes by peaceful means and to refrain from "threat or use of force against the territorial integrity or political independence of any state, or in any other manner inconsistent with the Purposes of the United Nations." [76] For the maintenance of international peace and security, the Charter requires Members "to take effective collective measures for the prevention and removal of threats to the peace, and for the suppression of acts of aggression or other breaches of the peace." [77]

In spite of this solemn obligation, Members have resorted to force on various grounds in order to achieve their national interests. The reasons more frequently given have been self-defense,[78] protection of vital interests as well as lives and property of nationals,[79] invitation by the legitimate government,[80] exercise of belligerent rights,[81] self-help,[82]

---

suit of World Order: U.S. Foreign Policy and International Organizations (New York, 1964), Pt. I; David C. Coyle, *The United Nations and How It Works,* rev. ed. (New York, 1966), pp. 88–142; Philip van Slyck, *Peace: The Control of National Power* (Boston, 1963), pp. 1–123; Lincoln P. Bloomfield, *Evolution or Revolution: The United Nations and the Problem of Peaceful Territorial Change* (Cambridge, 1957).

[75] For a survey of enforcement action and collective security under the United Nations, see U.S. Senate Committee on Foreign Relations, Subcommittee on the United Nations Charter, *Enforcement Action under the United Nations* (Washington, D.C., 1955); Joseph H. Ball, *Collective Security: The Why and How* (Boston, 1943).

[76] See Art. 2(3–4) of the Charter.

[77] Art. 1(1) of the Charter. The word 'aggression' is subject to variety of interpretations and definitions. See Rosalyn Higgins, pp. 178–179; Quincy Wright, "Conflict of Aggression," 29 *Am. Jour. Int. Law* (1935), pp. 377, 389.

[78] See *supra,* §73; *infra,* §196.

[79] This was one of the reasons given by the British and French governments for their intervention in the Suez Canal Zone in 1956. See SC *Official Records,* 11th year, 749th and 751st meetings.

[80] For instance, the landing of United States and British forces in Lebanon and Jordan, respectively, in 1958. The Soviet Union also used this reason for her intervention in Hungary in 1956. See GA *Official Records,* 2nd emergency sess., 564th meeting.

[81] Egypt justified her restrictions of Israeli shipping through the Suez Canal on this ground.

[82] Great Britain attempted to justify her minesweeping operations in the *Corfu Channel Case* on the ground of self-help, which was rejected by the International Court of Justice. I.C.J. Reports, 1950, p. 35.

and retaliation.[83] Throughout the history of the United Nations, the political organs have been busily occupied with the task of restoring peace after resort to force by the states concerned.

As the Security Council has the primary responsibility to maintain international peace and security, it is empowered to determine the existence of any threat to the peace, breach of the peace, or act of aggression. It is most difficult to ascertain that a certain situation constitutes a threat to peace even though force is not used. The Security Council may choose either of the following actions: (1) to make recommendations, or (2) to decide on enforcement measures.[84] Under the League system, military sanctions were at the discretion of Members, while economic sanctions against states violating the Covenant by resorting to war were automatically undertaken by Members without waiting for the decision of the League Council.[85] Members of the United Nations need not take any action before the decision of the Security Council. But once a decision on enforcement measures is made, it is binding on the Members whether the sanctions are economic or military.[86]

The term 'threat to peace' does not apply to a situation which may be a potential threat to peace. Such a contention was raised in connection with the Spanish question at the Security Council in 1946, but the majority opinion favored a restrictive interpretation of the term.[87] Whether a situation has developed to such a degree that international peace is threatened or breached constitutes another point of argument. This happened at the Security Council in connection with the Palestine question, and was decided in the affirmative at a meeting on July 15, 1948.[88]

On the basis of the principle of non-intervention by the United Nations in matters essentially within the domestic jurisdiction of a state,[89] Article 39 of the Charter is not applicable to a civil war. But the situation would be different if the civil war had reached such dimensions as to endanger international peace and security. This issue was raised throughout the consideration of the Indonesian question,

[83] The Security Council rejected Israeli action in Qibya under such a justification on November 24, 1953. See S/3139/Rev.2.

[84] See Art. 39 of the Charter.

[85] See Art. 16 of the Covenant.

[86] See Art. 25 of the Charter.

[87] For texts of different statements, see SC *Official Records,* 1st year, 1st Ser., No. 2.

[88] See *ibid.,* 3rd year, Nos. 67–75; Supp. for July 1948, pp. 76–77, S/902.

[89] See Art. 2(7) of the Charter.

especially concerning the decisions of August 1, 1947, and December 24, 1948,[90] and also of the Congo situation.

Generally, the Security Council first makes recommendations to the parties concerned in a situation involving threat to or breach of peace, or act of aggression. Upon failure to maintain or restore international peace and security, the Security Council may decide on enforcement measures. It may 'call upon' the disputants to comply with certain provisional measures, which are without prejudice to their rights, claims, or position.[91] The provisional measures may vary in different cases, but usually include cessation of hostilities, termination of retaliatory measures, or withdrawal of armed forces from certain areas. The words 'call upon' imply that enforcement measures will be undertaken by the Security Council if its first effort fails.

The Security Council did invoke Articles 39 and 40 of the Charter in the protracted Palestine dispute and, in July 1948, ordered the parties concerned to cease hostilities.[92] In its resolution of July 27, 1950,[93] the Security Council urged Members of the United Nations to furnish necessary assistance to the Republic of Korea to repel armed attack from North Korea, which failed to comply with the Council's previous resolution to withdraw invading forces and cease hostilities.[94] From the above-mentioned cases it can be seen that Article 39 on enforcement action is applicable to non-members.

A recent instance of United Nations enforcement action against a non-member can be found in the case of Southern Rhodesia. This unique situation was created by the declaration of independence from British rule by a government controlled by the whites, a little over one-twentieth of the country's population. To Prime Minister Ian D. Smith, this matter is entirely within the domestic jurisdiction of Southern Rhodesia, but Great Britain and other members of the United Nations hold an opposite view. After the failure of Prime Minister Harold Wilson's attempt to settle the dispute through direct negotiations, the Security Council deemed that the situation in Southern Rhodesia con-

[90] See SC *Official Records,* 2nd year, Nos. 67–68; 3rd year, Nos. 132–134.

[91] Art. 40 of the Charter.

[92] See SC *Official Records,* 3rd year, No. 97, p. 43.

[93] S/1511. After intervention by the Central People's Government of the People's Republic of China, the General Assembly adopted, on February 1, 1951, resolution 498 (V), condemning Chinese aggression in Korea.

[94] On the Korean situation, see also Leland M. Goodrich, *Korea: A Study of U.S. Policy in the United Nations* (New York, 1956); Leon Gordenker, *The United Nations and the Peaceful Unification of Korea* (The Hague, 1959).

stituted a threat to international peace and security. On December 16, 1966, it decided to impose mandatory economic sanctions by banning the purchase of twelve key Rhodesian exports and the supply of oil and oil products to Rhodesia by United Nations Members.[95]

According to the Charter, enforcement measures adopted by the Security Council can be non-military or military. It may decide and call upon members of the United Nations to apply specific measures not involving the use of armed force, including "complete or partial interruption of economic relations and of rail, sea, air, postal, telegraphic, radio, and other means of communication, and the severance of diplomatic relations." [96] The United Nations action against Southern Rhodesia is a collective economic sanction. Its effectiveness depends largely upon the willingness and support of United Nations Members. It remains to be seen what action the Security Council may take against Members which do not abide by its decision in the Rhodesian case.

Foreseeing that non-military measures may be inadequate in certain cases, the Charter further provides that the Security Council may take such military actions as "demonstrations, blockade, and other operations by air, sea, or land forces of Members of the United Nations." [97] The actual obligation of individual Members of the United Nations depends on the terms of their special agreements to be concluded with the Security Council with respect to "the numbers and types of forces, their degree of readiness, and general location, and the nature of the facilities and assistance to be provided." [98] Upon request of the Security Council to contribute military forces for enforcement measures, a Member of the United Nations not represented on the Council may be invited to participate in Council discussions of the

[95] SC res. 232 (1966). The resolution was adopted by a vote of 11 to 0, with 4 abstentions. For its text, see *The New York Times,* December 17, 1966. The Council's decision was criticized by former Secretary of State Dean Acheson, but vigorously defended by Ambassador Arthur J. Goldberg. For their views, see, respectively, *The Washington Evening Post,* December 11, 1966, and *The New York Times,* December 30, 1966. See also George A. Mudge, "Domestic Policies and UN Activities: The Cases of Rhodesia and Republic of South Africa," 21 *Int. Organization* (1967), pp. 24–54; C. G. Fenwick, "When Is There a Threat to the Peace?—Rhodesia," 61 *Am. Jour. Int. Law* (1967), pp. 753–755.

[96] Art. 41 of the Charter.

[97] Art. 42 of the Charter.

[98] Art. 43(2). See also Art. 45, which is supplementary to Art. 43. It should be noted that the Charter was adopted before the United States used the atomic bomb.

particular matter.[99] The major obstacle to the conclusion of such agreements has been disagreement among the permanent members of the Security Council on their respective military contributions, according to the report of the Military Staff Committee,[100] which was constituted under the provisions of the Charter to advise and assist the Security Council on all questions relating to "the employment and command of forces placed at its disposal, the regulation of armaments, and possible disarmament."[101] The Military Staff Committee has since become impotent, though it still holds regular meetings.[102]

By the Uniting for Peace Resolution adopted on November 5, 1950, the General Assembly urged the Security Council to "devise measures for the earliest application of Articles 43, 45, 46, and 47 of the Charter of the United Nations regarding the placing of armed forces at the disposal of the Security Council by the states Members of the United Nations and the effective functioning of the Military Staff Committee."[103] No action was taken by the Security Council on this recommendation. Probably the founders of the United Nations foresaw the difficulty of concluding special agreements on military contributions by Members, and thus entrusted China, France, Great Britain, the Soviet Union, and the United States, the five permanent members of the Security Council, with authority to consult with one another and other Members on joint action whenever necessary.[104]

From the wording of Articles 43 and 45 of the Charter, the United Nations force for enforcement action should be composed of the na-

[99] See Art. 44 of the Charter. This provision was made to satisfy some middle powers at San Francisco on the principle of no military contributions without representation, advocated by the Netherlands delegation.

[100] By a resolution adopted at its meeting on February 16, 1946, the Security Council directed the Military Staff Committee to study and make recommendations on the provisions of Art. 43. The Council examined the report submitted by the Committee on April 30, 1947, and was unable to agree on major points.

[101] Art. 47(1). See also Art. 46 of the Charter.

[102] For details, see *supra*, §154. Since 1947, Committee meetings have been held under a simple and interesting pattern: "In full uniform the officers gather in a scheduled room at the United Nations headquarters. The session is called to order by the current chairman—rotating each month. The agenda is adopted, the minutes of the last meeting are approved, the time of the next meeting is set and the meeting is adjourned. Sometimes there are brief speeches of welcome for new members." *The New York Times,* August 9, 1964.

[103] GA res. 377B (V).

[104] See Art. 106 of the Charter. No special agreements have been concluded by the Security Council with members of the United Nations.

tional contingents of individual states under a United Nations flag. This was the practice during the Korean War, the commander-in-chief being appointed by the United States at the request of the United Nations.[105] Enforcement measures may be taken either by all or some of the Members of the United Nations as determined by the Security Council,[106] with the assistance of other organs of the United Nations and the specialized agencies as called upon. In connection with the agenda item 'Complaint of Aggression upon the Republic of Korea,' the Security Council adopted a resolution on July 31, 1950, requesting "the Secretary-General, the Economic and Social Council . . . other appropriate United Nations principal and subsidiary organs, the specialized agencies . . . to provide such assistance as the Unified Command may request." [107]

In carrying out enforcement measures, Members are expected to afford mutual assistance; non-members may consult the Security Council with regard to special economic problems as a result of collective sanction.[108] Mutual assistance among United Nations Members is similar to that provided in the League Covenant.[109] As permanent members of the Security Council may exercise the veto power on substantive matters, no enforcement action can be taken against any of them. This double standard may have been motivated by practical considerations, but is in contradiction to the principle of equality of Members of the United Nations.

Peace-keeping operations of the United Nations For the maintenance or restoration of international peace and security, the United Nations has dispatched, on a number of occasions, peace-keeping forces to areas where there were threats to or breaches of peace. These forces, which have had a variety of strengths and responsibilities, have not been exactly for enforcement action, but for the maintenance of peace,[110] such as the United Nations Emergency Force in the Middle East (UNEF) in 1956 [111] and the United Nations Operations in the

[105] This was in accordance with a resolution adopted by the Security Council on July 7, 1950. See 9 United Nations *Bulletin* (1950), p. 96.

[106] See Art. 48 of the Charter.

[107] SC *Official Records,* 5th year, No. 21, p. 3. Under Art. 65 of the Charter, the Security Council may call upon the Economic and Social Council for necessary assistance.

[108] See Arts. 49, 50, of the Charter.

[109] See Art. 16(3) of the Covenant.

[110] 'Provisional measures' may be adopted by the Security Council under Art. 40 of the Charter.

[111] GA res. 1000(ES-1).

Congo (ONUC) in 1960.[112] In the execution of their duties, the United Nations forces could exercise the right of self-defense under compelling circumstances.[113] However, the presence and effectiveness of all peace-keeping operations depend "not only on the consent of the authorities in the area of their deployment but on the cooperation and goodwill of those authorities." [114] Here lies the important distinction between a peace-keeping operation and an enforcement action under Chapter VII of the United Nations Charter.[115]

In the past ten and a half years, UNEF has been a deterrent influence along the armistice demarcation line and the international frontier between Israel and the United Arab Republic. This mission was originally authorized by the General Assembly and accepted by the United Arab Republic to perform its buffer functions in the bordering areas under the latter's territorial jurisdiction. Because of the steady deterioration of relations between the Arab states and Israel in May 1967, the United Arab Republic deemed that the continuing presence of the United Nations forces would hinder her military action [116] and requested the prompt withdrawal of UNEF. Secretary-General U Thant considered the position of UNEF as untenable under the circumstances and on May 18 ordered its withdrawal from the Gaza Strip and the Sinai Peninsula.[117] It was most disturbing that, at this critical time, the

[112] S/4387.

[113] In pursuance of the United Nations instructions to ONUC troops in the Congo. See S/4451; also GA res. 3943, 4587.

[114] Report by Secretary-General U Thant to the Security Council on May 20, 1967. See *The New York Times,* May 21, 1967. In his report on the withdrawal of the United Nations Emergency Force to the General Assembly on June 27, 1967, the Secretary-General emphatically stated that UNEF "was a peace-keeping force, not an enforcement action," and that "its effectiveness was based entirely on voluntary cooperation." See *ibid.,* June 28, 1967.

[115] For the intricate problems of the United Nations peace-keeping role, see the Report to the Committee on Foreign Relations of the United States Senate (90th Cong., 1st Sess.), *The United Nations Peace-Keeping Dilemma* (Washington, D.C., 1967). The report was submitted by Senator Clifford P. Case, a member of the United States delegation to the twenty-first session of the General Assembly of the United Nations.

[116] For the growing tension between Syria and Israel, see the Secretary-General's Reports to the Security Council on January 15, 1967 (S/7683), and May 8, 1967 (S/7877).

[117] See the Special Report by the Secretary-General to the General Assembly on May 18, 1967. A/6669, Par. 12(c). UNEF consisted of approximately 3,400 men from India, Canada, Yugoslavia, Sweden, Brazil, Norway, and Denmark. It was said that Brazil and Canada questioned

United Nations had not been able to take more positive steps to prevent the outbreak of hostilities in that explosive region.[118]

Due to the refusal of certain Members of the United Nations to pay the costs of the peace-keeping operations, the General Assembly, by a resolution adopted on December 20, 1961, requested the International Court of Justice to deliver an advisory opinion on the question of *Certain Expenses of the United Nations (Art. 17, Par. 2 of the Charter*.[119] By a vote of 9 to 7, the Court delivered an opinion on July 20, 1962, that the expenditures authorized in certain General Assembly resolutions enumerated in the request for opinion, relating to United Nations operations in the Congo and in the Middle East undertaken in pursuance of Security Council and General Assembly resolutions likewise enumerated, were 'expenses of the Organization' within the meaning of Article 17, Paragraph 2, of the Charter of the United Nations.[120]

The General Assembly accepted the advisory opinion,[121] but the Soviet Union, France, and several other Members refused to pay their share of the expenses.[122] The Soviet position was that only the Security Council has the authority to impose such assessments for peace-keeping operations in opposition to the view that the General Assembly has the residual authority to maintain international peace and security. In fact, UNEF was set up with the consent of the disputing parties concerned

---

the authority of the Secretary-General to make the decision of its withdrawal at the closed meetings prior to his action. See *The New York Times*, May 20, 1967.

[118] In his statement on the Middle East on May 23, 1967, President Johnson frankly expressed United States dissatisfaction with the current development: "We are dismayed at the hurried withdrawal of the United Nations Emergency Force from Gaza and Sinai after more than 10 years of steadfast and effective service in keeping the peace, without action by either the General Assembly or the Security Council." *Ibid.*, May 24, 1967. Divergent opinions on the withdrawal of UNEF from the Gaza Strip and the Sinai Peninsula can be found in Israeli Foreign Minister Abba Eban's speech at the emergency special session of the General Assembly and Secretary-General Thant's reply, on June 19 and 20, 1967, respectively. Further reference on the subject may be made to Hammarskjöld's 'Good Faith' Aide-Mémoire of November 20, 1956, and U Thant's lengthy report to the General Assembly on June 27, 1967. See *ibid.*, June 19–21, 28, 1967.

[119] I.C.J. Reports (1962), p. 151.

[120] Art. 17(2) of the Charter reads: "The expenses of the Organization shall be borne by the Members as apportioned by the General Assembly." For a summary of the advisory opinion, see *Yearbook*, UN, 1962, pp. 473–477, 541–549.

[121] GA res. 1854A (XVII), adopted on December 19, 1962.

[122] For details, see *supra*, §52.

by the General Assembly under the Uniting for Peace Resolution on November 5, 1956,[123] and ONUC was initially authorized by the Security Council on July 13, 1960.[124] After reviewing the records of both operations, the Court concluded that they did not involve 'preventive or enforcement measures' against any state under Chapter VII of the Charter or 'action' in the sense of Art. 11(2).[125] The Court was further of the opinion that financial obligations incurred by the Secretary-General in accordance with the authority of either the Security Council or the General Assembly constituted obligations of the Organization for which the General Assembly was entitled to make provision under the authority of Article 17, Paragraph 2, of the Charter.

Because of serious arguments about the legal authority of the General Assembly and Security Council's peace-keeping operations and financial assessments, a new suggestion was made for the establishment of a United Nations military force. But the question of its constitution and authority remains unsolved.[126] The Soviet Union proposed that such a force should be under the supervision of the Security Council, with military units drawn from small powers.[127] Considering past difficulties and the existing international situation, a permanent international force may not at this time be feasible. Probably future peace-keeping forces will still be recruited whenever need arises, and expenses will be shared by the Members in favor of such resolutions.[128]

[123] GA res. 1000 (ES-I), adopted by the General Assembly. See *Yearbook*, UN, 1956, pp. 36–37.

[124] S/4387, adopted by the Security Council, by a vote of 8 to 0, with China, France, and Great Britain abstaining. See *ibid.*, 1960, p. 97.

[125] Art. 11(2) of the Charter reads: "The General Assembly may discuss any questions relating to the maintenance of international peace and security brought before it by any Member of the United Nations, or by the Security Council, or by a state which is not a Member of the United Nations in accordance with Article 35, paragraph 2, and, except as provided in Article 12, may make recommendations with regard to any such question to the state or states concerned or to the Security Council or to both. Any such question on which action is necessary shall be referred to the Security Council by the General Assembly either before or after discussion."

[126] For a comprehensive review of the situation arising out of differences of principle about the establishment, conduct, and financing of United Nations peace-keeping operations, see *Yearbook*, UN, 1964, pp. 3–59.

[127] See the memorandum submitted by the Soviet Union on July 7, 1964. For its excerpts and the Western reaction to the Soviet proposal, see *The New York Times*, July 8, 21, 1964.

[128] As different situations usually require different contingents, it is not advisable to have a standing United Nations force under present circum-

The effectiveness of enforcement measures in the future depends upon agreement on two conditions among the Members of the United Nations, especially the major powers: (1) establishing speedy procedures for the call-up of national contingents earmarked by different Member states for international action; (2) authorizing the General Assembly to direct peace-keeping operations if the Security Council is immobilized by a veto.[129] It should be recalled that the Uniting for Peace Resolution, adopted by the General Assembly on November 3, 1950,[130] was intended to fulfill that objective, because the failure of the Security Council to perform its functions does not relieve Member states or the United Nations of their obligations under the Charter.[131]

III. *RELATIONSHIP WITH REGIONAL ARRANGEMENTS AND AGENCIES* [132]

§194. PROVISIONS OF THE CHARTER

Unlike the League Covenant, the Charter specifically provides for recourse to regional arrangements and agencies as one of the methods

---

stances. Because of the veto power, no coercive action can be taken without the consent of the permanent members of the Security Council.

[129] For details of the voting procedure at the Security Council, see *supra,* §149.

[130] GA res. 377 (V). For its text, see *Yearbook,* UN, 1950, pp. 193–195. Under the Resolution, Members are urged to maintain within their national armed forces appropriate elements for service as a United Nations unit or units, and to cooperate fully with the Peace Observation Commission and the Collective Measures Committee, set up in accordance with the Resolution. For further details, see *supra,* §60.

[131] Further references on United Nations peace-keeping operations may be found in Arthur L. Burns and Nina Heathcote, *Peace-Keeping by United Nations Forces* (New York, 1962); Gabriella E. Rosner, *The United Nations Emergency Force* (New York, 1963); William R. Frye, *A United Nations Peace Force* (New York, 1957); Carnegie Endowment for International Peace, *Synopses of United Nations Cases in the Field of Peace and Security* (New York, 1966); Lincoln Bloomfield *et al.* (eds.), *International Military Forces* (Boston, 1964); King Gordon, *The United Nations in the Congo* (New York, 1962); David Brook, *Preface to Peace: The United Nations and the Arab-Israel Armistice System* (Washington, D.C., 1964); David W. Wainhouse and associates, *International Peace Observation: A History and Forecast* (Baltimore, 1966); H. G. Nicholas, *op. cit.,* pp. 58–69.

[132] General texts on the subject: Fenwick, *Principles,* Chs. X; XXVI, §P; XXVII, §K; Kelsen, pp. 519–522; Schwarzenberger, I, Chs. 7 (I–IV),

for the pacific settlement of international disputes and the maintenance of international peace and security.[133] Enforcement action on a regional basis is a new feature under the United Nations system.[134] Members of the United Nations and parties to regional arrangements or agencies are urged to settle their disputes through local channels before submitting them to the Security Council, but this stipulation in no way impairs the investigatory functions of the Security Council or the right of access by states to the United Nations with respect to disputes and situations.[135] Meanwhile, whatever activities undertaken or contemplated under regional arrangements or by regional agencies for the maintenance of international peace and security are to be fully reported to the Security Council at all times.[136]

§195. FUNCTIONS OF REGIONAL ORGANIZATIONS

Regional arrangements designate commitments made by interested states through multilateral instruments that establish agencies or organizations to fulfill such commitments.[137] These arrangements or agencies may be classified according to their purposes and objectives: (1) collective defense, such as NATO, SEATO, CENTO, and the organization of the Warsaw Pact nations; (2) economic and social objectives, such as the European Economic Community, the Council of Mutual Eco-

---

11 (II–III); Satow, Ch. XXXIII; Soviet *Text,* Ch. VIII, §§7–10; Schuschnigg, Ch. 18; Svarlien, Ch. 20; Claude, Ch. 6; Kelsen, *UN,* Ch. 12; Goodrich & Hambro, Ch. VIII; Clark & Sohn, Ch. VIII; Eagleton, Ch. 19; Jacob & Atherton, Chs. 5–6; Leonard, Ch. 17.

[133] See Arts. 33(1), 52(1), of the Charter. Regional arrangements are multilateral instruments signed by states essentially of, but not limited to, the same region. While regional arrangements may not necessarily create a specific organization to execute commitments, regional agencies are established as a result of the conclusion of regional arrangements. See Kelsen, *UN*, pp. 319–320.

[134] See Art. 53 of the Charter.

[135] For details, see Ch. VIII of the Charter. According to Art. 2 of the Inter-American Treaty of Mutual Assistance of 1947, member states of OAS are required to submit and settle their disputes in the Inter-American system before referring them to the United Nations. Thus contention was made at the time of the United Nations discussion of the Guatemalan complaint in 1954 that the complaint should be referred to OAS before submission to the Security Council.

[136] See Art. 54 of the Charter.

[137] For instance, NATO was created under the North Atlantic Treaty of 1949, by which member states are committed to collective defense against aggression.

nomic Assistance (COMECON), and the Colombo Plan. OAS has both functions. The Arab League and the Organization of African Unity are also comprehensive in nature. Although the motivation of certain arrangements is partly distrust of the United Nations as effective machinery for peace,[138] all of them should be encouraged to take an active part in pacific settlement of disputes.

As a consequence of modern power alignment, regional organizations for collective defense are sometimes under the leadership of a superpower outside the region. Although this practice was originally dictated by military necessity, it has created an uneasy relationship among member states. France's withdrawal from many NATO arrangements was partly due to resentment against the dominance of a European organization by an American power. In Southeast Asia, the same sentiment has been reflected in public statements and private conversations of Asian leaders.[139] Even in the same hemisphere, the hegemony of one state is not always well received by others. The attitude of Latin-American states toward the Monroe Doctrine is an instance.[140]

§196. SELF-DEFENSE AND REGIONAL AGENCIES

The right of self-defense as provided in Article 51 of the Charter essentially harmonizes the authority of the United Nations with regional arrangements and agencies. Self-defense, either individual or

[138] For a more detailed discussion of the relationship of regional arrangements or agencies with the United Nations, see Von Glahn, pp. 486–497; Fenwick, *Principles*, pp. 228–246, 630–633.

[139] Recently Foreign Minister Thanat Khoman of Thailand, one of the closest allies of the United States, told his colleagues from Malaysia and the Philippines at Bangkok that it was time for Asians "to take our destiny into our hands instead of letting others from far away mold it at their whim." His statement was made at the opening meeting of the newly revived Association of Southeast Asia, whose members are Thailand, Malaysia, and the Philippines, concerning Thailand's proposal for an Asian-sponsored peace conference on Vietnam. See *The New York Times*, August 4, 1966.

[140] Further references on regional arrangements and agencies can be found in K. M. Panikkar, *Regionalism and Security* (New York, 1948); Pierre Vellas, *Le Régionalisme international et L'Organisation des Nations Unies* (Paris, 1948); W. Eric Beckett, *The North Atlantic Treaty, the Brussels Treaty and the Charter of the United Nations* (London, 1950); Inis L. Claude, Jr., "The OAS, the UN, and the United States," *International Conciliation* (March 1964), No. 547; John C. Dreier, *The Organization of American States and the Hemisphere Crisis* (New York, 1962); Ernst B. Haas, *The Uniting of Europe* (Stanford, 1958). See also *supra*, Ch. 3, note 9.

collective, is considered an 'inherent right' of nations. This article was invoked by the representative of Egypt when the Security Council considered the agenda item 'Restrictions Imposed by Egypt on the Passage of Ships through the Suez Canal,' submitted by Israel on July 11, 1951. Egypt attempted to justify her restrictions on the passage through the Suez Canal of goods for Israel. But, in the opinion of the Security Council, Egypt could not invoke Article 51 to justify her exercise of belligerent rights of visit, search, and seizure nearly two and a half years after the conclusion of an armistice agreement with Israel. The Security Council, therefore, called upon Egypt "to terminate the restrictions on the passage of international commercial shipping and goods through the Suez Canal wherever bound and to cease all interference with such shipping beyond that essential to the safety of shipping in the Canal itself and to the observance of the international conventions in force." [141]

The compatibility of regional defense arrangements with the collective system of the United Nations was raised at the sixth session of the General Assembly in connection with the agenda item 'Measures to Combat the Threat of a new World War and to Strengthen Peace and Friendship.' The Soviet representative submitted a draft resolution declaring participation in the North Atlantic Treaty Organization incompatible with membership in the United Nations. The General Assembly did not share the view of the Soviet Union and rejected the draft resolution.[142]

According to the provisions of the Charter, regional arrangements or agencies are to be utilized chiefly for pacific settlement of disputes. Enforcement action may only be undertaken with the authority of the Security Council. The only exception is enforcement measures against any state which, during World War II, was an enemy of any signatory of the Charter.[143] This position was supported by both the United States and the Soviet Union at the Security Council at the time of its discussion of intervention of the Arab states in Palestine in 1947,[144] and of aggressive acts of the Dominican Republic against Venezuela in 1960.[145] The Soviet Union condemned OAS's expulsion of Cuba in 1962, but, in that case, no enforcement action was taken.[146]

[141] See SC *Official Records*, 558th meeting, Par. 5, S/2298/Rev.1.

[142] See UN Doc. A/C.1/698; 3 *Int. Organization* (1949), pp. 400–406. A similar draft resolution was submitted at the seventh session of the General Assembly by the representative from Poland, but he did not press for a vote. See UN Doc. A/C.1/L.39.

[143] See Art. 53 of the Charter.

[144] See SC *Official Records*, 2nd year, 299th and 302nd meetings.

[145] See S/4476, S/4477, S/4491.

[146] See S/5075, S/5086.

The right of individual or collective self-defense under Article 51 of the Charter is not unlimited, but restricted to the following conditions: (1) circumstances—an armed attack against a Member of the United Nations; [147] (2) time—before the action of the Security Council; (3) procedure—immediate report to the Security Council about measures already undertaken for self-defense; and (4) limit—no action of self-defense detrimental to the authority and responsibility of the Security Council.[148] Judged by the above standards, the French and British action in the Suez Canal Zone in 1956 [149] and the American operations in Vietnam are not in accord with the Charter.[150]

[147] Anticipatory self-defense is not within the meaning of Art. 51 of the Charter, which allows only self-defense against armed attack or aggression. For statements by French, Indian, and British delegates in debates of the Tunisian question in 1958, the Jammu-Kashmir case in 1950, and the restriction of Israeli shipping through the Suez Canal in 1951, see, respectively, SC *Official Records,* 13th year, S/3951; 5th year, 460th and 536th meetings; 6th year, 550th and 551st meetings. In any event, self-defense can only be resorted to under extremely urgent conditions and should be carried out with due proportion.

[148] For further discussion on self-defense, see D. W. Bowett, *Self-Defense in International Law* (New York, 1958).

[149] Unlike Israel's, the British and French action was chiefly based on the protection of vital interests and lives and property of nationals. See GA res. 997(ES–I), 999(ES–I); SC *Official Records,* 11th year, 849th meeting. For a brief review of the Suez Canal question, see *Yearbook,* UN, 1956, pp. 19–39. See also Quincy Wright, "Intervention," 51 *Am. Jour. Int. Law* (1957), pp. 257-276; Thomas T. F. Huang, "Some International and Legal Aspects of the Suez Canal Question," *ibid.,* pp. 277–307.

[150] Perhaps it is advisable to explain briefly the historical development of the present situation in Vietnam. After a prolonged war in Indochina, the French army lost Dienbienphu on May 7, 1954, to the Viet Minh troops led by Ho Chi Minh. As a result of the conclusion of the armistice agreements between France and the victorious Communist Command at Geneva on July 20, 1954, Laos, Cambodia, and Vietnam achieved their independence, with Vietnam partitioned along the 17th parallel into two states pending reunification through 'free elections' to be held by July 20, 1956. For the texts of the agreements, see U.S. Congress, 89th Congress, 1st Session, *Background Information relating to Southeast Asia and Vietnam* (Washington, D.C., 1965), pp. 28–42. The following countries were represented at the Geneva Conference: the Democratic Republic of Vietnam, the State of Vietnam, France, Cambodia, Laos, the People's Republic of China, the Soviet Union, Great Britain, and the United States. While refusing to join the Declaration of the Geneva Conference, Under-Secretary of State Bedell Smith, the American representative at the Conference, declared that

Probably in anticipation of possible exercise of the veto by the Soviet Union at the Security Council and North Vietnam's refusal to settle the dispute through the United Nations, the United States assumed the responsibility of applying military sanctions without the authority of the Security Council. Nor did she report to the Security Council until August 1964.[151] It would be more appropriate for the

---

the United States would refrain from disturbing the agreements. For texts of the Armistice Agreements of the Geneva Declaration and Smith's statement, see *ibid.*, pp. 28–42, 58–60, and 61, respectively. With the deposition of Bao Dai and the election of Ngo Dinh Diem as Chief of State in South Vietnam on October 26, 1955, American aid was rapidly increased. Because of increasing danger of Communist conquest since 1964, American military forces in South Vietnam have been taking direct action against the Viet Cong beyond the original scope of indirect assistance. On February 7, 1965, the United States Air Force started to bomb North Vietnam. It appears, however, that the determination of North Vietnam and the Viet Cong has been hardened and that a war of essentially political nature cannot be won by military means alone. Much commentary about the United States action has been published. While many have seriously questioned its legality, others have defended the American military operations on various grounds. Early in 1966, President Johnson received two letters from a number of international lawyers in support of the United States position. For texts, see *Congressional Record,* Appendix, January 27, 1966; February 23, 1966, pp. 3694–3695. The United States policy was fully explained in the memorandum on *The Legality of United States Participation in the Defense of Vietnam,* prepared by Leonard Meeker, Legal Adviser of the Department of State, and submitted to the Senate Committee on Foreign Relations on March 8, 1966 (Washington, D.C., 1966, a pamphlet, reprinted from the Department of State *Bulletin*). However, "this memorandum is obviously an adversary document stating 'our side' in the legal controversy and making very little effort to assess impartially the facts or the law in support of the other side." Richard A. Falk, "New Approaches to the Study of International Law," 61 *Am. Jour. Int. Law* (1967), p. 477. For divergent views on this subject, see Quincy Wright, "Legal Aspects of the Vietnam Situation," 60 *ibid.* (1966), pp. 750–769; John N. Moore, "The Lawfulness of Military Assistance to the Republic of Vietnam," 61 *ibid.* (1967), pp. 1–34; Wolfgang Friedmann, "Law and Politics in the Vietnamese War: A Comment," *ibid.*, pp. 776–785.

[151] Only after an attack on American naval vessels near the Gulf of Tonkin on August 2 and 4, 1964, did the United States bring the incident to the attention of the Security Council. According to Art. 51 of the Charter, any measure taken by a Member of the United Nations against an armed attack in the exercise of the right of self-defense "shall be immediately

United States to refer the Vietnam problem to SEATO [152] for proper action as she did to OAS after her initial intervention in the Dominican Republic in 1965. Again, regional agencies must report to and take orders from the United Nations for self-defense or enforcement action.[153] On the other hand, neither the Security Council nor SEATO has assumed the responsibility to take necessary action for the restoration of peace in Vietnam.[154]

---

reported to the Security Council and shall not in any way affect the authority and responsibility of the Security Council. . . ." The debates at the Security Council concerning the incident resulted in no action or recommendation. For details, see *Yearbook*, UN, 1964, pp. 147–149.

[152] The Signatories of the Southeast Asia Collective Defense Treaty of September 8, 1954, are Australia, France, New Zealand, Pakistan, the Philippines, Thailand, the United Kingdom, and the United States. While Cambodia, Laos, and South Vietnam are not parties to it, a separate protocol includes these states in the collective defense system as provided in Art. IV of the Treaty. Although the United States has kept SEATO informed about the Vietnam situation, her military action was initially taken independently of this regional organization. There is serious dissension among members of SEATO with respect to its policy toward Vietnam. Its internal weakness was fully revealed at a Council meeting in Washington in April 1967. France did not send a representative. Pakistan expressed dissatisfaction with the alliance over Vietnam policy. Great Britain disputed about the obligation of SEATO members to supply troops to Vietnam. Only Australia, New Zealand, the Philippines, and Thailand endorsed American policy. See *The New York Times,* April 20, 21, 1967

[153] The following comment by L. Oppenheim on self-defense is pertinent to the Vietnam situation: "It does not follow from the character of the right of self-defense—conceived as an inherent, a natural, right—that the states resorting to it possess the legal faculty of remaining the ultimate judges of the justification of their action." Oppenheim, II, p. 159. *Cf.* D. W. Bowett, *op. cit.,* Ch. IX, on self-defense under the United Nations Charter. See also McDougal and Feliciano, *Law and Minimum World Public Order,* pp. 121–260.

[154] Various proposals for peaceful settlement have been made from both official and unofficial quarters, including the reconvening of the Geneva Conference, but none has been proved acceptable to all the parties at dispute. In late January 1966, after the United States peace offensive and bombing pause, the Vietnam conflict was again brought before the Security Council, which did not, however, adopt any resolution. Although the Vietnam problem figured large in the general debate at its twenty-first session, this vital issue has never been on the agenda of the General Assembly.

IV. *WAR OR THE USE OF FORCE UNDER THE UNITED NATIONS SYSTEM* [155]

§197. THE CONCEPT OF WAR OR THE USE OF FORCE

The Charter of the United Nations prefers the term 'use of force' to 'resort to war,' as used in the League Covenant.[156] The founders of the United Nations probably hoped that World War II would be the last 'war to end war' and did not want to use the same terminology. Actually, there is no substantial difference between these two terms, because war is resort to force by one disputing party or parties in order to subdue the enemy for compulsory settlement of their differences.[157] But war in the legal sense traditionally implies the legal equality of the belligerents, which cannot be true under the United Nations system. While the right to make war or to use force was traditionally considered within the sovereign power of a state,[158] it is no longer permitted under the United Nations Charter except for individual or collective self-defense or for enforcement measures by the Organization.[159]

[155] General texts on the subject: Oppenheim, II, §§52fe–60; Fenwick, *Principles,* Ch. XXVIII; Brierly, Ch. IX; Hyde, III, §§596–601; Moore, *Digest,* VII, §§1100–1104; Hackworth, *Digest,* VI, §562; Von Glahn, Ch. 27; Schwarzenberger, I, Ch. 7 (XI); Jacobini, pp. 224–230; Jessup, Ch. VIII; Gould, Ch. 20; Soviet *Text,* pp. 401–405; Kaplan & Katzenbach, Ch. 8; Eagleton, Chs. 15–16, 18.

[156] Art. 2(4) of the Charter reads: "All Members shall refrain in their international relations from the threat or use of force against the territorial integrity or political independence of any state, or in any other manner inconsistent with the Purposes of the United Nations." The same phraseology is used in Art. 44 and other provisions in the Charter.

[157] In *Western Reserve Life Insurance Co. v. Meadows,* the Supreme Court of Texas laid down the definition in 1953 that "every forcible contest between two governments, *de facto,* or *de jure,* is war." 261 S.W.(2d) 554. According to Karl von Clausewitz, "war is nothing but a continuation of political intercourse, with a mixture of other means." Clausewitz, *On War* (London, 1940, translation by J. J. Graham), III, p. 121. In the words of Lenin, "war is a continuation of policy by other means." Lenin, *On Britain* (Moscow, English ed.), p. 340.

[158] See *United States v. Active,* United States, District Court, Territory of Mississippi, 1814. 24 *Federal Cases,* 755 (No. 14, 420). The Court ruled that individuals could not control operations of war or commit any hostility without sovereign order.

[159] See Arts. 51–52 of the Charter.

Whether certain forcible measures are war or measures short of war under traditional international law depends on their nature and intent. Pacific blockade or even sporadic border conflict is not considered war.[160] Recourse to propaganda, subversion, infiltration, or similar means to carry out so-called cold war is not war in the legal sense under traditional rules of international law; nor is it a use of force or armed attack under the United Nations Charter. The duration or scope of an armed conflict is not the determining factor, because certain wars are short and limited. Whether it is designated as the use of force, hostilities, or armed conflict, it is war in the material sense if it has reached considerable magnitude.[161] Attempts have been made to classify wars or armed conflicts as just and unjust or aggressive and defensive, but such distinctions can only be determined by particular circumstances and outcome.[162]

As rules of warfare and neutrality were formulated long before the emergence of the United Nations, the traditional term 'war' as adopted in previous conventions is used in this book for convenience of discussion, but it is intended to mean war in the material sense and not war in the legal sense as distinguished from traditional international law.[163] Because the drastic change in the concept of war began with the League Covenant and the Kellogg-Briand Pact, a brief review of

[160] Border conflicts can develop into war, depending on their scope and intensity, such as the armed clashes between Japan and the Soviet Union on the Manchurian frontier during the period 1935–1945, and also those between the People's Republic of China and India in 1962.

[161] For further discussion of the subject, see A. Appadorai, *The Use of Force in International Relations* (Bombay, 1958); Lothar Kotzsch, *The Concept of War in Contemporary History and International Law* (Geneva, 1956).

[162] Discussion of the justice of a war may easily enter the domain of international morality, which is viewed differently by states under varied circumstances. The military action of North Korea during the Korean War was deemed an act of aggression by the United Nations Commission in Korea in its report to the General Assembly on September 4, 1950, but the Communist countries held a different position and rejected this verdict. For an attempted definition of aggression, see the Draft Code of Offenses against the Peace and Security of Mankind, proposed by the International Law Commission, Ch. II. UN Doc. A/CN.4/44. For Grotius' concept of just cause of war, see *De jure belli ac pacis* (English translation), Bk. II, Ch. I, §II. Reference may also be made to C. A. Pompe, *Aggressive War an International Crime* (The Hague, 1953); Robert W. Tucker, *The Just War: A Study in Contemporary American Doctrine* (Baltimore, 1960).

[163] See *The Three Friends,* U.S. Supreme Court, 1897 (166 U.S. 1); Quincy Wright, *A Study of War*, pp. 8, 12, 685.

these documents will precede analysis of the Charter of the United Nations.

§198. WAR UNDER THE LEAGUE COVENANT

War as a last recourse to settle international disputes by individual states had never been questioned until the establishment of the League of Nations, even though the Hague Conventions laid down certain requirements and limitations. Under the League Covenant, any war or threat of war was deemed a matter of concern to the whole League, which was required to take necessary action to safeguard international peace. Should any Member of the League resort to war in disregard of pacific means to solve international differences, it would be considered to have committed an act of war against all other Members of the League. Upon the failure of other forcible measures, the League might recommend that individual Members contribute armed forces for the enforcement of peace.[164] However, if the League Council should fail to reach an agreement for settling a dispute, the Members concerned might "reserve to themselves the right to take such action as they shall consider necessary for the maintenance of right and justice."[165] Thus, war by individual states was not entirely outlawed under the League system.

§199. THE GENERAL TREATY FOR THE RENUNCIATION OF WAR

The Kellogg-Briand Pact of 1928 went one step further in that the Signatories renounced war as an instrument of national policy in their relations with one another,[166] and agreed to settle all disputes by peaceful means. It did not, however, preclude war for self-defense or against a non-signatory to the Pact. Nor did it provide any sanctions to ensure the observance of treaty obligations. The Treaty did not prevent invasions by Japan, Italy, and Germany in the following years. The right of self-defense was often claimed by the aggressors to justify their military actions, but the findings of the Lytton Commission, the League Assembly and Council, and the International Tribunals at Nuremberg and Tokyo proved the contrary.

§200. WAR OR THE USE OF FORCE UNDER THE PROVISIONS OF THE CHARTER

For the prevention of war and the maintenance of peace, the United Nations Charter requires Members to refrain from the use or threat of force; the Security Council is to determine threats to and

[164] See Arts. 11, 16, of the Covenant.

[165] Art. 15(7) of the Covenant.

[166] Art. 1 of the Pact.

breaches of peace or acts of aggression. Whenever the Security Council so determines and is unable to restore peace by 'provisional measures,' it must recommend or decide effective collective measures for enforcement action.[167] Thus, war as a means for settling international disputes by individual Members or even regional arrangements and agencies is not permitted under the United Nations system, except for self-defense to repel an armed attack and subject to conditions stipulated in the Charter.[168] Soviet authorities and legal experts have persistently advocated so-called national-liberation wars as just and sacred. They have at times suggested it was their duty to intervene on the Communist side in a civil strife. On the other hand, the United States has declared a policy of intervention on the non-Communist side to 'contain Communism.' Under such conditions, it is probable that civil strife between Communist and anti-Communist factions may extend to international war. If these policies are carried out without restraint, they can hardly be reconciled with the provisions of the Charter and the principle of coexistence.[169]

The Security Council is the proper authority to determine whether a war or the use of force is for self-defense or for aggression. Consequently, the United Nations is the only organ which has the power to recommend or decide the use of force as an enforcement measure.[170] It is doubtful, however, whether a non-member is bound by the provisions of the Charter, to which it is not a signatory.[171] In reply to an appeal from the Secretary-General of the United Nations to comply with economic sanctions against Rhodesia, the Swiss government stated on February 13, 1967, that, as a neutral state and a non-member of the United Nations, Switzerland could not agree to mandatory sanctions

[167] See Arts. 1(1), 39, of the Charter.

[168] See Art. 51 and Ch. VIII of the Charter. See also Arts. 1, 3(e), 6, of the Inter-American Treaty of Reciprocal Assistance of 1947, and Arts. 1, 3, 5, of the North Atlantic Treaty of 1949. By its resolution 2160 (XXI) of November 30, 1966, the General Assembly reminded all Members of their duty to observe strictly the prohibition of the threat or use of force in international relations.

[169] In the opinion of an expert on Soviet affairs, "if the United Nations is to mean anything, it can tolerate no differential standards for judging cases of outbreaks of international violence; and violence by ex-colonies against imperial nations is qualitatively indistinguishable from any other type of violence and therefore prohibited." George Ginsburg, " 'Wars of National Liberation' and the Modern Law of Nations—the Soviet Thesis," 29 *Law and Contemporary Problems* (1964), pp. 931–932.

[170] See Arts. 39, 42, of the Charter.

[171] Art. 2(6) of the Charter declares that non-members must observe the principles of the Charter "so far as necessary for the maintenance of international peace and security."

enforced by the Security Council since December 1966.[172] Furthermore, individual or collective sanctions through military action may also be taken against ex-enemy states of World War II.[173] Sometimes armed conflicts between individual states have occurred without being stopped by the United Nations, because of exercise of the veto by a permanent member of the Security Council or lack of majority vote in the Security Council or the General Assembly. Under these circumstances, war as a last resort to settle international disputes is still in practice whether it is called 'use of force' or any other term.

When North Korea attacked South Korea in June 1950, the Security Council condemned the action as a breach of peace and called for the immediate cessation of hostilities.[174] Then, by a resolution adopted on June 27, it recommended that members of the United Nations furnish necessary assistance to the Republic of Korea to repel the armed attack. Confronted with this grave situation, which was further complicated by the eventual intervention of Communist China,[175] the United Nations applied collective sanctions against the invaders by armed forces constituted by national contingents under a unified United Nations Command. The Korean conflict was a war in the material sense; it was not ended until the signing of the Armistice Agreement on July 27, 1953. This is a unique instance of collective sanction by armed force by the United Nations.

The peace-keeping operations of the United Nations in the Middle East and the Congo were not intended to wage war against the disputing parties, but to maintain or restore peace in these areas.[176] Other armed conflicts, for example, in Indochina in 1947–1954, the Suez Canal Zone in 1956, and the present conflict in Vietnam, are wars in the material sense.[177] Whatever the designation, the use of force without the authority of the United Nations is not in conformity with the letter and spirit of the Charter.

[172] See *The New York Times*, February 14, 1967.

[173] See Arts. 53, 107, of the Charter.

[174] By a resolution adopted by the Security Council on June 25, 1950.

[175] The Chinese forces used the designation 'Chinese People's Volunteers,' as distinguished from the regular army of the People's Republic of China.

[176] For further discussion on the subject, see Inis L. Claude, Jr., "The United Nations and the Use of Force," *International Conciliation* (March 1961), No. 532. See also A. E. Hindmarsh, *Force in Peace* (Cambridge, 1933).

[177] With respect to the hostilities in the Suez Canal Zone, the Lord Privy Seal of Great Britain interestingly commented, on November 1, 1956, that "there is no state of war, but there is a state of conflict." Starke, p. 394. Of course, in view of the circumstances of these conflicts, none can be called war in the legal sense.

C H A P T E R 1 4

WAR OR THE USE OF FORCE UNDER TRADITIONAL INTERNATIONAL LAW

I. *SOURCES OF THE TRADITIONAL LAWS OF WAR* [1]

§201. HISTORICAL DEVELOPMENT

War in the material sense is still in existence, whether it is called 'use of force,' 'armed conflict,' or 'hostilities'; it cannot be eliminated merely by avoiding the use of the term.[2] Although war in the legal sense

[1] General texts on the subject: Oppenheim, II, §§61–69a, 176–179, 214a–214c; Fenwick, *Principles,* Ch. XXX, §A; Hershey, pp. 545–556; Moore, *Digest,* II, §1164; Schwarzenberger, I, Ch. 7 (VI); Von Glahn, pp. 542–549, 581–585, 592–594, 602–604; Jacobini, pp. 230–232; Soviet *Text,* pp. 405–415, 436–442.

[2] See *supra,* §200. For the concept of permissible and impermissible resort to coercion, see McDougal and Feliciano, *Law and Minimum World Public Order,* pp. 143–260. For causes and controls of war, see Arthur L. Goodhart, "International Law and the Causes of War," 28 *Grotius Society* (1943), pp. 65–82; Julius Stone, *Legal Controls of International Conflict,* rev. ed. (London, 1959); Quincy Wright, *The Role of International Law in the Elimination of War* (Manchester, 1961). Some different approaches may be found in Ian Brownlie, *International Law and the Use of Force by States* (New York, 1963).

is outlawed under the United Nations system, many rules of traditional laws of war and neutrality will still apply where a belligerent treats hostilities as war in its own legislation.[3] The effective conduct of war, with due consideration of humanity, has been the basis of customary rules and regulations governing the rights and duties of belligerents and neutrals.[4]

Since the conclusion of the Thirty Years' War (1618–1648), usage and practice in the conduct of hostilities have gradually developed into procedural laws of war. The Declaration of Paris of 1856 for the regulation of maritime warfare marked the beginning of positive enactment through international conferences in the form of multilateral instruments.[5] Initiated by the Tsar of Russia, the two Hague Peace Conferences of 1899 and 1907 produced a series of conventions, regulations, and declarations, concerning opening of hostilities, laws of land and sea warfare, and rights and duties of neutrals.[6]

§202. LEGAL PROVISIONS ON INSTRUMENTS OF WARFARE

Though antiquated in the nuclear age, there are a number of conventions and declarations regulating instruments of warfare. The Declaration of St. Petersburg of 1868 prohibiting the use in war of certain projectiles was followed by the Hague Declarations, the signatories of which were to abstain from the use of expanding (dumdum) bullets, projectiles for the diffusion of asphyxiating or deleterious gases, and

[3] Because of this, the present tense is generally used here in describing laws of war and neutrality. It is understood that, with the exception of those for humanitarian purposes, many rules and regulations cannot possibly apply to United Nations enforcement action and to hostilities between aggressors and defenders on a basis of equality. See Report of Committee on Study of Legal Problems of the United Nations, "Should the Law of War Apply to United Nations Enforcement Action," Falk & Mendlovitz, III, p. 71. See also D. W. Bowett, *United Nations Forces: A Legal Study* (New York, 1964), pp. 484–516.

[4] On the relationship between war and international law, L. Oppenheim observed: "War is a fact recognized, but not established, by International Law." Oppenheim, II, p. 202.

[5] For details, see Francis R. Stark, *The Abolition of Privateering and the Declaration of Paris* (New York, 1897).

[6] Perhaps the Instructions for the Government of Armies of the United States in the Field of 1863 represented the first effort to codify and develop laws of war. For details of the Hague Conventions and commentaries, see A. P. Higgins, *The Hague Peace Conferences and Other International Conferences concerning the Laws and Usages of War* (Cambridge, England, 1909); J. B. Scott, *The Reports to the Hague Conferences of 1899 and 1907* (Oxford, 1917).

projectiles or explosives from balloons or other kinds of aircraft. There are also the Hague Convention of 1907 relating to the laying of automatic submarine contact mines; the Geneva Protocol of 1925 regulating the use of asphyxiating, poisonous, or other gases, and of all analogous liquids, materials, or other devices; and the London Protocol of 1936 concerning the use of submarines against merchant vessels.

§203. OTHER CONVENTIONS AND THEIR EFFECTIVENESS

For the amelioration of the condition of wounded soldiers, the Geneva Conventions of 1864 and 1906 were concluded for land warfare and later adapted for maritime warfare. In 1929, another convention was signed at Geneva concerning the treatment of sick and wounded and of prisoners of war. These conventions were replaced, as between the contracting parties, by a 1949 Geneva Convention for the Amelioration of the Condition of the Wounded and Sick in the Armed Forces in the Field, which was adopted together with three more conventions at the Geneva Conference, held from April 21 to August 12, 1949. The other three deal with treatment of prisoners of war, protection of civilian persons, and replacement of Hague Convention X as between the contracting parties, on amelioration of the condition of wounded, sick, and shipwrecked members of armed forces at sea. For the protection of cultural monuments in wartime, a special convention was signed at The Hague on May 14, 1954.[7]

A weakness of some of the Hague Conventions was the inclusion of the so-called 'general participation clause,' which stipulates that their binding force depends on whether the belligerents are signatories. However, most of the rules of warfare are merely declaratory of existing international law and are thus binding upon all states. This was also the position held by the International Military Tribunal in 1946.[8] During the two world wars, accusations of violations were made by belligerents on both sides, but most of the rules of warfare were observed except for urgent military necessity.[9] The misconception that

[7] For further details on the sources of the laws of war, see Oppenheim, II, pp. 226–236.

[8] Among other reasons, the Tribunal stated that "by 1939 these rules laid down in the Convention [on land warfare] were recognized by all civilized nations and were regarded as being declaratory of the laws and customs of war. . . ." Thus, the Tribunal ruled that the Convention was fully applicable to Czechoslovakia, which was not a party to it. Judgment of the Nuremberg International Tribunal, Cmd. 6964, p. 125.

[9] An exhaustive study of practice of the laws of war during World War I can be found in James W. Garner, *International Law and the World War* (London & New York, 1920). For war in general, consult Quincy Wright, *A Study of War* (Chicago, 1942; 2nd ed., 1965).

necessity knows no law is legally untenable and practically dangerous to all belligerents and neutrals.

There is no specific convention prohibiting the dropping of atomic bombs as the United States did on Hiroshima and Nagasaki near the end of World War II, but mass annihilation of civilians and wanton destruction of non-military objectives are in violation of other international conventions and customary rules of international law.[10] The Test Ban Treaty of October 6, 1963, which has not yet been adhered to by France and the People's Republic of China, only limits the means of tests.[11] It is imperative to conclude a multilateral treaty that prohibits the use of all nuclear and thermonuclear weapons as well as intercontinental ballistic missiles, which pose a major threat to civilians and undefended towns. Such a treaty should be initiated either by the nuclear powers or under the auspices of the United Nations.[12]

Question has been raised as to whether rules of warfare are applicable to 'armed conflict,' which is not under the designation of 'war.' The answer is in the affirmative in accordance with general practice and express statement in the Geneva Convention of 1949, even though there may be some divergencies in the effects of war. During the period of Korean hostilities, 1950–1953, both governments in Korea and the United Nations Command declared their intention to observe the laws of war.[13]

---

[10] Since atomic bombs contain poisonous substance, their use constitutes a violation of the Declaration of St. Petersburg of 1868 and the Geneva Protocol of 1925, in addition to Art. 23(a, e) of the Hague Regulations and other provisions relating to non-combatants and non-military objectives. The resolution unanimously adopted by the League Assembly in 1938 to limit air strikes to military objectives and avoid the civilian population reflected the general sentiment of the nations at the time toward air warfare. For further discussion on the legality of the use of nuclear weapons, see Georg Schwarzenberger, *The Legality of Nuclear Weapons* (London, 1958); Nagendra Singh, *Nuclear Weapons and International Law* (New York, 1959), particularly Pt. III; Richard A. Falk, "The Shimoda Case: A Legal Appraisal of the Atomic Attacks upon Hiroshima and Nagasaki," 59 *Am. Jour. Int. Law* (1965), pp. 759–793.

[11] For the text of the Treaty, see Department of State *Bulletin*, August 12, 1963, p. 239.

[12] On October 17, 1963, the General Assembly unanimously adopted a resolution prohibiting the placement of nuclear weapons in space vehicles. Much talk has been going on both in and outside the United Nations about the conclusion of a treaty to ban all nuclear weapons tests.

[13] 'Armed conflict' is used in the Geneva Conventions of 1949 and the Vienna Convention on Diplomatic Relations of 1961. See also 9 United Nations *Bulletin* (1950), p. 101; Starke, p. 398.

II. *THE COMMENCEMENT OF WAR*[14]

§204. THE HAGUE CONVENTION ON DECLARATION OF WAR

Commencement of hostilities has often been preceded by a declaration of war. The Hague Convention on Opening of Hostilities of 1907 required the contracting powers not to commence hostilities "without previous and explicit warning, in the form either of a reasoned declaration of war or of an ultimatum with conditional declaration of war."[15] Belligerents were obliged immediately to notify neutral powers of the existence of a state of war, but the latter could not rely on the absence of this communication if they had already been aware of the actual situation.[16] These provisions become obsolete after the conclusion of international treaties outlawing war.

§205. OUTBREAK OF WAR PRIOR TO DECLARATION

International practice does not always follow the Hague stipulation concerning the necessity of a declaration of war, chiefly in order to gain military advantages. There are many instances of the existence of war prior to declaration: Japan's attack on China in 1894 and on Russia in 1904, Italy's military operations against Ethiopia in 1935, and Germany's invasion of Poland in 1939 and the Soviet Union in 1941. Throughout the Sino-Japanese hostilities beginning on July 7, 1937, Japan never declared war, even though China did on December 9, 1941. It was war in the material sense, but Japan chose not to use the term through the omission of a declaration in order to avoid legal implications involving violation of treaty obligations.[17] Another reason

[14] General texts on the subject: Oppenheim, II, §§93–96; Fenwick, *Principles,* Ch. XXIX, §A; Hyde, III, §§602–604; Moore, *Digest,* VII, §§1106–1108; Hackworth, *Digest,* VI, §563; Hershey, pp. 559–562; Von Glahn, pp. 561–565; Soviet *Text,* pp. 419–420.

[15] Art. I of the Hague Convention. This Convention, adopted on October 18, 1907, was designed to prevent sudden attacks, such as that of the Japanese navy on Russian warships in Port Arthur in 1904.

[16] Art. 2 of the same Convention.

[17] Japan's invasion of China violated several treaties to which Japan was a party, including the Nine-Power Treaty of 1922, the League Covenant, and the Kellogg-Briand Pact. In *Kawasaki Kisen Kabushiki Kaisha of Kobe v. Banthan Steamship Co., Ltd.,* the British Court of Appeal decided, in 1939, that a state of war between China and Japan existed within the meaning of the charterparty despite the fact that the British government

was to induce third states not to enforce restrictions on export of war materials to Japan, because neutral rights and duties would be invoked in a state of war.[18] Which branch of government has the power to declare war is not the concern of international law, but is within the constitutional provisions of each state.[19] Thus war is an existing fact, with or without declaration.[20] In several instances, war was declared without the actual use of force.[21]

III. *EFFECTS OF WAR* [22]

§206. EFFECT ON DIPLOMATIC AND CONSULAR RELATIONS

War has vital effects on belligerents and neutrals. Although Anglo-Saxon and Continental practices have certain divergencies, general

---

considered the prevailing situation as indeterminate and anomalous. The Court rightly stated that "war may break out without His Majesty's Government recognizing it." [1939] 2 K.B. 544.

[18] On the status of belligerency in a civil war in *The Prize Cases* in 1862, the U.S. Supreme Court pointed out that "the condition of neutrality cannot exist unless there be two belligerent parties." 2 Black 635. The principle applies equally to a foreign war, whose existence justifies the proclamation of neutrality by third states. On civil war, see also James N. Rosenau (ed.), *International Aspects of Civil Strife* (Princeton, 1964).

[19] In *Western Reserve Life Insurance Co. v. Meadows,* the Supreme Court of Texas clarified this point, in 1953, as follows: "Congress alone may have power to 'declare' it [war] beforehand, and thus cause or commence it. But it may be initiated by other nations, or by traitors; and then it exists, whether there is any declaration of it or not. It may be prosecuted without any declaration; or Congress may, as in the Mexican war, declare its previous existence. In either case it is the fact that makes 'enemies,' and not any legislative Act. (*Dole v. Merchants' Mutual Marine Ins. Co.,* 51 Me. 465, 470.)" 261 S.W. (2d) 554. The Court ruled that there was war in Korea. See also *Rosenau et al. v. Idaho Mutual Benefit Ass'n,* U.S. Superior Court of Idaho, 1944. 65 Idaho 408, 145 P.(2d) 227.

[20] In *Louise C. Bennion v. New York Life Insurance Co.,* the U.S. Circuit Court of Appeal (10th District) ruled, in 1946, that the commencement of war with Japan dated back to the time of Japan's attack on Pearl Harbor. 41 *Am. Jour. Int. Law* (1947), pp. 680–689.

[21] *E.g.,* China's declaration of war against Germany during World War I, and several Latin-American states' against Germany during World War II.

[22] General texts on the subject: O'Connell, II, pp. 844–867; Oppenheim, II, §§93–102c; Hyde, III, §§605–637A; Schwarzenberger, I, Ch. 7

principles are basically the same. As a rule, diplomatic and consular relations are terminated. Whether diplomatic and consular officers are permitted to leave the country depends upon the circumstances and national policies of the belligerents. Diplomatic missions of some neutral countries are usually requested to protect the interests and archives of the belligerents.[23]

§207. EFFECT ON TREATIES

With the outbreak of war, treaty relationships between belligerents are immediately changed. International instruments concerning laws of war and neutrality, such as the Hague and Geneva conventions, come into actual application; while executory treaties, including political alliance, commerce, and navigation, are abrogated. Executed treaties recognizing independence and boundaries, as well as many multilateral treaties, are suspended for the duration of the war, but may be revived after the restoration of peace. In general, treaties become inoperative only when necessary.[24]

§208. EFFECT ON ENEMY ALIENS

Treatment of enemy aliens within a belligerent's territory is determined by their attitude and the belligerent's national interests. They may be allowed to leave the belligerent's territory or to remain at liberty, or be interned for the duration of the war. Practices varied during the two world wars.[25] In view of past abuses, the 1949 Geneva Convention provides extensive safeguards for enemy nationals.[26]

The former practice of preventing enemy aliens from taking or

---

(V); Moore, *Digest,* VII, §§1135–1142; Hackworth, *Digest,* VI, §§583–586, 589; Hershey, pp. 563–574; Starke, Ch. 16, §§1–2; Svarlien, Ch. 21; Von Glahn, pp. 549–551, 565–573; Jacobini, pp. 235–240; Soviet *Text,* pp. 420–421.

[23] See *supra,* Ch. 9, *passim.*

[24] See *Techt v. Hughes,* United States, Court of Appeals, 1920. 229 N.Y. 222. For further reference on the subject, see Stuart H. McIntyre, *Legal Effect of World War II on Treaties of the United States* (The Hague, 1958). See also *supra,* Ch. 11, *passim.*

[25] During World War I, belligerents allowed enemy nationals to remain in their territories. General internment was practiced in Germany, Austria-Hungary, France, and Great Britain. On entering World War II, the United States reversed her previous policy by interning not only a large number of aliens but also American nationals of Japanese descent, in flat violation of their constitutional rights.

[26] See Oppenheim, II, pp. 313–317.

defending proceedings in the court of the belligerent has been gradually discontinued, but has not yet vanished. In *Wells v. Williams,* a British court decided that an enemy alien residing in Great Britain could maintain an action in court.[27] The United States Supreme Court upheld the same principle in *Ex Parte Kumezo Kawato* in 1942.[28] However, enemy aliens not residing in England could neither sue nor be sued in an English court for the duration of the war.[29]

The right to sue of a corporation with its principal business at a place under enemy control is more complicated. In *Sovfracht v. Van Uden's Scheepvaart en Agentur Maatschappij,* the British House of Lords differed from the Court of Appeal and affirmed this right in 1943.[30] International lawyers, especially Continental writers, consider the effect of trading and contracts between nationals and belligerents to be within the competence of municipal laws of states. Except for special permission, traditional Anglo-American practice has been inclined to prohibit all intercourse and to treat contractual obligations as void or abrogated.[31] The enforcement of such regulations is bound to produce harsh effects. Unless dictated by military necessity, some relaxation is perhaps desirable.

§209. EFFECT ON PRIVATE ENEMY PROPERTY AND DEBTS

In spite of violations during the two world wars, modern customary law prohibits confiscation of enemy private property or debts due to enemy aliens.[32] In *Haw Pia v. China Banking Corporation,* the Supreme

[27] Great Britain, Court of King's Bench, 1697. 1 L. Raym. 282.

[28] 317 U.S. 69.

[29] See *Porter v. Freudenberg,* Great Britain, Court of Appeal, 1915. [1915] 1 K.B. 857.

[30] [1943] A.C. 203.

[31] For Anglo-American practice, see *The Hoop,* Great Britain, High Court of Admiralty, 1799 (1 C. Rob. 196); *The Rapid,* U.S. Supreme Court, 1814 (8 Cranch 155). Dissolution, as a result of war, of business partnership with enemy nationals was the ruling in *Nathaniel L. Griswold, etc. v. Joshua Waddington,* New York, Court of Errors, 1819 (16 Johnson 438); *Sutherland v. Mayer,* U.S. Supreme Court, 1926 (271 U.S. 272). In the latter case, the Court also ruled that the right of partners to an accounting was only suspended during the war. In *New York Life Insurance Co. v. Statham,* the U.S. Supreme Court held, in 1876, that insurance policies would lapse after outbreak of war if payment of premiums were discontinued. 93 U.S. 24. The right of inheritance by enemy nationals was not affected by war in accordance with the decision in *Clark v. Allen,* U.S. Supreme Court, 1947. 331 U.S. 503.

[32] See *In re Ferdinand, Ex-Tsar of Bulgaria,* Great Britain, Court of Appeal, 1920. [1921] 1 Ch. 107. In *Hanger v. Abbott,* the U.S. Supreme

Court of the Philippines ruled in 1948 that "such sequestration or seizure of properties is not an act for the confiscation of enemy property, but for the conservation of it, subject to further disposition by treaty between the belligerents at the end of the war." [33] Confiscation of enemy merchantmen in harbors of a belligerent by imposing an embargo was practiced in the past, but is not permitted by modern international law.[34] The trend seems to be in accord with the practice followed during the Crimean War by giving certain days of grace for their departure. The same principle will probably be applied to enemy civil airplanes, unless new rules of air warfare stipulate otherwise. It should be noted that enemy public property in a belligerent's territory is not exempt from confiscation, except possibly the premises owned by an enemy belligerent for the use of its diplomatic mission prior to the war.[35]

IV. *THE ENEMY CHARACTER* [36]

§210. ENEMY TERRITORY AND THE REGION OR THEATER OF WAR

A distinction should be made between enemy territory and the region or theater of war. The land, sea, and air domains under the

---

Court held in 1867 that belligerents could not confiscate debts owed to enemy aliens and that war merely suspended the collection of debts. 6 Wallace 532. After examining citations of Grotius, Vattel, Pufendorf, and others, in *Wolff v. Oxholm,* the British Court of King's Bench concluded in 1817 that confiscation of debts had never been generally recognized. 6 Maule & Selwyn 92. However, in an earlier case, the U.S. Supreme Court held that non-confiscation of property and debts was a matter of expediency, not of law, but that goods were not actually confiscated until declared so by an act of Congress. See *Brown v. United States,* 1814. 8 Cranch 110.

[33] 23 Phil. L.J. 575 (1949).

[34] The principle of non-confiscation is laid down in Arts. 2, 3, of Hague Convention VI of 1907. It is now general practice to allow a reasonable time for the departure of enemy private vessels.

[35] On enemy property, see Almá Latifi, *Effects of War on Property, Being Studies in International Law and Policy* (London, 1909). For effects of war in general, consult Lord McNair and A. D. Watts, *The Legal Effects of War* (Cambridge, England, 1967).

[36] General texts on the subject: Oppenheim, II, §§70–92; Fenwick, *Principles,* Ch. XXIX, §B; Hyde, III, §§648–654, 703-708, 783–796A; Hershey, pp. 577–579, 651–657; Moore, *Digest,* VII, §§1109–1110, 1183–1194; Hackworth, *Digest,* VI, §§599–609; Von Glahn, pp. 552–560; Soviet *Text,* pp. 421–424; Jacobini, pp. 247–248.

jurisdiction of an enemy belligerent are within the sphere of enemy territory. Whereas the region of war may extend far beyond enemy territory to the high seas and airspace above it, the theater of war designates only the area where hostilities are actually conducted.[37] Sometimes a war was waged in the territory of a neutral country without its consent in violation of the law of neutrality. This happened during the Russo-Japanese War in 1904–1905, when the belligerents carried out military operations in Korea and China's Manchuria in disregard of the territorial sovereignty of the neutrals. Germany's invasion of Belgium and Luxemburg in 1914 created world indignation, especially because their status of permanent neutrality had been guaranteed by the great powers.[38]

§211. ENEMY FORCES

Whereas the composition of the armed forces of a belligerent is essentially a matter of domestic discretion, all component units are required to observe the rules of warfare. In addition to army, navy, and air force, many states include militia and volunteers as regular armed forces. Under different designations, such as guerrillas, partisans, and underground resistance groups, they took an active part in military operations of certain Allied countries against the Axis Powers during World War II.[39]

Under the Hague Regulations of 1907 and the Geneva Convention of 1949, irregular forces are entitled to the same legitimate character as regular forces provided that they fulfill the following conditions: (1) being headed by a responsible commander, (2) wearing a fixed distinctive emblem, (3) carrying arms openly, and (4) conducting their operations in accordance with the laws and customs of warfare.[40] There is no question about the first of the four requirements, but the other three would put irregular forces at considerable disadvantage. In

[37] During the two world wars, Germany and Great Britain declared extensive areas in the open sea as war zones at the expense of neutral rights and the principle of freedom of the seas.

[38] For the status of neutralized states, see *supra*, §21. In 1940, Germany invaded Denmark and the Netherlands, both of which were neutrals during the early part of World War II.

[39] These irregular forces were very active in the Soviet Union and Yugoslavia. There was a strong resistance movement in France and the Netherlands against the enemy occupation.

[40] See Art. 1 of the Hague Regulations respecting the Laws and Customs of War on Land; Art. 4 of the Third Geneva Convention of 1949 on Treatment of Prisoners of War.

view of changing tactics of modern warfare, the legitimate character of certain measures of concealment by irregular forces should be granted. During the Korean War, the Chinese volunteers were recognized by the United Nations Command as regular forces of the People's Republic of China.

§212. COMBATANTS AND NON-COMBATANTS

All members of the armed forces are combatants, with the exception of doctors, nurses, chaplains, ambulance drivers, and the like. If captured, they will be treated as prisoners of war in accordance with the Hague Regulations of 1907 and the Geneva Convention of 1949.[41] The same right is extended to members of irregular forces unless they violate the conditions required by the laws and customs of warfare. In this connection, modern guerrilla warfare has definitely complicated the situation.

Inhabitants in areas under enemy occupation have to obey the laws enforced by the invading belligerent.[42] Any violent resistance, whether by individuals or in a levy *en masse,* is subject to severe punishment. Otherwise, civilian persons should be duly protected in wartime under rules and customs of warfare, especially the Geneva Convention of 1949. Although every civilian is a potential combatant in a modern war, distinction must be drawn between combatants and the civilian population by the belligerents.[43]

§213. ENEMY VESSELS AND GOODS

The enemy character of vessels and goods has been one of the most controversial subjects in wartime, and has often constituted a

[41] Prisoners of war must be humanely treated. It is specifically forbidden to kill or wound a surrendered enemy or to declare that no quarter will be given. The Hague Regulations of 1907 and the Geneva Convention of 1949 have detailed provisions on captivity. For a brief analysis, see Oppenheim, II, pp. 366–396. Prisoners of war must observe certain standards of discipline to maintain their status. See *Rex v. Brosig,* Canada, Ontario Court of Appeal, 1945. 2 D.L.R. 232.

[42] In *United States v. Rice,* the U.S. Supreme Court stated, in 1819, that "by surrender [of Castine], the inhabitants passed under a temporary allegiance to the British government and were bound by such laws, and such only, as it chose to recognize and impose." 4 Wheaton 246. In *Vicente Hilado v. Felix de la Costa and Philippine National Bank,* the Philippine Supreme Court held the same view in 1949. 46 *Official Gazette* 5472 (1950).

[43] Soviet writers strongly support this distinction. Meanwhile, they favor the recruitment of irregular forces. See Soviet *Text,* pp. 423–426.

serious issue between belligerents and neutrals. Generally, the flag of a vessel is the determining factor of her enemy character.[44] Such enemy character may also be attributed to a neutral vessel if it directly participates in hostilities, renders services to the enemy, or resists by force a belligerent's demand for visit and search. The so-called British rule of 1756 conferred enemy character on a neutral vessel engaging in a trade originally reserved by an enemy belligerent to its own vessels. Support by some maritime powers notwithstanding, this unilateral rule has never been universally accepted.

There were divergent views between Great Britain and Germany concerning the status of converted merchantmen during the two world wars. While Germany considered them as part of the regular navy, Great Britain refused to recognize the right of conversion on the high seas. Another problem in connection with captured enemy merchantmen was the status of the crew, who have generally been interned by the belligerents in recent wars.[45]

In spite of divergent practices, there are generally two guiding rules to determine the enemy character of goods: (1) being found on enemy vessels, and (2) belonging to enemy owners.[46] While the United States concluded several treaties at the turn of the nineteenth century to establish the rule of 'free ships, free goods' for the protection of her national interests as a neutral country, Chief Justice Marshall declared that "the goods of an enemy found in the vessel of a friend are prizes of war, and . . . the goods of a friend found in the vessel of an enemy are to be restored." [47] British practice is that neutral goods on enemy vessels or neutral goods on neutral vessels for delivery to any enemy belligerent are liable to forfeiture.[48]

[44] See *The Unitas,* Great Britain, Privy Council (in Prize), 1950. 2 All Eng. L.R. 219.

[45] See Arts. 2–5 of Hague Convention XI, adopted at the Second Hague Peace Conference in 1907. With respect to enemy merchant ships under Art. 1, Clause 1, and Art. 2 of Hague Convention VI, the High Prize Court of China ruled in *The Albenga No. 3* and *The Fortuna* in 1918 that an enemy merchant ship that ceased trade and took refuge in a port in order to escape capture by a belligerent could not be privileged under that Convention. *Judgment of the High Prize Court* (1919), pp. 25, 68; Tung, pp. 296, 242.

[46] In *The Venus,* the U.S. Supreme Court ruled, in 1814, that where a national of one belligerent was domiciled in another, the domicile should determine the national character of the goods. 8 Cranch 253. According to the practice of several European states, the nationality of the owner determines the character of the goods, no matter where the owner may reside.

[47] *The Nereide,* U.S. Supreme Court, 1815. 9 Cranch 388.

[48] See *The Sally,* Great Britain, the Lords Commissioners of Appeals, 1795. 3 C. Rob. 300.

§214. ENEMY NATIONALS AND CORPORATIONS

As a general rule, nationality is the common standard for ascertaining the enemy character of individuals. Although there is no rule of international law governing the status of a corporation, the place of its incorporation usually determines its enemy character.[49] This traditional principle was modified by the British House of Lords in 1916 in *Daimler Co., Ltd. v. Continental Tyre and Rubber Co., Ltd.* In this case, the court held that a corporation would obtain enemy character "if its agents or the persons in *de facto* control of its affairs are resident in an enemy country, or, wherever resident, are adhering to the enemy or taking instructions from or acting under the control of enemies." [50]

Perhaps the most complicated case concerning an enemy-dominated neutral corporation in recent years is the *Interhandel Case.* The Société internationale (Interhandel) was registered in Switzerland in 1928, on the initiative of I. G. Farbenindustrie of Frankfurt, Germany. The corporation owned some 90 percent of the shares of the General Aniline and Film Corporation (GAF) in the United States. In 1942, the United States government seized the assets of GAF on the ground that the shares were the property of Farbenindustrie or were held for that enemy alien. The seized assets were vested in the Office of Alien Property. The case was brought to the United States Supreme Court in 1952.[51] It was submitted by Switzerland in 1957 to the International Court of Justice, which ruled that the Swiss application was inadmissible because Interhandel had not yet exhausted local remedies available in the courts of the United States.[52] The controversy was eventually settled through direct negotiation by the parties concerned.[53]

[49] See *Janson v. Driefontein Consolidated Mines,* Great Britain, House of Lords, 1902. [1902] A.C. 484.

[50] [1916] 2 A.C. 307. This principle was also applied to *Sovfracht v. Van Uden's Scheepvarrt en Agentur Maatschappij,* Great Britain, House of Lords, 1942. [1943] A.C. 203.

[51] See *Kaufman v. Société internationale,* U.S. Supreme Court, 1952. 343 U.S. 156.

[52] *Interhandel (Preliminary Objections) Case,* International Court of Justice, 1959. I.C.J. Reports (1959), 6.

[53] In 1963, the United States government and the Interhandel agreed on an out-of-court settlement by selling the assets of GAF to private enterprise and distributing the proceeds between them on a 70–30 basis, respectively. For further information on the settlement, see *The New York Times,* April 16, 1964.

V. *ILLEGITIMATE AND PERMISSIBLE MEANS OF WARFARE*[54]

§215. PROHIBITION OF ILLEGITIMATE WARFARE

In war under traditional international law, there is no substitute for victory. Thus, every legitimate weapon and means may be used to subdue the enemy on land, in air, and at sea. The major objectives of the armed forces are to annihilate enemy combatants, occupy enemy territory, destroy enemy navy and aircraft, and bombard enemy fortifications and other military objectives. But the right of the belligerents in this respect is not unlimited. On the contrary, their conduct of warfare is governed by the Hague Conventions and Regulations, other international instruments, and customary rules of international law.[55] These regulations and limitations for humanitarian purposes still apply to all hostilities and remain valid under both traditional international law and the United Nations system.

According to the Hague Regulations, certain methods of warfare are declared to be illegitimate and are especially forbidden: (1) employing poison or poisoned weapons; (2) killing or wounding treacherously individuals of the hostile nation or army; (3) killing or wounding an enemy who, having laid down his arms, or no longer having means of defense, has surrendered at discretion; (4) declaring that no quarter will be given; (5) employing arms, projectiles, or material

[54] General texts on the subject: Oppenheim, II, §§103–117, 155–165, 173–191, 201–203, 210–211, 214–214h, 215–230; Fenwick, *Principles*, Chs. XXIX, §§C–D,G; XXX; Hyde, III, §§638–647A, 655–667, 710–751B; Moore, *Digest*, VII, §§1111–1126, 1157–1162, 1166–1176; Hackworth, *Digest*, VI, §§564–575, 591–598; Starke, Ch. 16, §3; Hershey, pp. 592–605, 626–647; Von Glahn, pp. 585–592, 604–618, 696–702; Schwarzenberger, I, Ch. 7(VII–X); Jacobini, pp. 255–264; Soviet *Text*, pp. 415–418, 424–427, 430–431, 441–442; Grotius, II, Bk. 1, Chs. 1–5; Bk. 2, Chs. 1, 22–25; Bk. 3, Chs. 13–24; Vattel, III, Bk. 3; Manning, pp. 131–133; Lawrence, §§135–180, 195–217; Le Fur, §§880–929, 956–960, 990–996; Westlake, *Chapters*, pp. 264–273; Holland, *War*, §16.

[55] See Hall, §17; Art. 22 of the Hague Regulations. In view of the intensification of the Vietnam war, the International Red Cross issued a seven-point statement on May 19, 1967. It appealed to all belligerents to assure proper and humane treatment of prisoners of war, to avoid causing death or injury to civilians during all ground, air, and naval operations, and to conclude a cease-fire agreement with a view to ending the "intolerable burden of human misery" imposed upon the Vietnamese. See *The New York Times*, May 20, 1967.

calculated to cause unnecessary suffering; (6) making improper use of a flag of truce, of the national flag, or of the military insignia and uniform of the enemy, as well as the distinctive badges of the Geneva Convention; (7) destroying or seizing enemy property, unless such destruction or seizure be imperatively demanded by necessity of war; (8) declaring abolished, suspended, or inadmissible in a court of law the rights and actions of the nationals of the hostile party.[56] While these regulations deal chiefly with land warfare, they also apply to air and maritime warfare wherever appropriate.

Four rules are laid down by the Declaration of Paris of 1856: (1) privateering is abolished; (2) a neutral flag covers enemy goods with the exception of contraband of war; (3) neutral goods, contraband of war excepted, are not liable to capture under the enemy flag; (4) blockade, to be binding, must be effective. The Hague Conventions of 1907 regulate naval bombardment, enemy merchantmen and their conversion into warships, right of capture, and other aspects of maritime warfare.[57]

Several conventions and declarations prohibit the use of projectiles and explosives from balloons, expanding bullets, and projectiles diffusing asphyxiating or deleterious gases. Chemical and bacteriological warfare is prohibited by the Hague Regulations and the Geneva Protocol of 1925.[58] There are no provisions expressly prohibiting atomic bombs; but, judging by atomic bombing's devastating effects on civilians and non-military objectives, it is not in conformity with the customary rules of international law.[59] In spite of the lack of precise

[56] Art. 23. Among the international instruments regulating land warfare, the 1907 Hague Convention IV and its annexed Regulations are most comprehensive. In editing *International Law Opinions* (Cambridge, England, 1956), 3 vols., Lord McNair deemed it important to include documents concerning questions of war and neutrality, because, among other reasons, their "legal principles remain fundamentally the same" notwithstanding "the continued changes in weapons and modes of warfare." III, p. 3.

[57] For details, see Hague Conventions VI–IX, XI, on maritime warfare.

[58] Art. 23(a) of the Hague Regulations provides that "in addition to the prohibitions provided by the special conventions, it is particularly forbidden to employ poison or poisoned weapons."

[59] On nuclear weapons in relation to customary international law, treaty law, and the Geneva Conventions of 1949, see Nagendra Singh, *Nuclear Weapons and International Law* (New York, 1959). Soviet writers on international law and delegates to the United Nations have denounced the use of nuclear weapons even though the Soviet government has exerted every effort for their development. See Peter B. Maggs, "The Soviet Viewpoint on Nuclear Weapons in International Law," 29 *Law and Contemporary Problems* (Autumn 1964), pp. 956–970. The Soviet delegation has

rules, air warfare is also regulated by pertinent rules governing land and maritime warfare.[60] The Geneva Conventions are applicable to war in general, whether on land, at sea, or in the air.[61] The often-quoted statement that necessity knows no law is solely for self-justification of wrongful acts, entirely lacking in legal foundation.[62]

§216. ATTACK AND BOMBARDMENT FROM LAND, SEA, AND AIR

Attack and bombardment by army, navy, and air force are legitimate means of winning a war, but undefended towns, villages, dwellings, or buildings must be exempted.[63] Every effort must be exerted to spare buildings dedicated to religion, art, science, or charitable pur-

---

supported various resolutions adopted by the General Assembly against the use of nuclear weapons, such as 1653 (XVI), November 24, 1961, and 1884 (XVIII), October 17, 1963. On the other hand, Soviet leaders have spoken of possible use of nuclear weapons under compelling circumstances. By the Sino-Soviet Agreement of October 15, 1957, the Soviet government was committed to deliver models of atomic bombs to Communist China, but the transaction was not actually carried out. See *Peking Review*, August 16, 1963, p. 14.

[60] Before World War I, the only rules exclusively about air warfare were the 1899 Hague Declaration prohibiting launching of projectiles and explosives and the 1907 Hague Regulations (Art. 25 on sieges and bombardment, and Art. 29 on spies). The draft code of air warfare proposed by a Commission of Jurists at The Hague in 1923 and the resolution adopted by the General Commission of the Disarmament Conference in 1932 did not have binding force upon the states. See LN Doc. 1932.IX.63. However, all these proposals were merely declaratory of the customary rules of international law. Aerial bombardment was extensively carried out during World War II, causing considerable damages to property and heavy civilian casualties, in violation of pledges by belligerents on both sides at the beginning of the war. "Although the charge of indiscriminate bombing of the civilian population was included in the indictment of the German major war criminals before the International Military Tribunal at Nuremberg, no conviction was recorded on that score." Oppenheim, II, p. 529.

[61] For a systematic discussion of the methods and instruments of land and air warfare, see Morris Greenspan, *The Modern Law of Land Warfare* (Berkeley, 1959), Ch. IX.

[62] For the German justification of military necessity, see James W. Garner, *International Law and the World War*, II, §§439–440.

[63] Naval bombardment can be directed only against fortifications, but the town or port where fortifications are located may be inevitably attacked if the enemy refuses to surrender. Art. 3 of the 1907 Convention IX also permits bombardment of undefended towns which refuse requisitions imposed by the enemy force for its immediate use. There is, thus far, no specific rule concerning siege.

poses, historical monuments, hospitals, and places where sick and wounded are collected, provided they are not being used at the time for military purposes.[64] Pillage of any town or place is prohibited,[65] but requisitions and contributions may be collected under prescribed conditions.[66] Civilians are entitled to special protection by the Geneva Convention of 1949 and the customary rules of international law.[67] Though exposed to all risks of military operations, non-combatants must not be directly attacked or killed. Except in case of assault, the commander of the attacking force must do all in his power to warn the authorities before the commencement of bombardment.[68]

The above regulations may be applied to attacks and bombardment from the sea and the air. The wanton destruction caused by German V-1 and V-2 missiles, as well as continuous air bombing of England during World War II, was in violation of international law. The extensive air strikes by the United States in North and South Vietnam may be militarily expedient but legally questionable, even though the American government promises to reconstruct the country after the restoration of peace.[69]

Attack and seizure of enemy ships in maritime warfare has been further complicated by the increasing effectiveness of submarine and aircraft. Attack may be directed from land, air, and sea against enemy warships, and also against enemy merchantmen upon the latter's refusal to submit to visit and search.[70] If a merchantman of a belligerent

[64] See Arts. 25, 27, of the Hague Regulations; the Hague Convention of 1954 on the protection of cultural monuments in the event of war. The besieged has the duty to indicate the presence of specially exempted buildings or places by visible signs and to notify the enemy beforehand. See also Arts. 1, 5, of the 1907 Hague Convention IX on naval bombardment. Again, the belligerents failed to observe these stipulations in the two world wars.

[65] See Art. 28 of the Hague Regulations.

[66] See Arts. 49, 51, 52, of the Hague Regulations; Arts. 3, 4, of the 1907 Hague Convention IX.

[67] Persons directly connected with military operations cannot be treated as part of the 'civilian population.' See *Christian Damson v. Germany*, United States-Germany, Mixed Claims Commission, 1925. 19 *Am. Jour. Int. Law* (1925), 815.

[68] See Art. 26 of the Hague Regulations.

[69] In a speech at a luncheon at the United Nations Correspondents' Association on June 20, 1966, Secretary-General U Thant denounced the war in Vietnam as "one of the most barbarous" in history. See *The New York Times*, June 21, 1966.

[70] Whether an enemy civil aircraft should be subject to attack is a controversial problem. According to the Hague Rules, it is liable to be fired upon unless under specific circumstances as stipulated in Art. 33.

takes the initiative in attacking public or private vessels of an opposing belligerent, this is considered a piratical act and can be punished as such. Without provocation, a private merchantman is not subject to attack by shore batteries and aircraft.

Privateering was abolished by the Declaration of Paris of 1856, but submarine warfare has become a serious threat since World War I. Its legality and practice will be discussed in connection with the doctrine of the freedom of the seas.[71] Merchantmen with defensive armaments were subject to attack during the war, because the distinction between defensive and offensive armaments could hardly be made.[72] Quarter must be given to an enemy public ship which surrenders. In case of an enemy merchantman, the ship and goods should be disposed according to the adjudication of the prize court of the capturing belligerent.[73]

Laying of automatic submarine contact mines is prohibited by the Hague Convention.[74] In spite of this rule, the belligerents in recent wars deposited mines far beyond their coasts, and eventually declared extensive war zones filled with mines. The immunity of certain ships not used for military purposes is either provided for by special conventions or is in accordance with customary rules of international law.[75] Belligerents are forbidden to launch attacks on ships used for religious, scientific, and philanthropic purposes, hospital ships,[76] cartel ships, and small vessels in fishing or coastal trade.

[71] See *infra,* §233.

[72] The position of the United States government has been inconsistent. First proposing the prohibition of any armament in early 1916, it soon adhered to the opposite view held by Great Britain. During World War II, attacks on enemy shipping were conducted by naval and air forces of both belligerents.

[73] See *infra,* §235. [74] See the 1907 Hague Convention VIII.

[75] *E.g.*, the 1907 Hague Convention X; Arts. 3–4 of Hague Convention XI; Arts. 22, 24, 33, of the 1949 Geneva Convention for the Amelioration of the Condition of Wounded, Sick, and Shipwrecked Members of Armed Forces at Sea. For the exemption of mail bags, see Art. 1 of the 1907 Hague Convention XI. The exemption of small fishing boats from capture is a customary rule of international law. See *The Paquete Habana,* U.S. Supreme Court, 1900. 175 U.S. 677.

[76] In deciding the *Case of Dithmar and Boldt* in 1921, the German Reichsgericht ruled that firing on a hospital ship and lifeboats was an offense against international law. 16 *Am. Jour. Int. Law* (1922), 708. In *The Orel* case, the Sasebo Prize Court of Japan decided, in 1905, that, if a hospital ship committed acts in aid of the military operations of the enemy, she could be captured and condemned. 2 Hurst & Bray's *Russian and Japanese Prize Cases* (1913), p. 354; Tung, p. 298.

The above is a brief description of the existing conventions, regulations, and declarations governing land, air, and maritime warfare. There are still many phases not yet covered by precise rules, especially the extent to which rules apply equally to the aggressor and the defender. So long as there is a possibility of war or armed conflict, further development and codification of international law in this field are necessary.[77]

§217. ESPIONAGE AND RUSES

Espionage is a common practice of states in peace and war.[78] Belligerents employ spies to collect necessary information which is likely to be vital to the conduct of war. According to the Hague Regulations, a spy is a person who, acting clandestinely or on false pretenses, obtains or endeavors to obtain information in the zone of operations of a belligerent, with the intention of communicating it to the enemy. Thus, soldiers who do not wear a disguise but penetrate the enemy zone of operations for the purpose of obtaining information are not spies. Nor are soldiers and civilians who carry out their mission openly, deliver dispatches intended for their own army or for the enemy's army, or are sent in balloons or aircraft for the purpose of carrying dispatches and maintaining communications between different parts of the armed forces or territories.[79]

A spy taken in the act cannot be punished without trial, in accordance with customary international law. His usual punishment is hanging or shooting. If he is captured after rejoining his own army, he is not to be held responsible for his previous acts of espionage, but is to be treated as a prisoner of war.[80] Espionage must not be confused with

[77] For instance, there is no rule prohibiting belligerents from interfering with or destroying submarine cables. See *Eastern Extension, Australasia and China Telegraph Co.,* United States-Great Britain, Claims Arbitration, 1923. Nielsen's Report, 73. In land warfare, there is no rule on siege. Rules on air warfare remain to be formulated. For further references on rules of warfare, consult Morris Greenspan, *The Modern Law of Land Warfare* (Berkeley, 1959); Department of the Army, *Law of Land Warfare* (Washington, D.C., 1956); J. M. Spaight, *War Rights on Land* (London, 1911); R. W. Rucker, *The Law of War and Neutrality at Sea* (Washington, D.C., 1957); J. M. Spaight, *Air Power and War Rights* (London, 1947); American Academy of Political and Social Science, "Unconventional Warfare," 341 *The Annals* (May 1962).

[78] For a general discussion of the subject, see Roland J. Stanger (ed.), *Essays on Espionage and International Law* (Columbus, Ohio, 1962).

[79] See Arts. 24, 29, of the Hague Regulations.

[80] Arts. 30–31 of the Hague Regulations.

war treason, which represents certain illegitimate acts of warfare committed within the enemy lines.[81] Ruses of war or stratagems are permissible, because any deceit employed to mislead the enemy serves the interest of military operations. Unlike stratagems, however, perfidy is prohibited.[82] Espionage and ruses may be employed by the army, navy, or air force.

§218. NON-HOSTILE RELATIONS BETWEEN BELLIGERENTS

Whereas normal intercourse between two or more states is ended at the commencement of war, special agreements may be made either directly by the belligerents or through neutrals for certain transactions in consideration of humanity, mutual convenience, or other factors. Thus, 'cartels' may be concluded for the exchange of prisoners of war, treatment of the sick and wounded, and specific means of communication. So-called cartel ships are commissioned for such purposes. 'Capitulations' are arranged by military commanders for the surrender of armed forces, fortresses, places, as well as war materials and equipments. Once concluded, they must be carried out in good faith.[83]

There are other temporary documents issued by a belligerent for the following purposes: (1) a passport, by which an enemy national or some other person may travel within the territory under its control; (2) a safe-conduct, by which he may go to a specific location for a defined purpose, or, in case of a ship or cargo, a special certificate for free movement; and (3) a safeguard, by which he or his property is given special protection. Mention should also be made of 'flags of truce.' The flag bearer and his entourage sent by one belligerent to enter into communication with the other have the right of inviolability; but this right should not be abused. In any event, the commander of the other belligerent is not obliged to receive them, and may resort to precautionary measures to keep them from taking advantage of the opportunity to collect information.[84]

[81] 'War treason' is different from the word 'treason' in the normal sense. The latter is an offense of attempting by overt acts to overthrow the government of a state to which the offender owes allegiance.

[82] For instance, violation of oaths and promises.

[83] See Art. 35 of the Hague Regulations. 'Sponsions' are capitulations concluded by military officers beyond their authority and subject to ratification by their superior officers. For armistice, truce, or suspension of arms, see *infra*, §223. Capitulations and armistices are provided for in Chs. IV and V of the Hague Regulations.

[84] See Ch. III of the Hague Regulations.

VI. *RULES GOVERNING ENEMY TERRITORY, PROPERTY, AND PERSONS* [85]

§219. OCCUPATION OF ENEMY TERRITORY

The occupation of the whole or a part of enemy territory by a belligerent represents the success of its military operations. Unlike invasion, occupation is to take possession and administer territory until the belligerent decides to withdraw or is driven out by the enemy.[86] A distinction must also be made between the belligerent occupation of enemy territory during the course of the war and the postwar occupation of Germany and Japan by the Allied Powers. Pending eventual settlement by a peace treaty, the occupant is forbidden to annex the territory or to set up an independent state as Japan did in Manchuria in 1932.[87] Except for military necessity, local laws prevailing in the occupied territory must be respected.

In the occupied area, regular taxes may be collected for local uses. Local inhabitants cannot be compelled to participate in military operations against their own country.[88] Public functionaries may be dis-

[85] General texts on the subject: Oppenheim, II, §§118–154, 166–172b, 192–209, 212–213; Fenwick, *Principles,* Chs. XXIX, §§E–F; XXX, §§A–B; Hyde, III, §§668–702A, 773–781; Moore, *Digest,* VII, §§1127–1134, 1143–1156, 1177–1178; Hackworth, *Digest,* VI, §§576–582, 587–588; Hershey, pp. 579–591, 612–623; Von Glahn, pp. 594–601, 666–694; Soviet *Text,* pp. 427–436, 440–441; Jacobini, pp. 248–255, 264–266; Gould, Ch. 21; Svarlien, Ch. 23; McNair, III, pp. 4–30, 61–100.

[86] Sometimes, on account of military necessity, belligerents temporarily occupy the territory of a non-enemy or even that of an ally, as in the Allied occupation of North Africa (1942–1943) and Greece (1944).

[87] In this respect, J. J. G. Syatauw attempted to make a distinction between enemy territory proper and colonies: "Traditional international law still holds that the Japanese had no authority to create an independent state in occupied territory. This might have been true in occupied China, but to hold such an opinion in the colonial case is to close one's eyes deliberately to the hard facts." On the basis of this reasoning, he concluded that "the creation of the Burmese state by Japan was not contrary to international law." Syatauw, *Some Newly Established States and the Development of International Law,* pp. 88, 92.

[88] See Art. 23 (1h, 2) of the Hague Regulations; Art. 51 of the pertinent Geneva Convention of 1949. As stated before, local inhabitants are obliged to obey occupant authorities under martial law. But, on approach of an enemy who has not taken actual possession of the territory, they may spon-

missed by the occupant, but cannot be forced to stay in office without urgent necessity.[89] During World War II, Germany and Japan repeatedly violated these customary rules of international law. When circumstances demand, local inhabitants may be asked to supply certain kinds of articles or services in the nature of requisitions or to pay some ready money as contributions, for which a receipt must be given.[90] As for what will happen to the various measures enforced by the occupant after the return of the original authority, the legitimate government should decide each case on its own merits.[91]

§220. DISPOSITION OF ENEMY PROPERTY

The destruction and damage of enemy property for military offense or defense is almost unavoidable, but general devastation is prohibited.[92] The disposition of enemy property depends upon its ownership and location. Modern rules concerning enemy public property is that public immovables, such as land and buildings, may not be confiscated by the military occupant, who may, however, appropriate the produce of such state property unless it belongs to municipalities, or religious, charitable, or educational institutions.[93] Under the same exceptions, public movables in the occupied territory can be appropriated for urgent necessity of military operations.[94]

---

taneously take arms to resist the invading force. See Art. 2 of the Hague Regulations; Arts. 67, 68, of the Geneva Convention on the Protection of Civilian Persons at War. This Geneva Convention does not incorporate the traditional concept of temporary allegiance of local inhabitants to the occupying authorities.

[89] See Art. 54 of the pertinent Geneva Convention of 1949. See also Morris Greenspan, *op. cit.*, Ch. IV.

[90] See Arts. 49, 51, 52, of the Hague Regulations.

[91] On occupation of enemy territory, see Gerhard von Glahn, *The Occupation of Enemy Territory: A Commentary on the Law and Practice of Belligerent Occupation* (Minneapolis, 1957); D. A. Graber, *The Development of the Law of Belligerent Occupation, 1863–1914* (New York, 1949); Odile Debbasch, *L'Occupation Militaire* (Paris, 1962); Ernst Fraenkel, *Military Occupation and the Rule of Law* (London & New York, 1914); Ernst H. Feilchenfeld, *International Economic Law of Belligerent Occupation* (Washington, D.C., 1942); McDougal and Feliciano, *Law and Minimum World Public Order*, pp. 732–832.

[92] Special care must be taken to protect historical monuments, and buildings and articles for scientific, educational, religious, and charitable purposes. See Arts. 23(g), 56, of the Hague Regulations.

[93] Arts. 55–56 of the Hague Regulations.

[94] See Art. 53 of the Hague Regulations.

All public and private enemy property found on the battlefield may be deemed war booty except valuable articles, cash, and correspondence of the prisoners of war.[95] The appropriation of private enemy immovables is strictly prohibited. Nor is it permissible to seize private enemy movables, except those necessary for military operations and on condition that they will be restored at the end of the war with due compensation.[96]

The final disposition of captured merchantmen and goods on board is determined by the decision of the prize court of the capturing belligerent. National in character, prize courts are established in the territory under the control of the belligerents to adjudicate all cases in accord with their own rules of procedure in conformity with customary international law.[97] A proposal for an international prize court of appeals was adopted by the Second Hague Conference, but the convention failed of ratification.[98]

A captured vessel is usually conducted by the captor to a nearby or convenient port for adjudication. It is difficult for submarines and impossible for aircraft to execute such a mission, but the prize law may be applied to aircraft as well. Pending a decision of the prize court, the

[95] See Arts. 4, 14, of the Hague Regulations; Art. 18 of the 1949 Geneva Convention of the Prisoners of War; Art. 16 of the 1949 Geneva Convention for the Amelioration of the Condition of Wounded and Sick.

[96] For prohibition of confiscation of private enemy property by the military occupant, see Arts. 46–47 of the Hague Regulations. Ownership of bonds during military occupation was clarified by the U.S. Court of Appeals (Second District) in *State of the Netherlands v. Federal Reserve Bank* in 1953. 201 F.2d 455.

[97] In deciding *The Odessa* in 1915, the British Judicial Committee of the Privy Council pronounced the following principle: "As the right to seize is universally recognized, so also is the title which the judgment of the court creates. The judgment is of international force, and it is because of this circumstance that courts of prize have always been guided by general principles of law capable of universal acceptance rather than by considerations of special rules of municipal law." [1916] A.C. 145. In *The Albenga No. 1*, the High Prize Court of China ruled, in 1918, that a prize court was solely concerned with the question whether or not a captured ship or cargo should be condemned; the question whether or not the thing condemned or its owner was burdened with a debt being only a civil matter outside the jurisdiction of the court. The Chinese prize court went further to state that "according to international law a belligerent has an absolute right to what has lawfully captured." *Judgments of the High Prize Court* (1919), p. 16; Tung, p. 316.

[98] Convention XII.

prize must not be destroyed unless military necessity so requires.[99] If destroyed, due compensation should be paid. The ownership of the prize is the criterion for determining its enemy character,[100] which has always been a controversial subject between neutrals and belligerents.[101] The right of requisition of a captured vessel and goods in custody of the prize court pending a final decision can only be exercised by the capturing belligerent under military necessity. This principle, as pronounced by the British Judicial Committee of the Privy Council in the case of *The Zamora* in 1916, is declaratory of customary international law.[102]

§221. TREATMENT OF ENEMY PERSONS

In war, it is legitimate to kill or wound as many combatants of the opposing belligerent as possible in accordance with rules of warfare, with the exception of those disabled, sick, or wounded.[103] In case of civilians, every care must be exercised to respect their lives and property, family honor and right, and religious freedom. It is absolutely forbidden to treacherously kill or wound enemy civilians.[104] Unless for urgent necessity of self-defense, private enemy individuals must not be taken into captivity.[105] Medical care, humanitarian treatment, and other necessary considerations are emphasized in the Geneva Conventions.[106]

[99] In *The Eorus*, the Japanese Prize Court at Sasebo ruled, in 1915, that the captor could destroy the prize if it hindered the military action of taking the captured ship into the captor's port. U.S. Naval College, *International Law Decisions* (1923), p. 169.

[100] This is the guiding rule for prize courts; *e.g.*, in *The Odessa*, just cited.

[101] In *The Miramichi*, the British High Court of Admiralty determined, in 1914, that the goods in question were still the property of the American claimants and had not yet passed to enemy buyers. It therefore decreed that neutral goods were not subject to seizure. [1915] Probate 71. This is the general rule of customary international law.

[102] [1916] 2 A.C. 77.

[103] See Art. 23(c, d) of the Hague Regulations; Morris Greenspan, *op. cit.*, Ch. IV.

[104] See Art. 23(h), 46, of the Hague Regulations.

[105] Germany violated this rule in 1914 in Belgium and other occupied areas by taking men of military age into captivity.

[106] The protection of civilians was prescribed in a special Geneva Convention of 1949 and two more conventions of the same year on the amelioration of the condition of the wounded and sick in the armed forces in the

§222. PRISONERS OF WAR

The humanitarian treatment of prisoners of war is one of the important features of modern laws of war. The ancient practices of killing and enslaving have long been abolished. Beginning with a bilateral treaty between the United States and Prussia in 1785,[107] followed by the 1907 Hague Regulations [108] and the Geneva Conventions of 1929 and 1949,[109] there are now detailed provisions on the treatment of prisoners of war. Consisting of 143 articles and in effect as of October 21, 1950, the Geneva Convention of 1949 replaces all earlier international instruments on the subject among parties to the Convention.[110]

The 1949 Geneva Convention enumerates a comprehensive list of persons who must be treated as prisoners of war after falling into the power of the enemy. They include militia, members of organized resistance movements and other volunteer corps, non-combatants of the armed forces, members of crews, and also persons in a levy *en masse* on the approach of the enemy.[111] They may be entrusted to a neutral country as the 'protecting power' by a belligerent whose nationals have been taken as prisoners of war in the territory under the control of its opposing belligerent. They must be supplied by the detaining belligerent with the normal standard of food, clothing, and shelter, and must also be protected from violence, intimidation, insults, medical and scientific experiments, and reprisals.[112] With the exception of officers, they may be assigned to do some work with pay, but such work must

---

field and at sea, and of those shipwrecked in the navy. For further details, see Morris Greenspan, *op. cit.*, Ch. VI.

[107] Art. 24 of the Treaty provides for proper treatment of prisoners of war.

[108] Arts. 4–20 in operation during World War I.

[109] The 1929 Convention consists of 94 articles, and incorporates practically all provisions of the 1907 Hague Regulations on this subject except Arts. 10–12 on parole. The 1929 Convention was in operation among most of the belligerents, with the exception of relations between Germany and Russia, during World War II. But these provisions are merely declaratory of customary international law and should be observed by all parties at war.

[110] The 1949 Geneva Convention does not contain the 'general participation clause' as provided in the Hague Conventions. Art. 2(3) of the Geneva Convention states: "Although one of the Powers in conflict may not be a party to the present Convention, the Powers who are parties thereto shall remain bound by it in their mutual relations. They shall furthermore be bound by the Convention in relation to the said Power, if the latter accepts and applies the provisions thereof."

[111] Art. 4. [112] Art. 13.

not be connected with war.[113] In case of insubordination or attempt of escape, they are subject to punishment through disciplinary measures and judicial proceedings.[114]

The captivity of prisoners of war may be terminated by their death, escape, or release on parole, direct repatriation of the sick and wounded, or transfer to neutral countries. Most important is release and repatriation at the cessation of hostilities.[115] The Soviet Union was accused of failing to repatriate promptly a large number of prisoners of war taken into custody during World War II.[116] Another repatriation problem came up at the cessation of the Korean hostilities, when thousands of Chinese and North Korean prisoners of war and a handful of Americans refused to be repatriated to their original countries. This unique situation necessitated the signing of an Agreement on Repatriation of Prisoners of War on June 8, 1953, and another supplementary agreement on July 27 of the same year.[117]

For amelioration of the condition of wounded and sick as well as humanitarian treatment of prisoners of war, the International Red Cross and its national organizations have done much to fulfill the purposes and objectives of the Geneva Conventions.[118]

[113] Art. 50. [114] See Arts. 82–107 in particular.

[115] See especially Arts. 109–119. The signatories agreed to refer disputes on the interpretation or application of the Convention to the International Court of Justice. On prisoners of war, see William E. S. Flory, *Prisoners of War: A Study in the Development of International Law* (Washington, D.C., 1942); Department of the Army, *Geneva Conventions of 12 August 1949 for the Protection of War Victims* (Washington, D.C., 1950); Morris Greenspan, *op. cit.*, Ch. V.

[116] See the *Report* published by the Information Section of NATO on July 1, 1952.

[117] These prisoners of war were eventually transferred to Taiwan and several other places. With the exception of one or two, the American turncoats have come back to the United States from Communist China. See Jaro Mayda, "The Korean Repatriation Problem," 47 *Am. Jour. Int. Law* (1953), pp. 414–438.

[118] The first Geneva Convention of 1864 was prompted by the publication, in 1862, of Henri Dunant's *Un Souvenir de Solférino.* Based upon his personal observations, Dunant, a Swiss, described the lack of care of the dead and wounded in the battle of Solférino in 1859 by Austria against France and Sardinia. Moved by public opinion, the Swiss government invited other European states to an international conference at Geneva in 1864. According to Soviet history, however, a Russian surgeon, Pirogov, initiated this idea earlier than Dunant. During the Crimean War, Pirogov realized the necessity of formulating rules for the care of the sick and wounded on the field, and published his *Course of Military Surgery* in 1862, calling for the es-

VII. *THE TERMINATION OF WAR*[119]

§223. CESSATION OF HOSTILITIES, ARMISTICES, AND PEACE TREATIES

A war may be ended in different ways, but cessation of hostilities is essential. Sometimes hostile acts may be simply discontinued, leaving everything uncertain in the future; although this has happened in the past,[120] the practice is almost obsolete. The term 'cease-fire' has frequently been used by United Nations organs to call on disputing parties to stop armed conflict.[121] War is terminated when the cease-fire agreement takes effect.[122]

A distinction must be made between suspension of arms and armistice: the former represents a cessation of hostilities for a short time agreed upon by the belligerents for specific military purposes, such as collection of wounded and dead or evacuation of a certain defended area; the latter in its broad sense means ceasing military operations in the whole region of war as a preliminary step for the negotiation of a peace treaty for the termination of war; an example is the Armistice of November 11, 1918.[123] Different from general armistice, partial armistice, often called 'truce,' covers only part of the theater of war.[124]

tablishment of an international agency to undertake the work. See Soviet *Text*, p. 407.

[119] General texts on the subject: Oppenheim, II, §§231–240, 261–284; Fenwick, *Principles*, Ch. XXXV; Hyde, III, §§904–923; Starke, Ch. 16, §4; Moore, *Digest*, VII, §1163; Hackworth, *Digest*, VI, §590; Hershey, pp. 606–610; Schwarzenberger, I, Ch. 7 (XII); Von Glahn, pp. 573–580; 702–718; Jacobini, pp. 232–235; Svarlien, Ch. 24; Soviet *Text*, pp. 447–452.

[120] The wars between France and Spain in 1720 and France and Mexico in 1867 ended this way.

[121] In its attempt to stop the armed conflict between the Netherlands and Indonesia in December 1948, the Security Council ordered a 'cease-fire' between the two disputing parties. This term was also applied to hostilities in Laos in 1962. Cease-fire orders were repeatedly issued by the Security Council for immediate termination of the armed conflict between Israel and several Arab States in June 1967.

[122] See *Shneiderman v. Metropolitan Casualty Co.*, U.S., Supreme Court of New York (Appellate Division), 1961. 220 N.Y.S.(2d) 947. In this case, the court ruled that the 'war' in the Suez Canal Zone ended on November 6, 1956, when the cease-fire agreement came into force.

[123] The war with Germany was formally terminated by the Treaty of Versailles of 1919.

[124] See Art. 37 of the Hague Regulations. The United Nations used the term 'truce' at the time of cessation of hostilities in Palestine in May and June 1948.

Even partial armistice bears political significance and has impact on the general course of war.

Technically speaking, "an armistice effects nothing but a suspension of hostilities," because "it is the treaty which terminates the war." [125] Before the conclusion of a peace treaty, war may be terminated for all practical purposes, but not in the legal sense.[126] Thus, an issue was raised whether the Armistice Agreement of 1945 between Israel and four Arab states [127] had terminated their state of war. Egypt contested the Israeli view that the Armistice Agreement produced such an effect.

In recent years, general armistice has led to cessation of hostilities and maintenance of the status quo after the war for a considerable length of time, chiefly due to difficulty in reaching a permanent political settlement. The most notable instances are the Korean Armistice Agreement of July 27, 1953,[128] and the Armistice Agreements of July 20, 1954, on the cessation of hostilities in Indochina.[129] The cold war delayed the conclusion of a peace treaty with Japan for six years and that with Germany almost indefinitely.[130]

§224. SUBJUGATION, CONQUEST, AND MILITARY OCCUPATION

Conquest, taking possession of a portion or an entire area of enemy territory by military force, is an effective means to overcome the will to resist of the enemy belligerent and bring about the end of the war.

[125] See *Commercial Cable Co. v. Burleson*, U.S. District Court, S.D.N.Y., 1919. 255 F. 99. See also *Kahn v. Anderson, Warden*, U.S. Supreme Court, 1921. 255 U.S. 1.

[126] If the conclusion of a peace treaty is not in sight after cessation of hostilities for a long time, the former belligerents may declare the legal termination of the state of war. Examples are Great Britain, France, and the United States with Germany on July 9, 1951, and the Soviet Union with Japan on October 19, 1956.

[127] Egypt, Jordan, Lebanon, and Syria.

[128] "A peaceful settlement at a political level" is the eventual aim of the Korean question as expressly stipulated in Art. 62 of the Korean Armistice Agreement.

[129] For details, see *supra*, Ch. 13, note 150.

[130] The war with Japan ended in August 1945, but the Peace Treaty was not concluded until September 8, 1951, in San Francisco. The anomalous status of Germany reflects deep-rooted distrust among the major powers during the postwar period. In deciding the case of *Rex v. Bottrill* in 1946, the British Court of Appeal was bound by the opinion of the Foreign Secretary, who certified that the state of war with Germany continued. [1947] 1 K.B. 41.

Conquest does not necessarily result in subjugation,[131] but subjugation is essential to the termination of a war.[132] It must be emphasized that conquest and subjugation by individual states are prohibited under the United Nations system. Unlike armistice, unconditional surrender means the victorious powers imposing dictated terms by unilateral declaration on the vanquished, which has no choice but to submit.[133] It was thus that Germany and Japan surrendered to the Allied Powers in 1945.[134] Both countries were under Allied military occupation for a long period in order to ensure complete fulfillment of post-surrender terms.[135]

§225. CONSEQUENCES OF THE TERMINATION OF WAR

The traditional rule of *uti possidetis* that each belligerent is entitled to what actually is in its possession at the end of the war has been gradually replaced by the modern practice of providing every phase of postwar relations in the peace treaty. Nor is the *jus postliminium* automatically applicable, because the restoration of prewar rights and ownership also depends on the terms agreed upon by the belligerents. While there is no definite standard of terms, the following steps are usually taken after the conclusion of peace: release and repatriation of prisoners of war,[136] resumption of diplomatic and consular relations,

[131] During the Sino-Japanese War (1937–1945), Japan conquered a large part of China without being able to subdue the enemy. Germany took military occupation of Belgium, the Netherlands, and several other countries, whose governments were forced into exile but continued their resistance against the enemy.

[132] Instances of termination of war in consequence of subjugation are the Two Sicilies, subjugated by Italy in 1859; Ethiopia, by Italy in 1936; and Goa, by India in 1961.

[133] See, *e.g.*, the text of the unconditional surrender instruments for Germany and Italy signed in May 1945. 39 *Am. Jour. Int. Law* (1945), Supp., pp. 168–171.

[134] Germany on May 8, and Japan on September 2.

[135] The ultimate objectives of the 'Basic Post-Surrender Policy for Japan' as formulated by the Far Eastern Commission in 1947 were to ensure that Japan would not again become a menace to the peace and security of the world and to bring about the earliest possible establishment of a democratic and peaceful government. To achieve these objectives, four principal means were laid down: limitation of territory, complete disarmament and demilitarization, respect for fundamental human rights and individual freedoms, and maintenance of a regulated economy.

[136] See Art. 118 of the Geneva Convention of 1949.

revival of certain treaties suspended for the duration of the war,[137] return or retention of enemy property seized during the war,[138] release of nationals in enemy territory from any legal disabilities on account of the war, and execution of the terms of the peace treaty. These terms usually include payment of indemnity and cession of territory. The official commencement of peace generally starts from the date of the conclusion of the peace treaty, unless it stipulates otherwise.[139]

§226. TRIAL OF WAR CRIMINALS

War crimes in the traditional sense are crimes committed by members of the armed forces and individuals in violation of the rules of legitimate warfare with or without superior orders.[140] Prior to World War I, an amnesty was usually proclaimed to relieve all persons of wrongful acts committed for the prosecution of the war. The Treaty of Versailles of 1919 established a precedent by providing for the trial and punishment of William II of Hohenzollern, formerly Emperor of Germany. In the view of the Allied and Associated Powers, the German Kaiser had committed "a supreme offense against international morality and sanctity of treaties." [141] It was originally decided to set up a special tribunal to try the former Emperor, who took political asylum in the Netherlands. The contemplated trial did not, however, materialize, because the government of the Netherlands declined the Allied request on the ground that, according to international law, political criminals are not subject to extradition.

In view of the unprecedented scale of war crimes committed by Germany and in pursuance of the Moscow Declaration of 1943, the United States, Great Britain, France, and the Soviet Union signed, on

[137] See *supra*, §171.

[138] The retention and disposal of German assets seized by the Allied Powers were specifically provided for in the Paris Agreement on German Reparation of January 24, 1946, and the Bonn Convention of May 26, 1952.

[139] See, *e.g.*, *Kotzias v. Tyser*, Great Britain, Court of Appeal, 1920. [1920] 2 K.B. 69.

[140] For a classification of war crimes, see Oppenheim, II, pp. 567–576. Espionage is punishable when a soldier or an individual involved is captured behind enemy lines. But international law permits belligerents to have recourse to it. According to the United States Army Field Manual on the Law of Land Warfare (1956), espionage is not a breach of international law (Par. 77). Superior orders may be considered as a mitigating factor in accordance with the Charter of the International Military Tribunal of 1945. (Art. 8).

[141] Art. 227 of the Treaty of Versailles.

August 8, 1945, the Agreement for the Prosecution and Punishment of the Major War Criminals for the European Axis.[142] An International Military Tribunal was consequently set up at Nuremberg.[143] The defendants indicted were persons who, acting in the interests of the European Axis countries, whether as individuals or as members of organizations, committed any of the following: crimes against peace, war crimes, and crimes against humanity.[144]

War crimes were violations of the laws and customs of war. They included but were not limited to murder, ill-treatment, or deportation to slave labor or for any other purpose of civilian population of or in occupied territory; murder or ill-treatment of prisoners of war or persons on the seas; killing of hostages; plunder of public or private property; wanton destruction of cities, towns, or villages, or devastation not justified by military necessity. All these stipulations were binding upon the Tribunal as the law to be applied in the trial of the cases.[145]

Among the accused who were convicted and sentenced by the Nuremberg Tribunal only a few were found guilty of crimes against peace or humanity alone. Most of them were convicted of war crimes in addition to others. The Tokyo trials were conducted by the International Military Tribunal for the Far East, which was established in 1946, to implement the Cairo Declaration of 1943, the Declaration of

[142] For details, see *International Conference on Military Trials, London, 1945* (Washington, D.C., 1949).

[143] The Tribunal consisted of four judges and four alternates. Each of the four Powers signatory to the Agreement chose one judge and one alternative. The Tribunal began to function on November 20, 1945. Sentences were pronounced on October 1, 1946.

[144] Art. 6 of the Charter of the Tribunal.

[145] Art. 6(b) of the Charter of the Tribunal. The following were listed as crimes against peace: planning, preparation, initiation, or waging of a war of aggression, or a war in violation of international treaties, agreements, or assurances, or participation in a common plan or conspiracy for the accomplishment of any one of the foregoing. There was also an extensive list of crimes against humanity: murder, extermination, enslavement, deportation, and other inhuman acts committed against any civilian population, before or during the war, or persecutions on political, racial, or religious grounds in execution of or in connection with any crime within the jurisdiction of the Tribunal, whether or not in violation of the domestic law of the country where perpetrated. Art. 6(a, c) of the Charter of the Tribunal. See also United Nations Secretariat, *Charter and Judgment of the Nürnberg Tribunal—History and Analysis.* UN Doc. A/CN.4/5. For details of the trials, reference can be made to *Trial of the Major War Criminals before the International Military Tribunal* (Nuremberg, 1947), 42 vols.

Potsdam of 1945, and other international instruments.[146] The defendants were charged with the same categories of crime. The Tokyo Tribunal cited at length from the judgments of the Nuremberg trials.

In addition to these two international tribunals, national courts and special military courts also had jurisdiction over defendants within their respective areas. The most discussed was the case of General Yamashita of Japan, who was convicted by the American Military Commission on account of his failure to prevent his troops from committing war crimes. The United States Supreme Court denied, in 1946, both habeas corpus and certiorari petitioned by the defendant.[147] In *Koki Hirota, et al. v. General of the Army Douglas MacArthur,* the United States Supreme Court held, in 1948, that the courts of the United States had no power or authority to review, affirm, set aside, or annul the judgments and sentences imposed on the defendants by the military tribunal set up as the agent of the Allied Powers.[148]

On December 11, 1946, the General Assembly of the United Nations adopted a resolution, which affirmed "the principles of international law recognized by the Charter of the Nürnberg Tribunal and the Judgment of the Tribunal." [149] According to the Nuremberg principle, "crimes against international law are committed by men, not by abstract entities, and only by punishing individuals who commit such crimes can the provisions of international law be enforced." [150] This reasoning is definitely a departure from the traditional rule of 'act of state,' and has become a subject of lively discussion among international lawyers.

Individual responsibility for war crimes as well as crimes against peace and humanity will certainly serve as a serious warning to political and military leaders of various nations, especially those who are in a position to decide their national destinies. This Nuremberg principle may exert some restraining influence on their actions; because they themselves may perish in case of recourse to war. However, the question has been raised whether fairness and justice can be achieved by *quasi* international tribunals and national courts of the victorious pow-

[146] Consisting of eleven judges, the Tokyo Tribunal began its proceedings on June 4, 1946, and pronounced sentences on November 4, 1948.

[147] *In re Yamashita,* U.S. Supreme Court, 1946. 323 U.S. 1. For various individual trials, see United Nations War Crimes Commission, *Law Reports of Trials of War Criminals* (1946–1949), 15 vols.

[148] 335 U.S. 876, 338 U.S. 197.

[149] GA res. 95(I). See *Yearbook,* UN, 1946–1947, p. 254.

[150] Judgment of the Nuremberg International Tribunal, September 30, 1946, *Transcript of Proceedings,* p. 16,878.

ers, which unilaterally determine the standard of law in an extremely emotional atmosphere.[151]

[151] For further discussion on war crimes and international tribunals, consult J. B. Keenan and B. F. Brown, *Crimes against International Law* (Washington, D.C., 1950); J. A. Appleman, *Military Tribunals and International Crimes* (Indianapolis, 1954); S. Cluck, *The Nuremberg Trial and Aggressive War* (New York, 1946); R. H. Jackson, *The Nuremberg Case* (New York, 1947); W. E. Benton (ed.), *Nuremberg: Some German Views of the War Trials* (Dallas, 1955); Morris Greenspan, Ch. XII; Sohn, Ch. VIII, §5; Robert K. Woetzel, *The Nuremberg Trials in International Law* (London & New York, 1960).

CHAPTER 15

RELATIONS BETWEEN BELLIGERENTS AND NEUTRALS UNDER TRADITIONAL INTERNATIONAL LAW

I. *THE CHANGING CONCEPT OF NEUTRALITY* [1]

§227. NEUTRALITY AS AN INSTITUTION AMONG NATIONS

As explained before, the Charter of the United Nations prefers the term 'use of force' to 'war.' For convenience and in view of the common use of 'war' in previous conventions and regulations, the traditional term is used but with the understanding that it means war in the material sense. It should also be noted that, under the United Nations system, neutrality is inconsistent with the letter and spirit of the Charter if the aggressor has been determined.[2]

[1] General texts on the subject: Oppenheim, II, §§285–306a; Fenwick, *Principles*, Ch. XXXII; Hackworth, *Digest*, VII, §§656, 662; Hershey, Ch. XXXI; Svarlien, Ch. 22; Schwarzenberger, I, Ch. 8 (I–III); Von Glahn, pp. 619–630; Jacobini, pp. 269–276; Soviet *Text*, pp. 442–446; McNair, III, pp. 133–158.

[2] See Art. 2(5) of the Charter.

Neutrality represents an impartial attitude or policy of a third state which, as a non-participant in a war, invokes special rights and duties in relation to the belligerents. Grotius, Bynkershoek, Vattel, and other writers on international law helped develop neutrality as a legal doctrine. While Grotius' distinction of just and unjust causes of war as a determining factor of a neutral's attitude has not always been followed in international practice, his concept serves as a prelude to the provision of collective sanctions in the League Covenant and the United Nations Charter.

The First Armed Neutrality, initiated by Catherine the Great of Russia on February 29, 1780, and adhered to by the principal European powers,[3] was an early attempt by neutral nations to use force for the protection of neutral commerce.[4] On the belligerents' side, France and Spain expressed respect for neutral rights and England declared her willingness to abide by treaty obligations. The United States intended, but failed, to join the Armed Neutrality, because she was not then a neutral country.[5]

Among all the nations, the United States was most persistent in upholding neutral rights during the Napoleonic wars and the early years of the two world wars, as well as neutral obligations during her Civil War.[6] Four neutrality acts were enacted by Congress between the two world wars,[7] but the American concept of neutrality was later

[3] The Netherlands, Prussia, the Holy Roman Empire, Portugal, and the Two Sicilies. Denmark and Sweden were bound by a defensive treaty. The Second Armed Neutrality, which was organized by Russia, Prussia, Sweden, and Denmark in 1800 against England, lasted only a year until the Danish fleet was destroyed by the British navy.

[4] The main principles of armed neutrality were: (1) right of neutral vessels to navigate freely from port to port and along the coasts of the belligerents; (2) effects owned by nationals of belligerents on board neutral vessels being free, except contraband of war; (3) contraband being defined according to the terms of the Treaty of Commerce of 1776 between Russia and England; (4) a blockaded port being one where the attacking power has stationed its vessels sufficiently near and in such a way as to render access thereto clearly dangerous; (5) the above principles serving as a rule for proceedings and judgments on the legality of prize.

[5] The United States sent Francis Dana to St. Petersburg to enter into negotiations with Russia, which was, however, determined not to grant recognition before Great Britain did so.

[6] The Neutrality Act of 1794 was the earliest one enacted by the United States. On American insistence on neutral obligations during the Civil War, see the Treaty of Washington, concluded by Great Britain and the United States in 1871.

[7] After the Italo-Ethiopian armed clash in the summer of 1935, Congress

changed from absolute impartiality to non-belligerency.[8] The transfer of fifty over-age destroyers to Great Britain in 1940 and the Lend-Lease Act of 1941 actually led the way to active belligerency. As regular participants in numerous wars, the major powers in Europe had inevitably made extreme claims to belligerent rights. Small states were generally anxious to stay out of war, but did not always succeed. Nevertheless, neutrality as a legal institution gradually received recognition in spite of repeated violations by belligerents.

§228. THE HAGUE CONVENTIONS ON NEUTRALITY

After the Armed Neutrality of 1780, no serious efforts were exerted to establish common principles of neutrality through international legislation. The Second Hague Conference made a long step toward this direction by adopting two conventions: (1) Convention V, respecting the Rights and Duties of Neutral Powers and Persons in War on Land, and (2) Convention XIII, respecting the Rights and Duties of Neutral Powers in Naval War. Although Great Britain ratified none of them, most provisions are merely declaratory of customary international law and worthy of recognition and observance by all nations. There are other conventions adopted by the Hague Conference indirectly related to neutral rights and duties.[9]

---

passed the First Neutrality Act on August 31, 1935, forbidding arms shipments to belligerents without distinction. At the time of the expiration of most provisions of the First Neutrality Act, a second one was enacted on February 29, 1936, including the prohibition of any form of loan to belligerent governments by any person within the United States, in order to avoid what American bankers did during World War I. The Third Neutrality Act of May 1, 1937, extending the main provisions of the two previous acts, forbade American citizens to travel on belligerent ships. When the United States was moving from strict neutrality to non-belligerency, the Fourth Neutrality Act was enacted on November 4, 1939, to enable Great Britain and her Allies alone to buy and carry away war goods from the United States. A most comprehensive study of the historical development of neutrality can be found in Philip C. Jessup and others, *Neutrality: Its History, Economics and Law* (New York, 1935–1936), 4 vols. See also C. G. Fenwick, *American Neutrality: Trial and Failure* (New York, 1940); N. Örvik, *The Decline of Neutrality, 1914–1941, with Special Reference to the United States and the Northern Neutrals* (Oslo, 1953).

[8] The term 'non-belligerency' describes an anomalous policy of the United States, moving from absolute impartiality to active belligerency. For further details, see Edwin M. Borchard, "War, Neutrality and Non-Belligerency," 35 *Am. Jour. Int. Law* (1941), pp. 618–625.

[9] These include Convention VII on the Conversion of Merchant Ships into Warships, Convention VIII on the Laying of Automatic Submarine

An extensive code of naval warfare was embodied in the Declaration of London of 1909, but it had not come into effect at the outbreak of World War I. Throughout the war, there were extreme claims of belligerent and neutral rights as well as accusations of violations by both sides. However, the neutral status of Switzerland, the Netherlands, and several other states survived the world catastrophe.

§229. NEUTRALITY UNDER THE SYSTEM OF COLLECTIVE SANCTIONS

The legal institution of neutrality has undergone a drastic change since the establishment of the League of Nations. Resort to war by any League Member in disregard of the provisions of the Covenant was deemed an act of war against all other League Members, which were to undertake immediate measures of economic sanctions against the Covenant-breaker.[10] By Article 17 of the Covenant, the same action was to be applied to a non-member. This is a definite departure from the traditional concept of impartiality. Although the Kellogg-Briand Pact had no enforcement provisions, its signatories were under a moral obligation not to be neutral in a war waged by one contracting party against another in violation of the letter and spirit of the Pact. However, neutrality provisions were still incorporated in other international instruments concluded at that time.[11]

The League system was brought to an end by World War II, when Switzerland and some other countries managed to maintain neutrality. Since the restoration of peace, the United Nations Charter again emphasizes collective responsibility of the United Nations Members.[12] The Security Council may call upon the Members to apply enforcement

---

Contact Mines, Convention XI on Certain Restrictions on the Exercise of the Right of Capture, and Convention XII on the Establishment of an International Prize Court, which never materialized.

[10] See Art. 16(1) of the Covenant.

[11] Generally based upon the Hague Conventions of 1907, the Havana Convention on Maritime Neutrality of 1928 has a special provision by which the signatories reserve freedom of action to fulfill international obligations under previous undertakings. This reservation evidently refers to the League Covenant.

[12] Before and immediately after the outbreak of World War II, certain regional arrangements for the maintenance of neutrality were made; for instance, a code of neutrality rules adopted by the Scandinavian states in 1938 and the Panama Declaration of Neutrality proclaimed by the twenty-one American states in October 1939. The establishment of a 300-mile safety zone around the American continent except Canada did not represent the prevailing rules of international law. The belligerents, including Germany, Great Britain, and France, challenged the validity of the Panama Declaration.

measures to give effect to its decisions, including military forces if necessary.[13] Under such circumstances, Members have no legal right to be neutral. On the other hand, there are still armed conflicts or wars which, for various reasons, may not involve the United Nations, as in the case of Vietnam. Members may stay neutral if they are not called upon by the United Nations to apply any form of collective sanctions, but they should do nothing to help the aggressor or to hamper the defender.[14] Most Members were not actually involved in the Korean War. Thus, neutrality as a legal institution is not entirely obsolete either in theory or in practice.[15]

II. *NEUTRAL RIGHTS AND DUTIES IN GENERAL*[16]

§230. CHARACTERISTICS OF NEUTRALITY

Neutrality as an institution exists only in wartime. The basic characteristic of neutrality is the impartial attitude of a third state which is not involved in a war.[17] So-called 'neutralism' or 'neutral bloc' is a peacetime term applied to states which do not belong to either side of the cold war conflict; they may not necessarily stay neutral in a future war.

[13] See Arts. 41, 42, of the Charter.

[14] See Art. 2(5) of the Charter.

[15] International treaties concluded in recent years, such as the 1949 Geneva Conventions, still recognize the status of neutrality. For an analysis of neutrality in connection with the maintenance of minimum order, see McDougal and Feliciano, *Law and Minimum World Public Order,* pp. 384–519. In the opinion of Louis Henkin, "Whether in or out of the United Nations, Members cannot, under the guise of neutralism approve, or even remain 'neutral' to, the threat or use of force." He stated further that "whether force is the force of Communism, or of others, whether it is blatant or coated, neutralists who remain neutral to such force challenge their own claim to independence, sow aggressive revolutions, increase the risks of escalating war." Falk & Mendlovitz, II, p. 350; reprinted from "Force, Intervention, and Neutrality in Contemporary International Law," *Proceedings* of Am. Society Int. Law, 1963, p. 162.

[16] General texts on the subject: Oppenheim, II, §§307–367; Fenwick, *Principles,* Chs. XXXIII-XXXIV; Hyde, III, §§844–889; Moore, *Digest,* VII, §§1287–1336; Hackworth, *Digest,* VII, §§656–691; Starke, Ch. 17, §§1–2; Hershey, Chs. XXXII–XXXIII; Schwarzenberger, I, Ch. 8 (IV); Von Glahn, pp. 630–648, 660–664; Jacobini, pp. 276–283; McNair, III, pp. 161–219.

[17] For a discussion of abstention and impartiality as characteristics of neutrality, see Quincy Wright, "The Present Status of Neutrality," 34 *Am. Jour. Int. Law* (1940), pp. 392–394.

The obligation of impartiality entitles a neutral state to claim corresponding rights from the belligerents. Yet a belligerent may not be satisfied with the status of a state which claims to be neutral but actually renders assistance to an opposing belligerent. Such an attitude, sometimes known as 'benevolent neutrality' or 'non-belligerency,' is not neutrality in the strict sense, and may be considered as a cause of war by the injured belligerent. The reason why Germany did not declare war against the United States after the latter's transfer of destroyers to Great Britain and the application of the Lend-Lease Act was not lack of legal ground but, for military expediency, to keep the United States from joining the war as long as possible.

The status of permanent neutrality or neutralization, such as Switzerland's, was guaranteed by the major powers and placed the neutralized state under the obligation to be neutral in any war.[18] A state may also be bound by a bilateral treaty to remain neutral if the other signatory is involved in a war with another state. Neutrality under these circumstances leaves the state concerned no alternative. Normally, states have freedom of choice to be neutral or not on the basis of their own national interests, unless directed by the decisions of the United Nations or under other international obligations.[19]

Neutrality begins with the commencement of war among other states. In case of a civil war, enforcement of neutrality usually follows the granting of the status of belligerency to the rebels.[20] Enactment of laws and decrees to effect neutrality is within the domestic competence of a neutral state.[21] Neutrality is automatically terminated at the end of hostilities between the belligerents. When a neutral state joins a war either by its own volition or by compulsion of circumstances, its status will then be transformed from neutrality to belligerency. For the duration of its neutrality, a state is, however, entitled to certain rights and bound by certain duties.[22]

§231. NEUTRAL RIGHTS

In order to maintain national sovereignty and strict impartiality, a neutral state must insist on respect by belligerents for its territorial

[18] See *supra,* §21.

[19] In treaties of mutual assistance and defense, the signatories are sometimes obligated to fight jointly and collectively under specific conditions. Thus, neutrality is ruled out by conventional commitments.

[20] See *supra,* §28.

[21] For instance, the American Proclamation of Neutrality of August 4, 1914, and several neutrality acts previously described.

[22] For details, see Morris Greenspan, *The Modern Law of Land Warfare,* pp. 532–584.

inviolability and legitimate right to protect its property and nationals.[23] Relinquishment of such a right to one belligerent may adversely affect the interests of the other and consequently result in partiality. Thus, invasion of neutral territory on whatever ground or compulsory passage of troops must be resisted.[24] Nor can the airspace above a neutral state be violated.[25]

It is impermissible for a neutral state to allow a belligerent to use its territory as a base of military operations or for the erection of any installations for war purposes.[26] The exercise of the belligerent right of visit, search, attack, and seizure of enemy ships in neutral waters, and the institution of prize courts in the land and water domain of a neutral state are prohibited.[27] If a neutral state has used all means at its disposal to defend its neutral right, it cannot be held responsible for its failure to prevent violation by superior force.[28]

[23] See Art. 1 of Hague Convention V.

[24] During the Soviet-Finnish War in 1940, Sweden and Norway as neutral states refused the request by Great Britain and France to send armed forces to Finland through their neutral territories.

[25] The intruding aircraft must be compelled to land and be interned. The Netherlands as a neutral state insisted on this right during World War I.

[26] See Art. 5 of Hague Convention XIII, and Art. 3 of Hague Convention V. The United States was correct in keeping French Minister Genêt from issuing commissions on American territory in 1793 and in maintaining strict neutrality by the enactment of the neutrality law of June 5, 1794.

[27] For regulation of the use of neutral ports for captured prizes, see Arts. 21–23 of Hague Convention XIII. In deciding the case of *The Appam* in 1917, the U.S. Supreme Court ruled that prizes could be brought into the territorial domain of a neutral state only because of unseaworthiness, stress of weather, or want of fuel or provisions. 243 U.S. 124. In *The Florida*, the same court upheld, in 1879, a Brazilian complaint against capture by a Union warship in a Brazilian port. 101 U.S. 37. In *The Pellworm*, the British Judicial Committee of the Privy Council ruled, in 1922, that the capture of enemy merchant vessels within neutral territorial waters was illegal and that the capturing state should return these vessels to the waters of the neutral state. [1922] 1 A.C. 292. If a belligerent's warship is in a neutral port at the outbreak of war, it must be ordered to leave neutral water within a prescribed period in accord with Art. 13 of Hague Convention XIII. See also Art. 10 of the same Convention, and Art. 2 of Hague Convention V.

[28] See *The General Armstrong*, United States-Portugal, Claims Arbitration, 1852. Moore, *Int. Arbitrations*, II, p. 1094. For controversy over the right of passage of warships in territorial waters in the case of *The Altmark*, see Hackworth, *Digest*, VII, pp. 568 ff. The Japanese capture of a Russian destroyer in the neutral port of Chefoo during the Russo-Japanese War was a violation of Chinese neutrality. In defense of the Japanese position, S. Takahashi, a Japanese jurist, argued that China had failed of neutral duty to prevent the intrusion of the Russian ship in her port. See his *International*

Under military necessity, a belligerent may requisition neutral ships and other property with due compensation. Whether neutrals will allow a belligerent to exercise such a right depends largely upon the urgency of circumstances.[29] The protection of neutral nationals in a belligerent's territory is also a controversial problem. Generally speaking, they are entitled to the same protection of the state of their domicile and hence subject to the same fate as the belligerent's nationals. If they are drafted by their domiciled belligerent, no complaint can be effectively made by their own countries. Arguments were raised during World War I about immunity of neutral nationals on board armed belligerent ships. So long as they were under the protection of a belligerent, they could hardly be immune from attack by an opposing belligerent.[30] The most conflicting claims of belligerent and neutral rights are, however, centered in neutral trading with belligerents.[31]

§232. NEUTRAL DUTIES

Impartiality is the maxim of neutrality. The Hague Conventions and customary rules of international law require that a neutral government perform certain duties essential to the maintenance of neutrality. It must abstain from supplying military and financial assistance to a belligerent as the United States did before entering into World War II. It must also prevent, by whatever means at its disposal, any belligerent act on its territorial domain. In deciding *The Santissima Trinidad and the St. Ander* in 1822, the United States Supreme Court applied the rule that a neutral state has the duty to prevent augumentation of force by a belligerent in its territory.[32]

A neutral state is further under the obligation to control the individual acts of its nationals, especially military assistance to one belligerent detrimental to the interests of the other. The United States was compensated by Great Britain in the *Alabama Claims* in 1872, because of British failure to prevent the fitting out of the *Alabama* and other ships which inflicted heavy loss on the commerce of the Union.[33]

Law Applied to the Russo-Japanese War, with the Decisions of the Japanese Prize Courts (New York, 1908), pp. 437–444. For the regulations governing neutral granting of asylum to belligerent warships, see Art. 9 of Hague Convention XIII.

[29] See *The Zamora,* Great Britain Judicial Committee of the Privy Council, 1916. [1916] 2 A.C. 77. See also *The Nereide,* U.S. Supreme Court, 1815. 9 Cranch 388.

[30] See E. M. Borchard and W. P. Lage, *Neutrality for the United States* (New Haven, 1940), *passim.*

[31] For details, see *infra,* §§233–235.

[32] 7 Wheaton 283.

[33] United States-Great Britain, Claims Arbitration, 1872. 4 *Papers relating to the Treaty of Washington,* p. 49.

The three rules laid down by the Treaty of Washington of May 8, 1871,[34] for the guidance of the Arbitration Tribunal to decide the *Alabama Claims* case fully illustrate the essential duties of a neutral. A neutral state is required to prevent (1) the fitting out, arming, or equipping, within its jurisdiction, of any vessel for the use of one belligerent against another; (2) the use by one belligerent of its territorial domain for the operation or augmentation of military forces; and (3) any violation by persons within its jurisdiction of the above obligations.

Judging by these rules, the American exchange of over-age destroyers for naval and air bases in 1940 was definitely in violation of the neutral duty of the United States.[35] In spite of their over-age, these destroyers were still useful to the British navy; otherwise, there was no purpose in their transfer. With respect to individual acts of trading, granting loans,[36] or committing other unneutral services,[37] a neutral state should adopt appropriate measures of control in order to avoid grave complications. Of course, individuals concerned will suffer the consequences for breach of blockade, sale of contraband of war,[38] and other actions hostile to either side of the belligerents.

[34] Malloy, *Treaties*, I, p. 717.

[35] Art. 6 of Hague Convention XIII provides: "The supply in any manner, directly or indirectly, by a neutral Power to a belligerent Power of warships, ammunition or war material of any kind whatever is forbidden." Notwithstanding arguments of the United States Attorney-General to the contrary, the transfer of destroyers and the Lend-Lease Act were serious violations of the law of neutrality.

[36] Although a neutral government must refrain from granting loans to a belligerent, its nationals may do so. For the concept of loans to belligerents as investments, see Vattel, III, §110.

[37] Unneutral services committed by neutral ships may include carrying of enemy dispatches, transmission of intelligence, and transportation of enemy forces. Such ships may be subject to capture and condemnation. However, if the unneutral service is not committed in bad faith and there is other recourse of redress by the injured belligerent, the capture of the ship is not deemed proper. This was the ruling of the Tribunal of the Permanent Court of Arbitration in *The Manouba* case in 1913. Wilson, *Hague Arbitration Cases* (1915), p. 341.

[38] In deciding *Pearson v. Allis-Chalmers Co.* in 1915, the Wisconsin Circuit Court examined prevailing statutes and concluded that the act of selling contraband of war to a belligerent was not an offense. 11 *Am. Jour. Int. Law* (1917), p. 883. See also Art. 7 of Hague Convention V. A neutral state is not required under international law to forbid its nationals to sell contraband of war to belligerents. See *In re Grazebrook*, Great Britain, Court of Appeals in Bankruptcy, 1865 (34 L.J.N.S., Bank. 17); *The Helen*, Great Britain, High Court of Admiralty, 1865 (L.R.I.A. and E.1).

III. *PROBLEMS OF NEUTRAL TRADING WITH BELLIGERENTS* [39]

§233. BELLIGERENT INTERFERENCE WITH THE FREEDOM OF THE SEAS

Freedom of the seas is an established principle of international law, but has often been infringed during wartime by the exercise of the belligerent right of visit and search, blockade, and confiscation of contraband of war. The United States was the champion of the doctrine of the freedom of the seas throughout the Napoleonic Wars. She was also determined to oppose commercial depredation of the Barbary powers and peacetime visit and search by the British navy for the suppression of African slave-trading.[40] After the outbreak of World War I, however, unrestricted submarine warfare and the declaration of extensive war zones by the belligerents considerably undermined neutral shipping and commerce. The sinking of the *Lusitania,* a British passenger ship, on May 7, 1915, by a German submarine without warning, resulting in a loss of over one thousand lives, intensified American indignation at Germany.[41]

Freedom to navigate the high seas in peace and war is one of the Fourteen Points declared by President Wilson on January 8, 1918, as a statement of war aims of the United States.[42] After the conclusion of

[39] General texts on the subject: Oppenheim, II, §§368–447a; Fenwick, *Principles,* Chs. XXXI, §C; XXXIII, §C; Starke, Ch. 17, §3; Hyde, III, §§752–772, 797–843, 890–903; Moore, *Digest,* VII, §§1179–1182, 1195–1214, 1222–1286; Hackworth, *Digest,* VII, §§610–655; Hershey, pp. 647–650, 692–740; Schwarzenberger, I, Ch. 8 (V–VI); Von Glahn, pp. 648–660; Jacobini, pp. 283–291; Soviet *Text,* pp. 438–440; McNair, III, pp. 223–347.

[40] On May 15, 1820, Congress branded slave-trading as piracy, which is an international crime. However, the United States rejected the right of visit and search by the British navy in peacetime.

[41] In deciding the case of *The Lusitania* in 1918, the U.S. District Court (Southern District of N.Y.) first examined the German proclamation of February 4, 1915, which did not mention sinking enemy merchant vessels without warning. It then concluded: "There is, of course, no doubt as to the right to make prize of an enemy ship on the high seas, and, under certain conditions, to destroy her, and equally no doubt of the obligation to safeguard the lives of all persons aboard, whether passengers or crews. . . ." 251 F. 715. See also the opinions of the United States-Germany Mixed Claims Commission, 1923. *Annual Digest,* 1923–1924, Case No. 113.

[42] Point 2. For belligerent excessive measures in detriment to the freedom of the seas, see James W. Garner, *International Law and the World War,* I, §§214, 227.

World War I, further efforts were made to restrict submarine warfare. The London Naval Treaty of 1930, signed by Great Britain, France, Italy, Japan, and the United States, asserted that submarines must conform to the established rules of international law as surface vessels in their action against merchant ships.[43] The five naval powers signed another Protocol on November 6, 1936, before the expiration of the 1930 Treaty, incorporating the submarine provisions. The Protocol was open to adherence by other states, and such adherents numbered forty-eight prior to World War II, including Germany and the Soviet Union.[44] During the Spanish civil war, several powers signed the "Nyon Arrangement," condemning unlimited submarine warfare and reaffirming the 1936 Protocol as declaratory of international law.[45]

When the United States adopted the policy of patrols in the early part of World War II, German submarines attacked American vessels escorting war supplies to Great Britain in retaliation against unneutral service. After the destroyer *Greer* was attacked in September 1941, President Roosevelt ordered the United States navy to fire at sight upon German and Italian submarines and surface vessels. Meanwhile, he reasserted the traditional doctrine of freedom of the seas. After the United States entered the war in December 1941, submarine warfare was intensified by belligerents on both sides in ever extended war zones.[46] Because of the range of modern ballistic missiles and bombers armed with nuclear weapons, no part of the seas would be free from attack in future major wars.

§234. BLOCKADE

A blockade is to prevent by force the ingress or egress of ships and aircraft of all nations along a part or the whole of an enemy coast for strategic and commercial purposes.[47] Since the latter part of the

[43] Pt. IV of the Treaty, which was not ratified by France and Italy.

[44] For the text of the Protocol, see LN *Treaty Series*, 1936, No. 29.

[45] The Signatories of the 'Nyon Arrangement' were Great Britain, France, the Soviet Union, Turkey, Bulgaria, Egypt, Greece, Rumania, and Yugoslavia.

[46] Admiral Doenitz was convicted by the Nuremberg Tribunal in 1947 for sinking neutral vessels in war zones unilaterally declared by Germany in violation of the 1936 Protocol.

[47] The blockading belligerent may exercise its discretion to exempt certain neutral warships for particular purposes or other neutral ships under special permission. During World War I, vessels were allowed into blockaded ports for lack of provisions, stress of weather, or urgent necessity of repairs. A blockade may be enforced for commercial reasons even under the

sixteenth century,[48] blockade has been gradually developed as a legitimate means of warfare, with profound effect on neutral shipping and commerce. According to the Declaration of Paris of 1856, a blockade to be binding must be effective. In other words, a sufficient force must be maintained to prevent access to the coast of the enemy. A blockading force, chiefly warships in the past, may be assisted by aircraft and submarines; but the latter two alone cannot effectively undertake the task.[49] A blockade may be considered effective if the forces employed are such that any breach of blockade will bring considerable risk to the ships involved. An ineffective or paper blockade is legally not binding.

As the Declaration of London of 1909 was not ratified, there are no conventional rules governing blockade other than what was stated in the Declaration of Paris. However, the institution of blockade through centuries of practice and development has been well recognized by customary international law. A notification of blockade by the blockading belligerent is desirable but not essential, because blockade is a fact which may be made known by the blockading commander to neutral ships approaching the enemy coast.[50] Neutral ships already in enemy ports must be given a few days' time to depart. Punishment for actual breach of blockade is confiscation of the ship or cargo or both

present collective system. In the *Oriental Navigation Co. Claim,* the United States-Mexico General Claims Commission stated, in 1928, that there would still be economic warfare in future wars; for instance, the provisions of Art. 16 of the League Covenant. *Opinions of Commissioners* (1929), p. 23.

[48] The first blockade was imposed by Holland against the ports of Flanders controlled by Spain during the period 1584–1630. See Westlake, *Papers,* pp. 325–337.

[49] It should be noted that Art. 2 of Hague Convention VIII forbids the laying of automatic contact mines off the coasts and ports of the enemy with the sole purpose of intercepting commercial shipping.

[50] Here there is a difference between Continental and Anglo-Saxon writers, with the former holding the necessity of notification. Hence comes the term 'notified blockade' as distinguished from '*de facto* blockade.' But, once the existence of blockade is known to neutral ships, the legal effect is practically the same. In *The Adula,* the U.S. Supreme Court ruled, in 1900, that "a *de facto* blockade was also recognized as legal by this court in the case of *The Circassian* [1864], 2 Wall. 135, 150, 17 L. Ed. 796." Using the terms 'simple blockade' and 'public blockade' to represent the above categories, the Court made a further clarification as follows: "A simple blockade may be established by a naval officer, acting upon his own discretion or under the direction of superiors, without governmental notification; while a public blockade is not only established in fact, but is notified, by the government directing it, to other governments." 176 U.S. 361.

through adjudication by the prize court.[51] Sometimes an attempted breach of blockade may also be subject to punishment.[52]

Blockade can only be applied to enemy territory or areas temporarily under the control of the enemy. Thus, international rivers, canals, straits, gulfs, and bays must not be blockaded, possibly with the exception of the belligerent part of the waters.[53] Long distance blockade over an extensive war zone by the belligerents during the two world wars was an excessive claim of belligerent rights at the expense of neutral commerce.

Doctrine of continuous voyage The so-called doctrine of continuous voyage,[54] developed during the American Civil War, applies to such neutral vessels carrying contraband of war first to neutral ports but ultimately destined for a belligerent port. In deciding the leading cases, *The Springbok* and *The Peterhoff* in 1866,[55] the United States Supreme Court concluded that broken voyages designed for the evasion of blockade to trade with the enemy were actually a continuous voyage and that cargo on these neutral ships was subject to condemnation on the basis of the doctrine of ultimate destination through continuous transportation. Challenged by British and Continental writers at that time, this doctrine was actually applied during World War I.

[51] While holding that evidence of blockade was not clear and decisive in *The Betsey* case, the British High Court of Admiralty delivered the opinion on breach of blockade in 1798 as follows: "On the question of blockade, three things must be proved, 1st, The existence of an actual blockade; 2dly, The knowledge of the party; and 3rdly, Some act of violation, either by going in, or by coming out with a cargo laden after the commencement of blockade. . . ." 1 C. Rob. 93. The crew of the captured vessel may have to be temporarily interned to serve as witnesses before the prize court pending its decision of the case.

[52] According to Anglo-Saxon practice, an attempt of a breach of blockade applies to vessels sailing for a blockaded port or found near it even if the attempt is not shown in the ship's papers or by a continuous voyage. The Continental interpretation is generally restricted to actual use of force or ruse by a neutral vessel near the line of blockade.

[53] See *The Frau Ilsabe,* Great Britain, High Court of Admiralty, 1801. 4 C. Rob. 63.

[54] This doctrine can be traced back to the British rule of 1756 and was used in *The Essex* case in 1805. The rule of 1756 had its origin in time of war between Great Britain and France, when the latter permitted vessels of Holland and later of other neutrals to carry on trade between France proper and her colonies. The British prize court condemned these vessels and cargo on the ground of their unneutral service and assistance to France.

[55] *The Springbok,* 5 Wallace 1; *The Peterhoff,* 5 Wallace 28.

It is on the issues of blockade and contraband of war that the belligerents and neutrals have the conflicting claims of rights to an extreme extent. Sometimes the attitude of a state toward these rights changes as soon as its status shifts from neutrality to belligerency, such as that of the United States during World War I. The settlement of such issues is not solely a legal matter, but is largely dictated by military necessity and political expediency. In deciding *The Prize Cases* in 1862, the United States Supreme Court recognized both positions in stating that neutrals "have a right to enter the ports of a friendly nation for the purposes of trade and commerce, but are bound to recognize the rights of a belligerent engaged in actual war, to use this mode of coercion, for the purposes of subduing the enemy." [56] This situation is, of course, applied to both civil and foreign wars.

During the Spanish and the Chinese civil wars, the term 'closure of ports' was used instead of blockade in order to avoid legal complications, because a proclamation of blockade would, in effect, recognize the status of belligerency of the insurgents.[57] The Spanish government on August 20, 1936, and the Chinese government on June 20, 1949, notified the American embassies in Madrid and Canton respectively that certain coasts and ports would be closed to foreign vessels. In both cases, the government of the United States replied that it could not admit the legality of such action unless the blockade was effectively maintained. Evidently the United States made no legal distinction between closure of ports and blockade.[58]

A blockade may be terminated by the blockading belligerent itself for any reason whatever or by the superior force of the enemy belligerent. The neutrals will then be released from obligations arising out of blockade. Naval forces employed by the belligerent for the enforcement of blockade must cease such operations.

§235. CONTRABAND OF WAR

Contraband of war designates goods as can be used for war purposes and are thus prohibited by either belligerent to be transported to its enemy. Contraband is subject to condemnation after its seizure and

[56] 2 Black 635. In the same case, the Court held that "neutrals have a right to challenge the existence of a blockade *de facto* and also the authority of the party exercising the right to institute it."

[57] See *supra*, §28.

[58] See U.S. Department of State *Press Releases*, XV (August 29, 1936), No. 361, p. 192; Department of State *Bulletin*, XXI (July 11, 1949), No. 523, p. 34; XXII (January 2, 1950), No. 548, p. 23.

adjudication by the prize court of the capturing belligerent.[59] Grotius' classification of absolute and conditional contrabands has been generally followed by Anglo-Saxon practice, but the Continental states have been inclined to limit the extent of contraband to articles absolutely essential to war. The moot question is how to set up a standard which can be agreed upon by belligerents and neutrals. In an early case, *The Jonge Margaretha*, the British High Court of Admiralty admitted, in 1799, that the catalogue of contraband had varied very much owing to change of circumstances and that "the most important distinction is, whether the articles were intended for the ordinary use of life, or even for merchantile ships' use; or whether they were going with a highly probable destination to military use." [60]

The nature of the cargo determines the character of contraband if destined for an enemy port, but neutral cargo destined for a neutral country is not contraband.[61] The Declaration of Paris of 1856 laid down the rule governing contraband of war in two articles: a neutral flag covers an enemy's goods, with the exception of contraband of war (Art. 2); neutral goods, with the exception of contraband of war, are not liable to capture under an enemy's flag (Art. 3).[62] In deciding *The*

[59] In *The Knight Commander* case in 1905, the Supreme Prize Court of Russia decided that a British ship conveying contraband to the enemy in quantity exceeding one-half of her cargo should be condemned together with the contraband. 1 Hurst & Bray's *Russian and Japanese Prize Cases* (1912), p. 54; Tung, p. 302. In recent wars, Germany often destroyed captured vessels in violation of the recognized rules of international law. The German action was also due to practical difficulty in bringing the prize to a German port for adjudication because of the Allied naval superiority. For further details on the law of prize and related subjects, consult C. H. Huberich, *The Law Relating to Trading with the Enemy* (New York, 1918); H. Reason Pyke, *The Law of Contraband of War* (Oxford, 1915); Archer Polson, *Principles of the Law of Nations, with Practical Notes and Supplementary Essays on the Law of Blockade, and on Contraband of War*, 2nd ed. (London, 1859); J. C. Colombos, *A Treatise on the Law of Prize*, 3rd ed. (London, 1949); James W. Garner, *Prize Law during the World War* (New York, 1927).

[60] 1 C. Rob. 189. In this case, the Court confiscated the cargo without enforcing the usual penalty of confiscation of the ship.

[61] In *The Imina* case, the British High Court of Admiralty ordered, in 1800, restitution of cargo because the voyage was destined to a neutral port. 3 C. Rob. 167. For further discussion on destination of the cargo, see J. C. Colombos, *op. cit.*, §§171–188.

[62] When contraband goods are found on a neutral vessel, the free goods of the same owner are also subject to condemnation. Long in practice, this so-called doctrine of infection was adopted by the Declaration of London in 1909.

Marine Carp case in 1949, the Prize Court of Alexandria, Egypt, invoked Article 2 of the Paris Declaration and ordered the release of four shipments seized on the ground that "the protection of the neutral flag is settled not only in favor of neutrals, but equally in favor of owners of merchandise who are enemy subjects." [63] Notwithstanding the eloquent reasoning by Secretary W. H. Seward in the *Trent* Affair in 1861 that "persons, as well as property, may become contraband," [64] international law limits contraband to goods only.

The Declaration of London of 1909 made an attempt to add a third class as a free list to be distinguished from absolute and conditional contraband.[65] When World War I broke out, the United States urged the belligerents to observe the provisions of the unratified Declaration of London, but Great Britain made sweeping additions to the list of absolute contraband and objected to the rule laid down by the Declaration that the blockading belligerent "must not bar access to the ports or to the coasts of neutrals." On March 11, 1915, the British government declared that goods "of enemy destination, ownership, or origin" would be forbidden to proceed to or from the enemy directly or indirectly. Meanwhile, the doctrine of continuous voyage through the operation of continuous transportation was invoked to confiscate contraband intended for ultimate destination to the enemy.[66] From April 1916 on,

[63] 5 *Revue égyptienne de droit international* (1949), pp. 155–157; translation from Hudson, pp. 707–709. This decision was in accord with that of the same court in *The Dirigo* in 1919.

[64] Secretary Seward's note of December 26, 1861, to Lord Lyons, British Minister to Washington. The *Trent* was a British mail steamer. In November 1861, James M. Mason and John Slidell, sent by the Confederate government as commissioners to Europe for secret negotiations, boarded the *Trent* at Havana. Captain Wilkes of a Union sloop halted the British steamer and removed the two men on his own initiative and without bringing the ship before a prize court. They were neither military personnel nor destined for enemy territory. The British government was outraged by the American arbitrary act. President Lincoln decided to release the prisoners to placate public opinion in England. For further details of the incident, see Julius W. Pratt, *A History of United States Foreign Policy*, pp. 306–309; Moore, *Digest*, VII, §1265.

[65] Certain articles should be free from confiscation under whatever circumstances, such as those exclusively used for the sick and wounded and also the vessels carrying them. For the sake of humanity, belligerents should all agree on this.

[66] In *The Kim*, the British High Court of Justice decided, in 1915, to confiscate conditional contraband bound to enemy destination. [1915] Probate 215. In contrast to the opinions of many British writers, the British government favored the doctrine of continuous voyage. This attitude was

the distinction between absolute and conditional contraband was practically dropped.

Despite all these severe regulations dictated by the necessity of war, the British court decided contraband cases with reason and care.[67] For instance, in the case of *The Bonna* in 1918, the judge of the High Court of Justice discussed at length the possible application of the doctrine of continuous voyage to confiscate the cargo, but finally ordered its release with the following opinion:

> I do not consider that it would be in accordance with international law to hold that raw materials on their way to citizens of a neutral country to be converted into a manufactured article for consumption in that country were subject to condemnation on the ground that the consequence might, or even would, necessarily be that another article of a like kind, and adopted for a like use, would be exported by other citizens of the neutral country to the enemy.[68]

To prevent the neutral countries adjacent to Germany from importing goods for ultimate delivery to the enemy, Great Britain arbitrarily imposed a rationing quota on these countries on the basis of prewar figures. Enforcement of contraband went further during World War II. By the order in council of July 31, 1940, the so-called 'navicerts' system was instituted by the British government. 'Cargo navicert' means a pass issuable to a shipment of goods consigned to any port or place from which they might reach the enemy, to the effect that, so far as known at the date of issue, there is no objection to the consignment. 'Ship navicert' represents a pass issuable to a vessel for a given voyage. Thus, neutral shippers were required to apply for such passes from the appropriate British or Allied authorities in the neutral countries concerned to ensure that no contraband would be shipped to the enemy.[69]

With the innovation of the navicert system, the application of the doctrine of continuous voyage, and the ever-increasing number of articles as contraband, interference with neutral commerce reached a climax during World War II. Germany was not in a position to challenge the superior power of the British navy. Her resort was to unrestricted submarine warfare, which caused further damage to neutral shipping. The United States, traditional champion of neutral rights

---

further evidenced by British seizure of the German vessels *Bundesrath*, *Herzog*, and *General* in 1900, during the South African War.

[67] See James W. Garner, *Prize Law during the World War* (New York, 1927), Nos. 391–418.

[68] [1918] Probate 123.

[69] See also *Harvard Research* (1939), pp. 505–530.

and freedom of the seas, vigorously protested against the excessive claims of belligerents' rights, but, after entering the war, resigned herself to military expediency. With the drastic revolution in the nature of war, the traditional law of neutrality has to be revised to meet changing circumstances.

IV. *ENFORCEMENT OF THE TRADITIONAL RULES OF WAR AND NEUTRALITY*

§236. ON THE NEUTRALS

To prevent the carrying of contraband and breach of blockade by neutral vessels, a belligerent warship may exercise the right of visit, search, and capture on the high seas.[70] The prize may be condemned after adjudication by a prize court. Under compelling circumstances, enemy and neutral merchandise on board may be destroyed.[71] Any deliberate attempt by a neutral vessel to resist legitimate visit and search by a belligerent's warship makes the vessel subject to condemnation in prize.[72] However, the belligerent right in this respect has to be exercised with extreme care.

Compensation must be given for capture and detention of a neutral vessel without sufficient reason. This principle was reasserted by the Tribunal of the Permanent Court of Arbitration in *The Carthage* case in 1913.[73] A belligerent is also responsible for damage to a neutral vessel as a consequence of reprisals against an enemy.[74] On the per-

[70] Ever since the nineteenth century, the practice of visitation has been limited to private vessels.

[71] See *The Indian Prince,* Germany, Oberprisengericht, 1916. 1 *Entscheidungen des Oberprisengerichts,* p. 87; translation from the French, Hudson, pp. 681–683. When the plaintiffs appealed from the decision of the German prize court that the destroyed ship and cargo were subject to seizure, the appeal was refused for the following reasons: "In the prize matter of the *Glitra,* the competent court has decided that when an enemy prize is lawfully destroyed, neutral merchandise found on board such enemy ship and destroyed along with her is not entitled to compensation for damages. This decision is to be followed in spite of the contrary assertions made in the present case."

[72] This principle was upheld by the Supreme Court of Sierra Leone in *The Indo-Chinois case* in 1941. 1 *Lloyd's Prize Cases,* 2d, p. 73.

[73] Scott, *Hague Court Reports,* p. 330.

[74] In deciding the case of *The Cysne* in 1930, the Portugal-Germany Mixed Arbitral Tribunal held Germany liable for compensation to Portugal for the sinking by a German submarine in May 1915 of a Portuguese steamer with a cargo of pit props, which was deemed by Germany as

formance of various unneutral services by neutral vessels and nationals, a belligerent has the legitimate right to impose a penalty on them according to the circumstances of individual cases.[75]

If a neutral government is directly responsible for the commission or omission of any act in violation of neutral duties, the injured belligerent may demand reparations. Likewise, a neutral government may make claims against intrusions on its rights by a belligerent. Under extreme circumstances, either may use force against the other. Because of this possibility and in consideration of national interest, both belligerents and neutrals refrain from violating the recognized rules.

The settlement of *The Trent* affair was prompted by American desire to maintain peace with England. Threat of war and reprisals by the Union strengthened the determination of the British government to prevent more raiders of *The Alabama* type from joining the Confederate navy. When the Washington Treaty was signed in 1871 for the arbitration of the *Alabama Claims,* there was a possibility of war between Russia and Great Britain. It was partly to avoid a precedent for the United States to build 'Alabamas' for Russia that Great Britain decided to make concessions.[76] Taking into consideration both legal and political implications, the two governments settled the intricate dispute.

§237. ON THE BELLIGERENTS

Complaints of illegitimate warfare by one belligerent against another have frequently been made during wars. Upon the enemy's failure to comply with rules of warfare regardless of warnings, the injured belligerent may resort to reprisals. Because of lack of any provisions in the Hague Regulations, reprisals can be arbitrarily carried out to extreme severity.[77] In the two world wars, both sides applied retaliatory measures by extension of contraband lists and war zones, enforcement of extensive blockade, recourse to unrestricted submarine warfare and

---

absolute contraband in a measure of reprisal against England. *Annual Digest,* 1929–1930, No. 287.

[75] In *The Industrie,* the Sasebo Prize Court of Japan decided, in 1905, that to watch one of the belligerents and report military secrets to the other constituted unneutral service and that international law allowed condemnation of a neutral vessel employed for such a purpose. 2 Hurst & Bray's *Russian and Japanese Prize Cases* (1913), p. 323; Tung, p. 273.

[76] For details, see Malloy, *Treaties,* I, p. 717.

[77] The former practice of taking hostages is prohibited under Art. 34 of the 1949 Geneva Convention on the Protection of Civilians in Time of War. See *United States v. List and Others (Hostages Case),* the Military Tribunal at Nuremberg, 1947–1948. 8 *War Crimes Trials Reports,* p. 39.

air strikes, and other means to compel the enemy's observance of the Hague Conventions and other international instruments.[78]

Direct reprisals may be met with counter-reprisals,[79] and do not always achieve the desired end. Thus, belligerents have often lodged complaints with neutral governments in past wars, in the hope that the latter would render good offices and mediation. On many occasions, neutrals did intervene on various grounds in civil and foreign wars. Sometimes neutral intervention was motivated by reasons other than the violation of rules of warfare.[80]

Fear of punishment for war crimes and payment of heavy indemnity subsequent to defeat may also serve as a strong deterring force against violations of rules of warfare.[81] Another important factor is the pressure of world public opinion and the possibility of collective sanctions. If a belligerent endangers international peace as a consequence of warfare, the United Nations may decide on enforcement action through economic and military measures. Of course, any threat to, or breach of, peace or act of aggression is a concern of the Organization,[82] which has the important responsibility of preventing war and maintaining or restoring peace.

The world may be distressed at the fact that, after the adoption of the United Nations Charter and the establishment of collective security, the traditional practices of war and neutrality are still pursued. Discussion of principles and rules governing hostile relations among nations is still necessary.[83] The extent of constructive influence exerted by international law and organization on the community of nations depends much on the will of mankind. Legal principles and institutions alone cannot create a warless world if determined human efforts do not seek to achieve this goal. Clear understanding of the provisions of treaties outlawing war, elaboration of the legal consequences of resort

[78] Art. 3 of Hague Convention IV prescribes payment of compensation as a means of redress for the violation of Hague provisions.

[79] British prohibition of all imports to and exports from Germany during World War II was a kind of counter-reprisal against the German extension of the war zone and unrestricted submarine warfare, which were aimed at Great Britain in retaliation against the latter's sweeping list of absolute contraband.

[80] For details, see *supra*, §72.

[81] War indemnity is a common practice, imposed on a defeated power as a kind of punishment. The word 'reparation' was used in the Treaty of Versailles of 1919 in the sense of compensation for war losses and damages.

[82] See *supra*, §193; Ch. VII of the Charter.

[83] On the enforcement of the rules of war and neutrality, see E. Castrén, *The Present Law of War and Neutrality* (Helsinki, 1954); Oppenheim, II, §§241–260; Fenwick, *Principles*, Ch. XXIX, §H.

to force, and further examination of the observance by states of the common standard and rules of international law may, with other steps, contribute to a realization of the purposes and principles of the United Nations Charter to free men from the scourge of war.[84]

[84] A comprehensive discussion of the subject may be found in Quincy Wright, *The Role of International Law in the Elimination of War* (Manchester, 1961).

BIBLIOGRAPHY

This bibliography does not include all the sources used in the book. References already cited in footnotes are not repeated here except those cited only in abridged forms and a limited number of others selected for their general interest or importance. It should not be difficult for readers to find in the footnotes special treatises, articles, and documentary materials pertinent to various topics, which are numbered in consecutive sections.

I. OFFICIAL PUBLICATIONS

A. LEAGUE OF NATIONS PUBLICATIONS

The *Official Journal* (cited as LN *Official Jour.*) and special *Supplements* to the *Official Journal* contain records and documents of the Assembly, the Council, and other bodies of the League of Nations. For proceedings of all League organs, reference may be made to its *Monthly Summary.* The *Treaty Series* of the League is indispensable for the study of treaty relations among states. Publications of the Permanent Court of International Justice and their abridged symbols are listed in A Note on Abbreviations. For further study of League documents, Marie J. Carroll's *Key to League of Nations Documents Placed on Public Sale, 1920–1929* and its four supplementary volumes (to 1936) are helpful. A compact book of the same nature is Hans Aufricht's *Guide to League of Nations Publications: A Bibliographical Survey of the Works of the League, 1920–1947* (New York, 1951).

B. UNITED NATIONS PUBLICATIONS

Each organ of the United Nations has its *Official Records.* Many documents are also printed as supplements to *Official Records.* The *Yearbook of the United Nations* (cited as *Yearbook,* UN), *Yearbook of the International Court of Justice* (cited as *Yearbook,* I.C.J.), *Yearbook of the International Law Commission* (cited as *Yearbook,* Int. Law Com.), and *Yearbook on Human Rights* are extremely useful. The *Treaty Series* is published continuously by the United Nations. A summary of the work of the United Nations each year is contained in the *Annual Report of the Secretary-General of the Work of the Organization. Everyman's United Nations* (cited as *Everyman's UN*) is a ready reference for the general public. An official monthly, the *United Nations Review* (formerly the semi-monthly United Nations *Bulletin*), comprises summaries of United Nations activities as well as articles of popular interest. The *Review* was replaced by the *UN Monthly Chronicle* in May 1964.

An analytical summary of the application of the United Nations Charter can be found in the *Repertory of Practice of United Nations Organs* (United Nations, 1955, cited as *Repertory,* UN), 5 vols., and its *Supplements* (one additional volume containing table of contents and subject index to vols. I–V, 1957; Supp. No. 1, 2 vols., 1958; Supp. No. 2, 3 vols., 1963–1964). Of the same nature but limited to the practice of the Security Council are the *Repertoire of the Practice of the Security Council, 1946–1951* (United Nations, 1954, cited as *Repertoire,* SC) and its *Supplements* (one volume each for 1952–1955, 1956–1958, 1959–1963). Reports of the International Court of Justice are cited as I.C.J. Reports. Rules of Procedure of the General Assembly, the Security Council, the Economic and Social Council, and the Trusteeship Council are indispensable references on the functioning of these principal organs of the United Nations.

The United Nations has published numerous volumes in legal, economic, social, educational, and other fields, which are essential for research on specific topics. For the study of jurisdiction over waters, for instance, the *United Nations Conference on the Law of the Sea* (7 vols., 1958) and the *Second United Nations Conference on the Law of the Sea* (1960) must be consulted. Likewise, *Documents of the United Nations Conference on International Organization, San Francisco, 1945* (16 vols., United Nations, 1945–1946, cited as *Documents,* UNCIO) is indispensable to research on the establishment of the United Nations. A summary of the United Nations deliberations and negotiations on disarmament in the past two decades can be found in *The United Nations and Disarmament 1945–1965,* which includes also a postscript on developments in 1966 and early 1967. Further information on documentary materials on the United Nations and specialized agencies can be found in Brenda Brimmer and others (eds.), *A Guide to the Use of United Nations Documents* (Dobbs Ferry, N.Y., 1962); *A Bibliography of the Charter of the United Nations* (United Nations, 1955).

C. GOVERNMENT PUBLICATIONS

This section is limited to publications frequently referred to in this work. Official gazettes and bulletins of different countries, already cited in the footnotes, are not repeated here.

Br. & For. St. Papers *British and Foreign State Papers,* 1812–. Compiled and edited by the Foreign Office, London.

Documents on Disarmament, 1945–1959. Washington, D.C.: Department of State Publication 7008, 1960, 2 vols.

Dumbarton Oaks Conversations on World Organization, August 21 to October 7, 1944. London: H.M. Stationery Office, 1944. Misc. No. 4 (1944), Cmd. 6560.

Dumbarton Oaks Documents on International Organization. Washington, D.C.: Department of State, Conf. Ser. 56, publication 2192.

Hackworth, *Digest* Hackworth, G. H., *Digest of International Law.* Washington, D.C.: Government Printing Office, 1940–1944, 8 vols.

International Military Tribunal, Nuremberg, *Trial of the Major War Criminals before the International Military Tribunal, Nuremberg, 1945–1946, Official Documents,* 1947–1949, 42 vols.

Malloy, *Treaties* Malloy, W. M., *Treaties, Conventions, Internal Acts, Protocols and Agreements between the United States and Other Powers.* Washington, D.C.: Government Printing Office, 1910–. Vols. I–II, 1776–1909 (1910); Vol. III, 1910–1923, by C. F. Redmond (1923); Vol. IV, 1923–1937, by Edward J. Trenwith (1938).

Moore, *Digest* Moore, J. B., *A Digest of International Law.* Washington, D.C.: Government Printing Office, 1906, 8 vols.

Moore, *Int. Arbitrations* Moore, J. B., *History and Digest of International Arbitrations to Which the United States Has Been a Party.* Washington, D.C.: Government Printing Office, 1898, 6 vols.

Opinions of Commissioners Claims Commission, United States and Mexico, *Opinions of Commissioners under the Convention Concluded September 8, 1923.* Washington, D.C.: Government Printing Office, 1927, 1929, 1931, 3 vols.

Ralston's *Report* *Venezuelan Arbitrations of 1903.* U.S. Senate Doc. 316, 58th Cong., 2nd Sess., 1904, Report of Jackson H. Ralston.

Report to the President on the Results of the San Francisco Conference by the Chairman of the United States Delegation, the Secretary of State, June 26, 1945. Department of State publication 2349, Conf. Ser. 71. Washington, D.C.: Government Printing Office, 1945.

U.S. For. Rel. *Papers relating to the Foreign Relations of the United States,* 1861–. Washington, D.C.: Government Printing Office.

U.S. Senate Committee on Foreign Relations (83rd Cong., 2nd Sess.), Subcommittee on the United Nations Charter, Review of the United Nations Charter, 1954–1955. 12 Staff Studies, Doc. No. 164; also issued separately. Washington, D.C.: Government Printing Office, 1954–1955.

Wharton Wharton, F., *A Digest of the International Law of the United States.* Washington, D.C.: Government Printing Office, 1886, 3 vols.

Whiteman, *Digest* Whiteman, M. M., *Digest of International Law.* Washington, D.C.: Government Printing Office, 5 vols. up to 1966.

II. UNOFFICIAL COLLECTIONS OF CASES, DOCUMENTS, AND OTHER MATERIALS

While law reports and documentary materials can be found in official sources, the following collections are most convenient references for students and general readers. Certain old editions of casebooks are included, chiefly because they contain cases and documents not easily available elsewhere. All casebooks appear in abbreviations as shown below.

Annual Digest *Annual Digest and Reports of Public International Law Cases.* 13 vols. to 1952, covering 1919–1946; appearing as *International Law Reports* since 1950. London: Butterworth, 1919–.

Bentwich Bentwich, N., *Students Leading Cases and Statutes on International Law.* London: Sweet & Maxwell, 1913.

Bishop Bishop, W. W., Jr., *International Law Cases and Materials.* 2nd ed. New York: Prentice-Hall, 1962.

Briggs Briggs, H. W., *The Law of Nations: Cases, Documents, and Notes.* 2nd ed. New York: Appleton-Century-Crofts, 1952.

Cobbett Cobbett, P., *Leading Cases and Opinions on International Law.* 4th ed. London: Sweet & Maxwell, 1913, 1922, 2 vols.

Dickinson Dickinson, E. D., *Cases and Materials on International Law.* Brooklyn: Foundation Press, 1950.

Evans Evans, L. B., *Leading Cases on International Law.* 2nd ed. Chicago: Gallaghan, 1922.

Feller, A. H., and M. O. Hudson, *Diplomatic and Consular Laws and Regulations of Various Countries.* Washington, D.C.: Carnegie Endowment for International Peace, 1933, 2 vols.

Fenwick Fenwick, C. G., *Cases on International Law.* 2nd ed. Chicago: Gallaghan, 1951.

Flournoy, R. W., and M. O. Hudson, *A Collection of Nationality Laws of Various Countries as Contained in Constitutions, Statutes and Treaties.* New York: Oxford University Press, 1929.

Green Green, L. C., *International Law Through Cases.* 2nd ed. New York: Praeger, 1955.

Hertslet, *Treaties* Hertslet, Edward, *Treaties, etc. between Great Britain and China; and between China and Foreign Powers; and Orders in Council, Rules, Regulations, Acts of Parliament, Decrees, etc. affecting British Interests in China.* 3rd ed. London: Harison, 1908. By Godfrey E. P. Hertslet, covering a period of 1689–1907, 2 vols.

Higgins, A. P., *The Hague Peace Conferences and Other International Conferences concerning the Laws and Usages of War.* Cambridge, England: At the University Press, 1909.

Hudson Hudson, M. O., *Cases and Other Materials on International Law.* 3rd ed. St. Paul: West Publishing Co., 1951.

Hudson, M. O., *International Legislation, 1919–1945*. Washington, D.C.: Carnegie Endowment for International Peace, 1931–1952, 9 vols.

Hudson, M. O., *World Court Reports, 1922–1942*. Washington, D.C.: Carnegie Endowment for International Peace, 1934–1943, 4 vols.

Jaeger & O'Brien Jaeger, H. E., and M. V. O'Brien, *International Law: Cases, Text Notes and Other Materials*. Washington, D.C.: Georgetown University Press, 1958.

MacMurray, *Treaties* MacMurray, J. V. A., *Treaties and Agreements with and concerning China, 1894–1919*. New York: Oxford University Press, 1921, 2 vols.

McNair McNair, A. D. (ed.), *International Law Opinions*. Cambridge, England: Cambridge University Press, 1956, 3 vols.

Mangone Mangone, G. J., *The Elements of International Law: A Casebook*. Homewood, Ill.: Dorsey Press, 1963.

Moore, J. B., *International Adjudications*. New York: Oxford University Press, 1929–1933, 6 vols.

Orfield Orfield, L. B., and E. D. Re, *Cases and Materials on International Law*. Indianapolis: Bobbs-Merrill Co., 1955.

Scott Scott, J. B., *Cases on International Law*. St. Paul: West Publishing Co., 1922.

Scott, J. B., *The Hague Conventions and Declarations of 1899 and 1907*. New York: Oxford University Press, 1915.

Scott, J. B., *Hague Court Reports*. Washington, D.C.: Carnegie Endowment for International Peace, 1916; 2nd ser., 1932.

Scott, J. B., *The Reports to the Hague Conferences of 1899 and 1907*. London & New York: Oxford University Press, 1917.

Sohn Sohn, L. B., *Cases and Materials on World Law*. New York: The Foundation Press, 1950, with a 1953 *Supplement* in a separate booklet.

Stowell & Munro Stowell, E. C., and H. F. Munro, *International Cases*. Boston: Houghton Mifflin, 1916, 2 vols.

Tung Tung, W. L., *Cases and Other Materials on International Law*. Shanghai: Evans Book Co., 1940.

Watkins & Robinson Watkins, J. T., and J. W. Robinson, *General International Organization*. Princeton: D. Van Nostrand, 1956.

III. TREATISES, YEARBOOKS, AND PERIODICALS

This section lists all general texts referred to in abbreviated form in this work. Special treatises on various topics except a few of general interest or importance are not listed here; their full titles and publishing data can be found in the footnotes. Articles cited in the footnotes are too numerous to be repeated here. Most of them are drawn from the *American Journal of International Law;* other important sources are *British Yearbook of International Law, Transactions of the Grotius Society, Proceedings* of the Annual Meetings of the American Society of International Law, *International Con-*

ciliation, and *International Organization.* Other law reviews and journals are indicated in the footnotes together with the articles appearing in them. A limited number of yearbooks (other than those published by the United Nations) and important periodicals are listed below.

Am. Jour. Int. Law *American Journal of International Law,* a quarterly, Washington, D.C., 1907–.

Blaisdell Blaisdell, D. C., *International Organization.* New York: Ronald Press, 1966.

Borchard, E. M., *Diplomatic Protection of Citizens Abroad.* New York: Bank Law Publishing Co., 1915.

Bowett, D. W., *The Law of International Institutions.* New York: Praeger, 1963.

Bowett, D. W., *United Nations Forces: A Legal Study.* New York: Praeger, 1964.

Brierly Brierly, J. L., *The Law of Nations* (edited by Sir Humphrey Waldock). 6th ed. Oxford: Clarendon Press, 1963.

British Yearbook of International Law, published since 1920.

Bynkershoek Bynkershoek, C. van, *De Mominio Maris Dissertatio (The Dissertation on the Sovereignty of the Sea).* Translated by Ralph van Deman Magoffin from the 1744 ed. Washington, D.C.: Carnegie Endowment for International Peace, 1923.

Calvo Calvo, C., *Le Droit international: théorique et pratique.* 5th ed. Paris: Arthur Rousseau, 1896, 6 vols.

Chowdhuri, R. N., *International Mandates and Trusteeship Systems.* The Hague: Martinus Nijhoff, 1955.

Clark & Sohn Clark, G., and L. B. Sohn, *World Peace through World Law.* 2nd ed. Cambridge: Harvard University Press, 1962.

Claude Claude, I. L., Jr., *Swords into Plowshares: The Problems and Progress of International Organization.* 3rd ed. New York: Random House, 1964.

Cohen, M. (ed.), *Law and Politics in Space.* Montreal: McGill University Press, 1964.

Commission to Study the Organization of Peace: *Reports* (9th, 1955; 17th, 1966).

Corbett Corbett, P. E., *Law in Diplomacy.* Princeton: Princeton University Press, 1959.

Davis Davis, G. B., *The Elements of International Law.* 4th ed. New York: Harper, 1916.

De Louter De Louter, J., *Le Droit international public positif.* French translation from the Dutch. Oxford: Imprimerie de L'Université, 1920, 2 vols.

De Visscher, C., *Theory and Reality in Public International Law.* Translation from the French by P. E. Corbett. Princeton: Princeton University Press, 1957.

Despagnet Despagnet, F., *Cour de droit international public.* 4th ed. Paris: Ancienne Maison L. Larose & Forcel, 1910.

Dunn, F. S., *The Practice and Procedure of International Conferences.* Baltimore: Johns Hopkins Press, 1929.

Dunn, F. S., *The Protection of Nationals.* Baltimore: Johns Hopkins Press, 1932.

Eagleton Eagleton, C., *International Government.* 3rd ed. New York: Ronald Press, 1957.

Falk, R. A., *Law and Morality and War in the Contemporary World.* New York: Praeger, 1963.

Falk & Mendlovitz Falk, R. A., and S. H. Mendlovitz (eds.), *The Strategy of World Order,* New York: World Law Fund, 1966, 4 vols.

Fauchille Fauchille, P., *Traité de droit international public.* 8th ed. Paris: Arthur Rousseau, 2 vols. Vol. I, Pt. 1 (1922), Pt. 2 (1925), Pt. 3 (1926); Vol. II (1921).

Fenwick, *Principles* Fenwick, C. G., *International Law.* 4th ed. New York: Appleton-Century-Crofts, 1965.

Fiore Fiore, P., *International Law Codified and Its Legal Sanction or the Legal Organization of the Society of States.* Translation from the 5th Italian ed. by Edwin M. Borchard. New York: Baker, Voorhis & Co., 1918.

Friedmann Friedmann, W., *The Changing Structure of International Law.* New York: Columbia University Press, 1964.

Garner, J. W., *International Law and the World War.* New York: Longmans, Green & Co., 1920, 2 vols.

Garner, J. W., *Recent Developments in International Law.* Calcutta: University of Calcutta Press, 1925.

Genet Genet, R., *Traité de diplomatie et de droit diplomatique.* Paris: Publications de la revue génerale de droit international public, 1931–1932, 3 vols.

Gidel Gidel, G., *Le Droit international public de la mer, le temps de paix.* Paris: Recueil Sirey, 1932–1934, 3 vols.

Goodrich Goodrich, L. M., *The United Nations.* New York: Thomas Y. Crowell Co., 1959.

Goodrich & Hambro Goodrich, L. M., and E. Hambro, *Charter of the United Nations: Commentary and Documents.* 2nd ed. Boston: World Peace Foundation, 1949.

Goodspeed Goodspeed, S. S., *The Nature and Function of International Organization.* New York: Oxford University Press, 1959; 2nd ed., 1967.

Gould Gould, W. L., *An Introduction to International Law.* New York: Harper, 1957.

Greenspan, M., *The Modern Law of Land Warfare.* Berkeley: University of California Press, 1959.

Grotius Grotius, H., *De Jure Belli ac Pacis, Libri Tres (The Law of War and Peace).* Translated by Francis W. Kelsey from the text of 1646 ed., 2 vols. Vol. I, photographic reproduction of 1646 ed.; Vol. II, translation. Washington, D.C.: Carnegie Endowment for International Peace, 1925.

Grotius Society *Grotius Society, Transactions of the,* published since 1915.

Hague *Recueil* *Recueil des cours de l'Académie de Droit International de la Haye.*

Haley, A. G., *Space Law and Government.* New York: Appleton-Century-Crofts, 1963.

Hall Hall, W. E., *A Treatise on International Law.* 8th ed. by A. P. Higgins. Oxford: Clarendon Press, 1924.

Halleck Halleck, H. W., *International Law.* 4th English ed. by G. S. Baker. London: Kegan Paul, Trench, Trubner & Co., 1908, 2 vols.

Harvard Research Harvard Research in International Law, under the auspices of the Harvard Law School. Draft Conventions prepared for the codification of international law, directed by M. O. Hudson. *Am. Jour. Int. Law, Special Supp.*, 1929, 1932, 1935, 1939. 1929: Nationality; Responsibility of States for Injuries to Aliens; Territorial Waters. 1932: Diplomatic Privileges and Immunities; Legal Position and Functions of Consuls; Competence of Courts in Regard to Foreign States; Piracy; A Collection of Piracy Laws of Various Countries. 1935: Extradition; Jurisdiction with Respect to Crime; Law of Treaties. 1939: Judicial Assistance; Rights and Duties of Neutral States in Naval and Aerial War; Rights and Duties of States in Case of Aggression.

Hazeltine Hazeltine, H. D., *The Law of the Air.* London: Hodder & Stoughton, 1911.

Hershey Hershey, A. S., *The Essentials of International Public Law and Organization.* New York: Macmillan, 1927.

Higgins, A. P., and C. J. Colombos, *The International Law of the Sea.* 4th ed. London & New York: Longmans, Green & Co., 1959.

Higgins, R., *The Development of International Law through the Political Organs of the United Nations.* New York: Oxford University Press, 1963.

Hoffmann, S. H. (ed.), *Contemporary Theory in International Relations.* Englewood Cliffs, N.J.: Prentice-Hall, 1960.

Holland, *Lectures* Holland, T. E., *Lectures on International Law.* Edited by T. A. Walker and W. L. Walker. London: Sweet & Maxwell, 1933.

Holland, *Studies* Holland, T. E., *Studies in International Law.* London: Oxford University Press, 1898.

Holland, *War* Holland, T. E., *The Laws of War on Land.* London: Oxford University Press, 1908.

Hovet, T., Jr., *Bloc Politics in the United Nations.* Cambridge: Harvard University Press, 1960.

Hudson, M. O., *The Permanent Court of International Justice, 1920–1942.* New York: Macmillan, 1943.

Hyde Hyde, C. C., *International Law Chiefly as Interpreted and Applied by the United States.* 2nd ed. Boston: Little, Brown & Co., 1945, 3 vols.

International Conciliation, published five times a year, New York, 1907–.

Int. Organization *International Organization,* published quarterly, Boston, 1947–.

Jacob & Atherton Jacob, P. E., and A. L. Atherton, *The Dynamics of International Organization: The Making of World Order.* Homewood, Ill.: Dorsey Press, 1965.

Jacobini Jacobini, H. B., *International Law.* Homewood, Ill.: Dorsey Press, 1962.

Jenks, C. W., *The Common Law of Mankind.* London: Stevens, 1958.

Jenks, C. W., *The Proper Law of International Organizations.* London: Stevens, 1962.

Jessup Jessup, P. C., *A Modern Law of Nations.* New York: Macmillan, 1948.

Jessup, P. C., *The Law of Territorial Waters and Maritime Jurisdiction.* New York: G. A. Jennings Co., 1927.

Jessup, P. C., *Transnational Law.* New Haven: Yale University Press, 1956.

Jessup, P. C., and H. J. Taubenfeld, *Controls for Outer Space and the Antarctic Analogy.* New York: Columbia University Press, 1959.

Jessup, P. C., F. Deak, W. A. Phillips, A. H. Reed, and E. Turlington, *Neutrality: Its History, Economics and Law.* New York: Columbia University Press, 1935–1936, 4 vols.

Kaplan & Katzenbach Kaplan, M. A., and N. DeB. Katzenbach, *The Political Foundations of International Law.* New York: John Wiley, 1961.

Kelsen Kelsen, H., *Principles of International Law.* 2nd ed., revised and edited by Robert W. Tucker. New York: Holt, Rinehart & Winston, 1966.

Kelsen, *UN* Kelsen, H., *The Law of the United Nations.* London: Stevens, 1950.

Koo, W., Jr., *Voting Procedures in International Political Organizations.* New York: Columbia University Press, 1947.

Korowicz Korowicz, M. St., *Introduction to International Law.* The Hague: Martinus Nijhoff, 1964.

Lauterpacht, H., *The Development of International Law by the International Court.* New York: Praeger, 1958.

Lauterpacht, H., *International Law and Human Rights.* London: Stevens, 1950.

Lawrence Lawrence, T. J., *The Principles of International Law.* 7th ed. edited by P. H. Winfield. New York: D. C. Heath, 1923.

Le Fur Le Fur, L., *Précis de droit international public.* 3rd ed. Paris: Librairie Dalloz, 1937.

Leonard Leonard, L. L., *International Organization.* New York: McGraw-Hill, 1951.

Lissitzyn, O. J., *The International Court of Justice: Its Role in the Maintenance of International Peace and Security.* New York: Carnegie Endowment for International Peace, 1951.

Lissitzyn, O. J., *International Law in a Divided World.* New York: Carnegie Endowment for International Peace, 1963. (*International Conciliation,* No. 542, March 1963.)

Liszt Liszt, F. V., *Le Droit international.* Translation from the 9th German ed. by Gilbert Gidel. Paris: A. Pedone, 1927.

McDougal, M. S., and associates, *Studies in World Public Order.* New Haven: Yale University Press, 1960.

McDougal, M. S., and W. T. Burke, *The Public Order of the Oceans.* New Haven: Yale University Press, 1962.

McDougal, M. S., and F. P. Feliciano, *Law and Minimum World Public Order.* New Haven: Yale University Press, 1961.

McDougal, M. S., H. D. Lasswell, and I. A. Vlasic, *Law and Public Order in Space.* New Haven: Yale University Press, 1963.

McFee, W., *The Law of the Sea.* Philadelphia: J. B. Lippincott Co., 1950.

McNair, A. D., *The Law of the Air,* 2nd ed. edited by M. R. E. Kerr and R. A. MacCrindle. London: Stevens, 1953.

McNair, A D., *The Law of Treaties—British Practice and Opinions.* Oxford: Clarendon Press, 1961.

McNair, Lord, and A. D. Watts, *The Legal Effects of War.* New York: Cambridge University Press, 1967.

Maine Maine, H. J. S., *International Law.* 2nd ed. New York: Henry Holt, 1894.

Mangone, G. J., *A Short History of International Organization.* New York: McGraw-Hill, 1954.

Manning Manning, W. O., *Commentaries on the Law of Nations.* Rev. ed. by Sheldon Amos. London: Macmillan, 1875.

Martens, F. de, *Traité de droit international.* Translation from the original Russian by A. Léo. Paris: Chevalier Marescq, 1883–1887, 3 vols.

Mendlovitz, S. H. (ed.), *Legal and Political Problems of World Order.* New York: World Law Fund, 1962.

Mérignhac Mérignhac, A., *Traité de droit international.* Paris: Librairie générale de droit et de jurisprudence, 3 vols. Vol. I, 1905; II, 1907; III, 1912.

Miller, D. H., *The Drafting of the Covenant.* New York: Putnam, 1928, 2 vols.

Morgenthau, H. J., *Politics among Nations.* 3rd ed. New York: Knopf, 1960.

Murray, J. N., Jr., *The United Nations Trusteeship System.* Urbana: University of Illinois Press, 1957.

Myers, D. P., *Handbook of the League of Nations since 1920.* Boston: World Peace Foundation, 1930.

Nussbaum, A., *A Concise History of the Law of Nations.* Rev. ed. New York: Macmillan, 1954.

Nys Nys, E., *Le Droit international.* 2nd ed. Bruxelles: A. Castiagne, 1912, 3 vols.

O'Brien, W. V. (ed.), *The New Nations in International Law and Diplomacy.* New York: Praeger, 1965.

O'Connell O'Connell, D. P., *International Law*. London: Stevens, 1965, 2 vols.

O'Connell, D. P., *The Law of State Succession*. Cambridge, England: Cambridge University Press, 1956.

Oppenheim Oppenheim, L., *International Law: A Treatise*. Edited by H. Lauterpacht. London: Longmans, Green & Co., 2 vols. Vol. I, 8th ed., 1955; Vol. II, 7th ed., 1952.

Örvik, N., *The Decline of Neutrality, 1914–1941, with Special Reference to the United States and the Northern Neutrals*. Oslo: Tanum, 1953.

Pastuhov, V. D., *A Guide to the Practice of International Conferences*. Washington, D.C.: Carnegie Endowment for International Peace, 1945.

Phillimore Phillimore, R., *Commentaries upon International Law*. 3rd ed. London: Butterworths, 4 vols. Vol. I, 1879; II, 1882; III, 1885; IV, 1889.

Phillipson, C., *Termination of War and Treaties of Peace*. London: Unwin, 1916.

Piédelièvre Piédelièvre, R., *Précis de droit international public ou droit des gens*. Paris: Librairie Cotillon, F. Piehon, 1894–1895, 2 vols.

Plischke Plischke, E., *Conduct of American Diplomacy*. New York: D. Van Nostrand, 1950.

Pompe, C. A., *Aggressive War an International Crime*. The Hague: Martinus Nijhoff, 1953.

Potter, P. B., *An Introduction to the Study of International Organization*. 5th ed. New York: Appleton, 1948.

Praag Praag, L. V., *Jurisdiction et droit international public*. La Haye: Librairie Belinfante Frères, 1915.

Pradier-Fodéré Pradier-Fodéré, P., *Traité de droit international public, européen et américain*. Paris: A. Durand et Pedone-Lauriel, 8 vols. Vol I, 1885; II, 1885; III, 1887; IV, 1888; V, 1891; VI, 1894; VII, 1897; VIII, 1906.

Proceedings of Am. Society Int. Law *Proceedings* of the Annual Meetings of the American Society of International Law, Washington, D.C., 1907–.

Pufendorf Pufendorf, S., *De Jure Naturae et Gentium (The Law of Nature and Nations)*. Translation from the 1688 ed. by C. H. Oldfather and W. A. Oldfather, 2 vols. Vol. I, photographic reproduction of 1688 ed.; Vol. II, translation. Washington, D.C.: Carnegie Endowment for International Peace, 1934.

Rivier Rivier, A., *Principes de droit des gens*. Paris: Arthur Rousseau, 1896, 2 vols.

Roth, A. H., *The Minimum Standard of International Law Applied to Aliens*. Leiden: A. W. Sijthoff, 1950.

Royal Institute of International Affairs, *International Sanctions*. London: Oxford University Press, 1938.

Russell, R. B., *A History of the United Nations Charter*. Washington, D.C.: The Brookings Institution, 1958.

Satow Satow, E., *A Guide to Diplomatic Practice.* 4th ed. edited by Sir Nevile Bland. New York: Longmans, Green & Co., 1957.

Schuschnigg Schuschnigg, K. von, *International Law: An Introduction to the Law of Peace.* Milwaukee: Bruce Publishing Co., 1959.

Schwarzenberger Schwarzenberger, G., *A Manual of International Law.* 4th ed. London: Stevens, 1960, 2 vols.

Sen Sen, B., *A Diplomat's Handbook of International Law and Practice.* The Hague: Martinus Nijhoff, 1965.

Singh, N., *Nuclear Weapons and International Law.* New York: Praeger, 1959.

Smedal, G., *Acquisition of Sovereignty over Polar Areas.* Oslo: Dybwad, 1931.

Smith, H. A., *The Law and Custom of the Sea.* 3rd ed. London: Stevens, 1959.

Soviet *Text* Academy of Sciences of U.S.S.R., Institute of State and Law, *International Law: A Textbook for Use in Law Schools.* Moscow: Foreign Languages Publishing House, n.d.

Soviet Yearbook of International Law, Moscow, Academy of Sciences of U.S.S.R., 1958–.

Spaight, J. M., *Air Power and War Rights.* London: Longmans, Green & Co., 1947.

Spaight, J. M., *Aircraft in Peace and the Law.* London: Macmillan, 1919.

Spaight, J. M., *War Rights on Land.* London: Macmillan, 1911.

Starke Starke, J. G., *An Introduction to International Law.* 5th ed. London: Butterworths, 1963.

Stockton Stockton, C. H., *Outlines of International Law.* New York: Charles Scribner's Sons, 1914.

Stoessinger, J. G., *The Might of Nations.* Rev. ed. New York: Random House, 1965.

Stoessinger, J. G., *The United Nations and the Superpowers.* New York: Random House, 1965.

Stoessinger, J. G., and associates, *Financing the United Nations System.* Washington, D.C.: The Brookings Institution, 1964.

Stone, J., *Legal Controls of International Conflict: A Treatise on the Dynamics of Disputes- and War-Law.* Rev. ed. London: Stevens, 1959.

Strupp & Blociszewski Strupp, K., and J. Blociszewski, *Eléments du droit international public, universel, européen et américain.* 2nd ed. Paris: Arthur Rousseau, 1930, 3 vols.

Stuart Stuart, G. H., *American Diplomatic and Consular Practice.* 2nd ed. New York: Appleton-Century-Crofts, 1952.

Svarlien Svarlien, O., *Introduction to the Law of Nations.* New York: McGraw-Hill, 1955.

Taracouzio, T. A., *The Soviet Union and International Law.* New York: Macmillan, 1935.

Taylor Taylor, H., *A Treatise on International Law.* Chicago: Callaghan, 1901.

Testa Testa, C., *Le Droit public international, maritime principes généraux—règles pratiques.* Translated from Portuguese into French by Ad. Boutiron. Paris: À Durand et Pedone-Lauriel, 1886.

Thayer Thayer, C. W., *Diplomat.* New York: Harper, 1959.

Toussaint, C. E., *The Trusteeship System of the United Nations.* New York: Praeger, 1956.

Toynbee, A. J., *Survey of International Affairs,* published annually since 1924. London: Humphrey Milford.

Triska, J. F., and R. M. Slusser, *The Theory, Law, and Policy of Soviet Treaties.* Stanford: Stanford University Press, 1962.

Tunkin, G. I., *Coexistence and International Law (Recueil).* The Hague: Academy of International Law, 1958.

Twiss Twiss, T., *The Law of Nations Considered as Independent Political Communities.* London: Oxford University Press, 2 vols. Vol. I, 1884; II, 1875.

Vattel Vattel, E. de, *Le Droit des gens ou principes de la loi naturelle (The Law of Nations or the Principles of Natural Law).* Translated by Charles G. Fenwick from the 1758 ed., 3 vols. Vols. I–II, photographic reproduction of 1758 ed.; Vol. III, translation. Washington, D.C.: Carnegie Endowment for International Peace, 1916.

Von Glahn von Glahn, G., *Law among Nations: An Introduction to Public International Law.* New York: Macmillan, 1965.

Walters, F. P., *A History of the League of Nations.* New York: Oxford University Press, 1952, 2 vols.

Westlake Westlake, J., *International Law.* 2nd ed. Cambridge, England: Cambridge University Press, 1910–1913, 2 vols.

Westlake, *Chapters* Westlake, J., *Chapters on the Principles of International Law.* Cambridge, England: Cambridge University Press, 1894.

Westlake, *Papers* Westlake, J., *The Collected Papers of John Westlake on Public International Law.* Edited by L. Oppenheim. Cambridge, England: Cambridge University Press, 1914.

Wheaton-Atlay Wheaton, H., *Elements of International Law.* 4th ed. by J. B. Atlay. London: Stevens, 1904.

Whitaker Whitaker, U. G., Jr., *Politics and Power: A Text in International Law.* New York: Harper, 1964.

Wilcox & Marcy Wilcox, F. O., and C. M. Marcy, *Proposals for Changes in the United Nations.* Washington, D.C.: The Brookings Institution, 1955.

Wilson, G. G., *Handbook of International Law.* 3rd ed. St. Paul: West Publishing Co., 1939.

Wilson, G. G., *International Law.* 9th ed. New York: Silver Burdett Co., 1935.

Wilson & Tucker Wilson, G. G., and G. F. Tucker, *International Law.* 5th ed. New York: Silver Burdett Co., 1910.

Wolff Wolff, C., *Jus Gentium Methodo Scientifica Pertractatum (The Law of Nations Treated according to a Scientific Method).* Translated by Joseph H. Drake from the 1764 ed., 2 vols. Vol. I, photographic reproduction of 1764 ed.; Vol. II, translation. Washington, D.C.: Carnegie Endowment for International Peace, 1934.

Woolsey Woolsey, Th. D., *Introduction to the Study of International Law*. 6th ed. revised and enlarged by Theodore S. Woolsey. New York: Charles Scribner's Sons, 1892.

Wright, Q., *Contemporary International Law: A Balance Sheet*. Rev. ed. New York: Random House, 1961.

Wright, Q., *International Law and the United Nations*. New York: Asia Publishing House, 1960.

Wright, Q., *Mandates under the League of Nations*. Chicago: University of Chicago Press, 1930.

Wright, Q., *Research in International Law since the War*. Washington, D.C.: Carnegie Endowment for International Peace, 1930.

Wright, Q., *The Role of International Law in the Elimination of War*. Manchester: Manchester University Press, 1961.

Wright, Q., *The Strengthening of International Law*. The Hague: Academy of International Law, 1960.

Wright, Q., *The Study of International Relations*. New York: Appleton-Century-Crofts, 1955.

Wright, Q., *A Study of War*. Chicago: University of Chicago Press, 1942, 2 vols.; 2nd ed., 1965.

Yearbook of the European Convention on Human Rights. The Hague: Martinus Nijhoff, 1959–.

Yearbook of World Affairs, published by the London Institute of World Affairs, 1947–.

Zimmern, A., *The League of Nations and the Rule of Law, 1918–1935*. London: Macmillan, 1936.

APPENDICES

APPENDIX I

COVENANT OF THE LEAGUE OF NATIONS*

THE HIGH CONTRACTING PARTIES,

In order to promote international co-operation and to achieve international peace and security

by the acceptance of obligations not to resort to war,

by the prescription of open, just and honourable relations between nations,

by the firm establishment of the understandings of international law as the actual rule of conduct among Governments,

and by the maintenance of justice and a scrupulous respect for all treaty obligations in the dealings of organized peoples with one another,

Agree to this Covenant of the League of Nations.

Article 1

1. The original Members of the League of Nations shall be those of the Signatories which are named in the Annex to this Covenant and also such of those other States named in the Annex as shall accede without reservation to this Covenant. Such accession shall be effected by a Declaration deposited with the Secretariat within two months of the coming into force of the Covenant. Notice thereof shall be sent to all other Members of the League.

2. Any fully self-governing State, Dominion or Colony not named in the Annex may become a Member of the League if its admission is agreed to by two-thirds of the Assembly, provided that it shall give effective guarantees of its sincere intention to observe its international obligations, and shall accept

* The text in italics is that of the amended provisions.

such regulations as may be prescribed by the League in regard to its military, naval and air forces and armaments.

3. Any Member of the League may, after two years' notice of its intention so to do, withdraw from the League, provided that all its international obligations and all its obligations under this Covenant shall have been fulfilled at the time of its withdrawal.

Article 2

The action of the League under this Covenant shall be effected through the instrumentality of an Assembly and of a Council, with a permanent Secretariat.

Article 3

1. The Assembly shall consist of Representatives of the Members of the League.

2. The Assembly shall meet at stated intervals and from time to time as occasion may require at the Seat of the League or at such other place as may be decided upon.

3. The Assembly may deal at its meetings with any matter within the sphere of action of the League or affecting the peace of the world.

4. At meetings of the Assembly, each Member of the League shall have one vote, and may have not more than three Representatives.

Article 4

1. The Council shall consist of Representatives of the Principal Allied and Associated Powers, together with Representatives of four other Members of the League. These four Members of the League shall be selected by the Assembly from time to time in its discretion. Until the appointment of the Representatives of the four Members of the League first selected by the Assembly, Representatives of Belgium, Brazil, Spain and Greece shall be members of the Council.

2. With the approval of the majority of the Assembly, the Council may name additional Members of the League whose Representatives shall always be Members of the Council; the Council, with like approval may increase the number of Members of the League to be selected by the Assembly for representation on the Council.

2bis. The Assembly shall fix by a two-thirds majority the rules dealing with the election of the non-permanent Members of the Council, and particularly such regulations as relate to their term of office and the conditions of re-eligibility.

3. The Council shall meet from time to time as occasion may require, and at least once a year, at the Seat of the League, or at such other place as may be decided upon.

4. The Council may deal at its meetings with any matter within the sphere of action of the League or affecting the peace of the world.

5. Any Member of the League not represented on the Council shall be

invited to send a Representative to sit as a member at any meeting of the Council during the consideration of matters specially affecting the interests of that Member of the League.

6. At meetings of the Council, each Member of the League represented on the Council shall have one vote, and may have not more than one Representative.

Article 5

1. Except where otherwise expressly provided in this Covenant or by the terms of the present Treaty, decisions at any meeting of the Assembly or of the Council, shall require the agreement of all the Members of the League represented at the meeting.

2. All matters of procedure at meetings of the Assembly or of the Council, including the appointment of Committees to investigate particular matters, shall be regulated by the Assembly or by the Council and may be decided by a majority of the Members of the League represented at the meeting.

3. The first meeting of the Assembly and the first meeting of the Council shall be summoned by the President of the United States of America.

Article 6

1. The permanent Secretariat shall be established at the Seat of the League. The Secretariat shall comprise a Secretary-General and such secretaries and staff as may be required.

2. The first Secretary-General shall be the person named in the Annex; thereafter the Secretary-General shall be appointed by the Council with the approval of the majority of the Assembly.

3. The secretaries and staff of the Secretariat shall be appointed by the Secretary-General with the approval of the Council.

4. The Secretary-General shall act in that capacity at all meetings of the Assembly and of the Council.

5. *The expenses of the League shall be borne by the Members of the League in the proportion decided by the Assembly.*

Article 7

1. The Seat of the League is established at Geneva.

2. The Council may at any time decide that the Seat of the League shall be established elsewhere.

3. All positions under or in connection with the League, including the Secretariat, shall be open equally to men and women.

4. Representatives of the Members of the League and officials of the League when engaged on the business of the League shall enjoy diplomatic privileges and immunities.

5. The buildings and other property occupied by the League or its officials or by Representatives attending its meetings shall be inviolable.

Article 8

1. The Members of the League recognize that the maintenance of peace requires the reduction of national armaments to the lowest point consistent with national safety and the enforcement by common action of international obligations.

2. The Council, taking account of the geographical situation and circumstances of each State, shall formulate plans for such reduction for the consideration and action of the several Governments.

3. Such plans shall be subject to reconsideration and revision at least every ten years.

4. After these plans have been adopted by the several Governments, the limits of armaments therein fixed shall not be exceeded without the concurrence of the Council.

5. The Members of the League agree that the manufacture by private enterprise of munitions and implements of war is open to grave objections. The Council shall advise how the evil effects attendant upon such manufacture can be prevented, due regard being had to the necessities of those Members of the League which are not able to manufacture the munitions and implements of war necessary for their safety.

6. The Members of the League undertake to interchange full and frank information as to the scale of their armaments, their military, naval and air programmes and the condition of such of their industries as are adaptable to warlike purposes.

Article 9

A permanent Commission shall be constituted to advise the Council on the execution of the provisions of Articles 1 and 8 on military, naval and air questions generally.

Article 10

The Members of the League undertake to respect and preserve as against external aggression the territorial integrity and existing political independence of all Members of the League. In case of any such aggression or in case of any threat or danger of such aggression, the Council shall advise upon the means by which this obligation shall be fulfilled.

Article 11

1. Any war or threat of war, whether immediately affecting any of the Members of the League or not, is hereby declared a matter of concern to the whole League, and the League shall take any action that may be deemed wise and effectual to safeguard the peace of nations. In case any such emergency should arise, the Secretary-General shall, on the request of any Member of the League, forthwith summon a meeting of the Council.

2. It is also declared to be the friendly right of each Member of the League to bring to the attention of the Assembly or of the Council any circumstance whatever affecting international relations which threatens to

disturb international peace or the good understanding between nations upon which peace depends.

Article 12

1. The Members of the League agree that if there should arise between them any dispute likely to lead to a rupture they will submit the matter either to arbitration or *judicial settlement* or to enquiry by the Council, and they agree in no case to resort to war until three months after the award by the arbitrators *or the judicial decision* or the report by the Council.

2. In any case under this Article the award of the arbitrators *or the judicial decision* shall be made within a reasonable time, and the report of the Council shall be made within six months after the submission of the dispute.

Article 13

1. The Members of the League agree that whenever any dispute shall arise between them which they recognize to be suitable for submission to arbitration *or judicial settlement,* and which cannot be satisfactorily settled by diplomacy, they will submit the whole subject-matter to arbitration *or judicial settlement.*

2. Disputes as to the interpretation of a treaty, as to any question of international law, as to the existence of any fact which, if established, would constitute a breach of any international obligation, or as to the extent and nature of the reparation to be made for any such breach, are declared to be among those which are generally suitable for submission to arbitration *or judicial settlement.*

3. *For the consideration of any such dispute, the court to which the case is referred shall be the Permanent Court of International Justice, established in accordance with Article 14, or any tribunal agreed on by the parties to the dispute or stipulated in any convention existing between them.*

4. The Members of the League agree that they will carry out in full good faith any award *or decision* that may be rendered, and that they will not resort to war against a Member of the League which complies therewith. In the event of any failure to carry out such an award *or decision,* the Council shall propose what steps should be taken to give effect thereto.

Article 14

The Council shall formulate and submit to the Members of the League for adoption plans for the establishment of a Permanent Court of International Justice. The Court shall be competent to hear and determine any dispute of an international character which the parties thereto submit to it. The Court may also give an advisory opinion upon any dispute or question referred to it by the Council or by the Assembly.

Article 15

1. If there should arise between Members of the League any dispute likely to lead to a rupture, which is not submitted to arbitration *or judicial*

settlement in accordance with Article 13, the Members of the League agree that they will submit the matter to the Council. Any party to the dispute may effect such submission by giving notice of the existence of the dispute to the Secretary-General, who will make all necessary arrangements for a full investigation and consideration thereof.

2. For this purpose, the parties to the dispute will communicate to the Secretary-General, as promptly as possible, statements of their case with all the relevant facts and papers, and the Council may forthwith direct the publication thereof.

3. The Council shall endeavour to effect a settlement of the dispute, and if such efforts are successful, a statement shall be made public giving such facts and explanations regarding the dispute and the terms of settlement thereof as the Council may deem appropriate.

4. If the dispute is not thus settled, the Council either unanimously or by a majority vote shall make and publish a report containing a statement of the facts of the dispute and the recommendations which are deemed just and proper in regard thereto.

5. Any Member of the League represented on the Council may make public a statement of the facts of the dispute and of its conclusions regarding the same.

6. If a report by the Council is unanimously agreed to by the members thereof other than the Representatives of one or more of the parties to the dispute, the Members of the League agree that they will not go to war with any party to the dispute which complies with the recommendations of the report.

7. If the Council fails to reach a report which is unanimously agreed to by the members thereof, other than the Representatives of one or more of the parties to the dispute, the Members of the League reserve to themselves the right to take such action as they shall consider necessary for the maintenance of right and justice.

8. If the dispute between the parties is claimed by one of them, and is found by the Council, to arise out of a matter which by international law is solely within the domestic jurisdiction of that party, the Council shall so report, and shall make no recommendation as to its settlement.

9. The Council may in any case under this Article refer the dispute to the Assembly. The dispute shall be so referred at the request of either party to the dispute provided that such request be made within fourteen days after the submission of the dispute to the Council.

10. In any case referred to the Assembly, all the provisions of this Article and of Article 12 relating to the action and powers of the Council shall apply to the action and powers of the Assembly, provided that a report made by the Assembly, if concurred in by the Representatives of those Members of the League represented on the Council and of a majority of the other Members of the League, exclusive in each case of the Representatives of the parties to the dispute, shall have the same force as a report by the Council concurred in by all the members thereof other than the Representatives of one or more of the parties to the dispute.

Article 16

1. Should any Member of the League resort to war in disregard of its covenants under Articles 12, 13 or 15, it shall *ipso facto* be deemed to have committed an act of war against all other Members of the League, which hereby undertake immediately to subject it to the severance of all trade or financial relations, the prohibition of all intercourse between their nationals and the nationals of the covenant-breaking State, and the prevention of all financial, commercial or personal intercourse between the nationals of the covenant-breaking State and the nationals of any other State, whether a Member of the League or not.

2. It shall be the duty of the Council in such case to recommend to the several Governments concerned what effective military, naval or air force the Members of the League shall severally contribute to the armed forces to be used to protect the covenants of the League.

3. The members of the League agree, further, that they will mutually support one another in the financial and economic measures which are taken under this Article, in order to minimise the loss and inconvenience resulting from the above measures, and that they will mutually support one another in resisting any special measures aimed at one of their number by the covenant-breaking State, and that they will take the necessary steps to afford passage through their territory to the forces of any of the Members of the League which are co-operating to protect the covenants of the League.

4. Any Member of the League which has violated any covenant of the League may be declared to be no longer a Member of the League by a vote of the Council concurred in by the Representatives of all the other Members of the League represented thereon.

Article 17

1. In the event of a dispute between a Member of the League and a State which is not a member of the League, or between States not members of the League, the State or States not members of the League shall be invited to accept the obligations of membership in the League for the purposes of such dispute, upon such conditions as the Council may deem just. If such invitation is accepted, the provisions of Articles 12 to 16 inclusive shall be applied with such modifications as may be deemed necessary by the Council.

2. Upon such invitation being given, the Council shall immediately institute an enquiry into the circumstances of the dispute and recommend such action as may seem best and most effectual in the circumstances.

3. If a State so invited shall refuse to accept the obligations of membership in the League for the purposes of such dispute, and shall resort to war against a Member of the League, the provisions of Article 16 shall be applicable as against the State taking such action.

4. If both parties to the dispute when so invited refuse to accept the obligations of membership in the League for the purposes of such dispute, the Council may take such measures and make such recommendations as will prevent hostilities and will result in the settlement of the dispute.

Article 18

Every treaty or international engagement entered into hereafter by any Member of the League shall be forthwith registered with the Secretariat and shall as soon as possible be published by it. No such treaty or international engagement shall be binding until so registered.

Article 19

The Assembly may from time to time advise the reconsideration by Members of the League of treaties which have become inapplicable and the consideration of international conditions whose continuance might endanger the peace of the world.

Article 20

1. The Members of the League severally agree that this Covenant is accepted as abrogating all obligations or understandings *inter se* which are inconsistent with the terms thereof, and solemnly undertake that they will not hereafter enter into any engagements inconsistent with the terms thereof.

2. In case any Member of the League shall, before becoming a Member of the League, have undertaken any obligations inconsistent with the terms of this Covenant, it shall be the duty of such Member to take immediate steps to procure its release from such obligations.

Article 21

Nothing in this Covenant shall be deemed to affect the validity of international engagements, such as treaties of arbitration or regional understandings like the Monroe doctrine, for securing the maintenance of peace.

Article 22

1. To those colonies and territories which as a consequence of the late war have ceased to be under the sovereignty of the States which formerly governed them and which are inhabited by peoples not yet able to stand by themselves under the strenuous conditions of the modern world, there should be applied the principle that the well-being and development of such peoples form a sacred trust of civilisation and that securities for the performance of this trust should be embodied in this Covenant.

2. The best method of giving practical effect to this principle is that the tutelage of such peoples should be entrusted to advanced nations who, by reason of their resources, their experience or their geographical position, can best undertake this responsibility, and who are willing to accept it, and that this tutelage should be exercised by them as Mandatories on behalf of the League.

3. The character of the mandate must differ according to the stage of the development of the people, the geographical situation of the territory, its economic conditions and other similar circumstances.

4. Certain communities formerly belonging to the Turkish Empire have reached a stage of development where their existence as independent nations

can be provisionally recognised subject to the rendering of administrative advice and assistance by a Mandatory until such time as they are able to stand alone. The wishes of these communities must be a principal consideration in the selection of the Mandatory.

5. Other peoples, especially those of Central Africa, are at such a stage that the Mandatory must be responsible for the administration of the territory under conditions which will guarantee freedom of conscience and religion, subject only to the maintenance of public order and morals, the prohibition of abuses such as the slave trade, the arms traffic and the liquor traffic, and the prevention of the establishment of fortifications or military and naval bases and of military training of the natives for other than police purposes and the defence of territory, and will also secure equal opportunities for the trade and commerce of other Members of the League.

6. There are territories, such as South West Africa and certain of the South Pacific Islands, which, owing to the sparseness of their population, or their small size, or their remoteness from the centres of civilisation, or their geographical contiguity to the territory of the Mandatory, and other circumstances, can be best administered under the laws of the Mandatory as integral portions of its territory, subject to the safeguards above mentioned in the interests of the indigenous population.

7. In every case of mandate, the Mandatory shall render to the Council an annual report in reference to the territory committed to its charge.

8. The degree of authority, control or administration to be exercised by the Mandatory shall, if not previously agreed upon by the Members of the League, be explicitly defined in each case by the Council.

9. A permanent Commission shall be constituted to receive and examine the annual reports of the Mandatories and to advise the Council on all matters relating to the observance of the mandates.

Article 23

Subject to and in accordance with the provisions of international conventions existing or hereafter to be agreed upon, the Members of the League:

(a) will endeavour to secure and maintain fair and humane conditions of labour for men, women and children, both in their own countries and in all countries to which their commercial and industrial relations extend, and for that purpose will establish and maintain the necessary international organisations;

(b) undertake to secure just treatment of the native inhabitants of territories under their control;

(c) will entrust the League with the general supervision over the execution of agreements with regard to the traffic in women and children, and the traffic in opium and other dangerous drugs;

(d) will entrust the League with the general supervision of the trade in arms and ammunition with the countries in which the control of this traffic is necessary in the common interest;

(e) will make provision to secure and maintain freedom of communications and of transit and equitable treatment for the commerce of all

Members of the League. In this connection, the special necessities of the regions devastated during the war of 1914–1918 shall be borne in mind;

(f) will endeavour to take steps in matters of international concern for the prevention and control of disease.

Article 24

1. There shall be placed under the direction of the League all international bureaux already established by general treaties if the parties to such treaties consent. All such international bureaux and all commissions for the regulation of matters of international interest hereafter constituted shall be placed under the direction of the League.

2. In all matters of international interest which are regulated by general conventions but which are not placed under the control of international bureaux or commissions, the Secretariat of the League shall, subject to the consent of the Council and if desired by the parties, collect and distribute all relevant information and shall render any other assistance which may be necessary or desirable.

3. The Council may include as part of the expenses of the Secretariat the expenses of any bureau or commission which is placed under the direction of the League.

Article 25

The Members of the League agree to encourage and promote the establishment and co-operation of duly authorised voluntary national Red Cross organisations having as purposes the improvement of health, the prevention of disease and the mitigation of suffering throughout the world.

Article 26

1. Amendments to this Covenant will take effect when ratified by the Members of the League whose Representatives compose the Council and by a majority of the Members of the League whose Representatives compose the Assembly.

2. No such amendments shall bind any Member of the League which signifies its dissent therefrom, but in that case it shall cease to be a Member of the League.

ANNEX TO THE COVENANT

I. ORIGINAL MEMBERS OF THE LEAGUE OF NATIONS, SIGNATORIES OF THE TREATY OF PEACE

United States of America
Belgium
Bolivia
Brazil
British Empire
    Canada
    Australia
    South Africa
    New Zealand
    India
China
Cuba
Ecuador
France
Greece
Guatemala
Haiti
Hejaz
Honduras
Italy
Japan
Liberia
Nicaragua
Panama
Peru
Poland
Portugal
Rumania
Serb-Croat-Slovene State
Siam
Czechoslovakia
Uruguay

STATES INVITED TO ACCEDE TO THE COVENANT

Argentine Republic
Chile
Colombia
Denmark
Netherlands
Norway
Paraguay
Persia
Salvador
Spain
Sweden
Switzerland
Venezuela

II. FIRST SECRETARY-GENERAL OF THE LEAGUE OF NATIONS.

THE HON. SIR JAMES ERIC DRUMMOND, K.C.M.G., C.B.

APPENDIX II

CHARTER OF THE UNITED NATIONS*

WE THE PEOPLES OF THE UNITED NATIONS DETERMINED

to save succeeding generations from the scourge of war, which twice in our lifetime has brought untold sorrow to mankind, and

to reaffirm faith in fundamental human rights, in the dignity and worth of the human person, in the equal rights of men and women and of nations large and small, and

to establish conditions under which justice and respect for the obligations arising from treaties and other sources of international law can be maintained, and

to promote social progress and better standards of life in larger freedom,

AND FOR THESE ENDS

to practice tolerance and live together in peace with one another as good neighbors, and

to unite our strength to maintain international peace and security, and

to ensure, by the acceptance of principles and the institution of methods, that armed force shall not be used, save in the common interest, and

to employ international machinery for the promotion of the economic and social advancement of all peoples,

* The passages in italics are the amended provisions in substitution for those enclosed in brackets.

HAVE RESOLVED TO COMBINE OUR EFFORTS TO ACCOMPLISH THESE AIMS.

Accordingly, our respective Governments, through representatives assembled in the city of San Francisco, who have exhibited their full powers found to be in good and due form, have agreed to the present Charter of the United Nations and do hereby establish an international organization to be known as the United Nations.

CHAPTER I

PURPOSES AND PRINCIPLES

Article 1

The Purposes of the United Nations are:

1. To maintain international peace and security, and to that end: to take effective collective measures for the prevention and removal of threats to the peace, and for the suppression of acts of aggression or other breaches of the peace, and to bring about by peaceful means, and in conformity with the principles of justice and international law, adjustment or settlement of international disputes or situations which might lead to a breach of the peace;

2. To develop friendly relations among nations based on respect for the principle of equal rights and self-determination of peoples, and to take other appropriate measures to strengthen universal peace;

3. To achieve international cooperation in solving international problems on an economic, social, cultural, or humanitarian character, and in promoting and encouraging respect for human rights and for fundamental freedoms for all without distinction as to race, sex, language, or religion; and

4. To be a center for harmonizing the actions of nations in the attainment of these common ends.

Article 2

The Organization and its Members, in pursuit of the Purposes stated in Article 1, shall act in accordance with the following Principles.

1. The Organization is based on the principle of the sovereign equality of all its Members.

2. All Members, in order to ensure to all of them the rights and benefits resulting from membership, shall fulfill in good faith the obligations assumed by them in accordance with the present Charter.

3. All Members shall settle their international disputes by peaceful means in such a manner that international peace and security, and justice, are not endangered.

4. All Members shall refrain in their international relations from the threat or use of force against the territorial integrity or political independence of any state, or in any other manner inconsistent with the Purposes of the United Nations.

5. All Members shall give the United Nations every assistance in any action it takes in accordance with the present Charter, and shall refrain from giving assistance to any state against which the United Nations is taking preventive or enforcement action.

6. The Organization shall ensure that states which are not Members of the United Nations act in accordance with these Principles so far as may be necessary for the maintenance of international peace and security.

7. Nothing contained in the present Charter shall authorize the United Nations to intervene in matters which are essentially within the domestic jurisdiction of any state or shall require the Members to submit such matters to settlement under the present Charter; but this principle shall not prejudice the application of enforcement measures under Chapter VII.

CHAPTER II

MEMBERSHIP

Article 3

The original Members of the United Nations shall be the states which, having participated in the United Nations Conference on International Organization at San Francisco, or having previously signed the Declaration by United Nations of January 1, 1942, sign the present Charter and ratify it in accordance with Article 110.

Article 4

1. Membership in the United Nations is open to all other peace-loving states which accept the obligations contained in the present Charter and, in the judgment of the Organization, are able and willing to carry out these obligations.

2. The admission of any such state to membership in the United Nations will be effected by a decision of the General Assembly upon the recommendation of the Security Council.

Article 5

A Member of the United Nations against which preventive or enforcement action has been taken by the Security Council may be suspended from the exercise of the rights and privileges of membership by the General Assembly upon the recommendation of the Security Council. The exercise of these rights and privileges may be restored by the Security Council.

Article 6

A Member of the United Nations which has persistently violated the Principles contained in the present Charter may be expelled from the Organization by the General Assembly upon the recommendation of the Security Council.

CHAPTER III

ORGANS

Article 7

1. There are established as the principal organs of the United Nations: a General Assembly, a Security Council, an Economic and Social Council, a Trusteeship Council, an International Court of Justice, and a Secretariat.

2. Such subsidiary organs as may be found necessary may be established in accordance with the present Charter.

Article 8

The United Nations shall place no restrictions on the eligibility of men and women to participate in any capacity and under conditions of equality in its principal and subsidiary organs.

CHAPTER IV

THE GENERAL ASSEMBLY

COMPOSITION

Article 9

1. The General Assembly shall consist of all the Members of the United Nations.

2. Each Member shall have not more than five representatives in the General Assembly.

FUNCTIONS AND POWERS

Article 10

The General Assembly may discuss any questions or any matters within the scope of the present Charter or relating to the powers and functions of any organs provided for in the present Charter, and except as provided in Article 12, may make recommendations to the Members of the United Nations or to the Security Council or to both on any such questions or matters.

Article 11

1. The General Assembly may consider the general principles of co-operation in the maintenance of international peace and security, including the principles governing disarmament and the regulation of armaments, and may make recommendations with regard to such principles to the Members or to the Security Council or to both.

2. The General Assembly may discuss any questions relating to the

maintenance of international peace and security brought before it by any Member of the United Nations, or by the Security Council, or by a state which is not a Member of the United Nations in accordance with Article 35, paragraph 2, and, except as provided in Article 12, may make recommendations with regard to any such questions to the state or states concerned or to the Security Council or to both. Any such question on which action is necessary shall be referred to the Security Council by the General Assembly either before or after discussion.

3. The General Assembly may call the attention of the Security Council to situations which are likely to endanger international peace and security.

4. The powers of the General Assembly set forth in this Article shall not limit the general scope of Article 10.

Article 12

1. While the Security Council is exercising in respect of any dispute or situation the functions assigned to it in the present Charter, the General Assembly shall not make any recommendation with regard to that dispute or situation unless the Security Council so requests.

2. The Secretary-General, with the consent of the Security Council, shall notify the General Assembly at each session of any matters relative to the maintenance of international peace and security which are being dealt with by the Security Council and shall similarly notify the General Assembly, or the Members of the United Nations if the General Assembly is not in session, immediately the Security Council ceases to deal with such matters.

Article 13

1. The General Assembly shall initiate studies and make recommendations for the purpose of:

a. promoting international cooperation in the political field and encouraging the progressive development of international law and its codification;

b. promoting international cooperation in the economic, social, cultural, educational, and health fields, and assisting in the realization of human rights and fundamental freedoms for all without distinction as to race, sex, language, or religion.

2. The further responsibilities, functions, and powers of the General Assembly with respect to matters mentioned in paragraph 1 (b) above are set forth in Chapters IX and X.

Article 14

Subject to the provisions of Article 12, the General Assembly may recommend measures for the peaceful adjustment of any situation, regardless of origin, which it deems likely to impair the general welfare or friendly relations among nations, including situations resulting from a violation of the provisions of the present Charter setting forth the Purposes and Principles of the United Nations.

Article 15

1. The General Assembly shall receive and consider annual and special reports from the Security Council; these reports shall include an account of the measures that the Security Council has decided upon or taken to maintain international peace and security.

2. The General Assembly shall receive and consider reports from the other organs of the United Nations.

Article 16

The General Assembly shall perform such functions with respect to the international trusteeship system as are assigned to it under Chapters XII and XIII, including the approval of the trusteeship agreements for areas not designated as strategic.

Article 17

1. The General Assembly shall consider and approve the budget of the Organization.

2. The expenses of the Organization shall be borne by the Members as apportioned by the General Assembly.

3. The General Assembly shall consider and approve any financial and budgetary arrangements with specialized agencies referred to in Article 57 and shall examine the administrative budgets of such specialized agencies with a view to making recommendations to the agencies concerned.

VOTING

Article 18

1. Each member of the General Assembly shall have one vote.

2. Decisions of the General Assembly on important questions shall be made by a two-thirds majority of the members present and voting. These questions shall include: recommendations with respect to the maintenance of international peace and security, the election of the non-permanent members of the Security Council, the election of the members of the Economic and Social Council, the election of members of the Trusteeship Council in accordance with paragraph 1 (c) of Article 86, the admission of new Members to the United Nations, the suspension of the rights and privileges of membership, the expulsion of Members, questions relating to the operation of the trusteeship system, and budgetary questions.

3. Decisions on other questions, including the determination of additional categories of questions to be decided by a two-thirds majority, shall be made by a majority of the members present and voting.

Article 19

A Member of the United Nations which is in arrears in the payment of its financial contributions to the Organization shall have no vote in the

General Assembly if the amount of its arrears equals or exceeds the amount of the contributions due from it for the preceding two full years. The General Assembly may, nevertheless, permit such a Member to vote if it is satisfied that the failure to pay is due to conditions beyond the control of the Member.

PROCEDURE

Article 20

The General Assembly shall meet in regular annual sessions and in such special sessions as occasion may require. Special sessions shall be convoked by the Secretary-General at the request of the Security Council or of a majority of the Members of the United Nations.

Article 21

The General Assembly shall adopt its own rules of procedure. It shall elect its President for each session.

Article 22

The General Assembly may establish such subsidiary organs as it deems necessary for the performance of its functions.

CHAPTER V

THE SECURITY COUNCIL

COMPOSITION

Article 23

1. The Security Council shall consist of [eleven] *fifteen* Members of the United Nations. The Republic of China, France, the Union of Soviet Socialist Republics, the United Kingdom of Great Britain and Northern Ireland, and the United States of America shall be permanent members of the Security Council. The General Assembly shall elect [six] *ten* other Members of the United Nations to be non-permanent members of the Security Council, due regard being specially paid, in the first instance to the contribution of Members of the United Nations to the maintenance of international peace and security and to the other purposes of the Organization, and also to equitable geographical distribution.

2. The non-permanent members of the Security Council shall be elected for a term of two years. In the first election of the non-permanent members [however, three shall be chosen for a term of one year] *after the increase of the membership of the Security Council from eleven to fifteen, two of the four additional members shall be chosen for a term of one year.* A retiring member shall not be eligible for immediate re-election.

3. Each member of the Security Council shall have one representative.

FUNCTIONS AND POWERS

Article 24

1. In order to ensure prompt and effective action by the United Nations, its Members confer on the Security Council primary responsibility for the maintenance of international peace and security, and agree that in carrying out its duties under this responsibility the Security Council acts on their behalf.

2. In discharging these duties the Security Council shall act in accordance with the Purposes and Principles of the United Nations. The specific powers granted to the Security Council for the discharge of these duties are laid down in Chapters VI, VII, VIII, and XII.

3. The Security Council shall submit annual and, when necessary, special reports to the General Assembly for its consideration.

Article 25

The Members of the United Nations agree to accept and carry out the decisions of the Security Council in accordance with the present Charter.

Article 26

In order to promote the establishment and maintenance of international peace and security with the least diversion for armaments of the world's human and economic resources, the Security Council shall be responsible for formulating, with the assistance of the Military Staff Committee referred to in Article 47, plans to be submitted to the Members of the United Nations for the establishment of a system for the regulation of armaments.

VOTING

Article 27

1. Each member of the Security Council shall have one vote.

2. Decisions of the Security Council on procedural matters shall be made by an affirmative vote of [seven] *nine* members.

3. Decisions of the Security Council on all other matters shall be made by an affirmative vote of [seven] *nine* members including the concurring votes of the permanent members; provided that, in decisions under Chapter VI, and under paragraph 3 of Article 52, a party to a dispute shall abstain from voting.

PROCEDURE

Article 28

1. The Security Council shall be so organized as to be able to function continuously. Each member of the Security Council shall for this purpose be represented at all times at the seat of the Organization.

2. The Security Council shall hold periodic meetings at which each of its members may, if it so desires, be represented by a member of the government or by some other specially designated representative.

3. The Security Council may hold meetings at such places other than the seat of the Organization as in its judgment will best facilitate its work.

Article 29

The Security Council may establish such subsidiary organs as it deems necessary for the performance of its functions.

Article 30

The Security Council shall adopt its own rules of procedure, including the method of selecting its President.

Article 31

Any Member of the United Nations which is not a member of the Security Council may participate, without vote, in the discussion of any question brought before the Security Council whenever the latter considers that the interests of that Member are specially affected.

Article 32

Any Member of the United Nations which is not a member of the Security Council or any state which is not a Member of the United Nations, if it is a party to a dispute under consideration by the Security Council, shall be invited to participate, without vote, in the discussion relating to the dispute. The Security Council shall lay down such conditions as it deems just for the participation of a state which is not a Member of the United Nations.

CHAPTER VI

PACIFIC SETTLEMENT OF DISPUTES

Article 33

1. The parties to any dispute, the continuance of which is likely to endanger the maintenance of international peace and security, shall, first of all, seek a solution by negotiation, enquiry, mediation, conciliation, arbitration, judicial settlement, resort to regional agencies or arrangements, or other peaceful means of their own choice.

2. The Security Council shall, when it deems necessary, call upon the parties to settle their dispute by such means.

Article 34

The Security Council may investigate any dispute, or any situation which might lead to international friction or give rise to a dispute, in order to determine whether the continuance of the dispute or situation is likely to endanger the maintenance of international peace and security.

Article 35

1. Any Member of the United Nations may bring any dispute, or any situation of the nature referred to in Article 34, to the attention of the Security Council or of the General Assembly.

2. A state which is not a Member of the United Nations may bring to the attention of the Security Council or of the General Assembly any dispute to which it is a party if it accepts in advance, for the purposes of the dispute, the obligations of pacific settlement provided in the present Charter.

3. The proceedings of the General Assembly in respect of matters brought to its attention under this Article will be subject to the provisions of Articles 11 and 12.

Article 36

1. The Security Council may, at any stage of a dispute of the nature referred to in Article 33 or of a situation of like nature, recommend appropriate procedures or methods of adjustment.

2. The Security Council should take into consideration any procedures for the settlement of the dispute which have already been adopted by the parties.

3. In making recommendations under this Article the Security Council should also take into consideration that legal disputes should as a general rule be referred by the parties to the International Court of Justice in accordance with the provisions of the Statute of the Court.

Article 37

1. Should the parties to a dispute of the nature referred to in Article 33 fail to settle it by the means indicated in that Article, they shall refer it to the Security Council.

2. If the Security Council deems that the continuance of the dispute is in fact likely to endanger the maintenance of international peace and security, it shall decide whether to take action under Article 36 or to recommend such terms of settlement as it may consider appropriate.

Article 38

Without prejudice to the provisions of Articles 33 to 37, the Security Council may, if all the parties to any dispute so request, make recommendations to the parties with a view to a pacific settlement of the dispute.

CHAPTER VII

ACTION WITH RESPECT TO THREATS TO THE PEACE, BREACHES OF THE PEACE, AND ACTS OF AGGRESSION

Article 39

The Security Council shall determine the existence of any threat to the peace, breach of the peace, or act of aggression and shall make recommendations, or decide what measures shall be taken in accordance with Articles 41 and 42, to maintain or restore international peace and security.

Article 40

In order to prevent an aggravation of the situation, the Security Council may, before making the recommendations or deciding upon the measures provided for in Article 39, call upon the parties concerned to comply with such provisional measures as it deems necessary or desirable. Such provisional measures shall be without prejudice to the rights, claims, or position of the parties concerned. The Security Council shall duly take account of failure to comply with such provisional measures.

Article 41

The Security Council may decide what measures not involving the use of armed force are to be employed to give effect to its decisions, and it may call upon the Members of the United Nations to apply such measures. These may include complete or partial interruption of economic relations and of rail, sea, air, postal, telegraphic, radio, and other means of communication, and the severance of diplomatic relations.

Article 42

Should the Security Council consider that measures provided for in Article 41 would be inadequate or have proved to be inadequate, it may take such action by air, sea, or land forces as may be necessary to maintain or restore international peace and security. Such action may include demonstrations, blockade, and other operations by air, sea, or land forces of Members of the United Nations.

Article 43

1. All Members of the United Nations, in order to contribute to the maintenance of international peace and security, undertake to make available to the Security Council, on its call and in accordance with a special agreement or agreements, armed forces, assistance, and facilities, including rights of passage, necessary for the purpose of maintaining international peace and security.

2. Such agreement or agreements shall govern the numbers and types of forces, their degree of readiness and general location, and the nature of the facilities and assistance to be provided.

3. The agreement or agreements shall be negotiated as soon as possible on the initiative of the Security Council. They shall be concluded between the Security Council and Members or between the Security Council and groups of Members and shall be subject to ratification by the signatory states in accordance with their respective constitutional processes.

Article 44

When the Security Council has decided to use force it shall, before calling upon a Member not represented on it to provide armed forces in fulfillment of the obligations assumed under Article 43, invite that Member, if the Member so desires, to participate in the decisions of the Security Council concerning the employment of contingents of that Member's armed forces.

Article 45

In order to enable the United Nations to take urgent military measures, Members shall hold immediately available national air-force contingents for combined international enforcement action. The strength and degree of readiness of these contingents and plans for their combined action shall be determined, within the limits laid down in the special agreement or agreements referred to in Article 43, by the Security Council with the assistance of the Military Staff Committee.

Article 46

Plans for the application of armed force shall be made by the Security Council with the assistance of the Military Staff Committee.

Article 47

1. There shall be established a Military Staff Committee to advise and assist the Security Council on all questions relating to the Security Council's military requirements for the maintenance of international peace and security, the employment and command of forces placed at its disposal, the regulation of armaments, and possible disarmament.

2. The Military Staff Committee shall consist of the Chiefs of Staff of the permanent members of the Security Council or their representatives. Any Member of the United Nations not permanently represented on the Committee shall be invited by the Committee to be associated with it when the efficient discharge of the Committee's responsibilities requires the participation of that Member in its work.

3. The Military Staff Committee shall be responsible under the Security Council for the strategic direction of any armed forces placed at the disposal of the Security Council. Questions relating to the command of such forces shall be worked out subsequently.

4. The Military Staff Committee, with the authorization of the Security Council and after consultation with appropriate regional agencies, may establish regional subcommittees.

Article 48

1. The action required to carry out the decisions of the Security Council for the maintenance of international peace and security shall be taken by all the Members of the United Nations or by some of them, as the Security Council may determine.

2. Such decisions shall be carried out by the Members of the United Nations directly and through their action in the appropriate international agencies of which they are members.

Article 49

The Members of the United Nations shall join in affording mutual assistance in carrying out the measures decided upon by the Security Council.

Article 50

If preventive or enforcement measures against any state are taken by the Security Council, any other state, whether a Member of the United Nations or not, which finds itself confronted with special economic problems arising from the carrying out of those measures shall have the right to consult the Security Council with regard to a solution of those problems.

Article 51

Nothing in the present Charter shall impair the inherent right of individual or collective self-defense if an armed attack occurs against a Member of the United Nations, until the Security Council has taken the measures necessary to maintain international peace and security. Measures taken by Members in the exercise of this right of self-defense shall be immediately reported to the Security Council and shall not in any way affect the authority and responsibility of the Security Council under the present Charter to take at any time such action as it deems necessary in order to maintain or restore international peace and security.

CHAPTER VIII

REGIONAL ARRANGEMENTS

Article 52

1. Nothing in the present Charter precludes the existence of regional arrangements or agencies for dealing with such matters relating to the maintenance of international peace and security as are appropriate for regional action, provided that such arrangements or agencies and their activities are consistent with the Purposes and Principles of the United Nations.

2. The Members of the United Nations entering into such arrangements or constituting such agencies shall make every effort to achieve pacific settlement of local disputes through such regional arrangements or by such regional agencies before referring them to the Security Council.

3. The Security Council shall encourage the development of pacific settlement of local disputes through such regional arrangements or by such regional agencies either on the initiative of the states concerned or by reference from the Security Council.

4. This Article in no way impairs the application of Articles 34 and 35.

Article 53

1. The Security Council shall, where appropriate, utilize such regional arrangements or agencies for enforcement action under its authority. But no enforcement action shall be taken under regional arrangements or by re-

gional agencies without the authorization of the Security Council, with the exception of measures against any enemy state, as defined in paragraph 2 of this Article, provided for pursuant to Article 107 or in regional arrangements directed against renewal of aggressive policy on the part of any such state, until such time as the Organization may, on request of the Governments concerned, be charged with the responsibility for preventing further aggression by such a state.

2. The term enemy state as used in paragraph 1 of this Article applies to any state which during the Second World War has been an enemy of any signatory of the present Charter.

Article 54

The Security Council shall at all times be kept fully informed of activities undertaken or in contemplation under regional arrangements or by regional agencies for the maintenance of international peace and security.

CHAPTER IX

INTERNATIONAL ECONOMIC AND SOCIAL COOPERATION

Article 55

With a view to the creation of conditions of stability and well-being which are necessary for peaceful and friendly relations among nations based on respect for the principle of equal rights and self-determination of peoples, the United Nations shall promote:

a. higher standards of living, full employment, and conditions of economic and social progress and development;

b. solutions of international economic, social, health, and related problems; and international cultural and educational cooperation; and

c. universal respect for, and observance of, human rights and fundamental freedoms for all without distinction as to race, sex, language, or religion.

Article 56

All Members pledge themselves to take joint and separate action in cooperation with the Organization for the achievement of the purposes set forth in Article 55.

Article 57

1. The various specialized agencies, established by intergovernmental agreement and having wide international responsibilities, as defined in their basic instruments, in economic, social, cultural, educational, health, and related fields, shall be brought into relationship with the United Nations in accordance with the provisions of Article 63.

2. Such agencies thus brought into relationship with the United Nations are hereinafter referred to as specialized agencies.

Article 58

The Organization shall make recommendations for the coordination of the policies and activities of the specialized agencies.

Article 59

The Organization shall, where appropriate, initiate negotiations among the states concerned for the creation of any new specialized agencies required for the accomplishment of the purposes set forth in Article 55.

Article 60

Responsibility for the discharge of the functions of the Organization set forth in this Chapter shall be vested in the General Assembly and, under the authority of the General Assembly, in the Economic and Social Council, which shall have for this purpose the powers set forth in Chapter X.

CHAPTER X

THE ECONOMIC AND SOCIAL COUNCIL

COMPOSITION

Article 61

1. The Economic and Social Council shall consist of [eighteen] *twenty-seven* Members of the United Nations elected by the General Assembly.

2. Subject to the provisions of paragraph 3, [six] *nine* members of the Economic and Social Council shall be elected each year for a term of three years. A retiring member shall be eligible for immediate re-election.

3. At the first election [eighteen members of the Economic and Social Council shall be chosen. The term of office of six members so chosen shall expire at the end of one year, and of six other members at the end of two years,] *after the increase in the membership of the Economic and Social Council from eighteen to twenty-seven members, in addition to the members elected in place of the six members whose term of office expires at the end of that year, nine additional members shall be elected. Of these nine additional members, the term of office of three members so elected shall expire at the end of one year, and of three other members at the end of two years,* in accordance with arrangements made by the General Assembly.

4. Each member of the Economic and Social Council shall have one representative.

FUNCTIONS AND POWERS

Article 62

1. The Economic and Social Council may make or initiate studies and reports with respect to international economic, social, cultural, educational, health, and related matters and may make recommendations with respect to

any such matters to the General Assembly, to the Members of the United Nations, and to the specialized agencies concerned.

2. It may make recommendations for the purpose of promoting respect for, and observance of, human rights and fundamental freedoms for all.

3. It may prepare draft conventions for submission to the General Assembly, with respect to matters falling within its competence.

4. It may call, in accordance with the rules prescribed by the United Nations, international conferences on matters falling within its competence.

Article 63

1. The Economic and Social Council may enter into agreements with any of the agencies referred to in Article 57, defining the terms on which the agency concerned shall be brought into relationship with the United Nations. Such agreements shall be subject to approval by the General Assembly.

2. It may coordinate the activities of the specialized agencies through consultation with and recommendations to such agencies and through recommendations to the General Assembly and to the Members of the United Nations.

Article 64

1. The Economic and Social Council may take appropriate steps to obtain regular reports from the specialized agencies. It may make arrangements with the Members of the United Nations and with the specialized agencies to obtain reports on the steps taken to give effect to its own recommendations and to recommendations on matters falling within its competence made by the General Assembly.

2. It may communicate its observations on these reports to the General Assembly.

Article 65

The Economic and Social Council may furnish information to the Security Council and shall assist the Security Council upon its request.

Article 66

1. The Economic and Social Council shall perform such functions as fall within its competence in connection with the carrying out of the recommendations of the General Assembly.

2. It may, with the approval of the General Assembly, perform services at the request of Members of the United Nations and at the request of specialized agencies.

3. It shall perform such other functions as are specified elsewhere in the present Charter or as may be assigned to it by the General Assembly.

VOTING

Article 67

1. Each member of the Economic and Social Council shall have one vote.

2. Decisions of the Economic and Social Council shall be made by a majority of the members present and voting.

PROCEDURE

Article 68

The Economic and Social Council shall set up commissions in economic and social fields and for the promotion of human rights, and such other commissions as may be required for the performance of its functions.

Article 69

The Economic and Social Council shall invite any Member of the United Nations to participate, without vote, in its deliberations on any matter of particular concern to that Member.

Article 70

The Economic and Social Council may make arrangements for representatives of the specialized agencies to participate, without vote, in its deliberations and in those of the commissions established by it, and for its representatives to participate in the deliberations of the specialized agencies.

Article 71

The Economic and Social Council may make suitable arrangements for consultation with non-governmental organizations which are concerned with matters within its competence. Such arrangements may be made with international organizations and, where appropriate, with national organizations after consultation with the Member of the United Nations concerned.

Article 72

1. The Economic and Social Council shall adopt its own rules of procedure, including the method of selecting its President.

2. The Economic and Social Council shall meet as required in accordance with its rules, which shall include provision for the convening of meetings on the request of a majority of its members.

CHAPTER XI

DECLARATION REGARDING NON-SELF-GOVERNING TERRITORIES

Article 73

Members of the United Nations which have or assume responsibilities for the administration of territories whose peoples have not yet attained a full measure of self-government recognize the principle that the interests of the inhabitants of these territories are paramount, and accept as a sacred trust the obligation to promote to the utmost, within the system of international peace and security established by the present Charter, the well-being of the inhabitants of these territories, and, to this end:

a. to ensure, with due respect for the culture of the peoples concerned, their political, economic, social, and educational advancement, their just treatment, and their protection against abuses;

b. to develop self-government, to take due account of the political aspirations of the peoples, and to assist them in the progressive development of their free political institutions, according to the particular circumstances of each territory and its peoples and their varying stages of advancement;

c. to further international peace and security;

d. to promote constructive measures of development, to encourage research, and to cooperate with one another and, when and where appropriate, with specialized international bodies with a view to the practical achievement of the social, economic, and scientific purposes set forth in this Article; and

e. to transmit regularly to the Secretary-General for information purposes, subject to such limitation as security and constitutional considerations may require, statistical and other information of a technical nature relating to economic, social, and educational conditions in the territories for which they are respectively responsible other than those territories to which Chapters XII and XIII apply.

Article 74

Members of the United Nations also agree that their policy in respect of the territories to which this Chapter applies, no less than in respect of their metropolitan areas, must be based on the general principle of good-neighborliness, due account being taken of the interests and well-being of the rest of the world, in social, economic, and commercial matters.

CHAPTER XII

INTERNATIONAL TRUSTEESHIP SYSTEM

Article 75

The United Nations shall establish under its authority an international trusteeship system for the administration and supervision of such territories as may be placed thereunder by subsequent individual agreements. These territories are hereinafter referred to as trust territories.

Article 76

The basic objectives of the trusteeship system, in accordance with the Purposes of the United Nations laid down in Article 1 of the present Charter, shall be:

a. to further international peace and security;

b. to promote the political, economic, social, and educational advancement of the inhabitants of the trust territories, and their progressive development towards self-government or independence as may be appropriate to the particular circumstances of each territory and its peoples and the freely expressed wishes of the peoples concerned, and as may be provided by the terms of each trusteeship agreement;

c. to encourage respect for human rights and for fundamental freedoms for all without distinction as to race, sex, language, or religion, and to encourage recognition of the interdependence of the peoples of the world; and

d. to ensure equal treatment in social, economic, and commercial matters for all Members of the United Nations and their nationals, and also equal treatment for the latter in the administration of justice, without prejudice to the attainment of the foregoing objectives and subject to the provisions of Article 80.

Article 77

1. The trusteeship system shall apply to such territories in the following categories as may be placed thereunder by means of trusteeship agreements:

a. territories now held under mandate;

b. territories which may be detached from enemy states as a result of the Second World War; and

c. territories voluntarily placed under the system by states responsible for their administration.

2. It will be a matter for subsequent agreement as to which territories in the foregoing categories will be brought under the trusteeship system and upon what terms.

Article 78

The trusteeship system shall not apply to territories which have become Members of the United Nations, relationship among which shall be based on respect for the principle of sovereign equality.

Article 79

The terms of trusteeship for each territory to be placed under the trusteeship system, including any alteration or amendment, shall be agreed upon by the states directly concerned, including the mandatory power in the case of territories held under mandate by a Member of the United Nations, and shall be approved as provided for in Articles 83 and 85.

Article 80

1. Except as may be agreed upon in individual trusteeship agreements, made under Articles 77, 79, and 81, placing each territory under the trusteeship system, and until such agreements have been concluded, nothing in this Chapter shall be construed in or of itself to alter in any manner the rights whatsoever of any states or any peoples or the terms of existing international instruments to which Members of the United Nations may respectively be parties.

2. Paragraph 1 of this Article shall not be interpreted as giving grounds

for delay or postponement of the negotiation and conclusion of agreements for placing mandated and other territories under the trusteeship system as provided for in Article 77.

Article 81

The trusteeship agreement shall in each case include the terms under which the trust territory will be administered and designate the authority which will exercise the administration of the trust territory. Such authority, hereinafter called the administering authority, may be one or more states or the Organization itself.

Article 82

There may be designated, in any trusteeship agreement, a strategic area or areas which may include part or all of the trust territory to which the agreement applies, without prejudice to any special agreement or agreements made under Article 43.

Article 83

1. All functions of the United Nations relating to strategic areas, including the approval of the terms of the trusteeship agreements and of their alteration or amendment, shall be exercised by the Security Council.

2. The basic objectives set forth in Article 76 shall be applicable to the people of each strategic area.

3. The Security Council shall, subject to the provisions of the trusteeship agreements and without prejudice to security considerations, avail itself of the assistance of the Trusteeship Council to perform those functions of the United Nations under the trusteeship system relating to political, economic, social, and educational matters in the strategic areas.

Article 84

It shall be the duty of the administering authority to ensure that the trust territory shall play its part in the maintenance of international peace and security. To this end the administering authority may make use of volunteer forces, facilities, and assistance from the trust territory in carrying out the obligations towards the Security Council undertaken in this regard by the administering authority, as well as for local defense and the maintenance of law and order within the trust territory.

Article 85

1. The functions of the United Nations with regard to trusteeship agreements for all areas not designated as strategic, including the approval of the terms of the trusteeship agreements and of their alteration or amendment, shall be exercised by the General Assembly.

2. The Trusteeship Council, operating under the authority of the General Assembly, shall assist the General Assembly in carrying out these functions.

CHAPTER XIII

THE TRUSTEESHIP COUNCIL

COMPOSITION

Article 86

1. The Trusteeship Council shall consist of the following Members of the United Nations:

a. those Members administering trust territories;

b. such of those Members mentioned by name in Article 23 as are not administering trust territories; and

c. as many other Members elected for three-year terms by the General Assembly as may be necessary to ensure that the total number of members of the Trusteeship Council is equally divided between those Members of the United Nations which administer trust territories and those which do not.

2. Each member of the Trusteeship Council shall designate one specially qualified person to represent it therein.

FUNCTIONS AND POWERS

Article 87

The General Assembly and, under its authority, the Trusteeship Council, in carrying out their functions, may:

a. consider reports submitted by the administering authority;

b. accept petitions and examine them in consultation with the administering authority;

c. provide for periodic visits to the respective trust territories at times agreed upon with the administering authority; and

d. take these and other actions in conformity with the terms of the trusteeship agreements.

Article 88

The Trusteeship Council shall formulate a questionnaire on the political, economic, social, and educational advancement of the inhabitants of each trust territory, and the administering authority for each trust territory within the competence of the General Assembly shall make an annual report to the General Assembly upon the basis of such questionnaire.

VOTING

Article 89

1. Each member of the Trusteeship Council shall have one vote.

2. Decisions of the Trusteeship Council shall be made by a majority of the members present and voting.

PROCEDURE

Article 90

1. The Trusteeship Council shall adopt its own rules of procedure, including the method of selecting its President.

2. The Trusteeship Council shall meet as required in accordance with its rules, which shall include provision for the convening of meetings on the request of a majority of its members.

Article 91

The Trusteeship Council shall, when appropriate, avail itself of the assistance of the Economic and Social Council and of the specialized agencies in regard to matters with which they are respectively concerned.

CHAPTER XIV

THE INTERNATIONAL COURT OF JUSTICE

Article 92

The International Court of Justice shall be the principal judicial organ of the United Nations. It shall function in accordance with the annexed Statute, which is based upon the Statute of the Permanent Court of International Justice and forms an integral part of the present Charter.

Article 93

1. All Members of the United Nations are *ipso facto* parties to the Statute of the International Court of Justice.

2. A state which is not a Member of the United Nations may become a party to the Statute of the International Court of Justice on conditions to be determined in each case by the General Assembly upon the recommendation of the Security Council.

Article 94

1. Each Member of the United Nations undertakes to comply with the decision of the International Court of Justice in any case to which it is a party.

2. If any party to a case fails to perform the obligations incumbent upon it under a judgment rendered by the Court, the other party may have recourse to the Security Council, which may, if it deems necessary, make recommendations or decide upon measures to be taken to give effect to the judgment.

Article 95

Nothing in the present Charter shall prevent Members of the United Nations from entrusting the solution of their differences to other tribunals by virtue of agreements already in existence or which may be concluded in the future.

Article 96

1. The General Assembly or the Security Council may request the International Court of Justice to give an advisory opinion on any legal question.

2. Other organs of the United Nations and specialized agencies, which may at any time be so authorized by the General Assembly, may also request advisory opinions of the Court on legal questions arising within the scope of their activities.

CHAPTER XV

THE SECRETARIAT

Article 97

The Secretariat shall comprise a Secretary-General and such staff as the Organization may require. The Secretary-General shall be appointed by the General Assembly upon the recommendation of the Security Council. He shall be the chief administrative officer of the Organization.

Article 98

The Secretary-General shall act in that capacity in all meetings of the General Assembly, of the Security Council, of the Economic and Social Council, and of the Trusteeship Council, and shall perform such other functions as are entrusted to him by these organs. The Secretary-General shall make an annual report to the General Assembly on the work of the Organization.

Article 99

The Secretary-General may bring to the attention of the Security Council any matter which in his opinion may threaten the maintenance of international peace and security.

Article 100

1. In the performance of their duties the Secretary-General and the staff shall not seek or receive instructions from any government or from any other authority external to the Organization. They shall refrain from any action which might reflect on their position as international officials responsible only to the Organization.

2. Each Member of the United Nations undertakes to respect the exclusively international character of the responsibilities of the Secretary-General and the staff and not to seek to influence them in the discharge of their responsibilities.

Article 101

1. The staff shall be appointed by the Secretary-General under regulations established by the General Assembly.

2. Appropriate staffs shall be permanently assigned to the Economic and Social Council, the Trusteeship Council, and, as required, to other organs of the United Nations. These staffs shall form a part of the Secretariat.

3. The paramount consideration in the employment of the staff and in the determination of the conditions of service shall be the necessity of securing the highest standards of efficiency, competence, and integrity. Due regard shall be paid to the importance of recruiting the staff on as wide a geographical basis as possible.

CHAPTER XVI

MISCELLANEOUS PROVISIONS

Article 102

1. Every treaty and every international agreement entered into by any Member of the United Nations after the present Charter comes into force shall as soon as possible be registered with the Secretariat and published by it.

2. No party to any such treaty or international agreement which has not been registered in accordance with the provisions of paragraph 1 of this Article may invoke that treaty or agreement before any organ of the United Nations.

Article 103

In the event of a conflict between the obligations of the Members of the United Nations under the present Charter and their obligations under any other international agreement, their obligations under the present Charter shall prevail.

Article 104

The Organization shall enjoy in the territory of each of its Members such legal capacity as may be necessary for the exercise of its functions and the fulfillment of its purposes.

Article 105

1. The Organization shall enjoy in the territory of each of its Members such privileges and immunities as are necessary for the fulfillment of its purposes.

2. Representatives of the Members of the United Nations and officials of the Organization shall similarly enjoy such privileges and immunities as are necessary for the independent exercise of their functions in connection with the Organization.

3. The General Assembly may make recommendations with a view to determining the details of the application of paragraphs 1 and 2 of this Article or may propose conventions to the Members of the United Nations for this purpose.

CHAPTER XVII

TRANSITIONAL SECURITY ARRANGEMENTS

Article 106

Pending the coming into force of such special agreements referred to in Article 43 as in the opinion of the Security Council enable it to begin the exercise of its responsibilities under Article 42, the parties to the Four-Nation Declaration, signed at Moscow, October 30, 1943, and France, shall, in accordance with the provisions of paragraph 5 of that Declaration, consult with one another and as occasion requires with other Members of the United Nations with a view to such joint action on behalf of the Organization as may be necessary for the purpose of maintaining international peace and security.

Article 107

Nothing in the present Charter shall invalidate or preclude action, in relation to any state which during the Second World War has been an enemy of any signatory to the present Charter, taken or authorized as a result of that war by the Governments having responsibility for such action.

CHAPTER XVIII

AMENDMENTS

Article 108

Amendments to the present Charter shall come into force for all Members of the United Nations when they have been adopted by a vote of two-thirds of the members of the General Assembly and ratified in accordance with their respective constitutional processes by two thirds of the Members of the United Nations, including all the permanent members of the Security by a vote of any [seven] *nine* members of the Security Council.

Article 109

1. A General Conference of the Members of the United Nations for the purpose of reviewing the present Charter may be held at a date and place to be fixed by a two-thirds vote of the members of the General Assembly and by a vote of any [seven] *nine* members of the Security Council. Each Member of the United Nations shall have one vote in the conference.

2. Any alteration of the present Charter recommended by a two-thirds vote of the conference shall take effect when ratified in accordance with

their respective constitutional processes by two-thirds of the Members of the United Nations including all the permanent members of the Security Council.

3. If such a conference has not been held before the tenth annual session of the General Assembly following the coming into force of the present Charter, the proposal to call such a conference shall be placed on the agenda of that session of the General Assembly, and the conference shall be held if so decided by a majority vote of the members of the General Assembly and by a vote of any [seven] *nine* members of the Security Council.

CHAPTER XIX

RATIFICATION AND SIGNATURE

Article 110

1. The present Charter shall be ratified by the signatory states in accordance with their respective constitutional processes.

2. The ratification shall be deposited with the Government of the United States of America, which shall notify all the signatory states of each deposit as well as the Secretary-General of the Organization when he has been appointed.

3. The present Charter shall come into force upon the deposit of ratifications by the Republic of China, France, the Union of Soviet Socialist Republics, the United Kingdom of Great Britain and Northern Ireland, and the United States of America, and by a majority of the other signatory states. A protocol of the ratifications deposited shall thereupon be drawn up by the Government of the United States of America which shall communicate copies thereof to all the signatory states.

4. The states signatory to the present Charter which ratify it after it has come into force will become original Members of the United Nations on the date of the deposit of their respective ratifications.

Article 111

The present Charter, of which the Chinese, French, Russian, English, and Spanish texts are equally authentic, shall remain deposited in the archives of the Government of the United States of America. Duly certified copies thereof shall be transmitted by that Government to the Governments of the other signatory states.

In faith whereof the representatives of the Governments of the United Nations have signed the present Charter.

Done at the city of San Francisco the twenty-sixth day of June, one thousand nine hundred and forty-five.

APPENDIX III

STATUTE OF THE INTERNATIONAL COURT OF JUSTICE

Article 1

The International Court of Justice established by the Charter of the United Nations as the principal judicial organ of the United Nations shall be constituted and shall function in accordance with the provisions of the present Statute.

CHAPTER I

ORGANIZATION OF THE COURT

Article 2

The Court shall be composed of a body of independent judges, elected regardless of their nationality from among persons of high moral character, who possess the qualifications required in their respective countries for appointment to the highest judicial offices, or are jurisconsults of recognized competence in international law.

Article 3

1. The Court shall consist of fifteen members, no two of whom may be nationals of the same state.

2. A person who for the purposes of membership in the Court could be regarded as a national of more than one state shall be deemed to be a national of the one in which he ordinarily exercises civil and political rights.

Article 4

1. The members of the Court shall be elected by the General Assembly and by the Security Council from a list of persons nominated by the national groups in the Permanent Court of Arbitration, in accordance with the following provisions.

2. In the case of Members of the United Nations not represented in the Permanent Court of Arbitration, candidates shall be nominated by national groups appointed for this purpose by their governments under the same conditions as those prescribed for members of the Permanent Court of Arbitration by Article 44 of the Convention of The Hague of 1907 for the pacific settlement of international disputes.

3. The conditions under which a state which is a party to the present Statute but is not a Member of the United Nations may participate in electing the members of the Court shall, in the absence of a special agreement, be laid down by the General Assembly upon recommendation of the Security Council.

Article 5

1. At least three months before the date of the election, the Secretary-General of the United Nations shall address a written request to the members of the Permanent Court of Arbitration belonging to the states which are parties to the present Statute, and to the members of the national groups appointed under Article 4, paragraph 2, inviting them to undertake, within a given time, by national groups, the nomination of persons in a position to accept the duties of a member of the Court.

2. No group may nominate more than four persons, not more than two of whom shall be of their own nationality. In no case may the number of candidates nominated by a group be more than double the number of seats to be filled.

Article 6

Before making these nominations, each national group is recommended to consult its highest court of justice, its legal faculties and schools of law, and its national academies and national sections of international academies devoted to the study of law.

Article 7

1. The Secretary-General shall prepare a list in alphabetical order of all the persons thus nominated. Save as provided in Article 12, paragraph 2, these shall be the only persons eligible.

2. The Secretary-General shall submit this list to the General Assembly and to the Security Council.

Article 8

The General Assembly and the Security Council shall proceed independently of one another to elect the members of the Court.

Article 9

At every election, the electors shall bear in mind not only that the persons to be elected should individually possess the qualifications required, but also that in the body as a whole the representation of the main forms of civilization and of the principal legal systems of the world should be assured.

Article 10

1. Those candidates who obtain an absolute majority of votes in the General Assembly and in the Security Council shall be considered as elected.

2. Any vote of the Security Council, whether for the election of judges or for the appointment of members of the conference envisaged in Article 12, shall be taken without any distinction between permanent and non-permanent members of the Security Council.

3. In the event of more than one national of the same state obtaining an absolute majority of the votes both of the General Assembly and of the Security Council, the eldest of these only shall be considered as elected.

Article 11

If, after the first meeting held for the purpose of the election, one or more seats remain to be filled, a second and, if necessary, a third meeting shall take place.

Article 12

1. If, after the third meeting, one or more seats still remain unfilled, a joint conference consisting of six members, three appointed by the General Assembly and three by the Security Council, may be formed at any time at the request of either the General Assembly or the Security Council, for the purpose of choosing by the vote of an absolute majority one name for each seat still vacant, to submit to the General Assembly and the Security Council for their respective acceptance.

2. If the joint conference is unanimously agreed upon any person who fulfils the required conditions, he may be included in its list, even though he was not included in the list of nominations referred to in Article 7.

3. If the joint conference is satisfied that it will not be successful in procuring an election, those members of the Court who have already been elected shall, within a period to be fixed by the Security Council, proceed to fill the vacant seats by selection from among those candidates who have obtained votes either in the General Assembly or in the Security Council.

4. In the event of an equality of votes among the judges, the eldest judge shall have a casting vote.

Article 13

1. The members of the Court shall be elected for nine years and may be re-elected; provided, however, that of the judges elected at the first election, the terms of five judges shall expire at the end of three years and the terms of five more judges shall expire at the end of six years.

2. The judges whose terms are to expire at the end of the above-mentioned initial periods of three and six years shall be chosen by lot to be drawn by the Secretary-General immediately after the first election has been completed.

3. The members of the Court shall continue to discharge their duties until their places have been filled. Though replaced, they shall finish any cases which they may have begun.

4. In the case of the resignation of a member of the Court, the resignation shall be addressed to the President of the Court for transmission to the Secretary-General. This last notification makes the place vacant.

Article 14

Vacancies shall be filled by the same method as that laid down for the first election, subject to the following provision: the Secretary-General shall, within one month of the occurrence of the vacancy, proceed to issue the invitations provided for in Article 5, and the date of the election shall be fixed by the Security Council.

Article 15

A member of the Court elected to replace a member whose term of office has not expired shall hold office for the remainder of his predecessor's term.

Article 16

1. No member of the Court may exercise any political or administrative function, or engage in any other occupation of a professional nature.

2. Any doubt on this point shall be settled by the decision of the Court.

Article 17

1. No member of the Court may act as agent, counsel, or advocate in any case.

2. No member may participate in the decision of any case in which he has previously taken part as agent, counsel, or advocate for one of the parties, or as a member of a national or international court, or of a commission of enquiry, or in any other capacity.

3. Any doubt on this point shall be settled by the decision of the Court.

Article 18

1. No member of the Court can be dismissed unless, in the unanimous opinion of the other members, he has ceased to fulfil the required conditions.

2. Formal notification thereof shall be made to the Secretary-General by the Registrar.

3. This notification makes the place vacant.

Article 19

The members of the Court, when engaged on the business of the Court, shall enjoy diplomatic privileges and immunities.

Article 20

Every member of the Court shall, before taking up his duties, make a solemn declaration in open court that he will exercise his powers impartially and conscientiously.

Article 21

1. The Court shall elect its President and Vice-President for three years; they may be re-elected.

2. The Court shall appoint its Registrar and may provide for the appointment of such other officers as may be necessary.

Article 22

1. The seat of the Court shall be established at The Hague. This, however, shall not prevent the Court from sitting and exercising its functions elsewhere whenever the Court considers it desirable.

2. The President and the Registrar shall reside at the seat of the Court.

Article 23

1. The Court shall remain permanently in session, except during the judicial vacations, the dates and duration of which shall be fixed by the Court.

2. Members of the Court are entitled to periodic leave, the dates and duration of which shall be fixed by the Court, having in mind the distance between The Hague and the home of each judge.

3. Members of the Court shall be bound, unless they are on leave or prevented from attending by illness or other serious reasons duly explained to the President, to hold themselves permanently at the disposal of the Court.

Article 24

1. If, for some special reason, a member of the Court considers that he should not take part in the decision of a particular case, he shall so inform the President.

2. If the President considers that for some special reason one of the members of the Court should not sit in a particular case, he shall give him notice accordingly.

3. If in any such case the member of the Court and the President disagree, the matter shall be settled by the decision of the Court.

Article 25

1. The full Court shall sit except when it is expressly provided otherwise in the present Statute.

2. Subject to the condition that the number of judges available to constitute the Court is not thereby reduced below eleven, the Rules of the Court may provide for allowing one or more judges, according to circumstances and in rotation, to be dispensed from sitting.

3. A quorum of nine judges shall suffice to constitute the Court.

Article 26

1. The Court may from time to time form one or more chambers, composed of three or more judges as the Court may determine, for dealing with particular categories of cases; for example, labor cases and cases relating to transit and communications.

2. The Court may at any time form a chamber for dealing with a particular case. The number of judges to constitute such a chamber shall be determined by the Court with the approval of the parties.

3. Cases shall be heard and determined by the chambers provided for in this Article if the parties so request.

Article 27

A judgment given by any of the chambers provided for in Articles 26 and 29 shall be considered as rendered by the Court.

Article 28

The chambers provided for in Articles 26 and 29 may, with the consent of the parties, sit and exercise their functions elsewhere than at The Hague.

Article 29

With a view to the speedy despatch of business, the Court shall form annually a chamber composed of five judges which, at the request of the parties, may hear and determine cases by summary procedure. In addition, two judges shall be selected for the purpose of replacing judges who find it impossible to sit.

Article 30

1. The Court shall frame rules for carrying out its functions. In particular, it shall lay down rules of procedure.

2. The Rules of the Court may provide for assessors to sit with the Court or with any of its chambers, without the right to vote.

Article 31

1. Judges of the nationality of each of the parties shall retain their right to sit in the case before the Court.

2. If the Court includes upon the Bench a judge of the nationality of one of the parties, any other party may choose a person to sit as judge. Such person shall be chosen preferably from among those persons who have been nominated as candidates as provided in Articles 4 and 5.

3. If the Court includes upon the Bench no judge of the nationality of the parties, each of these parties may proceed to choose a judge as provided in paragraph 2 of this Article.

4. The provisions of this Article shall apply to the case of Articles 26 and 29. In such cases, the President shall request one or, if necessary, two of the members of the Court forming the chamber to give place to the members of the Court of the nationality of the parties concerned, and, failing

such, or if they are unable to be present, to the judges specially chosen by the parties.

5. Should there be several parties in the same interest, they shall, for the purpose of the preceding provisions, be reckoned as one party only. Any doubt upon this point shall be settled by the decision of the Court.

6. Judges chosen as laid down in paragraphs 2, 3, and 4 of this Article shall fulfil the conditions required by Articles 2, 17 (paragraph 2), 20, and 24 of the present Statute. They shall take part in the decision on terms of complete equality with their colleagues.

Article 32

1. Each member of the Court shall receive an annual salary.

2. The President shall receive a special annual allowance.

3. The Vice-President shall receive a special allowance for every day on which he acts as President.

4. The judges chosen under Article 31, other than members of the Court, shall receive compensation for each day on which they exercise their functions.

5. These salaries, allowances, and compensation shall be fixed by the General Assembly. They may not be decreased during the term of office.

6. The salary of the Registrar shall be fixed by the General Assembly on the proposal of the Court.

7. Regulations made by the General Assembly shall fix the conditions under which retirement pensions may be given to members of the Court and to the Registrar, and the conditions under which members of the Court and the Registrar shall have their traveling expenses refunded.

8. The above salaries, allowances, and compensation shall be free of all taxation.

Article 33

The expenses of the Court shall be borne by the United Nations in such a manner as shall be decided by the General Assembly.

CHAPTER II

COMPETENCE OF THE COURT

Article 34

1. Only states may be parties in cases before the Court.

2. The Court, subject to and in conformity with its Rules, may request of public international organizations information relevant to cases before it, and shall receive such information presented by such organizations on their own initiative.

3. Whenever the construction of the constituent instrument of a public international organization or of an international convention adopted thereunder is in question in a case before the Court, the Registrar shall so notify the public international organization concerned and shall communicate to it copies of all the written proceedings.

Article 35

1. The Court shall be open to the states parties to the present Statute.

2. The conditions under which the Court shall be open to other states shall, subject to the special provisions contained in treaties in force, be laid down by the Security Council, but in no case shall such conditions place the parties in a position of inequality before the Court.

3. When a state which is not a Member of the United Nations is a party to a case, the Court shall fix the amount which that party is to contribute towards the expenses of the Court. This provision shall not apply if such state is bearing a share of the expenses of the Court.

Article 36

1. The jurisdiction of the Court comprises all cases which the parties refer to it and all matters specially provided for in the Charter of the United Nations or in treaties and conventions in force.

2. The states parties to the present Statute may at any time declare that they recognize as compulsory *ipso facto* and without special agreement, in relation to any other state accepting the same obligation, the jurisdiction of the Court in all legal disputes concerning:

a. the interpretation of a treaty;

b. any question of international law;

c. the existence of any fact which, if established, would constitute a breach of an international obligation;

d. the nature or extent of the reparation to be made for the breach of an international obligation.

3. The declarations referred to above may be made unconditionally or on condition of reciprocity on the part of several or certain states, or for a certain time.

4. Such declarations shall be deposited with the Secretary-General of the United Nations, who shall transmit copies thereof to the parties to the Statute and to the Registrar of the Court.

5. Declarations made under Article 36 of the Statute of the Permanent Court of International Justice and which are still in force shall be deemed, as between the parties to the present Statute, to be acceptances of the compulsory jurisdiction of the International Court of Justice for the period which they still have to run and in accordance with their terms.

6. In the event of a dispute as to whether the Court has jurisdiction, the matter shall be settled by the decision of the Court.

Article 37

Whenever a treaty or convention in force provides for reference of a matter to a tribunal to have been instituted by the League of Nations, or to the Permanent Court of International Justice, the matter shall, as between the parties to the present Statute, be referred to the International Court of Justice.

Article 38

1. The Court, whose function is to decide in accordance with international law such disputes as are submitted to it, shall apply:

a. international conventions, whether general or particular, establishing rules expressly recognized by the contesting states;

b. international custom, as evidence of a general practice accepted as law;

c. the general principles of law recognized by civilized nations;

d. subject to the provisions of Article 59, judicial decisions and the teachings of the most highly qualified publicists of the various nations, as subsidiary means for the determination of rules of law.

2. This provision shall not prejudice the power of the Court to decide a case *ex aequo et bono*, if the parties agree thereto.

CHAPTER III

PROCEDURE

Article 39

1. The official languages of the Court shall be French and English. If the parties agree that the case shall be conducted in French, the judgment shall be delivered in French. If the parties agree that the case shall be conducted in English, the judgment shall be delivered in English.

2. In the absence of an agreement as to which language shall be employed, each party may, in the pleadings, use the language which it prefers; the decision of the Court shall be given in French and English. In this case the Court shall at the same time determine which of the two texts shall be considered as authoritative.

3. The Court shall, at the request of any party, authorize a language other than French or English to be used by that party.

Article 40

1. Cases are brought before the Court, as the case may be, either by the notification of the special agreement or by a written application addressed to the Registrar. In either case the subject of the dispute and the parties shall be indicated.

2. The Registrar shall forthwith communicate the application to all concerned.

3. He shall also notify the Members of the United Nations through the Secretary-General, and also any other states entitled to appear before the Court.

Article 41

1. The Court shall have the power to indicate, if it considers that circumstances so require, any provisional measures which ought to be taken to preserve the respective rights of either party.

2. Pending the final decision, notice of the measures suggested shall forthwith be given to the parties and to the Security Council.

Article 42

1. The parties shall be represented by agents.

2. They may have the assistance of counsel or advocates before the Court.

3. The agents, counsel, and advocates of parties before the Court shall enjoy the privileges and immunities necessary to the independent exercise of their duties.

Article 43

1. The procedure shall consist of two parts: written and oral.

2. The written proceedings shall consist of the communication to the Court and to the parties of memorials, counter-memorials and, if necessary, replies; also all papers and documents in support.

3. These communications shall be made through the Registrar, in the order and within the time fixed by the Court.

4. A certified copy of every document produced by one party shall be communicated to the other party.

5. The oral proceedings shall consist of the hearing by the Court of witnesses, experts, agents, counsel, and advocates.

Article 44

1. For the service of all notices upon persons other than the agents, counsel, and advocates, the Court shall apply direct to the government of the state upon whose territory the notice has to be served.

2. The same provision shall apply whenever steps are to be taken to procure evidence on the spot.

Article 45

The hearing shall be under the control of the President or, if he is unable to preside, of the Vice-President; if neither is able to preside, the senior judge present shall preside.

Article 46

The hearing in Court shall be public, unless the Court shall decide otherwise, or unless the parties demand that the public be not admitted.

Article 47

1. Minutes shall be made at each hearing and signed by the Registrar and the President.

2. These minutes alone shall be authentic.

Article 48

The Court shall make orders for the conduct of the case, shall decide the form and time in which each party must conclude its arguments, and make all arrangements connected with the taking of evidence.

Article 49

The Court may, even before the hearing begins, call upon the agents to produce any document or to supply any explanations. Formal note shall be taken of any refusal.

Article 50

The Court may, at any time, entrust any individual, body, bureau, commission, or other organization that it may select, with the task of carrying out an enquiry or giving an expert opinion.

Article 51

During the hearing any relevant questions are to be put to the witnesses and experts under the conditions laid down by the Court in the rules of procedure referred to in Article 30.

Article 52

After the Court has received the proofs and evidence within the time specified for the purpose, it may refuse to accept any further oral or written evidence that one party may desire to present unless the other side consents.

Article 53

1. Whenever one of the parties does not appear before the Court, or fails to defend its case, the other party may call upon the Court to decide in favor of its claim.

2. The Court must, before doing so, satisfy itself, not only that it has jurisdiction in accordance with Articles 36 and 37, but also that the claim is well founded in fact and law.

Article 54

1. When, subject to the control of the Court, the agents, counsel, and advocates have completed their presentation of the case, the President shall declare the hearing closed.

2. The Court shall withdraw to consider the judgment.

3. The deliberations of the Court shall take place in private and remain secret.

Article 55

1. All questions shall be decided by a majority of the judges present.

2. In the event of an equality of votes, the President or the judge who acts in his place shall have a casting vote.

Article 56

1. The judgment shall state the reasons on which it is based.

2. It shall contain the names of the judges who have taken part in the decision.

Article 57

If the judgment does not represent in whole or in part the unanimous opinion of the judges, any judge shall be entitled to deliver a separate opinion.

Article 58

The judgment shall be signed by the President and by the Registrar. It shall be read in open court, due notice having been given to the agents.

Article 59

The decision of the Court has no binding force except between the parties and in respect of that particular case.

Article 60

The judgment is final and without appeal. In the event of dispute as to the meaning or scope of the judgment, the Court shall construe it upon the request of any party.

Article 61

1. An application for revision of a judgment may be made only when it is based upon the discovery of some fact of such a nature as to be a decisive factor, which fact was, when the judgment was given, unknown to the Court and also to the party claiming revision, always provided that such ignorance was not due to negligence.
2. The proceedings for revision shall be opened by a judgment of the Court expressly recording the existence of the new fact, recognizing that it has such a character as to lay the case open to revision, and declaring the application admissible on this ground.
3. The Court may require previous compliance with the terms of the judgment before it admits proceedings in revision.
4. The application for revision must be made at latest within six months of the discovery of the new fact.
5. No application for revision may be made after the lapse of ten years from the date of the judgment.

Article 62

1. Should a state consider that it has an interest of a legal nature which may be affected by the decision in the case, it may submit a request to the Court to be permitted to intervene.
2. It shall be for the Court to decide upon this request.

Article 63

1. Whenever the construction of a convention to which states other than those concerned in the case are parties is in question, the Registrar shall notify all such states forthwith.
2. Every state so notified has the right to intervene in the proceedings;

but if it uses this right, the construction given by the judgment will be equally binding upon it.

Article 64

Unless otherwise decided by the Court, each party shall bear its own costs.

CHAPTER IV

ADVISORY OPINIONS

Article 65

1. The Court may give an advisory opinion on any legal question at the request of whatever body may be authorized by or in accordance with the Charter of the United Nations to make such a request.

2. Questions upon which the advisory opinion of the Court is asked shall be laid before the Court by means of a written request containing an exact statement of the question upon which an opinion is required, and accompanied by all documents likely to throw light upon the question.

Article 66

1. The Registrar shall forthwith give notice of the request for an advisory opinion to all states entitled to appear before the Court.

2. The Registrar shall also, by means of a special and direct communication, notify any state entitled to appear before the Court or international organization considered by the Court, or, should it not be sitting, by the President, as likely to be able to furnish information on the question, that the Court will be prepared to receive, within a time limit to be fixed by the President, written statements, or to hear, at a public sitting to be held for the purpose, oral statements relating to the question.

3. Should any such state entitled to appear before the Court have failed to receive the special communication referred to in paragraph 2 of this Article, such state may express a desire to submit a written statement or to be heard; and the Court will decide.

4. States and organizations having presented written or oral statements or both shall be permitted to comment on the statements made by other states or organizations in the form, to the extent, and within the time limits which the Court, or, should it not be sitting, the President, shall decide in each particular case. Accordingly, the Registrar shall in due time communicate any such written statements to states and organizations having submitted similar statements.

Article 67

The Court shall deliver its advisory opinions in open court, notice having been given to the Secretary-General and to the representatives of Members of the United Nations, of other states and of international organizations immediately concerned.

Article 68

In the exercise of its advisory functions the Court shall further be guided by the provisions of the present Statute which apply in contentious cases to the extent to which it recognizes them to be applicable.

CHAPTER V

AMENDMENT

Article 69

Amendments to the present Statute shall be effected by the same procedure as is provided by the Charter of the United Nations for amendments to that Charter, subject however to any provisions which the General Assembly upon recommendation of the Security Council may adopt concerning the participation of states which are parties to the present Statute but are not Members of the United Nations.

Article 70

The Court shall have power to propose such amendments to the present Statute as it may deem necessary, through written communications to the Secretary-General, for consideration in conformity with the provisions of Article 69.

INDEX OF CASES

For the convenience of readers who wish to study cases referred to in this work, the following Index provides their pagination in different casebooks of international law. Names of arbitral and judicial tribunals are also indicated. Law reports in abridged form can be found either in the list of abbreviations or in the bibliography. Cases and incidents which were subjects of diplomatic discussion are listed in the Subject Index.

SUBJECT INDEX

For advisory opinions of international courts and decisions of arbitral or judicial tribunals, see the Index of Cases.

C

D

O

S

T

V

Y

Z